SALES MANAGEMENT
Analysis and Decision Making

—— **Second Edition** ——

SALES MANAGEMENT
Analysis and Decision Making

——— Second Edition ———

Thomas N. Ingram
Memphis State University

Raymond W. LaForge
University of Louisville

THE DRYDEN PRESS
A Harcourt Brace Jovanovich College Publisher
Fort Worth Philadelphia San Diego New York Orlando Austin San Antonio
Toronto Montreal London Sydney Tokyo

Acquisitions Editor: Rob Zwettler
Developmental Editor: Mary Beth Nelligan
Project Editor: Karen Hill
Art and Design Director: Jeanne Calabrese
Production Manager: Barb Bahnsen
Permissions Editor: Doris Milligan
Director of Editing, Design, and Production: Jane Perkins

Text and Cover Designer: Frances Hasegawa, Pil/Has Design + Construction
Copy Editor: Sally Jaskold
Indexer: Lois Oster
Compositor: The Clarinda Company
Text Type: 10/12 Janson

Library of Congress Cataloging-in-Publication Data

Ingram, Thomas N.
    Sales management : analysis and decision making / Thomas N.
Ingram, Raymond W. LaForge. — 2nd ed.
        p.   cm.
    Includes bibliographical references and index.
    ISBN 0-03-054168-9
    1. Sales management.   I. LaForge, Raymond W.   II. Title.
HF5438.4.I54   1992
658.8'1—dc20   90-29905

Printed in the United States of America
 23-040-98765432

Address orders:
The Dryden Press
Orlando, Florida 32887

Address editorial correspondence:
The Dryden Press
301 Commerce Street, Suite 3700
Fort Worth, TX 76102

The Dryden Press
Harcourt Brace Jovanovich

Cover Illustration: © Jud Guitteau

To our parents and to Jacque, Susan, and Alexandra.

THE DRYDEN PRESS *Series in Marketing*

PREFACE

Our objective in writing the second edition of *Sales Management: Analysis and Decision Making* was to continue to present comprehensive and rigorous coverage of contemporary sales management in a readable, interesting, and challenging manner. Findings from recent sales management research are blended with examples of current sales management practice into an effective pedagogical format. Topics are covered from the perspective of a sales management decision maker. This decision-making perspective is accomplished through a chapter format that typically consists of discussing basic concepts, identifying critical decision areas, and presenting analytical approaches for improved sales management decision making. Company examples from the contemporary business world are used throughout the text to supplement chapter discussion.

Changes in this Edition

Several elements have been added to or expanded upon in the second edition of *Sales Management:*

- Additional emphasis is given to ethical issues in sales management by featuring a boxed insert entitled "An Ethical Perspective" in each chapter.
- Two short cases have been added at the end of the chapters to allow additional discussion of concepts presented in the chapters. These cases will help the student to develop analytical skills, which can be further developed through analysis of the end-of-part and comprehensive cases in the text.
- Coverage of sales forecasting methods has been expanded to emphasize the importance of forecasting and to explain the way forecasts are developed and utilized.
- The microcomputer software package has been revised to include ten spreadsheet templates keyed to cases and a salesperson performance-evaluation exercise.
- The depiction of the sales process stresses the relationship-building aspects of personal selling.

Level and Organization

This text was written for the undergraduate student enrolled in a one-semester or one-quarter sales management class. However, it is sufficiently rigorous to be used at the MBA level.

A sales management model is used to present coverage in a logical sequence. The text is organized into six parts to correspond with the six stages in the sales management model.

Part One, "Describing the Personal Selling Function," is designed to provide students with an understanding of personal selling prior to addressing specific sales management areas. Colleagues across the country have suggested that available sales management texts do not provide enough coverage of personal selling. We decided to devote three chapters at the beginning of the text to this topic.

Part Two, "Defining the Strategic Role of the Sales Function," consists of two chapters that discuss important relationships between personal selling and organizational strategies at the corporate, business, marketing, and sales levels. Each chapter in this part focuses on how strategic decisions at different organizational levels affect sales management decisions and personal selling practices.

Part Three, "Designing the Sales Organization," addresses the key decisions required to establish an effective sales organization. The two chapters in this part investigate alternative sales organization structures and examine analytical methods for determining salesforce size, territory design, and the allocation of selling effort.

Part Four, "Developing the Salesforce," changes the focus from organizational topics to people topics. The two chapters in this part cover the critical decision areas in the recruitment and selection of salespeople and in training salespeople once they have been hired.

Part Five, "Directing the Salesforce," continues the people orientation by examining important areas of salesforce motivation and reward systems. The last of three chapters in this part discusses the general supervisory and leadership roles necessary for successful sales management.

Part Six, "Determining Salesforce Effectiveness and Performance," concludes the sales management process by addressing evaluation and control procedures. Differences in evaluating the effectiveness of the sales organization and the performance of salespeople are highlighted and covered in separate chapters. The three chapters in this part focus on evaluation approaches and the ways they can be used to diagnose problems and develop effective sales management solutions.

Pedagogy

The following pedagogical format is used for each chapter to facilitate the learning process.

Learning Objectives. Specific learning objectives for the chapter are stated in behavioral terms so that students will know what they should be able to do after the chapter has been covered.

Opening Vignettes. All chapters are introduced by an opening vignette that typically consists of a recent, real-world company example addressing many of the key points to be discussed in the chapter. These opening vignettes are intended to generate student interest in the topics to be covered and to illustrate the practicality of the chapter coverage.

Key Words. Key words are highlighted in bold type throughout each chapter and summarized in list form at the end of the chapter to alert students to their importance.

Boxed Inserts. Each chapter contains two boxed inserts titled "A Global Perspective" and "An Ethical Perspective." These items provide specific company examples illustrating important topics covered in the chapter and related to global and ethical sales management issues.

Figure Captions. Every figure in the text includes a summarizing caption designed to make the figure understandable without reference to the chapter discussion.

Chapter Summaries. A chapter summary recaps the key points covered in the chapter by restating and answering questions presented in the learning objectives at the beginning of the chapter.

Discussion Questions. Ten discussion questions are presented at the end of each chapter to review key concepts covered in the chapter. Some of the questions require students to summarize what has been covered, while others are designed to be more thought provoking and extend beyond chapter coverage.

Application Exercises. Three application exercises are supplied for each chapter, requiring students to apply what has been learned in the chapter to a specific sales management situation. Many of the application exercises require data analysis.

Cases. Each chapter concludes with two short cases. Most of these cases represent realistic and interesting sales management situations. Several require data analysis that can be performed with the accompanying spreadsheet software.

Cases

The book contains a mixture of short, medium, and long cases—54 in all. The 30 short cases at the end of chapters can be used as a basis for class discussion or short written assignments. The longer cases are more appropriate for detailed analysis and class discussions or presentations by individuals or student groups. The longer cases are located at the end of the six parts of the book. We have tried to match the major focus of each case with the appropriate chapter coverage in the book. In addition, four comprehensive cases that integrate multiple sales management decision areas are presented at the end of the book.

Ancillaries

Instructor's Manual, Test Bank, and Transparency Masters. A comprehensive package of ancillary materials is available to make it easy for professors to teach a rigorous and interesting sales management course. The *Instructor's Manual, Test*

Bank, and Transparency Masters, prepared by the authors, contains a separate section for each chapter as well as teaching notes for all of the cases. Each section includes a summary; examples, exercises, and materials not covered in the book that could be incorporated into class discussion; and answers to review questions and application exercises. The manual also contains sample course outlines. The *Test Bank* contains multiple-choice and true-false questions and is available in a computerized version for IBM microcomputers.

A large number of *Transparency Masters* are in the manual, more than half of which represent figures and tables that do not appear in the book. Finally, the manual concludes with a user-friendly discussion of the microcomputer software available with the book and the way this software can be used in a sales management class.

Microcomputer Software. A package containing two microcomputer disks has been developed for use with the book. The first disk contains spreadsheet templates that can be used in analyzing ten of the cases. The second disk contains a stand-alone computer exercise, SPREE, for evaluating salesperson performance. The software is designed to be very easy for students to use, and everything necessary to incorporate the microcomputer analysis into a sales management class is provided in the *Instructor's Manual*.

Sales Management Update. We have tried to make the book as current as possible by incorporating recent sales management examples and research results. However, sales management is a dynamic field with new examples and research findings continuously emerging. Therefore, we have decided to prepare a "Sales Management Update" that will be available each year in early January and early August. The update will be organized according to the chapters in the book and will include the latest company examples, new research findings, and other teaching aids geared to each chapter, making it easy for professors to incorporate this current information into their class sessions.

Acknowledgments

The writing of a book is a long and arduous task that requires the dedicated efforts of many individuals. The contributions of these individuals are greatly appreciated and deserve specific recognition. We are especially grateful for the efforts of the following colleagues, who provided many useful suggestions that improved this edition:

Karen Anderson, *Iowa State University*
Kenneth Anglin, *Central Michigan University*
John Coppett, *University of Houston—Clear Lake*
Kenneth Evans, *University of Missouri, Columbia*
Bruce MacNab, *California State University, Hayward*
Philip Mahin, *West Virginia University*
Bruce Pilling, *Georgia State University*

Michael Swenson, *Brigham Young University*
Frank Zuccaro, *Hofstra University*

We also wish to thank our colleagues who reviewed all or part of the manuscript for the last edition:

Ramon Avila, *Ball State University*
Steve Castleberry, *Northern Illinois University*
Steve Clopton, *Appalachian State University*
Cathy Cole, *University of Iowa*
Bob Collins, *University of Nevada, Las Vegas*
Bill Cron, *Southern Methodist University*
Ken Evans, *Arizona State University*
Sarah Gardial, *University of Tennessee, Knoxville*
Harrison Grathwol, *California State University, Chico*
David Good, *Central Missouri State University*
Jon Hawes, *University of Akron*
Vince Howe, *University of North Carolina, Wilmington*
Bill Moncrief, *Texas Christian University*
Walter Pachuk, *University of Scranton*
Hal Teer, *James Madison University*
Dan Weilbaker, *Bowling Green State University*

We sincerely appreciate the willingness of many individuals to allow us to include their cases in the book. These cases have substantially enhanced the effectiveness and interest of the text.

Interaction with sales and marketing executives has produced interesting examples and useful insights that have been incorporated in various ways throughout the book. Special thanks go to Jim Houts, *Xerox Corporation;* Dave Moore, *Ruddell's Associates, Inc.;* Brent Pennington, *Virginia State Lottery;* Don Hutson, *U.S. Learning;* Jim Shirah, *BellSouth;* and Russ Stavig, *Armstrong World Industries.* Valuable input was also provided by two long-time friends, Don Becker and Wesley Singleton, entrepreneurs whose extraordinary success is largely attributable to highly developed sales management skills. Sales and Marketing Executives International (SMEI) has also been of great assistance, particularly through support of the authors' research that is reflected in this book.

We would also like to thank Cliff Young *(University of Colorado at Denver)* for doing a terrific job in developing and refining all of the microcomputer software accompanying the book. Cliff also translated the bits and bytes into an excellent, user-friendly discussion of how to use the software in a sales management class.

A great deal of credit for this book should go to all of the wonderful people at The Dryden Press. Their expertise, support, and constant encouragement turned an extremely difficult task into a very enjoyable one. We would like to recognize specifically the tremendous efforts of the following professionals and friends: Rob Zwettler, Mary Beth Nelligan, Karen Hill, Jeanne Calabrese, Sally Jaskold, and Doris Milligan. However, we also want to thank the many individuals with whom we did not have direct contact but who assisted in the development and production of this book. We have been treated superbly by everyone at The Dryden Press during this project.

We are also very appreciative of the support provided by our colleagues at Memphis State University, James Madison University, and the University of Louisville.

Thomas N. Ingram
Raymond W. LaForge

September 1991

ABOUT THE AUTHORS

Thomas N. Ingram (PhD, Georgia State University) is Professor of Marketing and holder of the Sales and Marketing Executives Chair in Sales Excellence at Memphis State University. Dr. Ingram spent eight years at the University of Kentucky, where he received the National Alumni Association Great Teacher Award. Prior to entering academia, Dr. Ingram worked in sales, product management, and sales management with Exxon USA and Mobil Corporation. He is chairman of the Sales and Marketing Executives International (SMEI) Accreditation Institute and has been designated a Certified Sales Executive by SMEI. In 1990, he was named SMEI Marketing Educator of the Year. His articles have appeared in the *Journal of Marketing Research, Journal of Marketing, Journal of Personal Selling and Sales Management*, and many other journals and proceedings. Professor Ingram is editor of the *Journal of Personal Selling and Sales Management*.

Raymond W. LaForge (DBA, University of Tennessee) is Brown Forman Professor of Marketing at the University of Louisville. Dr. LaForge has been active in research, consulting, and seminar programs that focus on increasing sales productivity. His articles have appeared in a number of journals and proceedings, including the *Journal of Marketing Research, Decision Sciences, Journal of Business Research, Journal of Personal Selling and Sales Management*, and *Business Horizons*. He is founding editor of the *Marketing Education Review* and a member of the Editorial Review Board for the *Journal of Personal Selling and Sales Management*. Dr. LaForge holds the SMEI Certified Sales Executive designation.

BRIEF CONTENTS

CONTENTS

An Overview of Contemporary Sales Management

Chapter 1

Consider the following job announcement:

> WANTED: Need an individual that can plan, direct, and control the personal selling activities of a rapidly growing firm. Qualified applicant must be a sales forecaster, market analyst, strategic planner, student of buyer behavior, opportunity manager, intelligence gatherer, scarce-product allocator, accounts receivable collector, cost and profit analyst, budget manager, leader, and master communicator (both verbal and nonverbal). Duties will be performed in an environment characterized by high buyer expertise, high customer expectations, intense foreign competition, revolutionary changes in communications technology, and an influx of women and minorities into personal selling jobs.[1]

This job announcement provides an accurate description of a typical sales management position as we move through the 1990s to the twenty-first century. The days when a sales manager merely supervised the day-to-day activities of a few salespeople are long gone. Sales management today is a complex and demanding professional occupation, as evidenced by a day in the life of a top-level sales manager for a magazine publishing firm:

> I arrive at my office at 8:00 a.m., toss down my coffee, and begin the day. The first thing on my schedule is the reorganization of our sales operation to get better coverage of accounts, greater exposure of our products, and more effective monitoring of results. Then, the phone begins to ring with calls from regional and field sales managers concerning new sales opportunities, trade show plans, pricing questions, and a host of other issues. All of a sudden it is the afternoon, and I review some marketing research, tackle a stack of sales correspondence, review call reports, call a couple of our independent sales representatives, and examine sales commission printouts from the accounting department. Before I know it the day is over. I sit back and realize that as a sales manager, I am extremely active in recruiting, training, motivating, equipping, meeting, traveling with, compensating, evaluating, and rewarding our sales staffs.[2]

This exciting world of sales management is explored in the following manner in this text. First, the present chapter provides an overview of contemporary sales management, with a brief presentation of each stage in the sales management process, a discussion of different types of sales management positions and emerging sales management issues, and a description of the format used in the remaining chapters of the text. Then each area of sales management is covered in a separate chapter, with the goal of providing thorough, current, and interesting in-depth information and discussion.

FIGURE 1.1 ▪ *Sales Management Model*

The six major stages of sales management as presented in this model correspond to the six major parts of this textbook.

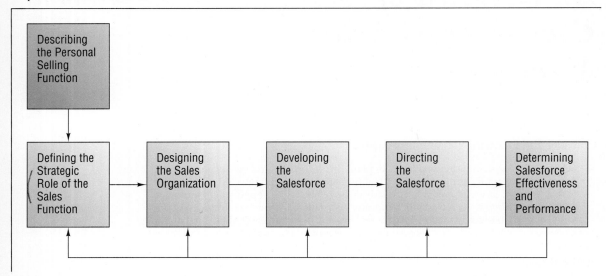

Sales Management Process

The promotional tools available to any firm are typically classified as personal selling, advertising, sales promotion, and publicity. *Personal selling* has been defined as direct communication with an audience through paid personnel of an organization or its agents in such a way that the audience perceives the communicator's organization as being the source of the message.[3] This definition differentiates personal selling from other promotional tools in two ways. First, personal selling is personal communication, whereas advertising and sales promotion are nonpersonal. Second, in personal selling the audience perceives the message as being delivered by the organization, whereas in publicity, even when it is in the form of personal communication, the audience typically perceives the media, not the organization, as being the source of the message.

Sales management is simply management of an organization's personal selling function. As the job announcement at the beginning of this chapter suggests, managing the personal selling function requires a large number of diverse activities. These activities can be classified into three major categories: planning, implementation, and control. Sales managers are involved in both the strategy (planning) and people (implementation) aspects of personal selling as well as in evaluating and controlling all personal selling activities. They must be able to deal effectively with people in the personal selling function, people in other functional areas in the organization, and with people outside the organization, especially customers. The sales management model presented in Figure 1.1 illustrates the major stages in the sales management process.

Describing the Personal Selling Function

Since sales managers are responsible for managing the personal selling function, they must thoroughly understand it. This text therefore devotes three chapters to that subject before discussing sales management activities. Chapter 2 ("An Overview of Personal Selling") presents a general discussion of contemporary personal selling, tracing its evolution from ancient times to the current era of the professional salesperson. The importance of personal selling to society, business firms, and customers is explained, and the diverse forms it can take are examined (that is, alternative approaches to selling and different types of sales jobs).

Chapter 3 ("Personal Selling: Job Activities and the Sales Process") investigates the various activities involved in personal selling in great detail. Although the basic job of salespeople is to sell, successful selling requires salespeople to be able to develop and maintain long-term relationships with accounts. Thus, salespeople perform management activities in their relationships with individual accounts and in managing their time and assigned territory. Salespeople are also normally engaged in various support activities for their firm, such as collecting market information, assisting in the recruitment and selection of salespeople, collecting past-due accounts, and so on. The selling activities of salespeople are presented as a series of interrelated steps used to initiate, develop, and enhance customer relationships.

The coverage of personal selling concludes with Chapter 4 ("Sales Careers: Characteristics, Qualifications, and Stages"), in which the basic characteristics of sales careers and the general qualifications for most sales positions are discussed. The progression of salespeople through different stages in a sales career is also examined. Then, the factors associated with promotion into sales management are investigated, along with an examination of typical career paths in personal selling and sales management.

Defining the Strategic Role of the Sales Function

Many firms in the contemporary business world consist of collections of relatively autonomous business units that market multiple products to diverse customer groups. These multiple-business, multiple-product firms must develop and integrate strategic decisions at different organizational levels. Chapter 5 ("Corporate, Business, and Marketing Strategies and the Sales Function") discusses the key strategic decisions at the corporate, business, and marketing levels and the basic relationships between these decisions and the personal selling and sales management functions. Corporate and business level strategic decisions typically provide guidelines within which sales managers and salespeople must operate. In contrast, personal selling is an important component of marketing strategies in specific product market situations. The role of personal selling in a given marketing strategy has direct and important implications for sales managers.

Strategic decisions at the corporate, business, and marketing levels must be translated into strategies for individual accounts. Chapter 6 ("Sales Strategy and the Sales Function") discusses two types of sales strategies: relationship strategy and sales channel strategy. Since personal selling is typically important in organizational marketing situations, an explanation of organizational buyer behavior is provided as a foundation for the development of sales strategies.

A *relationship strategy* entails decisions on developing, maintaining, and expanding relationships with accounts. Counselor, supplier, and systems designer relationship strategies are discussed. A *sales channel strategy* entails decisions on the best methods for providing selling effort coverage to accounts. In addition to regular field selling effort, firms might employ industrial distributors, independent representatives, team selling, telemarketing, and/or trade shows to provide selling effort coverage to different accounts.

Designing the Sales Organization

The development and integration of corporate, business, marketing, and sales strategies establishes the basic strategic direction for personal selling and sales management activities. However, an effective sales organization is necessary to implement these strategies successfully. Chapter 7 ("Organizing the Activities of Sales Managers and Salespeople") presents the basic concepts in designing an effective sales organization structure: specialization, centralization, span of control versus management levels, and line versus staff positions. Different decisions in any of these areas produce different sales organization structures. The appropriate structure for a firm depends upon the specific characteristics of a given selling situation. If major account selling programs are used, specific attention must be directed toward determining the best organizational structure for serving these major accounts.

Closely related to sales organization decisions are decisions on the amount and allocation of selling effort. Chapter 8 ("Allocating Selling Effort, Determining Salesforce Size, and Designing Territories") presents specific methods for making salesforce deployment decisions. Since the decisions on selling effort allocation, salesforce size, and territory design are interrelated, they should be addressed in an integrative manner. A number of different analytical approaches can assist in this endeavor, but "people" issues must also be considered.

Developing the Salesforce

The sales strategy, sales organization, and salesforce deployment decisions produce the basic structure for personal selling efforts and can be considered similar to the "machine" decisions in a production operation. Sales managers must also make a number of "people" decisions to ensure that the right types of salespeople are available and have the skills to operate the "machine" structure effectively and efficiently.

Chapter 9 ("Staffing the Salesforce: Recruitment and Selection") discusses the key activities involved in planning and executing salesforce recruitment and selection programs. These activities include determining the type of salespeople desired, identifying prospective salesperson candidates, and evaluating candidates to ensure that the best are hired. Legal and ethical issues are important considerations in the recruiting and selection process. The ramifications of this process for salespeople's subsequent adjustment to a new job (socialization) are also examined.

Chapter 10 ("Continual Development of the Salesforce: Sales Training") emphasizes the need for continuous training of salespeople and the important role that sales managers play in this activity. The sales training process consists of assessing training needs, developing objectives, evaluating alternatives, designing the training program, carrying it out, and evaluating it. Sales managers face difficult decisions at each stage of the sales training process, since it is not only extremely important but also expensive, and there are many sales training alternatives available.

Directing the Salesforce

Hiring the best salespeople and providing them with the skills required for success is one thing; directing their efforts to meet sales organization goals and objectives is another. Sales managers spend a great deal of their time in motivating, supervising, and leading members of the salesforce.

Chapter 11 ("Salesforce Motivation: Theories and Current Issues") presents several content and process theories of motivation that attempt to explain how individuals decide to spend effort on specific activities over extended periods of time. Sales managers can use these theories as a foundation for determining the best ways to get salespeople to spend the appropriate amount of time on the right activities over a period of time. Key issues in and general guidelines for salesforce motivation are also discussed.

Chapter 12 ("Managing Salesforce Reward Systems") builds on the previous discussion of motivation by focusing on the specific salesforce reward systems. Both the compensation type of rewards and the noncompensation types are examined. The advantages and disadvantages of different compensation programs are investigated as well as different methods for sales expense reimbursement. Specific guidelines for developing and managing a salesforce reward system are suggested.

Chapter 13 ("Sales Management Leadership and Supervision") distinguishes between the leadership and supervisory activities of a sales manager. *Leadership activities* focus on influencing salespeople through communication processes to attain specific goals and objectives. In contrast, *supervisory activities* are concerned with day-to-day control of the salesforce under routine operating conditions. The use of power and influence strategies is discussed in the context of an overall sales leadership model. Different styles of sales management are illustrated and key issues and problems in sales management leadership and supervision discussed.

Determining Salesforce Effectiveness and Performance

Sales managers must continually monitor the progress of the salesforce to determine current effectiveness and performance. This is a difficult task, since these evaluations should address both the effectiveness of different units within the sales organization as well as the performance of individual salespeople. Chapter 14 ("Developing Forecasts and Establishing Sales Quotas and Selling Budgets") provides the necessary background for effectiveness and performance evaluations. The different types of forecasts, the bottom-up and top-down forecasting approaches, and several sales forecasting methods are presented.

It is critically important that forecasts for developing sales quotas and selling budgets be accurate. *Sales quotas* represent specific sales goals that should be achieved by salespeople or sales organization units during a prescribed time period. *Selling budgets* consist of the financial resources that have been allocated to salespeople and sales organization units to achieve sales quotas and other objectives. Both sales quotas and selling budgets are often derived directly or indirectly from sales forecasts.

Chapter 15 ("Evaluating Sales Organization Effectiveness: Sales, Cost, Profitability, and Productivity Analysis") focuses on evaluating the effectiveness of sales organization units, such as territories, districts, regions, and zones. The *sales organization audit* is the most comprehensive approach for evaluating the effectiveness of the sales organization as a whole. Specific methods for assessing the effectiveness of different sales organization units with regard to sales, costs, profitability, and productivity are presented. Skill in using these different analyses helps a sales manager to diagnose specific problems and develop solutions to them.

Chapter 16 ("Evaluating Salesperson Performance and Job Satisfaction") changes the focus to evaluating the performance of people, both as individuals and in groups. These performance evaluations are used for a variety of purposes by sales managers. Specific criteria to be evaluated and different methods for providing the evaluative information are examined, and the use of this information in a diagnostic and problem-solving manner is described. A method for measuring salesperson job satisfaction, which is closely related to salesperson performance, is presented as well.

Sales Management Positions

The complexity of multibusiness, multiproduct firms and the diversity of strategies used by these firms result in many different types of sales management positions. Although these positions might be discussed in several ways, our discussion will be in terms of their level in the sales organization and the sales channel strategy.

Level in Sales Organization

Most sales organizations have hierarchical structures with different types of sales managers at different levels. One reasonably simple sales organization structure is illustrated in Figure 1.2. This structure has three levels of sales management and thus three different types of sales management positions. A firm with this structure would have to perform all of the sales management activities shown in Figure 1.1; sales managers at different levels would have different responsibilities and would focus on different activities.

Consider the example of David C. Moore, who has been a district sales manager, regional sales manager, and national sales manager for Drawing Board Greeting Cards. His experiences at each sales management level follow:[4]

The district sales manager represents the first level of "pure" sales management. As a district sales manager, I had no direct account responsibility (or, if you will, I had responsibility for *all* accounts in the district). I implemented/executed directives

FIGURE 1.2 ▪ *Example of Sales Organization Structure*

In this example of a sales organization structure, there are three levels of sales management and thus three different types of sales management positions.

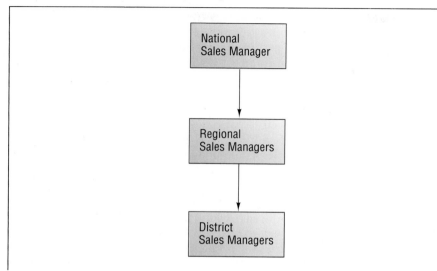

received from my regional sales manager. The majority of my time and effort was spent in building our district business by working with the salespeople in all types (and sizes) of accounts. I had hiring and firing responsibilities, subject to the approval of my regional sales manager. As a district manager, I, for the first time, faced the harsh reality that my success and continued career growth depended entirely upon my ability to motivate and manage salespeople rather than on my own efforts to secure and develop business for the company.

As a regional sales manager, I received my initial exposure to "chief decision-maker" status in the sales organization. For the first time, I had ultimate hiring and firing responsibilities. Direct contact via fieldwork with salespeople was less frequent, and most customer contacts occurred at the upper management echelons in major accounts. Because I was an interface/liaison between field district sales managers and corporate national sales management, the ability to communicate (both verbally and in written correspondence) became paramount in importance. One of the more difficult tasks associated with the regional sales manager position was maintaining a results-oriented environment while reinforcing the importance of the team concept to our mutual success. At least one day a week was occupied with strategic planning activities directed at improving the short- and long-term productivity of the territories and districts within the region.

The national sales manager is the chief head knocker in the field sales organization. The buck stops here! As national sales manager, I spent 75 percent of my working hours managing the salesforce and 25 percent on internal responsibilities ranging from product line reviews and sales forecasting to developing effective performance appraisals. I had little direct contact with salespeople but provided specific direction to the regional sales managers and would typically accompany them on major account calls when top management was in attendance. Personnel decisions made at the national sales manager level are extremely important (and I might add highly visible!) and impact large numbers of people and sales volume. One of my most difficult tasks at the national sales manager level was learning to delegate responsibility and authority effectively—and then holding subordinates accountable for their performance. This was made doubly difficult by the tremendous demands on my time from both the field sales organization and various support departments within the company.

As David C. Moore's experience attests, management skills increase in direct proportion to responsibilities within a sales organization. These skills are refined at lower sales management levels in preparation for promotions to senior level assignments with increased responsibilities. At the same time, the significance and importance of each decision is magnified the higher a person progresses up the corporate ladder.

Our focus in this text is typically on the position of *district sales manager* as a field sales manager working directly with salespeople in the field. Field sales managers perform a variety of different activities in monitoring, directing, evaluating, and rewarding the salespeople under their supervision. Exhibit 1.1 presents the results of a recent study that examined the importance of specific field sales management activities across 144 field salesforces in the United States. As indicated in the exhibit, the most important activities tend to be those related to close personal contact between field sales managers and salespeople.

This emphasis on field sales management does not restrict our coverage to the day-to-day activities of field sales managers. We think that it is important to understand the complete sales function and the basic relationships between different organizational strategies and the sales function. For example, the turbulent environment faced by many firms is forcing them to make major strategic changes on a continual basis. The success of these strategic changes often depends upon proper restructuring of the sales function. This restructuring can affect all levels of the sales function, including the activities performed by field sales managers and the salespeople they supervise. This close relationship between environmental turbulence, organizational strategic change, and restructuring of the sales function is exemplified by recent actions taken by Schaeffer Eaton, Campbell Soup, Xerox, and many other firms.[5] The importance of these relationships to field sales managers is illustrated in the discussion of sales channel strategy in the next section.

Sales Channel Strategy

Our description of sales management positions at different sales organization levels assumes that the personal selling effort is provided by a field salesforce that makes personal sales calls to accounts. This assumption is reasonable for most firms today, but many are beginning to employ sales channels other than the typical field personal selling. As these new sales channels replace field selling or are integrated with field selling, sales management responsibilities and activities will change. Oftentimes, new sales management positions must be created.

Recent research investigates the increasing use of major account and telemarketing sales channels by many firms.[6] These new sales channels are being employed as a means of controlling the rapidly rising costs of field selling, as a way to respond to the changing buying habits and service requirements of accounts, and as a potential avenue for securing competitive advantages. An example of using the information contained herein should prove extremely relevant to those who begin their careers in personal selling and progress through the ranks of sales management.

Notes

[1]The job characteristics and environmental situations are adapted from Rolph E. Anderson and Bert Rosenbloom, "Eclectic Sales Management: Strategic Response to Trends in the Eighties," *Journal of Personal Selling and Sales Management*, November 1982, 41–46; and Bert Rosenbloom and Rolph E. Anderson, "The Sales Manager: Tomorrow's Super Marketer," *Business Horizons*, March–April 1984, 50–56.

[2]Adapted from "Publisher's Side Pocket," *Sales and Marketing Management*, March 1990, 5.

[3]This definition is taken from David W. Cravens, Gerald E. Hills, and Robert B. Woodruff, *Marketing Management* (Homewood, Ill.: Irwin, 1987), 487.

[4]This description is taken from materials provided by David C. Moore in January 1991. Mr. Moore is no longer with Drawing Board Greeting Cards, and the company is now Carlton Cards, which is a wholly owned subsidiary of American Greetings Corporation.

[5]See David W. Cravens, Raymond W. LaForge, and Thomas N. Ingram, "Sales Strategy: Charting a New Course in Turbulent Markets," *Business*, October–December 1990, 3–9, for a more complete discussion and specific examples of these relationships.

[6]This discussion is taken from Richard N. Cardozo, Shannon H. Shipp, and Kenneth J. Roering, "Implementing New Business-to-Business Selling Methods," *Journal of Personal Selling and Sales Management*, August 1987, 17–26; Richard Cardozo and Shannon Shipp, "New Selling Methods Are Changing Industrial Sales Management," *Business Horizons*, September–October 1987, 23–28; and Rowland T. Moriarity and Ursula Moran, "Managing Hybrid Marketing Systems," *Harvard Business Review*, November–December 1990, 146–155.

[7]Reported in Richard Cardozo and Shannon Shipp, "New Selling Methods Are Changing Industrial Sales Management," *Business Horizons*, September–October 1987, 27.

Part One

Describing the Personal Selling Function

The three chapters in Part One describe the personal selling function. A clear understanding of personal selling is essential to gain a proper perspective of the issues facing sales managers. In Chapter 2, the historical evolution of selling is presented, along with a contemporary look at the contributions of personal selling to our economic and social system. In addition, classifications of the various approaches to personal selling and types of personal selling jobs are discussed.

Chapter 3 reviews the key job activities of salespeople. In addition to selling, salespeople are involved in time and territory management, assisting sales managers, and providing support for other organizational activities. This chapter also reviews the sales process.

In Chapter 4, sales careers are discussed, including the characteristics of sales jobs, the skills and human characteristics necessary for success in sales and sales management, and the career paths typical in sales.

An Overview of Personal Selling

A MAJOR SALE TO E.I. DU PONT DE NEMOURS & CO.
Guy Anderson, a sales executive with Atlanta-based Stockholder Systems Inc., spent almost two years selling Du Pont a new record-keeping system. Working hard throughout the prolonged period required to make the sale was well worth it for Anderson and his company, as the total sale was a million and a half dollars. Anderson established a strong relationship with Bob Kearney, Du Pont's manager of stockholder relations, to make the sale.

When a company the size of Du Pont decides to change its stockholder record-keeping system, the resulting sales situation is quite complex. In the beginning of the sales process, Du Pont analyzed all possible vendors in terms of how each could meet the company's needs. Guy Anderson used this time to get to know the key Du Pont decision makers and their specific requirements for the system. Anderson commented, "When you get into a complex sale, you're dealing with a lot of different personalities and the different objectives of the groups involved."

Kearney recalls Anderson's role: "Guy would call regularly and ask how we were progressing, if there was anything I needed, would I like him to bring anyone else in to talk with me, would we be able to get the funding we needed, etc. He introduced us to some of his clients and invited us to symposiums where we saw the product demonstrated."

By the end of the evaluation period, Anderson had built a competitive edge over the competition. He had sold Du Pont, not only on the product, but just as importantly on his ability to provide necessary follow-up and postsale service. Anderson beat out four competitors to earn the sale. "We had seen so much of Guy, we knew him well," said Kearney. "We felt very comfortable with him and his product."

After the contract was signed with Du Pont, Anderson focused on providing complete customer satisfaction. He does not want to lose his well-earned contract to competition, so he stays in touch regularly, providing appropriate information and service. Kearney notes that Guy "checks in like clockwork" to ensure that the system is working according to Du Pont's expectations. Noting that he has often gained business when a competitor's service falters, Anderson certainly understands the importance of customer follow-up and timely service throughout the sales process.

Source: *The Selling Advantage* 1, No. 6 (1989): 3.

Learning Objectives

After completing this chapter, you should be able to

1 *Describe the evolution of personal selling from ancient times to the modern era.*

2 *Explain the contributions of personal selling to society, business firms, and customers.*

3 *Discuss five alternative approaches to personal selling.*

4 *Describe different types of personal selling jobs.*

Evolution of Personal Selling

The successful professional salesperson of today and the future is quite likely a better listener than a talker, is more oriented toward developing long-term relationships with customers than placing an emphasis on high-pressure, short-term sales techniques, and has the skills and patience to endure lengthy, complex sales processes. In earning the Du Pont account, Guy Anderson displayed these qualities of a sales professional.

Personal selling, as represented by professionals like Guy Anderson, has evolved into a quite different activity than it was merely a few decades ago. Throughout this course you will learn about new technologies and techniques that have contributed to this evolution. This chapter provides an overview of personal selling, affording insight into the operating rationale of today's salespeople and sales managers. In the highly competitive, complex environment of the world business community, personal selling and sales management have never played more critical roles.

Early Origins of Personal Selling

Ancient Greek history documents selling as an exchange activity, and the term *salesman* appears in the writings of Plato.[1] However, true salespeople, those who earned a living only by selling, did not exist in any sizable number until the Industrial Revolution in England, from the mid-eighteenth century to the mid-nineteenth century. Prior to this time, traders, merchants, and artisans filled the selling function. These predecessors of contemporary marketers were generally viewed with contempt since deception was often employed in the sale of goods.[2]

In the latter phase of the Middle Ages, the first door-to-door salesperson appeared in the form of the peddler. Peddlers collected produce from local farmers, sold it to townspeople, and, in turn, bought manufactured goods in town for subsequent sale in rural areas.[3] Like many other early salespeople, they performed other important marketing functions—in this case, purchase, assembly, sorting, and redistribution of goods.

The emergence of the *guild system* represented an important development in the evolution of personal selling. Made up of associations of merchants and artisans, the guild system had the effect of uniting competition and discouraging sales expeditions into new geographic areas. However, it also made a positive contribution to personal selling because the high ethical standards espoused by the guilds elevated the social status of all business people.

Industrial Revolution Era

As the Industrial Revolution began to blossom in the middle of the eighteenth century, the economic justification for salespeople gained momentum. Local economies were no longer self-sufficient, and as intercity and international trade began to flourish, economies of scale in production spurred the growth of mass markets in geographically dispersed areas. The continual need to reach new customers in these dispersed markets called for an increasing number of salespeople.

While acting as an agent of innovation, the salesperson invariably encounters a strong resistance to change in the latter stages of the diffusion process. The status quo seems to be extremely satisfactory to many parties, even though, in the long run, change is necessary for continued progress or survival. By encouraging the adoption of innovative products and services, salespeople may indeed be making a positive contribution to society. For example, our educational system has been improved by the addition of computers to the classroom, a development that would have been delayed indefinitely without the efforts of salespeople.

Salespeople and the Employing Firm

A chapter in this book details the job activities of salespeople, but at this point, we will discuss the more general contributions of salespeople to their firms—as revenue producers, as sources of market research and feedback, and as candidates for management positions.

Salespeople as Revenue Producers. Sales managers and salespeople rally around the common slogan of "we bring in the money . . . everybody else is just overhead." This slogan has taken on literal meaning in recent years with corporations such as IBM and Digital Equipment Corporation, with massive redeployment to their sales organizations from other functional areas. Digital CEO Kenneth Olsen, commenting on the shift of 3,000 to 4,000 technicians and engineers into sales positions, said, "We want more salespeople with less overhead."[18]

Salespeople do occupy the somewhat unique role as the **revenue producers** in their firms. Consequently, they usually feel the brunt of that pressure along with the management of the firm. While accountants and financial staff are concerned with profitability in bottom-line terms, salespeople are constantly reminded of their responsibility to achieve a healthy "top line" on the profit and loss statement. Their goals are thus distinguished by their narrower focus on revenue production.

Market Research and Feedback. Since salespeople spend so much time in direct contact with their customers, it is only logical that they would play an important role in market research and in providing feedback to their firms. For example, salespeople for General Foods visit grocery stores in their territories daily, where they scan the shelves, collect data, and respond to specific questions furnished by their sales managers. They record the information on hand-held computers and transmit it back to headquarters where the information is integrated into the company's management information system.[19] This enables General Foods to utilize the most recent field information to design sales strategies and other promotional programs.

Some would argue that salespeople are not trained as market researchers, or that salespeople's time could be better utilized than in research and feedback activities. Many firms, however, refute this argument by finding numerous ways to capitalize upon the salesforce as a reservoir of ideas. It is not an exaggeration to say that many firms have concluded that they cannot afford to operate in the absence of salesforce feedback and research.

Salespeople as Future Managers. In recent years, marketing and sales personnel have been in strong demand for upper management positions. Recognizing the need for a top management trained in sales, many firms use the sales job as an entry-level position that provides a foundation for future assignments.[20] The dominance of former salespeople in top management has been cited as the key reason for the success of IBM, Frito-Lay, Procter and Gamble, and Domino's Pizza, among other top firms.[21] As progressive firms continue to emphasize customer orientation as a basic operating concept, it is only natural that salespeople who have learned how to meet customer needs will be good candidates for management jobs.

As competition intensifies, salespeople will continue to be valuable human resources. While they make important contributions as salespeople, many will make even more significant contributions as top managers in customer-oriented firms.

Salespeople and the Customer

Extensive research by Learning International, a large training and consulting firm, reveals the expectations that buyers have of salespeople. According to respondents of a Learning International survey, buyers like to deal with salespeople who

- Understand general business and economic trends, as well as the buyer's business
- Provide guidance throughout the sales process
- Help the buyer to solve problems
- Have a pleasant personality and a good professional appearance
- Coordinate all aspects of the product and service to provide a total package[22]

These expectations are consistent with other surveys of buyer expectations of salespeople that span several years.[23] The overall conclusion is that buyers expect salespeople to contribute to the success of the buyer's firm. Buyers value the information furnished by salespeople, and, more than ever before, they value the problem-solving skills of salespeople.

The importance of providing customers with knowledgeable, customer-oriented salespeople is well understood by Federal Express, one of the great success stories in recent business history. Bill Razzouk, vice-president of U.S. sales for Federal Express, points out that every employee of the company must fulfill a sales role. Mr. Razzouk says that Federal Express officers spend time in the field with salespeople and customers to learn more about what customers want and need. The benefits accrue to both customers and to Federal Express when customer needs are more closely met.[24]

As salespeople serve their customers, they simultaneously serve their employers and society. When the interests of these parties conflict, the salesperson can be caught in the midst. By learning to resolve these conflicts as a routine part of their jobs, salespeople further contribute to developing a business system based on progress through problem solving. An important part of resolving potential conflict between customers and salespeople is to have a customer-oriented code of ethics for salespeople. An example of such a code is shown in "An Ethical Perspective: The Equitable Financial Companies Policy Statement on Ethics."

Classification of Personal Selling Approaches

Over 20 years ago, four basic approaches to personal selling were identified: stimulus-response, mental-states, need-satisfaction, and problem-solving.[25] Since that time, another approach to personal selling, termed contingency selling, has gained popularity. All five approaches to selling are practiced today. Furthermore, many salespeople use elements of more than one approach in their own hybrids of personal selling.

Some salespeople use no conscious approach to their sales efforts. But most successful salespeople do benefit from at least a rudimentary working knowledge of the different views of selling.

Stimulus-Response Selling

Of the five views of personal selling, **stimulus-response selling** is the simplest. The theoretical background for this approach originated in early experiments with animal behavior. The key idea is that various stimuli can elicit predictable responses. Salespeople furnish the stimuli from a repertoire of words and actions designed to produce the desired response. This approach to selling is illustrated in Figure 2.1.

An example of the stimulus-response view of selling would be **continued affirmation,** a method in which a series of questions or statements furnished by the salesperson is designed to condition the prospective buyer to answering "yes" time after time, until, it is hoped, he or she will be inclined to say "yes" to the entire

---

AN ETHICAL PERSPECTIVE

The Equitable Financial Companies Policy Statement on Ethics   Policy statements and codes for ethical sales behavior are becoming a more integral part of sales training programs as salespeople and sales managers are increasingly being held accountable for their actions in the field. The following items were excerpted from The Equitable Financial Companies Policy Statement on Ethics:

▪ The Equitable's reputation for integrity is tested every day by the way you treat clients. Honesty, fairness, and keeping commitments must be hallmarks of the way you do business.

▪ Sell products on their merits. Describe them truthfully without exaggeration, pointing out their benefits but also making clear their risks and costs.

▪ Explain contracts, products, and investment opportunities clearly. Clients should not be surprised by finding provisions or conditions about which they were not informed.

▪ Ensure that commitments are honored and that all your clients receive the highest quality service that you can provide.

Source: The Equitable Financial Companies Policy Statement on Ethics.

FIGURE 2.1 ▪ *Stimulus-Response Approach to Selling*

The salesperson attempts to gain favorable responses from the customer by providing stimuli, or cues, to influence the buyer. After the customer has been properly conditioned, the salesperson tries to secure a positive purchase decision.

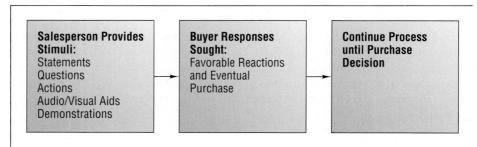

sales proposition. This method is often employed by telemarketing personnel, who rely on comprehensive sales scripts read or delivered from memory.

Stimulus-response sales strategies, particularly when implemented with a canned sales presentation, have some advantages for the seller. The sales message can be structured in a logical order. Questions and objections from the buyer can usually be anticipated and addressed before they are magnified during buyer-seller interaction. Inexperienced salespeople can rely on stimulus-response sales methods in some settings, and this may eventually contribute to sales expertise.

The limitations of stimulus-response methods, however, can be severe, especially if the salesperson is dealing with a professional buyer. Most buyers like to take an active role in sales dialogue, and the stimulus-response approach calls for the salesperson to dominate the flow of conversation. The lack of flexibility in this approach is also a disadvantage, as buyer responses and unforeseen interruptions may neutralize or damage the effectiveness of the stimuli.

Considering the net effects of this method's advantages and disadvantages, it appears most suitable for relatively unimportant purchase decisions, when time is severely constrained, and when professional buyers are not the prospects. As consumers in general become more sophisticated, this approach will become more problematic.

Mental-States Selling

Mental-states selling, or the *formula approach* to personal selling, assumes that the buying process for most buyers is essentially identical and that buyers can be led through certain mental states, or steps, in the buying process. These mental states are typically referred to as **AIDA** (attention, interest, desire, and action).[26] Appropriate sales messages provide a transition from one mental state to the next.

Like stimulus-response selling, the mental-states approach relies on a highly structured sales presentation. The salesperson does most of the talking, as feedback from the prospect could be disruptive to the flow of the presentation.

A positive feature of this method is that it forces the salesperson to plan the sales presentation prior to calling on the customer. It also helps the salesperson

EXHIBIT 2.2   ▪   *Mental-States View of Selling*

Mental State	Sales Step	Critical Sales Task
Curiosity	Attention	Get prospects excited, then get them to like you
Interest	Interest	Interview: needs and wants
Conviction	Conviction	"What's in it for me?" Product—"Will it do what I want it to do?" Price—"Is it worth it?" "The hassle of change?" "Cheaper elsewhere?" Peers—"What will others think of it?" Priority—"Do I need it now?" (sense of urgency)
Desire	Desire	Overcome their stall
Action	Close	Alternate choice close: which, not if!

Source: Adapted from D. Forbes Ley, *The Best Seller* (Newport Beach, Calif.: Sales Success Press, 1986).

recognize that timing is an important element in the purchase-decision process, and that careful listening is necessary to determine which stage the buyer is in at a given point in time. The mental-states approach to personal selling has been popular with sales trainers, perhaps because it is easy to formulate major selling points around the attention, interest, desire, and action states.

A problem with the mental-states method is that it is very difficult to determine which state a prospect is in. Sometimes a prospect is spanning two mental states or moving back and forth between two states during the sales presentation. Consequently, the heavy guidance structure the salesperson implements may be inappropriate, confusing, and even counterproductive to sales effectiveness. We should also note that this method is not customer-oriented. Although the salesperson tailors the presentation to each customer somewhat, this is done by noting customer mental states rather than needs.

The mental-states, or formula, approach to personal selling is very popular in consumer and industrial sales. One interesting account of this approach is furnished by the Glass Container Group of the Ball Corporation. This firm's sales strategy is based on moving through several stages over a time period that can extend into years. It is founded on the premise that the most important goal in communicating is getting the prospect to listen. This corresponds to the attention stage of AIDA. From the attention-gaining platform, Ball attempts to interest the potential customer in its company as a potential supplier, then it "moves the script along" to an ultimate "lift-off," where the buyer makes a positive decision regarding Ball.[27]

The mental-states method is illustrated in Exhibit 2.2. Note that this version includes "conviction" as an intermediate stage between interest and desire. Such minor variations are commonplace in different renditions of this approach to selling.

FIGURE 2.2 ▪ *Need-Satisfaction Approach to Selling*

The salesperson attempts to uncover customer needs that are related to the salesperson's product or service offering. This may require extensive questioning in the early stages of the sales process. After confirming the buyer's needs, the salesperson proceeds with a presentation based on how the offering can meet those needs.

Need-Satisfaction Selling

Need-satisfaction selling is based on the notion that the customer is buying to satisfy a particular need or set of needs. This approach is shown in Figure 2.2. It is the salesperson's task to identify the need to be met, then to help the buyer meet the need. Unlike the mental-states and stimulus-response methods, this method focuses on the customer rather than on the salesperson. The salesperson utilizes a questioning, probing tactic to uncover important buyer needs. Customer responses dominate the early portion of the sales interaction, and only after relevant needs have been established does the salesperson begin to relate how his or her offering can satisfy these needs.

Customers seem to appreciate this selling method and are often willing to spend considerable time in preliminary meetings to define needs prior to a sales presentation or written sales proposal. Also, this method avoids the defensiveness that arises in some prospects when a salesperson rushes to the persuasive part of the sales message without adequate attention to the buyer's needs.

As originally conceived, need-satisfaction selling was meant to create a friendly, low-pressure environment for communication between the buyer and seller in which the salesperson would be perceived as a trusted source of information and advice. In recent years, a version of need-satisfaction selling called *nonmanipulative selling* has gained favor with sales trainers. The conversational framework of this method directs salespeople to spend more time on determining prospect needs and wants than on any other part of the sales process.[28]

Although critics charge that the time expenditure in needs-satisfaction selling is too great in both training and time away from actual "selling," the method is nevertheless well entrenched in business practice today. One study attesting to its potency was conducted by Learning International and found that the more successful salespeople were able to[29]

▪ Ask questions to uncover needs
▪ Recognize when customers have real needs and show how their products or services could satisfy the needs
▪ Present the benefits of the product or service so that the customers see how their needs will be satisfied

grocery industry. There are strong similarities between sales missionaries and religious missionaries. Like their counterparts, sales missionaries are expected to "spread the word" with the purpose of conversion—to customer status. Once converted, the customer receives reinforcing messages, new information, and the benefit of the missionary's activities to strengthen the relationship between buyer and seller.

In the pharmaceutical industry, the **detailer** is a fixture. Major corporations utilize the detailer to support the sales effort at crucial junctures in the channel of distribution. Detailers working at the physician level furnish valuable information regarding the capabilities and limitations of medications in an attempt to get the physician to prescribe their product. Another sales representative from the same pharmaceutical company will sell the medication to the wholesaler or pharmacist, but it is the detailer's job to support the direct sales effort by calling on physicians.

Technical specialists are sometimes considered to be sales support personnel. These **technical support salespeople** may assist in design and specification processes, installation of equipment, training of the customer's employees, and follow-up service of a technical nature. They are sometimes part of a sales team that includes another salesperson who specializes in identifying and satisfying customer needs by recommending the appropriate product or service.

New Business

New business is generated for the selling firm by adding new customers or introducing new products to the marketplace. Two types of new-business salespeople are pioneers and order-getters.

Pioneers, as the term suggests, are constantly involved with either new products, new customers, or both. Their task requires creative selling and the ability to counter the resistance to change that will likely be present in prospective customers. Pioneers are well represented in the sale of business franchises, where the sales representatives travel from city to city seeking new franchisees. They are also found in consumer and industrial firms, where new accounts are turned over to another salesperson once the pioneer has established the buyer-seller relationship.

Order-getters are salespeople who actively seek orders, usually in a highly competitive environment. While all pioneers are also order-getters, the reverse is not true. An order-getter may serve existing customers on an ongoing basis, whereas the pioneer moves on to new customers as soon as possible. Order-getters may seek new business by selling an existing customer additional items from the product line. A well-known tactic is to establish a relationship with a customer by selling a single product from the line, then to follow up with subsequent sales calls for other items from the product line.

Most corporations emphasize sales growth, and salespeople operating as pioneers and order-getters are at the heart of sales-growth objectives. The pressure to perform in these roles is fairly intense; the results are highly visible. For these reasons, the new-business salesperson is often among the elite in any company's salesforce.

Existing Business

In direct contrast to new-business salespeople, other salespeople's primary responsibility is to maintain relationships with existing customers. These salespeople are no less valuable to their firms than the new-business salespeople, but creative selling skills are less important to this category of sales personnel. Their strengths tend to be reliability and competence in assuring customer convenience. Customers grow to depend on the services provided by this type of salesperson. As most markets are becoming more competitive, the role of existing business salespeople is sometimes critical to prevent erosion of the customer base.

Many firms, believing that it is easier to protect and maintain profitable customers than it is to find replacement customers, are reinforcing sales efforts to existing customers. A classic example of thwarting competitive efforts through stressing the importance of existing customers occurred when American Hospital Supply Corporation introduced its ASAP (analytical systems automated purchasing) systems. In a nutshell, these systems made it hard for hospitals to switch to another purchasing system after they had become accustomed to the superior features of the ASAP system.[33] In a slow market for hospital admissions, placing priority on serving existing business proved to be an astute move for American Hospital.

Salespeople who specialize in maintaining existing business include **order-takers.** These salespeople frequently work for wholesalers, and as the term *order-taker* implies, they are not too involved in creative selling. Route salespeople who work an established customer base, taking routine reorders of stock items, are order-takers. They sometimes follow a pioneer salesperson and take over the account after the pioneer has made the initial sale.

Inside Sales

In this text, **inside sales** refers to non-retail salespeople who remain in their employer's place of business while dealing with customers. The inside-sales operation has received considerable attention in recent years, not only as a supplementary sales tactic, but also as an alternative to field selling.

Inside sales can be conducted on an active or passive sales basis. Active inside sales include the solicitation of entire orders, either as part of a telemarketing operation or when customers walk into the seller's facilities. Passive inside sales imply the acceptance, rather than solicitation of, customer orders, although it is common practice for these transactions to include add-on sales attempts. We should note that customer service personnel sometimes function as inside-sales personnel as an ongoing part of their jobs.

Direct-to-Consumer Sales

Direct-to-consumer salespeople are the most numerous type. There are over 4 million retail salespeople in this country and perhaps another million selling real estate, insurance, and securities. Add to this figure another several million selling direct to the consumer for companies such as Tupperware, Mary Kay, and Avon.

This diverse category of salespeople ranges from the part-time, often temporary salesperson in a retail store to the highly educated, professionally trained stockbroker on Wall Street. As a general statement, the more challenging direct-to-consumer sales positions are those involving the sale of intangible services such as insurance and financial services.

Combination Sales Jobs

Now that we have reviewed some of the basic types of sales job, let us consider the salesperson who performs multiple types of sales jobs within the framework of a single position. We will use the case of the territory manager's position with Beecham Products, U.S.A., to illustrate the **combination sales job** concept. Beecham, whose products include Aqua-Fresh toothpaste, markets a wide range of consumer goods to food, drug, variety, and mass merchandisers. The territory manager's job blends responsibilities for developing new business, maintaining and stimulating existing business, and performing sales support activities.

During a typical day in the field, the Beecham territory manager is involved in sales support activities such as merchandising and in-store promotion at the individual retail store level. Maintaining contact and goodwill with store personnel is another routine sales support activity. The territory manager also makes sales calls on chain headquarters personnel to handle existing business and to seek new business. And it is the territory manager who introduces new Beecham products in the marketplace.

Summary

1. **Describe the evolution of personal selling from ancient times to the modern era.** The history of personal selling can be traced as far back as ancient Greece. The Industrial Revolution enhanced the importance of salespeople, and personal selling as we know it today had its roots in the early twentieth century. The current era of sales professionalism represents a further evolution.

2. **Explain the contributions of personal selling to society, business firms, and customers.** Salespeople contribute to society by acting as stimuli in the economic process and by assisting in the diffusion of innovation. They contribute to their employers by producing revenue, performing research and feedback activities, and by comprising a pool of future managers. They contribute to customers by providing timely knowledge to assist in solving problems.

3. **Discuss five alternative approaches to personal selling.** Alternative approaches to personal selling include stimulus-response, mental-states, need-satisfaction, problem-solving, and the contingency approach. Stimulus-response selling often utilizes the same sales presentation for all customers. The mental-states approach prescribes that the salesperson lead the buyer through stages in the buying process. Need-satisfaction selling focuses on relating benefits of the seller's products or services to the buyer's particular situation. Problem-solving selling extends need-satisfaction by concentrating on various alternatives

available to the buyer. In the contingency approach, the salesperson adapts to the situation, utilizing whichever sales methods are most appropriate.

4. **Describe different types of personal selling jobs.** Among the countless number of different personal selling jobs are the following six types: sales support, new business, existing business, inside sales (non-retail), direct-to-consumer sales, and combination jobs. Sales support positions include missionary or detail salespeople and technical support salespeople. Two types of new-business salespeople are pioneers and order-getters. The primary responsibility of existing-business salespeople is to maintain relationships with present customers through routine sales calls and follow-up. Inside sales in non-retail settings is typified in telemarketing operations and is also used to handle walk-in sales transactions. Direct-to-consumer sales include retail selling, as well as the sale of insurance, securities, and real estate. Combination sales jobs are commonplace and may combine new-business selling with sales support and existing-business responsibilities, as shown in the Beecham Products example. Other combinations are also frequently encountered.

Key Terms

- **Canned sales presentation**
- **Sales professionalism**
- **Cost per sales call index**
- **Economic stimuli**
- **Diffusion of innovation**
- **Revenue producers**
- **Stimulus-response selling**
- **Continued affirmation**
- **Mental-states selling**
- **AIDA**
- **Need-satisfaction selling**

- **Problem-solving selling**
- **Contingency approach**
- **Sales support personnel**
- **Missionary salespeople**
- **Detail salespeople**
- **Technical support salespeople**
- **Pioneers**
- **Order-getters**
- **Order-takers**
- **Inside sales**
- **Combination sales jobs**

Review Questions

1. What factors will influence the continued evolution of personal selling?
2. How do salespeople contribute to our society? Are there negative aspects of personal selling from a societal perspective?
3. What are the primary contributions made by salespeople to their employers?
4. Most businesses would have a difficult time surviving without the benefits of the salespeople who call on them. Do you agree?
5. Review the boxed insert in this chapter entitled "An Ethical Perspective: The Equitable Financial Companies Policy Statement on Ethics." What additional policies dealing with sales ethics could you suggest to ensure a customer-oriented, truthful sales approach?

6. How are need-satisfaction and problem-solving selling related? How do they differ?

7. The contingency approach to personal selling can incorporate the other approaches to selling within its framework. Give an example of how one of the other views of personal selling might be utilized within the contingency framework.

8. When do you think stimulus-response selling would be most effective?

9. What are the differences in key responsibilities of missionary salespeople and pioneer salespeople? What recurring problems would you expect each type to encounter as they call on their customers?

10. Review the boxed insert in this chapter entitled "A Global Perspective: Honeywell's Denzil Plomer Provides Right Solutions." Do you think that Mr. Plomer goes too far with the idea of being customer-oriented when he recommends a solution that his company could not currently provide?

Application Exercises

1. Assume you are a telemarketing sales representative for a residential lawncare company. Using the stimulus-response approach, plan a sales presentation designed to persuade a homeowner to utilize your service, which involves four equally priced applications of fertilizer and weed killer on an annual basis. The presentation, to be conducted by telephone, should not last over two minutes.

2. a. The contingency sales approach requires adapting to differing situations, including the buyer's personality. For each of the following personality traits, discuss how a salesperson might react to facilitate the sale.
 ▪ Argumentative
 ▪ Hesitant
 ▪ Impulsive
 ▪ Decisive
 ▪ Procrastinator

b. The need-satisfaction, problem-solving, and contingency approaches to selling recognize that customer motives may differ. For each of the following buyers of liquid carpet cleaner, list the most likely concerns or motives that must be addressed by the salesperson.
 ▪ Hardware store owner
 ▪ Purchasing agent for a janitorial-supplies wholesaler
 ▪ Manager of a municipal airport

3. Visit your library and locate five articles that portray negative aspects of salespeople and five that portray positive aspects. What factors seem to contribute to the image of salespeople in general? How does the image of salespeople affect sales management? (Note: To complete this assignment, consult popular magazines and newspapers rather than trade periodicals or academic journals.)

Notes

[1] Marjorie J. Caballero, Roger A. Dickinson, and Dabney Townsend, "Aristotle and Personal Selling," *Journal of Personal Selling and Sales Management* 4 (May 1984): 13–18.

[2] William T. Kelley, "The Development of Early Thought in Marketing," in *Salesmanship: Selected Readings*, ed. John M. Rathmell (Homewood, Ill.: Irwin, 1969), 3.

[3] Thomas L. Powers, Warren S. Martin, Hugh Rushing, and Scott Daniels, "Selling Before 1900: A Historical Perspective," *Journal of Personal Selling and Sales Management* 7 (November 1987): 5. For additional review of personal selling from the period 1600 to the present era, see Robert Desman and Terry E. Powell, "Personal Selling: Chicken or Egg," in *Proceedings*, 13th Annual Conference of the Academy of Marketing Science, ed. Jon M. Hawes (Orlando, 1989).

[4] Michael Bell, *The Salesman in the Field* (Geneva: International Labour Office, 1980), 1.

[5] Stanley C. Hollander, "Anti-Salesman Ordinances of the Mid-19th Century," in Rathmell, *Salesmanship*, 9.

[6] Ibid., 10.

[7]Jon M. Hawes, "Leaders in Selling and Sales Management," *Journal of Personal Selling and Sales Management* 5 (November 1985): 60.

[8]Charles W. Hoyt, *Scientific Sales Management* (New Haven, Conn.: George W. Woolson and Co., 1913), 3–4.

[9]Ibid., 4.

[10]Edward C. Bursk, "Low-Pressure Selling," *Harvard Business Review* 25 (Winter 1947): 227–242.

[11]Roy E. Chitwood, *Futuresell: A Selling Guide for the 21st Century Salesperson* (Max Sacks International, 1989), 1.

[12]Arthur Bragg, "Listen Up," *Sales and Marketing Management*, February 1990, 10.

[13]Synthesized from "Selling in the 1990s: A Sales Productivity Report" (Boston: The Forum Corporation, 1989); "How the Game Will Change in the 1990s," *Sales and Marketing Management*, June 1989, 52–61; David W. Cravens, Thomas N. Ingram, and Raymond W. LaForge, "Evaluating Multiple Sales Channel Strategies," *Journal of Business and Industrial Marketing* (forthcoming); and Thomas N. Ingram, "Improving Sales Force Productivity: A Critical Examination of the Personal Selling Process," *Review of Business* (forthcoming).

[14]William M. Pride and O. C. Ferrell, *Marketing*, 6th ed. (Boston: Houghton Mifflin Co., 1989) 512. For a survey that indicates the importance of personal selling, see Kenneth Traynor and Susan C. Traynor, "Marketing Approaches Used by High Tech Firms," *Industrial Marketing Management*, November 1989, 281–287.

[15]"1990 Survey of Selling Costs," *Sales and Marketing Management*, February 26, 1990, 79.

[16]Joseph A. Bellizzi, A. Frank Thompson, and Lynn J. Loudenback, "Cyclical Variations of Advertising and Personal Selling," *Journal of the Academy of Marketing Science* 11 (Spring 1983): 142–155.

[17]Allan J. McGrath, "The Preeminence of Selling," *Sales and Marketing Management*, January 1990, 16.

[18]Leslie Helm, "DEC Has One Little Word for 30,000 Employees: Sell," *Business Week*, August 1989, 86.

[19]Ed Rubenstein, "Food Manufacturers Discover the Value of Intelligence Systems," *Marketing News*, August 15, 1989, 11.

[20]Alan J. Dubinsky and Thomas N. Ingram, "Important First-Line Qualifications: What Sales Executives Think," *Journal of Personal Selling and Sales Management* 3 (May 1983): 18–26.

[21]Thomas J. Peters and Nancy K. Austin, *A Passion for Excellence* (New York: Random House, 1985), 107.

[22]"Profiles in Customer Loyalty," (Stamford, Conn.: Learning International, 1989), 22–24.

[23]Alvin J. Williams and John Seminerio, "What Buyers Like from Salesmen," *Industrial Marketing Management* 14 (May 1985): 75–78.

[24]Gerhard Gschwandter, "Secrets of Sales Success at Federal Express," *Personal Selling Power*, January–February 1990, 15.

[25]Robert F. Gwinner, "Base Theory in the Formulation of Sales Strategy," *MSU Business Topics*, Autumn 1968, 37–44.

[26]Allan L. Reid, *Modern Applied Selling* (Englewood Cliffs, N.J.: Prentice-Hall, 1990), 175–177.

[27]Clayton J. Reichard, "Industrial Selling: Beyond Price and Persistence," *Harvard Business Review* 63 (March–April 1985): 127–133.

[28]Tony Alessandra, Phil Wexler, and Rick Barrera, *Non-Manipulative Selling*, 2nd ed. (New York: Prentice-Hall, 1987).

[29] "Success Factors in Selling," (Stamford, Conn.: Learning International, 1989), 3.

[30]Kenneth N. Thompson, "Monte Carlo Simulation Approach to Product Profile Analysis: A Consultative Selling Tool," *Journal of Personal Selling and Sales Management* 9 (Summer 1989): 1–10.

[31]Empirical studies that show the importance of contingency selling include William R. Forrester, Jr., and William B. Locander, "Effects of Sales Presentation Topic on Cognitive Responses in Industrial Buying Groups," *Journal of the Academy of Marketing Science* 17, No. 4 (1989): 305–313; H. Michael Hayes and Steven W. Hartley, "How Buyers View Industrial Salespeople," *Industrial Marketing Management* 18 (May 1989): 73–80; and Robert E. Hite and Joseph A. Bellizzi, "Differences in the Importance of Selling Techniques Between Consumer and Industrial Salespeople," *Journal of Personal Selling and Sales Management* 5 (November 1985): 127–133.

[32]"Standing Tall on the Sales Call," *Sales and Marketing Management*, January 1987, 76.

[33]Collin Canright, "Seizing the Electronic Information Advantage," *Business Marketing*, January 1988, 81–86.

CASE 2.1 *Ecosystems Inc.*

Background

Ecosystems Inc. was founded in 1980 as a distributor of commercial trash compactors and accompanying products such as trash bags and chemicals to be used in the cleaning and maintenance of the compactors. With headquarters in Orlando, Florida, Ecosystems originally covered the state of Florida, selling primarily to condominiums, resort facilities, and restaurants.

The spectacular growth of the tourist business in Florida during the 1980s enabled Ecosystems to expand from first-year sales of $2 million to a current annual sales level of $50 million. Ecosystems now has sales coverage in eight southeastern states with a total of 35 sales representatives.

In 1989, Ecosystems began manufacturing its own line of compactor trash bags. The company hired Mark Kovar, formerly an experienced plant manager with one of the top plastic bag manufacturers, to manage Ecosystem's manufacturing operations. Trash bag sales were now tracking at an annual level of $5 million.

Current Situation

Ron Parrish had been with Ecosystems since the day the company was founded. Starting out as a truck driver, Parrish had worked his way through college and then began a sales career with Ecosystems. He is currently the Central Florida sales representative.

During the past weekend, Parrish had made an emergency phone call to Ernie Baxter, the Georgia/Florida district sales manager. Baxter had listened intently as Parrish outlined the problem:

"As you know, Ernie, we finally got the compactor bag business at Walden Homes, which is a large retirement community near Orlando. The residents at Walden Homes buy our compactor bags packed 50 to the case, break them down into packages of 5 and sell them to several retirement communities in the Orlando area. On our first shipment of 200 cases, 180 were anywhere from 1 to 3 bags short of the 50 count. I called Mark Kovar, who assured me that he had not been aware of any shortage prior to shipment. We smoothed the

situation over by sending Walden Homes 5 free cases of bags to cover the shortage. Kovar also guaranteed that we would not have any problem like this in the future.

"Competitors found out about our mistake and a couple of them started telling Walden Homes that Ecosystems had a reputation for poor quality and for charging the customer the full price although shortages were common. I was able to overcome all this until our second shipment arrived Friday. Every single case was short at least 2 bags, with some short as many as 5. The people at Walden Homes have given me until Monday morning to show them why they should not take the following steps: (1) switch all their trash bag business to another supplier, (2) warn all other retirement communities of the deceptive practices of Ecosystems, and (3) file a complaint with the Better Business Bureau and the state Consumer Protection Agency.

"To make matters worse, one of the residents of Walden Homes is a retired state senator whose son is running for the state House of Representatives from the Orlando district. He hinted to me on Friday that the problem could very easily become a political issue in the election campaign."

After Parrish had told him all the details, Baxter quickly took action. He called Martin Tyler, the president of Ecosystems, briefed him on the situation, and asked Tyler to meet him later in the day to review the situation. Next, he phoned Mark Kovar. After a brief discussion, they agreed to meet at the office within an hour to work on the problem.

After giving Kovar all the details, Baxter asked, "Mark, how could we ship the product with an incorrect count after you had been alerted to the same product on the first shipment by Ron Parrish?"

Kovar replied, "It is not as simple as counting the number of bags that go in the case. The mechanical counters do that. The problem is that we have been getting some variations on our manufacturing equipment which make the bags thicker than normal. As a result of increased thickness, 50 bags will not fit into the corrugated boxes we use to package our product."

Kovar went on to say that sometimes the manufacturing variation caused the customer to get more than 50 bags per case and that in the long run it "all averaged out." Kovar also said that the maximum variation to be expected should be plus or minus 3 percent of the specified thickness of the bag. He could not explain why some of the cases shipped to Walden Homes were up to 10 percent short of the specified 50 count.

Baxter relayed this information back to Parrish, who then called to make a Monday morning appointment at Walden Homes. As he hung up the phone, he hoped the weekend would provide enough time to answer the questions occupying his mind.

Questions

1. What can Parrish do to retain the Walden Homes business?
2. How badly has Ecosystems's credibility been damaged?
3. How will Ecosystems try to cope with adverse publicity if the problem cannot be solved?

CASE 2.2   *Tensile Strength Hanger Company*

Background

Tensile Strength Hanger Company has been a key supplier of clothes hangers to the uniform rental, laundry and dry cleaning, and garment manufacturing industries for the past ten years. Five years ago, Tensile added a direct salesforce to supplement its previous means of selling through a direct-mail catalog system. Its salesforce sold hangers to distributors, who in turn sold the hangers to individual dry cleaners, to uniform rental companies, and, in textile-producing areas, to garment manufacturers. Tensile salespeople fulfilled three fundamental roles in their jobs: gaining new distributors, maintaining and enhancing Tensile's sales to existing distributors, and building business and goodwill by calling on the end-user markets.

Current Situation

Barbara Masters, newly hired sales representative, has just completed her training program and has been assigned to the northern California territory. In her training program, Barbara was taught the mental states view of selling, which relies on leading the customer through five steps to make a sale: attention-interest-conviction-desire-close. She is plotting her strategy with Endocino Laundry Supply, owned by Paul Lang. Lang was known to his inner circle of friends as "the czar," due to his rather domineering way of conducting business.

Barbara had called on Lang three times in the past month in an attempt to reestablish Tensile's presence in the account. Lang had firmly (and often rudely) rebuffed her, reminding her that he stopped doing business "once and for all" with Tensile because a previous Tensile sales representative had (allegedly) sold him at a higher price than other distributors in the area. Lang did not seem interested in buying from Barbara, and she felt she had to do something rather dramatic to get his attention so she could ultimately sell him on the Tensile product line. Highlights of her most recent call on Lang follow:

Barbara: Good morning, Mr. Lang. I just came back from visiting one of your largest accounts, Bay Uniform Rental. While I was there, I noticed some problems with the hangers you are using. You know, those lightweight hangers don't hold up very well with those heavy uniform jackets.

Lang: Those hangers get the job done, and I have not received a single complaint! What's your point?

Barbara: My point is double-edged. First, after my visit today, I think you may indeed hear some complaints from Bay Uniform Rental. Second, I think Bay wants a higher-grade hanger, and if you can't provide it, some other distributor will.

Lang: Now wait just a minute! Bay is my customer, not yours. I'll decide what kind of hanger is best for them.

Barbara: Those days are gone, Mr. Lang. I'll be working this market at the end-user level to build our business through cooperative distributors. In fact, I am prepared to call on Bay Uniform's customers — the service stations, welding shops, whatever it takes — to show them a better hanger at approximately the same price.

Lang: Well, I thought I had seen it all, but this takes the cake! A brand-new rookie coming in here, threatening to turn my business upside down! By the time I'm through with you, you'll be lucky to have a job.

Barbara: Save it for somebody who scares easily, Mr. Lang. I had a feeling it might come to this, but I had no idea it would happen so quickly. I won't bother you again by calling on you, but you can rest assured that I'll be out there on the street, switching your business to distributors who really want to work with us.

On her way out of Lang's office, Barbara could not resist temptation. She shot Lang a glance over her shoulder and left him with these words: "No hard feelings, czar! See you on the battlefield."

Questions

1. Do you think Barbara has accomplished the "attention" step of mental-states selling?
2. What risks are inherent in Barbara's plan?
3. What are the chances that Barbara's strategy will work?

Personal Selling: Job Activities and the Sales Process

DEVELOPING A CUSTOMER RELATIONSHIP TAKES TIME, SKILL, AND PATIENCE Ken DeGruchy is a national accounts sales representative with Anixter Bros. Inc., a wiring specialist company headquartered in Skokie, Illinois. For a two-year period in the late 1980s, DeGruchy worked out of the company's New York office to pursue a major order for high-tech power cables manufactured in West Germany, warehoused in Wisconsin, delivered to Maryland for installation on steel work from South Korea, in a job run by a Japanese contractor. The contractor/customer was Sumitomo Heavy Industries, which eventually bought power cables from DeGruchy for seven high-speed cranes they were building for use in loading and unloading ships in the Port of Baltimore. DeGruchy met with Sumitomo officials 75 times in 24 months to establish the buyer-seller relationship.

When Mr. DeGruchy first called on Sumitomo, he did not know they were planning the Baltimore crane project. He discovered that Sumitomo was not familiar with Anixter's product line. DeGruchy had been instructed by his manage-

Learning Objectives

After completing this chapter, you should be able to

1 *Describe the key job activities of salespeople.*

2 *Explain how salespeople act as managers in certain situations.*

3 *Delineate the role salespeople play in supporting their organizations.*

4 *Discuss the sales process as a series of interrelated steps.*

ment to investigate opportunities in the East Coast crane market, and, quite fortuitously, he had walked head-on into a major opportunity. The meetings, conferences, and negotiations over the next 24 months required extensive planning. Most calls on the customer were intricate and lengthy, and multiple parties had to work on the basis of mutual cooperation to ensure success. DeGruchy credits the general manager of the cable division of Siemens-Allis, the West German manufacturer, who obtained cost savings, and one of Anixter's inside salespeople for their cooperative efforts.

Anixter stresses its role in becoming a partner with its customers. Their goal is to deliver the right product at the right time to the right place so that the customer can get the job done on schedule at less cost. In the case of the Port of Baltimore job, the goal was met, primarily due to careful planning and implementation of a Ken DeGruchy. As DeGruchy summarizes, "At Anixter we know how important it is to build relationships. After all, a customer isn't about to make a major investment with an unknown supplier."

Source: "A Powerful Story," *NAMA Journal* (Spring 1989): 1–3.

Ken DeGruchy's report on the Port of Baltimore project illustrates several points related to the job activities of professional salespeople, especially the establishment of relationships with customers. It often takes a long time and a lot of patience to establish a workable relationship with a customer. Other parties, both inside and outside the salesperson's company, may have a role in bolstering the sales effort. Numerous sales calls will require new strategies and new sales tactics to meet the evolving situation. It should also be noted that when it takes an extended period of time to establish a relationship with a customer, the salesperson and the salesperson's company are making a significant investment in time and money long before realizing any compensatory sales revenue.

In this chapter, we will examine the key job activities of salespeople, which include a lot more than making face-to-face sales calls. In fact, most salespeople only spend 25 to 40 percent of their time engaged in actual selling. The remainder of the time is spent on various other activities required to execute their sales duties or to support other organizational activities. As you read this chapter, use the combination sales job as a frame of reference. More specifically, picture an outside salesperson who is responsible for nurturing old business, developing new business, and performing sales support activities.

The management activities of salespeople will be discussed first. While salespeople do not usually supervise other employees of their firms, they are involved in time and territory management, managing company assets, and assisting sales management. Next, we will review the organization support activities of salespeople. Finally, the majority of the chapter will be devoted to the sales process, or how salespeople initiate, develop, maintain, and enhance relationships with customers.

Key Job Activities of Salespeople

A study of 1,393 salespeople in 15 manufacturing industries shows that the job activities of salespeople can be broken into the ten activity groups shown in Exhibit 3.1. The proportion of time spent on any given activity will probably vary from one salesperson to the next. For example, a survey of European salespeople found that Danish and German salespeople were rarely involved in recruiting and training new salespeople, in contrast to the information shown in Exhibit 3.1.[1] Although circumstances will understandably cause some variation in key job activities among salespeople, most salespeople will be involved to some degree with all ten activities. Many of the specific activities comprising these groups will be discussed in this chapter.

The Salesperson as Manager

Salespeople sometimes function in management roles—namely, time and territory management and sales management support as part of their regular sales jobs.

Time and Territory Management

Time and territory management (TTM) involves the planning, organizing, and implementing of sales activities to optimize sales performance. The essential task of TTM is to determine which activities are most conducive to sales success and to

EXHIBIT 3.1 ▪ *Activities of Salespeople*

Activity Name	Selected Activities
Selling function	Search out leads; prepare sales presentations; make sales calls; overcome objections.
Working with orders	Correct orders; expedite orders; handle shipping problems.
Servicing the product	Test equipment; teach safety instructions; supervise installation.
Information management	Provide feedback to superiors; receive feedback from clients.
Servicing the account	Inventory; set up point-of-purchase displays; stock shelves.
Conferences/meetings	Attend sales conferences; set up exhibitions, trade shows.
Training/recruiting	Recruit new sales representatives; train new sales representatives.
Entertaining	Take clients to lunch, golfing, fishing, tennis, etc.
Out-of-town traveling	Spend night on road; travel out of town.
Working with distributors	Establish relations with distributors; extend credit; collect past-due accounts.

Source: Adapted from William C. Moncrief, "Selling Activity and Sales Position Taxonomies for Industrial Salesforces," *Journal of Marketing Research* 23 (August 1986): 261–270, published by the American Marketing Association. These results have been supported in another study using data from 430 salespeople from 38 firms. See William C. Moncrief and David W. Finn, "Industrial Sales Jobs: A Replication of the Moncrief Taxonomy," in *Enhancing Knowledge Development in Marketing, 1989 AMA Educators' Proceedings*, eds. Paul Bloom et al. (Chicago: American Marketing Association, 1989), 66.

perform these activities on a priority basis. The importance of effective TTM is well articulated by Martin D. Shafiroff, a managing director of Shearson Lehman/American Express:

> Every salesperson worth his or her salt is a good time manager. There are only so many minutes in each day, and how well you make use of them is often what separates star sales performers from mediocre performers. Common sense dictates that if two salespersons have equal ability, and one gives twice as many presentations, he will produce at least twice as many sales. And when you consider the principle of synergy, his productivity may be far greater—resulting in three or four times as many sales. For this reason, every salesperson must carefully prepare his day in advance, making sure his prime selling time is used in front of the customer.[2]

Coming from Mr. Shafiroff, this advice should be easy to accept. He is a leading investment broker whose commissions have sometimes exceeded $10 million a year. Salespeople who wish to improve their TTM skills might start with a self-audit, as suggested in Exhibit 3.2. To be effective at TTM, salespeople must complete three major activities: prioritize and plan their work, execute their work in an efficient manner, and analyze their efforts and results to seek continual improvement.

EXHIBIT 3.2   ▪   *Self-Audit Time Analysis*

This method considers five major categories where salespeople spend their time—travel, office, service, personal, and face-to-face customer contact. Activities should be noted on a worksheet in 30-minute intervals over a period of several weeks.

1. *Travel:* Time spent traveling to and from work, time between calls, and time spent waiting to see customers.

2. *Office time and paperwork:* Time spent in the office reading, writing, listening or talking on the phone, planning calls, preparing proposals, attending meetings, or any other inside activities required to move correspondence in the office.

3. *Service:* Time spent servicing customers, including handling complaints, expediting orders, and resolving design problems.

4. *Personal:* Time spent on meals, coffee breaks, servicing the car, and other personal activities.

5. *Customers:* Time spent in the presence of one or more buyers in an organization where you are seeking an order.

For illustration purposes, say a salesperson spends two and one-half hours per day spending time in the fifth category, seeing customers. If the salesperson can allocate an additional 30 minutes of time to this category, a 20 percent increase in sales calls could be realized. Assuming a constant ratio between sales calls and orders written, this could result in a sales increase of 20 percent.

Source: Vince Pesce, *A Complete Manual of Professional Selling*, Rev. ed. (Englewood Cliffs, N.J.: Prentice-Hall, 1989), 126–127.

Setting Priorities. In many organizations, salespeople's priorities are set by annual objectives, which are then decomposed into quarterly, monthly, weekly, daily, and even individual sales-call objectives. Without clear-cut direction provided at least in part by measurable objectives, salespeople (like most people) tend to concentrate on the most pleasant job tasks, which may or may not be the most important tasks. As a result, sales managers have been heard to complain that they are supervising paid tourists rather than salespeople. Actually, the fault probably lies with sales management in such cases for neglecting to establish meaningful objectives for the salesforce.

Another part of setting priorities involves determining how to allocate the salesperson's time among his or her accounts. Pareto's Law, or the **80/20 rule,** which states that 80 percent of a company's volume will come from 20 percent of the customers, is so well known that it is almost a cliche. Nevertheless, it is surprisingly accurate and emphasizes the need to plan the time spent with various customers on a prioritized basis, recognizing that all customers are not equally important to the firm and that some warrant more sales attention than others.

Efficient Work Execution. In addition to prioritizing their work, salespeople must execute it efficiently. When travel is involved, this requires careful planning and scheduling to avoid inefficiencies such as retracing a route, or unnecessary zig-zagging. Plans can be devised with sophisticated computer algorithms, or they can be as simple as a city map indicating customer locations and the sales-call

FIGURE 3.1 ▪ *Travel Alternatives*

Travel plans such as these are designed to allow adequate account coverage on a regular basis without unnecessary zig-zagging or retracing of steps.

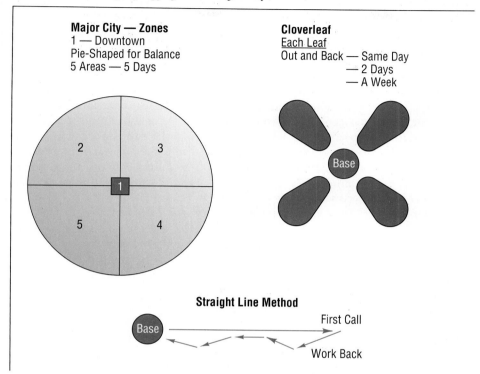

Source: Jim Rapp, *Time and Territory Management* (Orlando, Fla.: The National Society of Sales Training Executives, 1982), 17. Used with permission.

sequence to be followed. Three simple yet efficient travel plans are shown in Figure 3.1.

Travel plans include more than determining the route to be followed. It may be necessary to make motel or airline reservations, select a site for a business lunch, and handle other logistical details. Another factor in planning is the sales-call schedule, which must allow adequate coverage for all customers.

Salespeople should plan to see each customer on a regular basis, but **call frequency** will vary according to the priority assigned to each account. For example, key accounts might be called on monthly and secondary accounts only quarterly.

The average length of sales calls may vary according to the importance of the account and other situational factors. In planning the average length, salespeople should also consider their customers' preferences in scheduling sales calls. For example, some organizations will see salespeople only on certain days of the week or only during specified hours.

Increasingly, the questions of sales-call frequency and average duration of sales calls are being addressed with the assistance of the computer. A survey of firms that use computers in their sales activities reveals that over 25 percent use computers to plan sales calls, and almost 40 percent use computers for calendar scheduling and time and territory management.[3] Procedures for deciding how much sales effort should be allocated to various activities are presented in Chapter 8.

Analysis of Efforts and Results. Salespeople and sales managers should constantly analyze their efforts and results to try to improve the productivity of time spent on various activities. One standard tool for analyzing individual sales calls and, ultimately, sales calls taken collectively is the **call report.** The report may be completed in handwritten form, dictated to a portable tape recorder, or entered into a portable computer. Regardless of the means employed, the report should be recorded immediately after the call, since information from a sales call has proved highly perishable.

Call reports also vary in format. For example, some call reports use checklists so that salespeople can quickly record information about the sales call by simply checking off the appropriate items. Others require a written narrative or, in some cases, a memo from the salesperson to the sales manager. A sample call report that combines some checklist features and a narrative remarks section is shown in Exhibit 3.3. Information commonly requested in call reports includes:[4]

- Name, address, and key contact at customer or prospect contacted
- Outcome of call—that is,
  - Business gained (details)
  - Business lost (why?)
  - Business "on hold"
  - Date of next scheduled call
  - Competitive information obtained
  - More information needed, if any
  - Assistance required from other members of the selling team, including sales management

The analysis of sales calls on a regular basis by salespeople and sales managers can lead to improved time and territory management, which in turn leads to improved sales performance. For example, Hewlett-Packard analyzed where its salespeople were spending their time and found that only 30 percent of the time was spent on customer contact activities. As a result, Hewlett-Packard equipped their salesforce with personal computers and implemented a voice mail system, thereby significantly increasing salespeople's contact time with customers.

In summarizing the TTM responsibilities of salespeople, it is helpful to view salespeople as managers of valuable assets, the most valuable of which is the customer base, which could represent millions of dollars in actual and potential sales. Salespeople are expected to provide a return on the investment their companies have made in salaries, commissions, fringe benefits, and other selling costs. Efficient time and territory management can maximize this return by maximizing productive selling time.

EXHIBIT 3.3 ▪ *Example of a Call Report Form*

Sales Call Report

Salesperson _____ Date of Call ____/____/____

☐ Active Customer   ☐ Inactive Customer   ☐ New Customer   ☐ Prospect

Company _____ Phone _____

Address _____

City _____ State _____ Zip _____

Talked To _____ Title _____

Sold To _____ Amount of Order _____

Remarks and Special Notes

_____

_____

_____

_____

_____

                                        Follow-up Date   /   /

Add to Mailing List: ☐ Yes   ☐ No   Send: ☐ Catalog   ☐ Price List   ☐ Other

Assisting in Sales Management

As Exhibit 3.1 indicated, salespeople spend some of their time assisting sales managers. Typical sales management support activities carried out by salespeople are recruiting, training, managing warehouses, and supervising manufacturers' representatives.

In the recruiting and selection process, salespeople may be asked to conduct screening interviews or spend a day in the field with the recruit to provide a job preview for the prospective candidate. This may even become a major job activity for some salespeople, as in the case of Exxon salespeople in the retail division, who are responsible for recruiting independent service station operators for the company's leased outlets.

Training new salespeople is a common responsibility of salespeople in most industries. It has become a time-honored tradition for the rookie salesperson to spend some time with the seasoned veteran.

In some companies that use independent warehouses as part of the channel of distribution for their products, salespeople may monitor the operation of the warehouse to ensure prompt handling of orders and conscientious management of the inventory. Since independent warehouses are usually performing for more than one supplier, the salesperson is sometimes expected to encourage the warehouse operator to treat the salesperson's company as a priority supplier whose orders will be filled on a preferred basis.

Salespeople may also be responsible for supervising sales assistants and independent representatives who supplement the company's own salesforce. (Independent representatives are discussed in Chapter 6.)

All these activities contribute directly to the sales management function within a firm. Salespeople also are involved in activities that support other areas within the organization. We will now consider some of those activities.

Organization Support Activities

Three primary types of organization support activities are (1) administrative, (2) market information, and (3) meeting participation.

Administrative Duties

In addition to completing the aforementioned call reports, salespeople may be required to perform other administrative duties, such as tracking accounts receivable and being responsible for collecting past-due accounts. Also, they may be expected to file expense accounts on a regular basis to receive reimbursement for their sales expenses.

Market Information Activities

In Chapter 2 we discussed the role of salespeople in providing market research and feedback to their employers. Some of these activities assist not only sales management but other areas in the firm such as production, finance, or general management as well. Input from the salesforce may be utilized to formulate marketing strategy and support other marketing tools. For example, Frito-Lay, a division of Pepsico, has a sophisticated system in which the salespeople gather information in the field and transmit the information via computer back to headquarters. Recently, Frito-Lay salespeople discovered that a regional competitor had just introduced El Galindo, a white-corn tortilla chip that was taking market share away from Frito's traditional tortilla chip product, Tostitos. Frito-Lay responded with a competitive white-corn version of Tostitos and regained the lost market share within three months. Other major suppliers in the food industry, including Procter & Gamble and RJR Nabisco, also have information management systems that rely on input from their salesforces.[5]

Westinghouse provides another example of a firm which made a major investment in a system that integrates sales with other parts of the marketing system. In addition, Westinghouse links the marketing system with the engineering and production systems to form an integrated system. The system, which is shown in Figure 3.2, relies on the input of the Westinghouse sales representatives.

Examples of firms that have successfully integrated the salesperson into the market research system are plentiful. Even so, the authors would agree with the findings of empirical studies which indicate that there is, unquestionably, room for improvement in integrating the salesforce into marketing information systems.[6]

FIGURE 3.2   ▪   *Westinghouse Interactive Communications Network*

Salespeople provide key inputs into this interactive communications network. The network links sales, marketing, manufacturing, and other areas into one integrated communication system.

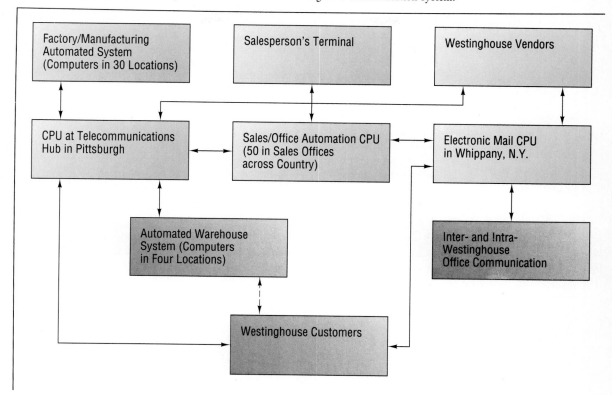

Source: Diane Lynn Kastiel, "New Tools for Enhanced Sales Force Productivity," *Business Marketing*, March 1986, 89.

Meeting Participation

As indicated in Exhibit 3.1, salespeople are routinely involved in attending meetings and conferences held for a variety of purposes, such as training, planning, reviewing performance, motivating the salesforce, or rewarding a job well done. Other activities in this area include teleconferences and one-on-one conferences with the sales manager.

The Sales Process

The nonselling activities on which most salespeople spend a majority of their time are essential for the successful execution of the most important part of the salesperson's job, the **sales process.** The sales process has traditionally been described as a series of interrelated steps beginning with locating qualified prospective customers. From there, the salesperson plans the sales presentation,

FIGURE 3.3 ▪ *The Sales Process*

Salespeople must possess certain attributes to develop trust in their customers and to be able to adapt their selling strategy to different situations. The three major phases of the sales process are initiating, developing, and enhancing customer relationships.

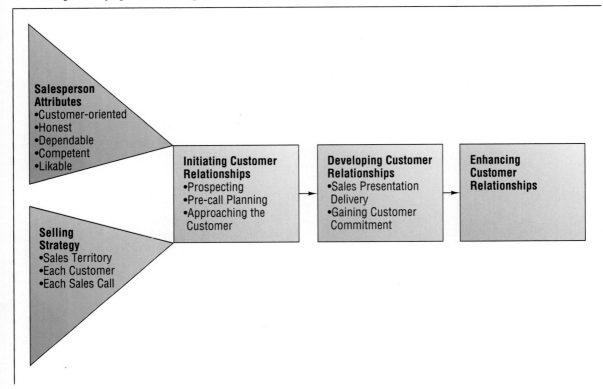

makes an appointment to see the customer, completes the sale, and performs postsale activities.

As you should recall from the discussion of the continued evolution of personal selling in Chapter 2 (refer to Exhibit 2.1), the sales process is increasingly being viewed as a relationship management process, as depicted in Figure 3.3. In this conceptualization of the sales process, salespeople strive to attain lasting relationships with their customers. The basis for such relationships may vary (see Chapter 6 for discussion of different types of relationships), but the element of trust between the customer and the salesperson is an essential part of enduring relationships. To earn the trust of customers, salespeople should be customer-oriented, honest, dependable, competent, and likable.[7] These attributes are reflected by Edwardo Ortega, a sales representative for the giant agricultural products manufacturer, Cargill Inc. Ortega is based in Tampa and has customers in Florida, the Caribbean area, Mexico, and South America. He says:

> In order to be a successful salesperson, I believe you must be responsible, trustworthy, act with integrity 100 percent of the time, have good follow-up skills, be very perceptive, and know the product you are selling so that you can speak

intelligently at all times. I think one of the biggest reasons that people buy from other people is because they [salespeople] can be trusted. If a buyer can trust you, then most of the time it also means that he or she likes you as a person. As we all know, or maybe we don't know, most of the time people like to buy from people they like. If you can be trusted, you are always going to be on firm ground.[8]

Gaining the customer's trust is sometimes made more difficult because of the unscrupulous activity of criminals who pose as salespeople. For a closer look at this problem, see "An Ethical Perspective: Overcoming Fraud in Telephone Selling."

Another important element of achieving sound relationships with customers is to recognize that individual customers and their particular needs must be addressed with appropriate selling strategies and tactics. In Chapters 5 and 6, we will discuss strategy at four levels: corporate, business unit, marketing department, and the overall sales function. An individual salesperson is strongly guided by strategy at these higher levels in the organization but must also develop selling strategies and tactics to fit the sales territory, each customer, and, ultimately, each sales call.

When studying the sales process, we should note that there are countless versions of the process in terms of number of steps and the names of the steps. If, however, you were to examine popular trade books on selling and training manuals used by different corporations, you would find that the various depictions of the sales process are actually more alike than truly unique. The sales process shown in Figure 3.3 is quite comparable to most versions of the sales process, with the exception of those versions that advocate high-pressure methods centering on how to get the customer to "say yes" rather than focusing on meeting the customer's

---

AN ETHICAL PERSPECTIVE

Overcoming Fraud in Telephone Selling   Unfortunately, it is apparently quite easy for telephone con artists to impress a willing public of their perceived legitimacy. The Secret Service estimates that thieves rake in at least $100 million each year through fraudulent scams. Official estimates are thought to be only a fraction of the true losses, as most victims are too embarrassed to contact legal authorities. The most popular products offered through illegal schemes are cut-rate vacations, credit card insurance, vitamins, cleaning products, rare coins, and water filtration systems. These high-pressure "salespeople" operate in true boiler-room fashion, although their modern offices feature the latest communications technologies, such as automatic dialing from computerized lists that may have been purchased from other scam operators.

Knowing that prospects may be a bit wary of salespeople on the telephone, the true professional salesperson can do several things to overcome the stigma created by unscrupulous salespeople. Company literature can be sent prior to the phone contact, to help establish credibility with the prospect. When calling, be straightforward about the purpose of the call. Do not use gimmicks (such as pretending to know the decision maker when you do not) to get past the secretary in order to speak to the prospect. Be patient, and be willing to fully discuss the sales proposition, rather than rushing to close the sale according to a high-pressure condensed sales script.

Source: Based in part on "Dialing for Dollars," *Aide Magazine*, December 1989, 36–37.

true needs. This version of the sales process suggests that salespeople must have certain attributes to develop trust in their customers and that salespeople should adapt their selling strategy to fit the situation. The three phases of the sales process are initiating, developing, and enhancing customer relationships. For discussion purposes, the first two phases have been subdivided into a total of five steps. The sixth and final step in the sales process is that of enhancing customer relationships, which, in many cases, extends over a prolonged time period.

Another point that should be stressed is that the sales process is broken into steps in order to facilitate discussion and sales training, not to suggest discrete lines between the steps. The steps are actually highly interrelated, and in some instances may overlap. Further, the step-wise flow of Figure 3.3 does not imply a strict sequence of events. Salespeople may move back and forth in the process with a given customer, sometimes shifting from step to step several times in the same sales encounter. Finally, completion of the sales process typically will require multiple sales calls.

As we proceed to discuss the steps in the sales process, we will present an overview of each step. The overviews will describe the objectives of each step and identify key issues to be dealt with in each step. Selected techniques and activities that are usually associated with each step will be presented as well.

Initiating Customer Relationships

Prospecting.   The term **prospecting** as used in the sales context is analogous to the prospecting process for gold as practiced in the 1800s. The prospector for gold would work a stream, separating the sludge and mud in a search for strains of the precious metal. The contemporary salesperson locates a pool of potential customers and then screens them to determine which ones are qualified prospects.

In some situations, such as in most retail operations, salespeople are only slightly involved in prospecting; usually, however, they play an important role. A survey of 2,500 manufacturers found that salespeople locate more prospects than any other prospecting means, including advertising and direct mail.[9] The importance of the salesperson's role in prospecting was further documented in a study of 170 consumer and industrial goods salespeople in which the prospecting method rated as "most important" was personal observation, where the salesperson looks and listens for evidence of good prospects.[10]

Locating Prospects.   The initial part of the prospecting process is the generation of a pool, or list, of potential customers. Various methods are used to locate potential prospects. As Exhibit 3.4 indicates, a salesperson may utilize sources outside the organization along with internal company sources. Exhibit 3.4 includes some methods in which the salesperson plays a fairly passive role in this part of prospecting and others where the salesperson is directly responsible for locating the potential customer.

Screening Prospects.   After potential prospects are located, they must be evaluated in terms of **screening criteria** to see whether they merit further sales attention.

EXHIBIT 3.4 ▪ *Prospecting Methods*

Category	*Prospecting Techniques*
1. External Sources	Referral approach: Ask each prospect for the name of another potential prospect. Community contact: Ask friends and acquaintances for the names of potential prospects. Introduction approach: Obtain introduction by one prospect to others via phone, by letter, or in person. Contact organizations: Seek sales leads from service clubs and chambers of commerce. Noncompeting salespeople: Seek leads from noncompeting salespeople. Cultivate visible accounts: Cultivate visible and influential accounts that will influence other buyers.
2. Internal Sources	Examine records: Examine company records, directories, telephone books, membership lists, and other written documents. Inquiries to advertising: Respond to customer inquiries generated from company advertising. Phone/mail inquiries: Respond to phone or mail inquiries from potential prospects.
3. Personal Contact	Personal observation: Look and listen for evidence of good prospects. Cold canvassing: Make cold calls on potential prospects (by phone or in person).
4. Miscellaneous	Hold/attend trade shows: Organize or participate in a trade show directed toward potential prospects. Bird dogs: Have junior salespeople locate prospects that senior salespersons will contact. Sales seminar: Prospects attend as group to learn about a topic in which the salesperson's product is involved.

Source: Adapted from A. J. Dubinsky, "A Factor Analytic Study of the Personal Selling Process," *Journal of Personal Selling and Sales Management* 1, No. 1 (Fall–Winter, 1980–81): 28. Used with permission.

These criteria vary from one sales organization to the next, but some that are commonly used follow:

▪ Compatibility—between the seller's product and the needs or wants of the prospect
▪ Accessibility—to the prospect
▪ Eligibility—in terms of geographic location and type of business the prospect is engaged in
▪ Authority—to make the purchase decision
▪ Profitability—as estimated based on the prospect's willingness and ability to pay and on predicted sales expenses

Questions involving these criteria may be hard to answer fully in the prospecting stage. As a case in point, consider the profitability element. A salesperson may not be able to estimate whether a prospect will prove profitable at some future point in time. It is certainly possible for a prospect to become an unprofitable customer in the future and subsequently lose customer and prospect status with the selling firm. However, the prospecting stage does not require irrevocable decisions regarding the suitability of a prospect, only sufficient indications that the prospect is worthy of sales pursuit.

Prospecting Issues. There are three managerial issues of extreme interest in the prospecting stage. One is the persistent question of which method or methods work best for locating qualified prospects. The second is the problem of **cold-call reluctance** in many salespeople. The third is the issue of using technology to complete the basic tasks of prospecting.

Which method or methods work best? There is no answer to this question without some experimentation by the selling firm. For one firm, a trade show may be a bonanza, while another will find it more profitable to rely exclusively on cold canvassing. With the costs of personal sales calls continuing to rise, sales managers and salespeople must experiment with new prospecting methods in an effort to reduce selling expenses and optimize personal contact activities. For example, there is an increasing amount of interest in experimenting with **teleprospecting,** or the use of telephone surveys to identify prospective buyers' needs and their sales potential.[11] Another example comes from a study in which prospects were notified that literature would be mailed to them prior to salespeople calling for an appointment. The prenotification produced an extraordinary number of qualified prospects.[12]

The subject of cold-call reluctance is especially important, since this method of locating prospects is crucial in many sales situations. Call reluctance experienced later in the sales process is generally not as acute as in the prospecting stage, where the salespeople are encountering strangers on their (the strangers') turf and may feel as if they are intruding. Many have a hard time dealing with the face-to-face rejection that often accompanies this prospecting method.

Noting that the origins of call reluctance are multiple and complex, experts in this phenomenon have reported that "the thick-skinned fearlessness expected in salespeople is more fiction than fact. It turns out that many salespeople are struggling with a bone-shaking fear of prospecting. This fear tends to persist regardless of what they have to sell, how well they have been trained to sell it, or how much they personally believe in their product's worth."[13] This problem is of sufficient magnitude that sales managers and sales trainers frequently address it in training and development programs.

Another prospecting topic that is generating considerable discussion among sales managers is the use of technology to perform some or all prospecting. In recent years, automated systems combining computers with communications equipment have become widely available. Some systems extend beyond prospecting to include other sales functions such as account tracking and postsale follow-up. An example of such a system is shown in Exhibit 3.5. The system uses the computer to screen prospects against qualifying criteria, select the appropriate literature for mailing, and schedule the proper follow-up action. As the quest for

EXHIBIT 3.5 ▪ *Automated Prospect Screening and Tracking System*

This exhibit illustrates a computerized system that coordinates all of the activities related to screening prospects, mailing appropriate literature, and scheduling follow-up by the salesforce.

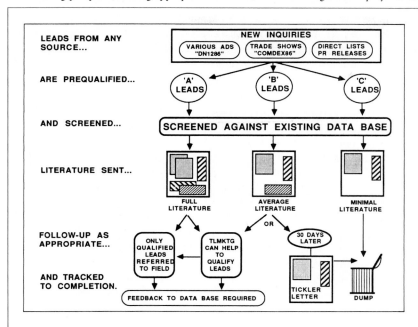

Source: Christopher Stockwell, "Be Concerned with Quality, Not Quantity, of Sales Leader," *Marketing News,* March 14, 1988, 11; published by the American Marketing Association.

improving sales productivity continues, the use of the latest technology to perform certain prospecting activities will become more commonplace.[14]

Pre-call Planning

Preapproach. In the **preapproach,** the salesperson gathers information about the prospect that will be used to formulate the sales presentation. During this step, the salesperson may determine buyer needs, buyer motives, and details of the buyer's situation that are relevant to the upcoming sales presentation.

Various information sources may be consulted in this undertaking. Published materials such as industry newsletters, magazine articles, and newspaper accounts may be useful. Another alternative is to call on the prospect for information-gathering purposes. This tactic is practiced by IBM, as illustrated in the following passage:

It's a matter of a rep doing enough fact-finding to fully understand what is giving the prospect the greatest challenges. Once this is identified, the rep can begin to take the appropriate IBM equipment and put it in the prospect's office, factory, or perhaps warehouse, and provide a solution to his problem. But the rep can't very well answer any problems unless he's able to draw out the necessary day-to-day bits of information from the prospect. As you can see, a lot of fact-finding is required before an IBM rep can properly do his or her job.[15]

In addition to gathering information to be used in the sales presentation, the preapproach offers other benefits. Because of the information it provides, the salesperson may avoid serious blunders based on false assumptions. Also, the self-confidence of the salesperson is increased by the acquisition of knowledge, and the salesperson's credibility with the prospect is enhanced.

The preapproach raises two issues worthy of management attention. First is the question of how extensive the preapproach should be. Second is the issue of invasion of privacy.

The extensiveness of the preapproach depends on the nature of the sales situation. Specifically, it has been suggested that a more extensive preapproach is appropriate when[16]

- Future interactions (after the initial sale) with the customer are anticipated.
- Customers are making complex, high-involvement decisions.
- The purchase decision will have significant impact on the salesperson.
- The salesperson has a range of alternatives to offer the customer.
- Customers encountered by the salesperson are heterogeneous in terms of their needs.

Sales managers and salespeople should also be sensitive to the issue of invasion of privacy when conducting the preapproach. There have been instances where surreptitious methods were used to learn personal details about prospects. Such tactics are unethical, and they often backfire if the prospect becomes aware of the practice. A related tactic is the use of so-called market research that purports to be "selling nothing" when in reality, selling is precisely the purpose. As was indicated in the previous chapter, straightforward sales techniques have proved more effective over the long run.

Sales-Presentation Planning. This step has become more important in recent years, as evidenced by increased coverage on the topic in sales training programs. The requirements of professional selling today make **sales-presentation planning** imperative, and it is often extensive, since it is increasingly viewed as a critical link in the sales process. Sales presentation planning becomes more complex when dealing with new customers, as illustrated in "A Global Perspective: Sales Planning for European Customers."

As with other planning processes, the salesperson must begin with a specifically stated objective, or perhaps multiple objectives, for each sales presentation. Typical objectives might be stated as order quantities, dollar values, or even in communications terms, such as reaching an agreement in principle with the prospect. Once a clearly stated objective has been formulated, the salesperson can focus on how the benefits of his or her offering can be related to the prospect in a competitively advantageous manner.

Taken to the ultimate, sales-presentation planning might actually result in a script to guide sales encounters. Not to be confused with a scripted sales message

A GLOBAL PERSPECTIVE

Sales Planning for European Customers As trade restrictions fall in the European countries and political reform allows more trade with the West, salespeople from U.S. companies will need to learn more about how Europeans prefer to do business. For example, Europeans are sensitive to any suggestion that their productivity levels might be lower than those of their U.S. counterparts. Thus, salespeople selling manufacturing equipment should not push for details such as hours required to do the job. Rather, they should communicate their capabilities and wait for the customer's reaction.

U.S. salespeople should also understand that typically it will take longer for a Euro-pean customer to make a decision than for the typical U.S. customer. Salespeople should be prepared to be patient and proceed cautiously when sales progress slows down.

Americans should remember that while Europeans have a sense of humor, it is often quite localized. The typical American approach to joviality does not play well in Europe. Also, U.S. salespeople should be careful to avoid the "ugly American" syndrome, keeping a quiet demeanor instead.

Source: David N. Burt, "Nuances of Negotiating Overseas," *Journal of Purchasing and Materials Management* 25 (Spring 1989): 56–62.

to be delivered over the telephone, this script would be more a guide to expected sales activities given a particular buying situation. Research has been conducted that suggests that scripts could help salespeople learn how to adapt to the customer and the selling situation, while developing their own personal style and sales tactics.[17]

Sales-Presentation Format. To plan the sales presentation, salespeople must decide on a basic presentation format. Alternatives include a canned sales presentation, an organized presentation, and the written sales proposal. A salesperson might utilize one or more of these formats with a particular customer. Each format has unique advantages and disadvantages.

The highly structured, inflexible, **canned sales presentation** does not vary from customer to customer. When properly formulated, it is logical, complete, and minimizes sales resistance by anticipating the prospect's objections. It can be utilized by relatively inexperienced salespeople and perhaps is a confidence builder for some salespeople.

The major limitation of the canned sales presentation is that it fails to capitalize on the strength of personal selling—the ability to tailor the message to the prospect. Further, it does not handle interruptions well, may be awkward to use with a broad product line, and may alienate buyers who want to participate in the interaction.

In spite of its limitations, the canned sales presentation has been shown to be effective in some situations.[18] If the product line is narrow and the salesforce is relatively inexperienced, the canned presentation may be quite suitable. Also, many salespeople may find it effective to use canned portions in a sales presentation to introduce their company, demonstrate the product, or for some other limited purpose.

According to survey data, presentations that are tailored to each prospect are far more popular with salespeople than are canned sales presentations. [19] In the **organized sales presentation,** the salesperson organizes the key points into a planned sequence that allows for adaptive behavior by the salesperson as the presentation progresses. Feedback from the prospect is encouraged, and therefore this format is less likely to offend a participation-prone buyer.

One reality of this presentation format is that it requires a knowledgeable salesperson who can react to questions and objections from the prospect. Further, this format may extend the time horizon before a purchase decision is reached and it is vulnerable to diversionary delay tactics by the prospect. Presumably, those who make these arguments feel that a canned presentation forces a purchase decision in a more expedient fashion.

Overall, however, most agree that the organized presentation is ideal for most sales situations. Its flexibility allows a full exploration of customer needs and appropriate adaptive behavior by the salesperson.

A written sales presentation, the **sales proposal,** may be developed after careful investigation of the prospect's needs; or, alternatively, a generic proposal may be presented. With the increasing prevalence of word processing, computer graphics, and desktop publishing, the written sales proposal is being used in an increasing number of situations. These technologies have minimized the traditional disadvantage of the written proposal—the time it takes to prepare it.

The sales proposal has long been associated with important, high-dollar-volume sales transactions. It is frequently used in competitive bidding situations and in situations involving the selection of a new supplier by the prospect. One advantage of the proposal is that the written word is usually viewed as being more credible than the spoken word. Written proposals are subject to careful scrutiny with few time constraints, and specialists in the buying firm often analyze various sections of the proposal.

Sales proposals are often combined with face-to-face presentations and question-and-answer periods. Their content is similar to other sales presentations, focusing on customer needs and related benefits offered by the seller. In addition, technical information, pricing data, and perhaps a timetable are included. Most proposals provide a triggering mechanism such as a proposed contract to confirm the sale, and some specify follow-up action to be taken if the proposal is satisfactory.

Sales Mix Model. To this point, our discussion of the sales presentation planning process should have clearly suggested a need for a specific objective for each presentation and a need to determine the basic format of the presentation. In general terms, we have spoken of blending information into a palatable sales message. This is best done within the context of the **sales mix model** shown in Figure 3.4. The model includes five variables that require planning effort: presentation pace, presentation scope, depth of inquiry, degree of two-way communication, and use of visual aids.

Presentation pace refers to the speed with which the salesperson intends to move through the presentation. The appropriate pace will be largely determined by the preference of the prospect and may be affected by variables such as

FIGURE 3.4 ▪ *Sales Mix Model*

Five variables require planning effort after the salesperson has set objectives for the presentation and selected a basic presentation format.

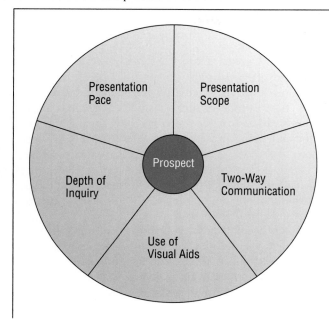

Source: John I. Coppett and William A. Staples, *Professional Selling: A Relationship Approach* (Cincinnati, Ohio: South-Western Publishing Co., 1990), 187.

complexity of the product or the number of products to be presented. Another determinant of pace would be past experiences with a particular customer, as a quicker pace may be possible with a familiar customer.

Presentation scope involves the selection of benefits and terms of sale to be included in the presentation. This narrowing-down process can be a challenge for the knowledge-laden salesperson, who may know more about the product than will be of interest to the prospect. Time and again, we see reports of jargon-spouting salespeople who have talked themselves out of a sale through indiscriminate use of their extensive product knowledge. An illustration of this problem comes from Charles O'Meara, an expert who advises customers on how to buy stereo equipment. O'Meara says that if a salesperson "tries to, say, inundate your aural sensibility with a plethora of polysyllabic terminology—watch out! Either the salesperson is trying to confuse you or he is a techie who can't relate to other human beings. The salesperson should talk technical only if the customer wants to talk technical."[20]

Depth of inquiry refers to the extent to which the salesperson goes to ascertain the prospect's needs and decision process. Some of this information may have been gained in the preapproach, and some probing is usually necessary during the presentation. The planning task is simply to identify gaps in needed information and plan the presentation accordingly.

The issue of **two-way communication** is partially addressed when the salesperson selects a basic format for the presentation. By definition, the canned presentation does not allow for significant two-way communication. The organized presentation allows for, and usually encourages, a two-way flow. The degree of interactive flow is often dictated by buyer expertise, with more allowance for two-way flow planned with expert buyers.

Visual aids to supplement the spoken word have become an important element in sales presentations, and their use must be carefully planned. Unless sales aids are utilized with caution, they may actually detract from rather than enhance the sales presentation. When properly orchestrated, visual aids ranging from flip charts to video demonstrations can be valuable tools during the sales presentation. The potential for enhancing presentations with relatively inexpensive desktop video productions is becoming an exciting reality. For example, salespeople with companies such as Textron, IBM, and Westinghouse use a PC-based system to construct and integrate all forms of information—including photographs, graphics, statistical data, and sound effects—into a video presentation.[21]

After the sales presentation is planned, the salesperson is ready to shift to an active selling mode. While the customer may have been contacted earlier in the sales process, the emphasis has been on information gathering and planning. Now the actual selling begins as the salesperson seeks an interview with the prospect.

Approaching the Customer

Approaching the customer involves two phases. The first phase is securing an appointment for the sales interview. The second phase covers the first few minutes of the sales call. Each step in the sales process is critical, and the approach is no exception. In today's competitive environment, a good first impression is essential to lay the groundwork for subsequent steps in the sales process. A bad first impression on the customer can be difficult or impossible to overcome.

Getting an Appointment. Most initial sales calls on new prospects require an appointment. Requesting an appointment accomplishes several desirable outcomes. First, the salesperson is letting the prospect know that the salesperson thinks the prospect's time is important. Second, there is a better chance that the salesperson will receive the undivided attention of the prospect during the sales call. Third, setting appointments is a good tool to assist the salesperson in effective time and territory management. The importance of setting appointments is clearly proclaimed in a survey of purchasing agents, who included "walking in without an appointment" as behavior common to "bad" salespeople.[22] Given this rather strong feeling of buyers, it is a good idea to request an appointment if there is any doubt about whether one is required.

Appointments may be requested by phone, mail, or personal contact. By far, setting appointments by telephone is the most popular method. Combining mail and telephone communications to seek appointments is also commonplace. Regardless of the communications vehicle used, salespeople can improve their chances of getting an appointment by following three simple directives: give the prospect a reason why an appointment should be granted; request a specific amount of time; suggest a specific time for the appointment. These tactics recognize that prospects are busy people who do not spend time idly.

In giving a reason why the appointment should be granted, a well-informed salesperson can appeal to the prospect's primary buying motive as related to one of the benefits of the salesperson's offering. Being specific is recommended. For example, it is better to say "you can realize gross margins averaging 35 percent on our product line" than "our margins are really quite attractive."

Specifying the amount of time needed to make the sales presentation alleviates some of the anxiety felt by a busy prospect at the idea of spending some of his or her already scarce time. It also helps the prospect if the salesperson suggests a time and date for the sales call. It is very difficult for busy people to respond to a question such as, "What would be a good time for you next week?" In effect, the prospect is being asked to scan his or her entire calendar for an opening. If a suggested time and date are not convenient, the interested prospect will typically suggest another.

Starting the Sales Call. Having secured an appointment with a qualified, presumably interested prospect, the salesperson should plan to accomplish some important tasks during the first few minutes of the call. First in importance is to establish a harmonious atmosphere for discussion. Common rules of etiquette and courtesy apply here. In addition, recent sales research reveals certain techniques for building rapport with a prospect. One interesting method is **neuro-linguistic programming,** or **NLP.** Originally developed by psychotherapists to help develop trust, rapport, and understanding with clients, NLP is being used in some sales training programs to teach salespeople how to do the same with customers. Body cues and word selection of the prospect are observed and responded to in specified ways.[23] Some preliminary small talk is usually part of the ritual, then the discussion should turn to business. Adaptive salespeople can learn how to interpret the prospect's signals and move into the sales message on cue.

Another important aspect in starting a sales call is to ascertain the customer's needs as related to the benefits of the salesperson's offering. In many cases, salespeople will ask questions pertaining to the prospect's situation and then, at the appropriate time, show the prospect how the salesperson's product or service can benefit the customer. Research has indicated that successful salespeople ask more questions than do less successful salespeople.[24] Further, successful salespeople focus on the benefits of their offering, rather than the features of the offering. For example, Frito-Lay salespeople can offer their customers next-day delivery, a feature of their offering. The benefits of next-day delivery include reduction of inventory cost, avoidance of out-of-stock situations, and fresher product for the consumer.

Gimmickry: An Issue in the Approach. An examination of some sales training materials uncovers the disturbing recommendation that to secure the prospect's attention and interest, salespeople should resort to the *shock approach*, which involves creating fear in the prospect, or the *premium approach*, where the salesperson gives the prospect a token gift to get the interview. It is somewhat comforting to note that these two methods were rated unimportant in a survey of professional salespeople.[25]

Developing Customer Relationships

Sales Presentation Delivery. During the **sales presentation,** the salesperson expands on the basic theme established in the first few minutes of the sales call or during previous sales calls. Specifically, more details are furnished regarding how offered benefits will meet customer needs. If the prior steps in the sales process have been properly implemented, the salesperson is now interacting with a qualified, interested prospect at a convenient time. Given these circumstances, three major goals remain: building credibility, achieving clarity, and coping with questions and objections raised by the prospect.

Building Credibility. With any major purchase, prospects perceive a considerable amount of risk. In order to be able to reduce that perception of risk in the prospect, the salesperson must appear a credible source of information. In a classic study, Harvard professor Theodore Levitt found *source credibility* for salespeople to be a function of three factors: the individual salesperson, the company image, and the product being sold.[26] Additional research has indicated that salespeople's credibility may be affected by their job title. For example, those salespeople holding the designation Chartered Life Underwriter were viewed as being more credible than other insurance salespeople in one study.[27] In our discussion of source credibility, we will concentrate on factors that can, to a significant degree, be controlled by the salesperson. These factors can be divided into two categories—personal behavior and sales techniques.

Personal Behavior. The basics of personal behavior that build credibility are dressing appropriately, showing common courtesy for all personnel in the prospect's organization, and being customer-oriented. As previously mentioned, all words and actions should be consistent with the traits of honesty and integrity. These findings confirm that building credibility is a very worthwhile activity for salespeople.

One approach to building credibility through personal behavior is to become a good listener. In a recent survey, 432 buyers were asked to identify the most impressive behavior of salespeople. The most frequently mentioned behavior was "really listening," followed by "answers questions well."[28] Obviously, there is a strong correlation between listening and being able to answer customer questions. Both skills are essential for building credibility with the customer. As the benefits of listening become more apparent, popular sales training programs have increased their coverage of this subject. Good listening skills enable the salesperson to learn more about the prospect and also keep the prospect interested in the sales proposition, since people are usually more interested in listening to someone else when they, too, are given the chance to talk. Moreover, by listening, the salesperson is, in effect, complimenting the prospect and showing respect for the prospect's point of view. The result is a reciprocation process in which the prospect repays the salesperson by listening to the sales presentation more attentively. The platform for credibility is built by the salesperson's willingness and ability to be an effective listener.

We discussed listening as a personal behavior since most effective listeners practice the art all the time, not just during sales presentations. We would not argue, however, with those who propose that listening is a sales technique rather than a personal behavior.

•*Sales Techniques.* One sales technique used to build credibility with prospects is that of **conservative claims** regarding the benefits of the offering. The idea is that prospects may expect claims to be exaggerated, so upon discovering that the salesperson has conservatively stated the claims, they tend to rate the credibility of the salesperson higher.

Another technique is to use **third-party evidence** to support a contention. **Testimonials** from satisfied customers are sometimes used for this purpose, as are research reports and product reviews from trade magazines. In the early stages of establishing credibility, salespeople often find that third-party information, particularly if it is written, may be more acceptable than the salesperson's spoken word.

Guarantees and warranties are other sales tools that can improve a salesperson's credibility. A strong warranty without a plethora of fine-print exceptions can go a long way toward eliminating the prospect's perceived risk and elevating the salesperson's credibility.

Another method is to let the prospect try the product or service under actual usage conditions. This can be as simple as a test-drive in a new automobile or as extensive as installing a computer system on a trial basis. This method permits the prospect to raise and answer questions without immediate persuasive pressure from the salesperson.

Even salespeople who work for companies with good reputations cannot assume that source credibility is a given. Further, they cannot assume that it will be easy to establish. They must recognize the skepticism and perceived risk in many sales situations and then combine appropriate personal behavior and sales techniques to overcome it.

Achieving Clarity. Salespeople begin the task of **achieving clarity** during sales-presentation planning. Recall the sales mix model, in which the salesperson plans such presentation elements as depth of inquiry, pace, and visual aids. The sales mix model also includes the presentation scope and the degree of two-way communication to be accomplished. At this point in the sales presentation, we are ready to implement those plans made with the assistance of the sales mix model.

To supplement the forethought given to achieving clarity as implied in the sales mix model, salespeople must adapt to the dynamics of the sales presentation. That is, as changes in the sales situation occur, salespeople must be adept at soliciting, interpreting, and reacting to feedback from the prospect. Again, listening skills emerge as important. Questioning skills are, too. Closed questions (those providing a series of potential responses) appear most effective for obtaining relevant information from the prospect.[29]

Sales aids such as charts, graphs, printed literature, photographs, films, slides, and portable computers are excellent tools in a number of sales situations for achieving clarity. Such sales aids should be employed only where they can make the presentation more effective, not merely to "put on a show." After all, the medium should not overpower the message.

Addressing Customer Concerns.   The solicitation of feedback from the prospect will usually raise concerns in the form of questions and objections related to the salesperson's offering. Addressing these concerns is a routine part of the salesperson-customer relationship. In some cases, these concerns represent an unwillingness to buy unless the problem is resolved. In other cases, the buyer is asking for clarification of a point, or seeking information, perhaps reassurance on a particular point. In still other cases, prospects raise objections and ask questions as a bargaining tactic in an attempt to negotiate a more favorable deal.

Regardless of the reasons for raising objections and asking questions, the salesperson must be ready to respond effectively. Veteran salespeople generally look forward to dealing with questions and objections, viewing them as indicators of interest and therefore of an imminent purchase decision. Accordingly, they treat objections and questions with respect, even when they must tell the prospect that he or she is in error on a point.

Gaining Customer Commitment

A successful relationship requires that all parties in the relationship make firm commitments to each other. Assuming that the earlier steps in the sales process have been properly conducted, a joint commitment is the next logical step. In a sales context, this means that both the customer and the salesperson agree to a course of action. This may involve a purchase agreement or other courses of action, such as agreements to continue sales negotiations, to conduct a product usage test, or perhaps to sign a long-term distribution contract.

The reality of a competitive marketplace dictates that salespeople actively seek a commitment, since more than one firm can usually meet the customer's needs adequately. Customers expect salespeople to seek commitments, but they do not appreciate being pressured into premature decisions, nor do they appreciate high-pressure gimmicks designed to force a positive decision. A passage from an executive newsletter addresses this issue:

> Sales training literature is filled with clever, contrived, manipulative, and gimmicky "closing" attempts. Happily, we are getting away from much of that in our more sophisticated selling procedures. Can you really imagine one of your sales rep's buyers who is hesitating on a buying decision suddenly responding to the blunt question, "What purchase order number do you want me to use on this order?" This will only work if the decision has already been made.[30]

The question of when to seek commitment remains open. The stock answer in days gone by was "early and often," meaning that salespeople should try to conclude the sale quickly by using repeated closing attempts. This approach is, however, risky; if the closing attempt is inappropriately early, a negative response is more likely; and once a negative response has been voiced by the prospect, principles of *cognitive consistency* dictate that the prospect will tend to reinforce the decision. The question of timing, therefore, is important in seeking commitment.

Although there are no unimpeachable guidelines to timing, if the presentation has been completed without questions or objections from the prospect, it is logical that commitment should be sought without delay. Likewise, if all questions and objections have been satisfactorily handled, seeking commitment is in order. In many instances, salespeople can interpret cues, or signals, from the prospect that indicate that gaining commitment is the next logical step. For example, the prospect might ask, "Can you deliver by next Tuesday?" Such a question would not be asked by an indifferent or unreceptive prospect. In the final analysis, the question of when to seek commitment is a judgment call to be made by the salesperson, sometimes with the assistance of the prospect.

Enhancing Customer Relationships

The importance of a diligent effort to maintain and enhance customer relationships is reflected in a survey of corporate buyers who were asked to identify their chief reason for switching vendors. Their response? "Sales rep is out of touch."[31] The emphasis on maintaining and enhancing customer relationships is definitely increasing, as suggested by the number of companies who tout their after-the-sale service as a competitive advantage. Such a claim is made in the advertisement shown in Exhibit 3.6. As we see the notion of providing superior customer-oriented service become more publicized, a reasonable question is, How sincere are these programs?

Some disciples of service-oriented follow-up are true believers, while others only masquerade as such. Consider this passage:

> All sales experts strongly believe that outstanding service is mandatory in today's selling world. Yet, while the importance of this is so obvious, sadly only a small percentage of salespeople are ready and willing to provide it. To the mass army of salespeople, "the customer always comes first" is a tired cliche, but to most successful salespeople it represents a code to live by. To them, making a sale and failing to follow up with the best possible service is tantamount to delivering damaged goods. The customer is cheated because he doesn't receive the true value that's due him for his money.[32]

Clearly, professional salespeople must view their customer base as far too valuable an asset to risk losing through neglect. In maintaining and enhancing customer relationships, salespeople are involved in performing routine postsale follow-up activities and in enhancing the relationship as it evolves by anticipating and adapting to changes in the customer's situation, competitive forces, and other changes in the market environment.

One objective in this step is to create a strong bond with the customer that will diminish the probability of the customer's terminating the relationship. In effect, the salesperson's firm earns the business through a number of successive trials and strengthens its position as time passes.

EXHIBIT 3.6   ▪   *Advertisement Featuring Service after the Sale*

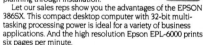

Relationship Enhancement Activities. Specific **relationship enhancement** activities vary substantially from company to company, but some of the more common ones are

▪ Entering orders
▪ Expediting orders
▪ Installing the product or service
▪ Training customer personnel
▪ Resolving complaints
▪ Correcting billing errors

To further enhance the relationship, salespeople should continually diagnose customer needs and recommend new solutions, products, and services when appropriate. Salespeople could hold formal status-of-the-business reviews with the customer on a regular basis, reinforcing the importance of the customer to the selling firm. During review sessions or regular sales calls or through surveys, salespeople can solicit feedback on how to improve the product and provide better service.

Salespeople can also enhance the relationship by reinforcing its value by providing the customer with information relating to how expectations have been met. For example, salespeople can identify and quantify contributions to cost savings and quality improvement programs. They should seek acknowledgment from the customer that the benefits and satisfaction that were sought have been delivered.

As mentioned at the beginning of our discussion on the sales process, **building trust** is an important element in a buyer-seller relationship. Throughout the sales process, the salesperson works to earn the trust of the customer. Sales technique is part of the trust-earning process, but the central truth of the matter is:

> While it is important to consciously work to convince the buyer that you can be trusted, in the long run nothing is likely to work better than doing what you say you will do, keeping all your promises, and always telling the truth. In the short run certain behaviors have been shown to speed this attribute of trustworthiness. But over the long run, nothing will earn the buyer's trust like being a trustworthy individual.[33]

Summary

1. **Describe the key job activities of salespeople.** In addition to actual selling, salespeople are involved in service activities, working with their sales managers, relaying information to and from their customers and their employers, travel and entertainment, and attending meetings and conferences. Exhibit 3.1 lists ten key activities. The typical salesperson spends only about 25 to 40 percent of his or her time engaged in actual selling and constantly tries to increase this percentage.

2. **Explain how salespeople act as managers in certain situations.** Salespeople are, in effect, performing management functions in two areas: They are time and territory managers, which requires setting priorities, efficient execution of work activities, and analysis of efforts and results. They also assist sales managers in recruiting, training, managing warehouses, and supervising manufacturers' representatives.

3. **Delineate the role salespeople play in supporting their organizations.** Salespeople are often relied upon to support the organization in administrative capacities such as collecting past-due accounts. They also are frequently called upon to provide market information used in marketing decisions such as pricing, packaging, and identifying test markets. They spend a fair amount of time participating in meetings and conferences for a variety of purposes.

4. **Discuss the sales process as a series of interrelated steps.** As presented in Figure 3.3, the sales process has six steps. The first three steps—prospecting, pre-call planning, and approaching the customer—are concerned

with initiating a relationship with the customer. The next two steps—sales-presentation delivery and gaining customer commitment—are related to developing the salesperson-customer relationship. The final step in the sales process, and in many cases the most important one, is enhancing the relationship with the customer. It is important to note that one step builds on the previous step and that it usually takes several sales calls to confirm an initial sale to a prospect.

Key Terms

- **Time and territory management (TTM)**
- **80/20 rule**
- **Call frequency**
- **Call report**
- **Sales process**
- **Prospecting**
- **Screening criteria**
- **Cold-call reluctance**
- **Teleprospecting**
- **Preapproach**
- **Sales-presentation planning**
- **Sales-presentation format**
- **Canned sales presentation**
- **Organized sales presentation**
- **Sales proposal**
- **Sales mix model**

- **Presentation pace**
- **Presentation scope**
- **Depth of inquiry**
- **Two-way communication**
- **Visual aids**
- **Approaching the customer**
- **Neuro-linguistic programming (NLP)**
- **Sales presentation**
- **Building credibility**
- **Conservative claims**
- **Third-party evidence**
- **Testimonials**
- **Guarantees and warranties**
- **Achieving clarity**
- **Relationship enhancement**
- **Building trust**

Review Questions

1. How does a salesperson act as a manager? Do all salespeople act as managers?
2. Describe the critical elements in time and territory management in terms of inputs, outputs, and controls.
3. What are typical organization support activities for salespeople?
4. What is the purpose of each step in the sales process?
5. Review the boxed insert entitled "An Ethical Perspective: Overcoming Fraud in Telephone Selling." How do the actions of unscrupulous salespeople and con artists affect the source credibility of legitimate salespeople?

6. Review the boxed insert entitled "A Global Perspective: Sales Planning for European Customers." What are the dangers of using cultural stereotypes for planning sales presentations?

7. Discuss the final step of the sales process as related to the evolution of personal selling, which was covered in Chapter 2.

8. Discuss the elements of the sales mix model shown in Figure 3.4.

9. Describe the three different sales-presentation formats in terms of their advantages and disadvantages.

10. Which do you feel is the most important—planning the sales presentation or delivering it?

Application Exercises

1. Successful salespeople are skilled at gathering information from their prospects during the sales process. Three types of questions that salespeople might use to gather information are verification questions, developmental questions, and evaluative questions.[34] Each is defined below.

a. *Verification questions* are designed to validate prior knowledge, assumptions, or impressions the salesperson has formed from either the prospect's previous statements or other sources of information.

b. *Developmental questions* are open-ended. They cannot be answered by "yes" or "no." They are used to encourage discussion by the prospect about ideas, feelings, or events introduced by the prospect or salesperson.

c. *Evaluative questions* ask the prospect for feedback concerning ideas or information provided by the salesperson.

Assume you are a salesperson for an automobile leasing firm. Your firm specializes in fleet leasing agreements, and you are planning a sales presentation for a fleet manager for a national firm. The firm currently owns its company cars, but you have heard that the company is considering a switch to leased automobiles. Using examples, illustrate how you might incorporate the three types of questions into your first sales call on the fleet manager.

2. Assume you are a salesperson and the following information applies to your territory:

Accounts Classified According to Anticipated Sales Volume

A: Large, 15 accounts
B: Medium, 10 accounts
C: Small, 8 accounts

Frequency and Length of Sales Call Per Account Class

A: 60 minutes/call × 48 calls/year
B: 30 minutes/call × 24 calls/year
C: 20 minutes/call × 12 calls/year

Workload in Hours Required for Account Coverage

A: 15 accounts × 48 hours/year = 720 hours
B: 10 accounts × 12 hours/year = 120 hours
C: 8 accounts × 4 hours/year = 32 hours
TOTAL = 872 hours/year

Assume you work 48 weeks per year and that 40 percent of your time is spent on actual selling. Further assume you work five days per week. How many hours per day must you work to provide the account coverage outlined in the preceding information? How many hours per day must be spent to complete all job activities? What recommendations can you make to salespeople who are trying to maximize selling time?

3. Assume you are selling PACSEAL, an automatic package-sealing device. One of your current prospects is a manufacturer of windshield wiper blades that ships approximately 5,000 boxes of blades per day to its customers. The cost of PACSEAL is $20,000. The customer can expect to save a penny per box shipped if PACSEAL is installed. The PACSEAL system has a guaranteed life of five years. How could you utilize this information in a sales proposal? How would you illustrate the key selling points derived from this information?

Notes

[1]"Selling in Europe," *Sales and Marketing Management*, November 1989, 25.

[2]Robert L. Shook, *The Perfect Sales Presentation* (New York: Bantam Books, 1986), 87–88.

[3]Thayer C. Taylor, "PCs Make Inroads, Yet Holdouts Persist," *Sales and Marketing Management*, November 1989, 119.

[4]For more information on call reports, see Gene Garofalo, *Sales Manager's Desk Book* (Englewood Cliffs, N. J.: Prentice-Hall, 1989), 63–69; and John P. Steinbrink, ed., *Sales Manager's Handbook*, 14th ed. (Chicago: Dartnell Corp., 1989), 940–944.

[5]Jeffrey Rothfeder, Jim Bartimo, Lois Therrien, and Richard Brandt, "How Software Is Making Food Sales a Piece of Cake," *Business Week*, July 2, 1990, 54–55.

[6]See Douglas M. Lambert, Howard Marmorstein, and Aron Sharma, "The Accuracy of Salesperson's Perceptions of Their Customers," *Journal of Personal Selling and Sales Management* 10 (Winter 1990): 1–9; and Kenneth R. Evans and John L. Schlacter, "The Role of Sales Managers and Salespeople in a Marketing Information System," *Journal of Personal Selling And Sales Management* 5 (November 1985): 57.

[7]Jon M. Hawes, Kenneth E. Mast, and John E. Swan, "Trust Earning Perceptions of Sellers and Buyers," *Journal of Personal Selling and Sales Management* 9 (Spring 1989): 1–8.

[8]Interview by the authors with Edwardo Ortega, sales representative with Cargill Inc.

[9]"The Computer in Sales and Marketing," *Sales and Marketing Management*, August 15, 1986, 71.

[10]Robert E. Hite and Joseph A. Belizzi, "Differences in the Importance of Selling Techniques Between Consumer and Industrial Salespeople," *Journal of Personal Selling and Sales Management* 5 (November 1985): 19–30.

[11]J. David Lichtenhal, Sameer Sikri, and Karl Folk, "Teleprospecting: An Approach for Qualifying Accounts," *Industrial Marketing Management* 18 (February 1990): 11–17.

[12]Marvin A. Jolson, "Prospecting by Telephone Prenotification: An Application of the Foot-in-the-Door Technique," *Journal of Personal Selling and Sales Management* 6 (August 1986): 39–42.

[13]George W. Dudley and Shannon L. Goodson, *The Psychology of Call Reluctance* (Dallas: Behavioral Science Research Press, 1986), 2.

[14]Robert H. Collins, "Microcomputer Systems to Handle Sales Leads: A Key to Increased Salesforce Productivity," *Journal of Personal Selling and Sales Management* 5 (May 1985): 77–83.

[15]Shook, *The Perfect Presentation*, 111.

[16]Barton A. Weitz, "A Critical Review of Personal Selling Research: The Need for Contingency Approaches," in *Sales Management: State-of-the-Art and Future Research Needs*, eds. Gerald Albaum and Gilbert A. Churchill, Jr. (Eugene, Oreg.: Division of Research, College of Business Administration, University of Oregon, 1979), 110.

[17]Thomas W. Leigh and Patrick F. McGraw, "Mapping the Procedural Knowledge of Industrial Sales Personnel: A Script-Theoretic Investigation," *Journal of Marketing* 53 (January 1989): 16–34.

[18]Marvin A. Jolson, "Canned Adaptiveness: A New Direction for Modern Salesmanship," *Business Horizons* 32 (January–February 1989): 7–12.

[19]Hite and Bellizzi, "Differences In," 25.

[20]Warren Burger, "Shopping Survival Skills," *Stereo Review*, February 1990, 70.

[21]Thayer C. Taylor, "Show and Tell That Sells," *Sales and Marketing Management*, April 1990, 78–85.

[22]"PAs Examine the People Who Sell to Them," *Sales and Marketing Management*, November 11, 1985, 38–41.

[23]William G. Nickels, Robert F. Everett, and Ronald Klein, "Rapport Building by Salespeople: A Neuro-Linguistic Approach," *Journal of Personal Selling and Sales Management* 3 (November 1983): 1–7.

[24]*Success Factors in Selling* (Stamford, Conn.: Learning International, 1989), 6–11.

[25]Hite and Bellizzi, "Differences In," 24.

[26]Theodore Levitt, *Industrial Purchasing Behavior: A Study in Communications* (Boston: Division of Research, Harvard School of Business, 1965).

[27]Edwin K. Simpson and Ruel C. Kahler, "A Scale for Source Credibility Validated in the Selling Context," *Journal of Personal Selling and Sales Management* 1 (Fall–Winter 1980–81): 17–25.

[28]"Talk, Talk, Talk: Try a Little Listening," *The Wall Street Journal*, March 22, 1990, B1.

[29]Camille P. Schuster and Jeffrey E. Danes, "Asking Questions: Some Characteristics of Successful Sales Encounters," *Journal of Personal Selling and Sales Management* 6 (May 1986): 17–28.

[30]George Lumsden, "What You Should Tell Your Sales Force About Closing the Sale," *Sales and Marketing Executive Report* (Chicago: Dartnell Corp., 1989), 7.

[31]"Talk, Talk, Talk," *The Wall Street Journal*, March 22, 1990, B1.

[32]Shook, *The Perfect Presentation*, 166–167.

[33]Hawes, Mast, and Swan, "Trust Earning Perceptions," 7.

[34]Thomas T. Ivy and Louis E. Boone, "A Behavioral Science Approach to Effective Sales Presentations," *Journal of the Academy of Marketing Science* 4 (June 1976): 456–466.

CASE 3.1   *Primo Tableware Inc.*

Background

Primo Tableware is a major nationwide supplier of cutlery and tablecloths to the restaurant industry. The Primo Tableware product line is sold by company sales representatives to restaurant supply wholesalers, who in turn sell to restaurants and institutional food service operations. Primo has 50 sales territories across the nation.

Current Situation

Bill Reed is the Primo Tableware sales representative for the Delaware territory. Bill has been with Primo Tableware for only eight months, but he has already shown tremendous promise as a salesperson. In fact, he is currently exceeding his year-to-date sales quota, and it is rumored that he has a good chance of being named "Rookie of the Year" at the year-end sales meeting.

Bill spends about three hours a week identifying and qualifying prospects and has been able to add six new accounts in the past two months. He was also encouraged by the response of prospective customers during the recently completed national restaurant trade show.

Bill thoroughly enjoyed the restaurant show, including the after-hours fraternizing with customers, other Primo Tableware salespeople, and sales-people from other companies whom he had met during the show. One evening Bill had planned to meet four prospects in the hotel lobby and then depart for dinner. When he arrived in the lobby, Bill was surprised to find Paul Hamlin, one of his major competitors, chatting with his prospects. Bill felt a little awkward but figured that Hamlin would soon depart and that dinner with the prospects would follow. After a couple of minutes, however, one of the prospects suggested that they leave for dinner and invited Hamlin to join them. Bill did not like the way the evening was unfolding but decided to be sociable and agreed to the prospect's suggestion.

At the end of the evening, Reed and Hamlin were alone on the hotel elevator, and the following conversation ensued:

Hamlin: Looks like we both will be getting some business from those four prospects.

Reed: I am not sure about you, but I definitely plan to sell all four of them.

Hamlin: Well, maybe we could split the business on the four of them, and   . . .

Reed: (Interrupting) Forget it, Hamlin. I try to get 100 percent of all my customers' business. May the best man win.

Hamlin: Hold on, Reed, I didn't mean to upset you. All I'm saying is why don't you take two and I'll take two, and we won't waste a lot of time fighting over the business.

Reed: I don't know . . . let me think it over, and I'll give you a call.

The next day, Bill had lunch with Hamlin, and they worked out an agreement on the four prospects. They agreed to take two prospects each and not to try to sell the other two prospects.

It was now 60 days after the trade show, and the enthusiasm for prospecting that Bill had felt when he left the show was beginning to fade. He had added the two prospects that he and Hamlin had agreed on, but that seemed to be his only bright spot. Knowing that he had not faced his major competitor in adding these accounts nagged Bill, but he was glad to have the new accounts.

The leads provided by the national restaurant show had proven to be disappointing. Bill had been following up with ten prospects that were in his territory by making cold calls in person as he traveled the territory. Much to his dismay, he found that most of these prospects were interested in free samples and little else. Only one had turned out to be a qualified prospect, who had not yet been converted to customer status.

Bill needed to add new accounts before year-end. He thought that if he could do this, he would certainly be named "Rookie of the Year." At this point, he decided to try the referral method of prospecting. After wrapping up a successful sales presentation with a wholesaler, Bill asked the buyer if he knew of other wholesalers in the area who might be interested in the Primo Tableware line. In a cold tone of voice, the buyer responded, "I thought you were selling all the wholesalers in Delaware already. No, I don't know of anyone who might be interested."

Questions

1. How would you evaluate the prospecting methods illustrated in this case?
2. What recommendations would you make for Primo Tableware and Bill Reed in particular for future prospecting activities?

CASE 3.2 *Nature's Delight Foods*

Background

Becky Sharpe had just recently been assigned to the central Kentucky territory by Nature's Delight Foods, an Illinois food processor. Nature's Delight specialized in sales to large institutional food users such as employee cafeterias, school systems, and government installations. One of her key target accounts was to be Fort Knox, Kentucky, which she hoped to sell on a direct basis. She had not yet made a sales call at Fort Knox, nor had she ever made a sales call to any military organization. Her prior experience with Nature's Delight had been selling to grocery chains.

Current Situation

From what Becky had heard, selling to a military organization could be a salesperson's nightmare because of bureaucratic red tape. Undaunted, she thought the best way to proceed was to go to Fort Knox, find the decision maker, and sell the product. After arriving at the main gate, Becky was told to contact a Major Lang, who agreed to see her in an hour. Upon arrival in Lang's office, Becky found a harried man who was deeply involved in trying to coordinate the arrival of a battalion of paratroopers who were returning earlier than expected from NATO maneuvers. This had created a minicrisis, as current food supplies were inadequate to feed the returning paratroopers. The phone was ringing constantly, and clerks scurried in and out of his office with stacks of requisitions to be approved and signed. When Becky got in to see Major Lang, he confirmed that he needed to make emergency food purchases to adequately handle the demands of the next few days. These purchases would be handled on a bid basis separate from the normal food procurement system. Because of the urgency of the situation, all qualified suppliers would have 24 hours to submit bids, and vendors would have to assure immediate delivery.

Because Nature's Delight Foods was not yet an approved supplier, he quickly dismissed Becky, telling her to see Captain Maxwell down the hall. When she located Maxwell, he told her, "I hate to pass the buck, but food purchases are not in my area of responsibility. If the major gives me the responsibility, I will be glad to talk with you, but he has not mentioned it to me." Becky persuaded Captain Maxwell to call Major Lang and clarify whose responsibility it would be to make the special food purchase. After several attempts, Maxwell got through to Major Lang. After hanging up, Maxwell told Becky that he would handle food purchases "until otherwise notified" but that Lang would have final approval of all purchases.

During the next hour, Becky convinced Captain Maxwell that her products could meet required specifications and delivery requirements at a competitive price. He had agreed to place Nature's Delight Foods on the approved supplier list, which meant that Becky could bid on the food items to be purchased for this special situation. Captain Maxwell had concluded the conversation by saying, "Looks like all is in order. Let me walk your bid down to Major Lang for his reaction."

In a few minutes, Maxwell returned with bad news. First, Nature's Delight Foods normally packaged their vegetables in 5-pound packages. Major Lang had decided to specify 10-pound packages to cut down on handling time preparing the food. One 10-pound package can be opened and placed in cooking utensils faster than could two 5-pound packages. Second, Captain Maxwell had told Becky, "This is unofficial, but it looks like Major Lang is going to favor local suppliers."

Unsure of how to react, she told Captain Maxwell, "Thank you for your time, Captain. I will let you know of our bid intentions well before the deadline tomorrow."

As she left the base, Becky was considering two possibilities to increase her chances of getting the bid: (1) have a local food wholesaler bid her products and (2) have the products repackaged to meet the new specifications. If the local wholesaler bid attempt was successful, Becky would sell to the wholesaler, who would then sell to Fort Knox. On the question of repackaging, Becky recalled a statement made by her sales manager when she had requested repackaging on an earlier order: "I am not going to say no without some specifics. We are basically a stock products outfit, but if the volume is high enough and you can get an acceptable price, I'll consider it."

Questions

1. Up to this point, how would you evaluate Becky Sharpe's sales effort? How could she have improved her chances of a successful sale?
2. What do you think Becky should do next?

Sales Careers: Characteristics, Qualifications, and Stages

RUSS STAVIG: PROFILE OF A CAREER SALES EXECUTIVE   Russ Stavig's career with Armstrong World Industries spans two decades and has seen him progressively move through a variety of sales and sales management positions. Stavig, a native of South Dakota, joined Armstrong shortly after graduation from the University of South Dakota in 1970. His first assignment, after receiving an intensive 16-week sales training, was as a sales representative in Dallas, where he sold Armstrong's Floor Division products to wholesalers and other markets, including builder, do-it-yourself, commercial, and residential remodel/replacement markets.

From Dallas, Mr. Stavig moved through several positions of increasing sales responsibilities in Phoenix and New York, broadening his customer experience to include architects, specifiers, and large end users such as hospitals and schools. His territory in New York included Manhattan, the Bronx, Brooklyn, and Long Island. While on assignment in New York, he received the President's Award for Outstanding Floor Division Marketing Representative.

After completing a major wholesaler assignment in New York, Stavig moved to Houston, where he concentrated on commercial flooring products. He was promoted to contract manager in Houston, which gave him full sales and marketing responsibilities in a large portion of the Southwest. While in Houston, Russ married Joanie, a Braniff flight attendant.

Since 1985, Russ Stavig has been in Lancaster, Pennsylvania, the international headquarters for Armstrong. He has been responsible for recruiting, selecting, and training floor division marketing representatives. In addition, he is heavily involved in ongoing training for Armstrong salespeople, wholesalers, and retailers. In the late 1980s, and again in early 1990, Stavig's responsibilities were expanded to include support services such as merchandising and customer service operations.

Russ Stavig embodies the characteristics of a successful sales executive. He is dedicated to his work, yet finds time for his family and recreational interests. His enthusiasm is contagious and certainly inspires others in the Armstrong sales organization to reach their full potential.

Source: Personal interview with Russell R. Stavig, Manager, Services Support, Floor Division, Armstrong World Industries, Lancaster, Pennsylvania.

Chapter 4

Learning Objectives

After completing this chapter, you should be able to

1 *Discuss the characteristics of sales careers.*

2 *List the skills and characteristics required for success in most sales positions.*

3 *Discuss the concept of career stages as applied to salespeople.*

4 *Describe the technical, human, and conceptual skills needed in sales management.*

5 *Name the factors associated with promotion into sales management.*

6 *Explain the existence of different career paths in sales and sales management.*

As illustrated in the case of Russ Stavig, sales can be an excellent place to pursue a career that can provide job advancement based on performance. The successful salesperson typically will have opportunities to move into management, as shown in the account of Mr. Stavig's career. To fully realize these opportunities, an individual must not only perform well but also be willing to tackle assignments enthusiastically, even if it means moving the family from one location to another.

Some salespeople choose to remain in sales rather than move into management, and others pursue entrepreneurial ventures. Regardless of what may develop later in an individual's career, gaining a sound understanding of the sales function is worthwhile during the formative years of a career. Sales offers a variety of career paths, and successful salespeople have the privilege of making a choice based on individual preference.

In this chapter, we will discuss the characteristics of, qualifications for, and stages of sales careers. Their wide diversity forces us to generalize, but a look at several typical career paths should give the reader an idea of whether sales is a suitable place for him or her to start a career in business.

While individual opinions will vary, the ideal career for most people offers a bright future, including good opportunities for financial rewards and job advancement. In addition, it offers jobs that are interesting and fulfilling. A recent survey of over 1,100 college students who were seeking sales positions confirms these thoughts, as the top attributes sought in entry-level sales jobs included

- The job itself—interesting, challenging, substantial variety, and autonomy
- Pay—enough to cover normal living expenses and some luxury items
- Advancement—based on ability
- Sense of achievement—seeing results of one's work
- Personal development—opportunity to develop and refine new skills
- Recognition—from peers, supervisors, and subordinates
- Job security—within the company[1]

As you read the following sections on the characteristics of sales careers, you might think about what you expect from a career and how your expectations compare with the students whose opinions were summarized in the previous listing.

Characteristics of Sales Careers

In this discussion, we treat salespeople and sales managers as one occupational group. The characteristics to be discussed are

- Job security
- Advancement opportunities
- Immediate feedback
- Prestige
- Job variety
- Independence
- Compensation
- Boundary-role effects

EXHIBIT 4.1 ▪ *Occupational Outlook for Salespeople*

Job Type	1984 Employment	1995 Employment	Percent Increase 1984–1995
Insurance	423,000	482,000	14
Manufacturer and Wholesale	1,883,000	2,316,000	23
Real Estate	422,000	494,000	17
Retail	4,571,000	5,485,000	20
Securities/Financial	200,000	310,000	55
Miscellaneous Services	481,000	697,450	45
Travel Agents	142,000	218,680	54

Source: *Occupational Outlook Quarterly*, 34 (Spring 1990): 32.

Job Security

Salespeople are revenue producers and thus enjoy relatively good job security compared with other occupational groups. A national survey of hiring practices concluded that "field salespeople seem to be leaders of the pack in job security."[2] Certainly, individual job security depends on the individual performance, but, in general, salespeople are usually the last group to be negatively affected by personnel cutbacks. For example, as IBM headed into the 1990s, the corporation planned to eliminate 10,000 jobs in the United States, which would affect every area except sales.[3] In fact, many of those cut from other jobs with IBM would be redeployed in sales and marketing positions. A similar development was taking place at U S West Communications, where over 1,000 people were redeployed from areas such as human resources, marketing staffs, and public relations into field selling positions.[4]

Competent salespeople also have some degree of job security based on the universality of their basic sales skills. In many cases, salespeople are able to successfully move to another employer, maybe even change industries, because sales skills are largely transferrable. For salespeople working in declining or stagnant industries, this is heartening news.

Furthermore, projections by the U.S. Department of Labor indicate strong demand for salespeople in all categories in the future (see Exhibit 4.1). And growth in the number of salespeople should bring a corresponding growth in the numbers of sales management positions. According to Exhibit 4.1, there are particularly good opportunities in financial services, the travel industry, and wholesale trades.

Advancement Opportunities

The opportunity for salespeople to advance their careers through promotion into management is one of the chief advantages of sales jobs. Evidence of advancement opportunities for salespeople comes from multiple sources:

1,100 newly promoted executives polled by the University of Michigan found sales/marketing to be the best preparation for top management positions.[5]

A GLOBAL PERSPECTIVE

A Fast-Track Sales Executive

At 31, London-based Michael Camp is the youngest national account manager ever to handle major grocery accounts for Britain Lyons Tetley. Camp is responsible for Sainsbury, one of the largest and most prestigious grocery chains and, in contrast, Kwik Save, a no-frills price discounter. These accounts require diverse strategies and constant attention to yield the impressive sales results with the confectionary product "Cluster" that have become routine for Mr. Camp.

Since entering the sales field at 21, Camp has served three employers. Always advancing rapidly based on records of solid results, he has advanced through eight positions of increasing responsibility. Along the way, he has been involved in field sales, sales training, and sales management. According to Camp, his success is based on developing the right strategy for each customer, then diligently pursuing the strategy to reach sales goals he has set for himself.

Observers of Camp's sales career stress that he was not a "born salesperson" but rather that he made himself a top salesperson by learning the tools of the trade. His presentations are meticulously crafted to bring mundane trade data to life, and he understands the importance of continuing to work toward sales goals over extended periods of time.

Source: Adapted from Christine Harvey, *Secrets of the World's Top Sales Performers* (Holbrook, Mass.: Bob Adams Inc., 1990), 11–125.

- A worldwide executive-search firm concludes that sales/marketing is the most traveled route to the top and has increased its lead over other functions since 1979.[6]
- A survey of CEOs of the 1,200 largest U.S. firms showed 58 percent want their successors to have a sales/marketing background.[7]
- A best-selling book, profiling "excellent" companies, says such companies promote a disproportionate share of salespeople to general management.[8]

As the business world continues to become more competitive, the advancement opportunities for salespeople will continue to be an attractive dimension of sales careers. In highly competitive markets, individuals and companies that are successful in determining and meeting customer needs will be rewarded. Mark DeAngelis, a sales engineer for General Electric in Buffalo, New York, points out the importance of acquiring sales skills as a desirable factor to enhance career advancement: "Everyone should go into sales when they join a company. The best way to learn a business is to be in front of the customer. If I were to move on in the company, this experience would help me remember what it's like from the customer's point of view."[9] For an illustration of how selling skills can lead to job advancement, see "A Global Perspective: A Fast-Track Sales Executive."

Immediate Feedback

Salespeople receive constant, immediate feedback on their job performance. Usually, the results of their efforts can be plainly observed by both salespeople and their sales managers—a source of motivation and job satisfaction.

One interesting study of 500,000 workers found salespeople to have the highest levels of job satisfaction for any occupational group, with immediate feedback being cited as a key reason. The study concluded that job satisfaction is high among salespeople because they "see the results of their efforts almost instantly, instead of having to wait years to obtain some satisfaction for a job well done."[10]

Prestige

Traditionally, sales has not been a prestigious occupation in the eyes of the general public. There are some indications that college students are viewing sales as a more prestigious career than did their predecessors. Yet we cannot say that sales is clearly a prestigious career. More recently, the negative stereotypical images of salespeople have begun to slowly disappear.

The struggling, down-and-out huckster depicted as Willy Loman in Arthur Miller's 1949 classic *Death of a Salesman* is hardly typical of the professional salesperson of today and the future. It has been noted that professional salespeople destroy such unfavorable stereotypes and that they are "far cries from the fast-talking tub-thumpers of yesteryear."[11] These perceptions are especially true in the business world, where encounters with professional salespeople are common-place. As members of society at large become more aware of the activities of professional salespeople, the prestige of selling as a career is likely to continue to improve.

Job Variety

Salespeople rarely vegetate due to boredom. Their jobs are multifaceted and dynamic. For a person seeking the comfort of a well-established routine, sales might not be a good career choice. In sales, day-to-day variation on the job is the norm. Customers change, new products and services are developed, and competition introduces new elements at a rapid pace. Joyce Nardone of Amfax America in Needham, Massachusetts, says that the large amount of variety in her job lets her create her own job. She handles a national accounts program, coordinates Amfax's newspaper advertising, arranges trade show exhibitions, and arranges installation of fax machines in her Boston-area territory.[12]

The opportunity to become immersed in the job and bring creativity to bear is reflected in the thoughts of Jerry Della Femina, one of the most successful advertising executives in the country:

> Selling—both in and out of the advertising industry—has become highly special-ized. The science of demographics has been refined to an art. Technology has impacted on advertising as well as on every other industry. If you want to sell—products, services, yourself—you've got to keep current. You've got to know what's happening today. . . . It's hard work, and you've got to be creative—and original. Creativity is the key ingredient in all selling—not only in adver-tising.[13]

Independence

Sales jobs often allow independence of action. This independence is frequently a by-product of decentralized sales operations in which salespeople live and work away from headquarters, therefore working from their homes and making their own plans for extensive travel.

Independence of action is usually presented as an advantage that sales positions have over tightly supervised jobs. Despite its appeal, however, independence does present some problems. New recruits working from their homes may find the lack of a company office somewhat disorienting. They may need an office environment to relate to, especially if their past work experience provided regular contact in an office environment.

Work-related travel sounds more exciting than most salespeople find it to be. The realities of extensive travel include boredom, diet modification, adjusting to ever-changing sleep environments, lack of exercise, and loneliness. These negative consequences of travel can be minimized by careful planning, and life on the road need not be drudgery. Nevertheless, a fair summary statement would be that travel more closely approximates demanding work than leisurely recreation. Extensive travel also places some demands on salespeople's personal lives, whether they are married or not.

The independence of action traditionally enjoyed by salespeople is apparently being scrutinized by sales managers more heavily now than in the past. The emphasis on sales productivity, accomplished in part through cost containment, is encouraging sales managers to take a more active role in dictating travel plans and sales-call schedules.

Compensation

Salesforce compensation will be discussed in detail in a later chapter, but a few generalizations are in order now. Compensation is generally thought to be a strong advantage of sales careers. Pay is closely tied to performance, especially if commissions and bonuses are part of the pay package. For example, one study found that salespeople who work solely on commission earn four times as much as what straight-salary salespeople earn.[14]

Starting salaries for inexperienced salespeople with a college degree typically range from $25,000 to $30,000. Between the extremes of the highly experienced salesperson and the inexperienced recruit, an average salesperson earns approximately $45,000 to $50,000 per year.[15]

Boundary-Role Effects

Salespeople are **boundary-role performers.** That is, they occupy boundary-spanning positions between their employers and their customers. Their loyalties are sometimes torn between customer demands and the expectations of their company or their sales manager. For example, the company may want to sell at list price, while the customer demands a discount. The salesperson is caught between the two parties and somehow must resolve the situation. This is but one example of the **role conflict** routinely experienced by salespeople.

Another dimension of boundary-spanning jobs such as sales jobs is **role ambiguity.** It occurs when the salesperson is unsure about what to do in a situation where no policy or procedure applies. This is not an uncommon event, given the variable nature of sales situations which sometimes require innovative problem solving.

The uncertainty arising from a lack of direction can contribute to **role stress.** Role conflict may also contribute to role stress, which salespeople, sales managers, organizational psychologists, and sales researchers all agree is strongly associated with sales careers. There is no escaping the conclusion that sales is a high-visibility, "spotlight" position. The revenue-production responsibilities of salespeople create considerable pressure to perform. When customer expectations are at odds with the employer's expectations, the pressure rises.

Some salespeople thrive in stressful situations. Catherine Hogan, an account manager with Bell Atlantic Network in Maryland, is one salesperson who enjoys the challenge of her sometimes-stressful job. She started her career as a temporary employee in marketing but sought a field sales assignment to "get out there and feel the heat—take risks, handle customers, and be responsible for their complaints."[16] For most salespeople, stress is a large part of the job. Some handle it satisfactorily, and some do not.

Qualifications and Skills Required for Success by Salespeople

Since there are so many different types of jobs in sales, it is rather difficult to generalize about the qualifications and skills needed for success. This list would have to vary according to the details of a given job. Even then, it is reasonable to believe that for any given job, different people with different skills could be successful. These conclusions have been reached after decades of research that has tried to correlate sales performance with physical traits, mental abilities, personality characteristics, and the experience and background of the salesperson.[17]

It should also be noted that many of the skills and characteristics leading to success in sales would do the same in practically any professional business occupation. For example, the *Occupational Outlook Handbook* published by the U.S. Department of Labor points out the importance of various personal attributes for success in sales, including the following: outgoing, enthusiastic personality; self-confidence; and self-discipline.[18] Who could dispute the value of such traits for any occupation?

Having made these introductory, rather cautionary, remarks, let us consider some of the skills and qualifications that are thought to be especially critical for success in most sales jobs.

Five factors that seem to be particularly important for success in sales are empathy, ego drive, ego strength, verbal communication skills, and enthusiasm.

These factors have been selected after reviewing three primary sources of information:

- A study of over 750,000 salespeople in 15,000 companies (Greenberg and Greenberg)[19]
- A review of 30 years of research on factors related to sales success (Comer and Dubinsky)[20]
- Surveys of sales and marketing executives[21]

Empathy. In a sales context, **empathy** (the ability to see things as others would see them) includes being able to read cues furnished by the customer to better determine the customer's viewpoint. An empathetic salesperson is presumably in a better position to tailor the sales presentation to the customer during the planning stages. More importantly, empathetic salespeople can adjust to feedback during the presentation. Though not verified by research, it is reasonable to link empathy with listening skills. The importance of effective listening was confirmed in a survey of sales and marketing executives conducted by the Princeton Research and Consulting Center, which rated it as the most critical skill for salespeople.[22]

The research of Greenberg and Greenberg found empathy to be a significant predictor of sales success. This finding was partially supported in the review by Comer and Dubinsky, who found empathy to be an important factor in consumer and insurance sales but not in retail or industrial sales.

Ego Drive. In a sales context, **ego drive** (an indication of the degree of determination a person has to achieve goals and overcome obstacles in striving for success) is manifested as an inner need to persuade others in order to achieve personal gratification. Greenberg and Greenberg point out the complementary relationship between empathy and ego drive that is necessary for sales success. The salesperson who is extremely empathetic but lacks ego drive may have problems in taking active steps to confirm a sale. On the other hand, a salesperson with excessive ego drive relative to empathy may ignore the customer's viewpoint in an ill-advised, overly anxious attempt to gain commitment from the customer.

Ego Strength. The degree to which a person is able to achieve an approximation of inner drives is **ego strength.** Salespeople with high levels of ego strength are likely to be self-assured and self-accepting. Salespeople with healthy egos are better equipped to deal with the possibility of rejection throughout the sales process. They are probably less likely to experience sales call reluctance and are resilient enough to overcome the disappointment of inevitable lost sales.

Kathy Serfilippi, a sales representative with American Airlines, understands the importance of ego strength in selling. When she first tried to book the national convention of the Veterans of Foreign Wars (VFW), she was turned down. Since she was not afraid to go back and ask again, she was successful the next year in having the VFW designate American as the official airline of the national convention, to be attended by 25,000 VFW members.[23]

Verbal Communication Skills. Executives who recruit salespeople cite **verbal communication skills,** including listening, as being essential for sales success. Closely related to listening is another important verbal communication skill, questioning. Chris Greene, district manager for J. Strickland and Company, a national supplier of health and beauty aids, offers these comments on questioning: "I encourage the use of questions to get the buyer involved, so that we can reach an understanding of what he or she needs. Sometimes buyers are not really sure what they want, and we can help them express their desires with questions. I tell my salespeople that they should use questions, even if they already know the answers, so that the buyer can go through a self-realization process with regard to what they want in a given transaction."[24]

The importance of verbal communication skills is borne out in surveys of executives, who rate this skill area among the top five attributes of potential new hires in sales and marketing.[25] Students who are in the job market corroborated the importance of these skills in a parallel survey, ranking verbal communication skills as the most important personal attribute in finding a job.[26]

Research on communication styles in selling indicates that salespeople can be more effective by recognizing different communication styles utilized by their customers and then adapting their own styles of communication. Empirical study has confirmed the role of verbal communication styles in successful sales interactions.[27]

The importance of verbal skills has been recognized by sales managers, recruiters, and sales researchers. These skills can be continually refined throughout a sales career, a positive factor from both a personal and a career-development perspective.

Enthusiasm. When sales executives and recruiters discuss qualifications for sales positions, they invariably include **enthusiasm.** They are usually referring to dual dimensions of enthusiasm—an enthusiastic attitude in a general sense and a special enthusiasm for selling. On-campus recruiters have told us that they seek students who are well beyond "interested in sales" to the point of truly being enthusiastic about career opportunities in sales. Recruiters are somewhat weary of "selling sales" as a viable career, and they welcome the job applicant who displays genuine enthusiasm for the field.

One survey of sales executives found enthusiasm to be the most important characteristic sought in newly hired salespeople.[28] Further evidence of the importance of enthusiasm in sales comes from Peters and Austin, who observed in top companies: "Early in their career, young men and women on the move clamor for an opportunity to be in sales."[29]

Comments on Qualifications and Skills

The qualifications and skills needed for sales success are quite different today from those required for success two decades ago. As the popularity of relationship

EXHIBIT 4.2 ▪ *Skills Needed for Success in Sales*

Traditional Selling	*Relationship Selling*
"Me"-oriented	"We"-oriented
Persuasion	Communication
Showmanship	Interviewing
Aggressiveness	Questioning
Thick skin	Cooperation
Competitiveness	Sensitivity
Killer instinct	Helping instinct

Source: Jim Cathcart, "Traditional vs. Relationship Selling," *The Selling Advantage* 1, No. 24 (February 1990): 2.

selling grows, the skills necessary for sales success will evolve to meet the needs of the marketplace. For example, Greenberg and Greenberg's research has identified what they call an "emerging factor" for sales success, a strong motivation to provide service to the customer.[30] They contrast this **service motivation** with ego drive by noting that while ego drive relates to persuading others, service motivation comes from desiring the approval of others. For example, a salesperson may be extremely gratified to please a customer through superior postsale service. Greenberg and Greenberg conclude that most salespeople will need both service motivation and ego drive to succeed, although they note that extremely high levels of both attributes are not likely to exist in the same individual. Other skills associated with success in relationship selling are shown in Exhibit 4.2.

Our discussion of factors related to sales success is necessarily brief, as a fully descriptive treatment of the topic must be tied to a given sales position. Veteran sales managers and recruiters can often specify with amazing precision what qualifications and skills are needed to succeed in a given sales job. These assessments are usually based on a mixture of objective and subjective judgments that will be discussed in the chapter on recruitment and selection later in the book.

Salesperson Career Stages

An interesting way to examine sales careers is to consider the various stages that salespeople pass through over the course of their careers. The **salesperson career cycle** was first discussed by Jolson in 1974.[31] Jolson theorized that salespeople pass through career stages in the same fashion that a product might move through its life cycle. He linked performance to the various stages in the career cycle—improving to a plateau, then declining as the salesperson approached the end of his or her career. The usefulness of the career cycle concept was in its recognition that the

EXHIBIT 4.3 ▪ *Salesperson's Career Stages*

	Career Stage Characteristics			
	Exploration	*Establishment*	*Maintenance*	*Disengagement*
Career Concerns:	Finding an appropriate occupational field.	Successfully establishing a career in a certain occupation.	Holding on to what has been achieved. Reassessing career, with possible redirection.	Completing one's career.
Developmental Tasks:	Learning the skills required to do the job well. Becoming a contributing member of an organization.	Using skills to produce results. Adjusting to working with greater autonomy. Developing creativity and innovativeness.	Developing broader view of work and organization. Maintaining a high performance level.	Establishing a stronger self-identity outside of work. Maintaining an acceptable performance level.
Personal Challenges:	Must establish a good initial professional self-concept.	Producing superior results on the job in order to be promoted. Balancing the conflicting demands of career and family.	Maintaining motivation though possible rewards have changed. Facing concerns about aging and disappointment over what one has accomplished. Maintaining motivation and productivity.	Acceptance of career accomplishments. Adjusting self-image.
Psychosocial Needs:	Support. Peer acceptance. Challenging position.	Achievement. Esteem. Autonomy. Competition.	Reduced competitiveness. Security. Helping younger colleagues.	Detachment from organization and organizational life.

Source: William L. Cron, "Industrial Salesperson Development. A Career Stages Perspective." Reprinted from *Journal of Marketing* 48 (Fall 1984): 45, published by the American Marketing Association.

challenges and desires relevant for a salesperson would change as the salesperson progressed through the stages.

Ten years after Jolson introduced the concept to sales management, other researchers refined the concept and began empirical research on career stages likely to be encountered by salespeople. Cron offered a modified perspective, summarized in Exhibit 4.3. As shown in Exhibit 4.3, salespeople's careers can be broken down into four distinct stages: exploration, establishment, maintenance, and disengagement. For each of the four stages, there will be different career concerns, developmental tasks, personal challenges, and psychosocial needs.

Exploration

In the **exploration stage,** people are most concerned with finding the right occupational field. They aspire to be accepted as productive members of the organization, and they must learn the basic skills of the job.

Establishment

In the **establishment stage,** salespeople commit to the sales field as an occupation of choice. Their skills are increasing, and they may begin to concentrate on producing better results. They become more autonomous on the job as they no longer rely heavily on direction from supervisors.

Maintenance

The **maintenance stage** is characterized by holding on to achievement levels and perhaps reassessing future career direction. At this point, performance has reached a satisfactory plateau, and the salesperson strives to maintain the plateau.

Disengagement

The **disengagement stage** is the transition from work to retirement. Salespeople's perspectives become more oriented toward factors outside the organization, such as retirement planning and establishing an identity outside the work environment.

Conclusions on Concept of Salesperson Career Stages

The career stages concept as applied to salespeople has begun to generate considerable research interest. Cron and Slocum studied 446 salespeople in six industrial firms and found that salespeople in the exploration stage often were not convinced they had made the right occupational choice. Salespeople in later stages, however, reported higher levels of job satisfaction. Further, salespeople in the maintenance stage reported quite positive attitudes toward their work and had the highest performance levels of any of the salespeople in the study.[32] In a study of 336 insurance agents, Hafer also reported higher sales levels in the latter stages of the career cycle.[33]

These studies imply that a sales career is not right for everyone, but those who do continue in sales find it rewarding. One reason for this result is that poor performers in the sales field usually exit, leaving those who will prosper, and thus enjoy, their work.

Another important finding from the research on career stages is that salespeople can move into various stages irrespective of their age or job tenure. Cron and Slocum's study found, for example, that salespeople in their forties might be grappling with exploration issues, or alternatively might be concerned with disengagement.[34] Another study found little connection between job tenure and a career-stage indicator, vocational maturity.[35]

A considerable number of salespeople will spend their entire career without advancing into management. Often, these career salespeople form the foundation of a company's salesforce. Other salespeople move into management, with the first assignment quite likely being in sales management. While similarities exist between selling and sales management positions, there are substantial differences in the two types of jobs. A discussion of the skills and characteristics required for success in sales management follows.

Qualifications and Skills Required for Success in Sales Management

Sales management positions are relatively more complex than personal-selling positions, as suggested by sales executive David Moore in Chapter 1. Sales managers frequently are charged with motivating and supervising salespeople they see on an irregular basis. Moreover, they often retain sales responsibility for designated accounts in addition to their managerial duties such as recruiting, training, and evaluating performance. Sales managers are also involved in planning, forecasting, and budgeting activities to a greater degree than the salespeople they supervise.

The overall perspective of salespeople as compared with sales managers is different. Salespeople have an individual perspective, and they focus on sales development. Salespeople are subordinates within the organization, typically having no supervisory responsibilities. Compared with sales managers, salespeople's jobs are narrowly defined and in many cases extremely specialized. In contrast, sales managers focus on getting results through the efforts of other people. They have a team perspective in two ways—they see their salesforce as a team of which they are leaders, and they view themselves as being part of a management team. Finally, sales managers' roles as superiors and as subordinates complicate their job.[36]

Figure 4.1 depicts three categories of skills required of sales managers: technical, human, and conceptual. The triangular representation in the figure suggests that more candidates for sales management positions acquire the requisite technical skills than acquire the necessary human skills. The narrowing process continues in that fewer still master the conceptual skills needed for sales management.

Technical Skills

The basic foundation of **technical skills** required for sales managers is acquired in the personal selling position. While sales managers generally agree that the best salesperson does not always make the best sales manager, incompetent salespeople are rarely promoted into sales management.

It is essential that salespeople learn the basic technical skills of the selling job before moving into sales management because they must prove their competence in that area in order to be able to influence subordinates. Also, they must be able to transfer technical knowledge to their salesforce. Fundamental skills must be

FIGURE 4.1   ▪   *From Selling to Sales Management: A Developmental Model*

Three categories of skills are necessary in sales management: technical, human, and conceptual. The technical skills required for sales management are acquired primarily as a result of experience gained as a salesperson. Human skills are more difficult to attain than technical skills, and conceptual skills are the most difficult to attain.

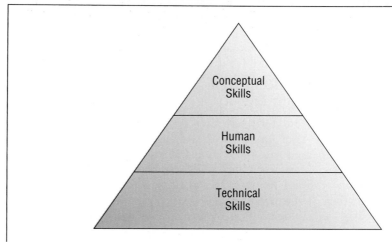

Source: *Harvard Business Review*, "Skills of an Effective Administrator" by Robert L. Katz (September/October 1974).

acquired in product, market, and company knowledge, sales techniques, and time and territory management before a salesperson is ready for promotion. Further, salespeople are wise to begin developing abilities in managerially oriented technical activities such as sales forecasting while still functioning in a personal selling job.

Human Skills

Human skills, those related to the development and management of effective working relationships, are critical for sales managers. As Figure 4.1 indicates, these skills are more difficult to attain than the technical skills needed for sales management. Three human skills required of sales managers are verbal communication skills, written communication skills, and leadership skills.

We previously noted the importance of verbal communication skills in personal selling positions. These skills become even more important as individuals move into sales management. Group presentations are given more frequently—to customers, to members of the management team, and to the salesforce. Sales managers must become adept at communicating sensitive information relating to matters such as performance appraisals and termination of employment for salespeople.

Written communications are stressed more in sales management than in most sales positions. Producing communications for the entire salesforce as opposed to writing for a single recipient requires a different approach, and planning documents must be precise and clear. Salespeople are being called upon more often to produce credible written communications, but for the most part, the scope of their written communications is much narrower than for sales managers. Salespeople concentrate on sales proposals, sales letters, and reports requested by management. Sales managers must prepare a far wider range of materials and require more versatility in written communication.

Leadership skills are those related to the interpersonal relationships between the sales manager and members of the salesforce. Sales managers act as leaders as they seek to accomplish organizational goals with the support of the salesforce. A later chapter will consider salesforce leadership in detail.

Conceptual Skills

As Figure 4.1 implies, only a relatively small number of salespeople master the final level of skills necessary for successful sales management, **conceptual skills.** Within a sales management context, conceptual skills refer to understanding the operational rationale of the organization, problem solving, adopting a systems approach, and utilizing a strategic planning perspective.

Understanding the *operational rationale* (why we do what we do) is the foundation for developing other important conceptual skills needed in sales management. This foundation is inextricably linked to the other conceptual skills. Problems cannot be logically solved without understanding the operational rationale of the organization. The *systems approach* dictates that the interactions between various elements in the organization, such as marketing, manufacturing, finance, and personnel, be taken into account as sales managers perform their jobs. A *strategic planning perspective* begins with an understanding of the organization's mission, which is highly suggestive of the operational rationale of the organization.

Success Factors Ranked by Sales Executives

In summarizing the technical, human, and conceptual skills necessary for sales management, it becomes readily apparent that competence in a selling job is a necessary, but not sufficient, condition for successful sales management. To gain further insight into the skills and characteristics thought to be important in sales management, we will review the findings of two surveys that asked sales executives and human resource managers their opinions. The factors deemed important for promotion into sales management by both sales executives and human resource managers are shown in Exhibit 4.4.

The sales executives survey disputed the conventional wisdom that sales managers should be highly extroverted, have keen political instinct, and have "workaholic" tendencies.[37] In one conflicting finding between the two surveys, human resource managers in Fortune 500 companies did feel that the combination

EXHIBIT 4.4 ▪ *Factors Associated with Promotion to Sales Management*

1. Intellectual ability, mental skills
2. Self-motivation
3. Human relations skills, handling people
4. Persuasiveness
5. Personal impact, has respect of others
6. Behavior flexibility, mature and cooperative
7. Ambition, desires advancement

Source: Compiled from Donald B. Guest and Havva J. Meric, "The Fortune 500 Companies' Selection Criteria for Promotion to First Level Sales Management," *Journal of Personal Selling and Sales Management* 9 (Fall 1989): 47–52; and Alan J. Dubinsky and Thomas N. Ingram, "Important First-line Sales Management Qualifications: What Sales Executives Think," *Journal of Personal Selling and Sales Management* 3 (May 1983): 18–25.

of a high energy level and workaholic tendencies was an important factor in gaining promotion into sales management.[38]

In the sales executives survey, respondents also identified integrity as an important factor in being promoted into sales management. For more discussion on integrity in sales management, see "An Ethical Perspective: The Sales Manager as a Role Model."

As you look over the factors thought to be associated with opportunities to enter sales management, it may occur to you that these characteristics would be desirable for managers in any area. This is true, and perhaps this explains, at least in part, why sales and sales management is a solid preparation for upper-management positions.

AN ETHICAL PERSPECTIVE

The Sales Manager as a Role Model   When unethical sales practices are investigated, often the sales manager has failed to provide proper guidance to salespeople or, worse yet, has encouraged the unethical behavior.

One example of unethical sales behavior that was apparently condoned by management occurred in Hollywood, Florida, where salespeople surreptitiously listened in on customers' conversations. By eavesdropping, salespeople were better prepared to overcome customer questions and objections. The customers had been lured to the showroom of Space Tech Industries with promises of free gifts after they had completed marketing surveys. Once in the showroom, the custom-

ers received a high-pressure sales presentation that encouraged them to buy a six-year supply of soap products. The products had not been mentioned in the surveys. It is hard to imagine that these events could have taken place without the knowledge of sales management.

Sales managers must realize that one of their major job responsibilities is to serve as a role model for their salespeople. Further, sales managers must be prepared to provide strong guidance in sales ethics and to discipline salespeople who violate ethical policies.

Source: "Sales Reps Allegedly Listened in on Customers," *Marketing News*, January 21, 1991.

FIGURE 4.2 ▪ *Career Paths in Sales and Sales Management*

The career paths shown are for illustrative purposes only. In the career sales path, the individual concentrates directly on actual selling activities throughout the career path. The management path includes jobs where directing the efforts of others in addition to actual selling are key activities.

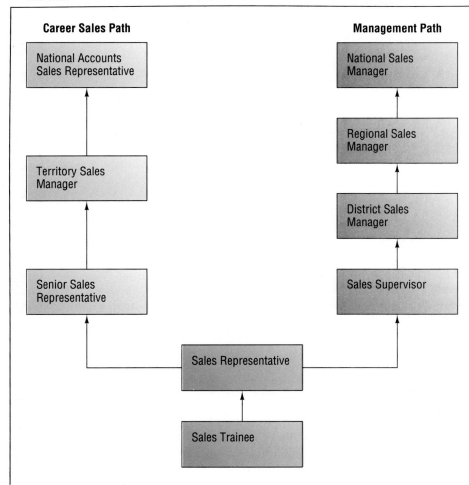

Source: Danny N. Bellenger and Thomas N. Ingram, *Professional Selling* (New York: Macmillan Publishing Company, 1984), p. 8.

Career Paths in Sales and Sales Management

Generic Career Paths

Individuals who begin their careers as salespeople may pursue any of an almost endless variety of **career paths.** As previously indicated, many salespeople move into management and perhaps entrepreneurial ventures. Two typical generic (that is, not company-specific) career paths, one for career salespeople and one for those who enter management after beginning in sales, are shown in Figure 4.2. Some

FIGURE 4.3 ▪ *E. J. Gallo Career Path*

This career path illustrates the first few years in the career of an individual hired as a sales representative for E. J. Gallo Winery. Of course, another individual hired in this capacity might have an entirely different career path.

Source: E. J. Gallo, Modesto, California. Used with permission.

salespeople become managers, then return to the job of a salesperson. Career paths vary not only from company to company but also sometimes within the same company. The path followed depends on the individual's strengths, successes, and preferences as well as various circumstantial factors beyond the control of the individual. The career paths shown are for illustrative purposes only. In the career sales path, the individual concentrates directly on actual selling activities throughout the career path. The management path includes jobs where directing the efforts of others in addition to actual selling are key activities.

Company-Specific Examples of Career Paths

Figure 4.3 illustrates the early stages of a potential career path for E. J. Gallo Winery of Modesto, California. This path would lead an individual through three phases—sales representative, first-level sales manager, and field-marketing manager-in-training. Those who succeed during the first two phases will become field-marketing managers-in-training in approximately two to three years.

In addition to actual selling, a Gallo sales representative would be involved in a variety of other tasks, including territory management, merchandising, servicing, product distribution, and working with distributors. With Gallo, a first-level sales manager begins sales management and executive training with the opportunity to manage other people. In Phase III, Gallo marketing managers are responsible for developing and implementing various marketing programs. Marketing managers are involved in pricing, advertising, new product decisions, and assuring growth in Gallo's markets.

The career path illustrated in Figure 4.3 is relatively simple since it extends only a few years into the future of a newly hired sales representative. A more complex career path is shown in Figure 4.4 for Beecham Products, whose products include Aqua-Fresh toothpaste, Sucrets lozenges, and Cling-Free fabric softener. In the Beecham career path, the territory manager position corresponds closely to

FIGURE 4.4 ▪ *Beecham Products Company Career Path*

Salespeople might progress in a straight path as indicated by the shaded boxes, or hold other jobs, examples of which are shown in the nonshaded boxes, as their careers advance. This career path at Beecham Products Company, like the one shown in Figure 4.3 for E. J. Gallo Winery, is only one example of several possible paths.

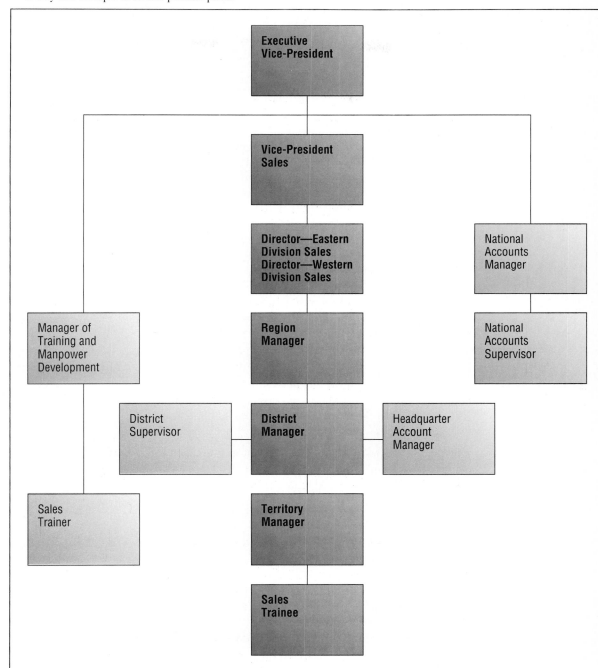

Source: Courtesy of Beecham Products, U.S.A. Training & Manpower Development Department.

Phase I in the Gallo career path. The Beecham district manager holds a first-level sales management position comparable to Phase II in the Gallo career path. While the successful Gallo first-level sales manager would move into marketing management, the Beecham first-level sales manager would continue into other sales management positions, such as sales trainer, regional sales manager, and national accounts manager.

Summary

1.   Discuss the characteristics of sales careers. Sales careers are characterized by relatively good job security and reasonable opportunities for advancement. Salespeople get immediate feedback on the job, and this may explain why job satisfaction for salespeople is higher than in many other occupational groups. The prestige of selling seems to be improving gradually. An advantage of sales careers is that they offer the salesperson the chance to become totally involved in a creative, dynamic occupation where boredom is rare. Sales careers have long been associated with independence of action, although sales managers lately are monitoring sales activities more closely to improve sales productivity. Salespeople are paid fairly well, with those receiving incentive pay such as commissions being paid better than those on a straight salary. Salespeople occupy boundary roles between their customers and their employers. These roles often produce conflict and stress due to pressure to perform well for multiple parties.

2.   List the skills and characteristics required for success in most sales positions. While there is not a universal profile of the successful salesperson, research indicates certain characteristics may be associated with sales success, namely, empathy, ego drive, ego strength, verbal communication skills, and enthusiasm.

3.   Discuss the concept of career stages as applied to salespeople. Research indicates that salespeople move through four stages in their careers — exploration, establishment, maintenance, and disengagement. Job performance and attitudes vary as salespeople pass through the career stages. One major study found that salespeople in the maintenance stage generally had the highest levels of job performance.

4.   Describe the technical, human, and conceptual skills needed in sales management. There are fundamental differences in the job responsibilities of salespeople and sales managers. It is common for salespeople to be promoted into sales management. The technical skills necessary for sales management have been largely acquired in the sales position. Various human skills involving communications and leadership must be developed. Conceptual skills dealing with strategic planning and problem solving must also be developed by sales managers.

5.   Name the factors associated with promotion into sales management. The limited research into this area is summarized in Exhibit 4.4. According to this exhibit, both sales executives and human resource managers agree that intellectual skills and mental abilities are important factors in earning a promotion. Human relations skills are also quite important, as witnessed by several factors shown in the exhibit. Quite logically, it is also important for the candidate for promotion to display a strong ambition to be promoted into sales management. Sales executives also feel that integrity is important, while human resource managers think that being a high-energy workaholic is a key factor in being promoted into sales management.

6. Explain the existence of different career paths in sales and sales management. Many different sales career paths are possible within an industry and even, sometimes, within a company. Career paths of successful salespeople can include management positions and entrepreneurial ventures.

Key Terms

- **Boundary-role performers**
- **Role conflict**
- **Role ambiguity**
- **Role stress**
- **Empathy**
- **Ego drive**
- **Ego strength**
- **Verbal communication skills**
- **Enthusiasm**
- **Service motivation**

- **Salesperson career cycle**
- **Exploration stage**
- **Establishment stage**
- **Maintenance stage**
- **Disengagement stage**
- **Technical skills**
- **Human skills**
- **Conceptual skills**
- **Career paths**

Review Questions

1. How would you assess sales in terms of the criteria for an ideal career presented in this chapter?
2. Review the story of Michael Camp in "A Global Perspective: A Fast-Track Sales Executive." What are the pros and cons of making frequent job changes during a career?
3. Salespeople enjoy relatively good job security and opportunities for advancement into management. Why is this so, and will these conditions hold true in the foreseeable future?
4. Explain what is meant by the statement that "salespeople are boundary-role performers."
5. What factors contribute to job stress for salespeople?
6. Describe the balance between empathy and ego drive required for sales success.
7. Explain the concept of the salesperson career cycle. Which stages can you identify in the profile of Russ Stavig at the beginning of the chapter?

8. What are the fundamental differences between sales jobs and sales management jobs?

9. Describe the technical, human, and conceptual skills required for sales management.

10. Review the boxed insert entitled "An Ethical Perspective: The Sales Manager as a Role Model." What factors contribute to the difficulty of ensuring ethical sales behavior?

Application Exercises

1. Arrange interviews with several sales executives to solicit their opinions about sales careers. Develop a list of questions before you call for an interview appointment. Suggested questions follow:

- What is the most positive aspect of a career in sales?
- What is the most negative aspect of a career in sales?
- What factors are related to sales success in your field?
- Can a successful salesperson succeed in any selling job?
- What is the future outlook for women in sales management?
- Would you recommend selling to a close friend or family member?

Summarize your findings, focusing on differences of opinions among the executives, and be prepared to discuss the results of your interviews in class.

2. An excellent way to learn about career opportunities in sales is to gain experience through an internship in sales. It may be possible for you to earn academic credit through your university for internships. Check with your academic advisor. Even if academic credit is not feasible, you might want to pursue an internship as a sales assistant or as a sales trainee. Contact likely employers (any firm with a salesforce), offering to work as a sales assistant. Stress that you are interested in learning about sales careers. Be flexible on the matter of compensation, as some of the best learning opportunities come in the form of unpaid internships. Clarify job duties and the objectives of the internship with your employer before you start the internship. Keep a daily log of your activities, and write a report at the end of the internship detailing your learning experience. A multitude of organizations that offer internships are identified in *Internships, Volume I: Advertising, Marketing, Public Relations, and Sales*, ed. Ronald W. Fry (Hawthorne, N.J.: Career Press Inc., 1988).

3. Ethical dilemmas are frequently encountered in all occupational settings, including sales. Some college students encounter their first occupational ethical dilemma during their pursuit of an entry-level job upon graduation. What would you do if you were Rick Gibson in the following scenario?

Rick Gibson will graduate from a university in the Midwest in two weeks, and he has been seeking an entry-level sales position. His first choice for an employer is Xerox. His interviews with Xerox have gone well, but Xerox has informed Rick that a reorganization of the salesforce is occurring and that hiring has been suspended for 60 days. Xerox management is telling Rick that it is likely that he will receive an offer, but there are no guarantees. Meanwhile, Rick has a firm offer from E. J. Gallo to begin work immediately upon graduation. Gallo has given Rick a week to decide on its offer, which would involve a relocation to its California headquarters. Gallo is an attractive company to Rick, but he has wanted to work for Xerox since he completed a favorable internship with the company last summer. At this point, Rick is considering accepting the Gallo offer but switching to Xerox if an offer materializes.

Notes

[1] Stephen B. Castleberry, "The Importance of Various Motivational Factors to College Students Interested in Sales Positions," *Journal of Personal Selling and Sales Management* 10 (Spring 1990): 67–72.

[2] "The Job Market: Quick, Get Me a Field Sales Manager," *Sales and Marketing Management*, May 1987, 27.

[3] John W. Verity, "A Slimmer IBM May Still Be Overweight," *Business Week*, December 18, 1989, 107–108.

[4] "At U S West, A Chance to Shift into Selling," *Sales and Marketing Management*, April 1989, 28.

[5] "Marketing Newsletter," *Sales and Marketing Management*, December 9, 1985, 29.

[6] "Marketing Newsletter," *Sales and Marketing Management*, February 1987, 27.

[7] "CEO Survey Finds Marketers Sought for Their Successors," *Marketing News*, January 30, 1987, 5.

[8] Thomas J. Peters and Nancy K. Austin, *A Passion for Excellence* (New York: Random House, 1985), 107.

[9] Martin Everett, "Selling's New Breed: Smart and Feisty," *Sales and Marketing Management*, October 1989, 54.

[10] "Industrial Newsletter," *Sales and Marketing Management*, July 1986, 43.

[11] Marc Hequet, "No More Willy Loman," *Training*, May 1989, 11.

[12] Everett, "Selling's New Breed," 59.

[13] William J. Birnes and Gary Markham, *Selling at the Top* (New York: Harper and Row, 1985), ix.

[14] "Commissioned Reps Make Out," *Business Marketing*, March 1987, 42.

[15] "Survey of Selling Costs," *Sales and Marketing Management*, February 26, 1990, 76.

[16] Everett, "Selling's New Breed," 52.

[17] Gilbert A. Churchill, Jr., Neil M. Ford, Steven W. Hartley, and Orville C. Walker, Jr., "The Determinants of Salesperson Performance: A Meta-Analysis," *Journal of Marketing Research* 22 (May 1985): 103–118.

[18] *Occupational Outlook Handbook, 1986–87 Edition* (Washington, D.C.: U.S. Department of Labor Statistics, April 1986), 253.

[19] See Herbert M. Greenberg and Jeanne Greenberg, *What It Takes to Succeed in Sales* (Homewood, Ill.: Dow-Jones Irwin, 1990).

[20] James M. Comer and Alan J. Dubinsky, *Managing the Successful Sales Force* (Lexington, Mass.: D.C. Heath and Co., 1985), 5–22.

[21] See Ralph M. Gaedeke and Dennis H. Tootelian, "Employers Rate Enthusiasm and Communication as Top Job Skills," *Marketing News*, March 27, 1989, 14.

[22] Arthur Bragg, "Listen Up," *Sales and Marketing Management*, February 1990, 10.

[23] Everett, "Selling's New Breed," 60–61.

[24] Personal interview with Chris Greene, District Manager, J. Strickland and Company, St. Louis, Mo.

[25] Ralph M. Gaedeke and Dennis H. Tootelian, "Gap Found Between Employers' and Students' Perceptions of Most Desirable Job Attributes," *Marketing News*, May 22, 1989, 42.

[26] Ibid.

[27] Kaylene C. Williams and Rosann L. Spiro, "Communication Style in the Salesperson-Customer Dyad," *Journal of Marketing Research* 22 (November 1985): 434–442.

[28] Gaedeke and Tootelian, "Employers Rate."

[29] Peters and Austin, *A Passion for Excellence*, 108.

[30] Greenberg and Greenberg, *What It Takes*, 38–42.

[31] Marvin A. Jolson, "The Salesman's Career Cycle," *Journal of Marketing* 38 (July 1974): 39–46.

[32] William L. Cron and John W. Slocum, Jr., "The Influence of Career Stages on Salespeople's Job Attitudes, Work Perceptions, and Performance," *Journal of Marketing Research* 23 (May 1986): 119–129.

[33] John C. Hafer, "An Empirical Investigation of the Salesperson's Career Stages Perspective," *Journal of Personal Selling and Sales Management* 6 (November 1986): 1–7.

[34] Cron and Slocum, "The Influence of Career Stages," 119–129.

[35] Alan J. Dubinsky, Thomas N. Ingram, and Charles H. Fay, "An Empirical Investigation of the Assumed Job Tenure-Vocational Maturity Linkage in the Industrial Sales Force," *Journal of the Academy of Marketing Science* 12 (Fall 1984): 52–62.

[36] Based on Alan J. Dubinsky and Thomas N. Ingram, "From Selling to Sales Management: A Developmental Model," *Journal of Business and Industrial Marketing* 2 (Spring 1987): 27–36.

[37]Alan J. Dubinsky and Thomas N. Ingram, "Important First-Line Sales Management Qualifications: What Sales Executives Think," *Journal of Personal Selling and Sales Management* 3 (May 1983): 18–25.

[38]Donald B. Guest and Havva J. Meric, "The Fortune 500 Companies' Selection Criteria for Promotion to First Level Sales Management," *Journal of Personal Selling and Sales Management* 9 (Fall 1989): 47–52.

CASE 4.1 *Bill Hanson's Career Change*

Background

Six months ago, Bill Hanson was passed over for promotion into sales management. Bill, a five-year sales veteran with Rap-Bat, a sporting goods manufacturer, had registered his displeasure with John Blackstone, district sales manager and Hanson's immediate supervisor. Blackstone had advised Hanson to keep working hard and a future promotion might be a possibility. Blackstone was careful, however, to stress that there were no guarantees that Hanson would get a promotion. A month later, Blackstone assigned Hanson to a special project that would require Hanson to spend 50 percent of his time working in Miami rather than in his Atlanta-based territory. During these 90 days, Hanson's regular accounts would receive supplemental sales coverage from Blackstone to reinforce Hanson's "part-time" coverage. Blackstone advised Hanson that if he did a good job with the temporary assignment in Miami, it would bolster his chances of being promoted, but he reminded Hanson that there were no firm assurances of a future promotion.

Current Situation

Blackstone has been told by one of Hanson's Atlanta-based customers that Hanson is planning to leave his current job to pursue a job with a Rap-Bat competitor. According to the customer, Hanson has been quite vocal in sharing his unhappiness with his current situation with Rap-Bat. The customer, an old college friend of Blackstone's, has told Blackstone: "Obviously, Hanson is not aware of our past connections. I'm not kidding, John, the man comes in here and all he can talk about is how he has been shafted, and now it's his turn to get even. He left here 15 minutes ago, and I was glad to see him leave. Could you come by later this week to handle an order for me?"

Somewhat shaken by this information, Blackstone decides to take action. Coincidentally, the phone rings, and it is Hanson. Blackstone asks him where he is calling from, and Hanson replies that he is in Miami. Given his conversation with the Atlanta customer, Blackstone is infuriated. He decides on the spot to fire Hanson but wants to take steps to recover the Miami customer records from him. Consulting his airline schedule guide, he gives Hanson an Eastern Airlines flight number and instructs Hanson to meet him at the airport in Miami at 4:00 p.m. later in the day. Hanson protests that he is too busy to make the extra trip to the airport, but Blackstone insists. Eventually Hanson agrees, and Blackstone ends the conversation by saying, "By the way, Bill, bring along your customer records — I have a couple of questions for you."

After hanging up the phone, Blackstone once again consults his airline guide and finds that Hanson has only one alternative for arriving in Miami early enough to meet Blackstone's plane. A Delta Airlines flight arrives at 3:15 p.m. Blackstone waits a half hour, then calls Delta. Pretending to be Hanson, he is able to confirm that Hanson is indeed booked on the Delta flight to Miami.

Questions

1. What would you recommend that John Blackstone do after meeting Hanson in Miami?
2. What ethically questionable actions can you identify in this case?
3. Can Hanson's behavior be justified? How do you think Hanson rationalizes his actions?

CASE 4.2 *Gina Bradley: Sales Job Applicant*

Gina Bradley will graduate from the University of Florida at the end of this semester, and she is seeking an entry-level sales position with a major pharmaceutical company such as SmithKline Beckman Corporation, Eli Lilly and Company, or Pfizer Inc. She worked in the pharmacy of a large hospital in Jacksonville in the summer months during college, which gave her some valuable industry experience. Gina has completed her initial interviews with SmithKline, Lilly, and Pfizer. The first company to contact her after the initial interviews was Eli Lilly, which extended an offer to visit their corporate center in Indianapolis. Gina was in the process of preparing for the visit, which would include an extensive round of interviews with Lilly executives.

Prior to her initial interview with Eli Lilly, Gina had researched the company and carefully read the information that was available in the campus placement center. At this juncture, however, she felt compelled to learn more about Lilly prior to her visit to their headquarters. She found more information about the company in a book entitled *The 100 Best Companies to Sell For.* As she read about Eli Lilly, she progressively became more excited about the prospect of going to work for the firm. For example, she read that sales and profits were on the upswing and that Lilly's emphasis on research and product development was at the forefront of the industry. Further, she discovered that Lilly's sales training was highly rated and that their employee benefits package was generous.

Gina also found that Lilly's sales representatives generally worked alone but that they are part of a district team. She read that the salespeople in larger metropolitan areas traveled infrequently, whereas those in smaller cities had overnight travel as a routine part of their jobs. According to *The 100 Best Companies to Sell For,* Lilly views its salespeople as a primary source of talent and promotes from within. In fact, all of the current vice presidents in sales and marketing divisions began their careers as sales representatives.

The only troublesome thing that Gina encountered in her research on Eli Lilly was that the company preferred to hire sales trainees who had earned a degree in pharmacy. Gina's degree was in marketing. Other than the matter of the degree, Gina fit the published profile of the Lilly sales trainee — she had good grades and good communication skills and had demonstrated her leadership qualities throughout college. She reasoned that the pharmacy degree must not be all that important, since she had passed the initial interview screening. As she looked forward to her visit, Gina was trying to figure out how to make the most of what appeared to be a great opportunity.

Questions

1. What suggestions can you make to help Gina prepare for her upcoming visit to the Lilly corporate center?
2. How reliable is information gleaned from published sources in preparing a job candidate for a job interview?
3. What kinds of questions should Gina ask the interviewers, assuming she is given the opportunity to ask questions?

Source: Information on Eli Lilly and Company based on Michael David Harkaway and the Philip Lief Group, *The 100 Best Companies to Sell For* (New York: John Wiley, 1989), 262–266.

Royal Corporation

As Mary Jones, a third-year sales representative for the Royal Corporation, reviewed her call plans for tomorrow, she thought about her sales strategy. It was only July, 1983, but Jones was already well on her way toward completing her best year, financially, with the company. In 1982, she had sold the largest dollar volume of copiers of any sales representative in the northeast and was the tenth most successful rep in the country.

But Jones was not looking forward to her scheduled activities for the next day. In spite of her excellent sales ability, she had not been able to sell the Royal Corporate Copy Center (CCC). This innovative program was highly touted by Royal upper management. Jones was one of the few sales reps in her office who had not sold a CCC in 1982. Although Jones had an excellent working relationship with her sales manager, Tom Stein, she was experiencing a lot of pressure from him of late because he could not understand her inability to sell CCCs. Jones had therefore promised herself to concentrate her efforts on selling CCCs even if it meant sacrificing sales of other products.

Jones had five appointments for the day—9:00 a.m., Acme Computers; 9:45, Bickford Publishing; 11:45, ABC Electronics; 12:30, CG Advertising; and 2:00 p.m., General Hospital. At Acme, Bickford, and ABC, Jones would develop CCC prospects. She was in various states of information gathering and proposal preparation for each of the accounts. At CG, Jones planned to present examples of work performed by a model 750 color copier. At General Hospital, she would present her final proposal for CCC adoption. Although the focus of her day would be on CCCs, she still needed to call and visit other accounts that she was developing.

Royal Introduces CCC Concept

In 1980, Royal had introduced its Corporate Copy Center facilities management program (CCC). Under this concept, Royal offered to equip, staff, operate, and manage a reproduction operation for its clients, on the clients' premises (see Exhibit I). After analyzing the needs of the client, Royal selected and installed the appropriate equipment and provided fully trained, Royal employed operators. The CCC equipment also permits microfilming, sorting, collating, binding, covering, and color copying, in addition to high-volume copying.

The major benefits of the program include: reproduction contracted for at a specified price, guaranteed output, tailor-made capabilities, and qualified operators.

As she pulled into the Acme Computers parking lot, she noticed that an unexpected traffic jam had made her ten minutes late for the 9:00 a.m. appointment. This made her uncomfortable as she valued her time, and assumed that her clients appreciated promptness. Jones had acquired the Acme Computers account the prior summer and had dealt personally with Betty White, Director of Printing Services, ever since. She had approached White six months earlier with the idea of purchasing a CCC, but had not pursued the matter further until now because Betty had seemed very unreceptive. For today's call, Jones had worked several hours preparing a detailed study of Acme's present reproduction costs. She was determined to make her efforts pay off.

Jones gave her card to the new receptionist, who buzzed White's office and told her that Jones was waiting. A few minutes later, Betty appeared and led Jones to a corner of the lobby. They always met in the lobby, a situation that Jones found frustrating but it was apparently company policy.

"Good morning, Betty, it's good to see you again. Since I saw you last, I've put together the complete analysis on the CCC that I promised. I know you'll be excited by what you see. As you are aware, the concept of a CCC is not that unusual anymore. You may

Source: Copyright © 1983. This case was prepared at Babson College by Professor Hubert Hennessey and Barbara Kalunian, graduate student, as the basis for discussion rather than to illustrate either effective or ineffective sales performance. Names and locations have been disguised.

EXHIBIT I

To see what Royal Corporate Copy Center can do for you—and for your operating budget—take a minute to explore the *true* cost of your *present* system, outlined in the chart below. As you can see, it includes those "hidden" reprographic expenses that *many* organizations fail to consider . . .

The CCC concept is a familiar one, of course . . . many progressive organizations are now utilizing similar arrangements for their food service and data processing programs.

Labor

Operator (Hrs × 4.3 Wks)
Secretary (Hrs × 4.3 Wks)
Executive (Hrs × 4.3 Wks)
Supervisor (Hrs × 4.3 Wks)

CCC provides expert operators and experienced reprographic managers so all labor costs are included in one convenient monthly invoice.

Paid Benefits

Social Security
Vacations
Sick Leave
Pensions
Medical Plans

CCC eliminates all "people problems"—your repro staff is on our payroll, and we pay for their benefits.

Recruiting & Training

Advertising Costs
Personnel Time
Interviewer Time
Operator Time
Supervisor Time

No more recruiting and training . . . we handle that job, and we cover all related expenses!

Administrative Time

Purchase Orders
Filing Work
Calling Service People
Talking to Sales People

We handle all repro management—you receive a single monthly invoice for your entire repro system (and supplies)!

Waste

Operator Negligence
Unauthorized Copies
Equipment Malfunction

You only pay for the copies you use . . .

Downtime

Resulting In . . .
Vendor Charges
Overtime Costs
Missed Deadlines

Comprehensive back-up capabilities at your local Royal Reproduction Center—job turnaround times are guaranteed at no extra cost to you!

Price Increases

Labor
Materials
Overhead
Interest

The CCC price includes everything and it's guaranteed for the length of our agreement!

Space Requirements

Inventory
File Cabinets
Additional Equipment

Equipment and supplies are our responsibility, eliminating the need for anything extra on your part . . .

Chargeback Control

Clients
Departments
Individuals

At no charge, we maintain a log of all copies made . . . for clients, departments and individuals.

recall from the first presentation that I prepared for you, the CCC can be a tremendous time and money saver. Could you take a few moments to review the calculations that I have prepared exclusively for Acme Computers?" Betty flipped through the various pages of exhibits that Jones had prepared, but it was obvious that she had little interest in the proposal. "As you can see," Jones continued, "the savings are really significant after the first two years."

"Yes, but the program is more expensive the first two years. But what's worse is that there will be an outsider here doing our printing. I can't say that's an idea I could ever be comfortable with."

Jones realized that she had completely lost the possibility of White's support, but she continued.

"Betty, let me highlight some of the other features and benefits that might interest Acme."

"I'm sorry, Mary, but I have a 10:00 meeting that I really must prepare for. I can't discuss this matter further today."

"Betty, will you be able to go over these figures in more depth a little later?"

"Why don't you leave them with me, I'll look at them when I get the chance," White replied.

Jones left the proposal with White hoping that she would give it serious consideration, but as she pulled out of the driveway to Acme Computers, she could not help but feel that the day had gotten off to a poor start.

The Royal Corporation established the Royal Reproduction Center (RRC) Division in 1956. With 51 offices located in 24 states in the United States, the RRC specializes in high quality quick-turnaround copying, duplicating, and printing on a service basis. In addition to routine reproduction jobs, the RRC is capable of filling various specialized requests including duplicating engineering documents and computer reports, microfilming, color copying, and producing overhead transparencies. In addition, the RRC sales representatives sell the Royal 750 color copier (the only piece of hardware sold through RRCs) and the Royal Corporate Copy Center program (CCC). Although the RRC accepts orders from "walk ins," the majority of the orders are generated by the field representatives who handle certain named accounts which are broken down by geographic territory.

At 9:45 a.m., Jones stopped at Bickford Publishing for her second sales call of the day. She waited in the lobby while Joe Smith, Director of Corporate Services, was paged. Bickford Publishing was one of Jones's best accounts. Last year her commission from sales

to Bickford totaled 10 percent of her pay. But her relationship with Joe Smith always seemed to be on unstable ground. She was not sure why, but she had always felt that Smith harbored resentment towards her. However, she decided not to dwell on the matter as long as a steady stream of large orders kept coming in. Jones had been calling on Bickford ever since Tim McCarthy, the sales representative before her, had been transferred. Competition among the RRC sales reps for the Bickford account has been keen. But Stein had decided that Jones's performance warranted a crack at the account, and she had proven that she deserved it by increasing sales 40 percent within six months.

"Good morning, Miss Jones, how are you today?" Smith greeted her. He always referred to her formally as Miss Jones.

"I'm fine, Mr. Smith," Jones replied. "Thank you for seeing me today. I needed to drop by and give you some additional information on the CCC idea that I reviewed with you earlier."

"Miss Jones, to be perfectly honest with you, I reviewed the information that you left with me, and although I think that your CCC is a very nice idea, I really don't believe it is something that Bickford would be interested in at this particular point in time."

"But Mr. Smith, I didn't even give you any of the particulars. I have a whole set of calculations here indicating that the CCC could save Bickford a considerable amount of time, effort, and money over the next few years."

"I don't mean to be rude, Miss Jones, but I am in a hurry, I really don't care to continue this conversation."

"Before you go, do you think that it might be possible to arrange to present this proposal to Mr. Perry [Tony Perry, V.P. of Corporate Facilities, Joe Smith's immediate supervisor] in the near future? I'm sure that he would be interested in seeing it. We had discussed this idea in passing earlier, and he seemed to feel that it warranted serious consideration."

"Maybe we can talk about that the next time you are here. I'll call you if I need to have something printed. Now I really must go."

As Jones returned to her car, she decided that in spite of what Smith had told her about waiting until next time, she should move ahead to contact Mr. Perry directly. He had seemed genuinely interested in hearing more about the CCC when she had spoken to him earlier, even though she had mentioned it only briefly. She decided that she would return to the office and send Perry a letter requesting an appointment to speak with him.

Although Jones was not yet aware of it, Joe Smith had returned to his desk and immediately began drafting the following memo to be sent to Tony Perry:

To: Tony Perry, V.P. Corporate Facilities
From: Joe Smith, Corporate Services
Re: Royal CCC

Tony:

I spoke at length with Mary Jones of Royal this morning. She presented me with her proposal for the adoption of the CCC program at Bickford Publishing. After reviewing the proposal in detail, I have determined that the program: (a) is not cost effective, (b) has many problem areas that need ironing out, and (c) is inappropriate for our company at this time.

Therefore, in light of the above, my opinion is that this matter does not warrant any serious consideration or further discussion at this point in time.

Royal 750 Color Copier

The Royal 750 color copier made its debut in 1973 and was originally sold by color copier specialists in the equipment division of Royal. But sales representatives did not want to sell the color copier exclusively and sales managers did not want to manage the color copier specialists. Therefore, the 750 was not a particularly successful product. In 1979, the sales responsibility for the color copier was transferred to the RRC division. Since the RRC sales representatives were already taking orders from customers needing the services of a color copier, it was felt that the reps would be in an advantageous position to determine when current customer requirements would justify the purchase of a 750.

Jones arrived back at her office at 10:45. She checked her mailbox for messages, grabbed a cup of coffee, and returned to her desk to draft the letter to Tony Perry. After making several phone calls setting up appointments for the next week and checking on client satisfaction with some jobs that were delivered that day, she gathered up the materials that she needed for her afternoon sales calls. Finishing her coffee, she noticed the poster announcing a trip for members of the "President's Club." To become a member, a sales representative had to meet 100% of his or her sales budget, sell a 750 color copier, sell a CCC program, and sell a short-term rental. Jones believed that making

budget would be difficult but attainable, even though her superior performance in 1982 led to a budget increase of 20% for 1983. She had already sold a color copier and a short-term rental. Therefore, the main thing standing in her way of making the President's Club was the sale of a CCC. Not selling a CCC this year would have even more serious ramifications, she thought. Until recently, Jones had considered herself the prime candidate for the expected opening for a senior sales representative in her office. But Michael Gould, a sales rep who also had three years experience, was enjoying an excellent year. He had sold two color copiers and had just closed a deal on a CCC to a large semiconductor manufacturing firm. Normally everyone in the office celebrated the sale of a CCC. As a fellow sales rep was often heard saying, "it takes the heat off all of us for a while." Jones, however, found it difficult to celebrate Michael's sale. For not only was he the office "Golden Boy" but now, in her opinion, he was also the prime candidate for the senior sales rep position as well. Michael's sale also left Jones as one of the few reps in the office without the sale of a CCC to his or her credit. "It is pretty difficult to get a viable CCC lead," Jones thought, "but I've had one or two this year that should have been closed." Neither the long discussions with her sales manager, nor the numerous inservice training sessions and discussions on how to sell the CCC had helped. "I've just got to sell one of these soon," Jones resolved.

On her way out, she glanced at the clock. It was 11:33. She had just enough time to make her 11:45 appointment with Sam Lawless, operations manager, at ABC Electronics. This was Jones's first appointment at ABC and she was excited about getting a foot in the door there. A friend of hers was an assistant accountant at ABC. She had informed Jones that the company spent more than $15,000 a month on printing services and that they might consider a CCC proposal. Jones knew who the competition was, and although their prices were lower on low-volume orders, Royal could meet or beat their prices for the kind of volume of work for which ABC was contracting. But Jones wasn't enthusiastic about garnering the account for reproduction work. She believed she could sell ABC a CCC.

Jones's friend had mentioned management dissatisfaction with the subcontracting of so much printing. Also, there had been complaints regarding the quality of work. Investment in an in-house print shop had been discussed. Jones had assessed ABC's situation and had noticed a strong parallel with the situation at Star

Electronics, a multi-division electronics manufacturing firm that had been sold CCCs for each of their four locations in the area. That sale, which occurred over a year ago, was vital in legitimatizing the potential customers in the Northeast. Jones hoped to sell ABC on the same premise that Fred Myers had sold Star Electronics. Myers had been extremely helpful in reviewing his sales plan with Jones and had given her ideas on points he felt had been instrumental in closing the Star deal. She felt well prepared for this call.

Jones had waited four months to get an appointment with Lawless. He had a reputation for disliking to speak with salespeople, but Jones's friend had passed along to him some CCC literature and he had seemed interested. Finally, after months of being unable to reach him by telephone, or get a response by mail, she had phoned two weeks ago and he had consented to see her. Today she planned to concentrate on how adoption of the CCC program might solve ABC's current reproduction problems. She also planned to ask Lawless to provide her with the necessary information to produce a convincing proposal in favor of CCC. Jones pulled into a visitor parking space and grabbed her briefcase. "This could end up being the one," she thought as she headed for the reception area.

Jones removed a business card from her wallet and handed it to the receptionist. "Mary Jones to see Sam Lawless, I have an appointment," Jones announced.

"I'm sorry," the receptionist replied, "Mr. Lawless is no longer with the company."

Jones tried not to lose her composure, "But I had an appointment to see him today. When did he leave?"

"Last Friday was Mr. Lawless's last day. Mr. Bates is now operations manager."

"May I see Mr. Bates, please?" Jones inquired, knowing in advance, the response.

"Mr. Bates does not see salespeople. He sees no one without an appointment."

"Could you tell him that I had an appointment to see Mr. Lawless? Perhaps he would consider seeing me."

"I can't call him. But I'll leave him a note with your card. Perhaps you can contact him later."

"Thank you, I will." Jones turned and left ABC, obviously shaken. "Back to square one," she thought as she headed back to her car. It was 12:05 p.m.

Jones headed for her next stop, CG Advertising, still upset from the episode at ABC. But she had long since discovered that no successful salesperson can dwell on disappointments. "It interferes with your whole attitude," she reminded herself. Jones arrived at

the office park where CG was located. She was on time for her 12:30 appointment.

CG was a large, full-service agency. Jones's color copy orders from CG had been increasing at a rapid rate for the past six months, and she had no reason to believe that their needs would decrease in the near future. Therefore she believed the time was ripe to present a case for the purchase of a 750 color copier. Jones had been dealing primarily with Jim Stevens, head of Creative Services. They had a good working relationship, even though on certain occasions Jones had found him to be unusually demanding about quality. But she figured that characteristic seemed to be common in many creative people. She had decided to use his obsession with perfection to work to her advantage.

Jones also knew that money was only a secondary consideration as far as Stevens was concerned. He had seemingly gotten his way on purchases in several other instances, so she planned her approach to him. Jones had outlined a proposal which she was now ready to present to Jim.

"Good morning, Jim, how's the advertising business?"

"It's going pretty well for us here, how's things with you?"

"Great, Jim," Jones lied, "I have an interesting idea to discuss with you. I've been thinking that CG has been ordering large quantities of color copies. I know that you utilize them in the presentations of advertising and marketing plans to clients. I also know that you like to experiment with several different concepts before actually deciding on a final idea. Even though we have exceptionally short turnaround time, it occurred to me that nothing would suit your needs more efficiently and effectively than the presence of one of our Royal 750 color copiers right here in your production room. That way, each time that you consider a revision one of your artists will be able to compose a rough, and you can run a quick copy and decide virtually immediately if that is the direction in which you want to go, with no need to slow down the creative process at all."

"Well, I don't know; our current situation seems to be working out rather well. I really don't see any reason to change it."

"I'm not sure that you're fully aware of all the things that the 750 color copier is capable of doing," Jones pressed on. "One of the technicians and I have been experimenting with the 750. Even I have discovered some new and interesting capabilities to be applied in your field, Jim. Let me show you some of them."

She reached into her art portfolio and produced a wide variety of samples to show Stevens. "You know that the color copier is great for enlarging and reducing as well as straight duplicating. But look at the different effects we got by experimenting with various sizes and colors. Don't you think that this is an interesting effect?"

"Yes, it really is," Stevens said loosening up slightly.

"But wait," Jones added, "I really have the ultimate to show you." Jones produced a sheet upon which she had constructed a collage from various slides that Stevens had given her for enlarging.

"Those are my slides! Hey, that's great."

"Do you think that a potential client might be impressed by something like this? And the best part is you can whip something like this up in a matter of minutes, if the copier is at your disposal."

"Hey, that's a great idea, Mary, I'd love to be able to fool around with one of those machines. I bet I'd be able to do some really inventive proposals with it."

"I'm sure you would, Jim."

"Do you have a few minutes right now, I'd like to bounce this idea off of Bill Jackson, Head of Purchasing, and see how quickly we can get one in here."

Jones and Stevens went down to Jackson's office. Before they ever spoke, Jones felt that this deal was closed. Jim Stevens always got his own way. Besides, she believed she knew what approach to use with Bill Jackson. She had dealt with him on several other occasions. Jackson had failed to approve a purchase for her the prior fall, on the basis that the purchase could not be justified. He was right on that account. Their present 600 model was handling their reproduction needs sufficiently, but you can't blame a person for trying, she thought. Besides, she hadn't had Stevens in her corner for that one. This was going to be different.

"How's it going, Bill. You've met Mary Jones before, haven't you?"

"Yes, I remember Miss Jones. She's been to see me several times, always trying to sell me something we don't need," he said cynically.

"Well, this time I do have something you need and not only will this purchase save time, but it will save money, too. Let me show you some figures I've worked out regarding how much you can save by purchasing the 750 color copier." Jones showed Jackson that, at their current rate of increased orders of color

copies, the 750 would pay for itself in three years. She also stressed the efficiency and ease of operation. But she knew that Jackson was really only interested in the bottom line.

"Well, I must admit, Miss Jones, it does appear to be a cost-effective purchase."

Stevens volunteered, "Not only that, but we can now get our artwork immediately, too. This purchase will make everyone happy."

Jones believed she had the order. "I'll begin the paperwork as soon as I return to the office. May I come by next week to complete the deal?"

"Well, let me see what needs to be done on this end, but I don't foresee a problem," Jackson replied.

"There won't be any problem," Stevens assured Jones.

"Fine, then. I'll call Jim, the first of next week to set up an appointment for delivery."

Jones returned to her car at 1:00. She felt much better having closed the sale on the 750. She had planned enough time to stop for lunch.

During lunch, Jones thought about her time at Royal. She enjoyed her job as a whole. If it weren't for the pressure she was feeling to sell the corporate copy center program, everything would be just about perfect. Jones had been a straight "A" student in college where she majored in marketing. As far back as she could remember, she had always wanted to work in sales. Her father had started out in sales, and enjoyed a very successful and profitable career. He had advanced to sales manager and sales director for a highly successful Fortune 500 company and was proud that his daughter had chosen to pursue a career in sales. Often they would get together, and he would offer suggestions that had proven effective for him when he had worked in the field. When Jones's college placement office had announced that a Royal collegiate recruiter was visiting the campus, Jones had immediately signed up for an interview. She knew several recent graduates that had obtained positions with Royal and were very happy there. They were also doing well financially. She was excited at the idea of working for an industry giant. When she was invited for a second interview, she was ecstatic. Several days later, she received a phone call offering her a position at the regional office. She accepted immediately. Jones attended various pre-training workshops for 6 weeks at her regional office preparing her for her 2-week intensive training period at the Royal Training Headquarters. The training consisted of product training and sales training.

She had excelled there, and graduated from that course at the head of her class. From that point on everything continued smoothly . . . until this problem with selling the CCC.

After a quick sandwich and coffee, Jones left the restaurant at 1:30. She allowed extra time before her 2:00 appointment at General Hospital, located just four blocks from the office, to stop into the office first, check for messages, and check in with her sales manager. She informed Tom Stein that she considered the sale of a 750 to CG almost certain.

"That's great, Mary, I never doubted your ability to sell the color copiers, or repro for that matter. But what are we going to do about our other problem?"

"Tom, I've been following CCC leads all morning. To tell you the truth, I don't feel as though I've made any progress at all. As a matter of fact, I've lost some ground." Jones went on to explain the situation that had developed at ABC Electronics and how she felt when she learned that Sam Lawless was no longer with the company. "I was pretty excited about that prospect, Tom. The news was a little tough to take."

"That's okay. We'll just concentrate on his replacement, now. It might be a setback. But the company's still there, and they still have the same printing needs and problems. Besides, you're going to make your final presentation to General Hospital this afternoon, and you really did your homework for that one." Stein had worked extensively with Jones on the proposal from start to finish. They both knew that it was her best opportunity of the year to sell a CCC.

"I'm leaving right now. Wish me luck."

He did. She filled her briefcase with her personals and CCC demonstration kit that she planned to use for the actual presentation and headed toward the parking lot.

Jones's appointment was with Harry Jameson of General Hospital. As she approached his office, his receptionist announced her. Jameson appeared and led her to the board room for their meeting. Jones was surprised to find three other individuals seated around the table. She was introduced to Bob Goldstein, V.P. of operations, Martha Chambers, director of accounting, and Dr. J. P. Dunwitty, chairman of the board. Jameson explained that whenever an expenditure of this magnitude was being considered, the hospital's executive committee had to make a joint recommendation.

Jones set up her demonstration at the head of the table so that it was easily viewed by everyone and began her proposal. She presented charts verifying the merits of the CCC (Exhibit II, III) and also the financial calculations that she had generated based upon the information supplied to her by Jameson.

Forty minutes later, Jones finished her presentation and began fielding questions. The usual concerns were voiced regarding hiring an "outsider" to work within the hospital. But the major concern seemed to revolve around the loss of employment on the part of two present printing press operators. One, John Brown, had been a faithful employee for more than five years. He was married and had a child. There had never been a complaint about John personally, or with regard to the quality or quantity of his work. The second operator was Peter Dunwitty, a recent graduate of a nearby vocational school and nephew of Dr. Dunwitty. Although he had been employed by the hospital for only three months, there was no question about his ability and performance.

In response to this concern, Jones emphasized that the new equipment was more efficient, but different, and did not require the skills of experienced printers

---

EXHIBIT II ▪ *Why Royal Corporate Copy Center?*

▪ No Hidden Costs	▪ Allows You to Devote Full Time to Your Business
▪ No Downtime	▪ Departmental Budget Control
▪ No Capital Investment	▪ RRC Full Center Support
▪ No Recruiting or Training	▪ Tailor Made System
▪ No People Problems	▪ Full Write Off
▪ No Inventory Problems	▪ Guaranteed Cost Per Copy
▪ Increased Quality	▪ Short Term Agreement
▪ Expert Operators—Plus	▪ Trial Basis
▪ Guaranteed Turnaround Time	

EXHIBIT III   ▪ *What is Royal Corporate Copy Center?*

Royal Corporate Copy Center is the means whereby Royal will equip, staff, operate and manage a reproduction operation for you on your own premises. First, we analyze your needs, then we select and install the appropriate equipment. Secondly, we provide two fully trained Royal employed operators and professional reproduction management. Finally, we schedule all work, and protect you with comprehensive back-up capabilities at our Royal Reproduction Center . . . and you receive just one monthly bill for the entire package.

General Hospital Copying Objectives

1. To lower on-hand inventory of forms
2. To be able to upgrade or relocate equipment if needed
3. To have a competent full-time operator as well as back-up operators
4. To increase productivity
5. To be more cost efficient
6. 89-day trial option period
7. To eliminate downtime
8. To eliminate waste
9. To assure fast turnaround
10. To establish an inventory control system for paper and copier supplies
11. To install an accurate departmental charge-back system
12. To improve copy quality
13. To eliminate queuing time
14. To allow administrative support personnel to devote their full time to General Hospital's daily business
15. To eliminate having to worry about service on machines

General Hospital Offset vs. Printing

1. You won't eliminate all your related printing problems such as:
   A. You will still have to keep Savins for short-run lengths.
   B. You will still have waste problems.
   C. You still need plates and printing supplies.
   D. It is messy and complicated.
   E. You must have a dependable operator every day, and someone for vacations.
   F. You will have to vend some printing.
   G. You won't be able to cut down inventory of forms on hand, and you will have to have long-run lengths to be profitable and long turnaround for two-sided copying.
   H. You will be running a copying print shop, but this is still not state of the art.
   I. It is very noisy. You wouldn't be able to put it in this building. You might have to find another location or keep it in the old building.
   J. Only 3 out of about 15 hospitals on the North Shore area have printing presses—those that do have large duplicators that do 100,000 to 200,000 in volume per month besides long-run lengths on presses.

2. You would lose all of the extra benefits the Royal Corporate Copy Center would give you. (See Attached)

3. For the first full year because of expense for press, your cost would be $14,890 higher than Royal Corporate Copy Center, and your estimated price increases over the next two years would not be fixed, thus still costing you more for a less efficient operation.

EXHIBIT III ▪ *(Continued)*

Royal Corporate Copy Center Will Satisfy These Objectives in the Following Manner:

1. By having a high-speed duplicator and professional operator, you will be able to order forms on an as-needed basis. This will lower your present inventory by at least 80%, thus freeing up valuable space for other use.

2. Because of the flexibility that Royal Corporate Copy Center gives you, you have the opportunity to change or upgrade equipment at any time. If relocation of equipment is necessary because of changes in the hospital's structure, this can be done also.

3. Royal Corporate Copy Center will provide a trained, professional operator whose hours will conform to General Hospital's. Regardless of vacation schedules, sickness, or personal absences, a competent operator will report to General Hospital every day. If these operators do not meet with General Hospital's satisfaction, they can be changed within 24 hours' time. Because Royal will supply the operators, you will be relieved of this person as a staff member. Benefits, sick time, and vacation will be taken care of by Royal. You will receive operators for your facility 52 weeks a year.

4. Our people will report directly to your supervisor for their assignment the same as any other employee under your supervision. These people will be able to sort incoming jobs as we have discussed or may be used for other work in the copy center at non-peak times. These people would also be available to pick up copying work from various central locations throughout General Hospital at specified times, thus eliminating the need for people to come to the copy center. These people may also be used to operate other various types of equipment that General Hospital has.

5. By having a Royal Corporate Copy Center program at General Hospital and letting Royal take care of all your duplicating needs in a professional manner, your copying costs will become much more cost efficient. We believe that the cost savings alone in the first year could be upwards of 10–15% and would increase as your copy volume grows with you. Your present system does not offer several of the important benefits that Royal Corporate Copy Center offers that now will be included in one fixed cost—in dollars and cents, by not having to pay for these services, this is where the additional 10–15% cost savings per year could come in. We also will give you a fixed reproduction cost so that you can budget more accurately. We will also fix all of your cost for the next three years (that includes supplies, machine, support and operators) if you sign a three-year agreement at the end of the trial period. This will enable you to save upwards of another 10% per year.

6. We at Royal feel very confident about this program and its success. We, therefore, wish to minimize our customers' risk for installing a new program. We feel we are able to do this by offering a trial option period of up to 89 days. This program works in the following way: General Hospital must sign a trial option pricing addendum and a three-year agreement. This will put into action the following:

   A. $1,050.00 per month credit off the original pricing for the first partial month, the first full month, and the second full month (total of $3,150.00).

   B. At the end of the trial option period General Hospital can elect to:

      a. Remain on the three-year agreement date May 1, 1983.

      b. Execute a 90-day, one-year, or two-year agreement with applicable pricing.

      c. Cancel the agreement date May 1, 1983, without liquidation damages.

7. With Royal Corporate Copy Center you will never experience downtime. Your work will always be done timely. We will back up the machines with a back-up copier running the work there or send it to our closest center to be completed and returned. By being a Royal Corporate Copy Center customer, General Hospital will always receive priority on service. Also, our operators will be able to handle more extensive types of service to the equipment.

8. General Hospital will be charged only for the copies ordered. This will eliminate all of your present waste that is involved with offset.

9. Trained Royal operators should reduce turnaround time on work. These operators will know how to run jobs on the equipment properly and in the fastest way so that productivity will increase and turnaround time will decrease.

(continued)

EXHIBIT III ▪ *(Continued)*

10. Royal will order all toner and developer, thus eliminating the need for General Hospital to make large commitments and maintain large inventories. We will order paper also for you on a weekly basis if you so choose.

11. Royal will install an accurate departmental charge-back system, allowing General Hospital to accurately account for all copies. You will receive a copy of this breakdown each month.

12. Royal will provide trained operators, guaranteeing high-quality copies. By using a Xerographic process, you will always have consistently high-quality copies.

13. By providing General Hospital with skilled operators, copying and duplicating requirements will be met in a timely fashion, eliminating the need for General Hospital employees to stand and wait to use other equipment. In essence, General Hospital employees will be free to do General Hospital business; Royal will fulfill the copying and duplicating requirements.

14. Administrative personnel will no longer have to worry about sales people, service problems, obtaining purchase orders, or buying supplies.

15. All machines used will be the responsibility of Royal for service and maintenance.

General Hospital Cash Flow (One-Year Period) Royal Corporate Copy Center vs. Present System

Corporate Copy Center		Hospital
Royal 900	Equipment	Obsolete presses & mimeo
$ 6,500.00	Supplies and Paper	$ 42,189.00
Included	Toner and Developer	-0-
Included	Labor	$ 22,496.00
Included	Benefits	$ 2,681.00
Included	Administrative Time	-?-
Included	Management Time	-?-
Included	CCC Benefits	None
Eliminated	Savin 680 Rental	$ 4,534.00
Eliminated	Smaller Savin I Rental	$ 1,080.00
Eliminated	Smaller Savin II Rental	$ 1,320.00
Eliminated	Savin Copying Cost	$ 2,400.00
Eliminated	Vending	$ 7,000.00
	(Forms that could be kept in-house)	
Eliminated	Issuing of P.O.s	$ 500.00
Eliminated	Expense for Present Building	$ 2,500.00
$ 80,310.00	Royal Facilities Management	—
($.029 per copy)	(200,000 copies)	
$ 86.810.00	TOTAL CASH FLOW	$ 86,700.00

	Fixed	*Price Increases*	*Est.*	
$ 86,810.00	0	15 months	5%	$ 91,035.00
$ 89,414.00	3%	2nd year	9%	$ 99,228.00
$ 91,202.00	2%	3rd year	9%	$108,158.00
$267,426.00		PROJECTED 3-YEAR COST		$298,421.00
$ 30,995.00		PROJECTED 3-YEAR SAVINGS		None

EXHIBIT III ▪ *(Continued)*

Recommendation

Royal feels at this time that it would be very beneficial for General Hospital to change from its present reproduction system of two offset presses, mimeograph equipment, several smaller copiers, and a collator to a Royal 900 and a professional operator under the Royal Corporate Copy Center program. Royal feels it would be beneficial for General Hospital to effect this change presently for the following reasons:

1. Professional people would replace a part-time operator (20 hours) and an operator that is on leave (20 hours).

2. State-of-the-art equipment would replace the present presses, which are very old and outdated.

3. The large amount of waste presently experienced would be eliminated.

4. The high maintenance cost for the presses would be eliminated.

5. Hand collating and off-line collating would be eliminated.

6. Poor and inconsistent quality in the copies would be eliminated.

7. The back-up problem would be eliminated.

8. You would have better turnaround and accountability.

9. Some of the smaller copiers, and lower copy volumes on the smaller copiers, would be eliminated.

10. You would receive all other Royal Corporate Copy Center benefits unattainable with your present program.

In the following pages I hope to show you how we will accomplish these goals by installing the Royal Corporate Copy Center at General Hospital.

---

like Brown and Dunwitty. She knew, however, that this was always the one point about the adoption of a CCC program that even she had the most difficulty justifying. She suddenly felt rather ill.

"Well, Miss Jones, if you'll excuse us for a few minutes, we'd like to reach a decision on this matter," said Jameson.

"There's no need to decide right at this point. You all have copies of my proposal. If you'd like to take a few days to review the figures, I'd be happy to come by then," said Jones, in a last-ditch attempt to gain some additional time.

"I think that we'd like to meet in private for a few minutes right now, if you don't mind," interjected Dunwitty.

"No, that's fine," Jones said as she left the room for the lobby. She sat in a waiting room and drank a cup of coffee. She lit a cigarette, a habit that she seldom engaged in. Five minutes later, the board members called her back in.

"This CCC idea is really sound, Miss Jones," Jameson began. "However, here at General Hospital, we have a very strong commitment to our employees. There really seems to be no good reason to put two fine young men out of work. Yes, I realize that from the figures that you've presented to us, you've indicated a savings of approximately $30,000 over three

years. But I would have to question some of the calculations. Under the circumstances, we feel that maintaining sound employee relations has more merit than switching to an unproven program right now. Therefore, we've decided against purchasing a CCC."

Jones was disappointed. But she had been in this situation often enough not to show it. "I'm sorry to hear that, Mr. Jameson, I thought that I had presented a very good argument for participation in the CCC program. Do you think that if your current operators decided to leave, before you filled their positions, you might consider CCC again?"

"I can't make a commitment to that right now. But feel free to stay in touch," Jameson countered.

"I'll still be coming in on a regular basis to meet all your needs for other work not capable of being performed in your print shop," Jones replied.

"Then you'll be the first to know if that situation arises," said Jameson.

"Thank you all for your time. I hope that I was of assistance even though you decided against the purchase. If I may be of help at any point in time, don't hesitate to call," Jones remarked as she headed for the door.

Now, totally disappointed, Jones regretted having scheduled another appointment for that afternoon. She would have liked to call it a day. But she knew she had an opportunity to pick up some repro work and develop a new account. So she knew she couldn't cancel.

Jones stopped by to see Paul Blake, head of staff training at Pierson's, a large department store with locations throughout the state. Jones had made a cold call one afternoon the prior week and had obtained a sizable printing order. Now she wanted to see whether Blake was satisfied with the job, which had been delivered earlier in the day. She also wanted to speak to him about some of the other services available at the RRC. Jones was about to reach into her briefcase for her card to offer to the receptionist when she was startled by a "Hello, Mary" coming from behind her.

"Hello, Paul," Jones responded, surprised and pleased that he had remembered her name. "How are you today?"

"Great! I have to tell you that report that you printed for us is far superior to the work that we have been receiving from some of our other suppliers. I've got another piece that will be ready to go out in about an hour. Can you have someone come by and pick it up then?"

"I'll do better than that. I'll pick it up myself," Jones replied.

"See you then," he responded as he turned and headed back towards his office.

"I'm glad I decided to stop by after all," Jones thought as she pressed the elevator button. She wondered how she could best use the next hour to help salvage the day. When the elevator door opened, out stepped Kevin Fitzgerald, operations manager for Pierson's. Jones had met him several weeks earlier when she had spoken with Ann Leibman, a sales rep for Royal Equipment Division. Leibman had been very close to closing a deal that would involve selling Pierson several "casual" copying machines that they were planning to locate in various offices to use for quick copying. Leibman informed Jones that Tom Stein had presented a CCC proposal to Pierson's six months earlier but the plan was flatly refused. Fitzgerald, she explained, had been sincerely interested in the idea. But the plan involved a larger initial expenditure than Pierson's was willing to make. Now, Leibman explained, there would be a much larger savings involved, since the "casual" machines would not be needed if a CCC were involved. Jones had suggested to Fitzgerald that the CCC proposal be reworked to include the new machines so that a current assessment could be made. He had once again appeared genuinely interested and suggested that Jones retrieve the necessary figures from

Jerry Query, Head of Purchasing. Jones had not yet done so. She had phoned Query several times, but he had never responded to her messages.

"Nice to see you again, Mr. Fitzgerald. Ann Leibman introduced us, I'm Mary Jones from Royal."

"Yes, I remember. Have you spoken with Mr. Query, yet?"

"I'm on my way to see him right now," Jones said as she thought that this would be the perfect way to use the hour.

"Fine, get in touch with me when you have the new calculations."

Jones entered the elevator that Fitzgerald had been holding for her as they spoke. She returned to the first floor and consulted the directory. Purchasing was on the third floor. As she walked off the elevator on the third floor, the first thing that she saw was a sign that said, "Salespeople seen by appointment only. Tuesdays and Thursdays, 10 a.m.–12 noon."

"I'm really out of luck," Jones thought, "not only do I not have an appointment, but today's Wednesday. But I'll give it my best shot as long as I'm here."

Jones walked over to the receptionist who was talking to herself as she searched through a large pile of papers on her desk. Although Jones knew she was aware of her presence, the receptionist continued to avoid her.

"This could be a hopeless case," Jones thought. Just then the receptionist looked up and acknowledged her.

"Good afternoon. I'm Mary Jones from Royal. I was just speaking to Mr. Fitzgerald who suggested that I see Mr. Query. I'm not selling anything. I just need to get some figures from him."

"Just a minute," the receptionist replied as she walked towards an office with Query's name on the door.

"Maybe this is not going to be so bad after all," Jones thought.

"Mr. Query will see you for a minute," the receptionist announced as she returned to her desk.

Jones walked into Mr. Query's plushly furnished office. Query was an imposing figure at 6 feet, 4 inches, nearly 300 pounds, and bald. Jones extended her hand, which Query grasped firmly. "What brings you here to see me?" Query inquired.

Jones explained her conversations with Ann Leibman and Kevin Fitzgerald. As she was about to ask her initial series of questions, Query interrupted. "Miss Jones, I frankly don't know what the hell you are doing here!" Query exclaimed. "We settled this issue over six months ago, and now you're bringing it up again. I really don't understand. You people came in with a proposal that was going to cost us more money than we were spending. We know what we're doing. No one is going to come in here and tell us our business."

"Mr. Query," Jones began, trying to remain composed, "the calculations that you were presented with were based upon the equipment that Pierson's was utilizing six months ago. Now that you are contemplating additional purchases, I mentioned to Mr. Fitzgerald that a new comparison should be made. He instructed me to speak with you in order to obtain the information needed to prepare a thorough proposal," Jones tried to explain.

"Fitzgerald! What on earth does Fitzgerald have to do with this? This is none of his damn business. He sat at the same table as I six months ago when we arrived at a decision. Why doesn't he keep his nose out of affairs that don't concern him? We didn't want this program six months ago, we don't want it now!" Query shouted.

"I'm only trying to do my job, Mr. Query. I was not part of the team that presented the proposal six months ago. But from all the information that is available now, I still feel that a CCC would save you money here at Pierson's."

"Don't you understand, Miss Jones? We don't want any outsiders here. You have no control over people that don't work for you. Nothing gets approved around here unless it has my signature on it. That's control. Now I really see no need to waste any more of my time or yours."

"I appreciate your frankness," Jones responded, struggling to find something positive to say.

"Well, that's the kind of man I am, direct and to the point."

"You can say that again," Jones thought. "One other thing before I go, Mr. Query. I was noticing the color copies on your desk."

"Yes, I like to send color copies of jobs when getting production estimates. For example, these are of the bogs that we will be using during our fall promotion. I have received several compliments from suppliers who think that by viewing color copies they get a real feel for what I need."

"Well, it just so happens that my division of Royal sells color copiers. At some time it may be more efficient for you to consider a purchase. Let me leave you some literature on the 750 copier which you can review at your leisure." Jones removed a brochure from her briefcase. She attached one of her business cards to it and handed it to Query. As she shook his hand and left the office, Jones noted that she had half an hour before the project of Blake's would be ready for pick-up. She entered the donut shop across the street and as she waited for her coffee, she reviewed her day's activities. She was enthusiastic about the impending color copier sale at CG Advertising, and about the new repro business that she had acquired at Pierson's. But the rest of the day had been discouraging. Not only had she been "shot down" repeatedly, but she'd now have to work extra hard for several days to insure that she would make 100% of budget for the month. "Trying to sell the CCC is even harder than I thought it was," Jones thought.

Hewlett-Packard Sales Force Automation: "What If . . ."

Where It Started

Karl Kiefer, Manager of the Rocky Mountain Sales Area, was reviewing sales performance and selling expenses from the past fiscal period in preparation of the area's new budget which was due in a couple of weeks. At first glance, Karl was surprised to see that the company total for selling was $380 million. In his analysis, he noted two areas in particular that were quite disturbing: First, the average cost of a sales call had been increasing substantially in recent years to where it now was costing HP $500 a day to keep a sales rep on the road. This is parallel to the rising costs throughout personal selling as indicated by data compiled by McGraw-Hill Research Department. For example, in 1983 the average cost of an industrial sales call was $205.40, up 50% from 1979 when an average call cost $137.02.

Secondly, nearly 60 percent of a sales rep's day was spent traveling (15%), processing paperwork (31%), and attending meetings (13%)—all nonselling activities (See Figure 5). Compounding this was HP's profit growth, which in 1985 fell below historic average although the company withstood a significant industry downturn. Karl's thoughts centered upon his own company's products and high tech industry—computers. He questioned,

> What if . . . we were to look toward computer-based solutions. Could HP develop new sales systems to bring together data from many sources providing sales reps access to the most up-to-date information?

As Karl began to formulate ideas about sales force automation (SFA) he projected that automation could reduce administrative communication tangles so sales professionals have more time for customers, and improve information accuracy and timeliness for more effective time usage.

> Maybe we could use our own technology (computers to provide the salesforce immediate information on order status, pricing, availability of items, electronic mail, spread sheets, account and territory profiles, etc.) to manage information and improve communications among the sales rep, sales manager, corporate marketing personnel, and the customer.

Background

Hewlett-Packard (HP) is one of the 100 largest industrial corporations in America, with revenues of $6.51 billion and earnings of $489 million recorded for 1985. Headquartered in Palo Alto, California, HP employs more than 84,000 people. Forty-eight percent of HP's business is carried out overseas, with 275 worldwide sales and support offices located in 75 countries, utilizing more than 28,000 personnel.

HP had its beginnings in 1939 in a small, neighborhood garage in Palo Alto as a partnership between two aspiring and innovative Stanford engineering graduates, William Hewlett and David Packard. Among the customers for their first product, an electronic test instrument known as an audio oscillator, was Walt Disney Studios which purchased eight for use in developing the sound track for the movie classic, "Fantasia."

Hewlett-Packard hired their first employees during 1940, and completed construction of their first plant in 1942. In just ten years, HP grew to 200 employees, 70 products and $2 million in annual sales.

HP entered their second decade strongly focused upon sustained and substantial growth, expanding the product line still further. By the end of 1959 they had entered the international market, with operational headquarters in Switzerland and a manufacturing plant in West Germany. Overseas plants continued to blossom through the years in such areas as Japan, England, Spain, Singapore, and France. From the 1985 total company sales of $6.51 billion, slightly less than half were generated outside the U.S., thus ranking the company as one of the top 20 American exporters.

From the time of its humble beginning, Hewlett-Packard had adhered to a predominately decentralized business structure operating around small product divisions, rarely numbering more than 2,000 people. Each division designs, manufactures and maintains marketing responsibility for its own products. A simplified organizational chart, Figure 1, depicts the refined structure which is currently in effect within HP.

Source: Allen J. Wedell, Colorado State University, and Les Carson, Augustana College, "Hewlett-Packard Sales Force Automation: What If . . .," Midwest Case Writers Association, March 1988. Copyright © 1988.

FIGURE 1 ▪ *Organizational Chart*

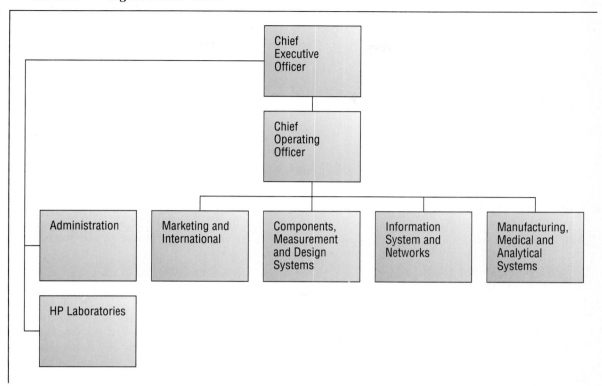

Source: Hewlett-Packard—In Brief, January 1986.

Fueling this decentralized body is an informal, non-authoritarian corporate atmosphere. Esprit de corps fosters individual dignity, pride in accomplishment and the motivation to produce quality work. Management by Objectives (MBO) provides guidance for both group and individual goals. This is achieved through the seven written corporate objectives:

1) Achieve sufficient profit to finance company and to meet corporate objectives.
2) Provide the highest quality products and services with the greatest value to the customer, thus gaining the customer's respect and loyalty.
3) Build strengths in the company's traditional fields of interest, entering new fields only when consistent with basic purpose of business and only when we are assured of making a needed and profitable contribution.

4) Limit growth only by our profits and ability to develop innovative products that satisfy real customer needs.
5) To help HP people share in the company's success, insure them safe and pleasant work environment, recognize individual achievements, job security based upon performance, and enable them to gain a sense of satisfaction and accomplishment in their work.
6) Foster initiative and creativity and provide great freedom of action in attaining well-defined objectives.
7) Honor our obligation to society, by being an economic, intellectual and sound asset.

This style, illustrated in Figure 2, has gained the active participation of all employees.

FIGURE 2   ▪ *HP Management by Objectives*

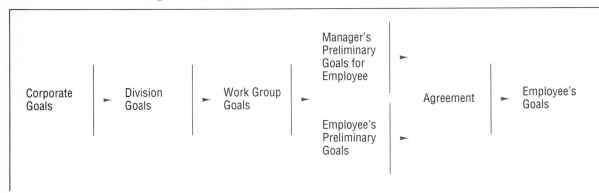

Employees share in the company's success through regular cash profit-sharing and stock purchase programs. HP has committed to financing its growth primarily through a "pay as you go" philosophy; acquiring capital from profits and from shareholders' stock purchases. HP shares have been traded on the New York and Pacific Stock Exchanges since 1961, with 257 million shares held by more than 74,000 stockholders.

Quality products and a commitment to research and development (R&D) have also contributed to HP's growth and stability over the years. Each year, 8–10 percent of sales revenues ($685 million in 1985) are earmarked for R&D. Producing quality products means more than just engineering excellence—HP has learned to produce every product so that it is considered a superior value by the customer. Product failure levels have been reduced to one-tenth of what they were a decade ago through the discovery that 25 percent of manufacturing costs were attributable to not doing things right the first time. HP's commitment to new product development is reflected by the company's orders in 1985—well over half were for products introduced during the three previous years.

Sales and Earnings

Adding to Karl's dilemma of rising selling costs and inefficiency in the selling process, was the realization that HP's 1985 orders increased only one percent as compared to a 29 percent increase in 1984. In a similar pattern, 1985 revenues increased only 8 percent (to $6.51 billion) compared to a revenue growth of 28 percent in 1984 as shown in Figure 3. Earnings in 1985, however, decreased 10 percent from the previous year

($489 million) compared to a 20 percent increase in 1984. A percent of change in revenues and earnings is illustrated in Figure 4.

Pilot Project in Sales Force Automation

Karl presented his ideas about sales force automation to James Arthur, vice president of U.S. Field Operations (a division of the Marketing and International sector as shown in Figure 1). Impressed with the opportunities of such a program, Mr. Arthur challenged Karl to come up with a project for giving sales reps productivity tools that would produce demonstratable results in six months.

Immediately Karl set up a steering committee to help him with this monumental task. The first order of business was to outline the goals and objectives for the project, and also to identify the resources that will be needed, not just financially, but equipment and support personnel too.

The committee agreed upon three fundamental objectives that could evaluate the effectiveness of the project, now called the "Field Productivity Program." The project's goals were:

1) To increase sales productivity and effectiveness by 25 percent (measured by customer contact time),
2) To increase customer visibility of HP's automation solutions through HP's own use of these solutions (measured by sales rep feedback),
3) To increase sales rep job satisfaction, confidence and motivation throughout the U.S. sales organization (measured by sales rep feedback).

FIGURE 3   ▪   *HP Net Revenue and Earnings from Sales*

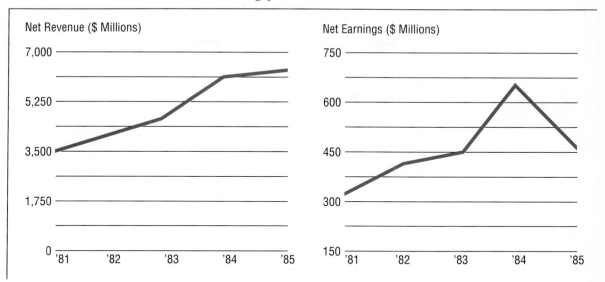

FIGURE 4   ▪   *HP Percent of Change in Revenue and Earnings*

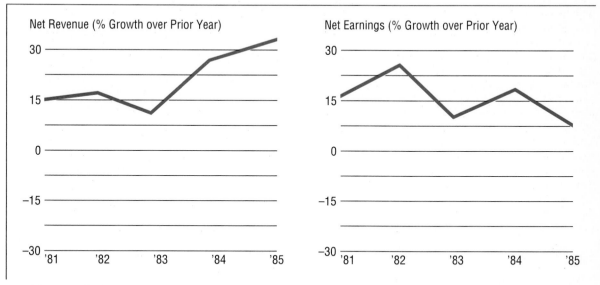

To meet all three objectives, the committee agreed that they needed to provide sales reps with tools that would not only impress customers, but would make their non-selling tasks easier to perform. "We can increase productivity in a variety of ways," Karl expressed to the rest of the committee, "but we also have to make the sales reps' job more enjoyable."

The resulting productivity tools consisted of:

1)   hardware—HP's Portable PLUS computer, Thinkjet printer and disc drive,

2)   software—word processing, Lotus 1-2-3, and time management programs for personal productivity solutions on the portable, and price and availabil-

FIGURE 5 ▪ *How HP Sales Reps Spend Their Time*

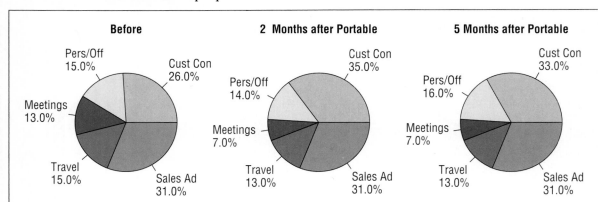

ity, order status and electronic mail through area miniframe computers,

3) cellular telephones—to take advantage of often wasted driving and out-of-the-office time.

Looking back to Mr. Arthur's original challenge—produce results in six months—four regional areas including 100 sales reps were chosen to participate in the Field Productivity Program's pilot-study.

While the programming was underway to create the software needed to link the sales reps' portable computers into HP's computer network, the committee was busy developing training formats and locating the hardware needed to set the project into motion.

Four-hour training sessions were held for the sales reps in the pilot-study to demonstrate how the system works and to gain hands-on experience. The reps were supported with a 24-hour help line and a dedicated specialist at each area to help solve problems the reps may encounter along the way.

To collect hard data on how sales reps spend their time, each rep was given a beeper watch that went off at odd intervals. When the beeper sounded, the reps marked off the activity they were involved in on a tally sheet. This process provided the committee with a large number of observations in a short period of time. Control groups in each area participated in the data collection, as did the experimental groups; however, the control groups *did not* receive the productivity tools.

Field Productivity Program Results

Activity measurements were collected three weeks prior to the introduction of the productivity tools to have a baseline level of sales reps' activities. Data was collected two months after the sales reps received the tools and again after five months. The results for the experimental groups are shown in Figure 5 and the results of the control groups are shown in Figure 6.

Karl had solicited feedback during the pilot-study from the sales reps using the productivity tools in an attempt to measure the impact upon customers, orders, and sales rep motivation, confidence and enthusiasm.

The response was overwhelming on both accounts. Almost all of the reps involved felt the tools helped to reduce their paperwork load and provide better response to customers' needs. Even the customers were impressed, often asking for demonstrations and surprised at the quick and easy access to information. However, Karl could not identify an increase in sales directly attributable to the automation project.

Karl's six months for the project were almost up. He had a meeting with James Arthur in three days, and he knew that Arthur wanted documentable results. As Karl looked over the information collected, he knew he had a tough three days ahead in deciding the fate of automating HP's sales force. While they had already spent $500,000 on the Field Productivity Program, it would cost $7–8 million to outfit HP's entire U.S. Sales Organization with just portables alone. Cellular telephones would cost an additional $5–6 million each year. Karl didn't know if his results could justify such a substantial investment. "Where do we go from here?" Karl asked, as much to himself as to the other committee members. If the decision to proceed is made, equipment and personnel resources had to be allocated, the project's direction mapped out, and payback periods estimated for the capital invested.

FIGURE 6 ▪ *Control Group*

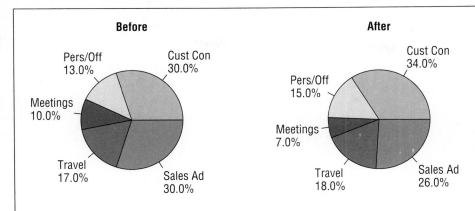

Part Two

Defining the Strategic Role of the Sales Function

The two chapters in Part Two discuss the sales function from a strategic perspective. Chapter 5 investigates strategic decisions at different levels in multibusiness, multiproduct firms. The key elements of corporate strategy, business strategy, and marketing strategy are described, and important relationships between each strategy level and the sales function are identified. Special attention is directed toward the role of personal selling in a marketing strategy. Chapter 6 changes the strategic focus to the sales function level. A discussion of organizational buyer behavior is presented to provide a foundation for sales strategy development. Relationship strategy and sales channel strategy are examined as the key types of sales strategies.

Corporate, Business, and Marketing Strategies and the Sales Function

STRATEGIC CHANGE AND THE SALES FUNCTION: THE NEW PROCTER & GAMBLE   The old Procter & Gamble was once the envy of consumer marketers. Well-known brands, extensive distribution, massive advertising, and an often-copied brand management system put P&G at the pinnacle of consumer marketing. Despite these marketing advantages, in 1985 P&G posted its first decline in annual earnings since 1952. What happened?

Slow market growth and increased competitive intensity are partially responsible, but the evidence suggests that P&G had also become bureaucratic, stodgy, arrogant, and old-fashioned. As stated by Shelly Zimbler, general sales manager for health and beauty aids: "The old way of doing business — good products with good advertising copy — is history. We need to work creatively with customers to find out what they need to move our products."

In recent years P&G has engaged in a major strategic restructuring designed to push authority downward, speed up decision making, and get closer to its customers. Initial results from the restructuring are encouraging based on an 18 percent increase in profits to $1.21 billion in fiscal 1989. What were the key elements in the strategic restructuring?

Strategic changes were made at all organizational levels. Corporate strategy changes included entering new business areas through internal development, acquisitions, and joint ventures. The old brand management system was updated by organizing the more than 92 brand managers into 39 product categories that are each operated as a separate business.

The category managers are now responsible for the development and execution of a business strategy for all the brands in their product category. Marketing strategies for individual brands are now coordinated and rely heavily on close relationships with retailers. The development and nurturing of these relationships is largely the responsibility of the sales function.

Until 1987, P&G had 4,000+ salespeople organized into 11 national salesforces each selling a specific product line. Retailers hated dealing with so many different salespeople, so P&G reorganized the salesforce so that individual salespeople or multifunctional sales teams are responsible for specific retailers. This change has helped P&G develop closer relationships with its retailers, especially the larger chains such as Wal-Mart and Kroger. The basic change was summarized by Mike Milligan, a top sales executive: "We're switching from a product to a customer approach."

Source: Excerpted from William Keenan, Jr., "America's Best Sales Forces: Six at the Summit," *Sales and Marketing Management*, June 1990, 66–72; Brian Dumaine, "P&G Rewrites the Marketing Rules," *Fortune*, November 6, 1989, 34–48; and Alecia Swasy, "In a Fast-Paced World, Procter & Gamble Sets Its Store in Old Values," *The Wall Street Journal*, September 21, 1989, A1–A2.

Chapter 5

Learning Objectives

After completing this chapter, you should be able to

1 *Define the different strategy levels for multibusiness, multiproduct firms.*

2 *Discuss how corporate strategy decisions affect the sales function.*

3 *Explain the relationships between business strategy and the sales function.*

4 *List the advantages and disadvantages of personal selling as a promotional tool.*

5 *Specify the situations where personal selling is typically emphasized in a marketing strategy.*

6 *Describe ways that personal selling, advertising, and other promotion tools can be blended into effective promotional strategies.*

The Procter & Gamble situation described in the opening vignette illustrates an important reality in the contemporary business world: most firms are really collections of relatively autonomous businesses that market multiple products to diverse customer groups. Strategy development in these multibusiness, multiproduct firms is extremely complex. Different types of strategic decisions must be made at different levels of the organization. However, the different strategies must be consistent with each other and integrated for the firm to perform successfully. As the P&G situation suggests, strategic changes at one organizational level can have profound effects on strategies at other organizational levels. For example, the success of P&G's strategic changes at the corporate, business, and marketing levels is dependent on strategic changes at the sales function level, such as the move from a product- to customer-oriented sales organization.

Since our focus is on personal selling and sales management, it is important to discuss the different types of organizational strategy and their relationships with the sales function. We will discuss corporate strategy, business strategy, and marketing strategy in this chapter.

Organizational Strategy Levels

The key strategy levels for multibusiness, multiproduct firms are presented in Exhibit 5.1. **Corporate strategy** consists of decisions that determine the mission, business portfolio, and future growth directions for the entire corporate entity. A separate **business strategy** must be developed for each *strategic business unit* (SBU) (discussed later in this chapter) in the corporate family, defining how that SBU plans to compete effectively within its industry. Since an SBU typically consists of multiple products serving different markets, each product/market combination requires a specific **marketing strategy.** Each marketing strategy includes the selection of target market segments and the development of a marketing mix to serve each target market. A key consideration is the role that personal selling will play in the promotional mix for a particular marketing strategy.

The corporate, business, and marketing strategies represent strategy development from the perspective of different levels within an organization. Although sales management may have some influence on the decisions made at each level, the key decision makers are typically from higher management levels outside the sales function. Sales management does, however, play the key role in sales strategy development. Sales strategy will be discussed in detail in Chapter 6.

Corporate Strategy and the Sales Function

Strategic decisions at the topmost level of multibusiness, multiproduct firms determine the corporate strategy for a given firm, which is what provides direction and guidance for activities at all organizational levels. The process of developing a corporate strategy consists of the following steps:[1]

1. Analyzing corporate performance and identifying future opportunities and threats.
2. Determining corporate mission and objectives.

Firms must continually evaluate their SBU definitions and make changes when warranted. One study of multibusiness corporations found that[9]

1. When there are too few SBUs, it is difficult to support each product or line of products.
2. When there are too many SBUs, it creates expensive duplication within the corporation.

The P&G example illustrates the situation where there were too many SBUs and expensive duplication in the marketing of individual brands.

The definition of SBUs is an important element of corporate strategy. Changes in SBU definition may increase or decrease the number of SBUs, and these changes typically affect the sales function in many ways. Salesforces may have to be merged, new salesforces may have to be established, or existing salesforces may have to be reorganized to perform different activities. These changes may affect all sales management activities from the type of salespeople to be hired to how they should be trained, motivated, compensated, and supervised.

Objectives for Strategic Business Units

Once strategic business units have been defined, corporate management must determine appropriate strategic objectives for each. Many firms view their SBUs collectively as a portfolio of business units. Each business unit faces a different competitive situation and plays a different role in the **business unit portfolio.** Therefore, specific strategic objectives should be determined for each SBU.

Several analytical tools are available to help management evaluate its business unit portfolio and to provide guidelines for determining strategic objectives. The two most popular methods are the growth-share matrix developed by the Boston Consulting Group and the multiple factor screening method developed by General Electric Company.[10] Both of these analytical tools provide a means for classifying SBUs into categories based upon market opportunity and competitive strength considerations. Each category represents a different environmental situation and suggests different strategic objectives. For example, an SBU classified into a category of high market opportunity and high competitive strength signifies a favorable environmental situation. The analytical methods would recommend market share building objectives for all SBUs in this category.

Although the growth-share matrix, multiple factor screening method, and other analytical approaches can provide useful information, they have been overused by many firms.[11] Corporate management has ultimate responsibility for establishing strategic objectives for each SBU whether analytical tools are used or not. As illustrated in Exhibit 5.4, the strategic objective assigned to a business unit has a direct effect on personal selling and sales management activities.

Different market share objectives for an SBU (build, hold, harvest, divest/liquidate) lead to different objectives for the sales organization. Achieving these different sales organization objectives requires that salespeople perform sales tasks appropriate for the objective. Sales management activities must also be consistent with the objectives and tasks as indicated by the recommended compensation system for each market share objective.

EXHIBIT 5.4 ▪ *SBU Objectives and the Sales Organization*

Market Share Objectives	Sales Organization Objectives	Primary Sales Tasks	Recommended Compensation System
Build	Build sales volume Secure distribution outlets	Call on prospective and new accounts Provide high service levels, particularly pre-sale service Product/market feedback	Salary plus incentive
Hold	Maintain sales volume Consolidate market position through concentration on targeted segments Secure additional outlets	Call on targeted current accounts Increase service levels to current accounts Call on new accounts	Salary plus commission or bonus
Harvest	Reduce selling costs Target profitable accounts	Call on and service most profitable accounts only and eliminate unprofitable accounts Reduce service levels Reduce inventories	Salary plus bonus
Divest/Liquidate	Minimize selling costs and clear out inventory	Inventory dumping Eliminate service	Salary

Source: Adapted from William Strahle and Rosann L. Spiro, "Linking Market Share Strategies to Salesforce Objectives, Activities, and Compensation Policies," *Journal of Personal Selling and Sales Management*, August 1986, 14 and 15. Used with permission.

Determining strategic objectives for each SBU is an important aspect of corporate strategy. These strategic objectives affect the development of the sales organization's objectives, the selling tasks performed by salespeople, and the activities of sales managers.

Corporate Growth Orientation

Another important aspect of corporate strategy is determining how the corporation will grow and develop over the long term. Most firms begin operations in a core business, then as growth opportunities in this core business diminish over time, management must expand the scope of operations to ensure long-term corporate growth. For example, Kodak (Figure 5.1) could no longer achieve corporate growth objectives within its core photographic business. Therefore, it moved into the pharmaceutical business, data storage business, and other areas.[12]

The basic corporate growth orientations, presented in Figure 5.1, are **intensive growth** in existing businesses or **diversification growth** by entering new business areas. Corporate strategists can use **internal development** or **acquisition** methods to achieve both intensive growth and diversification growth. Kodak provides a good example of multiple orientations toward corporate growth. The firm has grown intensively by introducing new products for existing markets and by diversifying into new businesses. These growth directions were accomplished both through internal development and acquisition.[13]

FIGURE 5.1 ▪ *Corporate Growth Orientation for Kodak*

Kodak has chosen to grow in both intensive and diversification directions and by means of both internal development and acquisition.

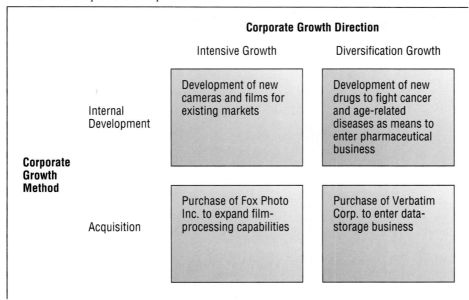

Source: Leslie Helm, "Why Kodak Is Starting to Click Again," *Business Week*, February 23, 1987, 134–138.

The corporate growth orientation of a firm has a direct impact on sales management activities. The specific effects depend upon the growth directions and methods employed. Examples of some specific differences in sales management activities for each growth direction and method are presented in Figure 5.2.

Intensive growth through internal development requires sales managers to increase selling effort in existing business areas. This is typically achieved by increasing the size of the salesforce and/or improving the productivity of salespeople. Productivity improvement is normally attempted through training and motivational programs directed toward increased market penetration and by the use of new technologies in sales operations. For example, firms such as Du Pont, Ciba Geigy, John Hancock Mutual Life, GTE, and the Wrangler Division of VF Corp. are equipping salespeople with cellular telephones, laptop computers, and/or hand-held order entry computers to improve their productivity.[14]

Diversification through internal development represents an entirely different sales management challenge. Instead of increasing selling effort in current business areas, sales operations must be developed for new business areas. Since the salesforce must sell different products to different customers, new methods and procedures for recruiting/selecting, training, and motivating salespeople must often be established. The situation faced by Tandy Corp. illustrates some of the difficulties involved. In 1986 Tandy decided to diversify into the business market for personal computers. The Tandy plan was to develop a salesforce of 1,500 to

FIGURE 5.2 ▪ ***Corporate Growth Orientation and Sales Management Activities***
Sales management activities differ considerably depending upon the corporate growth orientation (internal development or acquisitions, intensive growth or diversification growth). Acquisitions present a variety of sales management problems regardless of whether they are used for intensive or diversification growth.

		Corporate Growth Direction	
		Intensive Growth	Diversification Growth
Corporate Growth Method	Internal Development	Increase selling effort in current business areas; improve selling productivity; training programs for selling new products and penetrating current accounts; motivational programs to focus on new product sales to current accounts	Development of sales organization to operate in new business area; recruiting and selection of appropriate salespeople for new business area; development of appropriate training and motivational programs
	Acquisition	Determine best way to integrate sales organizations of acquiring and acquired firm; reorganize salesforce operations; consistent efforts to effectively communicate salesforce changes during transition period; communication with customers during transition period to ensure continued business	

compete against the likes of IBM in the personal computer business market. Tandy expected to be able to apply the retail methods used in its Radio Shack stores to direct sales to business customers. Results for the first year were disappointing. Sales did not meet objectives, turnover was 64 percent for salespeople and 25 percent for store managers, and problems in the sales training and motivational programs were identified. Although Tandy has improved direct sales operations in recent years, their initial problems serve as an example of diversification bringing difficult and complex sales management problems.[15]

Acquisitions present a different set of problems regardless of whether growth is intensive or by diversification. The key challenge is to determine the best way to integrate the selling operations of the acquiring and acquired firm. Options include a complete merging of the two salesforces, partial merging, or keeping both salesforces separate.

The keys to successful salesforce integration appear to be the development of a specific plan and the effective communication of this plan to salespeople and sales managers from both salesforces and to key customers.[16] One of the major problems during the acquisition and merger process is that rumors abound between the two salesforces and customers, if not addressed effectively by sales managers. Consider the successful approach taken by James River Corp. when acquiring the Northern and Dixie divisions of the then American Can Co. (now Primerica Corp.):

> As soon as the acquisition was announced, key managers were assembled and a personal letter sent to all salespeople to detail what was happening. Every effort was made to communicate with the field salesforce and key customers. Top sales executives met frequently with their sales managers and salespeople to address any and all rumors. Once the integration plan was finalized, sales management began the implementation process. Again, extensive communication between sales management and salespeople and customers was the key to a successful transition.[17]

Although internal development and acquisitions are the basic methods for corporate growth, the use of collaborative ventures has become increasingly popular in recent years. **Collaborative ventures,** often called strategic alliances, strategic partnerships, or joint ventures, represent various types of arrangements between firms to jointly produce and/or market products and services. Collaborative ventures possess some of the characteristics of both internal development and acquisitions.

An example of a collaborative venture is the agreement between Du Pont Co. and Merck & Co. for collaboration on the research and marketing of specific pharmaceutical products. Merck will help Du Pont reduce the development time for several new pharmaceutical products and will use its veteran salesforce to help market the products when final FDA approval is received. In exchange, Du Pont receives exclusive rights to sell several of Merck's existing, mature products. This collaborative arrangement allows the Merck salesforce to concentrate efforts on newer products and gives the Du Pont salesforce more pharmaceutical products to sell while awaiting approval of their newer products.[18]

Since collaborative ventures can take on many different forms, their effects on the sales function depend on the details of each specific arrangement. However, all collaborative ventures require that two or more separate firms work together in various ways. Collaborative ventures are becoming a favorite method for firms to expand globally, as illustrated in "A Global Perspective: Expanding through Collaborative Ventures."

Corporate Strategy Summary

Strategic decisions at the topmost levels of multibusiness corporations provide guidance for strategy development at all lower organizational levels. Even though the sales function is often far removed from the corporate level, corporate strategy has both direct and indirect impacts on personal selling and sales management. The corporate mission, definition of strategic business units, determination of strategic business unit objectives, and the establishment of corporate growth orientation all affect sales organization operations. However, corporate strategy decisions have their most immediate impact on business unit strategies.

Business Strategy and the Sales Function

Whereas corporate strategy addresses decisions across business units, a separate strategy must be designed for each SBU. The essence of business strategy is competitive advantage: How can each SBU compete successfully against compet-

A GLOBAL PERSPECTIVE

Expanding through Collaborative Ventures Many firms that are trying to expand globally to take advantage of the potential opportunities offered by consolidation of Western Europe in 1992, the move to market economies by Eastern European countries, and growth markets in other areas of the world are using collaborative ventures as a preferred corporate growth method. Consider the following examples:

▪ AT&T is negotiating a variety of computer sales partnerships with medium-sized computer software and systems-integration companies in France, Germany, Italy, Belgium, and The Netherlands.

▪ General Mills has announced plans for a joint venture with Swiss-based Nestle SA to form a separate company for marketing breakfast cereal throughout Europe.

▪ Chrysler Corp. is involved in a number of strategic alliances including one with Hyundai Motor Co. to sell specific Chrysler products in South Korea.

Source: Richard L. Hudson, "AT&T's Computer Business is Planning to Build Sales Partnerships in Europe," *The Wall Street Journal*, May 11, 1990, B5; John Sterlicchi and Charlotte Klopp, "Europe Faces Invasion by U.S. Cereal Makers," *Marketing News*, June 11, 1990, 2; and Bradley A. Stertz, "Chrysler's Search for Broader Alliances Intensifies Amid Strong Internal Debate," *The Wall Street Journal*, June 19, 1990, A4.

itive products and services? What differential advantage will each SBU try to exploit in the marketplace? What can each SBU do better than competitors? Answers to these questions provide the basis for business strategies.

Business Strategy Types

Although developing a business unit strategy is a complex task, several classification schemes have been developed to aid in this endeavor. One of the most popular is Porter's **generic business strategies,**[19] presented in Exhibit 5.5. Each of these generic strategies—**low cost, differentiation,** or **niche**—emphasizes a different type of competitive advantage. For example, Zenith Laboratories follows a low cost strategy by marketing generic drugs in the pharmaceutical industry.[20] IBM, on the other hand, employs a differentiation strategy that focuses on providing excellent customer service. They try to compete through high-quality products and superior customer service, not low price. Businesses using niche strategies achieve their competitive advantage by focusing on a specific target market and specializing in meeting the needs of target customers better than competitors. Nichers may also use a low cost or differentiation strategy to appeal to their target segments.

Another useful business strategy typology, suggested by Miles and Snow and presented in Exhibit 5.6,[21] classifies business strategies as prospectors, defenders, or analyzers. **Prospectors** are businesses that are continually introducing new products. **Defenders** concentrate on maintaining their current market position. Finally, **analyzers** represent strategies intended to both defend existing business and prospect for new business.

Both of the business strategy classification schemes are useful, but both oversimplify the situation. Each strategy category actually consists of many

EXHIBIT 5.5 ▪ *Generic Business Strategies and Salesforce Activities*

Strategy Type	*Role of the Salesforce*
Low Cost Supplier Aggressive construction of efficient-scale facilities, vigorous pursuit of cost reductions from experience, tight cost and overhead control, usually associated with high relative market share.	Servicing large current customers, pursuing large prospects, minimizing costs, selling on the basis of price, and usually assuming significant order-taking responsibilities.
Differentiation Creation of something perceived industrywide as being unique. Provides insulation against competitive rivalry because of brand loyalty and resulting lower sensitivity to price.	Selling nonprice benefits, generating orders, providing high quality of customer service and responsiveness, possibly significant amount of prospecting if high growth industry, selecting customers based on low price sensitivity. Usually requires a high-quality salesforce.
Niche Service of a particular target market, with each functional policy developed with this target market in mind. Although market share in the industry might be low, the firm dominates a segment within the industry.	To become experts in the operations and opportunities associated with the target market. Focusing customer attention on nonprice benefits and allocating selling time to the target market.

Source: Adapted from William L. Cron and Michael Levy, "Sales Management Performance Evaluation: A Residual Income Perspective," *Journal of Personal Selling and Sales Management*, August 1987, 58. Used with permission.

different business strategies. For example, firms following a differentiation strategy can attempt to differentiate themselves in any number of ways (customer service, product quality, innovativeness, etc.).

Business Strategy Execution

The sales function plays an important role in executing a specific business strategy. As indicated in Exhibit 5.5, the activities of sales managers and salespeople differ depending upon whether the business unit is employing a low cost, differentiation, or niche business strategy. Oftentimes, the sales function can provide the basis for differentiation.

The computer business at NCR provides a good example. NCR is changing the focus of its computer business to incorporate the standard chip designs and software used by competitors. Since NCR will now be using industry rather than proprietary standards, they might be expected to compete on price with a low cost strategy. However, Chairman and Chief Executive Charles E. Exley states that NCR will be price-competitive with high end rivals such as IBM and Compaq but will differentiate itself through the service and support provided by the NCR sales organization.[22]

The role of the sales function also differs when prospector, defender, or analyzer business strategies are used (see Exhibit 5.6). For example, an empirical study of the Miles and Snow typology in the financial services industry found that

EXHIBIT 5.6   ▪   *Miles and Snow Business Strategies and Salesforce Activities*

Strategy Type	*Role of the Salesforce*
Prospector	
Attempt to pioneer in product/market development. Offer a frequently changing product line and be willing to sacrifice short-term profits to gain a long-term stronghold in their markets.	Primary focus is on sales volume growth. Territory management emphasizes customer penetration and prospecting.
Defender	
Offer a limited, stable product line to a predictable market. Markets are generally in the late growth or early maturity phase of the product life cycle. Emphasis is on being the low-cost producer through high volume.	Maintain the current customer base. Very little prospecting for new customers is involved. Customer service is emphasized along with greater account penetration.
Analyzer	
Choose high growth markets while holding on to substantial mature markets. Analyzers are an intermediate type of firm. They make fewer and slower product/market changes than prospectors, but are less committed to stability and efficiency than defenders.	Must balance multiple roles: servicing existing customers, prospecting for new customers, uncovering new applications, holding on to distribution of mature products and support campaigns for new products.

Source: Adapted from William L. Cron and Michael Levy, "Sales Management Performance Evaluation: A Residual Income Perspective," *Journal of Personal Selling and Sales Management*, August 1987, 58. Used with permission.

the importance of the sales function declined when moving from prospector to analyzer to defender strategies. Prospectors were found to place a high emphasis on personal selling and sales management and a moderate emphasis on sales training. Analyzers placed a high emphasis on personal selling but only a moderate emphasis on sales management and a low emphasis on sales training. Defenders focused moderate attention to personal selling but placed a low emphasis on sales management and sales training.[23]

Business Strategy Summary

Business strategies determine how each SBU plans to compete in the marketplace. Several strategic approaches are available, placing different demands on the sales function. The role of the sales function depends upon how an SBU plans to compete in the marketplace with the activities of sales managers and salespeople being important in executing a business strategy successfully.

Marketing Strategy and the Sales Function

Since SBUs typically market multiple products to different customer groups, separate marketing strategies are often developed for each of an SBU's target markets. These marketing strategies must be consistent with the business strategy. For example, marketers operating in an SBU with a differentiation business

FIGURE 5.3 ▪ *Marketing Strategy and Personal Selling*

Personal selling is an important element of a promotion strategy. The promotion strategy is one element of a marketing mix designed to appeal to a defined target market. A marketing strategy can be defined in terms of target market and marketing mix components.

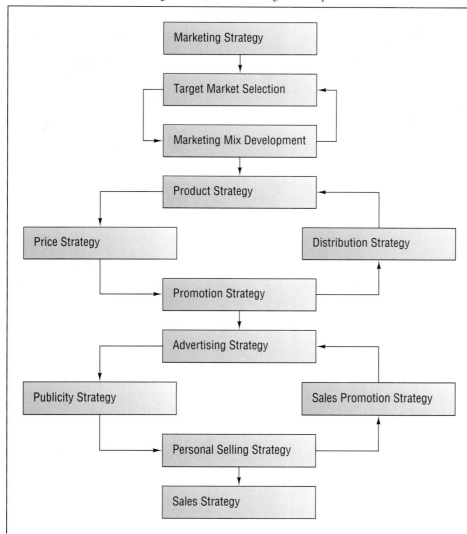

strategy would probably not develop marketing strategies that emphasize low price. The marketing strategies for each target market should reinforce the differentiation competitive advantage sought by the SBU.

Figure 5.3 illustrates the major components of a marketing strategy and highlights the position of personal selling within the promotional portion of a marketing strategy. The key components of any marketing strategy are the selection of a **target market** and the development of a **marketing mix.** Target market selection requires a definition of the specific market segment to be served.

The marketing mix then consists of a marketing offer designed to appeal to the defined target market. This marketing offer contains a mixture of product, price, distribution, and promotional strategies. The critical task for the marketing strategist is to develop a marketing mix that satisfies the needs of the target market better than competitive offerings.

Personal selling may be an important element in the promotional portion of the marketing mix. The promotional strategy consists of a mixture of personal selling, advertising, sales promotion, and publicity, with most promotional strategies emphasizing either personal selling or advertising as the main communication tool. Sales promotion and publicity are typically viewed as supplemental promotional tools. Thus, a key strategic decision is to determine when promotional strategies should be personal selling-driven or advertising-driven. This decision should capitalize on the relative advantages of personal selling and advertising for different target markets and different marketing mixes.

Advantages and Disadvantages of Personal Selling

Personal selling is the only promotional tool that consists of personal communication between seller and buyer, and the advantages and disadvantages of personal selling thus accrue from this personal communication. The personal communication between buyer and seller is typically viewed as more credible and has more of an impact (or impression) than messages delivered through advertising media. Personal selling also allows for better timing of message delivery, and it affords the flexibility of communicating different messages to different customers or changing a message during a sales call based on customer feedback. Finally, personal selling has the advantage of allowing a sale to be closed. These characteristics make personal selling a powerful promotional tool in situations where the benefits of personal communication are important (see Figure 5.4).

The major disadvantage of personal selling is the high cost to reach each member of the audience. *Sales and Marketing Management* reported that the median cost of an industrial sales call was $250.54 in 1990.[24] Contrast this with the pennies that it costs to reach an audience member through mass advertising. The benefits of personal selling do not come cheap. They may, however, outweigh its costs for certain types of target market situations and for specific marketing mixes.

Target Market Situations and Personal Selling

The characteristics of personal selling are most advantageous in specific target market situations. Personal selling-driven promotional strategies are appropriate when (1) the market consists of only a few buyers that tend to be concentrated in location, (2) the buyer needs a great deal of information, (3) the purchase is important, (4) the product is complex, and (5) service after the sale is important. The target market characteristics that favor personal selling are similar to those found in most industrial purchasing situations. Thus, personal selling is typically the preferred promotional tool in **industrial marketing,** while advertising is normally emphasized in consumer marketing situations (see Figure 5.5).

The target market characteristics presented in Figure 5.5 are only guidelines and not hard-and-fast rules. Sometimes firms can gain a competitive advantage by

FIGURE 5.4 ▪ *Personal Selling–Driven versus Advertising-Driven Promotion Strategies*

Personal selling–driven promotion strategies are most appropriate in situations where the benefits of personal communications are important.

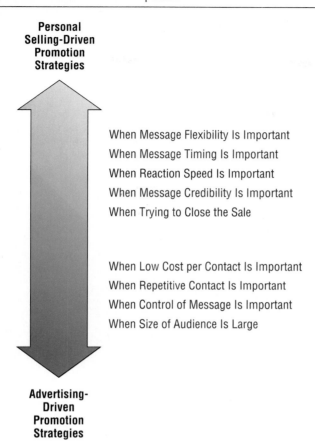

Personal Selling-Driven Promotion Strategies

When Message Flexibility Is Important
When Message Timing Is Important
When Reaction Speed Is Important
When Message Credibility Is Important
When Trying to Close the Sale

When Low Cost per Contact Is Important
When Repetitive Contact Is Important
When Control of Message Is Important
When Size of Audience Is Large

Advertising-Driven Promotion Strategies

FIGURE 5.5 ▪ *Target Market Characteristics and Promotion Strategy*

Personal selling–driven promotion strategies are most appropriate for target markets that have the typical characteristics of industrial markets.

Industrial Target Markets → **Personal Selling–Driven Promotion Strategies**

Characteristics
- Few Buyers
- Buyers Concentrated Geographically
- Purchase Information Needs High
- Purchases Made in Large Amounts
- High-Importance Purchases
- Complex Products Purchased
- Postpurchase Service Important

Consumer Target Markets → **Advertising-Driven Promotion Strategies**

Characteristics
- Many Buyers
- Buyers Dispersed Geographically
- Purchase Information Needs Low
- Purchases Made in Small Amounts
- Low-Importance Purchases
- Low-Complexity Products Purchased
- Postpurchase Service Not Important

EXHIBIT 5.7 ▪ *Marketing Mix Elements and Personal Selling*

Marketing Mix Area	Characteristics	Marketing Mix Area	Characteristics
Product or service	Complex products requiring customer application assistance (computers, pollution control systems, steam turbines) Major purchase decisions, such as food items purchased by supermarket chains Features and performance of the product requiring personal demonstration and trial by the customer (private aircraft)	Channels	Channel system relatively short and direct to end users Product and service training and assistance needed by channel intermediaries Personal selling needed in "pushing" product through channel Channel intermediaries available to perform personal selling function for supplier with limited resources and experience (brokers or manufacturers' agents)
Price	Final price negotiated between buyer and seller (appliances, automobiles, real estate) Selling price or quantity purchased enable an adequate margin to support selling expenses (traditional department store compared to discount house)		

Source: David W. Cravens, Gerald E. Hills, and Robert B. Woodruff, *Marketing Management* (Homewood, Ill.: Irwin, 1987), 546.

developing nontraditional promotional strategies. Take the direct selling industry as an example. Firms such as Avon, Amway, Mary Kay, and others market low-priced consumer products. The typical promotional strategy for these types of target markets would be advertising-driven. Yet, the direct selling firms emphasize personal selling and gain much of their competitive advantage from offering the convenience of shopping at home and the personal attention of a salesperson. Retail sales by these direct selling firms reached over $9.6 billion in 1988.[25]

An effective promotional mix capitalizes on the advantages of each promotional tool. Moreover, characteristics of the target market must be considered, and the promotional mix must also be consistent with the other elements of the marketing mix to ensure a coordinated marketing offer.

Marketing Mix Elements and Personal Selling

One of the most difficult challenges facing the marketing strategist is making sure that decisions concerning the product, distribution, price, and promotion areas result in an effective marketing mix. There are any number of different ways that these elements can be combined to form a marketing mix. However, there tend to be some combinations that represent logical fits. Exhibit 5.7 shows when a personal selling emphasis might fit well with the other marketing elements. Again, these suggestions should be considered only as guidelines, since the development of unique marketing mixes may produce competitive advantages in the market-place.

An interesting example of the unique emphasis on personal selling in a marketing strategy is the marketing of hosiery products by Hanes Hosiery Inc. Since hosiery products are low-priced and sold through retailers, the typical promotion strategy would be advertising-driven. Hanes, however, has achieved success by emphasizing personal selling. As stated by Steve Jolley, manager of field system sales: "Being in a store on a regular basis helps us present Hanes in a better light. That helps both the store and us succeed."

Hanes salespeople regularly visit each retail store, straighten the stock, fill in displays, and help manage the inventory for the retailer. The salespeople use hand-held computers with UPC-reading wands to compare the store's current inventory with the target stock level. They then use laptop computers to generate new orders and electronically transmit them to Hanes's main office. The services provided by the Hanes salespeople have allowed them to develop strong relationships with retailers as a way to increase sales of hosiery products.[26]

Integrating Personal Selling and Promotion Tools

Our discussion to this point has focused on general marketing strategies with an emphasis on when marketing and promotional strategies should be personal selling-driven or advertising-driven. Most firms, however, employ personal selling, advertising, and other promotion tools in their promotional mixes. When this is the case, it is important to determine the most effective way to integrate personal selling and other promotion tools.

One typical approach is to use advertising to generate company and product awareness and to identify potential customers. These sales leads are then turned over to the salesforce for personal selling attention. The basic objective is to use low cost-per-contact advertising to identify prospects, while more expensive personal selling efforts are used to turn prospects into customers. The effectiveness of this type of promotional strategy was documented by a study of 2,500 salespeople that found more than 85 percent of the salespeople had received leads from advertising during the past year.[27]

A specific example of effective use of advertising and personal selling is the promotional strategy used by NCR to introduce its Tower computer line into the business market. This promotional strategy had four objectives: (1) to increase brand awareness by 50 percent; (2) to generate high-quality leads for the salesforce; (3) to increase sales by 10 percent in six months; and (4) to improve salesforce morale. Although a typical approach would be to advertise in trade publications to increase awareness and generate leads, NCR found these publications to be cluttered with ads from competitors. Therefore, they decided to advertise on television in their largest markets. Ads on programs such as "60 Minutes," "20/20," and major sporting events produced a flood of inquiries, increased brand awareness by more than 50 percent, and improved salesforce morale dramatically. The high-quality leads were turned over to a motivated salesforce that then increased sales by 25 percent. NCR Tower computers are now one of the hottest-selling brands.[28]

EXHIBIT 5.8 ▪ *Environmental, Strategy, and Sales Function Changes*

	Schaeffer Eaton	*Campbell Soup*	*Xerox*
Market Served	Organizations and consumers	Household and institutional markets	Business and government markets
Product Mix	Writing and business products	Food products	Office equipment
Business Environment Changes	Competitive pressures	Fragmentation of food markets	Changes in customer needs and competitive pressures
Organizational Strategy Changes	Retrenchment by selling several business units	Changing the product mix by developing new products for geographic market segments	Repositioning as supplier of total business system needs for customers
Sales Function Changes	Change from company salesforce on salary/bonus/expenses to straight commission salesforce and addition of independent representatives	Reorganize salesforce to reflect geographic market differences Introduce product specialists Have salespeople develop promotional programs for individual retailers	Change from product specialized salesforce to specialization by account size Salespeople responsible for all products to assigned accounts
	Redeployment	Redeployment	Redeployment

Source: Adapted from David W. Cravens, Raymond W. LaForge, and Thomas N. Ingram, "Sales Strategy: Charting a New Course in Turbulent Markets," *Business*, October–December 1990, 7.

Another example of a rather unique integration of personal selling and other promotion tools is provided by BMW of North America Inc. In 1989 BMW sales in the United States were 33 percent below their 1986 peak. As a way to turn around this trend, the new president, Karl H. Gerlinger, instituted a new strategy for BMW dealers. It consists of a mixture of aggressive personal selling, promotional events, and direct marketing. BMW salespeople are moving out of their showrooms to find buyers. Once prospects are identified, promotional videotapes are sent to them. Then, a salesperson drops off a car at the potential buyer's home for test-driving. Negotiations to sell the car may take place via a fax machine. This type of aggressive promotion strategy represents an interesting blend of promotion tools for the automobile industry.[29]

Marketing Strategy Summary

Selecting target markets and developing marketing mixes are the key components in marketing strategy development. Marketing strategies must be developed for the target markets served by an SBU and must be consistent with the business unit strategy. One important element of the marketing mix is the promotional mix. The critical task is designing a promotional mix that capitalizes on the advantages of each promotional tool. Personal selling has the basic advantage of personal communication and is emphasized in target market situations and marketing mixes where personal communication is important.

The Turbulent Business Environment

The contemporary business environment is becoming increasingly turbulent. Consumer needs are continuously shifting, competitive pressures are causing the restructuring of many industries, new methods of distribution are being introduced, and an uncertain international and domestic environment is forcing many firms to make major strategic changes frequently. The success of these organizational strategy changes typically requires appropriate adjustments in the sales function.

The close relationships between the business environment, organizational strategy, and the sales function are illustrated in Exhibit 5.8. Schaeffer Eaton, Campbell Soup, and Xerox faced different pressures from their business environments. Each firm responded by making major changes in organizational strategy. Implementing the new organizational strategies required specific changes in each firm's sales function.

All indications are that the business environment of the future will be increasingly dynamic and uncertain. Firms must constantly change their strategies to take advantage of the opportunities and avoid the threats created by a turbulent business environment. Strategic changes at the corporate, business unit, and marketing levels require appropriate changes in the sales function. These changes affect the role and activities of sales managers and salespeople.

Summary

1.   **Define the different strategy levels for multibusiness, multiproduct firms.** Multibusiness, multiproduct firms must make strategic decisions at the corporate, business, marketing, and account levels. Corporate strategy decisions determine the basic scope and direction for the corporate entity through formulating the corporate mission statement, defining strategic business units, setting strategic business unit objectives, and determining corporate growth orientation. Business strategy decisions determine how each business unit plans to compete effectively within its industry. Marketing strategies consist of the selection of target markets and the development of marketing mixes for each product market. Personal selling is an important component of the promotional mix portion of marketing strategies and a key element in sales strategies.

2.   **Discuss how corporate strategy decisions affect the sales function.** Corporate strategy decisions provide direction for strategy development at all organizational levels. The corporate mission statement, definition of strategic business units, determination of strategic business unit objectives, and establishment of the corporate growth orientation provide guidelines within which sales managers and salespeople must operate. Changes in corporate strategy typically lead to changes in sales management and personal selling activities.

3.   **Explain the relationships between business strategy and the sales function.** Business strategy decisions determine how each strategic business unit intends to compete. Different business strategies place different demands on the sales organization.

4.   **List the advantages and disadvantages of personal selling as a promotional tool.** Personal selling is the only promotional tool that involves personal communication between buyer and seller. As such, personal selling has the advantage of being able to tailor the promotional message to the specific needs of each customer and to deliver complicated messages. The major disadvantage of personal selling is the high cost to reach individual buyers.

5.   **Specify the situations where personal selling is typically emphasized in a marketing strategy.** Marketing strategies tend to be either personal selling-driven or advertising-driven. Personal selling is normally emphasized in industrial markets where there are relatively few buyers, in concentrated locations, who make important purchases of complex products and require a great deal of information and service. Personal selling is also typically emphasized in marketing mixes for complex, expensive products that are distributed through direct channels or through indirect channels using a "push" strategy and when the price affords sufficient margin to support the high costs associated with personal selling.

6.   **Describe ways that personal selling, advertising, and other promotion tools can be blended into effective promotional strategies.** Effective promotional strategies typically consist of a mixture of personal selling, advertising, and other promotion tools. Oftentimes, firms use advertising to generate company and brand awareness and to identify potential customers. Personal selling is then used to turn these prospects into customers of the firm's products or services. Other promotion tools are normally used to supplement the advertising and personal selling efforts.

Key Terms

- **Corporate strategy**
- **Business strategy**
- **Marketing strategy**
- **Corporate mission statement**
- **Strategic business unit (SBU)**
- **Business unit portfolio**
- **Intensive growth**
- **Diversification growth**
- **Internal development**
- **Acquisition**
- **Collaborative venture**

- **Generic business strategies**
- **Low cost strategy**
- **Differentiation strategy**
- **Niche strategy**
- **Prospectors**
- **Defenders**
- **Analyzers**
- **Target market**
- **Marketing mix**
- **Industrial marketing**

Review Questions

1. Discuss how different organizational strategies affect the activities of salespeople and sales managers.

2. How does the corporate mission statement affect personal selling and sales management activities?

3. Refer to the study results presented in "An Ethical Perspective: A Study of Salesperson Ethics." What do you think companies and sales managers should do to increase the ethical behavior of new salespeople and salespeople compensated on a straight commission basis?

4. How can sales promotion and publicity be used to supplement a personal selling-driven promotional strategy?

5. Why is personal selling typically emphasized in industrial markets and advertising emphasized in consumer markets?

6. What are the critical problems faced by sales managers during and after an acquisition of another firm?

7. Why do most firms employ both personal selling and advertising in their promotional strategies?

8. How would sales management activities differ for an SBU following a differentiation strategy versus an SBU employing a low cost strategy?

9. Consider the examples presented in "A Global Perspective: Expanding through Collaborative Ventures." Compare the sales management problems associated with these collaborative ventures with those that would have been encountered had each company used internal development or acquisitions as their corporate growth method.

10. What are the major sales management problems for firms that are diversifying through internal development?

Application Exercises

1. Identify a recent feature article about a multibusiness, multiproduct corporation from the business press (*Business Week, Forbes, Fortune, Sales and Marketing Management,* etc.). Use the information in the article to describe the firm's corporate strategy, business strategy, marketing strategy, and sales function.

2. Identify three companies that you think employ unique and creative promotional strategies. Explain how each company's promotional strategy is unique and creative. Be sure to highlight the personal selling element in your discussion.

3. Assume that you are the national sales manager for an industrial products firm. Your company's business strategy is to develop a competitive advantage based on excellent customer service. What are five things that you might do as national sales manager to ensure that this competitive advantage is developed throughout the sales organization?

Notes

[1]David W. Cravens, *Strategic Marketing* (Homewood, Ill.: Irwin, 1991), 37–44.

[2]John A. Pearce II and Fred David, "Corporate Mission Statements: The Bottom Line," *Academy of Management Executive,* May 1987, 109.

[3]See Donald P. Robin and R. Eric Reidenbach, "Social Responsibility, Ethics, and Marketing Strategy: Closing the Gap between Concept and Application," *Journal of Marketing,* January 1987, 44–58, for an interesting discussion concerning the integration of ethical considerations into strategic planning.

[4]Gene R. Laczniak and Patrick E. Murphy, "Incorporating Marketing Ethics into the Organization," in *Marketing Ethics: Guidelines for Managers,* eds. Gene R. Laczniak and Patrick E. Murphy (Lexington, Mass.: Lexington Books, 1985), 104.

[5] Lawrence B. Chonko and Shelby D. Hunt, "Ethics and Marketing Management: An Empirical Investigation," *Journal of Business Research*, August 1985, 339–359.

[6] Daniel B. Moskowitz and John A. Byrne, "Where Business Goes to Stock Up on Ethics," *Business Week*, October 14, 1985, 66.

[7] Federal Industries, *Corporate Long Range Plan 1987/1995*, v.

[8] Cravens, *Strategic Marketing*, 43.

[9] National Analysts, *Marketing Organization Structure in Large Multiproduct/Multiservice Companies*, October 1985, 10.

[10] See Cravens, *Strategic Marketing*, 45–51, for a more complete discussion of these analytical tools.

[11] "The New Breed of Strategic Planner," *Business Week*, September 17, 1984, 63.

[12] Leslie Helm, "Why Kodak is Starting to Click Again," *Business Week*, February 23, 1987, 134–138.

[13] Helm, "Why Kodak," 135.

[14] A. J. Magrath, "Are You Overdoing 'Lean and Mean'?" *Sales and Marketing Management*, January 1988, 47–50.

[15] Todd Mason and Geoff Lewis, "Tandy Finds a Cold, Hard World Outside the Radio Shack," *Business Week*, August 31, 1987, 68–70.

[16] Kate Bertrand, "When Silence Isn't Golden," *Business Marketing*, February 1987, 62–69; and Kevin E. Carey, "Merging Two Salesforces Into One," *Sales and Marketing Management*, March 1987, 102–104.

[17] James H. Huguet, Jr., "Blending Sales Forces After Acquisition," *Mergers and Acquisitions*, Summer 1984, 57.

[18] Richard Koenig, "Du Pont Signs Agreement with Merck in Effort to Speed Up Drug Marketing," *The Wall Street Journal*, September 29, 1989, B3.

[19] Michael E. Porter, *Competitive Strategy* (New York: The Free Press, 1980), 34–46.

[20] Bill Kelley, "Zenith Labs on a New Product High," *Sales and Marketing Management*, October 1986, 42–45.

[21] Raymond E. Miles and Charles C. Snow, *Organizational Strategy, Structure, and Process* (New York: McGraw-Hill, 1978).

[22] John R. Wilke, "NCR is Revamping Its Computer Lines in Wrenching Change," *The Wall Street Journal*, June 20, 1990, A1–A6.

[23] Stephen W. McDaniel and James W. Kolari, "Marketing Strategy Implications of the Miles and Snow Strategic Typology," *Journal of Marketing*, October 1987, 19–30.

[24] "Hey, Where's My Survey of Selling Costs," *Sales and Marketing Management*, March 1991, 42.

[25] Direct Selling Association, *A Statistical Study of the Direct Selling Industry in the United States: 1980–1985* (Washington, D.C.: Direct Selling Association, October 1986), 3.

[26] Cyndee Miller, "Hanes Takes the Snags Out of Maintaining Hosiery Inventories," *Marketing News*, May 14, 1990, 23.

[27] Reported in "Salespeople Find Advertising Works," *Sales and Marketing Management*, January 1987, 20–22.

[28] David Perry, "Award-Winning Marketing That Sells," *Business Marketing*, March 1987, 129–131.

[29] Bruce Hager and John Templeman, "Now, They're Selling BMWs Door-to-Door—Almost," *Business Week*, May 14, 1990, 65.

CASE 5.1   *Stapro Manufacturing*

Background

Stapro is a manufacturer of high-quality, commercial-grade staplers. The firm markets the staplers to organizational customers in the western United States through a network of distributors. Stapro's business strategy has always been to differentiate itself from competitors by offering high-quality products and excellent service to both distributors and end-user customers. This high product and service quality image is communicated in all advertising and has allowed Stapro to charge prices 10 percent higher than competitors.

Current Situation

Lee France is the district sales manager for the state of California. Lee has recently hired Barbara Mason to be the salesperson for the northern California territory. Barbara is a recent graduate of UCLA and is in the last week of Stapro's three-week training program for new sales representatives.

The northern California territory had not had a full-time salesperson for the past 12 months. Sporadic sales coverage had been provided by Lee during this period, but by Lee's own account his coverage had been less than ideal: "Being a sales manager is enough to keep me busy — I just simply could not spend all the time necessary in northern California to do a good job."

Lee was in the process of visiting all of Stapro's distributors in the northern California territory to tell them that Barbara would begin full-time coverage of the territory in about two weeks. Lee's first call was to Brad Langford, owner and president of Langford Supply. The highlights of the sales call follow.

Lee: Good morning, Mr. Langford. I've got some really good news. We have hired Barbara Mason as the salesperson to provide full-time support to you and our other distributors in the northern California area. Barbara was an excellent student at UCLA and is doing very well in our training program for new sales representatives.

Brad: Well, it's about time. We haven't had much support from your company for over 12 months.

Lee: I realize that, but things will change drastically in two weeks when Barbara comes on board.

Brad: I'm going to take a wait-and-see attitude — actions speak louder than words. We like the quality of your products and their high margins but can't get the service and support we need to sell them. You should know that we've switched a large portion of our stapler business to a competitor because their service has been much better than yours.

Lee: I understand your concern, but when I bring Barbara by in two weeks I think you will see a tremendous increase in our service.

Brad: Well, we'll see. I'm not sure that an inexperienced salesperson can provide the type of support that we require.

Questions

1. What should Lee and Barbara do to regain the lost business with Langford Supply?
2. What should Lee tell Barbara about Brad Langford's comment concerning inexperienced salespeople?
3. What should Barbara do during the first sales call to Brad Langford?

CASE 5.2 *PolyWrap Inc.*

PolyWrap Inc. had just completed its tenth year of business as a manufacturer and marketer of polyethylene film to agricultural and industrial markets. Their primary product is a shredded polyethylene film that is used for soil erosion control by farmers and commercial landscapers. Sales of this product had increased at a rate of 20 percent per year for the first eight years. However, sales growth during the past two years had slowed to 3 percent, and sales forecasts for the next five years expected growth to remain in the 3 to 5 percent range.

Top management at PolyWrap had decided that the company should move into the pallet overwrap business, where polyethylene film is used to secure products to pallets for shipping. Growth prospects for this business were in the 10 to 15 percent per year range. Management was, however, considering two alternatives for entering the business. The first alternative was to develop the manufacturing capability for the pallet overwrap film internally and to market the product through the firm's existing sales organization. The second alternative was to acquire Pallet Wrap Inc., a small manufacturer and marketer of the pallet overwrap film. This alternative would give PolyWrap production facilities, a customer base, and a 30-person salesforce.

Top management had asked Bob Johnson, PolyWrap's national sales manager, to prepare an analysis of the sales organization implications of each alternative. Bob called a meeting of all district sales managers to discuss the alternatives. Excerpts from this meeting follow.

Johnson: Well, I guess all of you have heard the rumors about the move into the pallet overwrap business. Unfortunately, many of the rumors are false. We do not contemplate terminating any of our salespeople — in fact, we are probably going to need more salespeople, regardless of which alternative management selects.

Smith: My people are not as concerned about losing their jobs as they are about losing some of their key customers if their territory is redesigned. Some of my salespeople have been calling on the same account for over ten years. They don't want to have to start all over in developing new relationships with new customers.

Jones: Everyone in my district is against any move into the pallet overwrap business. We think that the poor sales in shredded film are largely due to the lack of sales support from the company during the last two years. If we move into another business area, we'll probably get less support in the future.

Winters: You both bring up good points, but I think we're going to lose some of our salespeople no matter which way management goes. Even if some of our salespeople are not terminated, some — and probably the best ones — are going to leave. I'm pretty sure that two of my best people are already talking to competitors about sales jobs.

Questions

1. How would you evaluate the comments made by each of the district sales managers?
2. Based on these comments, what would you recommend that Bob Johnson do?
3. In addition to the points made by the district managers, what other sales organization factors should Bob Johnson consider in evaluating the two alternatives and reporting to top management?

Sales Strategy and the Sales Function

A SUCCESSFUL SALES STRATEGY: ALPHA WIRE CORP.
Alpha Wire Corp. produces and markets electronic cable to customers for maintenance, repair, and operational uses, such as linking computer terminals. In 1986, the company developed new organizational and sales strategies to revive declining sales revenue. Since 1986, sales have grown from $50 million to $75 million, almost twice the industry growth rate. What strategic changes produced this impressive growth?

The key organizational strategy change was to focus efforts on customers who wanted quick delivery of small quantities of cable products and were willing to pay a higher price for this service. A sales strategy was developed to implement the organizational strategy effectively. The key elements of the sales strategy were to sell products only through the electronic distributor channel and to develop long-term relationships with the 1,000 electronic distributors nationwide.

Many of Alpha's competitors sold through multiple sales channels, such as through electronic distributors and direct to customers through their own field salesforce. Thus, these firms often competed directly with their distributors for sales to end users. Since Alpha's salesforce did not sell directly to customers, it was easier for them to build close relationships with the electronic distributors.

Alpha built effective distributor relationships by understanding the needs of the distributors and developing programs to satisfy those needs. For example, the distributors wanted their suppliers to help them sell products to end-user customers. Therefore, Alpha's salesforce changed from pushing products to providing service to distributors by expediting orders, answering technical questions, and making joint sales calls with distributor salespeople.

The successful organizational and sales strategies developed by Alpha Wire Corp. were based on an understanding of the buyer behavior of electronics distributors and end-user customers. This understanding of buyer behavior helped Alpha formulate sales strategies that were effective in meeting the needs of distributors and customers.

Source: Adapted from Tom Eisenhart, "Restless Revivalist," *Business Marketing*, March 1990, 12–17.

Chapter 6

Learning Objectives

After completing this chapter, you should be able to

1 *Discuss the important concepts behind organizational buyer behavior.*

2 *Explain the different types of relationship strategies.*

3 *Describe the different sales channel strategies.*

4 *Discuss the basic interrelationships between relationship strategy and sales channel strategy.*

Corporate, business, and marketing strategies view customers as aggregate markets or market segments. These organizational strategies provide direction and guidance for the sales function, but then sales managers and salespeople must translate these general organizational strategies into specific strategies for individual customers. As illustrated in the Alpha Wire Corp. example, effective sales strategies are necessary for successful firm performance.

In most cases, sales managers, who play merely a supporting role in the development of corporate, business, and marketing strategies, are the major players in the development and execution of sales strategy. Therefore, this entire chapter is devoted to discussing the key types of sales strategy, which is important for two basic reasons. First, it has a major impact on a firm's sales and profit performance. Second, it influences many other sales management decisions. Salesforce recruiting/selecting, training, compensation, and performance evaluations are all affected by the sales strategies employed by a firm.

This chapter is organized in the following manner: First, a sales strategy framework is presented for the chapter, showing the close relationship between sales strategy and organizational buyer behavior. Next, each element of this framework is examined, beginning with organizational buyer behavior. Then, two basic areas of sales strategy are covered: relationship strategy and sales channel strategy.

The Sales Strategy Framework

Since personal selling-driven promotion strategies are typical in industrial marketing, our discussion of sales strategy focuses on organizational (also called industrial or business) customers. Specific customers will be referred to as *accounts*. Thus, a sales strategy must be based on the important and unique aspects of organizational buyer behavior. A framework that integrates organizational buyer behavior and sales strategy is presented in Figure 6.1.

Organizational Buyer Behavior

Organizational buyer behavior refers to the purchasing behavior of organizations. Although there are unique aspects in the buying behavior of any organization, specific types of organizations tend to share similarities in their purchasing procedures (see Exhibit 6.1). Most of our attention is focused on business or industrial organizations classified as **users** or **original equipment manufacturers (OEMs).** However, we provide examples of **resellers, government organizations,** and **institutions** throughout the book.

One of the key distinguishing characteristics of organizational buyer behavior is that the organizational purchasing process is often long and complex. Consider the following example:[1]

Pilot Air Freight was awarded a three-year contract for air freight services by GTE. It took Pilot Air Freight more than three years and over 100 sales calls to GTE plants and offices across the country to obtain the contract. The final decision was made by a traffic council consisting of 25 decision makers from different GTE installations. After all of the preliminary work was completed, Pilot was given four minutes to

FIGURE 6.1 ▪ *The Sales Strategy Framework*

Salesperson interaction with different accounts is directed by a sales strategy. The sales strategy, which defines how the account is to be managed and how it is to be covered, must be based on an understanding of the buying situation, buying center, buying process, and buying needs of the account.

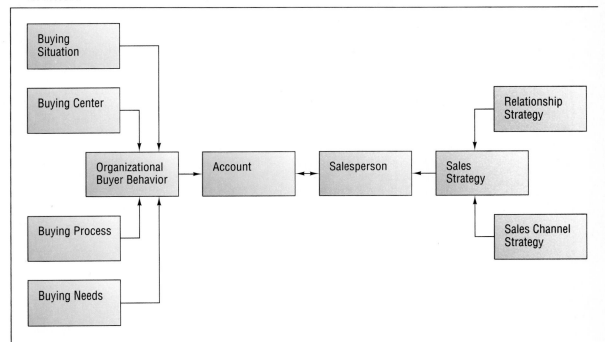

make a final presentation to the traffic council in Kansas City. The company's president, vice-president of sales and marketing, and account manager participated in the presentation and answered questions. The contract was awarded a few hours after the presentation.

Although this example represents a somewhat extreme situation, it illustrates how long and complex an organizational purchasing process might be.

As indicated in Figure 6.1, the development of sales strategy requires an understanding of organizational buyer behavior. The unique aspects of organizational buyer behavior revolve around the buying situation, buying center, buying process, and buying needs.

Buying Situation

One of the key determinants of organizational buyer behavior is the buying situation faced by an account. Three major types are possible, each representing its own problems for the buying firm and each having different strategic implications for the selling firm.

A **new task buying situation,** in which the organization is purchasing a product for the first time, poses the most problems for the buyer. Since the account has little knowledge or experience as a basis for making the purchase decision, it

EXHIBIT 6.1 ▪ *Types of Organizations*

Major Category	Types	Example
Business or industrial organizations	Users—purchase products and services to produce other products and services	IBM purchasing facsimile machines from Sharp for their corporate offices
	Original Equipment Manufacturers (OEM)—purchase products to incorporate into products	IBM purchasing microcomputer chips from Intel to incorporate into their personal computers
	Resellers — purchase products to sell	Businessland purchasing IBM personal computers to sell to organizations
Government organizations	Federal, state, and local government agencies	The Virginia State Lottery purchasing IBM personal computers for managers
Institutions	Public and private institutions	The United Way purchasing IBM personal computers for their offices

Source: Adapted from Michael D. Hutt and Thomas W. Speh, *Business Marketing Management* (Hinsdale, Ill.: The Dryden Press, 1989), 14–18.

will typically use a lengthy process to collect and evaluate purchase information. The decision making process in this type of situation is often called **extensive problem solving** and is illustrated in the example of GTE's purchase of air freight services from Pilot Air Freight.

A **modified rebuy buying situation** exists when the account has previously purchased and used the product. Although the account has information and experience with the product, it will usually want to collect additional information and may make a change when purchasing a replacement product. The decision making process in this type of situation is often referred to as **limited problem solving.** When the three-year contract between GTE and Pilot is over, GTE will probably use a limited problem solving process in awarding a new contract to Pilot or another firm.

The least complex buying situation is the **straight rebuy buying situation,** wherein the account has considerable experience in using the product and is satisfied with the current purchase arrangements. In this case the buyer is merely reordering from the current supplier and engaging in **routinized response behavior.**

The buying situation faced by an account affects all aspects of organizational buyer behavior and has important implications for sales strategy development. In general, as organizations move from new task buying situations to modified rebuy and straight rebuy situations, fewer members of the organization are involved in the buying process. The buying process itself also becomes less involved. Selling organizations must adjust sales strategy depending upon the account's buying situation. For example, the sales strategy used by Pilot Air Freight in a modified rebuy situation with GTE is likely to be different than the sales strategy used in the original new task situation. Although unlikely, it is possible that GTE will be sufficiently satisfied with Pilot to award them a new contract in a straight rebuy situation. In either case, Pilot will be in a better position than competitors, since they are the current supplier.

Buying Center

One of the most important characteristics of organizational buyer behavior is the involvement of the many individuals from the firm that participate in the purchasing process. The term **buying center** has been used to designate these individuals. The buying center is not a formal designation on the organization chart, but rather an informal network of purchasing participants. (However, members of the purchasing department are typically included in most buying centers and are normally represented in the formal organizational structure.) The difficult task facing the selling firm is to identify all the buying center members and to determine the specific role of each.

The possible roles that buying center members might play in a particular purchasing decision are

- *Initiators*, who start the organizational purchasing process
- *Users*, who use the product to be purchased
- *Gatekeepers*, who control the flow of information between buying center members
- *Influencers*, who provide input for the purchasing decision
- *Deciders*, who make the final purchase decision
- *Purchasers*, who implement the purchasing decision

Each buying center role may be performed by more than one individual, and each individual may perform more than one buying center role.

Take, for example, the roles for the telecommunications purchase illustrated in Exhibit 6.2. In this example, the corporate telecommunications department and vice-president of data processing both perform influencer roles, while the corporate purchasing and telecommunications departments act as gatekeepers. The telecommunications department is active in this purchasing decision as influencers, gatekeepers, and users. Additionally, consider the large number of GTE personnel at plants and offices around the country who were involved in the air freight service purchase. The final decision was made by 25 decision makers.

The strategic implications of the buying center concept are that sales strategy must be based on a comprehensive understanding of the buying center for a particular purchasing situation. This includes an identification of all members of the buying center and of the specific purchasing role performed by each member. It is important to define the buying center in terms of departments and individuals within departments; therefore, the buying center description in Exhibit 6.2 provides only a general framework—more information is needed to identify the specific individuals within each department who are involved in the buying center.

EXHIBIT 6.2 ▪ *Buying Center Role for Telecommunications Purchase*

Initiator	Division general manager proposes to replace the company's telecommunications system.
Decider	Vice-president of administration selects, with influence from others, the vendor the company will deal with and the system it will buy.
Influencers	Corporate telecommunications department and the vice-president of data processing have important say about which system and vendor the company will deal with.
Purchaser	Corporate purchasing department completes the purchase according to predetermined specifications by negotiating or receiving bids from suppliers.
Gatekeeper	Corporate purchasing and corporate telecommunications departments analyze the company's needs and recommend likely matches with potential vendors.
Users	All division employees who use the telecommunications equipment.

Source: *Harvard Business Review,* "Major Sales: Who Really Does the Buying?" by Thomas V. Bonoma (May–June 1982).

Buying Process

Organizational buyer behavior can be viewed as a **buying process** consisting of several phases. Although this process has been presented in different ways, the following phases represent a general consensus:[2]

Phase 1. Recognition of problem or need
Phase 2. Determination of the characteristics of the item and the quantity needed
Phase 3. Description of the characteristics of the item and quantity needed
Phase 4. Search for and qualification of potential sources
Phase 5. Acquisition and analysis of proposals
Phase 6. Evaluation of proposals and selection of suppliers
Phase 7. Selection of an order routine
Phase 8. Performance feedback and evaluation

These buying phases may be formalized for some organizations and/or for certain purchases. In other situations, this process may only be a rough approximation of what actually occurs. For example, government organizations and institutions tend to have more formal purchasing processes than most business or industrial organizations. Even though the GTE purchase of air freight services from Pilot was long and complex, it was probably not a completely formal, step-by-step process. Nevertheless, viewing organizational buying as a multiple-phase process is helpful in developing sales strategy. A major objective of any sales strategy is to facilitate an account's movement through this process in a manner that will lead to a purchase of the seller's product.

Using the organizational buying process as a basis for sales strategy development requires an understanding of who and what is involved at each phase for a particular account. Although detailed analyses of specific accounts is desirable, there are often general patterns used by similar types of firms. For

EXHIBIT 6.3 ▪ *Personal and Organizational Needs*

Personal Goals	*Organizational Goals*
Want a feeling of power	Control cost in product use situation
Seek personal pleasure	Few breakdowns of product
Desire job security	Dependable delivery for repeat purchases
Want to be well liked	Adequate supply of product
Want respect	Cost within budget limit

Source: David W. Cravens, Gerald E. Hills, and Robert B. Woodruff, *Marketing Management* (Homewood, Ill.: Irwin, 1987), 161.

example, a study in the metalworking industry found that different departments had more influence at different phases. The findings from this study suggested that the typical buying center for firms in the metalworking industry consists of individuals from engineering, purchasing, production, and corporate management. These buying center members do not participate equally throughout the entire decision process. Engineering and production personnel have most influence in the earlier stages, while corporate management and purchasing are most influential at the later stages.[3] From a sales strategy perspective, this suggests the need to spend effort on different individuals at different phases of the organizational purchasing process.

Buying Needs

Organizational buying is typically viewed as goal-directed behavior intended to satisfy specific **buying needs.** Although the organizational purchasing process is made to satisfy organizational needs, the buying center consists of individuals who are also trying to satisfy individual needs throughout the decision process. Exhibit 6.3 presents examples of individual and organizational needs that might be important in a purchase situation. Individual needs tend to be career related, while organizational needs reflect factors related to the use of the product.

Even though organizational purchasing is often thought to be almost entirely objective, subjective personal needs are often extremely important in the final purchase decision. For example, an organization may want to purchase a computer to satisfy data-processing needs. Although a number of suppliers might be able to provide similar products, some suppliers at lower cost than others, buying center members might select the most well known brand to reduce purchase risk and protect job security.

The personal and organizational needs vary in importance across members of the buying center. A study of the different organizational needs for different buying center members in the heating and air conditioning industry indicated that production engineers and plant managers were most interested in operating cost, corporate engineers with the initial product cost, and top management with state-of-the-art technology.[4] As another example, think about the likely differences in organizational and personal needs across the many members of the GTE buying center, especially the 25 decision makers.

We discussed how the influence of buying center members varies at different buying phases in the last section. Couple this with the different needs of different buying center members, and the complexity of organization buying behavior is evident. The complexity of organizational buyer behavior becomes even more complicated when ethical considerations are introduced, as evident in "An Ethical Perspective: Gift Giving." Nevertheless, sales managers must understand this behavior in order to develop sales strategies that will satisfy the personal and organizational needs of buying center members.

Sales Strategy

Sales managers and salespeople are typically responsible for strategic decisions at the account level. Although the firm's marketing strategy provides basic guidelines —an overall game plan—the battles are won on an account-by-account basis. Without the design and execution of effective sales strategies directed at specific accounts, the marketing strategy cannot be successfully implemented.

Take, for example, the highly competitive minicomputer industry, where Digital Equipment Corp. has taken market share from IBM in the financial services

---

AN ETHICAL PERSPECTIVE

Gift Giving The practice of salespeople giving gifts to buyers is widespread but has ethical implications for both the salesperson and the buyer. The ethical difficulty from the salesperson's perspective is the fine line between giving a gift and attempting to unduly influence or bribe a buyer. The buyer accepting a gift must be concerned about being perceived as favoring salespeople that provide gifts and not making purchasing decisions in the best interests of the firm. Although some firms have policies concerning the giving and receiving of gifts, gift giving still presents complex ethical dilemmas for salespeople and buyers.

A study of 186 purchasing professionals in different industries investigated the ethics of giving gifts of different value to customers of varied status. The important results of the study were as follows:

1. The giving of gifts of any value was viewed as more ethically appropriate when the gifts were given to current customers rather than to prospects. A gift to a current customer was viewed as a reward for past business and not an attempt to obtain future business.

2. Whether to a current customer or a prospect, highly valued gifts were viewed as less ethical than low-valued gifts. The higher the value of a gift, the more indebted the buyer felt to the salesperson.

3. The situation perceived as most ethical was when a low-value gift was given to a current customer.

The results of this study suggest the complex ethical considerations involved in gift giving and the need for sales managers and salespeople to be prepared to deal with these ethical situations.

Source: I. Frederick Trawick, John E. Swan, and David Rink, "Industrial Buyer Evaluation of the Ethics of Salesperson Gift Giving: Value of the Gift and Customer vs. Prospect Status," *Journal of Personal Selling and Sales Management*, Spring 1989, 31–38.

EXHIBIT 6.4 ▪ *Relationship Selling versus Traditional Selling*

Relationship Selling	*Traditional Selling*
Less common, but more valuable	The most familiar
Selling is a service	Selling is a contest
Selling is helping	Selling is persuading
Customers love to buy	Customers must be sold
Buyers want a trusted salesperson	Buyers are liars
The follow-through is number one	The close is number one
Great sellers truly care	Great sellers are manipulators
"We"-oriented	"Me"-oriented
It works—again and again!	It works—once!

Source: Adapted from Jim Cathcart, "Traditional vs. Relationship Selling," *The Selling Advantage*, February 1990, 1–2.

and data-processing markets. IBM has responded by changing its marketing strategy through the introduction of new products and the addition of services. The success of these strategic changes, however, depends upon IBM's ability to develop, maintain, and expand relationships with individual accounts. Evidence of this ability is suggested by the $200 million contract recently negotiated with Ford Motor Co.[5]

Our framework suggests two basic sales strategies: relationship strategy and sales channel strategy. We will consider each of these as a separate, but related, strategic decision area. Sales strategies are ultimately developed for each individual account; however, the strategic decisions are often made by classifying individual accounts into similar categories.

Relationship Strategy

As discussed in several previous chapters, the trend toward relationship selling by many firms is one of the most exciting developments of the 1990s. A direct comparison of relationship selling to traditional selling is presented in Exhibit 6.4. The implementation of a relationship selling perspective requires a totally different approach from the traditional selling perspective.[6]

The effectiveness of relationship selling has been documented by research conducted by several organizations:

- A study by Learning International found that successful salespeople "maintain long term relationships with customers by solving problems and providing quality service."[7]
- Ongoing research by the Forum Corporation suggests that successful salespeople "develop partnership relationships with their customers."[8]
- Research at the Pecos River Learning Center concludes that customers are "looking for a different, higher level, long term relationship with the salespeople and companies serving them."[9]

- Research by the Acclivus Corporation indicates that successful selling "depends upon a salesperson's ability to develop long term relationships or partnerships with customers and to bring selling skills to a higher level."[10]

The growing trend toward relationship selling is evident from the large number of manufacturers, wholesalers, and even retailers that are emphasizing the importance of customer relationships. Consider the following examples:

- Du Pont, the large chemical manufacturer, focuses a large portion of sales training efforts on teaching its technical sales representatives the importance of and procedures for developing customer relationships.[11]
- Bergen Brunswig, the pharmaceutical wholesaler, has pioneered the concept of *single supplier* by using computers and various services provided by salespeople to develop long-term relationships with independent, chain, and hospital pharmacies.[12]
- Nordstrom, the soft goods retailer, has been extremely successful by developing customer relationships through exceptional service by retail salespeople. As one salesperson explained, "Nordstrom tells me to do whatever I need to do to make you [the customer] happy. Period."[13]
- Charles F. Terasi has been a direct salesperson for the Fuller Brush Co. for 49 years. He has developed relationships with customers that have lasted over 15 years by providing personalized service and recommending the best products for each customer's specific needs.[14]

Because of the increasing importance of customer relationships, sales organizations need to develop **relationship strategies** as part of their sales strategy. We will examine three types of relationships between sellers and buyers and the types of activities required for successful relationships of each type (see Exhibit 6.5).[15]

Counselor Relationships

Counselor relationships are those where the seller firm provides expert advice and personalized attention to the buyer. The buyer typically has defined objectives to reach or problems to solve but does not know how to reach the objectives or solve the problems. The seller helps the buyer develop solutions to the problems and objectives. Counselor relationships are typically desired in the financial services, insurance, real estate, and many other industries. For example, salespeople from Northwestern Mutual Life Insurance Co. provide advice to help organizational customers determine the types and amounts of insurance needed.

Sellers attempting to develop counselor relationships must be able to apply their products or services to the specific needs of individual customers. This requires that their salespeople possess expert knowledge of the firm's products and services and that they have an in-depth understanding of each customer's situation. Salespeople must provide personalized attention, be continuously available to customers, and constantly monitor the customer and business environment to be able to anticipate and respond to changing needs. Finally, the counselor relationship must be based on trust and integrity between the seller and buyer.

EXHIBIT 6.5   ▪   *Relationship Types and Salesperson Activities*

Type of Relationship	Customer Situation	Salesperson Activities
Counselor	Knows general objective or desired condition but doesn't know how to implement a solution.	In-depth understanding of the customer's desired goals and objectives.
	Places high value on personalized attention and easy access to the salesperson.	Extensive expertise in various solutions to customer's problems and objectives.
		Keeps solutions matched to changing needs and goals of customers in a dynamic environment.
Supplier	Knows the objective he/she wants to attain.	Secures specific brands of goods and services the customer has indicated are needed.
	Knows what type of product/service will be needed to achieve objective.	Solves any logistical problems that occur such as shipping, billing, or replacing damaged goods.
	Needs assistance in procuring specific product or service.	Keeps buyer informed of new offerings and their availability.
Systems designer	Unaware of ways to perform an activity or function in a more efficient way.	Conceptualizes a better system for performing a function the customer is now performing.
	Expects total solution to a problem once it has been established that a better approach exists.	Implements the new system in the customer's environment.
		Upgrades the system to optimize its efficiency, when necessary.

Source: Adapted from John I. Coppett and William A. Staples, *Professional Selling: A Relationship Management Process* (Cincinnati, Ohio: South-Western Publishing Co., 1990), 54.

Supplier Relationships

Supplier relationships are those where the seller provides an ongoing supply of products and services to a buyer. The buyer in this situation typically knows the products and services needed to reach objectives or solve problems but is concerned with obtaining a supply of the identified products and services; the seller provides the buyer with these. Supplier relationships are typically desired by companies that sell to original equipment manufacturers and resellers, as well as in other situations. For example, Procter & Gamble salespeople desire to develop supplier relationships with the wholesalers and retailers that resell their products to final consumers.

   Sellers attempting to develop supplier relationships must provide a dependable supply of the desired products and services. Salespeople are more concerned with providing excellent service after the sale, rather than on closing individual sales. The salespeople must take care of any problems related to getting the products and services to the customer, ensuring customer satisfaction with the products and services, helping the buyer use or resell the products and services, and making the buyer aware of new products and services that might satisfy their needs better.

Systems Designer Relationships

Systems designer relationships are those where the seller provides complete solutions to help a buyer reach objectives or solve problems. These complete solutions may entail the integration of products and services from different vendors. The buyer in this situation has little knowledge concerning the integration of products and services to reach objectives or satisfy needs. Systems designer relationships are complex and often desired in the information and telecommunications industries as well as many others. For example, AT&T salespeople would desire to develop systems designer relationships with customers establishing telemarketing operations. The AT&T salespeople would design the complete telemarketing operation for a buyer by integrating the necessary AT&T and other products and services.

Salespeople desiring to develop systems designer relationships must be skilled in devising complete solutions to help buyers reach objectives or solve problems. They must be knowledgeable of their company's and other companies' products and services and of the way they can be applied to provide complete solutions. The salespeople must also be imaginative in devising specific solutions for each buyer, must provide assistance in implementing the solution, and must continuously look for ways to improve the system.

Relationship Strategy Summary

Our discussion has focused on three basic types of relationships and the salesperson activities required by each type. The type of desired relationship between seller and buyer is an important element in sales strategy. Different types of relationships require different salesperson activities and have different implications for sales managers in the areas of recruiting/selecting salespeople, sales training, motivation and compensation, supervision and leadership, and performance evaluation.

Sales Channel Strategy

Sales channel strategy—ensuring that accounts receive selling effort coverage in an effective and efficient manner—is a necessary component of sales strategy. Various methods are available to provide selling coverage to accounts, including a company salesforce, industrial distributors, independent representatives, team selling, telemarketing, and trade shows. Many firms employ multiple distribution channels and multiple sales channels for their products. For example, IBM markets its personal computers directly to larger customers using its own salesforce and indirectly to smaller customers through distributors that might use inside and/or outside salesforces as well as telemarketing.

However, as the Alpha Wire Corp. example in the opening vignette suggests, sometimes a single sales channel strategy can facilitate the development of desired relationships with organizational customers. Since most of this book is concerned with management of a company field salesforce, our discussion of sales channel strategy will focus on alternatives to the typical company field salesforce.

Industrial Distributors. One alternative sales channel is to employ **industrial distributors**—channel middlemen that take title to the goods that they market to end users. These distributors typically employ their own field salesforce and may carry (1) the products of only one manufacturer, (2) related but noncompeting products from different manufacturers, or (3) competing products from different manufacturers. Firms that use industrial distributors normally have a relatively small company salesforce to serve and support the efforts of the distributor.

The use of distributors is prevalent and increasing in the industrial marketplace. One study found that only 24 percent of industrial marketers used direct distribution exclusively, while 76 percent used some type of intermediary to reach end users, with industrial distributors being the most prominent.[16] Another study found that 25 percent of responding firms expect to be more dependent upon industrial distributors during the next five years.[17]

Industrial distributors can provide a cost-effective means for covering accounts in certain situations. A study of 297 firms from 58 different industries found that industrial distributors tended to be used when a firm's products were standard and nontechnical, when the product's gross margin was large, and when the firm served large markets containing geographically dispersed customers that order frequently and require short order lead times.[18]

The use of industrial distributors adds another member to the distribution channel. Although these distributors should not be considered as final customers, they should be treated like customers. Developing positive, long-term relationships with distributors is necessary for success. Indeed, the development of a partnership with distributors can be the key to success. As one marketing executive noted,

> If manufacturers develop loyal partnerships with distributors in this country, they probably can hold off or neutralize foreign competition. I'm not sure a lot of manufacturers realize that, but it's a very viable defense.[19]

Black and Decker's U.S. Power Tool Group is one firm that apparently recognizes the importance of distributor relationships as a means to combat foreign competition. Despite intense competition from overseas manufacturers, Black and Decker's sales have grown from $1.1 billion to $1.8 billion during the past four years. Much of this success can be attributed to improved relationships with distributors. Black and Decker has started distributor advisory councils, a formal sales training program for distributors, and is making joint sales calls with distributors' salespeople. The net effect of these efforts is that more than 4,000 distributor salespeople, rather than just the company's 275 salespeople, are actively pushing Black and Decker's products.[20]

Many firms are using advanced technology to strengthen relationships with distributors. For example, Apple Computer has developed AppleLink as a two-way electronic message system between distributors and the corporate office. The system is handling approximately 5,000 inquiries each month.[21] Ford Motor Company uses the Truck Order and Pricing System (TOPS) as an electronic communications program for industrial vehicle distributors to process orders, check the compatibility of orders, and produce price quotes. Training of

EXHIBIT 6.6   ■   *Company Salesforce and Industrial Distributors*

Salesperson and Tasks	*Key Skills*
Teacher of selling skills; ROI selling; product applications knowledge, market knowledge; display techniques (walk-in business).	Excellent presenter; listener; counselor; coach
Reviewer of sales by product mix; sales vs. forecasted quota; competitive activity in distributor's area; inventory stocking vs. targets; distributor's participation in promotions.	Analyzer; prober; trader of information; forecaster
Working partner on joint "buddy calls" to end-user accounts; sales blitzes at targeted industries; trade show activity at shared booths; lead program follow-up; distributor showroom programs on demo day.	Hands-on demonstrator; leader by showing sales professionalism
Ambassador about terms of sale, credit, warranties, and leasing; promotions, contests, new product launches; co-op plans on advertising; ordering policies and assortments; pricing schedules and margins.	Motivator; selling-in of programs
Ombudsman for distributor complaints on product performance; distributor credit and accounts receivable problems; distributor dissatisfaction about deliveries and backorders; distributor problems on order mixups, policies on assortments, minimums, and nonstandard products.	Negotiator; conciliator; empathetic confidante to distributor

Source: Reprinted by permission of the publisher from Allan J. Magrath and Kenneth G. Hardy, "Factory Salesmen's Roles with Industrial Distributors," *Industrial Marketing Management*, 16, 1987, 165. Copyright 1987 by Elsevier Science Publishing Co., Inc.

distributor salespeople is also being performed effectively using advanced technology with Eastman Kodak sending videotapes to disk-drive distributors and Caterpillar Tractor employing teleconferences to communicate with distributor salespeople.[22]

The use of industrial distributors presents unique challenges for sales managers and company salespeople. As indicated in Exhibit 6.6, company salespeople must play different roles in their interactions with distributors—roles requiring a variety of specific skills. Company sales managers are charged with the responsibility of hiring and developing a company salesforce that can work effectively with industrial distributors.

One area of potential conflict exists when firms employ both industrial distributors and a direct company salesforce. Care must be taken to develop specific policies and procedures that are fair and equitable to both the industrial

EXHIBIT 6.7 ▪ *Profile of Independent Representatives*

A study of the 9,000 member Manufacturers' Agent National Association (MANA) produced the following profile of an independent representative agency:	
Average number of offices	1.5
Average number of states covered	5.2
Average number of manufacturers represented	10.1
Average number of salespeople employed	3.5
Average gross sales	$4,402,986

Source: Jon M. Hawes, Kenneth E. Mast, and John E. Swan, "Trust Earning Perceptions of Sellers and Buyers," *Journal of Personal Selling and Sales Management*, Spring 1989, 3.

distributors and direct salespeople. Enormous problems can arise otherwise. For example, distributors for Wang Laboratories protested vigorously and even filed lawsuits when commissions to direct salespeople were lowered for sales made jointly with distributors. This put the direct salespeople in competition with the distributors and severely damaged distributor relations.[23] In another situation, Kroy angered distributors of electronic lettering machines by adding a direct salesforce to call on certain customers. A smaller competitor, Varitronics, was able to take advantage of this situation by courting the angry distributors using strong support programs. Varitronics achieved a 15 to 20 percent market share in two years through this industrial distributor network.[24] As suggested by these examples, developing and maintaining positive relationships with industrial distributors is an important and challenging sales management task.

Independent Representatives. Firms employing personal selling can choose to cover accounts with **independent representatives** (also called *manufacturers' representatives* or just *reps*). Reps are independent sales organizations that sell complementary, but noncompeting, products from different manufacturers. In contrast to industrial distributors, independent representatives do not normally carry inventory or take title to the products they sell. Manufacturers typically develop contractual agreements with several rep organizations. Each rep organization consists of one or more salespeople (see Exhibit 6.7) and is assigned a geographic territory. It is compensated on a commission basis for products sold.

Approximately 50,000 U.S. manufacturers use some of the approximately 30,000 rep agencies in the United States.[25] Why would so many manufacturers use reps instead of company salesforces?[26] As indicated in Exhibit 6.8, reps have certain advantages over company salesforces, especially for small firms or for smaller markets served by larger firms. Since reps are paid on a commission basis, selling costs are almost totally variable, whereas a large percentage of the selling costs of a company salesforce are fixed. Thus, at lower sales levels a rep organization is more cost efficient to use than a company salesforce. However, at some level of sales the company salesforce will become more cost efficient, since reps typically receive higher commission rates than company salespeople (see Figure 6.2).[27]

EXHIBIT 6.8   ▪   *Advantages of Independent Representatives*

Independent sales representatives offer several advantages over company salesforces:

▪ Reps provide a professional selling capability that is difficult to match with company salespeople.

▪ Reps offer in-depth knowledge of general markets and individual customers.

▪ Reps offer established relationships with individual accounts.

▪ The use of reps provides improved cash flow since payments to reps are typically not made until customers have paid for their purchases.

▪ The use of reps provides predictable sales expenses since most of the selling costs are variable and directly related to sales volume.

▪ The use of reps can provide greater territory coverage since companies can employ more reps than company salespeople for the same cost.

▪ Companies can usually penetrate new markets faster using reps because of the reps' established customer relationships.

Source: Adapted from Harold J. Novick, "The Case for Reps vs. Direct Selling: Can Reps Do It Better?" *Industrial Marketing*, March 1982, 90–98; and "The Use of Sales Reps," *Small Business Report*, December 1986, 72–78.

FIGURE 6.2   ▪   *Independent Representatives versus Company Salesforce Costs*

Independent representatives are typically more cost efficient at lower sales levels, since most of the costs associated with reps are variable. However, at higher sales levels (beyond point A) a company salesforce becomes more cost efficient.

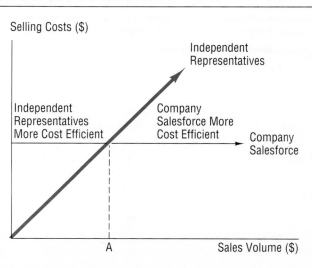

Although reps may cost less in many situations, management also has less control over their activities. The basic trade-off is cost versus control. There are two aspects to control. First, since reps are paid a commission on sales, it is difficult to get them to engage in activities not directly related to sales generation. Thus, if servicing of accounts is important, reps may not perform these activities as well as a company salesforce. Second, the typical rep represents an average of ten different manufacturers or principals. Each manufacturer's products will therefore receive 10 percent of the rep's time if it is divided equally. Usually, however, some products receive more attention than others. The biggest complaints that manufacturers seem to have with reps is that they don't spend enough time with their products and thus don't generate sufficient sales. The use of reps limits the amount of control that management has over the time spent selling their products.

The task facing sales management here is similar to the one involving industrial distributors: how to develop successful, long-term relationships. The general approach is to provide reps with support and assistance. Consider Joy Manufacturing's Air Moving Products Division, which has been using reps since 1965 to sell products to the heating, ventilating, and air conditioning market. Stan Harris, manager of marketing administration, describes the company's orientation toward reps as follows:

> We believe that we're faced with a two-edged competitive situation in the field. On the one hand, we compete with other fan manufacturers, but we also compete with the other principals for the rep's time. If we don't make it easy for the rep to make money on our products, Joy becomes a sideline to him and we lose the rep's time and effort.

Joy successfully implements this philosophy by providing training and technical assistance in the field to the reps.[28]

NEC America Inc.'s Broadcast Equipment Division uses independent representatives to sell video broadcast and transmitter products in the United States. Richard Dienhart, national sales manager for NEC, communicates constantly with the independent representatives by telephone, face-to-face communication, and a sales newsletter. He also goes on joint sales calls with reps to build trust and observe the rep's relationship with customers. According to Mr. Dienhart, "Anything that comes under the heading of supporting the sales effort is appropriate and due the manufacturers' rep."[29]

Two of the key challenges facing sales management are to get good rep agencies to carry their product lines and to motivate these independent representatives to spend sufficient time selling the firm's products. Sales managers need to know the factors that rep agencies consider when determining whether to carry a manufacturer's product line. A study by Lavin Associates found that these factors in descending order of importance were: the marketability of the manufacturer's products; the reputation of the products; fair commissions and timely payment; compatibility with present products; and competitive pricing, delivery, and service.[30]

Once contracts with independent representatives have been established, sales management must motivate the reps to spend sufficient time selling their products. One study found that reps spent more time with a principal's products when

A GLOBAL PERSPECTIVE

Master Representatives Firms trying to enter new international markets have a difficult time identifying, contracting, and managing independent representatives in different countries. Master representatives function as sales and marketing managers for their principals in these countries by providing services such as market identification, establishing and managing relationships with independent representatives in each country, and providing international risk management. They are compensated by sales commissions, fees, markups on merchandise, or combinations of these forms of payment.

The major advantage of master representatives to manufacturers is suggested by Bruno Rocca, president of Tecmos Group:

> Instead of dealing with 20 worldwide reps, the manufacturer deals directly with us. We know the markets, the cultural differences of the customers, and the intricacies of foreign business practice. . . . Master reps maximize the communication between customer and manufacturer. . . . We represent the manufacturer to the customer.

Source: Lois C. DuBois and Roger H. Grace, "Master Reps: Value-Added Distribution," *Business Marketing*, December 1987, 62–63.

(1) they perceived a higher marginal sales return for effort spent, (2) there was a strong partnership between the rep and principal (frequent communication, mutual participation, and frequent feedback), (3) there was synergy between the different principals' products, and (4) the principal was actively involved in the management of the rep agency.[31] Interestingly, higher commission rates were found to have a diminishing effect on reps' time. These results highlight the importance of selecting the appropriate rep agencies and then establishing and nurturing mutually beneficial relationships between reps and principals. An interesting type of independent representative for firms entering global markets is presented in "A Global Perspective: Master Representatives."

Team Selling. Our earlier discussion of organizational buyer behavior presented the concepts of buying centers and buying situations. If we move to the selling side of the exchange relationship, we find analogous concepts. Firms often employ multiple-person sales teams to deal with the multiple-person buying centers of their accounts. Figure 6.3 illustrates the basic relationships between sales teams and buying centers. A company salesperson typically coordinates the activities of the sales team, while the purchasing agent typically coordinates the activities of the buying center. Both the sales team and buying center can consist of multiple individuals from different functional areas. Each of these individuals can play one or more roles in the exchange process. Just as the type of *buying situation* is a major determinant of the size and activities of the buying center, the type of *selling situation* is a major determinant of the size and activities of the sales team. Three different situations are possible, corresponding to the three different buying situations.

From the selling firm's perspective, the **new task selling situation,** in which the seller is either introducing new products or calling on new accounts, is the most difficult and uncertain one. Due to the complexity of this situation, the sales team will typically be large, with participation from many different functional areas. The **modified resell selling situation** has less uncertainty and typically involves

FIGURE 6.3 ▪ *Team Selling and Buying Centers*

The salesperson coordinates the activities of a sales team to interact with the members of an account's buying center. The size, composition, and activities of the sales team depend upon whether the seller is facing a new task selling situation, modified resell selling situation, or routine resell selling situation.

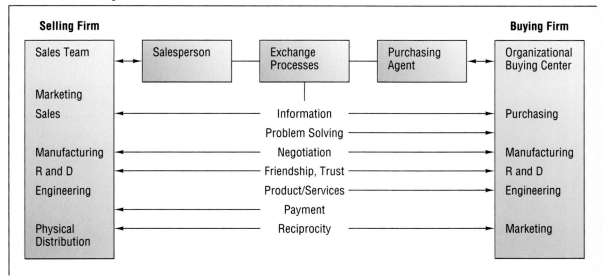

Source: Adapted from Michael D. Hutt, Wesley J. Johnston, and John R. Rouchelto, "Selling Centers and Buying Centers: Formulating Strategic Exchange Patterns," *Journal of Personal Selling and Sales Management*, May 1985, 34. Used with permission.

a smaller, less involved sales team. The **routine resell selling situation** may consist of interaction only between the salesperson and the purchasing agent.

The use of team selling is increasing in many firms. Developing successful relationships with accounts often requires the participation of many individuals from the selling firm. The approach employed by Metaphor Computer Systems is an example. Metaphor markets a specially designed workstation and customized software to help marketing people interpret statistical information. The company employs team selling with a sales team consisting of a salesperson, an applications consultant, and a systems engineer. Although this is an expensive approach, chairman David Liddle says it is necessary "because we take responsibility for the whole problem of data use and want to control the situation."[32]

Two specific types of **team selling** deserve mention. **Multilevel selling** is a variation of team selling in which the emphasis is to match functional areas between the buying and selling firm. Thus, individuals from a specific functional area or management level in the selling firm deal with their counterparts in the buying firm. For example, Reynolds Metals Company assembled a team of sales and marketing people, graphic designers, and engineers who educated members of a similar team from Campbell Soup Co. on the virtues of aluminum cans. Reynolds was selected to supply Campbell Soup with aluminum cans for their packaged foods.[33]

Major account selling represents the development of specific programs to serve a firm's largest and most important accounts. Although different approaches to major account selling will be presented in Chapter 7, one popular approach is to employ major account sales teams. For example, Gus Maikish is an IBM account executive who is assigned a major New York City bank as a single account. Mr. Maikish heads a 21-member sales team consisting of 2 sales managers, 4 salespeople, 2 trainees, and 13 technical people. The sales team works throughout the entire bank to solve the bank's problems with IBM equipment.[34]

Telemarketing. An increasingly important sales channel is **telemarketing,** which consists of using the telephone as a means for customer contact, to perform some or all of the activities required to develop and maintain account relationships. This includes both outbound telemarketing (the seller calls the account) and inbound telemarketing (the account calls the seller). The importance of telemarketing in business-to-business selling is illustrated by the following statistics:[35]

- Over 65 million business telemarketing sales calls are made per day by 224,000 firms.
- The average business-to-business sale by telemarketing is about $1,100.
- Annual business-to-business telemarketing sales are approximately $115 billion.

Firms typically use telemarketing to replace field selling for specific accounts or integrate telemarketing with field selling to the same accounts (see Figure 6.4). The major reason for replacing field selling with telemarketing at specific accounts is the low cost of telemarketing selling. Telemarketing salespeople are able to serve a large number of smaller accounts. This lowers the selling costs to the smaller accounts and frees the field salesforce to concentrate on the larger accounts. For example, Merrell Dow Pharmaceutical found that its cost of a field sales call was $225 but that a telemarketing sales call cost only $20. A telemarketing program was established where each telephone sales rep handles 500 of the smaller independent drug stores. This frees the field salesforce to call on 10,000 new accounts.[36]

Telemarketing is also being integrated with field selling operations.[37] One study of firms that were integrating telemarketing and field salesforces found that the major benefits of this integration were related to improved communication with and service of accounts. The lowering of selling costs was important but secondary. Surprisingly, 97.6 percent of the firms in this study indicated the use of shared accounts, where telemarketing and field salespeople served the same accounts and actively exchanged information concerning sales and service activity with each account. Telemarketing salespeople were found to be most involved in customer service, order taking, and handling complaints. However, most activities were performed by both the telemarketing and field salesforces, with customer preference often being the deciding factor as to which salesforce performed which activities.[38]

Some of the variety of ways that telemarketing is being used are illustrated in the following examples:[39]

FIGURE 6.4 ▪ *Uses of Telemarketing*

Telemarketing is typically used to either replace field selling or be integrated with field selling by performing specific activities.

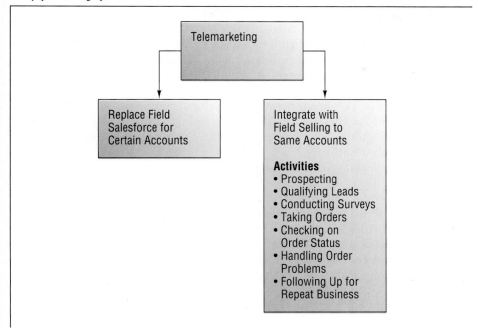

▪ Wing-Lynch Inc. markets photographic processing equipment and electronic temperature controls through industrial distributors. Distributor salespeople use the inbound telemarketing line to get product and technical information during sales calls or when equipment is being installed. Customers order replacement parts directly by phone.

▪ Glendo Corp. markets diamond grinding wheels and engraving equipment. Five years ago the firm had no telemarketers and 70 industrial distributors. Today, the firm has 4 telemarketers and 23 distributors concentrated in large metropolitan areas. Sales have increased 30 percent annually for the past five years due to the fact that the telemarketers typically convert 25 percent of leads into sales, compared to 12.5 percent for the industrial distributors.

▪ Westinghouse Electric Co.'s Voice Systems Division uses telemarketing to generate and qualify sales leads that are passed on to the field salesforce for on-site demonstrations. Approximately 95 to 99 percent of these qualified leads have been converted into sales.

▪ Dylakor sells data retrieval systems for IBM mainframes and compatibles to companies with large volume information processing needs. The firm's entire sales effort is through telemarketing. Dylakor employs 12 telemarketing salespeople that make 30 to 40 sales calls a day and employ a computerized database system to track prospects and clients.[40]

▪ General Electric has more than 45 different telemarketing centers manned by 2,000 employees who sell everything from $1.98 medical accessories to high-tech energy systems.[41]

The development of telemarketing salesforces to replace or support field selling operations can be a difficult task for sales managers. One of the keys to success appears to be consistent communication with the field salesforce throughout all stages of telemarketing development. Field salespeople must be assured that the telemarketing operations will help them improve their performance. Specific attention must also be directed toward developing appropriate compensation programs for both salesforces and devising training programs that provide the necessary knowledge and skills for the telemarketing and field salesforces to be able to work effectively together.

As the costs of selling continue to increase and technology develops, the use of telemarketing is likely to expand. The telephone will become a potent and cost-effective tool for communicating with accounts. Many firms will likely develop innovative uses of telemarketing; for example, one firm in a recent study reported using three telemarketing groups to make a single sale. The first group was located at corporate headquarters and used leads from trade shows to prospect for potential customers. Qualified prospects were turned over to a second telemarketing group located in the regional office closest to the prospect. These telemarketing salespeople prepared quotes, gathered technical specifications, and set an appointment for a salesperson presentation. If the sale was made, a third telemarketing group at corporate headquarters provided technical support for product installation and usage.[42]

Trade Shows. The final sales channel to be discussed here, **trade shows,** are typically industry-sponsored events where companies utilize a booth to display products and services to potential and existing customers. Because a particular trade show is only held once a year and only lasts for a few days, trade shows should be viewed as supplemental methods for account coverage, not to be used by themselves but integrated with other sales channels.

Statistics show that trade shows are popular. U.S. marketers spent more than $21 billion to participate in more than 9,000 trade shows in 1989.[43] One study of 9,000 executives found that 82 percent had attended a trade show during the previous 18 months and nearly 70 percent indicated that they had made a purchase decision as a result of visiting a trade show. Interestingly, almost 90 percent of the booth visitors had not been called on by a salesperson from the exhibiting company during the 12 months before the show.[44] The average total cost to reach a visitor at a trade show for the 1987–1989 period was $141.52.[45]

A recent study found that trade shows are used to achieve both selling and nonselling objectives. Relevant selling objectives are to test new products, to close sales, and to introduce new products. Nonselling objectives include servicing current customers, gathering competitive information, identifying new prospects, and enhancing corporate image. Successful trade shows tend to be those where firms exhibit a large number of products to a large number of attendees, where specific written objectives for the trade show are established and where attendees match the firm's target market.[46]

An interesting variation from the typical trade show is the corporate trade show used by one multidivisional company:[47]

We find often that 10–20 of our divisions may sell, or wish to sell, to a particular customer. In these instances, we may set up a standard trade show series of display booths at a hotel ballroom close to the customer's plant, with each of the 10–20 representing a different division of our company. During the show, approximately 100–600 representatives from the customer's plant—technical, sales, marketing, manufacturing, and management personnel—will visit the booths. It's an elegant method of getting behind the purchasing agent.

The use of trade shows places unique demands upon sales managers and salespeople, since they are typically taken out of the field to man company booths at a trade show. Interacting with attendees at a trade show is considerably different than calling on accounts in the field. Therefore, special training is normally required to equip sales managers and salespeople to achieve specific trade show objectives. Many firms also develop specific incentive programs for a trade show. For example, General Electric Silicon Systems Technology Department rewarded the salesperson that garnered the most qualified leads each day with a paperweight decorated with the department's logo. Although the paperweight only cost $10, an elaborate awards ceremony provided recognition that motivated salespeople to double the number of leads that were expected.[48]

Essential to effective use of trade shows is determining the specific results from each show. Firms such as Caterpillar Inc. and Combustion Engineering Inc. conduct multiple-phase studies to pinpoint the specific benefits from trade show participation.[49] The results from their studies and other available evidence suggest that trade shows can be a valuable supplement to other sales channels.

Sales Channel Strategy Summary

Developing a sales channel strategy is a difficult task for sales managers. Although some firms, such as Alpha Wire, can achieve a competitive advantage using a single sales channel, many firms are moving to multiple sales channel strategies as one way to serve customers and lower selling costs. Determining the appropriate sales channel mix requires a comparative evaluation of the firm's customer base and relationship strategy against the efficiency, effectiveness, and adaptability offered by the different sales channel alternatives.[50] Sales managers must continually assess their sales channel strategy and make necessary changes to adapt to the increasingly complex and dynamic business environment.

Summary

1. Discuss the important concepts behind organizational buyer behavior.
The key concepts behind organizational buyer behavior are buying situation, buying center, buying process, and buying needs. Buying situations can be characterized as new task, modified rebuy, or straight rebuy. The type of

buying situation affects all other aspects of organizational buyer behavior. The buying center consists of all of the individuals from a firm involved in a particular buying decision. These individuals may come from different functional areas and may play the role of initiators, users, gatekeepers, influencers, deciders, and/or buyers. Organizational purchasing should be viewed as a buying process with multiple phases. Different members of the buying center may be involved at different phases of the buying process. Organizational purchases are made to satisfy specific buying needs, which may be both organizational and personal. These concepts are highly interrelated and interact to produce complex organizational purchasing phenomena.

2.   **Explain the different types of relationship strategies.** The different types of relationship strategies are counselor, supplier, and systems designer. Counselor relationships involve the salesperson in providing advice to the customer about products and services. In supplier relationships, the salesperson provides a dependable supply of products and services to the customer. Systems designer relationships are the most complex, since the salesperson integrates different products and services to provide complete solutions for customers.

3.   **Describe the different sales channel strategies.** A sales channel strategy consists of decisions as to how to provide selling effort coverage to accounts. The sales channel strategy depends upon the firm's marketing strategy. If indirect distribution is used, then industrial distributors become the main focus of selling effort coverage. Firms might decide to employ independent representatives instead of having a company salesforce. The concept of team selling is analogous to the buying center concept. Depending upon whether the seller faces a new task selling situation, a modified resell situation, or a routine resell situation, different individuals will be included in the sales team. Multilevel selling and major account selling are different types of team selling strategies. Telemarketing is a sales channel that can be used to replace or support field selling operations. Finally, trade shows can be used to achieve specific objectives and supplement the other sales channels.

4.   **Discuss the basic interrelationships between relationship strategy and sales channel strategy.** Relationship strategy and sales channel strategy are separate but interrelated. Strategic decisions in one area often have an impact on strategies in other areas. The key is to develop an effective and integrated sales strategy.

Key Terms

- **User**
- **Original equipment manufacturer (OEM)**
- **Reseller**
- **Government organization**
- **Institution**

- **New task buying situation**
- **Extensive problem solving**
- **Modified rebuy buying situation**
- **Limited problem solving**
- **Straight rebuy buying situation**

▪ **Routinized response behavior**

▪ **Buying center**

▪ **Buying process**

▪ **Buying needs**

▪ **Relationship strategy**

▪ **Counselor relationships**

▪ **Supplier relationships**

▪ **Systems designer relationships**

▪ **Sales channel strategy**

▪ **Industrial distributors**

▪ **Independent representatives**

▪ **New task selling situation**

▪ **Modified resell selling situation**

▪ **Routine resell selling situation**

▪ **Team selling**

▪ **Multilevel selling**

▪ **Major account selling**

▪ **Telemarketing**

▪ **Trade shows**

Review Questions

1. Discuss how the type of buying situation affects the buying center, buying process, and buying needs.
2. How might the personal needs of engineers, purchasing agents, and marketing personnel affect the buying process for a product?
3. Consider the results of the study presented in "An Ethical Perspective: Gift Giving." Assume you are the national sales manager for a firm selling consumer products through various types of retailers. Develop specific policies to guide the gift-giving behavior of the salespeople in your firm.
4. How should management decide whether to employ a company-owned salesforce or to use independent representatives?
5. What are the key considerations in developing a telemarketing salesforce?
6. How is the management of relationships with industrial distributors different from the management of relationships with end-user customers?
7. How can trade shows be used to supplement other sales channels?
8. Review the role of master representatives discussed in "A Global Perspective: Master Representatives." What specific things should principals do to develop long-term relationships with master distributors?
9. How might telemarketing be used when accounts are covered by distributors?
10. What are the most important organizational buyer behavior trends, and how might these trends affect sales strategies in the future?

Application Exercises

1.   XYZ Food Products markets several food products to retail accounts. The firm's salesforce currently calls on all types of food retailers from small mom-and-pop operations to large superstores. You are considering the establishment of an in-house telemarketing operation to manage the smaller accounts. This would allow the field salesforce to spend more time with larger accounts and reduce the selling costs to smaller accounts. What problems do you foresee in developing the telemarketing operations? What would you do to minimize or solve these problems?

2.   ABC Manufacturing markets a small line of industrial products through independent sales representatives. Although your products serve a small market, you are the

dominant firm, with over 50 percent market share. Your reps typically represent four other principals. Each of these principals has a relatively small market share but operates in markets much larger than yours. You do not feel that the reps spend enough time trying to sell your products. What would you do to motivate the reps to increase their emphasis on your products?

3.   LM Salt Company sells bulk salt to various industrial customers. Some of the accounts purchase all of their salt from LM. However, several accounts want to maintain three suppliers of salt. For these accounts, LM has only a 33 percent share of their salt business. Since the salt market is experiencing slow overall growth, LM must increase its penetration of existing accounts to achieve sales and profit objectives. As the national sales manager, what would you do to increase account penetration?

Notes

[1]Martin Everett, "This Is the Ultimate in Selling," *Sales and Marketing Management*, August 1989, 28–30.

[2]Michael D. Hutt and Thomas W. Speh, *Business Marketing Management* (Hinsdale, Ill.: The Dryden Press, 1989), 14–18.

[3]Gary L. Lilien and M. Anthony Wong, "An Exploratory Investigation of the Structure of the Buying Center in the Metalworking Industry," *Journal of Marketing Research*, February 1984, 3.

[4]Hutt and Speh, *Business Marketing Management*, 18.

[5]Alex Beam and Geoff Lewis, "The IBM-DEC Wars: It's 'The Year of the Customer'," *Business Week*, March 30, 1987, 86–88.

[6]See F. Robert Dwyer, Paul H. Schurr, and Sejo Oh, "Developing Buyer-Seller Relationships," *Journal of Marketing*, April 1987, 11–27, for a more complete discussion of relationship and transaction exchange orientations.

[7]Reported in Kate Bertrand, "What Makes a Winning Sales Rep," *Business Marketing*, March 1989, 42.

[8]"Selling in the 1990s: A Sales Productivity Report," in *A Forum Special Issues Report* (The Forum Corporation, 1988), 1–19.

[9]Larry Wilson, *Changing the Game: The New Way to Sell* (New York: Simon and Schuster, 1987), 21–22.

[10]Gerhard Gschwandtner, "The Foundation for Sales Excellence in the 1990s," *Personal Selling Power*, September 1989, 32–33.

[11]"Dupont Turns Scientists into Salespeople," *Sales and Marketing Management*, June 1987, 57.

[12]"Bergen Brunswig Locks in Sales with Service," *Sales and Marketing Management*, June 1987, 48.

[13]Joan Hamilton and Amy Dunkin, "Why Rivals Are Quaking as Nordstrom Heads East," *Business Week*, June 15, 1987, 99–100.

[14]"Fuller Brush Man Uses Soft Sell, Humor to Boost Sales," *Marketing News*, January 18, 1988, 3.

[15]This section is based on material presented in John I. Coppett and William A. Staples, *Professional Selling: A Relationship Management Process* (Cincinnati, Ohio: South-Western Publishing Co., 1990), 55–64.

[16]Reported in James A. Narus and James C. Anderson, "Turn Your Industrial Distributors into Partners," *Harvard Business Review*, March–April 1986, 67.

[17]Howard Sutton, *Rethinking the Company's Selling and Distribution Channels* (New York: The Conference Board, 1986), 3.

[18]Donald M. Jackson and Michael F. d'Amico, "Products and Markets Served by Distributors and Agents," *Industrial Marketing Management*, 18, 1989, 27–33.

[19]Reported in Sutton, *Rethinking the Company's Channels*, 3.

[20]"Black and Decker Rebuilds," *Sales and Marketing Management*, June 1987, 49.

[21]"Apple's Instant Link with Dealers," *Sales and Marketing Management*, June 1987, 23–24.

[22]See Diane L. Kastiel, "Electronic Communications Avoid Short Circuits to Distributors," *Business Marketing*, July 1987, 70–75, for an expanded discussion of these and other examples.

[23]Diane L. Kastiel, "Wang's Retail Hopes Hinge on Plan's Success," *Business Marketing*, April 1987, 43–44.

[24]Sue Kapp, "Face-Off: An Optimist and a Realist Take on an Industry Goliath," *Business Marketing*, May 1987, 12–16.

[25]Lois C. DuBois and Roger H. Grace, "The Care and Feeding of Manufacturers' Reps," *Business Marketing*, December 1987, 56.

[26]See Thomas L. Powers, "Switching from Reps to Direct Salespeople," *Industrial Marketing Management*, 16, 1987, 169–172, for a systematic method for determining when to switch from independent representatives to a company salesforce.

[27]See Erin Anderson, "The Salesperson as Outside Agent or Employee: A Transaction Cost Analysis," *Marketing Science*, Summer 1985, 234–254, for a thorough discussion and empirical test of using independent representatives versus a company salesforce.

[28]Reported in Earl Hitchcock, "What Marketers Love and Hate About Their Manufacturers' Reps," *Sales and Marketing Management*, September 10, 1984, 60–65.

[29]Kate Bertrand, "They Don't Get No Respect," *Business Marketing*, June 1987, 38–40.

[30]"What's Their Line?" *Business Marketing*, July 1990, 19.

[31]Erin Anderson, Leonard M. Lodish, and Barton A. Weitz, "Resource Allocation Behavior in Conventional Channels," *Journal of Marketing Research*, February 1987, 85–97.

[32]"Metaphor's High-Cost Sell Pays Off," *Sales and Marketing Management*, April 1987, 25–26.

[33]William Keenan, Jr., "America's Best Sales Forces: Six at the Summit," *Sales and Marketing Management*, June 1990, 72–74.

[34]Everett, "This is the Ultimate," 32.

[35]Reported in "Toward More Successful Selling," *TeleProfessional*, Spring 1989.

[36]"Telemarketing Takes the Top Spot," *Direct Marketing*, September 1987, 120.

[37]William C. Moncrief, Charles W. Lamb, and Terry Dielman, "Developing Telemarketing Support Systems," *Journal of Personal Selling and Sales Management*, August 1986, 43–49.

[38]Geri Gantman, "Exclusive Survey," *Business Marketing*, September 1987, 57, 63–75.

[39]See Kate Bertrand, "The Inside Story," *Business Marketing*, September 1987, 51–62, for a more complete discussion of these and other telemarketing examples.

[40]Richard T. Brock, "Sharpening Your Telemarketing Edge through Automation," *Sales and Marketing Management*, May 1990, 156–157.

[41]Bill Kelley, "Is There Anything That Can't Be Sold by Phone?" *Sales and Marketing Management*, April 1989, 60–64.

[42]William C. Moncrief, Shannon H. Shipp, Charles W. Lamb, and David W. Cravens, "Examining the Roles of Telemarketing in Selling Strategy," *Journal of Personal Selling and Sales Management*, Fall 1989, 1–12.

[43]Reported in "Trade Shows Still Fighting a Rodney Dangerfield Image," *Marketing News*, May 14, 1990, 27.

[44]Reported in Edward Chapman, "Plan Your Exhibit Around the Motives of Attendees," *Marketing News*, June 11, 1990, 10.

[45]Reported in Richard K. Swandby, Jonathan M. Cox, and Ian K. Sequeira, "Trade Shows Poised for 1990s Growth," *Business Marketing*, May 1990, 46–52.

[46]See Roger A. Kerin and William L. Cron, "Assessing Trade Show Functions and Performance: An Exploratory Study," *Journal of Marketing*, July 1987, 87–94, for a more complete presentation of study results and more detailed discussion of research implications.

[47]Kate Bertrand, "Rewarding Ways to Build Trade Show Sales," *Business Marketing*, April 1987, 104–105.

[48]See Kate Bertrand, "Talking Turkey on Trade Shows," *Business Marketing*, March 1987, 94–103, for a detailed description of these trade-show evaluation methods.

[49]Earl L. Bailey, *Getting Closer to the Customer* (New York: The Conference Board, 1989), 6.

[50]See David W. Cravens, Thomas N. Ingram, and Raymond W. LaForge, "Evaluating Multiple Sales Channel Strategies," *Journal of Business and Industrial Marketing*, Summer/Fall 1991 (forthcoming); and Allan J. Magrath and Kenneth G. Hardy, "Selecting Sales and Distribution Channels," *Industrial Marketing Management*, 16, 1987, 273–278, for different procedures for evaluating sales channel alternatives.

CASE 6.1   *Microcomputer Corp.*

BUSINESS COMPUTING INC.
P.O. Box 1492
Richmond, VA 22801

September 14, 1991

Mr. Jack Sanderson
Vice-President of Sales
Microcomputer Corp.
P.O. Box 456
Atlanta, GA 44501

Dear Jack:

As you know, we have been a loyal distributor of your microcomputer products for the past five years. Until about two years ago, most of our sales were to small firms who purchased a few microcomputers from our inside salespeople. In 1989, cost and competitive pressures forced us to expand our focus to larger firms that purchase larger quantities. To serve these larger firms, we established an outside salesforce.

This strategy has been very successful, since our sales and profits have increased substantially over the past two years with approximately 40 percent of total sales and profits generated by our outside salesforce. Despite our satisfaction with this performance to date, we have recently become concerned about the increasing number of times that our salespeople are competing directly with your field salesforce for orders. Just this week, three of our salespeople complained about direct competition against your salesforce for large orders at three different accounts.

Trends in the microcomputer business lead us to believe that our future growth will be through outside sales to larger firms. Therefore, we think that it is important for our two companies to develop specific policies that eliminate direct competition between our salesforces. I would like to suggest two options:

1. Our salespeople would receive part of any commissions earned by your salespeople for sales in our market area.
2. We devise a procedure to assign exclusive rights for selling to all large accounts to either your salesforce or our salesforce.

Either of these options would be agreeable to us.

Please give me a call when you decide which option you would like to pursue. Maybe we could discuss the options over a round of golf.

Sincerely,

Ralph Zwettler

Ralph Zwettler
General Sales Manager

Questions

1. Are either of the options proposed by Ralph Zwettler acceptable to Jack Sanderson? Why or why not?
2. What is another solution to the problem that Jack should propose to Ralph?

CASE 6.2 *Franklin Chemical*

Background

Franklin Chemical produced and marketed various chemical products to industrial firms throughout the United States. The firm employed 100 salespeople that were each assigned a geographic sales territory and were responsible for selling Franklin products to all accounts in their territory. Although Franklin's sales had been growing in recent years, profits had declined. Management blamed the decline on the increasingly high level of selling costs. National sales manager Ken Williamson was given the responsibility to come up with a plan to reduce selling costs while maintaining sales growth.

Current Situation

Ken had come up with the following two alternatives:

1. Reduce the size of the field salesforce from 100 to 95. The current 100 sales territories would then be redesigned into 95. The elimination of 5 salespeople would reduce selling costs by approximately $625,000.
2. Develop and implement a telemarketing program. The telemarketing salespeople would be given all accounts with sales of less than $4,000 per year and would be responsible for maintaining and increasing sales to these accounts. They would also focus on generating sales from new, smaller accounts. The field salesforce would remain the same. Since the field salespeople would not have to call on the smaller accounts, their selling expenses would be reduced. In addition, they would also have more time available to generate more business from the larger accounts in their territories.

Ken was not sure which alternative he should recommend.

Questions

1. What are the advantages and disadvantages of each alternative?
2. Which alternative should Ken recommend? Why?
3. Can you devise a better alternative for Ken to consider?

CASES FOR PART TWO

United Tire Company

Phil Hart, Vice President of Sales for United Tire Company, hung up the phone and heaved a sigh of fatigue. He had just concluded a conversation with Jay Johnson, a regional division sales manager in Atlanta. Johnson had described the growing morale problem among his field sales representatives. Many of them had heard about a new telemarketing program that was being adopted by the company which, in their opinion, would cause significant reductions in the salesforce. Other rumors that were circulating indicated that those salespersons who did keep their jobs would find their compensation reduced significantly as a result of United's use of telemarketing to achieve sales.

Background

United Tire Company, a manufacturer of a full line of automotive tires, sells on a nationwide scale to car manufacturers in the United States as well as retail tire dealers. The number of automotive and tire dealers that United serves is approximately 20,000. Among these retailers are a wide variety of types and sizes of businesses. Some of United's customers are chains like K mart and Target. Others are small garages owned and operated by one person. The customers of United are distributed across the United States in a pattern closely resembling the national population distribution. Sales figures for United Tire Company are listed in Table 1.

The salesforce consists of 340 sales representatives managed by 20 district managers who, in turn, report to 5 division managers whose offices are in White Plains, New York; Atlanta, Georgia; St. Louis, Missouri; Denver, Colorado; and Los Angeles, California. The salesforce is organized on a geographic basis with each person assigned a number of counties, an SMSA (Standard Metropolitan Statistical Area), or a portion of an SMSA that provided each salesperson with an approximately equal sales potential.

Compensation of the sales personnel is a combination salary plus commission. Commissions were calculated on the percentage of a gross dollar volume that a sales representative attains each month. Average com-

TABLE 1 ▪ *1986 Gross Sales for United Tire Company*

$50 million	Automotive manufacturers purchasing tires for use on new cars and trucks
$200 million	Sales to retailers which included: $40 million—1,000 of the largest United customers $160 million—sales made to the remaining 19,000 customers
$250 million gross sales	

pensation for the salesforce is $38,000 per year. The lowest paid sales representative received $25,000 and the highest paid received $70,000. As a result of the above-average compensation and benefits package, the salesforce turnover rate was low. Over the past four years the average was less than 10% a year.

United Tire Company is facing the same forms of pressure that confront other domestic tire manufacturers. Foreign brands such as Bridgestone and Michelin have entered the U.S. market during the past ten years. The foreign marketers have introduced high-quality products while also keeping prices at or below the U.S. tire prices. This factor coupled with rising sales costs (see Table 2) caused United's profits to slump by approximately 3% a year for the past 4 years. United's top management has embarked on a vigorous campaign to cut costs and raise employee productivity.

Mr. Hart sensed the need to adopt significant cost-saving practices that would show that the Sales Department was aggressively attacking the problems of high costs. Therefore, when an invitation to attend a seminar on telemarketing was extended to Hart by the telephone company, he accepted it.

Source: This case was prepared by John I. Coppett, Associate Professor of Marketing, and William A. Staples, Professor of Marketing, University of Houston—Clear Lake. Reprinted with permission.

TABLE 2   ▪   *Average Cost of a Sales Call for a United Tire Representative*

1975	$ 64.14
1977	$ 87.11
1979	$123.32
1981	$160.20
1983	$184.86
1985	$206.73

The leaders of the seminar emphasized several points which were new to most of the executives attending the program. First, the audience was told that telemarketing was much more than just selling over the telephone to private consumers. Some of the other telemarketing applications that were of immediate interest to Hart involved the qualification of sales leads prior to turning the leads over to a field representative for a face-to-face visit. One of the many diagrams shown to the audience illustrated how the sales lead qualification program worked (see Figure 1).

The average cost to qualify a lead through the telemarketing program was $5.00, which included all of the costs associated with paying salaries, telephone service, and other overhead costs. An example the seminar leader provided to support her claim about the effectiveness of this program involved an adopter of the program who had improved the ratio of sales-closed to sales-calls-made from 1 out of 10 to 5 out of 10. A .500 batting average is fantastic in the sales world!

In addition to the sales lead qualification possibilities, Hart was also intrigued by another application

FIGURE 1   ▪   *A Sales Lead Qualification Program Using Telemarketing*

Sequence of Steps in Qualification Process:
1. Firm sponsors advertising of various kinds to stimulate inquiries from people who may be prospective customers.
2. Prospects respond by using (in this case) an 800 number to acquire more information and are then "qualified" by a telemarketing specialist.
3. Prospect's names which have been acquired during the qualification process are passed to field sales.
4. Field sales representatives call on only those consumers or businesses that have been submitted as qualified prospects.

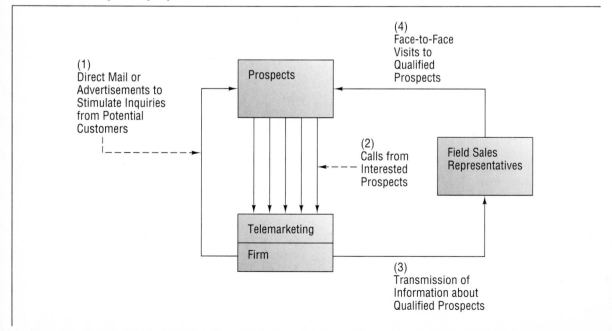

called "marginal account handling." The seminar example featured a situation in which a well-known greeting card manufacturer used telemarketing to continue to serve the thousands of small retail establishments where greeting cards were sold. In this situation, the greeting card marketer had realized almost ten years ago that there was no way to economically continue to achieve intensive distribution and serve all of the small accounts through face-to-face contact. By turning the marginally profitable accounts over to the new telemarketing center to handle, more frequent contact was maintained with the small gift shops, drug stores, and grocery stores. Presently, the greeting card marketer served almost 90 percent of its customer base through the telemarketing center. Although Hart's firm sold tires, the parallel to his problem did not escape his attention.

Shortly after attending the seminar, Mr. Hart received a call from a telephone company person who proposed a meeting to discuss the United Tire Company's situation. At the meeting, the telephone representative offered to work with Hart and his people to establish a telemarketing pilot program to test the feasibility of using telemarketing at United Tire Company. The initial test was designated for White Plains, New York. Three people were hired and trained to take incoming calls from prospects who were making inquiries to various advertisements, brochures, and direct mail (i.e., the "raw material" for sales leads).

In addition, to maximize the productivity of the three telemarketing specialists, each specialist was given 100 dormant accounts to contact. The telemarketing personnel were to attempt to sell tires that had been priced at a very attractive level for this situation. The purpose of this arrangement was to revive the accounts. The offer featured not only low-priced tires but also a two-day maximum delivery time plus a toll-free "hot line" for dealers to get instant service on any

problems they were having with the United Tire Company's products or services.

The success of the pilot was apparent within three weeks. After tracking the success of the field salespeople who followed up on the qualified leads furnished to them, Hart discovered that their sales-closed to sales-visits-made ratio exceeded 3.3 out of 10. This was compared to the national average of United's salesforce, which was 2 out of 10. The marginal, or dormant, account situation was also doing quite well. Twenty percent of the accounts contacted had responded favorably, with purchases that averaged $2,000 per customer.

As a by-product of some of the conversations the telemarketing specialists had had with customers, Hart learned that several customers had indicated they had not been contacted by a field salesperson from United Tire in many months. Some of the customers revealed their desire to continue to do business via the telemarketing program rather than having a field representative call on them.

After witnessing the pilot program results in White Plains for two months, Hart submitted a request for $300,000 to develop a telemarketing program in each of the other regional offices. After reviewing the proposal, Hart's superiors approved the request.

During the weekly teleconference Phil Hart had with the regional sales managers, he announced that within the next three months each regional office would have a sales lead qualification program and a marginal account program. The division managers were told to come to White Plains for additional briefing on the telemarketing program that would be implemented at United Tire Company.

It was two weeks after the division managers' meeting in White Plains that Hart received the call from Jay Johnson.

Morgantown Inc.

In November 1986 Morgantown Inc. merged with Lea-Meadows Industries, a manufacturer of upholstered furniture for living and family rooms. The merger was not planned in a conventional sense. Charlton Bates's father-in-law died suddenly in August 1986, leaving his daughter with controlling interest in the firm. The merger proceeded smoothly, since the two firms were located on adjacent properties and the general consensus was that the two firms would maintain as much autonomy as was economically justified. Moreover, the upholstery line filled a gap in the Morgantown product mix, even though it would retain its own identity and brand names.

The only real issue that continued to plague Bates was merging the selling effort. Morgantown had its own salesforce, but Lea-Meadows Industries relied on sales agents to represent it. The question was straightforward, in his opinion: "Do we give the upholstery line of chairs and sofas to our salesforce, or do we continue using the sales agents?" Mr. John Bott, Morgantown's sales vice-president, said the line should be given to his sales group; Mr. Martin Moorman, national sales manager of Lea-Meadows Industries, said the upholstery line should remain with sales agents.

Lea-Meadows Industries

Lea-Meadows Industries is a small manufacturer of upholstered furniture for use in living and family rooms. The firm is over seventy-five years old. The company has some of the finest fabrics and frame construction in the industry, according to trade sources. Net sales in 1986 were $3 million. Total industry sales of 1,500 upholstered furniture manufacturers in 1986 were $4.4 billion. Company sales had increased 15 percent annually over the last five years, and company executives believed this growth rate would continue for the foreseeable future.

Lea-Meadows Industries employed fifteen sales agents to represent its products. These sales agents also represented several manufacturers of noncompeting furniture and home furnishings. Often a sales agent found it necessary to deal with several buyers in a store in order to represent all lines carried. On a typical sales call, a sales agent would first visit buyers. New lines, in addition to any promotions being offered by manufacturers, would be discussed. New orders were sought where and when it was appropriate. A sales agent would then visit a retailer's selling floor to check displays, inspect furniture, and inform sales people on furniture. Lea-Meadows Industries paid an agent commission of 5 percent of net company sales for these services. Moorman thought sales agents spent 10 to 15 percent of their in-store sales time on Lea-Meadows products.

The company did not attempt to influence the type of retailers that agents contacted. Yet it was implicit in the agency agreement that agents would not sell to discount houses. All agents had established relationships with their retail accounts and worked closely with them. Sales records indicated that agents were calling on furniture and department stores. An estimated 1,000 retail accounts were called on in 1986.

Morgantown Inc.

Morgantown Inc. is a manufacturer of medium- to high-priced living and dining room wood furniture. The firm was formed in 1902. Net sales in 1986 were $50 million. Total estimated industry sales of wood furniture in 1986 were $7.1 billion at manufacturers' prices.

The company employed 10 full-time sales representatives who called on 1,000 retail accounts in 1986. These individuals performed the same function as sales agents, but were paid a salary plus a small commission. In 1986 the average Morgantown sales representative received an annual salary of $50,000 (plus expenses) and a commission of 0.5 percent on net company sales. Total sales administration costs were $112,500.

The Morgantown salesforce was highly regarded in the industry. The salesmen were known particularly for their knowledge of wood furniture and willingness to work with buyers and retail sales personnel. Despite these points, Bates knew that all retail accounts did not carry the complete Morgantown furniture line. He had therefore instructed John Bott to "push the group a little harder." At present, sales representatives were making ten sales calls per week, with the average sales call running three hours. Remaining time was accounted for by administrative activities and travel. Bates recommended that the call frequency be increased to seven calls per account per year, which was consistent with what he thought was the industry norm.

Source: This case is used with the permission of its author, Roger A. Kerin, Edwin L. Cox School of Business, Southern Methodist University, Dallas, Texas.

Merging the Sales Effort

In separate meetings with Bott and Moorman, Bates was able to piece together a variety of data and perspectives on the question. These meetings also made it clear that Bott and Moorman differed dramatically in their views.

John Bott had no doubts about assigning the line to the Morgantown salesforce. Among the reasons he gave for this approach were the following. First, Morgantown had developed one of the most well respected, professional sales groups in the industry. Sales representatives could easily learn the fabric jargon, and they already knew personally many of the buyers who were responsible for upholstered furniture. Second, selling the Lea-Meadows line would require only about 15 percent of present sales call time. Thus he thought the new line would not be a major burden. Third, more control over sales efforts was possible. He noted that Charlton Bates's father-in-law had developed the sales group twenty-five years earlier because of the commitment it engendered and the service "only our own people are able and willing to give." Moreover, our people have the Morgantown "look" and presentation style that is instilled in every person. Fourth, he said it wouldn't look right if we had our representatives and agents calling on the same stores and buyers. He noted that Morgantown and Lea-Meadows Industries overlapped on all their accounts. He said, "We'd be paying a commission on sales to these accounts when we would have gotten them anyway. The difference in commission percentages would not be good for morale."

Martin Moorman advocated keeping sales agents for the Lea-Meadows line. His arguments were as follows. First, all sales agents had established contacts and were highly regarded by store buyers, and most had represented the line in a professional manner for many years. He, too, had a good working relationship with 15 agents. Second, sales agents represented little, if any, cost beyond commissions. Moorman noted, "Agents get paid when we get paid." Third, sales agents were committed to the Lea-Meadows line: "The agents earn a part of their living representing us. They have to service retail accounts to get the repeat business." Fourth, sales agents were calling on buyers not contacted by Morgantown sales representatives. He noted, "If we let Morgantown people handle the line, we might lose these accounts, have to hire more sales personnel, or take away 25 percent of the present selling time given to Morgantown product lines."

As Bates reflected on the meetings, he felt that a broader perspective was necessary beyond the views expressed by Bott and Moorman. One factor was profitability. Existing Morgantown furniture lines typically had gross margins that were 5 percent higher than those for Lea-Meadows upholstered lines. Another factor was the "us and them" references apparent in the meetings with Bott and Moorman. Would merging the sales efforts overcome this, or would it cause more problems? Finally, the idea of increasing the sales force to incorporate the Lea-Meadows line did not sit well with him. Adding a new salesperson would require restructuring of sales territories, potential loss of commission to existing people, and "a big headache."

Adjeleian and Associates (A)

By October 1983, John A. Adjeleian, founder and president of Adjeleian and Associates consulting structural engineers in Ottawa, had invested over sixteen months evaluating state-of-the-art computer assisted design and drafting (CADD) systems. Mr. Adjeleian more than liked the technical capabilities of the new systems. Proposals from the three most promising vendors sat on his desk, each with a six-figure price tag that could not pass any reasonable test of financial return. It was decision time.

The Structural Consulting Business

The design and construction of a commercial or industrial building usually took several years from the decision to proceed by the owner to the polishing of the doorknobs by the cleanup crew. During the project several key parties were involved: 1) the owner, 2) the chief architect, who produced spatial and aesthetic drawings and specifications, 3) the chief structural engineering consultant, who produced drawings and specifications for the building's "skeleton," 4) the mechanical and electrical engineering consultants, who produced drawings and specifications for the building's systems, and 5) the general contractor who was responsible for material procurement and construction. In addition, the general contractor would normally issue several subcontracts to the subtrades. Drawings and specifications conformed to the rigid requirements of the National Building Code. At all stages of the project it was vitally important to keep all parties notified of changes to drawings or specifications because mistakes tended to be extremely costly.

Fees for structural engineering firms were generally derived from services provided directly to the building owner or chief architect. Even though the fee for a structural engineer's services might amount to less than 1% of a building's total cost to the owner (Exhibit 1), in general, engineering firms could not raise prices for their services because of the number of qualified competitors. In 1983, for example, 220 of the 850 member firms of the Association of Consulting Engineers of Canada (ACEC) listed Structural Engineering as a company specialty, and twenty-four of these had offices in Ottawa.

The competitive nature of the consulting engineering industry was reflected in modest salaries and narrow profit margins. According to Statistics Canada Catalogue 63-537 (1982), $1.30 billion of the industry's $2.23 billion fee revenue was paid to 39,352 employees, for an average salary of $33,000. Average company revenue was $997,000 with a profit margin of about 4% before tax. There was, however, variation in this margin. Many of the larger firms, with annual revenues exceeding $5 million, were operating at a slight

Source: This case was prepared as the basis for classroom discussion by David Large and Professor Donald W. Barclay, School of Business Administration, The University of Western Ontario, October 1990. Copyright © The University of Western Ontario.

EXHIBIT 1 ▪ *Adjeleian and Associates (A): Typical Building Project Cost Breakdown*

The following is an approximate cost breakdown for a "typical" 25 floor office building (including parking levels) located in downtown Ottawa, 1983.

Land, 30,000 square feet @ $200/square foot	$6,000,000
Building, 250,000 square feet	
"Hard Costs" (for Contractor) @ $80/square foot	20,000,000
"Soft Costs" (for permits and contingencies) @ 3%	600,000
Architect's design fee @ 5%	1,000,000
Structural design fee @ 0.9%	180,000
Mechanical design fee @ 0.8%	160,000
Electrical design fee @ 0.3%	60,000
Grand Total to Owner (before financing)	$28,000,000

loss. Smaller firms, with revenues under $1 million, had operating margins of 8 to 15%. Structural engineering was one of the most competitive fields.

The number of employees in a consulting engineering firm varied widely. A firm specializing in structural engineering could range from a single professional engineer to a dozen staff engineers or more, plus drafting and administrative personnel. Staff engineers were responsible for structural design, i.e., specification of the structural materials and structural plans, and calculation of the final dimensions of the structural components. Working in parallel with the engineers, drafting personnel were then responsible for translating the designs into finished detailed drawings. Because company revenues were directly related to the activity levels of the engineers and draftspersons, there was considerable pressure to keep idle time to a minimum. If company managers were unsuccessful in generating business, layoffs commonly ensued.

A tremendous amount of computer calculation was involved in arriving at a final structural design. Patterns of structural components were often highly complex, and the structural material could be any combination of steel, concrete, masonry, or timber.

Adjeleian and Associates Incorporated

John Adjeleian graduated from MIT in 1954 with a Masters degree in Civil Engineering and moved to Montreal to begin work with a combined architectural and engineering firm. The following year he accepted an invitation to move to Ottawa to assist an architect on two major building projects. In doing so, he became the first specialized structural engineering consultant to locate in Ottawa. Previously, structural design services had been provided by moonlighting civil servants, or had been included "free of charge" by steel supply companies.

Mr. Adjeleian then experimented with a multidisciplinary civil/mechanical/electrical engineering team but decided in 1961 to return to the structural specialist role. "Adjeleian and Associates," consulting structural engineers, opened a ground level office on Bank Street, a main street in Ottawa, and put a drafting table in the store front window so passers-by could watch the company in action. The initial office staff included Mr. Adjeleian, Mr. Charlie Fenton (a structural engineer), and Leo Bortolotti (an architectural technologist). The company's expertise was enhanced shortly thereafter when Mr. Adjeleian retained Dr.

Leslie Jaeger as a senior academic advisor. Dr. Jaeger, a structural engineering professor at McGill University in Montreal, was to play a key role in the company's adoption of successive generations of computer technology. This relationship between Adjeleian and Associates (A + A) and Dr. Jaeger was the first stage of Mr. Adjeleian's plan to maintain a permanent bridge between his company and the academic community.

The reputation of A + A was quickly established. This was by virtue of its expertise and computing capability, but especially because of Mr. Adjeleian's ability to understand and solve architects' problems. Above all, he emphasized client satisfaction and flexibility. Contracts were always negotiated to comply with the client's wishes. His firm could deliver a spectrum of structural designs in different materials and configurations, and original drawings and corrections were available quickly. Furthermore, A + A offered a wide range of related services such as feasibility studies, project management, on-site project supervision and damage assessment.

As a result, between 1961 and 1983 the firm was involved in over 2000 projects, from small to large (Exhibit 2), from the commonplace to the unusual (Exhibit 3), mainly in Ottawa but also in many other cities. Such became the visibility of his company's work in Ottawa that one of Mr. Adjeleian's favourite marketing approaches was to escort a potential client to the restaurant atop Place de Ville to sweep his arm across the Ottawa skyline pointing out projects in which A + A had been involved. Among A + A's more visible contributions were several public and private sector landmarks: Place de Ville, the National Arts Centre and the National Aviation Museum in Ottawa; the Harbour Castle Hotel in Toronto; la Cité in Montreal; and the Fathers of Confederation complex in Charlottetown (Exhibit 4). During this period there were two other corporate milestones: A + A's incorporation in 1972, and expansion to include a Toronto office in 1981.

Mr. Adjeleian constantly recognized the importance of finding and keeping the best people. High quality graduates were attracted to A + A by the company's exciting work and its career employment policy. A + A was "fussy on hiring, but once you're in, you stay." This policy was in contrast to the practice of many competitors, who tended to hire and fire according to fluctuating work levels. By 1983 A + A employed 28 people including 9 professional engineers, and enjoyed annual fee revenues of "mid six figures plus."

EXHIBIT 2 ▪ *Adjeleian and Associates (A):*
A + A Projects — Small and Large

(a) Public Elementary School, Kanata, Ontario

(b) Harbour Castle Hotel, Toronto, Ontario

EXHIBIT 3 ▪ *Adjeleian and Associates (A):*
A + A Projects —
Commonplace and Unusual

(a) Government of Canada, Booth St., Ottawa, Ontario

(b) Civic Centre, Ottawa, Ontario

Computing Evolution at A + A

The slide rule was the engineering tool of the day in the 1950s. A + A quickly adopted electronic calculators when they became available in the 60s. However, A + A's introduction to "real" computing occurred in 1966 with the strong encouragement of Dr. Jaeger when the firm connected to IBM's Quicktran computing service in Toronto. Via a terminal in Ottawa, A + A engineers were able to carry out limited calcula-

tions using IBM software and to develop and employ additional proprietary software. Administrative personnel also had access to general accounting packages. In 1970 A + A switched its computing to Systems Dimension Limited (SDL) in Ottawa, an independent computer service bureau. SDL supported a wider range of A + A's on-line design software, and provided punched card access to advanced structural design pro-

EXHIBIT 4 ▪ *Adjeleian and Associates (A):*
A + A List of Sample
Projects 1961–1983

Ottawa/Hull	Place de Ville, office and hotel complex
	National Arts Centre
	National Aviation Museum
	The Journal Towers
	Lansdowne Park Civic Centre
	NRC Fire Research Laboratory
	Ottawa Civic Hospital (several buildings)
	Carleton University (several buildings)
	Les Terrasses de la Chaudiere
	Children's Hospital of Eastern Ontario
Toronto	Harbour Castle Hotel
Montreal	la Cité office and residential complex
Charlottetown	Fathers of Confederation Provincial Buildings
International	Ocean Trail Condominium, West Palm Beach
	Samis National Computer Centre, Riyadh
	Canadian Embassy, Riyadh

grams. This proved to be a satisfactory arrangement for several years.

A significant milestone in A + A's computing history occurred in 1975 when Mr. Adjeleian accepted the position of Chair of Civil Engineering at Carleton University, a position he retained through 1982. It had been Mr. Adjeleian's longstanding ambition to return to the academic environment in a teaching capacity. However, as an unexpected bonus he gained valuable experience and contacts within the university computing community. In the Civil Engineering faculty, Mr. Adjeleian met Dr. Jagmohan Humar. "Jag" was a professor of structural engineering who had considerable talent in computer-based design and who would go on to collaborate with A + A on several complex projects. Among the graduate students in Structures was Don Duchesne, who also had considerable computer skills, and who would go on to join A + A after graduation in 1980. Mr. Adjeleian himself gained some firsthand experience with computers when the Department of Civil Engineering purchased a Digital Equipment Corporation PDP system. This association with leading-edge people and technology was to prove valuable for

A + A's future ability to evaluate the continuous advances in computing technologies.

In 1982, A + A recognized that a major crossroads had been reached regarding the company's computing approach. Due primarily to one particularly complex project, the National Aviation Museum, A + A's annual computer design charges from SDL were rapidly approaching $40,000. Furthermore, the engineering analysis required highly repetitive use of cumbersome punched cards for input, and the 24 hour turnaround was driving staff frustration up to unacceptable levels. In June, with the Museum design far from complete, and given the firm's desire to attract more complex projects, Mr. Adjeleian decided to become a "serious buyer" of a complete inhouse computer system.

The Search for an Inhouse Computer System

Mr. Adjeleian immediately put together a team which included himself, Jag Humar and Don Duchesne. The veteran and sophomore computer specialists were ideal complements for Mr. Adjeleian's business and negotiation skills, and the team operated well together from the beginning. By involving Mr. Duchesne early, Mr. Adjeleian was also starting the grooming process for a future Systems Manager.

After preliminary discussions, the team envisioned a computer system that would be capable of handling all of A + A's engineering design needs, as well as office administration functions. Engineers required a user-friendly system which was compatible with public software and A + A's proprietary software, and with no major restrictions on program or database size. Administrative personnel required word processing, accounting, job costing and aging of accounts. In addition, the team specified that the system must: be state-of-the-art, but field tested and proven; be backed by a "big league" company with staying power; have growth capabilities that could keep pace with the company's strategic plans; be capable of supporting time-sharing with several active terminals and printers; be capable of servicing both the Ottawa and Toronto offices; have local maintenance personnel; and be competitively priced. Mr. Adjeleian was willing to give special consideration to a Canadian computing systems supplier if the supplier was able to meet all or most of these requirements.

Such a system would probably be anchored by a minicomputer from a major manufacturer such as IBM, Hewlett-Packard (HP), or Digital Equipment Corporation (DEC). Other primary components would include operating, design and administrative software, about six design/administration terminals, two worksheet printers, and a letter quality printer. The team estimated from experience that an investment of $100,000 would be sufficient. Additional one-time costs would include about $10,000 for physical site preparation and $50,000–100,000 in foregone engineering billings as engineers received training on the system and converted programs and databases. Ongoing operating costs would have to be considered as well. Hardware and software maintenance charges, leased telephone lines, and supplies might run $2,000–3,000 per month.

A + A's financial situation would allow the purchase, but financial justification appeared tenuous. There was the immediate saving of $40,000 per annum in service bureau charges; this amount was expected to increase, but that in itself was not completely compelling. In its favour, the inhouse system would permit an immediate improvement in productivity and the ability to respond to design changes, which suggested higher billing potential. Furthermore, the improved working environment would ease the growing frustration with the limitations of the current approach and would maintain the company's ability to attract top engineering graduates. There was also the possibility of selling timesharing services to other architects and engineers in the Ottawa area. Finally, Mr. Adjeleian wanted to be able to continue to promote his company as continually innovative, able to provide the best service, and able to complete the most challenging projects.

Not long after the team had begun to identify its requirements, team members began to attend computer trade shows in Ottawa and Toronto. At a show in Toronto, Mr. Adjeleian witnessed for the first time a demonstration of a computer assisted structural *drafting* system, as opposed to a *design* system. The quality of the computer graphics compared favourably with that of professional manual graphics (Exhibit 5). It took only a few minutes for Mr. Adjeleian to adjust his thinking towards a completely integrated administration/design/draft system. Such systems existed in industries such as aerospace, but the first appearance of a drafting system designed specifically for building structures signalled that it might be time for A + A to act.

At the next meeting of the search team, the new concept was discussed. Mr. Adjeleian could foresee several advantages to a computer drafting capability. If drafting efficiency were improved, A + A might be able to boost contract drafting fees. Further, if terminals were placed in the offices of several major archi-

EXHIBIT 5 ▪ *Adjeleian and Associates (A): Manual vs. Computer Assisted Drafting*

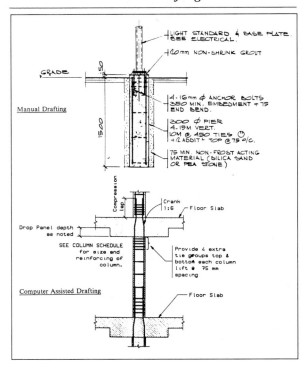

tects, delays and errors in the communication of revisions could be substantially reduced in joint projects. Some architects might also be interested in paying timesharing fees for the use of the system in unrelated projects. To be useful, a drafting software package would: enable preparation of intermediate and finished drawings; permit drawing storage, retrieval and updates; and allow the transfer of drawings to and from other systems.

Information gathering on drafting systems began in earnest. All of the major computer manufacturers had offices in Ottawa and Mr. Adjeleian began to talk to representatives from IBM, HP and DEC, among others. Quickly, word "hit the street" that A + A was serious about a purchase, and Mr. Adjeleian's phone began to ring. Among all the competitors, three received the most serious consideration.

Competitor #1 — Systemhouse. Systemhouse, an Ottawa-based software house and service bureau, invited A + A to view their design and drafting system supplied to them by Holguin and Associates, a well-established civil engineering firm in Texas. Mr. Adjeleian accepted the invitation to view the system because he'd heard that Stanley and Associates, a large multidisciplinary engineering firm in Edmonton, was using the same system with considerable success. Furthermore, it ran on an HP9000 minicomputer which enjoyed a solid reputation for product quality and maintenance, and which was definitely capable of supporting all of A + A's design and administration requirements. Systemhouse was offering to install and maintain a complete hardware/software system for $175,000.

This system "seemed OK" to Mr. Adjeleian and in fact it was quite attractive because the drafting software was well-established and tested. To further investigate the Holguin and Associates drafting software, Mr. Adjeleian attended a computer trade show in Dallas during the first quarter of 1983. He spent considerable time at the Holguin and Associates booth and learned that the company considered itself to be at the leading edge of structural design and drafting software development. Indeed, the graphics system was impressive in terms of retrieving, displaying, correcting and manipulating drawings. However, Mr. Adjeleian was disappointed with the small size of the terminal display unit, which would substantially limit the amount of viewable information. Of even greater significance, the booth attendant could not draw a basic floor plan starting with a blank screen.

A cursory inspection of the other booths at the trade show revealed that none of the other integrated systems on display could meet all of A + A's performance requirements with one possible exception. That one exception, Mr. Adjeleian noted, was the McDonnell Douglas "McAuto" system located in the largest booth. He didn't take the opportunity to initiate more probing conversations with the McDonnell Douglas representatives but filed a mental note to investigate that option at some later date.

Competitor #2 — Omnitech. Back in Ottawa, a reputable but young computer company named Omnitech had successfully convinced A + A to pay closer attention to its offering. Its graphics software was a byproduct of a Government of Canada Department of Public Works project, and it currently ran on a computer manufactured by a small company in Boston. Conversations with Omnitech's president followed. It appeared to both Dr. Humar and Mr. Duchesne that A + A's requirements could be substantially, but not entirely, satisfied for an investment of about $150K. In its favour, Omnitech strongly promoted its service orientation. Also, Mr. Adjeleian very much liked the fact that Omnitech was an Ottawa company. In particular he saw the potential of linking Omnitech with Orcatech, a local computer hardware manufacturer with proven capability.

However, there were some important concerns. The main drawback was the system's single user capacity which prevented timesharing by multiple users. Privately, members of the search team expressed concern about Omnitech's long term corporate survival and the relatively unknown reputation of the Boston computer manufacturer. Would it be dangerous to adopt a prototype system supported only by two small and relatively inexperienced companies?

Competitor #3 — ARC. In the summer of 1983, the three members of the search team attended an exhibition of computer drafting and mapping systems in Hull, Quebec. They were treated to a private demonstration by Applied Research of Cambridge (ARC) of their General Drafting System (GDS) software. It ran on a Prime 2250 minicomputer and appeared highly user friendly. According to Dr. Humar, "We were impressed—it could do the drafting job." Mr. Duchesne commented that it was "better than anything I'd seen." Mr. Adjeleian was pleased that ARC's representative could draw a basic floor plan beginning with a blank screen, and that the system had the potential to fulfill all of A + A's current and foreseeable administration, design and drafting requirements.

In conversation with the sales representative, the team learned that ARC had been in business in England for over 12 years, and that GDS was being employed by over 50% of English architects. Further, the U.S. rights to the GDS software had been purchased by McDonnell Douglas and was being marketed in the U.S. under the name "McAuto." The drafting software appeared to be well-established and supported in North America by a large reputable company.

The A + A team was not familiar with the Prime minicomputer because it had not yet entered the Ottawa market. However, the members were aware that Prime was listed in the Fortune 500 and was considered to be a high quality company. All technical factors considered, the ARC system appeared to be "the Cadillac" of all the CADD systems on the market. However, ARC had yet to make its first GDS sale in Canada. The price of $300,000 for a complete hardware/software system, including $60,000 for the GDS software alone, was probably a factor. Besides the high price, the team was concerned that the GDS software was not yet programmed with North American structural steel shapes. Furthermore, there was only one ARC representative in Canada and he was located in Toronto.

The team continued to examine other options for several more months until the members were convinced that no viable system existed or was on the verge of being announced. During this time, intensive efforts were made by all vendors to develop close working relationships with Mr. Adjeleian and other A + A personnel. In Appendix 1, an abridged account of one such relationship is provided from the perspective of the sales representative from one of the three leading contenders.

Assessing the Vendors

In October 1983, the A + A team paused to take stock of its position. Quotations had been received at various times from the three strongest contenders: 1) Systemhouse at $175,000, 2) Omnitech at $150,000, and 3) ARC at $300,000. The quotations were still valid, so no formal tendering process was contemplated. All three proposals had both positive and negative features, and for various reasons Mr. Adjeleian felt that all three would be willing to negotiate further.

The incremental capital cost for augmenting the administration/design system with a computer assisted drafting capability (graphics software, graphics terminal, plotters) appeared to be at least $50,000, plus $50,000–100,000 in lost drafting productivity during the learning phase. Incremental operating and salary costs to support the drafting application would probably amount to $2,000–3,000 per month. Financial justification for this incremental capability was as highly questionable as it was for the original administration/design concept. In certain drafting situations involving high repetition or geometrically complex shapes, the computer drafting system would increase drafting production by a factor of 2 to 10. However, in low repetition or one-off drawings the system would have little positive, or possibly a detrimental, effect. Also, if a hundred drawings for a complex project all required simultaneous changes, the two plotters would be tied up for days. Furthermore, much less expensive microcomputer-based drafting software packages such as AutoCAD appeared to be developing rapidly.

Countering this financial analysis was Mr. Adjeleian's enthusiasm for innovation and the desire for

A + A to be positioned as leaders. If A + A bought an integrated system, they would be the first structural engineering specialist in Canada to do so. Also, an integrated design/drafting system would provide A + A with a powerful marketing tool which would appeal to owners or architects involved in highly complex projects. This might be consistent with A + A's long term strategic plans.

Appendix 1:
Adjeleian and Associates (A)— A Buyer/Seller Relationship from a Sales Rep's Perspective

"I followed up a week after our first meeting, and there was a definite interest. Then at that point in time it became a fairly long process inasmuch as you sit down with a client and try and figure out what it is he wants to do. I saw John as the driving force, very much the businessman first. Then he had a technical person, Don Duchesne, whose responsibility was to make sure that whatever system John was going to buy was going to be suitable for the application.

"We hit it off, I think, very well right away. He took me around to an art gallery one day because I expressed an interest in art. He took me to lunch and dinner at his club. So I would say those were very positive signs of the beginning of a relationship.

"John was an innovator. He was a leader. He wanted to have a high profile look to his company, nothing second rate. He recognized well in advance of his other peers that in order to be competitive in his own industry, and also to show off in his own industry, that he had to have a really good CADD system. John was also paying for computer time for his structural analysis programs with somebody else. That was running him a lot of money. There was even some thought that maybe as master of his own destiny he could begin to rent out time as well.

"The company I was representing, in my opinion, was the leader in CADD minicomputer software. However, at that time there was an increasing technology change of going away from the glorified big system and going to a micro-based system for $50,000. We were beginning to fight that. So John was looking at buying from us knowing that we were hungry for our first Canadian sale, and that we needed somebody who would be willing to demonstrate our product in the Ottawa area if we so asked.

"Out of all the companies that he saw, we were the only one I think, who expressed a real interest in solving his problems. We would provide what we called a turnkey system. We would supply the drafting software, plus the computer, the terminals, and the plotter. (We could get a 20% discount on the hardware as a reseller.) We would stress our strengths very very heavily. I'm not someone to bad mouth somebody else's product. I would play up the service end on our part very heavily, and the genuine interest in making him succeed. In fact, although our firm was not located in Canada, I moved to the Toronto area as soon as I came on board. Providing the total solution, the integrated package, was a big sales feature.

"In this type of selling it was a team approach. My boss would have to approve all deals, but she was as hungry as I was. Then you had the salesperson, myself, as the lead seller, going in and talking to the president of the company. (I had quite a bit of experience in CADD myself. I had been in it three or four years at that time. I was recognized as a knowledgeable person.) But if John's technical person came to me

with technical questions, I would pass them on to my technical expert. Then he and I would discuss what went on. After the sale, we would bring in some installation and training expertise. Our training, as crude as it was, was the best that was available at that time. It was user friendly. We tried to make the prospective client feel at home. If I had any complaint, it was with our marketing people who were very very technically driven in those days. We were always short of marketing material. Always short. There were always these technical pamphlets to be handed out but there was no structured marketing philosophy or strategy.

"It was rare that you would have the employees as enthusiastic as the decision maker. The owner's fear is 'How am I going to pay for this?' The user's fear is 'How am I going to learn this new technology?' I spent as much time as I could with John's drafting employees assuring them that they would not lose their jobs with this new technology, that everybody would benefit, and it would make their job more pleasant."

Adjeleian and Associates (B)

On November 3, 1983, John Adjeleian signed Contract No. H001 with Applied Research of Cambridge (ARC) for the delivery of a complete administration/design/drafting computer system (Exhibit 1). Even though ARC had finally offered a substantial discount from its original $300,000 proposal, Mr. Adjeleian thought that "No way financially is it viable . . . . it's strictly visionary." Adjeleian and Associates (A + A) had just become the first structural engineering specialist in Canada to purchase such an integrated system.

The system was installed in January and debugged by February, 1984. Engineering personnel adopted the new design capability immediately. Compared to previous computer analysis procedures, which often involved punched cards and 24-hour turnaround from a computer service bureau, access to an inhouse computer facility proved irresistible. All functional criteria were met by the new system and it appeared as if the design portion of the system would pay out in 3 or 4 years.

Drafting personnel were understandably more hesitant to adopt the General Drafting System (GDS). Several had honed their manual drafting skills over a period of 10 or 20 years, none had any previous computer drafting experience, and the heavy demands from new jobs precluded any dedicated training time. Mr. Adjeleian and Mr. Duchesne, Systems Manager, refrained from a heavy-handed approach to encouraging their drafting staff to use the system. Instead, two additional personnel with some computer drafting experience were hired to initiate system use. Unfortunately, only the two new personnel and Mr. Duchesne ever developed any effective GDS expertise. Part of the explanation, according to Mr. Duchesne, was that ARC's sales team failed to follow through with their promises of training sessions for inexperienced drafting personnel. By the end of 1984, Mr. Adjeleian felt that GDS had been only moderately successfully implemented, and was still highly underutilized. The cost effectiveness of GDS was not in doubt: "Coldly, it [GDS] was an absolute loser."

Early in 1985, Mr. Adjeleian received a call from Rod Robbie, a Toronto architect whom Mr. Adjeleian had known personally and professionally for thirty years. Mr. Robbie had just heard of Toronto's intention to construct a large sports stadium with a retractable roof. He was wondering if Mr. Adjeleian might be interested in forming a consortium to submit a proposal to the stadium competition. Mr. Robbie knew of A + A's outstanding engineering reputation and also felt that A + A's new integrated computing capability would be a very strong selling feature in a proposal. He felt that interorganizational communications effectiveness would be maximized by minimizing design and drafting errors, thereby increasing the probability of conforming to tight schedules. Mr. Adjeleian agreed, and together with NORR and Ellis-Don they entered the competition (Exhibit 2). As part of their proposal, A + A produced a 5-minute animated video showing the stadium roof in the process of opening as if viewed by a pilot in a small plane circling and entering the stadium. The video, edited by Mr. Duchesne from a series of stills produced on A + A's new GDS software, was extremely well received by the adjudicators.

When the four finalists were announced that Fall, the Robbie/Adjeleian/NORR (RAN) consortium was excited but cautious. Even though its name was on that short list, most observers and critics viewed the RAN consortium as a distant underdog. That attitude prevailed because none of the members of the team had yet achieved the level of Toronto recognition that most observers seemed to think essential. On December 12, 1985, when it was announced that RAN would be the consortium to construct the Skydome, RAN's competitors were stunned. RAN's members, following a jubilant celebration, got right to work. By the end of January all offices of the consortium were in full production aiming for a christening date of April, 1989.

In reflecting on the success of the Skydome proposal, Mr. Adjeleian knew that the combined visual, human and structural design was unsurpassed. However, in his words, "If we hadn't had the system, we wouldn't have won the dome." As for the future, John Adjeleian knew that two or three northern U.S. National Football League stadium corporations were just beginning to consider the possibility of retractable roofs . . . .

Source: This case was prepared as the basis for classroom discussion by David Large and Professor Donald W. Barclay, School of Business Administration, The University of Western Ontario, October 1990. Copyright © The University of Western Ontario.

EXHIBIT 1 ∎ *Adjeleian and Associates (B): Components of the New System*

Computer	Prime 2250 super minicomputer (32 bit virtual memory cpu, 1.5 Mb RAM memory, convertible to 4 Mb)
Engineering/Administration Terminals	6 Falco TS100/132, with 80 or 132 column capabilities
Bond/Worksheet Printers	2 Mannisman Tally dot matrix printers 1 Diablo 620 letter quality printer
Drafting/Graphics Terminal	Tektronix 4109, with 19 inch screen, colour graphics, moderate resolution (640*40 pixel), local pan and zoom
Drawing Plotters	1 Nicolet-Zeta 3653sx 4 pen plotter 1 Tektronix ink jet screen printer
Communications	Datapac 3101 dedicated 1200 baud port, permitting Toronto office to use system, and employees to log in with home Hyperions
Software	PRIMOS operating system FORTRAN EMACS text edit Public domain design software (e.g. TABS80, SAPIV) Proprietary design software Proprietary financial cost accounting ARC's General Drafting System (GDS)

EXHIBIT 2 ∎ *Adjeleian and Associates (B): Key Parameters of RAN's Stadium Proposal*

Partners

Architects	Robbie Architects Inc. Neish Owen Rowland and Roy (NORR)
Senior Structural Engineer	Adjeleian and Associates Ltd.
Struct/Mech/Elect Engineer	Carr and Donald and Associates
General Contractor	Ellis-Don Ltd.

Parameters

Number of Seats	52,000 for baseball, 54,000 for football
Free Span	208 meters (same as Louisiana Superdome)
Free Height	> 30 floor office tower
Time to Open or Close	20 minutes
Serviceable Life	100 years
Quoted Price	$225 million

Information Sources

Barr, Greg (1985), "Dome Stadium Design Crowning Achievement for Ottawa Firm," *The Citizen* (Ottawa), Monday Dec. 16, B7.

Lasker, David (1985), "Field of Choice Narrows for Dome," *Canadian Building*, Nov/Dec, 19–23.

"The Skydome Retractable Roof System" (1988), *Engineering Digest*, Volume 35, Number 3, June, 24–28.

Buckeye Glass Company:
Chinese Culture and Negotiating Styles in the People's Republic of China

In November, 1988, Buckeye Glass sent a highly skilled team to Qinhuangdao, People's Republic of China to negotiate a joint venture for the manufacture of glassware. The team consisted of John Brickley, President; Bob Caines, Vice-President of Marketing; Steve Miller, Production Manager and Head Engineer. Brickley had carefully selected an interpreter, Lin Sida, who knew Mandarin Chinese, the dialect spoken in north China as he was concerned that a language barrier might arise. All of the members of the team had been with Buckeye Glass for at least 20 years, and had been rotated through the various departments in order to enable them to develop a broad perspective of the company and its strengths. Thus they were well qualified for this negotiating venture in the PRC.

Company Background

Buckeye Glass, headquartered in Columbus, Ohio, produced glassware, including wide and narrow mouth containers, and glass prescription ware. It had over 25,000 customers worldwide in diverse industries such as food processing, liquor, beer, wine, cosmetics, soft drinks, and proprietary and prescription drugs. Its ten-month worldwide sales in 1988 were $3.0 billion, and had plants in Europe, Asia, [and] North and South America, employing 44,000 people. Its earnings have been flat for the past 5 years and management was exploring new avenues for growth of sales and earnings. The plant being considered for construction in China would produce all types of glassware under the name of Buckeye, its brand name worldwide. It is known as a high quality producer and a leader in its field. It had only one plant in the Pacific Rim and thus could not serve these emerging markets well, and John Brickley was convinced that a plant in the PRC would give it a strategic position in this global market.

	Sales (Billion)	Profits (Million)
1988*	$3.0	$120
1987	$3.4	$138
1986	$3.0	$140
1985	$3.0	$136
1984	$2.8	$135

*10 months

Qinhuangdao

Qinhuangdao is a Chinese international port city in Northern China. Located on the Bohai Sea, it is only 277 kilometers (166 miles) northeast of Beijing and serves as the gateway to the capital as it has a large, modern harbor, which is ice and salt-free. The weather is milder than inland, and its beaches at Beidaihe attract thousands annually, including leading government officials from Beijing.

By 1988 Qinhuangdao had developed into an important economic center and was the glass capital of The People's Republic of China. It is one of 14 coastal cities opened to the outside world in 1984; and has a new economic and technical development site which has attracted foreign investors from the United States, Australia, and several other countries. There were 25 glass factories in the area producing laminated glass, thermal glass, medical glassware, fiberglass, and heat-absorbing glass. These companies have lateral economic cooperation and pool technologies, information and skilled personnel, thereby enhancing the quality and efficiency of production. The area is rich in quartz, a major ingredient in the manufacturing of glass.

Preliminaries. The Buckeye Glass team had flown for 26 hours and stayed overnight in Beijing at the Great Wall Hotel. The next morning they traveled by train for a 6 hour trip to Qinhuangdao. Enroute they discussed their plans and were anxious to meet the Chinese and begin negotiating as soon as possible.

When they arrived there, they were greeted warmly by their Chinese hosts and escorted to the Jinshan Hotel, expressly reserved for foreigners. They found to their surprise that their accommodations were comparable to those of first-class hotels in the United States. The rooms were complete with comfortable beds, baths, TV, and telephones. Wake-up service and

Source: This case was prepared by James A. Brunner of the University of Toledo as the basis for class discussion concerning the effects of Chinese customs and negotiations styles upon negotiations for a joint venture. © 1989. All rights reserved to the author and the North American Case Research Association. Permission to publish the case should be obtained from the author and the North American Case Research Association.

a dining room were available for meals, which were served in both Chinese and Western styles.

Pleased by their surroundings and encouraged by the congeniality of their hosts at dinner that night they retired; confident that the meeting scheduled for the next day would establish a beneficial working relationship with the Chinese. At 10 P.M. strains of Brahm's lullaby flowed from the intercom system, and the negotiators slept peacefully after their arduous journey as they began to adjust to their jet lag.

The Chinese arrived promptly at 9 a.m. The Chinese delegation was led by Tien Chao, mayor of Qinhuangdao and also the General Secretary of the Communist Party in this province. Thus he was responsible for making the final evaluation of the joint venture and its benefit for the PRC. The other Chinese respected his views and sought his approval before making their recommendations. Through their interpreter, he introduced Poh Jiwei, the Managing Director of the Xia Xian Glass Factory, the leading glass manufacturer in China. After formal introductions and an exchange of pleasantries, the group left for a tour of Xia Xian Glass Factory's manufacturing facilities. Tien Chao excused himself from the tour as he had other pressing governmental problems requiring his immediate attention.

Factory Tour. Arriving at the factory, the group was greeted by Pi Zhao, the Assistant Director, who escorted them on a tour of the facilities. The Americans were surprised by what awaited them. The floor of the factory was dirty, and there was a large number of glass container crates located haphazardly on the floor. Groups of employees were loitering, playing cards, conversing, and laughing, while others were engaged in various work activities. Surprised at the minimal level of activity in the plant, Brickley asked through their interpreter, Lin Sida, "Why aren't all these people working or are some of them on break?"

Poh Jiwei smiled and replied proudly, "Our plant has met its production quota for the year; but these men report in each day to be with their friends and do whatever work is planned for that day. You know, in China we provide jobs for all our people and unemployment is nonexistent. When we receive our new quota from the government, production will begin again at a higher level."

Brickley, still perplexed, replied, "Wouldn't it be more profitable to close down some of the production facilities and lay off at least some of the workers until the new quotas are announced and thereby increase the profits of the company?"

Poh Jiwei replied politely as he smiled, "In China, we do what is best for the workers in order to give them steady incomes. Our concern is more about the workers than the income of the factory."

Brickley, noting that some workers were arriving late, asked, "I've known that Chinese factories practice this 'iron rice bowl' concept whereby all workers are assured they will have jobs. But some of them are late in arriving for work. Aren't they expected to be on time?" Poh Jiwei smiled and replied, "Well, in the past we have not enforced your Western-style work ethic of being punctual, but we are beginning to change. But please understand that the middle-aged and elderly workers are hard to change and they resist this new approach. The younger workers, however, agree that punctuality should lead to increased productivity, and are willing to accept these changes. In fact we now give bonuses to those who exceed their quotas and stay on their jobs until closing time. You may be interested to know that our workers retire when they reach the age of 55, and we have only a few older workers in the factory."

As the tour progressed, Brickley continued to be amazed by the antiquated machinery in operation, but was startled when they came to an installation which had the latest container glass manufacturing technology. When he openly praised the equipment, Poh Jiwei smiled broadly and replied humbly to the surprise of the Americans, "Oh, our factory is very ill-equipped, with few modern machines unlike those you have in your country." Brickley, confused by Poh Jiwei's statement since they had just viewed a great deal of modern machinery, quickly assured Poh that the plant was indeed impressive and very well equipped.

Post Factory Tour Meeting. After the tour of the plant, the Buckeye executives were escorted to a conference room. They were invited to be seated at a table, and were served tea by their hosts. Pi Zhao thanked the Buckeye Team for visiting the plant and commented for five minutes upon their proposed relationship with Buckeye Glass. He elaborated upon the economic development plans of the People's Republic of China and noted that even though the government had not given top priority to glass container production he assured them it looked favorably upon the possibility of building a plant in Qinhuangdao for that purpose. He stressed the need for the development of a long term relationship and hoped those present could become 'old friends.' After elaborating further for twenty minutes, he sat down.

John Brickley immediately stood up and responded by expressing his sincere appreciation for the plant tour, and also his hope that a close relationship could be developed with the Chinese. He stressed how a glass manufacturing plant would be beneficial to the economic progress of the country as well as the living standards of the Chinese.

Sightseeing Tour. Tien Chao then proposed that after lunch they should tour Qinhuangdao and visit the eastern section of the Great Wall of China. He proudly stated that the sea end of the wall was in Qinhuangdao and at one time had been over 23,000 meters long, but that only 2300 meters of it still existed. He then announced, "We should visit other features of interest, such as the 'Old Dragon's Head' at the sea end of the wall, the park and, of course, the beach in Beidaihe."

The rest of the afternoon was, therefore, spent touring the area. A photographer went with the party to photograph the Americans at the various points of interest. Brickley was frustrated as he wanted to discuss the proposed joint venture. He attempted to conceal his impatience, and expressed interest in the special features of the region. They returned to the hotel and the Chinese joined them for dinner and left promptly at 8 p.m.

Initial Formal Meeting. The next morning, the Chinese delegation arrived promptly and escorted the Buckeye team to the hotel's meeting room. The Chinese delegation now consisted of twelve members including Poh Jiwei, Managing Director of Xia Xian Glass Factory, its plant manager, two assistant plant managers, several engineers, and the interpreter. The Chinese arranged themselves on one side of the table and the Buckeye Glass team seated opposite them. After they were served tea, Brickley rose, thanked the Chinese for inviting them, and described the services of his company.

Brickley then introduced Caines who elaborated for approximately 20 minutes upon the history of Buckeye Glass, its premier position in the worldwide market in the production of containers for a wide range of industries such as food, soft drinks, beer, cosmetics, and pharmaceuticals, and how profitable they had been internationally. He then turned to Steve Miller. Miller presented a slide presentation of the company's production and sales facilities, and a statistical review of sales and profits for the previous decade. He then elaborated upon the capabilities of Buckeye Glass. Brickley then rose and commented at length about its strong managerial team. He elaborated upon the integration of the marketing, finance and production activities at Buckeye Glass, which he explained had been highly effective in thrusting the company into a leading position in the global glass container industry.

He commented briefly upon his opinions concerning observations made the previous day in the factory, and noted that his company could assist the Chinese by introducing their production workers and managers to Western concepts of production and marketing. He emphasized the need to introduce Western management know-how and methods in the Xia Xian Glass Factory in order for it to serve effectively the needs of the Chinese people.

During his presentation, the Chinese seemed somewhat passive, but occasionally asked questions and probed for information. Brickley and the other members of the Buckeye Glass team carefully and patiently answered the questions raised. They also endeavored to sense the priorities of the Chinese concerning the various types of problems that they had and what they wanted the American team to do. In their discussions, it became evident that breakage was a major problem as the Chinese workers were not well trained in the use of the equipment. Further, they learned that Xia Xian's customers wanted different types of glass containers than were being produced in this plant, and that it had a sizable overaged inventory of these containers.

Further, the Chinese noted that their products were not meeting the quality specifications demanded by foreign buyers. Thus, it was evident that the quality control training program was essential. Poh Jiwei observed further that the corregated shipping containers for the glass products were inferior and oftentimes broke in shipment, which resulted in damaged ware.

As Brickley became aware of these problems, he couldn't decide the order in which the Chinese would prioritize them, and specifically, which Buckeye's services were considered to be the most important to the Chinese.

After the discussion had continued for three hours, Poh Jiwei suggested that they break for lunch; and that after lunch they should go on a sightseeing tour of Yanshan University, a new educational institution founded in the 1980s to train engineering and technical students in the latest scientific developments and technology. Poh Jiwei assured the Buckeye team that they would like to meet the next day to discuss the possibility of signing a letter of intent. The meeting then adjourned.

Letter of Intent Conference

The next morning, Pi Zhao and Poh Jiwei arrived with their interpreter and three engineers. They escorted the Buckeye Glass executives to the conference room. Through his interpreter, Poh Jiwei expressed his appreciation to the Americans for their informative presentation and announced that they were interested in signing a letter of intent. Poh Jiwei observed that the Xia Xian Glass Factory had inadequate equipment, and elaborated on a low level of skill possessed by the production workers as well as the managers. Brickley silently concurred with his observations concerning the workers, but he was surprised to hear this comment concerning the managers as some of them were present at the meeting. Further, Poh Jiwei expressed his admiration of the Buckeye Glass executives, acknowledging that the company was one of the leading glass manufacturers in the world, and that his company was humbly appreciative of the opportunity to join them in a joint venture. Brickley was amazed by this sense of humbleness as he didn't feel that they were as inferior as Poh Jiwei was suggesting.

Poh continued, "We feel that the time has arrived for us to sign a letter of intent and to express the general principles under which our venture will operate. Our objective is the modernization of the Xia Xian plant in Qinhuangdao and we propose that it be located in the new economic and technical development zone." He paused and then announced, "Further, Buckeye Glass will provide for the transfer of technology to improve the product's quality and performance, reduce production costs, and conserve energy and materials."

Brickley was silently pleased. On second thought, he was somewhat perplexed as the objectives proposed were very broad and outlined the general principles of the accord without spelling out the specific details. He was concerned that no specifics were mentioned about who was responsible for training the employees and managers, specifically what technology was involved and who was responsible for obtaining the raw materials and for marketing the output in China and the global markets. Nevertheless, he thanked Poh Jiwei and added, "I think it's important that we also include the

specific details of our mutual obligations in order to avoid any misunderstandings in the future."

Poh Jiwei smiled and replied, "We appreciate your concern, but it is not necessary to specify the particulars of the joint venture at this point. But we need to reach a general agreement on the principles in your letter of interest."

As the executives of Buckeye Glass were surprised at the Chinese proposed letter of intent, they began to fire questions concerning the specific details. Poh Jiwei again smiled and asserted, "The details can be worked out later, but first we must come to an agreement on general principles. We propose that we break for a period of time in order that you may have an opportunity to review our broad objectives. I propose that we meet again after lunch."

The meeting adjourned and the two groups went to separate meeting rooms. The Buckeye team met in Brickley's room and after pouring each a cup of tea, Brickley, exasperated, stated, "Well this certainly isn't what I expected. I thought we could reach some general agreement on the specific details. Evidently the Chinese are only interested in general principles. Frankly, I'm concerned we didn't specify the time period for the joint venture and the financial details. How much each of us is going to have to put up front is also up in the air. What products are to be produced? This is certainly different than any joint venture I've ever written in the United States. I propose that we come up with recommendations so that we can get this show on the road." Brickley noted further, "After listening to their monologue, I'm sure glad that I took notes, but I'm not certain what their priorities are. There is a lot we can bring to the table, but it would be helpful if we knew their priorities. I will press that issue after lunch."

Luncheon. At noon, Poh Jiwei and his team met Brickley and his associates and they went to the dining room. While the Chinese remained reserved and occasionally talked among themselves, the atmosphere was still friendly. After lunch they adjourned again to the conference room and Brickley stated their concern about the missing details and made some specific suggestions. Poh Jiwei commented, "I know we are old friends, but you are insisting upon being very specific about the details, and are not willing to agree only on the general principles. We regret this and don't understand why." Brickley's interpreter told him the Chinese felt he was behaving dishonorably and acted as though he did not trust the Chinese. Brickley feeling intimidated quickly responded, "I'm disappointed we can't agree. However, if it is not customary in China to be specific in a letter of agreement but only to reach agreement only on the general principles we will go along to demonstrate our sincerity. After we have signed it, I would like to give it to the press in order that my company may publicize it in the United States as it will be good publicity and will demonstrate Buckeye's interest in economic development in the People's Republic."

Poh Jiwei agreed, but asked that no dates be stated concerning when it was to commence, and that no mention be made of the investment that would be involved, nor the city in China in which it was to be located.

Brickley knew that the <u>Chinese had mixed feelings about publicity and preferred to maintain secrecy</u> in the negotiating process as they had a mistrust of publicity and perceived it as a form of pressure. Moreover, he sensed that they were concerned that their superiors might feel they were endeavoring to promote themselves. On the other hand, he thought that if he didn't publicize the agreement, the Chinese might be offended. He was aware that they might sense a violation of confidentiality if he revealed too much. It was a minor dilemma for him. Brickley paused, and then agreed to all of these stipulations with the exception that the city should be specified [because] it was known in the United States that his company had representatives in Qinhuangdao. Poh Jiwei agreed reluctantly.

The next day they met again and signed a joint agreement, which Brickley recognized was not binding on either parties, but at least served as a basis for commencing the substantive negotiations. He personally felt quite gratified with the progress made as the Chinese indicated that they were now willing to work out the specific details.

Formal Banquet. That evening the Chinese team escorted the Buckeye Glass representatives to a Chinese banquet to celebrate the signing of the letter of intent. Brickley was surprised to observe that placecards had been arranged on the tables in order to facilitate the seating arrangements. He was seated next to Tien Chao's left and the Chinese were interspersed among the Americans around two tables. When the first course consisting of braised prawns were served, the Chinese to the right of a Buckeye executive served him a portion of the prawns. While they were awaiting the second course, Poh Jiwei gave a speech lauding Sino-

American relations and the signing completed that afternoon. As he closed he offered a toast of Mao Tai wine to the Buckeye Glass team. Brickley, aware of the effect of Mao Tai which has a 40% alcoholic content, toasted cautiously.

Following this, in sequence, scallops fried in tomato sauce, sauteed conch, fillet of fish stir-fried, pork steak fried, crabmeat stir-fried, heart of rape with mushroom, and sea slugs were served. During each of these seven courses, the Chinese served the Americans saying, "Quing, Quing" ("please, please").

During the course of the two hour banquet, innumerable toasts were made by the Chinese and the Buckeye team reciprocated, oftentimes going from table to table to present toasts. Both teams used the white wine on the table for their toasts on these occasions rather than the Mao Tai. However when Poh Jiwei offered his toasts, Brickley followed protocol, and emptied the complete glass of wine, on the urging by Poh Jiwei, who proposed, "Ganbei" (bottoms-up).

During the dinner, the conversation naturally turned to the different cuisines of the various regions of the People's Republic of China. Miller asked facetiously if it was true that the Chinese in south China ate dog, snake and monkey brains. Poh Jiwei smiled broadly and replied affirmatively. Encouraged by Poh Jiwei's smile, Miller began joking about some of the other delicacies that appeared on the menu; such as heart of rape on mushrooms and the sea slugs. The Chinese apparently enjoyed this humorous approach as they were grinning and nodding their heads in response. Encouraged, the Americans began to tell Western jokes. Apparently, the atmosphere was friendly and relaxed.

Brickley, encouraged by this feeling of cordiality, sensed that the time was appropriate to again address the subject of the joint venture. Turning to Poh Jiwei, he said, "With our technology and investment Buckeye Glass can pull China from its backwardness and make it a world power." Poh Jiwei replied, "Yes, yes, Buckeye Glass is world leader, and a very powerful company from the United States. Xia Xian certainly must make use of a liaison with it."

Encouraged by Poh Jiwei's reply, Brickley continued, expounding upon the mutual benefit which this joint venture would provide both parties. He observed that Buckeye Glass could train the management of Xia Xian in moderate managerial techniques and assist them in training their workers to use Western technology. He noted further that their close contacts would enable Buckeye to establish a foothold in the Chinese market and become a major power in the glass industry in the Pacific Basin countries.

While the guests were eating the stir-fried crabmeat course, Tien Chao rose and commented on the close ties being established with Buckeye Glass. He then presented Brickley a gift of two Chinese exercise balls, which he stated had been in use in China since the 14th Century and were used to stimulate important acupressure points below the wrist. He then demonstrated that they emitted soft chiming sounds in two different pitches to calm the nerves and soothe the soul. Tien Chao then gave Brickley a 4' × 6' tapestry of the Great Wall. Brickley thanked him profusely, but was embarrassed as he had no gifts to reciprocate this show of friendship and cordial relations.

After the pastry had been served, the next course consisted of soup, rice and fruit. The Americans found the soup to be delicious and each took two servings of the rice as they especially enjoyed it. Tien Chao listened politely as Brickley sipped his tea. After a third cup, Tien Chao rose and thanked the Buckeye executives for attending the dinner. The hosts escorted them back to their room and quickly departed.

Political and Economic Environment

That night, Brickley reflected on the economic and political environment of China in order to gain a broader perspective. He was aware that the PRC had a population of over a billion, and that its economic system was being developed aggressively by the government. He noted that labor was inexpensive, and quite abundant without any problem of labor strikes. Further, he was aware that although raw materials and other supplies were less costly than in some countries, there were some difficulties in their procurement. He had heard that in the PRC the availability of materials and supplies was oftentimes dependent upon "connections" which one had with others. These relationships in China were referred to as guanxi and Brickley was aware that if one formed such ties, they signified close bonding. This permitted either party to call upon the other for any favors if they were within the power of a guanxi member to grant and he would be obligated to do so. Further he knew that guanxi ties were also important for getting things done when working with the governmental bureaucracy as the PRC does not have an institutionalized legal system. Therefore, getting favorable interpretations by bureaucrats was dependent largely upon whom one knew and who had guanxi with whom.

Moreover, he noted that the PRC had a culture which traditionally shunned legal considerations and stressed rather the ethical and moral principles of everyday living; and that formal agreements were based more upon moral obligations than the law. He also recognized that although the People's Republic was a socialist country it suffered from political instability, and the recent "open door" policy was primarily the endeavor of their senior leader Deng Xiaoping. Brickley knew that in November, 1983, Deng had launched a movement to put his mark on China's new emerging economic development. He had devised [a] five year plan to purge the Communist party's forty million members of one million leftists, most of whom were ill educated. This had been accomplished through a reedification program of self-criticism and prescribed study. Deng endeavored to clear the way for his proteges to rise to positions of power in order to ensure continuation of its economic, political and open door policies.

In October, 1987, Zhao Ziyang became the party's General Secretary succeeding Deng and a sixth five year plan was announced. Deng, however, remained a paramount figure in the decision making process and was encouraging some capitalistic practices to be adopted in China, such as using quotas and holding managers accountable for the profitability of their factories.

In general, China's semi-closed economy was modified to an open economy with international exchanges encouraged. In moving toward a market mechanism for setting prices, however, inflation surged in 1988 to an unofficial but acknowledged annual rate of nearly 50% in cities. There was evidence that government officials were capitalizing on entrepreneurism by accepting bribes and engaging in other unsavory activities. The economy was clearly overheated and industrial output had risen 7% in the first half, and investment in capital construction had increased 14%. China's inefficient factories were unable to keep up with the demand for goods and thereby added to the inflationary pressures. Demand for consumer goods was far outstripping supply and black market activities were thriving with inflationary price rises as a consequence.

The government attempted to slow the economy by controlling the money supply, but this had proven to be ineffective as the money supply rose 30% in the first five months of 1988. Finally, in order to get better control on the economy and slow down the inflationary pressures, the state council in October 1988 announced that as of December 1, it would reduce investment in a variety of nonessential industries, ranging from textiles processing to consumer electronics and plastics. However this would not apply to projects involving foreigners or those in priority areas such as energy and transportation. It was anticipated that the rollback would be huge, and that Beijing would cut back capital investment in 1989 by 50 billion Chinese yuan (13.5 billion dollars). Fortunately for Buckeye Glass, this would not pertain to glass containers but rather involved such products as cotton textiles, rubber goods, tractors, television sets, and those which consumed too much energy such as irons, vacuum cleaners and rice cookers. The crux of the problem was that the Chinese enterprises were state owned and the managers not inclined to think in terms of economic efficiency.

Substantive Negotiations. Negotiations commenced promptly the next day and continued for two days. Both teams had copies of the Law of the People's Republic of China on Joint Ventures. On occasion, the Chinese would engage in detailed questioning about topics which apparently were not too significant. Brickley sensed that this stalling tactic was used to gain time to enable the Chinese to elicit the comments of their superiors concerning various phases of the contract. He observed that when points requiring clarification arose, the Chinese during informal breaks would gather around the Buckeye Glass interpreter in order to attempt to persuade her to get concessions for the Chinese or to clarify Buckeye's proposals. Further, when the Americans expressed their views on a point under negotiation, Poh Jiwei would say, "We'll take note of your position," but then go on to the next issue under discussion. Brickley sensed that this indicated that the Chinese did not agree, but wished to avoid confrontations.

He also noted that the Chinese were extremely sensitive when pricing was being discussed and were apparently concerned that they might be given unfavorable treatment or [were] being cheated. From his interpreter, Brickley learned that this was true and that the Chinese were apprehensive that their superior would deal with them harshly if favorable terms were not obtained. Brickley also noted that in order to gain concessions from the Chinese, it was necessary to give one in return, thereby engaging in a *face*-saving action.

American Hosted Dinner. That evening, the Buckeye Glass executive hosted a dinner for the Chinese. The menu was simpler than the Chinese banquet as the Buckeye executives felt that the Chinese meal was too exotic for their tastes and digestion. Speeches were again given by Poh Jiwei and Brickley and frequent toasts were offered. Miller again told some Western jokes accompanied by friendly back slapping. The Buckeye executives attempted to lighten the ongoing formal conversation by steering it to familiar topics, such as the families of the Chinese, personal tastes and ideas, and sexual patterns in China. The Chinese responded with much smiling and laughter even though their replies to the questioning were vague.

Proposed Joint Venture Contract

After a long week-end during which the Americans and Chinese separately developed proposals for the joint venture, the Buckeye team were the first to present their terms for negotiators. Brickley submitted the financial requirements as he and his team perceived them (Exhibit 1) and their terms for the joint venture (Exhibit 2).

Negotiations Concluded. As Brickley was willing to negotiate and make concessions, he was puzzled that the Chinese did not present their terms. He commented on the key issues of the joint venture agreement and the Chinese listened intently. As they were passive and remained silent, Brickley couldn't tell whether they agreed or not with his proposal, and the team was perplexed about how to cope with these periods of silence. Poh Jiwei thanked him and proposed they continue their discussions at 2 p.m. that afternoon. He was most concerned about the confidentiality transfer of technology in China as he knew there were no comprehensive commercial laws to protect his company, and China did not have trade secret laws. He had been told that the Chinese, on occasion, take technology and copy it. Moreover, he was aware margins initially would be nonexistent for goods sold on the world markets, and the joint venture would undoubtedly incur losses until the company could become more efficient.

In the afternoon session, the Chinese were cordial but remained passive. Poh Jiwei observed, "We have reviewed your proposal and can agree on most of its provisions. However, the value placed on the technology is far greater than we believe can be justified. As you have already paid for its development, we insist that in the spirit of friendship, a much lower figure be used. Further, we believe that Buckeye Glass should contribute all of the money for the investment in in-

EXHIBIT 1 ▪ *Proposed Joint Venture: Buckeye Glass Company Financial Requirements (US $000)*

First Year Capital			Loan from Bank of China	$200
Working Capital	$898		Long-term debt	400
Installations and Equipment	490		Total Liabilities	600
New $450			Net Worth:	
Old 40			First 2-year loss	($200)
Factory	800		Initial Capital	2338
Land				
Technology	550			
TOTAL	$2738		TOTAL	$2738

Partners' Investments:

Xia Xian Glass Company	55%		Buckeye Glass	
Factory	$400		Factory	$400
Installations and Equipment	490		Technology	550
New 450			Cash/Equivalent	102
Old 40				
Cash/Equivalent	396			
TOTAL	$1286		TOTAL	$1052

stallations and equipment as we are providing labor at a considerably lower level than can be obtained elsewhere. We will cover the cost of the factory in our investment. We believe that 80% of the goods should be sold in the export market. Before proceeding, we wish to resolve these issues."

Brickley then endeavored to explain that although his company had already invested in the glass technology, that on world markets it would be valued at this level. Further, he was quite puzzled by the large percentage of output which was to be destined for the export market as he had assumed the Chinese were interested in raising the standards of living of the people in the PRC. Obviously the need for foreign hard currency was more paramount. Discussion continued for another hour, at which time Poh Jiwei then proposed they adjourn and meet the next morning.

Xia Xian's Proposal

At the morning meeting Poh Jiwei presented Xia Xian's proposal. Buckeye Glass was to invest 55% of the capital in the form of cash, installations, and technology. He specified that the technology must be advanced, lead to improved product quality and performance, and contribute to export expansion.

Brickley thereupon assured him that the technology proposed would do all these things, but insisted that the most advanced technology would not be appropriate at this time in China. He agreed that the value of the property in the buildings should be fixed by the People's government of Qinhuangdao according to a relative industry index. When Brickley inquired concerning the availability of silica and other raw materials for this project the Chinese were evasive, but assured him their "connections" [would] be able to find the necessary materials at reasonable prices.

To relieve some of the tension, Mr. Brickley and his team avoided the topics about which the two groups were in most disagreement; and again emphasized the great mutual benefits which would result from this venture. The afternoon meeting ended well. There were still some disagreements remaining. However, much ground had been covered. The remaining differences were considered by the Buckeye Glass negotiators to be minor, and they agreed to go back over them for the discussion on the next day, but Brickley was becoming impatient as he thought about the considerable investment his company had made in order to conduct these negotiations in Qinhuangdao. Buckeye had already committed over $25,000 for lodging, food, transportation and other expenses, and at least another million could be required for the equity capital.

EXHIBIT 2 ▪ *Proposed Joint Venture*

NAME: BUCKEYE GLASS COMPANY

CAPITAL CONTRIBUTIONS: 55% of the capital for the venture should be provided by the Xia Xian Glass Factory and 25% by the Buckeye Glass Company. In meeting this requirement, the Chinese were to obtain the right to use a site in the Qinhuangdao Economic Development Zone. It was agreed that the joint venture should rent the property from the Chinese government. Buckeye Glass was to invest $400,000 in the building and installations.

TRAINING: Buckeye Glass was also to provide for training of the joint venture's managers and engineers in the United States for a period of three months.

MARKETING: Buckeye Glass shall be the sole sales agent in the world market and provide for the maximum market penetration by its products internally in China and in the Pacific Basin countries, with the objective of 40% being sold domestically and the remaining 60% in the export market.

PRICING: The prices established in the world market would provide a 20% after tax return on the total investment of each party to the contract.

TECHNOLOGY: Technology provided by Buckeye Glass shall comply with the technology transfer regulations of the People's Republic of China and provide for the improvement of product quality and performance, reduce production costs, and increase foreign revenues. The value of the technology in the first year shall be $550,000.

IMPORTED MATERIALS: All silica and related production materials imported will not be subject to the standard 12% import duty if used for exported products, but a duty will be applied to those used for glassware produced for domestic sales. An 18% tax value added nature on domestic sales shall be levied. Sales in the world market shall provide a 20% after-tax return on the total investment of each party to the contract.

WORK FORCE: The work force shall consist of the normal staff of production workers and include staff employees including engineers, office workers and managers. The joint venture shall not hire additional workers for the factory or office workers without the approval of the Board of Directors.

The initial work force for the plant shall be limited to 200 factory workers and 50 service employees in the offices, including the managers.

WAGE COMPENSATION: The direct salary and benefits for the workers shall be determined by the Chinese government. The range for factory workers in the first year will be for 1200 Yuan and in the second year 1800 Yuan and will be for 2,000 hours annually.

The annual wage rate for the production workers will include direct and fringe benefits. The wage rate will be modified after the first year in conformity with those paid in other Chinese corporations for production workers by the Board of Directors.

TECHNOLOGY CONFIDENTIALITY: The joint venture partners will be obliged to maintain confidentiality of the technology and shall be required during the life of the joint venture and beyond. Damages for the breach of contract will be pursuant to the Foreign Economic Contract Law and recoverable against a contract transferee who discloses the confidential information.

EXPANSION: The joint venture should secure from the Chinese government an additional ten acres for expansion of this manufacturing facility.

BOARD OF DIRECTORS: The management of the joint venture shall consist of seven members of a Board of Directors, 4 of whom will be appointed by the Chinese and 3 by the Buckeye Glass Company. The board will follow modern management principles and establish a five-year marketing and production plan. A planning budget shall be developed for the same period of time. It will be the responsibility of the joint venture board to specify the types and numbers of workers and managers for the venture.

TAXATION: With approval of the tax authorities the joint venture may be exempt from taxation for the first two profitable making years and granted a 50 per cent tax reduction for the following five years. A profit making year shall be defined as the year in which a joint venture realizes profits after the accumulated operating losses from prior years have been deducted. Further, as this joint venture is in a Special Investment Zone, the tax rate applicable to the enterprise shall be 15%, and no withholding tax on repatriated profits shall be levied.

CURRENCY: This joint venture will use Reminbi (RMB) to calculate its income and tax liabilities. It may maintain its accounting records and books in dollars.

The next morning the negotiators met again and to Brickley's dismay, the Chinese were adamant and refused to modify their terms. However, Poh Jiwei proposed that production be expanded to include containers for the wine and soft drink industries rather than only for food. This astounded Brickley as these industries were expanding rapidly and naturally he wanted to be involved in the early phase of development of these markets. He knew that the Chinese had strong loyalty to their initial suppliers and it was essential to establish these relationships before other foreign competitors entered the Chinese market. "What do we do now to break this impasse?" he agonized to his team. "What concessions can we make to enable the Chinese to save *face*—and alter this position?"

Alternatives

Brickley was aware that any joint agreement proposal would be subject to review by not only the Chinese government but also his legal department. At least another year would be required to formalize the agreement. His team had been in China for two weeks and the potential for profit in the long run was in the millions after the shakedown period in the first two years. He perceived several options at this point. They could drop the idea and move on to more promising ventures in the short run, make some concessions, bring in an agent who resided on a permanent basis in Beijing who had strong Chinese ties as he was a successful Chinese negotiator, they could offer to invite the Chinese to come to America as Buckeye's guests in order to visit the corporate plant and observe the technology and training facilities, or they could set a date for departure with the objective of forcing the Chinese to move off dead center and reach an agreement on the terms. He murmured to himself, "Patience, John, getting a joint venture signed in the PRC is like building Rome—it takes longer than a day! Freight trains move faster than negotiations in the PRC!"

Appendix 1:
Chinese Culture and Negotiating Styles

A. Face. Paramount to an understanding of Chinese behavior in relationships is an understanding of *face* behavior. In China, *face* has two forms: *lien* and *mien-tzu*. *Lien* refers to one's moral character and is a person's most precious possession. Without it, one cannot function in society. It is earned by fulfilling one's duties and other obligations. *Mien-tzu* refers to a person's reputation or prestige and is based on personal accomplishments, political status or bureaucratic power. It also refers to one's ability to deal smoothly with people face-to-face. *Face* enhancement can be attained by acts of generosity in terms of time or gifts, or praise of others.

Face is the cooperative manner in which people behave toward one another in order to avoid loss of self-respect or prestige by either party. While the concept of *face* is often a fiction in practice, it retains its importance in actual dealings. For example, given a situation where two people are bargaining with each other, one must "win" and the other must "lose." Each side expects that the other will consider *face* in the transaction. In reality, both sides know at the end who has won and who has lost, but the winner makes token concessions to save the loser's *face*. This is important in that it allows the loser to "win" in that he/she has been respected by the other, the winning party. Without the saving of *face*, the loser will be justly offended and avoid dealing with the winner in the future. This avoidance reaction carries with it obvious consequences and hinders any potential ongoing business relationship.

Another aspect of *face* is similar to the Western concept of "being a good sport," or "being a good winner." Modesty over one's own achievement and appreciation of the loser's skill and effort are central to saving *face*. *Face* most often requires little effort but merely an attention to courtesy in relationships with others, yet will have a great positive effect upon the recipient. If lost, *face* will have a negative effect; which, if shown by the loser, results in still further loss of *face*. With the exception of a show of controlled anger by a person in authority, such as by a policeman, loss of self-control, sulking, and displays of anger or frustration create further loss of *face* rather than drawing respect or conciliation.

Once *face* has been lost, the loser will prefer to avoid the winner and ignore the *face*-losing incident as though it never occurred. In circumstance where the two parties must continue a relationship, the loser will return to formal and polite etiquette, pretending that the incident had not occurred. The other party should accommodate the loser's preference and not refer again to the incident. *Face* involves a high degree of self-control, social consciousness, and concern for others.

B. Smiling and Laughter. Laughter and smiling in Chinese culture represent the universal reaction to pleasure and humor. In addition, they are also a common response to negative occurrences, such as death and other misfortunes. When embarrassed or in the wrong, the Chinese frequently respond with laughter or smiling which will persist if another person continues to speak of an embarrassing topic or does not ignore the wrong. Westerners are often confused and shocked by this behavior, which is alien to them. It is important to remember that smiling and laughter in the above situations are not exhibitions of glee, but are rather a part of the concept of *face* when used in response to a negative or unpleasant situation.

C. *Guanxi:* **The Value of an Ongoing Relationship.**

Guanxi is the word that describes the intricate, pervasive network of personal relations which every Chinese cultivates with energy, subtlety and imagination. *Guanxi* is the currency of getting things done and getting ahead in Chinese society. *Guanxi* is a relationship between two people containing implicit mutual obligation, assurances and intimacy, and is the perceived value of an ongoing relationship and its future possibilities that typically govern Chinese attitudes toward long-term business. If a relationship of trust and mutual benefit is developed, an excellent foundation will be built to future business with the Chinese. *Guanxi* ties are also helpful in dealing with the Chinese bureaucracy as personal interpretations are used in lieu of legal interpretations.

Due to cultural differences and language barriers, the visitors to China are not in a position to cultivate *guanxi* with the depth possible between two Chinese. Regardless, *guanxi* is an important aspect of interrelations in China and deserves attention so that good friendly relations may be developed. These "connections" are essential to get things accomplished.

D. Formal and Informal Relations.

At present it is likely that the majority of social contacts foreigners have with the Chinese are on a more formal than informal level. Informality in China relates not to social pretension or artifice, but to the concept of *face*. Great attention is paid to observance of formal, or social behavior and corresponding norms. The social level is the level of form and proper etiquette where *face* is far more important than fact. It is considered both gauche and rude to allow one's personal feelings and opinions to surface here to the detriment of the social ambience. It is much more important to compliment a person or to avoid an embarrassing or sensitive subject than it is to express an honest opinion if honesty is at the ex-

pense of another's feelings. Directness, honesty, and individualism that run counter to social conventions and basic considerations of politeness have no place on the social level; emotions and private relationships tend to be kept private in Chinese society.

E. Chinese Etiquette for Social Functions.

Ceremonies and rules of ceremony have traditionally held a place of great importance in Chinese culture. Confucianism perpetuated and strengthened these traditions by providing the public with an identity, mask, or persona with which a person is best equipped to deal with the world with a minimum of friction. Confucianism consists of broad rules of conduct evolved to aid and guide interpersonal relations. Confucius assembled all the details of etiquette practiced at the courts of the feudal lords during the period c. 551–479 B.C. These rules of etiquette are called the *li* and have long since become a complete way of life for the Chinese.

The *li* may appear overly formalistic to Westerners at first glance. Upon closer inspection it is apparent that the rules of etiquette play a very important role in regulating interpersonal relations. Some basic rules of behavior are:

- A host should always escort a guest out to his car or other mode of transportation and watch until guest is out of sight.
- Physical expression is minimal by Western standards. A handshake is polite, but backslapping and other enthusiastic grasping is a source of embarrassment.
- At cultural functions and other performances, audience approval of performers is often subdued by American standards. Although the accepted manner of expressing approval varies between functions and age groups, applause is often polite, rather than roaring and "bravo"-like cheers.
- A person should keep control over his temper at all times.
- One should avoid blunt, direct, or abrupt discussion, particularly when the subject is awkward; delicate hints are often used to broach such a topic.
- It is a sign of respect to allow another to take the seat of honor (left of host), or to be asked to proceed through a door first.
- The serving of tea often signals the end of an interview or meeting. However, it is also served during extended meetings to quench the thirst of the negotiators.

—— **Part Three** ——

DESIGNING THE SALES ORGANIZATION

The two chapters in Part Three discuss sales organization design issues. Chapter 7 investigates different approaches for organizing the activities of sales managers and salespeople. The key concepts of specialization, centralization, span of control versus management levels, and line versus staff positions are emphasized as the basic elements of sales organization structure. Special attention is directed toward the increasingly important area of major account management.

Chapter 8 continues the sales organization discussion by addressing issues related to allocating selling effort to accounts, determining the appropriate salesforce size, and designing sales territories. The key considerations in each of these areas are discussed, and different decision-making approaches are presented.

Organizing the Activities of Sales Managers and Salespeople

RESTRUCTURING THE SALES ORGANIZATION: DIGITAL EQUIPMENT CORP.   Digital Equipment Corp. (DEC) is the number two computer maker in the United States, with 1989 sales of $12.7 billion. However, DEC has been losing market share and has posted several quarters of lackluster earnings. The company is trying to improve performance by introducing an array of new products targeted to the specific needs of specific industries. Implementing this strategy successfully requires a restructuring of the DEC sales organization.

Currently, DEC employs over 3,500 salespeople organized by geographic area. These salespeople are responsible for all accounts located in their geographic area and are supervised by area sales managers. The new sales organization structure replaces the geographic orientation with an industry orientation to focus selling effort more directly to specific customer needs.

DEC has targeted 27 key industries consisting of some 12,000 companies at 30,000 locations. Salespeople and sales managers are being organized according to these industries rather than the previous geographic areas. For example, area sales managers have been converted to national sales managers for targeted industries. Thus, the Boston sales manager may now be the sales manager for the electronics industry. These organizational changes are intended to change the perspective of salespeople and sales managers from serving geographic areas to satisfying the needs of customers in specific industries.

In addition to the industry-specialized regular salesforce, DEC has a major account program for its 200 top accounts. Corporate account managers are assigned to these top accounts and are responsible for the entire relationship between DEC and the account worldwide. These corporate account managers must utilize all of DEC's international resources to serve the top accounts.

As a way to coordinate the activities of an industry-specialized salesforce and major account program, DEC has developed a network-based personal computer system called Easynet. Easynet links all sales, marketing, and service personnel in 500 offices in 33 countries. DEC sales managers and salespeople can access the system from their offices, from customer sites, or at home. Over 50 sales and marketing programs and 100 utility-type programs are available on the Easynet network.

Source: Thayer C. Taylor, "DEC Gets Its House in Order," *Sales and Marketing Management*, July 1990, 59–66.

— Chapter 7 —

Learning Objectives

After completing this chapter, you should be able to

1 *Define the concepts of specialization, centralization, span of control versus management levels, and line versus staff positions.*

2 *Describe the different ways that salesforces might be specialized.*

3 *Evaluate the advantages and disadvantages of different sales organization structures.*

4 *Name the important considerations in organizing major account management programs.*

5 *Explain how one determines the appropriate sales organization structure for a given selling situation.*

Chapters 5 and 6 discussed the close relationships between corporate, business, marketing, and sales strategies. The different strategic levels must be consistent and integrated to be effective. Strategic changes at one organizational level typically require strategic changes at other organizational levels.

The development of effective strategies is one thing, successfully implementing them another.[1] In one sense, the remainder of this book is concerned with the development and management of a sales organization to implement organizational strategies successfully. This chapter begins the journey into successful implementation by investigating the key decisions required in developing a sales organization structure.

The DEC example in the opening vignette illustrates the close link between organizational strategy and sales organization structure. As DEC changed its strategic focus to developing new products to satisfy the needs of specific industries, the sales organization structure had to be revised. A geographically oriented sales organization could not implement the new strategic focus successfully. An industry-oriented sales organization was needed to satisfy the needs of customers in different industries. Strategic changes almost always require adjustments in sales organization structure.

Our coverage of sales organization structure begins with discussing the basic concepts underlying all sales organization structures. Situational factors that should be considered in making decisions on sales organization structure are then examined. The chapter concludes by presenting and analyzing several different sales organization structures, with special attention to major account organizations.

Sales Organization Concepts

The basic problem in sales organization structure can be presented in very simple terms. The corporate, business, marketing, and sales strategies developed by a firm prescribe specific activities that must be performed by salespeople for these strategies to be successful. Sales managers are also needed to recruit, select, train, motivate, supervise, evaluate, and control salespeople. In essence, the firm has salespeople and sales managers that must engage in a variety of activities for the firm to perform successfully. A sales organization structure must be developed to help salespeople and sales managers perform the required activities in an effective and efficient manner. This structure provides a framework for sales organization operations by indicating what specific activities are performed by whom in the sales organization. The sales organization structure is the vehicle through which strategic plans are translated into selling operations in the marketplace.

The important role of a sales organization structure for a firm has been described as follows:

> The role of organization in sales has been compared to that of the skeleton in the human body; it provides a framework within which normal functions must take place. There is, however, a degree of uniformity in the human skeleton that does not characterize the sales organization. Each firm has its own objectives and problems, and the structure of the sales organization reflects this diversity.[2]

Developing a sales organization structure is difficult. Many different types of structures might be used, and many variations are possible within each basic type.

FIGURE 7.1 ▪ *Salesforce Specialization Continuum*

There is a broad range of alternatives for specializing salesforce activities.

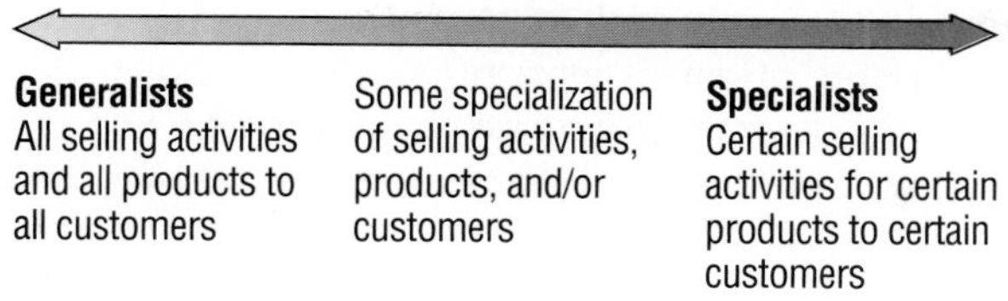

Generalists
All selling activities
and all products to
all customers

Some specialization
of selling activities,
products, and/or
customers

Specialists
Certain selling
activities for certain
products to certain
customers

Often the resultant structure is extremely complex with many boxes and arrows. The basic concepts involved are specialization, centralization, span of control versus management levels, and line versus staff positions.[3]

Specialization

Our earlier discussion suggested that a sales organization structure must ensure that all required selling and management activities are performed. In the simplest case, each salesperson could perform all selling tasks, and each sales manager could perform all management activities. Most sales organizations, however, are too complex for this structure and require instead some degree of **specialization,** in which certain individuals concentrate on performing some of the required activities to the exclusion of other tasks. Thus, certain salespeople might sell only certain products or call on certain customers. Some sales managers might concentrate on training, others on planning. The basic idea behind specialization is that by concentrating on a limited number of activities, individuals can become experts on those tasks, leading to better performance for the entire organization.

A useful way to view salesforce specialization is from the perspective of the continuum presented in Figure 7.1. At one extreme salespeople act as generalists, performing all selling activities for all of the company's products to all types of customers. Moving toward the right of the continuum, salespeople begin to specialize by performing only certain selling tasks, selling only certain types of products, or calling on only specific types of accounts. The old DEC sales organization would be located at the generalist end of the continuum. The new DEC sales organization would be located more toward the specialist end, since salespeople and sales managers now specialize by type of industry.

Centralization

An important characteristic of the management structure within a sales organization is its degree of **centralization**—that is, the degree to which important decisions and tasks are performed at higher levels in the management hierarchy. A centralized structure is one where authority and responsibility are placed at higher management levels. An organization becomes more decentralized as tasks become the responsibility of lower-level managers. Centralization is a relative concept in that no organization is totally centralized or totally decentralized. Organizations typically centralize some activities and decentralize others. However, most organizations tend to have a centralized or decentralized orientation.

Changing to a more centralized management structure is one way to help integrate the activities of specialized units. A decentralized structure provides less integration capability but promotes more responsive decision making and is usually preferable when there is little salesforce specialization. For example, Herman Miller markets office furniture to different customer types. The salesforce was organized by geographic area. The company added more managers at the sales director and sales district levels. The purpose of these changes was to "decentralize the decision making so you get ownership and accountability in the field."[4] Thus, the centralization and specialization decisions are interrelated and must be considered together in designing a sales organization structure.

Span of Control versus Management Levels

Span of control refers to the number of individuals that report to each sales manager. The larger the span of control, the more subordinates a sales manager must supervise. **Management levels** define the number of different hierarchical levels of sales management within the organization. Typically, span of control is inversely related to the number of sales management levels. This relationship is illustrated in Figure 7.2.

In the flat sales organization structure, there are relatively few sales management levels, with each sales manager having a relatively large span of control. Conversely, in the tall structure, there are more sales management levels and smaller spans of control. Flat organization structures tend to be used to achieve decentralization, while tall structures are more appropriate for centralized organizations. The span of control also tends to increase at lower sales management levels. Thus, as one moves down the organization chart from national sales manager to regional sales manager to district sales manager, the number of individuals to be supervised directly increases.

Line versus Staff Positions

Sales management positions can be differentiated as to line or staff positions. **Line sales management** positions are part of the direct management hierarchy within the sales organization. Line sales managers have direct responsibility for a certain number of subordinates and report directly to management at the next highest level in the sales organization. These managers are directly involved in the sales-generating activities of the firm and may perform any number of sales management activities. **Staff sales management** positions, on the other hand, are not in the direct chain of command in the sales organization structure. Instead, those in staff positions do not directly manage people, but they are responsible for certain functions (e.g., recruiting and selecting, training, etc.) and are not directly involved in sales-generating activities. Staff sales management positions are more specialized than line sales management positions.

A comparison of line and staff sales management positions is presented in Figure 7.3. The regional and district sales managers all operate in line positions. The district sales managers directly manage the field salesforce and report to a

FIGURE 7.2 ▪ *Span of Control versus Management Levels*

The flat sales organization has only two sales management levels, giving the national sales manager a span of control of 5. The tall sales organization has three sales management levels, giving the national sales manager a span of control of only 2.

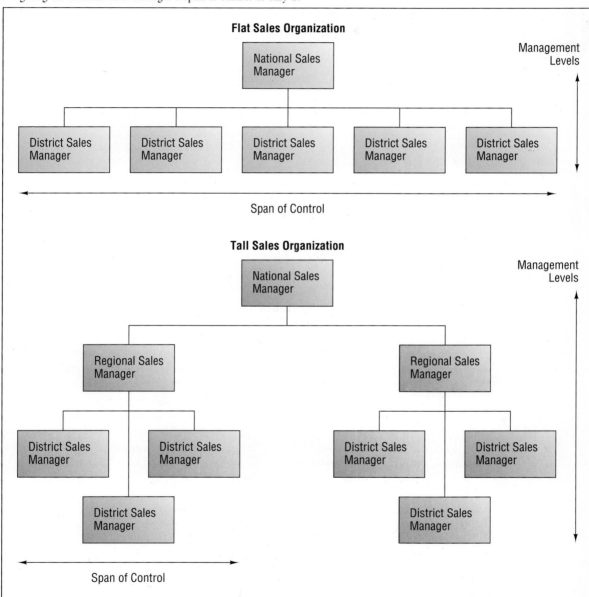

FIGURE 7.3 ▪ *Line versus Staff Positions*

The national, regional, and district sales managers occupy line positions, while the sales training managers represent staff positions.

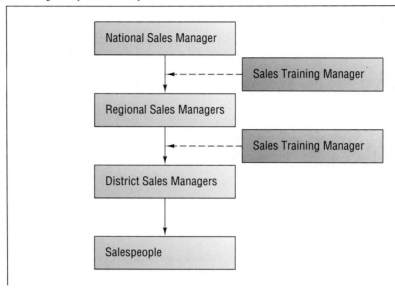

specific regional sales manager. The regional sales managers manage the district sales managers and report to the national sales manager. Two staff positions are represented in the figure. These training managers are located at both the national and regional levels and are responsible for sales training programs at each level. The use of staff positions results in more specialization of sales management activities. Staff managers specialize in certain sales management activities.

In sum, designing the sales organization is an extremely important and complex task. Decisions concerning the appropriate specialization, centralization, span of control versus management levels, and line versus staff positions are difficult. These decisions should be based on evaluations of certain characteristics of each selling situation.

Selling Situation Contingencies

Determining the appropriate type of sales organization structure is as difficult as it is important. There is no one best way to organize a salesforce. The appropriate organization structure depends or is contingent upon the characteristics of the selling situation. As a selling situation changes, the type of sales organization structure may also need to change. The DEC reorganization provides a good illustration of the way one firm altered its sales organization in response to changes in business and marketing strategies.

One of the key decisions in sales organization design relates to specialization. Two basic questions must be addressed:

EXHIBIT 7.1 ▪ *Selling-Situation Factors and Organizational Structure*

Organization Structure	Environmental Characteristic	Task Performance	Performance Objective
Specialization	High environmental uncertainty	Nonroutine	Adaptiveness
Centralization	Low environmental uncertainty	Repetitive	Effectiveness

Source: Robert W. Ruekert, Orville C. Walker, Jr., and Kenneth J. Roering, "The Organization of Marketing Activities: A Contingency Theory of Structure and Performance," *Journal of Marketing*, Winter 1985, 20–21.

1. Should the salesforce be specialized or not?
2. If the salesforce should be specialized, what type of specialization is most appropriate?

The decision on specialization hinges on the relative importance to the firm of selling skill versus selling effort. There is some empirical support for the notion that a generalized salesforce should be used when selling effort is more important than selling skill and a specialized one for the reverse case.[5] Thus, if sales management wants to emphasize the amount of selling contact, a generalized salesforce should be used. If sales management wants to focus on specific skills within each selling contact, then a specialized salesforce should be used. Obviously, there must be some balance between selling effort and selling skill in all situations. But sales management can skew this balance toward selling effort or selling skill by employing a generalized or specialized salesforce.

Research results also suggest that environmental characteristics, task characteristics, and performance objectives are important considerations in sales organization design. Some guidelines for sales organization structure and these selling situation factors are presented in Exhibit 7.1. This exhibit suggests that a specialized structure is best when there is a high level of environmental uncertainty, when salespeople and sales managers must perform creative and nonroutine activities, and when adaptability is critical to achieving performance objectives. Centralization is most appropriate when environmental uncertainty is low, sales organization activities are routine and repetitive, and the performance emphasis is on effectiveness.

Two of the most important factors in determining the appropriate type of specialization are the similarity of customer needs and the complexity of products offered by the firm. Figure 7.4 illustrates how these factors can be used to suggest the appropriate type of specialization. For example, when the firm has a simple product offering, but customers have different needs, a market-specialized salesforce is recommended. If, however, customers have similar needs and the firm sells a complex range of products, then a product-specialized salesforce is more appropriate.

Although these types of general guidelines are useful, sales managers need to perform more detailed analyses before deciding on the type of specialization for

FIGURE 7.4 ■ *Customer and Product Determinants of Salesforce Specialization*

Analysis of the similarity of customer needs and the complexity of a firm's product offering can provide general guidelines for determining the appropriate type of salesforce specialization.

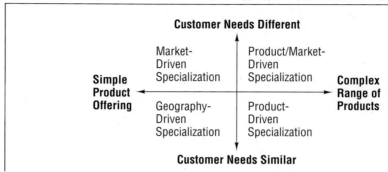

Source: David W. Cravens, *Strategic Marketing* (Homewood, Ill.: Irwin, 1991), 541.

their sales organization. One suggested approach is to compare the different alternatives against the criteria of affordability and payout, coverage and credibility, and flexibility.[6] For example, a $100 million manufacturer of numerically controlled machine tools used these criteria to examine alternative types of specialization. The analysis for the affordability and payout criteria are summarized in Exhibit 7.2.

This analysis suggests that when comparing the expected gross margin and the direct costs associated with each option, the major account specialization promises the highest net payout. However, both the product and market specialization options promise higher net payouts than the generalist option. This type of result is typical, since it almost always costs more to specialize, yet it almost always generates higher levels of sales than a generalist approach.

The firm then compared the alternatives with the credibility and coverage and flexibility criteria. Because the company served specific industry types with customized applications, the market specialization option was evaluated as the best on the credibility and coverage criteria. Market specialization provided the best means for the sales organization to identify and satisfy specific customer needs that differed by industry. Had the company served many different types of customers, a product specialization approach might have provided the best credibility and coverage.

The company also evaluated the market specialization option as second to the generalist option on the flexibility criterion. Since all types of specialization promised higher payouts than the generalist approach and the market specialization option was the best specialization option on the credibility and coverage and flexibility criteria, the firm decided to change to a market-specialized salesforce. The company plan was to restructure into separate salesforces for each major industry group served by the firm.

Decisions concerning centralization, span of control versus management levels, and line versus staff positions require analysis of similar selling situation

EXHIBIT 7.2 ▪ *Affordability and Payout Analysis*

	Generalist Option	Product Specialization Option	Market Specialization Option	Major Account Option
Expected Gross Margin	$405,000	$495,000	$500,000	$576,000
Expected Costs	$ 76,500	$ 95,000	$ 96,000	$ 99,000
Net Payout	$328,500	$400,000	$404,000	$477,000

Source: Adapted from example in Allan J. Magrath, "To Specialize or Not to Specialize?" *Sales and Marketing Management*, June 1989, 64–65.

factors. Decisions in these areas must be consistent with the specialization decision. For example, decentralized organization structures with few management levels, large spans of control, and the use of staff positions may be consistent with a specialized salesforce in some selling situations but not in others. The appropriate sales organization structure depends upon the specific characteristics of a firm's selling situation. The resulting structure can influence the ethical behavior of salespeople, as illustrated in "An Ethical Perspective: Sales Organization Structure and Salesperson Ethical Behavior."

AN ETHICAL PERSPECTIVE

Sales Organization Structure and Salesperson Ethical Behavior The formal structure of a sales organization can have an important effect on the ethical behavior of salespeople. Consider the following example:

> Steve has just completed the company's training program successfully but is having trouble generating large sales. Finally, one of his customers is interested in placing a major order with him but demands a kickback. Steve talks to his sales manager about the kickback and is told that this is normal and expected. Steve had never heard of this in his sales training and does not know what to do.

Since Steve's immediate supervisor seems to condone the kickback, this is likely to influence his decision. The formal sales organization structure is such that Steve may feel that he can go ahead with the kickback since he doesn't report to "anybody but my sales manager."

Many firms realize the restrictive nature of the formal sales organization structure and are establishing procedures to help salespeople like Steve with complex ethical situations. One approach is to have formal codes of ethics (as previously discussed in Chapter 5) to explicitly state acceptable behavior and to cover these codes in sales training programs. Had Steve's company done this, he would have known what the company wanted him to do without having to ask his sales manager. Other approaches are to have ethics committees or other procedures where salespeople can go outside the direct reporting relationships in the sales organization structure to get assistance in resolving ethical problems.

Source: Adapted from William T. Finn, "How to Make the Sale and Remain Ethical," *Sales and Marketing Management*, August 1988, 8.

Sales Organization Structures

Designing the sales organization structure requires integration of the desired degree of specialization, centralization, span of control, management levels, line positions, and staff positions. Obviously, there are a tremendous number of different ways that a sales organization might be structured. Our objective is to review several of the basic and most often used ways and to illustrate some variations in these basic structures.

In order to provide continuity to this discussion, each type of sales organization will be discussed from the perspective of the ABC Company. The ABC Company markets office equipment (typewriters, furniture, etc.) and office supplies (paper, pencils, etc.) to commercial and government accounts. The firm employs 200 salespeople who operate throughout the United States. The salespeople perform various activities that can be characterized as being related either to sales generation or account servicing. Examples of different types of sales organization structures that the ABC Company might use are presented and discussed.

Geographic Sales Organization

Most salesforces use some type of **geographic specialization.** This is the least specialized and most generalized type of salesforce. Salespeople are typically assigned a geographic area and are responsible for all selling activities to all accounts within the assigned area. There is no attempt to specialize by product, market, or function. For example, Herman Miller markets office furniture to dealers, specifiers in the architectural and design community, and end users. The company has 245 salespeople who perform all selling functions for all products and accounts within an assigned geographic area.[7] An example of a geographic sales organization for the ABC Company is presented in Figure 7.5. Again, note that this type of organization provides no salesforce specialization except by geographic area. Because of the lack of specialization, there is no duplication of effort. All geographic areas and accounts are served by only one salesperson.

The structure in this example is a rather tall one and thus somewhat centralized. There are four levels of line sales management with relatively small spans of control: national sales managers (2), regional sales managers (4), zone sales managers (5), and district sales managers (5). Note the sales management specialization in the sales training staff position. Since this staff position is located at the national sales manager level, training activities tend to be centralized.

Product Sales Organization

Product specialization has been popular in recent years, but it seems to be declining in importance, at least in certain industries. Salesforces specializing by product assign salespeople selling responsibility for specific products or product lines. The objective is for salespeople to become experts in the assigned product categories. For example, Gillette has separate salesforces for its personal care products and for its writing products.[8] Salespeople might also specialize by brands

FIGURE 7.5   ▪   *Geographic Sales Organization*

This geographic sales organization structure has four sales management levels, small spans of control, and a staff position at the national level.

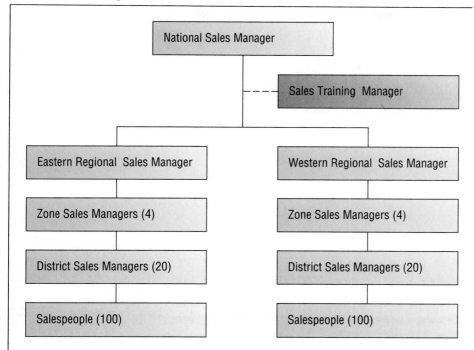

of the same type of product. This type of product specialization is exemplified by Cooper Tire and Rubber's use of separate salesforces for Cooper brands, Falls brands, and house brands of tires.[9]

An example of a product sales organization for the ABC Company is presented in Figure 7.6. This organization structure indicates two levels of product specialization. There are two separate salesforces: one salesforce specializes in selling office equipment, while the other specializes in selling office supplies. Each of the specialized salesforces performs all selling activities for all types of accounts. The separate salesforces are each organized geographically. Thus, there will be duplication in the coverage of geographic areas, with both office equipment and office supplies salespeople operating in the same areas. In some cases, the salespeople may call on the same accounts.

The example structure in Figure 7.6 is flat and decentralized, especially when compared with the example presented in Figure 7.5. There are only three line management levels with wide spans of control: national sales managers (2), product sales managers (10), and district sales managers (10). This structure has no staff positions and thus no management specialization beyond product specialization. The office equipment and office supplies salesforces are organized in exactly the same manner.

FIGURE 7.6 ▪ *Product Sales Organization*

This product sales organization structure has three sales management levels, large spans of control, and no staff positions.

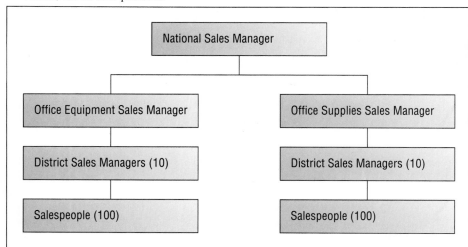

Market Sales Organization

An increasingly important type of specialization is **market specialization.** Salespeople are assigned specific types of customers and are required to satisfy all needs of these customers. Market specialization can take several forms:

1. *Broad market specialization.* Goodyear Tire & Rubber Co. has restructured into a salesforce that specializes in sales of passenger car tires to consumers through independent dealers and a salesforce that specializes in sales to commercial accounts, such as truck and auto fleets.[10]
2. *Specific industry specialization.* Novell Inc. employs separate salesforces to market network computer software to specific industry groups such as government agencies, educational institutions, distributors and retailers, and original equipment manufacturers and systems integrators.[11]
3. *Specialization by type of distributor.* Kimberly-Clark's U.S. Consumer Sales Division employs separate salesforces to market diapers, tissues, and feminine products to consumers through grocery stores, mass merchandisers, and Military PXs.[12]
4. *Specialization by account size.* Xerox redesigned its sales organization into a national account manager salesforce to serve the largest accounts with national operations, a major account manager salesforce to serve accounts that are large in certain regions, an account representative salesforce for medium-sized businesses, and a salesforce of marketing representatives for the remaining accounts, especially small businesses.[13]

The basic objective of market specialization is to ensure that salespeople understand how customers use and purchase their products. Salespeople should then be able to direct their efforts to satisfy customer needs better.

FIGURE 7.7 ▪ *Market Sales Organization*

This market sales organization structure organizes its commercial accounts salesforce differently from its government accounts salesforce. The commercial accounts salesforce has three sales management levels, small spans of control, and a staff position. The government accounts salesforce has two sales management levels, large spans of control, and no staff positions.

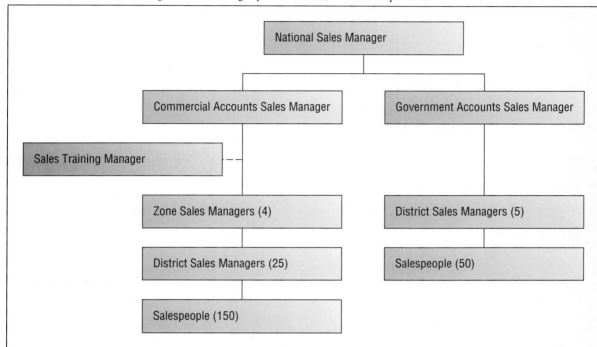

The market sales organization shown for the ABC Company in Figure 7.7 focuses on account types. Separate salesforces have been organized for commercial and government accounts. Salespeople perform all selling activities for all products but only for certain accounts. This arrangement avoids duplication of sales effort, since salespeople will never call on the same accounts. They may, however, operate in the same geographic areas.

The example in Figure 7.7 presents some interesting variations in sales management organization. The commercial accounts salesforce is much more centralized than the government accounts salesforce. This centralization is due to more line management levels, shorter spans of control, and a specialized sales training staff position. This example structure illustrates the important point that the specialized salesforces within a sales organization do not have to be structured in the same manner.

Functional Sales Organization

The final type of specialization is **functional specialization.** Most selling situations require a number of selling activities, so there may be efficiencies in having salespeople specialize in performing certain of these required activities.

telemarketing

FIGURE 7.8 ▪ *Functional Sales Organization*

This functional sales organization structure organizes its field salesforce differently from its telemarketing salesforce. The field salesforce has three sales management levels with small spans of control, while the telemarketing salesforce has two sales management levels with large spans of control. Neither salesforce utilizes staff positions.

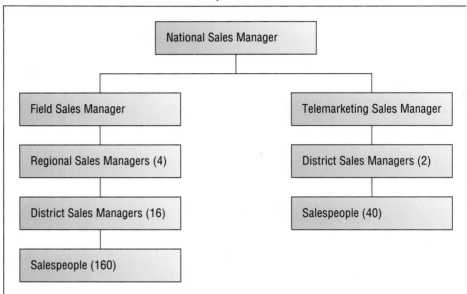

Gillette, for example, uses its direct salespeople to sell products and to talk with buyers about pricing, distribution, promotion, and display. A separate group of merchandisers is used to make sure that everything goes well at the point of sale by stocking shelves, checking on displays, and performing other in-store activities. As already discussed in Chapter 6, many firms are using a telemarketing salesforce to generate leads, qualify prospects, monitor shipments, and so forth, while the outside salesforce concentrates on sales-generating activities. These firms are specializing by function.

An example of a functional sales organization for ABC Company is presented in Figure 7.8. This is a structure where a field salesforce is used to perform sales-generating activities and a telemarketing salesforce is used to perform account-servicing activities. Although the salesforces will cover the same geographic areas and the same accounts, the use of telemarketing helps to reduce the cost of this duplication of effort. The more routine and repetitive activities will be performed by the inside, telemarketing salesforce. The more creative and nonroutine sales-generating activities will be performed by the outside, field salesforce.

The field salesforce is more centralized than the telemarketing salesforce, but both salesforces tend to be decentralized. The cost effectiveness of telemarketing is illustrated by the need for only two management levels and three managers to supervise 40 salespeople. This example does not include any staff positions for sales management specialization.

FIGURE 7.9   ▪   *Identifying Major Accounts*

Major accounts are both large and complex. They are extremely important to the firm and require specialized attention.

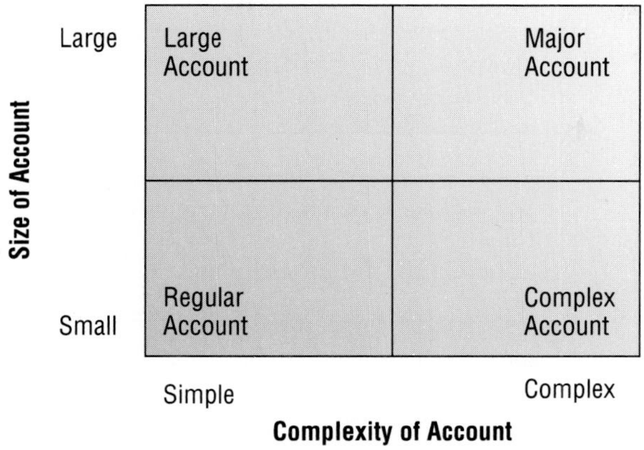

Source: Adapted from Benson P. Shapiro and Rowland T. Moriarity, *National Account Management: Emerging Insights* (Cambridge, Mass.: Marketing Science Institute, March 1982), 6.

Major Account Organizations

Many firms receive a large percentage of their total sales from relatively few accounts. These large-volume accounts are obviously extremely important and must be considered when designing a sales organization. The term *major account* is used to refer to large, important accounts that should receive special attention from the sales organization. Some firms use the term *national account* instead. Others use both terms, with national accounts representing large accounts with multiple buying locations and major accounts representing large customers with single buying locations. We will use the term *major account* to refer to all large, important accounts in this text. A **major account organization** represents a type of market specialization by account size.

Major account organization has become increasingly important in both domestic and international markets. Although major account programs differ considerably across firms, all firms must determine how to identify their own major accounts and how to organize for effective coverage of them.[14]

Identifying Major Accounts.   All large accounts do not qualify as major accounts. As illustrated in Figure 7.9, a major account should be of sufficient size and complexity to warrant special attention from the sales organization. An account can be considered complex under the following circumstances:[15]

▪ Its purchasing function is centralized.
▪ Top management heavily influences its purchasing decisions.
▪ It has multi-site purchasing influences.
▪ Its purchasing process is complex and diffuse.

FIGURE 7.10 ▪ *Major Account Options*

Once identified, major accounts can be served in three basic ways. The development of a major account salesforce is the most comprehensive approach and is being employed increasingly often for customers in domestic and international markets.

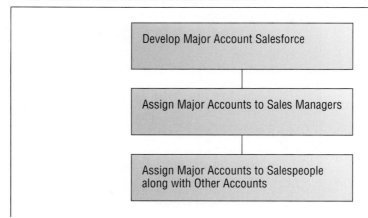

Source: Adapted from Benson P. Shapiro and Rowland T. Moriarity, *Organizing the National Account Force* (Cambridge, Mass.: Marketing Science Institute, April 1984), 1–37.

▪ It requires special price concessions.
▪ It requires special services.
▪ It purchases customized products.

Organizing for Major Account Coverage. Accounts that are not both large and complex are typically served adequately through the basic sales organization structure, but those identified as major accounts pose problems for organization design that might be handled in a variety of ways. The basic options are shown in Figure 7.10. In one option, major accounts, although identified, are assigned to salespeople, as are other accounts. This approach may provide some special attention to these accounts but is not a formal major account management program.

Many firms have found that formal major account management programs can strengthen account relationships and improve communications between buyers and sellers.[16] These formal programs are designed in several ways.[17] One approach is to assign major accounts to sales executives, who are responsible for coordinating all activities with each assigned account. This major account responsibility is typically in addition to the executives' normal management activities.

An increasingly popular approach is to establish a separate major accounts salesforce. This approach is a type of market specialization where salespeople specialize by type of account based on size and complexity. An example of this approach is the major account salesforce used by AT&T. Because of the complexity of the major accounts served by AT&T, each major account team consists of a direct marketing specialist, sales specialist, telemarketing account executive, and major account executive. Each member of the major account team focuses on specific activities for specific individuals within the account. AT&T has found this approach to result in more revenue from major accounts at lower selling costs than traditional major account approaches.[18]

One study found that firms tend to use four different major account sales organization structures (see Figure 7.11). Research suggests that firms currently using major account management programs can be profiled in the following manner:[19]

- Total company sales are $1.1 billion.
- Major account program is eight years old.
- Major account revenues represent 30 percent of company sales.
- Major account organization serves 95 customers.
- Major account organization consists of seven salespeople.
- Each major account salesperson is assigned 12 customers.
- A major account salesperson generates $34 million in total sales, or $3 million per customer.

Evidence also suggests that a typical major account manager is likely to be in touch with about 300 people—180 at customer locations, 45 in prospect accounts, and 75 in various departments within the major account manager's firm.[20]

Comparing Sales Organization Structures

The sales organization structures described in the last section represent the basic types of salesforce specialization and some examples of the variations possible. A premise of this chapter is that there is no one best way to structure a sales organization. The appropriate structure for a given sales organization depends upon the characteristics of the selling situation. Some structures are better in some selling situations than in others. Exhibit 7.3 summarizes much of what has been discussed previously by directly comparing the advantages and disadvantages of each basic sales organization structure.

As is evident from this exhibit, the strengths of one structure are weaknesses in other structures. For example, the lack of geographic and customer duplication is an advantage of a geographic structure but a disadvantage of the product and market structures. Because of this situation, many firms employ **hybrid sales organization** structures that incorporate several of the basic structural types. The objective of these hybrid structures is to capitalize on the advantage of each type while minimizing the disadvantages.

An example of a hybrid sales organizational structure is presented in Figure 7.12. This structure is extremely complex in that it includes elements of geographic, product, market, function, and major account organizations. Although Figure 7.12 represents only one possible hybrid structure, it does illustrate how the different structure types might be combined into one overall sales organization structure. The example also illustrates the complex nature of the task of determining sales organization structure. As noted before, the task is an extremely important one; sales management must develop the appropriate sales organization structure for its particular selling situation to ensure the successful implementation of organizational and account strategies. This task becomes

FIGURE 7.11 ▪ *Major Account Sales Organization Structures* Major account salesforces are being organized in four basic ways today. The most popular is to have the major account organization report to the highest sales management level.[a]

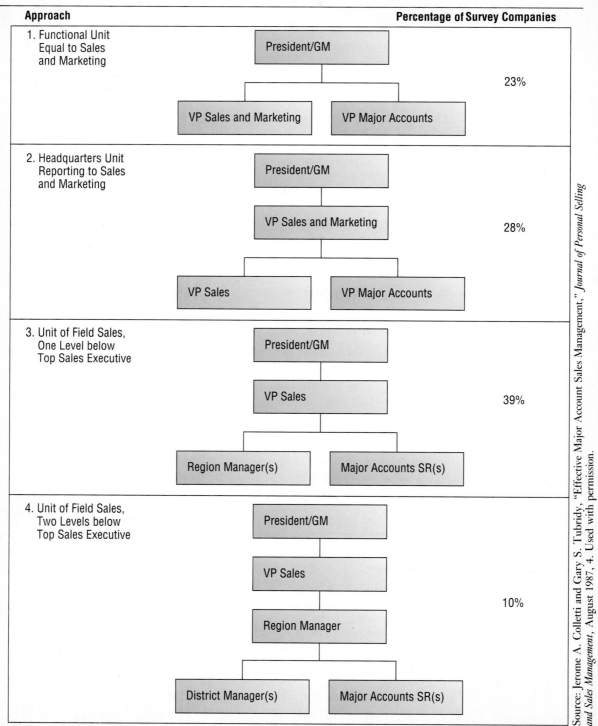

Approach	Percentage of Survey Companies

1. Functional Unit Equal to Sales and Marketing

President/GM
→ VP Sales and Marketing
→ VP Major Accounts

23%

2. Headquarters Unit Reporting to Sales and Marketing

President/GM
→ VP Sales and Marketing
→ VP Sales
→ VP Major Accounts

28%

3. Unit of Field Sales, One Level below Top Sales Executive

President/GM
→ VP Sales
→ Region Manager(s)
→ Major Accounts SR(s)

39%

4. Unit of Field Sales, Two Levels below Top Sales Executive

President/GM
→ VP Sales
→ Region Manager
→ District Manager(s)
→ Major Accounts SR(s)

10%

Source: Jerome A. Colletti and Gary S. Tubridy, "Effective Major Account Sales Management," *Journal of Personal Selling and Sales Management*, August 1987, 4. Used with permission.

[a]The study shown in this figure used the VP Sales title for the highest sales. In this textbook we use the National Sales Manager title when referring to the highest sales management level.

EXHIBIT 7.3 ▪ *Comparison of Sales Organization Structures*

Organization Structure	Advantages	Disadvantages
Geographic	▪ Low cost ▪ No geographic duplication ▪ No customer duplication ▪ Fewer management levels	▪ Limited specialization ▪ Lack of management control over product or customer emphasis
Product	▪ Salespeople become experts in product attributes and applications ▪ Management control over selling effort allocated to products	▪ High cost ▪ Geographic duplication ▪ Customer duplication
Market	▪ Salespeople develop better understanding of unique customer needs ▪ Management control over selling effort allocated to different markets	▪ High cost ▪ Geographic duplication
Functional	▪ Efficiency in performing selling activities	▪ Geographic duplication ▪ Customer duplication ▪ Need for coordination

FIGURE 7.12 ▪ *Hybrid Sales Organization Structure*

This complex sales organization structure incorporates market, product, functional, and geographic specialization.

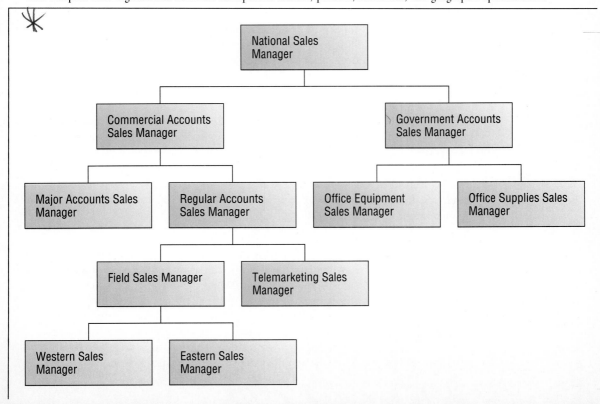

A GLOBAL PERSPECTIVE

International Sales Organization Structures   A study of the international sales organization structures of 27 U.S. firms operating in 45 different countries produced the following results:

- Companies often use the same sales organization structure in international markets that they use in the U.S. market.
- Companies tend to employ simple, generalized structures when entering a foreign market and switch to more complex, specialized structures when sales increase.
- Industry habits account for many of the differences in sales organization structure

in foreign markets. For example, companies in high technology industries typically use product-specialized structures to compete on technology, while consumer goods companies typically organize geographically to satisfy consumer needs in different geographic markets.

- Simple sales organization structures are used in less-developed countries, while more complex structures are employed in more-developed countries.

Source: John S. Hill and Richard R. Still, "Organizing the Overseas Sales Force: How Multinationals Do It," *Journal of Personal Selling and Sales Management*, Spring 1990, 57–66.

increasingly more difficult as firms operate globally (see "A Global Perspective: International Sales Organization Structures").

Summary

1.   Define the concepts of specialization, centralization, span of control versus management levels, and line versus staff positions. *Specialization* refers to the division of labor such that salespeople or sales managers concentrate on performing certain activities to the exclusion of others. *Centralization* refers to where in the organization decision-making responsibility exists. Centralized organizations locate decision-making responsibility at higher organizational levels than decentralized organizations. Any sales organization structure can be evaluated in terms of the types and degrees of specialization and centralization afforded by the structure. Sales management organization design also requires decisions concerning the number of management levels, spans of control, and line versus staff positions. In general, more *management levels* result in smaller *spans of control* and more *staff positions* result in more sales management specialization.

2.   Describe the different ways that salesforces might be specialized. A critical decision in designing the sales organization is determining whether the salesforce should be specialized, and if so, the appropriate type of specialization. The basic types of salesforce specialization are geographic, product, market (including major account organization), and functional. The appropriate type of specialization depends upon the characteristics of the selling situation. Important selling situation characteristics include the similarity of customer needs, the complexity of the firm's product offering, the market environment, and the professionalism of the salesforce. Specific criteria of importance are affordability and payout, credibility and coverage, and flexibility. The use of different types and levels of specialization typically requires the establishment of separate salesforces.

3. **Evaluate the advantages and disadvantages of different sales organization structures.** Since each type of sales organization structure has certain advantages and disadvantages, many firms use hybrid structures that combine the features of several types. Usually, the strengths of one structure are weaknesses in other structures.

4. **Name the important considerations in organizing major account management programs.** Identifying major accounts (which should be both large and complex) and organizing for coverage of them are the important considerations in major account management.

5. **Explain how one determines the appropriate sales organization structure for a given selling situation.** There is no one best way to structure a sales organization. The appropriate way to organize a salesforce and sales management depends upon certain characteristics of a particular selling situation. Also, since the sales organization structure decision is dynamic, it must be adapted to changes in a firm's selling situation that occur over time.

Key Terms

- **Specialization**
- **Centralization**
- **Span of control**
- **Management levels**
- **Line sales management**
- **Staff sales management**

- **Geographic specialization**
- **Product specialization**
- **Market specialization**
- **Functional specialization**
- **Major account organization**
- **Hybrid sales organization**

Review Questions

1. Discuss the situational factors that suggest the need for specialization and centralization. Provide a specific example of each factor discussed.
2. What are the basic disadvantages of salesforce specialization?
3. Why do you think there is a trend toward more salesforce specialization in the future?
4. Consider the ethical situation facing Steve in "An Ethical Perspective: Sales Organization Structure and Salesperson Ethical Behavior." As the national sales manager for this firm, what specific policies and procedures would you implement to assist salespeople like Steve with ethical problems?
5. Based on the study results presented in "A Global Perspective: International Sales Organization Structures," what type of sales organization structure would you recommend that DEC use when initially developing a salesforce in a developed country? In a less-developed country?
6. How should sales organizations be structured to serve accounts that are complex but small in size?

7. What are the advantages and disadvantages of structuring a sales organization for major account management?

8. What is meant by a contingency approach to sales organization structure?

9. What are some problems that a firm might face when undertaking a major restructuring of its sales organization?

10. What are the important relationships between span of control, management levels, line positions, staff positions, specialization, and centralization?

Application Exercises

1. Obtain the formal sales organization structure of any firm. Evaluate this structure in terms of specialization, centralization, span of control, management levels, and line and staff positions. Name any sales organization structural changes your analysis suggests. Be sure to support fully each of your recommended changes.

2. The EMI Corporation markets language labs to secondary schools and colleges/universities. The firm currently employs two salespeople to cover the entire United States. The basic strategy has been to use direct mail to generate requests for proposals and to send salespeople to schools only to present these proposals. The firm is considering the establishment of a field salesforce to call on schools to try to develop more penetration of the market. You have been hired as a consultant to determine the appropriate sales organization structure for EMI. Prepare a proposal that discusses exactly what you would do to arrive at a recommended sales organization structure. Be sure to include all of the factors that you would consider and discuss how these factors will help you determine the most appropriate structure.

3. Figure 7.12 presents a hybrid sales organization structure that includes elements of geographic, product, market, function, and major account structures. Prepare an alternative hybrid sales organization structure that also incorporates the same elements. Compare your hybrid structure to the one presented in Figure 7.12.

Notes

[1]See Thomas V. Bonoma, *The Marketing Edge: Making Strategies Work* (New York: The Free Press, 1985), for a more complete presentation of the importance of and problems in successfully implementing organizational strategies.

[2]Reported in "Structuring the Sales Organization," in *Sales Manager's Handbook*, ed. John P. Steinbrink (Chicago: The Dartnell Corporation, 1989), 90.

[3]See Robert W. Ruekert, Orville C. Walker, Jr., and Kenneth J. Roering, "The Organization of Marketing Activities: A Contingency Theory of Structure and Performance," *Journal of Marketing*, Winter 1985, 13–25, for a more complete presentation of structural characteristics and relationships. The discussion in this section borrows heavily from this article.

[4]Rayna Skolnik, "Battling for the Power of the Seats," *Sales and Marketing Management*, April 1987, 46–49.

[5]Ram C. Rao and Ronald E. Turner, "Organization and Effectiveness of the Multiple-Product Salesforce," *Journal of Personal Selling and Sales Management*, May 1984, 24–30.

[6]This section and the example are adapted from Allan J. Magrath, "To Specialize or Not to Specialize?" *Sales and Marketing Management*, June 1989, 62–68.

[7]Skolnik, "Battling for the Power," 46–49.

[8]"Gillette Hones Salespower to a Fine Edge," *Sales and Marketing Management*, June 1987, 59.

[9]"At Cooper Tire, Sales Are Rarely Flat," *Sales and Marketing Management*, June 1986, 56.

[10]"Marketing Unit Revamped, Staff Cutback May Follow," *The Wall Street Journal*, April 9, 1990, A5.

[11]Kate Bertrand, "Reorganizing for Sales," *Business Marketing*, February 1990, 30.

[12]"Kimberly-Clark: Do It Right the First Time," *Sales and Marketing Management*, June 1987, 62.

[13]"Xerox's Makeover," *Sales and Marketing Management*, June 1987, 68.

[14]See Michael W. Hunter, "Getting Started in National Account Marketing," *Business Marketing*, November 1987, 61–64; and Kate Bertrand, "National Account Marketing," *Business Marketing*, November 1987, 43–52, for examples of different approaches for major account organizations.

[15]Benson P. Shapiro and Rowland T. Moriarity, *National Account Management: Emerging Insights* (Cambridge, Mass.: Marketing Science Institute, 1982), 19.

[16]John Barrett, "Why Major Account Selling Works," *Industrial Marketing Management*, 15, 1986, 63–73.

[17]Benson P. Shapiro and Rowland T. Moriarity, *Organizing the National Account Force* (Cambridge, Mass.: Marketing Science Institute, 1983).

[18]Merrill Tutton, "Segmenting a National Account," *Business Horizons*, January–February 1987, 61–67.

[19]See Jerome A. Colletti and Gary S. Tubridy, "Effective Major Account Sales Management," *Journal of Personal Selling and Sales Management*, August 1987, 1–10, for a more complete presentation of these profiles and other research results.

[20]Reported in Martin Everett, "This Is the Ultimate in Selling," *Sales and Marketing Management*, August 1989, 32.

CASE 7.1 *Postal Products*

Background

Postal Products is a manufacturer and marketer of various types of mailing and shipping products. Although sales had been increasing in recent years, profits had been stagnant. The Postal Products salesforce called on many different types of accounts. The salesforce was organized geographically, with each salesperson assigned 200 accounts of various types and sizes.

Mr. Harold Teer was the national sales manager for the 400-member salesforce. He had recently examined sales and cost figures for the past few years and found that salesforce costs had been increasing faster than sales volume had been increasing. This analysis convinced him that specific actions needed to be taken to reduce salesforce costs and improve sales productivity.

Current Situation

Mr. Teer sent the following memo to all of his regional sales managers:

> To: Regional Sales Managers
> From: Harold Teer, National Sales Manager
> Subject: Sales Productivity Proposals
> Date: March 14, 1991
> Enclosed are my analyses of salesforce sales and costs for the past few years. I think the results indicate that we must take specific actions to re-

> duce selling costs and to improve sales productivity. Please have specific and detailed proposals ready for discussion at our meeting on March 30, 1991. We need to decide on a course of action and begin implementation as soon as possible.

Bob Reid, regional sales manager for the West region, had been convinced for some time that Postal Products should restructure the sales organization into a major account salesforce for the largest accounts with multiple locations and two salesforces for regular accounts. One of these salesforces would specialize in selling postal products, while the other salesforce would specialize in shipping products. He decided that it was time to introduce this proposal at the March 30 meeting. He knew that it would be difficult to sell his idea to Mr. Teer, since establishing specialized salesforces would raise selling costs, especially in the short run. However, he was convinced that his idea would produce substantial sales and profit increases over the long run.

Questions

1. Prepare a proposal for Bob Reid to present at the March 30 meeting.
2. Should Mr. Teer agree with Reid's idea?
3. How would you implement the specialization suggested by Reid?

CASE 7.2 *United Food Service Company*

United Food Service Company (UFSC) has recently introduced a new line of plastic disposable food service items (plates, bowls, cups, and tumblers) to be sold to hospitals. In the past, UFSC had introduced new products through its regular salesforce.

However, since it often took a long time before new products were adopted by many hospitals, it was often difficult to get salespeople to spend much time selling new products when they were introduced.

Dan Spitzer, vice-president of sales and marketing, had decided to try a new approach with the plastic disposable food service items. He was going to develop a detailer salesforce to help with the new product introduction. The detailer would

1. Call on hospitals to familiarize them with the concept of disposable food service items
2. Perform administrative duties such as corresponding with potential customers, reporting call results, and working on market research studies

The basic job of the detailer would be to show a 25-minute film to hospital administrators and dieticians concerning the disposable food service items. The detailer could not close a sale but would close each presentation by informing the hospital that a sales representative would be calling on them in the near future.

Approximately one week after the film presentation, the regular UFSC salesperson calls on the hospital to get them to test the disposable products against their current nondisposable food service products. Then, the salesperson makes an appointment for a sales call to the hospital to get them to purchase the product.

Questions

1. What are the advantages and disadvantages of the use of detailers as suggested by Dan Spitzer?
2. What type of specialization do the detailers represent?
3. How do you think the regular salesforce will respond to the use of detailers?

Allocating Selling Effort, Determining Salesforce Size, and Designing Territories

DESIGNING TERRITORIES: PERDUE FREDERICK CO. Perdue Frederick Co. is a pharmaceutical manufacturer with 240 salespeople, generating annual sales in excess of $100 million. Sales managers used to spend up to a full day defining the boundaries for a single territory. The manual process was very time consuming, as indicated by Stephanie Thompson, manager of marketing programs: "We used to sit down with our district managers for days and do a ton of manual calculations to put together our territories."

Because of rapid growth in the late 1980s, the company added 100 salespeople. Redesigning territories to accommodate these new salespeople and to ensure proper selling effort to their physician customers would have been extremely difficult with their manual approach. Realizing this, the company introduced microcomputer software to help with territory design. The software package integrated mapping software with spreadsheet functions containing data at the ZIP code level.

The basic data input was current sales, market potential, and targeted sales calls for each ZIP code. The software then realigned the territories to achieve nearly equal levels of market potential. These territories were then adjusted to equalize sales and targeted sales calls. The output from this process was then reviewed by sales managers and salespeople, and adjustments were made to reflect unique situations, such as important relationships between specific salespeople and customers.

When the complete process was finished in October 1988, each salesperson received a map of his or her assigned territory and a listing of the physicians within the territory. Adjustments were easily made throughout 1989 by entering ZIP code changes that shifted customer histories and potential prospects from one territory to another. The initial territory realignment cost $150,000, but it is expected to generate sales increases well in excess of this cost. Current plans are to expand the software to include information about retail pharmacies in the territory design process.

Source: Adapted from Tom Eisenhart, "Drawing a Map to Better Sales," *Business Marketing*, January 1990, 59–61.

Learning Objectives

After completing this chapter, you should be able to

1 *Discuss the different areas involved in salesforce deployment.*

2 *Explain three different analytical approaches for determining allocation of selling effort.*

3 *Describe three different methods for calculating salesforce size.*

4 *Explain the importance of sales territories from the perspective of the sales organization and from the perspective of the salespeople.*

5 *List the steps in the territory design process.*

6 *Describe a method for assigning salespeople to sales territories.*

7 *Discuss the important "people" considerations in salesforce deployment.*

A GLOBAL PERSPECTIVE

Deploying a Salesforce in Japan Deploying a company salesforce in international markets is often a difficult task because of the lack of available information for determining the appropriate salesforce size, territory design, or allocation of selling effort to accounts and prospects. Therefore, many firms use distributors or agents to supply their selling effort in many international markets. In Japan, however, companies are faced with complex distribution systems that are difficult to understand and penetrate. Coca-Cola solved this problem by using the capital of local bottlers to re-create the kind of salesforce it used in the United States. Coke has achieved a 70 percent soft drink market share in Japan by using its own salesforce instead of the typical independent distributors. The success of this approach in soft drinks provides a foundation for Coca-Cola to expand its business in Japan into fruit juices, sports drinks, and other related areas.

Source: Kenichi Ohmae, *The Borderless World: Power and Strategy in the Interlinked Economy* (New York, NY: Harper Business, 1990), 28.

The important sales management decisions involved in allocating selling effort, determining salesforce size, and designing territories are often referred to as **salesforce deployment.** These decisions are closely related to the organizational strategy and sales organization structure decisions. Changes in strategy and structure often require adjustments in all three areas of salesforce deployment—selling effort allocation, salesforce size determination, and territory design. In the case of international markets, the salesforce deployment task becomes even more difficult (see "A Global Perspective: Deploying a Salesforce in Japan").

The size of a salesforce determines the total amount of selling effort that a firm has available. This selling effort must be sufficient to provide adequate selling coverage to all of the firm's accounts and prospects. The use of territories is one way to ensure that selling effort is used effectively. Typically, each salesperson is assigned a specific territory as a basic work unit. Therefore, changes in the allocation of selling effort to accounts often require that salesforce size be increased or decreased and that territories be redesigned. Deployment decisions at Perdue Frederick reflected a situation where more selling effort became available due to large increases in salesforce size. This increased selling effort was allocated to specific accounts and salesperson territories redesigned. In other situations, firms might decide to reduce total selling effort by decreasing salesforce size. This also would require changes in allocation of selling effort to accounts and territory redesign.

Since the salesforce deployment decisions are highly interrelated, our discussion will begin by addressing them in an integrated manner. Then, specific discussions of each deployment area will focus on describing the deployment decisions facing sales management and examining different analytical approaches for making these decisions.

Salesforce Deployment

Salesforce deployment decisions can be viewed as providing answers to three interrelated questions:

FIGURE 8.1 ▪ *Interrelatedness of Salesforce Deployment Decisions*

Determining how much selling effort should be allocated to various accounts provides a basis for calculating the number of salespeople required to produce the desired amount of selling effort. The salesforce size decision then determines the number of territories that must be designed. Thus, decisions in one deployment area affect decisions in other deployment areas.

1. How much selling effort is needed to cover accounts and prospects adequately so that sales and profit objectives will be achieved?
2. How many salespeople are required to provide the desired amount of selling effort?
3. How should territories be designed to ensure proper coverage of accounts and to provide each salesperson with a reasonable opportunity for success?

The interrelatedness of these decisions is illustrated in Figure 8.1. Decisions in one salesforce deployment area affect decisions in other areas. For example, the decision of allocation of selling effort provides input for determining salesforce size, which provides input for territory design.

The potential value of addressing the areas of salesforce deployment in an integrated and sequential manner is supported by the results of deployment studies reported in Exhibit 8.1.[1] These studies indicate the impressive sales and profit increases that might be expected from a comprehensive deployment analysis.

Despite the importance of salesforce deployment and the need to address the deployment decisions in an interrelated manner, many sales organizations use simplified analytical methods and consider each deployment decision in an isolated manner—an approach not likely to result in the best deployment decisions. Even such simplified approaches, however, can typically identify deployment changes that will increase sales and profits. The basic objectives of and approaches for determining selling effort allocation, salesforce size, and territory design are discussed separately in the remainder of this chapter.

Allocation of Selling Effort

The allocation of selling effort is one of the most important deployment decisions, since the salesforce size and territory decisions are based on this allocation decision. Regardless of the method of account coverage, determining how much selling effort to allocate to individual accounts is an extremely important decision strategically speaking, because selling effort is a major determinant of account sales

EXHIBIT 8.1   ▪ *Results of Salesforce Deployment Studies*

Study	*Type of Product*	*Deployment Recommendation*	*Estimated Productivity Improvement*
1. Lambert and Kniffin (1970)	Medical X-ray film	Redeployment of salespeople across sales districts	$131,000 increase in gross profits
2. Lodish (1971)	Industry commodity	Redeployment of selling effort	20% sales increase
3. Montgomery, Silk, and Zaragoza (1971)	Ethical drugs	Reallocation of sales call time across products	$85,000 profit improvement for one year; $139,000 profit improvement over two-year period
4. Lodish (1975)	Advertising	Redeployment of selling effort and reassignment of salespeople to accounts	17%–21% profit increase
5. Beswick and Cravens (1977)	Appliances	Redeployment of selling effort across trading areas	$830,000 sales increase
		Increase in salesforce size and redeployment	$1,400,000 sales increase
6. Fudge and Lodish (1977)	Airline travel and cargo	Redeployment of selling effort to accounts	8.1% sales increase (actual results from implementation)
7. Parasuraman and Day (1977)	Consumer products	Reduction in and redeployment of selling effort to accounts	Maintain current sales levels with nearly 50% reduction in selling effort
8. Zoltners and Sinha (1980)	Consumer products	Redeployment of salespeople across regions and distribution channels	7% sales increase
9. LaForge and Cravens (1985)	Grocery products	Redeployment of selling effort to accounts	8%–30% sales improvement
10. Cravens, Dielman, Lamb, and Moncrief (1986)	Transportation services	Reduction in and redeployment of selling effort	Maintain current sales levels with 10%–20% reduction in salesforce size

Source: Adapted from Raymond W. LaForge, David W. Cravens, and Clifford E. Young, "Using Contingency Analysis to Select Selling Effort Allocation Methods," *Journal of Personal Selling and Sales Management*, August 1986, 23. Used with permission.

and a major element of account selling costs. For example, the cost of field sales calls has been estimated to be as high a $452.60 in the computer industry and as low as $99.10 in the petroleum and coal products industry.[2] These selling costs have commanded the attention of top management. A survey of top-level executives found that of 36 activities, improving salesforce productivity was rated as the fourth most important.[3] And the way in which sales calls are allocated to accounts has a major impact on salesforce productivity.

FIGURE 8.2 ▪ *Analytical Approaches to Allocation of Selling Effort*

The single factor, portfolio, and decision model approaches for performing a deployment analysis differ in terms of analytical rigor and in ease of development and use. Typically, the more rigorous the approach, the more difficult it is to develop and use.

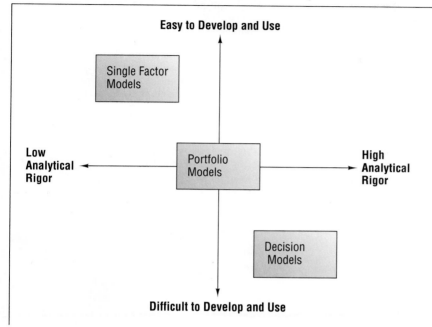

Source: David W. Cravens and Raymond W. LaForge, "Salesforce Deployment," in *Advances in Business Marketing*, ed. Arch G. Woodside (Greenwich, CT: JAI Press, 1986), 76.

Although decisions on the allocation of selling effort are difficult, several analytical tools are available to help. The three basic analytical approaches are single factor models, portfolio models, and decision models. These three are compared in Figure 8.2 and discussed in detail throughout the remainder of this section.

Single Factor Models. Easy to develop and use, **single factor models** do not, however, provide a very comprehensive analysis of accounts. The typical procedure is to classify all accounts on one factor, such as market potential, and then to assign all accounts in the same category the same number of sales calls. An example of using a single factor model for sales call allocation is presented in Exhibit 8.2.

Although single factor models have limitations, they do provide sales managers with a systematic approach for determining selling effort allocation. Sales managers are likely to make better allocation decisions using single factor models than when relying totally on judgment and intuition. Because of their ease of development and usage, single factor models are probably the most widely used analytical approach for making these allocation decisions.

EXHIBIT 8.2 ▪ *Example of Single Factor Model*

The XYZ Company markets a line of food products to ultimate consumers through different grocery wholesalers and retailers. The firm's salesforce calls on the grocery retailers to generate orders, develop sales promotions, and stock shelves. The salespeople are very important to the success of XYZ, and the company's account effort allocation strategy is a major determinant of salesforce productivity. A study was conducted to evaluate the current allocation and to suggest an improved strategy for the future. The study consisted of collecting information on a random sample of accounts, then using portions of the information to provide examples of the use of single factor models (this exhibit), portfolio models (Exhibit 8.3), empirical decision models (Exhibit 8.4), and judgment-based decision models (Exhibit 8.5).

The single factor model was applied to evaluate the market potential of each account and then classify all accounts into A, B, C, and D market potential categories. The average number of sales calls to an account in each market potential category was calculated and evaluated. Based on this analysis, changes in the account effort allocation strategy were made. A summary of the results follows:

Market Potential Categories	Average Sales Calls to an Account Last Year	Average Sales Calls to an Account Next Year
A	25	32
B	23	24
C	20	16
D	16	8

Portfolio Models. A more comprehensive analysis of accounts is provided by **portfolio models,** but they are somewhat more difficult to develop and use than single factor models. In a portfolio model each account served by a firm is considered as part of an overall portfolio of accounts. Thus, accounts within the portfolio represent different situations and receive different levels of selling effort attention. The typical approach is to classify all accounts in the portfolio into categories of similar attractiveness for receiving sales call investment. Then, selling effort is allocated so that the more attractive accounts receive more selling effort.[4] The typical attractiveness segments and basic effort allocation strategies are presented in Figure 8.3.[5]

Account attractiveness is a function of account opportunity and competitive position for each account. *Account opportunity* is defined as an account's need for and ability to purchase the firm's products (e.g., grocery products, computer products, financial services, etc.). *Competitive position* is defined as the strength of the relationship between the firm and an account. As indicated in Figure 8.3, accounts are more attractive the higher the account opportunity and the stronger the competitive positions are.

Using portfolio models to develop an account effort allocation strategy requires that account opportunity and competitive position be measured for each account. Based on these measurements, accounts can be classified into the attractiveness segments. The portfolio model differs from the single factor model in that many factors are normally measured to assess account opportunity and competitive position. The exact number and types of factors depend upon a firm's

FIGURE 8.3 ▪ *Portfolio Model Segments and Strategies*

Accounts are classified into attractiveness categories based upon evaluations of account opportunity and competitive position. The selling effort strategies are based on the concept that the more attractive an account, the more selling effort it should receive.

Competitive Position

	Strong	**Weak**
High (Account Opportunity)	**SEGMENT 1** **Attractiveness:** Accounts are very attractive because they offer high opportunity, and sales organization has strong competitive position. **Selling Effort Strategy:** Accounts should receive a heavy investment of selling effort to take advantage of opportunity and maintain/improve competitive position.	**SEGMENT 2** **Attractiveness:** Accounts are potentially attractive due to high opportunity, but sales organization currently has weak competitive position. **Selling Effort Strategy:** Additional analysis should be performed to identify accounts where sales organization's competitive position can be strengthened. These accounts should receive heavy investment of selling effort, while other accounts receive minimal investment.
Low (Account Opportunity)	**SEGMENT 3** **Attractiveness:** Accounts are moderately attractive due to sales organization's strong competitive position. However, future opportunity is limited. **Selling Effort Strategy:** Accounts should receive a selling effort investment sufficient to maintain current competitive position.	**SEGMENT 4** **Attractiveness:** Accounts are very unattractive; they offer low opportunity, and sales organization has weak competitive position. **Selling Effort Strategy:** Accounts should receive minimal investment of selling effort. Less costly forms of marketing (for example, telephone sales calls, direct mail) should replace personal selling efforts on a selective basis, or the account coverage should be eliminated entirely.

Source: Raymond W. LaForge, David W. Cravens, and Clifford E. Young, "Improving Salesforce Productivity," *Business Horizons*, September–October 1985, 54. Copyright 1985 by the Foundation for the School of Business at Indiana University. Reprinted by permission.

EXHIBIT 8.3 ∎ *Example of Portfolio Model*

The portfolio model is applied here to measure the account opportunity and competitive position for each account. Based on these measures, accounts are classified into segments on the portfolio grid (see Figure 8.3). Then the average sales calls and average sales for accounts in each segment are calculated and evaluated according to the portfolio strategies presented in Figure 8.3. Based on this analysis, changes in selling effort allocation are made for next year. Portions of the results follow:

Results for last year:

		Competitive Strength	
		Strong	Weak
Account Opportunity	High	Segment 1 Average Sales Calls: 27 Average Sales: 2,438 cases Number of Accounts: 97	Segment 2 Average Sales Calls: 21 Average Sales: 1,248 cases Number of Accounts: 15
	Low	Segment 3 Average Sales Calls: 23 Average Sales: 1,017 cases Number of Accounts: 26	Segment 4 Average Sales Calls: 17 Average Sales: 402 cases Number of Accounts: 66

Effort allocation changes for next year:

Portfolio Segment	Average Sales Calls to an Account Last Year	Average Sales Calls to an Account Next Year
1	27	36
2	21	24
3	23	12
4	17	6

A comparison of the single factor model (Exhibit 8.2) with the portfolio model suggests similarities in the basic approach and reasonably consistent results. However, since the portfolio model incorporates both account opportunity and competitive position, the portfolio results should provide better allocation guidelines than the single factor models.

specific selling situation. Thus, the portfolio approach provides a comprehensive account analysis that can be adapted to the specific selling situation faced by any firm. An example of a portfolio model is presented in Exhibit 8.3.[6]

Portfolio models can be valuable tools for helping sales managers improve their account effort allocation strategy. They are relatively easy to develop and use (though more difficult than single factor models) and provide a more comprehensive analysis than single factor models. Also, the portfolio model has been adapted for microcomputer use.[7]

An interesting recent development is the expansion of the portfolio model approach to incorporate sales channel decisions. As illustrated in Figure 8.4,

FIGURE 8.4   ▪   *Portfolio Model for Sales Channel and Selling Effort Decisions*
The portfolio model has been expanded to address both sales channel and selling effort decisions
for accounts.

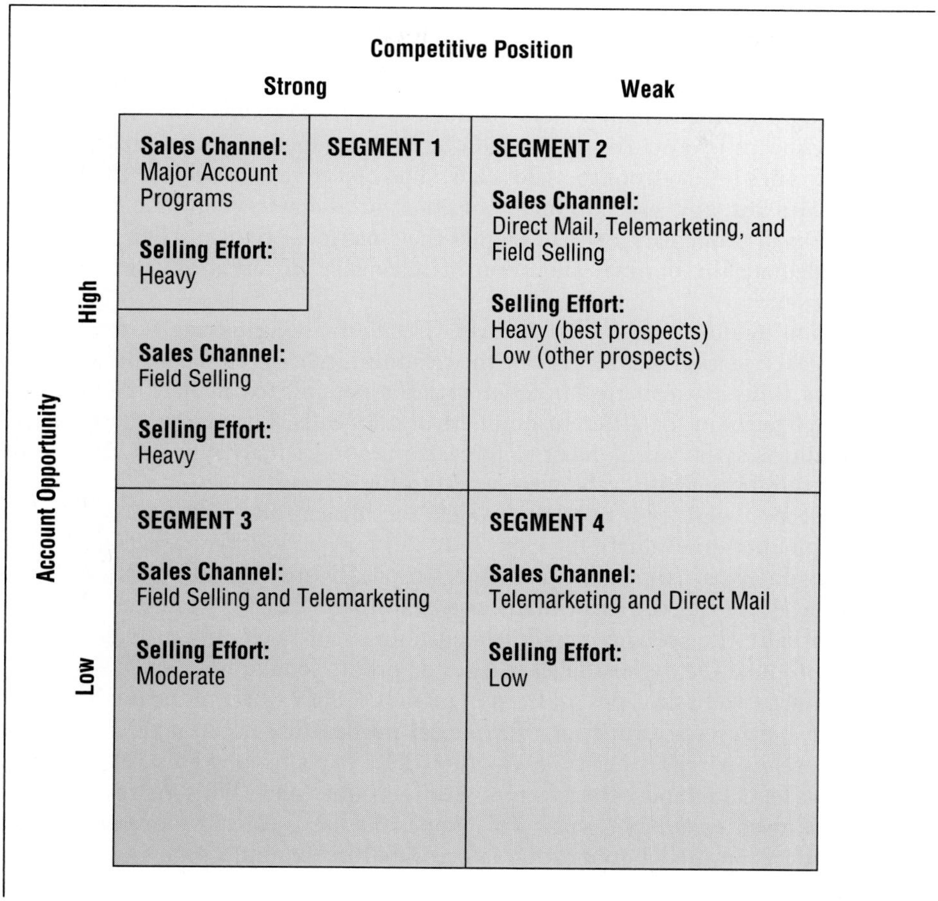

Competitive Position

	Strong	Weak

SEGMENT 1

Sales Channel:
Major Account
Programs

Selling Effort:
Heavy

Sales Channel:
Field Selling

Selling Effort:
Heavy

SEGMENT 2

Sales Channel:
Direct Mail, Telemarketing, and
Field Selling

Selling Effort:
Heavy (best prospects)
Low (other prospects)

SEGMENT 3

Sales Channel:
Field Selling and Telemarketing

Selling Effort:
Moderate

SEGMENT 4

Sales Channel:
Telemarketing and Direct Mail

Selling Effort:
Low

Account Opportunity — High / Low

Source: David W. Cravens, Thomas N. Ingram, and Raymond W. LaForge, "Evaluating Multiple
Sales Channel Strategies," *Journal of Business and Industrial Marketing*, Summer/Fall 1991 (forthcoming).

accounts are still classified into categories based on account opportunity and
competitive position considerations. However, accounts are first assigned sales
channel coverage based on their position in the portfolio model. This is followed
by determining the appropriate amount of selling effort from each sales channel for
each account. For example, the portfolio model can be used to determine the
specific amount of selling effort from telemarketing and from field selling that
accounts in Segment 3 should receive. This integration of sales channel assignment
and selling effort allocation decisions in a portfolio model is a promising
advancement, since (as discussed in Chapter 6) many sales organizations are
employing multiple sales channels to cover their accounts.

Decision Models. The most rigorous and comprehensive method for determining an account effort allocation strategy is by means of a **decision model.** Because of their complexity, decision models are somewhat difficult to develop and use. However, today's computer hardware and software make decision models much easier to use than before. Research results have consistently supported the value of decision models in improving effort allocation and salesforce productivity.[8]

Although the mathematical formulations of decision models can be complex, the basic concept is quite simple—to allocate sales calls to accounts that promise the highest sales return from the sales calls. The objective is to achieve the highest level of sales for any given number of sales calls and to continue increasing sales calls until their marginal costs equal their marginal returns. Thus, decision models calculate the optimal allocation of sales calls in terms of sales or profit maximization.

Decision models consist of two parts. The first, the **response function,** is a mathematical equation that represents the relationship between sales calls and sales to accounts. This mathematical function makes it possible to calculate the expected sales to each account for different numbers of sales calls. For example, a response function allows sales management to forecast sales to each account if 5, 10, 15, or any other number of sales calls were made to the account.

The second part of a decision model, the **allocation procedure,** uses the response function to evaluate the expected sales for many different account effort allocation strategies. Allocation procedures typically are able to rapidly evaluate the total level of sales the firm might expect from all feasible strategies. The net result is usually the specific recommended number of sales calls to each account that will produce the highest level of sales or profits for the firm.

There are two basic types of decision models.[9] They differ in the method used to develop the response function. **Empirical models** use account data from the past to develop a regression-type equation that explains previous relationships between sales calls (and other factors) and account sales. This regression-type equation is used to predict what will happen in the future. An example of an empirical decision model application is presented in Exhibit 8.4.

Judgment-based models use estimates from salespeople to develop separate response functions for each account. The typical procedure is to ask salespeople what they think sales to an account would be if they made the same number of sales calls to the account as made last year, if they decreased sales calls by 50 percent, if they increased sales calls by 50 percent, if they made no sales calls, and if they made the maximum possible number of sales calls. These estimates are used to develop a mathematical response function for each account that represents the expected relationship between sales calls and sales to the account. An example of a judgment-based decision model application is presented in Exhibit 8.5.

Comparison of Account Effort Allocation Analytical Methods. In sum, sales managers might employ single factor models, portfolio models, or decision models to help them develop an account effort allocation strategy. The approaches differ in the comprehensiveness of the account analysis, the rigor used to evaluate effort allocation alternatives, and the ease with which they can be developed and used.

EXHIBIT 8.4 ▪ *Example of Empirical Decision Model*

This empirical decision model is applied to measures of the account opportunity, competitive position, territory location, number of sales calls, and length of a sales call for each of the accounts. A regression-type procedure is used to develop an equation (response function) that uses measures of the variables just mentioned to predict sales to a retail account. An allocation procedure is then employed to use the response function to evaluate different effort allocation alternatives and to suggest the specific number of sales calls to each account that promises to produce the highest level of total sales. An example of the output of this procedure for five accounts follows:

Account	Actual Sales Calls Last Year	Actual Sales Last Year	Recommended Sales Calls Next Year from Model	Forecasted Sales Next Year from Model
AAA	25 sales calls	1,376 cases	38 sales calls	1,919 cases
BBB	50	1,404	25	1,309
CCC	20	700	14	696
DDD	26	1,213	39	1,988
EEE	20	585	10	506
	141 sales calls	5,278 cases	126 sales calls	6,418 cases

As indicated in this example application, decision models focus on effort allocation to individual accounts, whereas single factor models and portfolio models typically concentrate on effort allocation to groups of accounts. Decision models also provide a sales forecast for the suggested account effort allocation strategy. This is not possible with single factor or portfolio models. It is interesting to note that the portfolio models and empirical decision models use similar types of data. The approaches differ, however, in how this data is processed.

A detailed comparison of the different approaches is presented in Exhibit 8.6. Firms should not always use the most complex approach but should use the method that best fits their market situation and company capabilities.[10]

Salesforce Size

Research results have consistently shown that many firms could improve their performance by changing the size of their salesforce (see Exhibit 8.1).[11] In some situations the salesforce should be increased, as was the case for Perdue Frederick. In other situations, however, firms are employing too many salespeople and could improve performance by reducing the size of their salesforces. Determining the appropriate salesforce size requires an understanding of several key considerations as well as a familiarity with different analytical approaches that might be employed.

Key Considerations. The size of a firm's salesforce determines the total amount of selling effort that is available to call on accounts and prospects. The decision of salesforce size is analogous to the decision on advertising budget. Whereas the

EXHIBIT 8.5 ▪ *Example of Judgment-based Decision Model*

In this judgment-based decision model, salespeople predict what the sales to each account would be for next year if (1) the same number of sales calls are made as last year, (2) 50 percent more sales calls are made, and (3) 50 percent fewer calls are made. These estimates are used to develop a response function for each account. Each response function consists of a mathematical function that represents the relationship between sales calls and sales for a specific account. An allocation procedure is then used to search these response functions for the specific number of sales calls that would produce the highest level of total sales. The results of this procedure for five accounts follow:

Account	Actual Sales Calls Last Year	Actual Sales Last Year	Recommended Sales Calls Next Year from Model	Forecasted Sales Next Year from Model
AAA	25 sales calls	1,376 cases	44 sales calls	2,200 cases
BBB	50	1,404	23	1,375
CCC	20	700	10	675
DDD	26	1,213	40	2,050
EEE	20	585	5	475
	141 sales calls	5,278 cases	122 sales calls	6,775 cases

The major difference between the empirical decision model (Exhibit 8.4) and the judgment-based decision model is in the way the response function is developed. Data concerning what has happened in the past provides the basis for response functions in empirical models. Response functions in judgment-based models are based on estimates of what will happen in the future. The results of the two decision models for the same accounts in our example produced reasonably similar results. For example, both decision models suggest that fewer sales calls could produce more sales if changes were made in the account effort allocation strategy to the five accounts in the application example.

advertising budget establishes the total amount that the firm has to spend on advertising communications, the salesforce size determines the total amount of personal selling effort that is available. Since each salesperson can make only a certain number of sales calls during any period, the number of salespeople times the number of sales calls per salesperson defines the total available selling effort. For example, a firm with 100 salespeople that each make 500 sales calls per year has a total selling effort of 50,000 sales calls. If the salesforce is increased to 110 salespeople, then total selling effort is increased to 55,000 sales calls. Two of the key considerations in determining salesforce size are productivity and turnover.

Productivity. In general terms, *productivity* is defined as a ratio between outputs and inputs. One way the **sales productivity** of a salesforce is calculated is the ratio of sales generated to selling effort employed. Thus, productivity is an important consideration for all deployment decisions. However, selling effort is oftentimes expressed in terms of number of salespeople. Exhibit 8.7 presents sales productivity calculations for the computer industry. It shows IBM with the highest sales productivity and the largest salesforce. This suggests that the critical

EXHIBIT 8.6 ▪ *Comparison of Account Effort Allocation Analytical Methods*

Factor	Single Factor Model	Portfolio Model	Judgment-based Model	Empirical Model
Deployment Decisions	Appropriate for most deployment decisions	Appropriate for most deployment decisions	Best suited for within-territory deployment decisions	Best suited for across-territory deployment decisions
Analytical Rigor	Low	Moderate	High	High
Data Requirements	Minimal	Substantial—multiple factors are evaluated	Substantial—multiple response estimates are required	Substantial—multiple factors are evaluated
Computer Requirements	Minimal—does not require computer analysis	Ideally suited for microcomputer applications	Can be substantial, depending upon the size and complexity of the selling situation	Can be substantial, depending upon the size and complexity of the selling situation
Ease of Implementation	Relatively easy to implement	Moderately easy to implement	Somewhat difficult to implement, but incorporation of model user throughout the process aids implementation	Difficult to implement due to management's lack of understanding the complex nature of the analysis
Expenses	Low	Moderate, but depends upon firm's information system	Moderate out-of-pocket costs, but substantial time commitment required to obtain response estimates	Can be substantial, but depends upon firm's information system
Model Output	Classifications based on analysis of one factor	Classifications based on multiple factors and recommended effort deployment based on relative attractiveness	The "optimal" deployment of selling effort that will "maximize" the sales or profit objective	The "optimal" deployment of selling effort that will "maximize" the sales or profit objective

Source: Raymond W. LaForge, David W. Cravens, and Clifford E. Young, "Using Contingency Analysis to Select Selling Effort Allocation Methods," *Journal of Personal Selling and Sales Management*, August 1986, 21. Used with permission.

consideration is the *relationship* between selling effort and sales, not just the total amount of selling effort or the total level of sales.

Sales will generally increase with the addition of salespeople, but not in a linear manner. With some exceptions, costs tend to increase directly with salesforce size. This produces the basic relationship presented in Figure 8.5. In early stages, the addition of salespeople increases sales considerably more than the selling costs. However, as salespeople continue to be added, sales increases tend to decline until a point is reached where the costs to add a salesperson are more than

EXHIBIT 8.7 ▪ *Sales Productivity in the Computer Industry*

Company	1985 Revenue (Millions of Dollars)	No. of Sales Reps	Revenue per S/R (Thousands of Dollars)	S/R% of Total Employment
IBM	$50,056	20,000	$2,500	4.9%
Honeywell[a]	1,825	1,000	1,825	6.7
Sperry	3,423	2,000	1,712	5.0
NCR	4,317	3,000	1,439	4.8
Wang	2,352	2,000	1,176	6.3
DEC	6,686	6,000	1,114	8.6
Burroughs	5,038	5,500	916	9.1
Prime	770	860	900	10.6

[a]Information Systems, United States only.

Source: "Where IBM Still Leads the Way," *Sales and Marketing Management*, May 1987, 27.

the revenues that that salesperson can generate. In fact, the profit maximization point is where the marginal costs of adding a salesperson are equal to the marginal profits generated by that salesperson. It typically becomes more difficult to maintain high sales productivity levels at larger salesforce sizes. This makes it imperative that management consider the relationship between sales and costs when making decisions on salesforce size.

Turnover. It has been estimated that when a salesperson quits, the costs associated with recruiting, training, and managing a new salesperson, together with the opportunity costs from lost sales, may be as high as $50,000 to $75,000.[12] **Salesforce turnover** is extremely costly. A recent study reported that salesforce turnover has tripled in five years, from an average 7.6% in 1983 to 27% in 1988.[13] Of course, rates of turnover vary by industry and firm.

Since some turnover is going to occur for all firms, it should always be considered when determining salesforce size. Once the appropriate salesforce size is determined—that is, one sufficient for salespeople to call on all of the firm's accounts and prospects in a productive manner—this figure should be adjusted to reflect expected turnover. If an increase or maintenance of current salesforce size is desired, excess salespeople should be in the recruiting-selecting-training pipeline. If a decrease is desired, turnover might be all that is necessary to accomplish it. For example, a grocery products marketer who found that its salesforce should be reduced from 34 to 32 salespeople achieved the 2-salesperson reduction through scheduled retirements in the near future instead of firing 2 salespeople.

Analytical Tools. The need to consider sales, costs, productivity, and turnover makes salesforce size a difficult decision. Fortunately, some analytical tools are available to help management process relevant information and evaluate salesforce size alternatives more fully. Before describing these analytical tools, we want to

FIGURE 8.5 ▪ *Sales and Cost Relationships*

Although costs tend to increase in a linear manner with the addition of salespeople, the associated sales increases are typically nonlinear. In general, the increases in sales tend to decrease as more salespeople are added. A point (A) is reached where the sales from adding a salesperson are not sufficient to cover the additional costs.

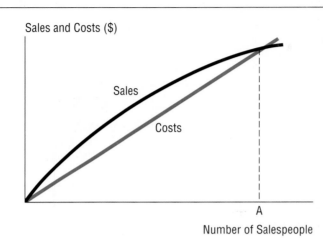

make it clear that there are different types of salesforce size decisions (see Figure 8.6). The most straightforward situation is when a firm has one, generalized salesforce. However, as discussed in Chapter 7, many firms employ multiple, specialized salesforces, in which case both the total number of salespeople employed by the firm and the size of each individual salesforce are important. Both generalized and specialized salesforces are normally organized into geographic districts, zones, regions, and so on. The number of salespeople to assign to each district, zone, region, and so on is a type of salesforce size decision.

These different types of decisions are similar conceptually and can be addressed by the same analytical tools, provided that the type of salesforce size decision being addressed is specified. Unless stated otherwise, you can assume the situation of one, generalized salesforce in the following discussion.

Breakdown Approach. A relatively simple approach for calculating salesforce size, the **breakdown approach** assumes that an accurate sales forecast is available. This forecast is then "broken down" to determine the number of salespeople needed to generate the forecasted level of sales. The basic formula is

Salesforce size = Forecasted sales/Average sales per salesperson

Assume that a firm forecasts sales of $50 million for next year. If salespeople generate an average of $2 million in annual sales, then the firm needs 25 salespeople to achieve the $50 million sales forecast:

Salesforce size = $50,000,000/$2,000,000 = 25 salespeople

The basic advantage of the breakdown method is its ease of development. The approach is very straightforward and the mathematical calculations very simple.

FIGURE 8.6   ▪   *Different Salesforce Size Decisions*

Depending upon the sales organization structure of a firm, sales managers may be faced with several different types of salesforce size decisions. Each requires the same basic concepts and analytical methods.

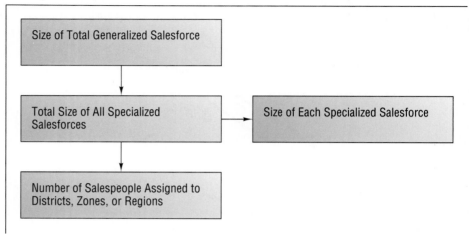

However, the approach is very weak conceptually. The concept underlying the calculations is that sales determine the number of salespeople needed. This puts "the cart before the horse," since the number of salespeople employed by a firm is an important determinant of firm sales. A sales forecast should be based on a given salesforce size. The addition of salespeople should increase the forecast, while the elimination of salespeople should decrease it.

Despite this weakness, the breakdown method is probably the most often used for determining salesforce size. It is best suited for relatively stable selling environments where sales change in slow and predictable ways and no major strategic changes are planned, also for organizations that use commission compensation plans and keep their fixed costs low. However, in many selling situations the costs of having too many or too few salespeople are high. More rigorous analytical tools are recommended for calculating salesforce size in these situations.

Workload Approach.   The first step in the **workload approach** is to determine how much selling effort is needed to adequately cover the firm's market. Then the number of salespeople required to provide this amount of selling effort is calculated. The basic formula is

$$\text{Number of salespeople} = \frac{\text{Total selling effort needed}}{\text{Average selling effort per salesperson}}$$

For example, if a firm determines that 37,500 sales calls are needed in its market area and a salesperson can make an average of 500 annual sales calls, then 75 salespeople are needed to provide the desired level of selling effort:

$$\text{Number of salespeople} = 37{,}500/500 = 75 \text{ salespeople}$$

EXHIBIT 8.8 ▪ *Incremental Approach*

Number of Salespeople	Marginal Salesperson Profit Contribution	Marginal Salesperson Cost
100	$85,000	$75,000
101	$80,000	$75,000
102	$75,000	$75,000
103	$70,000	$75,000

The key factor in the workload approach is the total amount of selling effort needed. Several workload methods can be used, depending upon whether single factor, portfolio, or decision models were used for determining the allocation of effort to accounts. Each workload method offers a different way to calculate how many sales calls to make to all accounts and prospects during any time period. When the sales call allocation strategies are summed across all accounts and prospects, the total amount of selling effort for a time period is determined. Thus, the workload approach integrates the salesforce size decision with account effort allocation strategies.

The workload approach is also relatively simple to develop, although this simplicity depends upon the specific method used to determine total selling effort needs. The approach is also sound conceptually, since salesforce size is based on selling effort needs established by account effort allocation decisions. Note, however, we have presented the workload approach in a simplified manner here by considering only selling effort. A more realistic presentation would incorporate nonselling time considerations (e.g., travel time, planning time, etc.) in the analysis. Although incorporating these considerations does not change the basic workload concept, it does make the calculations more complex and cumbersome.

The workload approach is suited for all types of selling situations. Sales organizations can adapt the basic approach to their specific situation through the method used to calculate total selling effort. The most sophisticated firms can use decision models for this purpose, while other firms might use portfolio models or single factor approaches.

Incremental Approach. The most rigorous approach for calculating salesforce size is the **incremental approach.**[14] Its basic concept is to compare the marginal profit contribution to the marginal selling costs for each incremental salesperson. An example of these calculations is provided in Exhibit 8.8. At 100 salespeople, marginal profits exceed marginal costs by $10,000. This relationship continues until salesforce size reaches 102. At 102 salespeople, the marginal profit equals marginal cost, and total profits are maximized. If the firm added one more salesperson, total profits would be reduced, because marginal costs would exceed marginal profits by $5,000. Thus, the optimal salesforce size for this example is 102.

The major advantage of the incremental approach is that it quantifies the important relationships between salesforce size, sales, and costs, making it possible to assess the potential sales and profit impacts of different salesforce sizes. It forces management to view the salesforce size decision as one that affects both the level of sales that can be generated and the costs associated with producing each sales level.

The incremental method is, however, somewhat difficult to develop. Relatively complex response functions must be formulated to predict sales at different salesforce sizes (sales = f[salesforce size]). Developing these response functions requires either historical data or management judgment. Thus, the incremental approach cannot be used for new salesforces where historical data and accurate judgments are not possible.

Turnover. All of the analytical tools incorporate various elements of sales and costs in their calculations. Therefore, they directly address productivity issues but do not directly consider turnover in the salesforce size calculations. When turnover considerations are important, management should adjust the recommended salesforce size produced by any of the analytical methods to reflect expected turnover rates. For example, if an analytical tool recommended a salesforce size of 100 for a firm that experiences 20 percent annual turnover, the effective salesforce size should be adjusted to 120. Recruiting, selecting, and training plans should be based on the 120 salesforce size.

Failure to incorporate anticipated salesforce turnover into salesforce size calculations can be costly. Evidence suggests that many firms may lose as much as 10 percent in sales productivity due to the loss in sales from vacant territories or low initial sales when a new salesperson is assigned to a territory. Thus, the sooner that sales managers can replace salespeople and get them productive in their territories, the less loss in sales within the territory.[15]

Designing Territories

As discussed earlier, the size of a salesforce determines the total amount of selling effort that a firm has available to generate sales from accounts and prospects. The effective use of this selling effort often requires that sales **territories** be developed and each salesperson be assigned to a specific territory. A territory consists of whatever specific accounts are assigned to a specific salesperson. The overall objective is to ensure that all accounts are assigned salesperson responsibility and that each salesperson can adequately cover the assigned accounts. Although territories are often defined by geographic area (e.g., the Oklahoma territory, the Tennessee territory, etc.), the key components of a territory are the accounts within the specified geographic area.

The territory can be viewed as the work unit for a salesperson. The salesperson is largely responsible for the selling activities performed and the performance achieved in a territory. Salesperson compensation and success are normally a direct function of territory performance; thus, the design of territories is extremely important to the individual salespeople of a firm as well as to management.

Territory Considerations. The critical territory considerations are illustrated in Exhibit 8.9. In this example, Andy and Sally are salespeople for a consumer durable goods manufacturer. They have each been assigned a geographic territory

EXHIBIT 8.9 ▪ *Territory Design Example*

	Trading Area[a]	*Present Effort (%)*[b]	*Recommended Effort (%)*[b]
Andy	1	10	4
	2	60	20
	3	15	7
	4	5	2
	5	10	3
Total		100	36
Sally	6	18	81
	7	7	21
	8	5	11
	9	35	35
	10	5	11
	11	30	77
Total		100	236

[a]Each territory is made up of several trading areas.
[b]The percentage of salesperson time spent in the trading area (100% = 1 salesperson). Thus, the deployment analysis suggests that Andy's territory requires only 0.36 salespeople, while Sally's territory needs 2.36 salespeople for proper coverage.
Source: Raymond W. LaForge, David W. Cravens, and Clifford E. Young, "Improving Salesforce Productivity," *Business Horizons*, September/October 1985, 57.

consisting of several trading areas. The exhibit compares the percentage of their time currently spent in each trading area with the percentages recommended from a decision model analysis. A review of the information provided in the exhibit highlights territory design problems from the perspective of the firm and of each salesperson.

The current territory design does not provide proper selling coverage of the trading areas. The decision model analysis suggests that the trading areas in Andy's territory should require only 36 percent of his time, yet he is spending all of his time there. Clearly, the firm is wasting expensive selling effort in Andy's territory. The situation in Sally's territory is just the opposite. Proper coverage of Sally's trading areas should require more than two salespeople, yet Sally has sole responsibility for these trading areas. In this situation the firm is losing sales opportunities because of a lack of selling attention.

From the firm's perspective, the design of Andy's and Sally's territories limits sales and profit performance. Sales performance in Sally's territory is much lower than it might be if more selling attention were given to her trading areas. Profit performance is low in Andy's territory because too much selling effort is being expended in his trading areas. The firm is not achieving the level of sales and profits that might be achieved if the territories were designed to provide more productive market coverage. Thus, one key consideration in territory design is the productive deployment of selling effort within each territory.

From the perspective of Andy and Sally, the poor territory design affects their level of motivation. Andy is frustrated. He spends much of his time making sales

FIGURE 8.7 ▪ *Territory Design Procedure*

Designing territories requires a multiple-stage approach. Although most territory design approaches follow the stages presented in this figure, the methods used at each stage differ considerably depending upon the analytical tools employed.

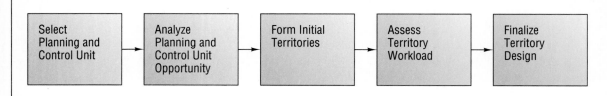

calls in trading areas where there is little potential for generating additional sales. Andy's motivational level is low, and he may consider resigning from the company. In contrast, Sally's territory has so much sales potential that she can limit her sales calls to the largest accounts or the easiest sales. She is not motivated to develop the potential of her territory, but can merely "skim the cream" from the best accounts. The situations facing Andy and Sally illustrate how territory design might affect salesperson motivation, morale, and even turnover. These potential effects are important considerations when designing territories.

Procedure for Designing Territories. A general procedure for designing territories is presented in Figure 8.7. Each step in the procedure can be performed manually or by using computer models. We will illustrate the procedure manually using Andy's and Sally's territories as an example application. The basic problem is to organize the 11 trading areas into 3 territories that provide proper market coverage of accounts in each territory and equal performance opportunities for each salesperson. We are developing 3 territories because the decision model results presented in Exhibit 8.9 indicate that two salespeople cannot adequately cover these trading areas. The data needed to design the sales territories is presented in Exhibit 8.10.

Select Planning and Control Unit. The first step in territory design is to select the **planning and control unit** that will be used in the analysis—that is, some entity that is smaller than a territory. The total market area served by a firm is divided into these planning and control units, then they are analyzed and grouped together to form territories.

Examples of potential planning and control units are illustrated in Figure 8.8. In general, management should use the smallest unit feasible. However, data are oftentimes not available for small planning and control units, and the computational task becomes more complex as more units are included in the analysis. The selection of the appropriate planning and control unit therefore represents a trade-off between what is desired and what is possible under the given data or computational conditions. In our example trading areas have been selected as the planning and control unit. As presented in the opening vignette, Perdue Frederick used ZIP codes as the planning and control unit for its territory design approach.

EXHIBIT 8.10 ▪ *Territory Design Data*

Trading Area	Market Potential	Number of Sales Calls
1	$ 250,000	25
2	$ 700,000	100
3	$ 350,000	35
4	$ 150,000	15
5	$ 200,000	20
6	$2,000,000	175
7	$ 750,000	65
8	$ 500,000	50
9	$1,000,000	100
10	$ 500,000	50
11	$1,750,000	175

Analyze Opportunity of Planning and Control Unit. First determine the amount of opportunity available from each planning and control unit. Specific methods for performing these calculations will be covered in Chapter 14. However, the most often used measure of opportunity is *market potential.* The market potentials for the 11 trading areas in our example are provided in Exhibit 8.10. Everything else being equal, the higher the market potential, the more opportunity is available.

Form Initial Territories. Once planning and control units have been selected and opportunity evaluated, initial territories can be designed. The objective is to group the planning and control units into territories that are as equal as possible in opportunity. This step may take several iterations as there are probably a number of feasible territory designs. It is also unlikely that any design will achieve complete equality of opportunity. The best approach is to design several different territory arrangements and evaluate each alternative. Each alternative must be feasible in that planning and control units grouped together are contiguous. This can be a cumbersome task when done manually but is much more efficient when computer modeling approaches are used, as indicated in the Perdue Frederick example.

FIGURE 8.8 ▪ *Potential Planning and Control Units*

Planning and control units represent the unit of analysis for territory design. Accounts are the preferred planning and control unit. However, oftentimes it is not possible to use them as such, in which case a more aggregate type of planning and control unit is employed.

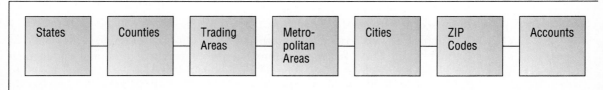

EXHIBIT 8.11 ▪ *Initial Territory Designs*

	Alternative 1		Alternative 2	
	Trading Area	*Market Potential*	*Trading Area*	*Market Potential*
Territory 1	1	$ 250,000	1	$ 250,000
	2	$ 700,000	2	$ 700,000
	3	$ 350,000	5	$ 200,000
	4	$ 150,000	8	$ 500,000
	5	$ 200,000	9	$1,000,000
		$1,650,000		$2,650,000
Territory 2	6	$2,000,000	6	$2,000,000
	7	$ 750,000	7	$ 750,000
	8	$ 500,000		
		$3,250,000		$2,750,000
Territory 3	9	$1,000,000	3	$ 350,000
	10	$ 500,000	4	$ 150,000
	11	$1,750,000	10	$ 500,000
			11	$1,750,000
		$3,250,000		$2,750,000

Two alternative territory designs for our example are presented and evaluated in Exhibit 8.11. Although the first design is feasible, the territories are markedly unequal in opportunity. However, a few adjustments produce reasonably equal territories.

Assess Territory Workloads. The preceding step produces territories of nearly equal opportunity. It may, however, take more work to realize this opportunity in some territories than in others. Therefore, the workload of each territory should be evaluated by (1) the number of sales calls required to cover the accounts in the territory, (2) the amount of travel time in the territory, (3) the total number of accounts, and (4) any other factors that measure the amount of work required by a salesperson assigned to the territory. In our example, workload for each trading area and territory is evaluated by the number of sales calls required. This information is presented in Exhibit 8.12.

Finalize Territory Design. The final step is to adjust the initial territories to achieve equal workloads for each salesperson. The objective is to achieve the best possible balance between equal opportunity and equal workload for each territory. Typically, both of these objectives cannot be completely achieved, so management must decide upon the best trade-offs for its situation. Any inequalities in the final territories can be addressed when quotas are established. These procedures will be discussed in Chapter 14.

Achieving workload and opportunity balance for our example is illustrated in Exhibit 8.13. The equal opportunity territories resulted in somewhat unequal workloads (see Exhibit 8.12). The final territory design moved Trading Area 7 to Territory 1 and Trading Area 2 to Territory 2. This produces territories that are reasonably equal in both opportunity and workload.

EXHIBIT 8.12 ▪ *Workload Evaluations*

	Trading Area	Sales Calls
Territory 1	1	25
	2	100
	5	20
	8	50
	9	100
		295
Territory 2	6	175
	7	65
		240
Territory 3	3	35
	4	15
	10	50
	11	175
		275

EXHIBIT 8.13 ▪ *Final Territory Design*

	Trading Area	Market Potential	Sales Calls
Territory 1	1	$ 250,000	25
	5	$ 200,000	20
	7	$ 750,000	65
	8	$ 500,000	50
	9	$1,000,000	100
		$2,700,000	260
Territory 2	2	$ 700,000	100
	6	$2,000,000	175
		$2,700,000	275
Territory 3	3	$ 350,000	35
	4	$ 150,000	15
	10	$ 500,000	50
	11	$1,750,000	175
		$2,750,000	275

Performing territory design analyses manually is difficult and time consuming. Fortunately, advances in computer hardware and software make it possible to consider multiple factors and rapidly evaluate many alternatives when designing territories.

Assigning Salespeople to Territories. Once territories have been designed, salespeople must be assigned to them. Salespeople are not equal in abilities and will perform differently with different types of accounts or prospects. Some sales managers consider their salespeople to be either *farmers* or *hunters*. Farmers are effective with existing accounts but do not perform well in establishing business with new accounts. Hunters excel in establishing new accounts but do not fully develop existing accounts. Based on these categories, farmers should be assigned to

EXHIBIT 8.14 ▪ *Salesperson Indices*

Salesperson	Territory		
	1	*2*	*3*
Andy	1.4	1.0	0.8
Sally	0.6	0.9	1.2
Sam	1.2	0.6	1.0

territories that contain many ongoing account relationships, while hunters should be assigned to territories in new or less-developed market areas.

One way to quantify the territory assignment decision is to develop salesperson indices for each territory. Management evaluates the potential effectiveness of each salesperson for each territory, with an index value of 1 for the norm. Values less than 1 indicate poor performance and values greater than 1 superior performance in a territory. The objective is to assign salespeople to territories in a manner that maximizes total firm performance.

As an illustration, let's continue our example. Exhibit 8.13 presents the three territories that have been designed. The task is to assign Andy, Sally, and another salesperson (Sam) to these territories. The first step is for management to develop ability indices for each salesperson and each territory. These indices are presented in Exhibit 8.14. As evident from the exhibit, performance is expected to differ substantially depending upon how the salespeople are assigned to the territories.

The next step is to use the indices to adjust the sales potential for each territory to reflect different salesperson assignments. Whereas the market potential evaluations used to design territories represent assessments of opportunity available to all competing firms, sales potential is an evaluation of the opportunity available to a specific firm. The sales potential figures are smaller than the market potential numbers and change depending upon the salesperson that is assigned to the territory. These calculations are presented in Exhibit 8.15. Since we are performing this task manually, we can calculate the total sales potential for alternative territory assignments. The results of this analysis for three alternatives are shown in Exhibit 8.16. The best alternative is the second one, where Sam is assigned to Territory 1, Andy is assigned to Territory 2, and Sally is assigned to Territory 3. No other alternative will produce a higher total sales potential, so this territory design is the one that maximizes total sales potential for the firm.

Two important points should be emphasized. First, assigning three salespeople to three territories is a simplified version of the typical territory assignment task. This manual procedure would be very cumbersome if management had to assign hundreds or thousands of salespeople. However, the procedure is readily adaptable to computerization. Once the salesperson indices and territory sales potentials are established, computer algorithms can rapidly evaluate assignment alternatives to determine the specific assignment of salespeople to territories that will maximize sales potential for the firm.

Second, maximizing the sales potential for individual salespeople will not necessarily maximize sales potential for the firm. As illustrated in Exhibit 8.15, Andy has the highest index for the highest sales potential territory. However, if

EXHIBIT 8.15   ▪   *Territory Assignment Calculations*

	Sales Potential	Andy	Sally	Sam
Territory 1	$500,000	× 1.4 = $700,000	× 0.6 = $300,000	× 1.2 = $600,000
Territory 2	$475,000	× 1.0 = $475,000	× 0.9 = $427,500	× 0.6 = $285,000
Territory 3	$450,000	× 0.8 = $360,000	× 1.2 = $540,000	× 1.0 = $450,000

EXHIBIT 8.16   ▪   *Evaluating Territory Assignment Alternatives*

		Alternatives				
		1		2		3
Andy	Territory 1 =	$700,000	Territory 2 =	$475,000	Territory 1 =	$700,000
Sally	Territory 2 =	$427,500	Territory 3 =	$540,000	Territory 3 =	$540,000
Sam	Territory 3 =	$450,000	Territory 1 =	$600,000	Territory 2 =	$285,000
		$1,577,500		$1,615,000		$1,525,000

Andy is assigned to Territory 1, Sally and Sam must be assigned to either Territory 2 or 3. In either case, the total sales potential is less than when Andy is assigned to Territory 2 (see Exhibit 8.16). The key implication is that management should consider all salespeople when making territory assignments. Focusing on only óne or two salespeople will not normally produce the best decisions.

"People" Considerations

Our discussion of salesforce deployment decisions has, to this point, focused entirely on analytical approaches. This analytical orientation emphasizes objective sales and cost considerations in evaluating different allocations of sales calls to accounts, different salesforce sizes, different territory designs, and different assignments of salespeople to territories. Although such analytical approaches are valuable and should be employed by sales managers, final deployment decisions should also be based on "people" considerations and should address potential ethical questions (see "An Ethical Perspective: Ethical Considerations in Territory Design and Assignment").

Statistics are numbers, whereas sales managers, salespeople, and customers are people. Analysis of statistical data provides useful but incomplete information for deployment decisions. Models are only representations of reality, and no matter how complex, no model can incorporate all of the people factors that are important in any salesforce deployment decision. Accordingly, while employing the appropriate analytical approaches, sales managers should temper the analytical results with people considerations before making final deployment decisions.

What are the important people considerations in salesforce deployment? The most important ones concern personal relationships between salespeople and customers and between salespeople and the sales organization. Consider the allocation of selling effort to accounts. The analytical approaches for making this decision produce a recommended number of sales calls to each account based on some assessment of expected sales and costs for different sales call levels. Although these approaches may incorporate a number of factors in developing the recommended sales call levels, there is no way that any analytical approach can utilize the detailed knowledge that a salesperson has about the unique needs of individual accounts. Therefore, an analytical approach may suggest that sales calls should be increased or decreased to a specific account, while the salesperson serving this account may know that the account will react adversely to any changes in sales call coverage. In this situation a sales manager would be wise to ignore the analytical recommendation and not change sales call coverage to the account, because of the existing relationship between the salesperson and customer.

Salesforce size decisions also require consideration of people issues. A decision to reduce the size of a salesforce means that some salespeople will have to be removed from the salesforce. How this reduction is accomplished can affect the relationship between salespeople and the sales organization. Achieving this reduction through attrition or offering salespeople other positions is typically a better approach than merely firing salespeople.

Increasing salesforce size means that the new salespeople must be assigned to territories. Consequently, some accounts will find themselves being served by new salespeople. These changes in assignment can have a devastating effect on the existing customer-salesperson relationship. Not only should that relationship be considered but also the issue of fairness in taking accounts from one salesperson and assigning them to another. The situation can be a delicate one, requiring careful judgment as to how these people considerations should be balanced against analytical results.

AN ETHICAL PERSPECTIVE

Ethical Considerations in Territory Design and Assignment

Our discussion of territory design and assignment has focused entirely on analytical considerations. However, the final territory design and assignment decisions typically incorporate additional factors and may result in some decisions with ethical consequences. Conversations with David C. Moore, Vice-President of Sales for Ruddell & Associates, produced the following ethical situations that he has witnessed:

- A sales manager reassigns a low performing salesperson to a poor territory as a punishment rather than directly addressing the salesperson's performance problem or taking definitive action and terminating the salesperson.

- A rookie salesperson is assigned an extremely difficult territory with little chance for him or her to be successful and no indication upon hire of how challenging and precarious the territory assignment is.

- A sales manager takes the easy way out in designing territories by giving each salesperson a state (or some other easily divisible area) without any consideration of differences in market potential or workload.

- A manufacturer's representative agency has done a terrific job in developing a territory. The company then takes the territory from the agency and hires direct salespeople to assume the sales responsibility.

Source: Based on conversations with David C. Moore, February 1991.

In sum, sales managers should integrate the results from salesforce deployment analysis with people considerations before implementing changes in sales call allocation, salesforce size, or territory design. A good rule of thumb is to make salesforce deployment changes that are likely to have the least disruptive effect on existing personal relationships.

Summary

1.   Discuss the different areas involved in salesforce deployment. Salesforce deployment decisions entail allocating selling effort, determining salesforce size, and designing territories. These decisions are highly interrelated and should be addressed in an integrated, sequential manner. Improvements in salesforce deployment can produce substantial increases in sales and profits.

2.   Explain three different analytical approaches for determining allocation of selling effort. Single factor, portfolio, and decision models can be used as analytical tools to determine appropriate selling effort allocations. The approaches differ in terms of analytical rigor and ease of development and use. Sales organizations should employ the approach that best fits their particular selling situation.

3.   Describe three different methods for calculating salesforce size. The breakdown method for calculating salesforce size is the easiest method to use but the weakest conceptually. It uses the expected level of sales to determine the number of salespeople. The workload approach is sounder conceptually, since it bases the salesforce size decision on the amount of selling effort needed to cover the market appropriately. The incremental method is the best approach, although it is often difficult to develop. It examines the marginal sales and costs associated with different salesforce sizes.

4.   Explain the importance of sales territories from the perspective of the sales organization and from the perspective of the salespeople. Territories are assignments of accounts to salespeople. Each becomes the work unit for a salesperson, who is largely responsible for the performance of the assigned territory. Poorly designed territories can have adverse effects on the motivation of salespeople. From the perspective of the firm, territory design decisions should ensure that the firm's market area is adequately covered in a productive manner.

5.   List the steps in the territory design process. The first step in the territory design process is to identify planning and control units. Next, the opportunity available from each planning and control unit is determined, initial territories are formed, and the workloads of each potential territory are assessed. The final territory design represents management's judgment concerning the best balance between opportunity and workload.

6.   Describe a method for assigning salespeople to sales territories. Once territories are designed, each salesperson must be assigned to a specific territory. The basic objective is to assign salespeople to territories in a manner that maximizes total firm performance. Ability indices can be used as a method for determining appropriate territory assignment. The indices are combined with territory sales potentials to calculate the total sales potential from alternative territory assignments. Then the territory assignment alternative that maximizes total sales potential can be selected.

7.   Discuss the important "people" considerations in salesforce deployment. Although analytical approaches provide useful input for salesforce deployment decisions, they do not address "people" considerations adequately. Sales managers should always consider existing relationships between salespeople and customers and between salespeople and the sales organization before making salesforce deployment changes. Many of these "people" considerations have ethical consequences.

Key Terms

- **Salesforce deployment**
- **Single factor models**
- **Portfolio models**
- **Decision models**
- **Response function**
- **Allocation procedure**
- **Empirical models**
- **Judgment-based models**

- **Sales productivity**
- **Salesforce turnover**
- **Breakdown approach**
- **Workload approach**
- **Incremental approach**
- **Territory**
- **Planning and control unit**

Review Questions

1. How are salesforce deployment decisions related to decisions on sales organization structure?
2. Referring to "A Global Perspective: Deploying a Salesforce in Japan," what potential difficulties and alternatives for deploying a salesforce in Eastern European countries can you suggest?
3. How do decisions on allocation of selling effort, salesforce size, and territory design affect salesforce productivity?
4. How can the incremental method be used to determine the number of salespeople to assign to a sales district?
5. How are salesforce size decisions different for firms with one generalized salesforce versus firms with several specialized salesforces?
6. Review the situations described in "An Ethical Perspective: Ethical Considerations in Territory Design and Assignment." Do you consider these practices to be unethical? Why or why not?
7. Discuss the advantages and disadvantages of the single factor, portfolio model, and decision models for allocating selling effort.
8. How can computer modeling assist sales managers in designing territories?
9. What are the key analytical and "people" considerations in assigning salespeople to territories?
10. Should firms always try to design equal territories? Why or why not?

Application Exercises

1. The XYZ Corporation is concerned about the productivity of its salesforce. As sales planning manager, you have been asked to prepare a proposal to evaluate current sales productivity and to suggest improvements for increasing sales productivity. Prepare a proposal that describes exactly what you would do and how you would do it. Use a flowchart to illustrate the sequence of steps you would take and how the steps are interrelated.

2. Assume that you are a district sales manager for ABC Company. You supervise six salespeople and are pleased with the performance of your district and the territories assigned to your salespeople. However, your regional sales manager has hired a new salesperson and assigned her to your district. You complain to the regional sales manager that your district does not need an additional salesperson. The regional sales manager indicates that you must accept this salesperson into your district and assign her to a territory. What would you do? Be sure to address the analyses you would perform and how you would use the new territories that you have designed to incorporate the new salesperson.

3. As the national sales manager for the PC Corporation, you are concerned about the productivity of your salesforce. You think that an improved account effort allocation strategy would increase sales productivity and have collected the following information:

Account	Account Opportunity	Competitive Position	Sales Calls	Sales
AAA	High	Strong	50	$25,000
BBB	High	Weak	25	$20,000
CCC	High	Weak	35	$ 5,000
DDD	Low	Strong	50	$10,000
EEE	Low	Strong	20	$10,000
FFF	High	Strong	25	$20,000
GGG	Low	Weak	20	$ 3,000
HHH	Low	Strong	35	$15,000
III	Low	Strong	30	$10,000
JJJ	High	Weak	25	$ 7,500

Assume that this is a large enough sample of accounts to be representative of all accounts. Develop a portfolio model and assess current effort allocation. Based on your analysis, suggest a more productive effort allocation strategy.

Notes

[1]See the following studies for more detailed results from deployment studies: Zarrel V. Lambert and Fred W. Kniffin, "Response Functions and Their Application in Sales Force Management," *Southern Journal of Business* 5 (January 1970): 1–11; Leonard M. Lodish, "Callplan: An Interactive Salesman's Call Planning System," *Management Science* 18 (December 1971): 25–40; David B. Montgomery, Alvin J. Silk, and Carlos E. Zaragoza, "A Multiple-Product Sales Force Allocation Model," *Management Science*, 18, 1971, 3–24; Leonard M. Lodish, "Sales Territory Alignment to Maximize Profit," *Journal of Marketing Research* 12 (February 1975): 30–36; Charles A. Beswick and David W. Cravens, "A Multistage Decision Model for Sales-force Management," *Journal of Marketing Research* 14 (May 1977): 134–144; William K. Fudge and Leonard M. Lodish, "Evaluation of the Effectiveness of a Model Based Salesman's Planning System by Field Experimentation," *Interfaces*, 8, 1977, 97–106; A. Parasuraman and Ralph L. Day, "A Management-Oriented Model for Allocating Sales Effort," *Journal of Marketing Research* 14 (February 1977): 22–23; Andris A. Zoltners and Prabhakant Sinha, "Integer Programming Models for Sales Resource Allocation," *Management Science*, 26, 1980, 242–260; Raymond W. LaForge and David W. Cravens, "Empirical and Judgment-Based Salesforce Decision Models: A Comparative Analysis," *Decision Sciences*, Spring 1985, 177–195; David W. Cravens,

Terry Dielman, Charles W. Lamb, Jr., and William C. Moncrief, "Sequential Modeling for Selling Effort Deployment in Reorganized Salesforces," *Working Paper Series*, Texas Christian University, 1986.

[2]"Surprise! Some Call Costs Decline," *Sales and Marketing Management*, November 1986, 24.

[3]Louis A. Wallis, *Marketing Priorities* (New York: The Conference Board, 1987), 5.

[4]See Renato Fiocca, "Account Portfolio Analysis for Strategy Development," *Industrial Marketing Management*, 11, 1982, 53–62; and Alan J. Dubinsky and Thomas N. Ingram, "A Portfolio Approach to Account Profitability," *Industrial Marketing Management*, 13, 1984, 33–41, for slightly different applications of the portfolio concept.

[5]See Raymond W. LaForge, David W. Cravens, and Clifford E. Young, "Improving Salesforce Productivity," *Business Horizons*, September–October 1985, 50–59, for more detailed discussion of the portfolio approach.

[6]See Raymond W. LaForge and David W. Cravens, "Steps in Selling Effort Deployment," *Industrial Marketing Management*, July 1982, 183–194; Raymond W. LaForge, Clifford E. Young, and B. Curtis Hamm, "Increasing Sales Productivity through Improved Sales Call Allocation Strategies," *Journal of Personal Selling and Sales Management*, November 1983, 52–59; and Raymond W. LaForge and Clifford E. Young, "A Portfolio Model for Planning Sales Call Coverage," *Business*, April–June 1985, 10–16, for additional portfolio model applications.

[7]See Raymond W. LaForge, David W. Cravens, and Clifford E. Young, "Developing Research-Based Selling Strategies," *Proceedings*, 1986 American Marketing Association Winter Educators' Conference, 154–157.

[8]See Raymond W. LaForge, David W. Cravens, and Clifford E. Young, "Using Contingency Analysis to Select Selling Effort Allocation Methods," *Journal of Personal Selling and Sales Management*, August 1986, 23, for a summary of productivity improvements from decision model applications.

[9]See Raymond W. LaForge and David W. Cravens, "Empirical and Judgment-Based Salesforce Decision Models: A Comparative Analysis," *Decision Sciences*, Spring 1985, 177–195, for a comparative discussion and test of the empirical and judgment-based decision model approaches.

[10]An approach for determining the appropriate method for a particular firm can be found in LaForge, Cravens, and Young, "Using Contingency Analysis," 19–27.

[11]See LaForge, Cravens, and Young, "Using Contingency Analysis," 23, for a summary of these research results.

[12]Reported in George H. Lucas, Jr., A. Parasuraman, Robert A. Davis, and Ben M. Enis, "An Empirical Study of Salesforce Turnover," *Journal of Marketing*, July 1987, 34.

[13]Reported in Lynn G. Coleman, "Sales Force Turnover Has Managers Wondering Why," *Marketing News*, December 4, 1989, 6.

[14]See Arthur Beidan, "Optimizing the Number of Industrial Salespersons," *Industrial Marketing Management*, 11, 1982, 63–74, for a detailed presentation of incremental methods for determining salesforce size.

[15]James W. Obermayer, "Don't Risk Sales Leakage!" *Business Marketing*, February 1990, 44–48.

CASE 8.1   *Fiber Tubing Inc.*

Background

Fiber Tubing Inc. is a small but growing firm that markets fiberglass tubing to many different types of industrial customers. The company is developing strategic plans for the 1990s. One of the major areas of concern for National Sales Manager Fred Wynn is whether the firm has sufficient selling effort in each district to meet the firm's growth objectives. Bill Johnson, a recent MBA, has just been added to Fred's sales planning staff. Bill has been given the assignment to analyze the situation and make recommendations concerning the number of salespeople needed in each district. Bill has assembled the following information for last year from company records:

District	Number of Salespeople in District	District Market Potential	District Sales
1	4	$10,000,000	$2,661,075
2	5	$12,000,000	$3,125,000
3	3	$ 8,000,000	$2,425,025
4	3	$ 7,500,000	$2,133,675
5	6	$15,000,000	$3,925,550
6	4	$11,000,000	$3,375,500

He has also used similar historical company data to develop the following model:

$$\text{District sales} = 25 \times \text{District market potential}^{.65} \times \text{Number of district salespeople}^{.55}$$

EXHIBIT 4 ▪ *Barro Stickney, Inc.: Statement of Income for the Year Ending December 31, 1991*

Revenue:	
Commission income	$302,362.00
Expenses:	
Salaries for Sales and Bonuses (includes Barro & Stickney)	$130,250.00
Office manager's salary	$ 20,000.00
Total non-personnel expenses[a]	$128,279.00
Total expenses	$278,529.00
Net Income:[b]	**$23,833.00 (7.9% of revenue)**

Notes:

[a]Includes travel, advertising, taxes, office supplies, retirement, automobile expenses, communications, office equipment, and miscellaneous expenses.

[b]Currently held in negotiable certificates of deposit in a Harrisburg bank.

Kruger-Montini Manufacturing Company

The management of Kruger-Montini Manufacturing Company had just entered a new fiscal year and was rethinking its specific policies and general position on transfers of sales representatives. The decision was the responsibility of the sales manager.

Founded many years earlier, this well-established corporation was a medium-sized manufacturer of several related industrial products in rather wide use. The majority of customers were manufacturers. For quite a few years Kruger-Montini did not do its own personal selling. Starting about twenty years ago, it gradually phased out the various intermediaries and manufacturers' agents. After about five years of difficult transition, Kruger-Montini relied strictly on sales representatives who were on the company's payroll and who worked for no one else. Kruger-Montini was not truly national in coverage in its early years but became so nine years ago when it added five sales representatives in one year and relocated thirteen.

The size of the sales force had increased as the company grew and prospered and had now reached thirty-eight. The sales manager had found it necessary to divide his organization into four geographical regions because of span of control difficulties as Kruger-Montini grew. Because the product line was fairly narrow, it was decided that geography, not type of products, would be the best basis for the organization structure. Thus each sales representative sold all products. A contributing reason for deciding against product specialization as the basis for organizing selling efforts was that it would have resulted necessarily in a larger geographical territory for each employee to cover. That would have meant his being away from home overnight much more than under the policy adopted. The present sales manager, Henry Rosas, estimated that the average person on his sales force spent six nights a month away from home. This figure was a little lower, he knew, for people in the highly industrialized and densely populated areas of the Northeast, the Michigan, Ohio, Indiana, Illinois, Wisconsin region in the Middle West, and parts of California. The figure was a little higher for his people in all other areas. Rosas estimated that the difference was about five versus eight nights per month. During the past few years the company had noticed a sizable number of its customers relocate to the Sun Belt and many customers open branch factories in those milder climate areas of the nation. The demand for Kruger-Montini's products was slowly becoming more evenly spread across the country, and this trend was expected to continue.

Rosas had been with the organization about three years. He had been a successful salesman with one company and then assistant sales manager with another company before coming with Kruger-Montini. He had a good personality and was well liked by the sales representatives.

The company had always used a salary plus commission pay plan. For the average representative the commission provided 25 percent of his compensation.

Kruger-Montini manufactured nine products, two of which had been introduced only in the past three years. Prior to that three-year period there had been no new product introductions for a great many years. It appeared highly probable that Kruger-Montini would introduce two more new products, closely related to the existing product line, and delete one during the next two years.

During the most recent fiscal year Kruger-Montini had transferred six sales representatives to different territories. In the four years previous to that, the company had transferred seven each year. Each was moved because of company need and/or the assigning of better territories to deserving sales representatives. See Exhibit 1 for earlier years and additional data on size of the sales force and average distances people were transferred. The mean distance of a relocation at Kruger-Montini had shown a downward trend for several years.

Every person on the sales force had moved at least once. The longest time in one place anyone on the present sales force had experienced with Kruger-Montini was seven years. Rosas was tentatively thinking about moving from five to seven members of the sales force later this year.

The management did not know much about the geographical preferences of its sales representatives or their family life. Rosas could not legally inquire systematically about whether the spouses were also employed and whether that work was professional and managerial, which might make one less willing to move. Dual careers made it difficult for couples to handle relocations well, and some probably would not consider it at all. However, Rosas and his four regional

Source: Reprinted with permission of Macmillan Publishing Company from *Cases in Marketing,* fourth edition by Thomas V. Greer. Copyright © 1987 by Thomas V. Greer.

cent men. In contrast, most Japanese life insurance companies rely on salesforces dominated by women. For example, Nippon Life Insurance has a salesforce of 69,000, of which 90 percent are female.

Prudential, America's largest insurance company, plans to sell a much broader mix of products in Japan than will Equitable. Prudential does not plan on hiring female salespeople in Japan. According to U.S.-educated Kiyofumi Sakaaguchi, president of Prudential's Japanese subsidiary, "Our approach was to develop a very sophisticated financial planning-type salesforce — only career-oriented males. We're shooting for three to four times the productivity of typical Japanese salespersons."

The difficult task of expanding sales in foreign markets is hardly a matter of choice for U.S. insurance companies. The insurance world of the future will be dominated by a few multinational giants, and there will only be a few lucrative niches. By investing in their salesforces now, American companies are attempting to buy insurance on their own futures.

Source: Resa King, Larry Armstrong, and Steven J. Dryden, "Who's That Knocking on Foreign Doors? U.S. Insurance Salesmen," *Business Week*, March 6, 1989, 84–85.

Learning Objectives

After completing this chapter, you should be able to

1 *Explain the critical role of recruitment and selection in building and maintaining a productive salesforce.*

2 *Identify the key activities in planning and executing a program for salesforce recruitment and selection.*

3 *Discuss the legal considerations in salesforce recruitment and selection.*

4 *Discuss the ethical concerns of salesforce recruitment and selection.*

5 *Name some additional special issues to be aware of in salesforce recruitment and selection.*

6 *Describe how recruitment and selection affects salesforce socialization and performance.*

The account of U.S. insurance companies' expansion of their global salesforces illustrates several points. First, recruiting and selecting salespeople must be coordinated with the firm's marketing strategy and objectives. In the case of both Prudential and Equitable, the expansion of global sales is necessary to meet sales and profit objectives. The types of insurance to be sold and the positioning strategies have led both Prudential and Equitable to develop unique recruiting strategies based on hiring men rather than women as salespeople. It should also be noted that recruiting and selection takes a sizable investment, not only in money but in time. Established in 1989, Prudential's Japanese subsidiary is not expected to return a profit until 1995.

Not only is recruiting costly, but it is difficult to forecast the return on investment of newly hired salespeople. It is also difficult to predict with precision which prospective salespeople will turn out to be successful. While other factors also influence sales performance, sales managers cannot survive without doing a competent job in recruiting and selecting salespeople. The vital and complex nature of the job is summarized by Munson and Spivey:

> The process is complicated by various conflicting factors—the need to select applicants with characteristics related to job success, the difficulty of determining these characteristics, inadequacies inherent in the various selection techniques themselves, and the need to simultaneously insure that the selection process satisfies existing governmental regulations pertaining to discrimination in hiring practices.[1]

In the 1990s the recruitment and selection process will have to be adjusted to new demographics of an older salesforce with a higher proportion of women than in the past.[2] Sales managers are expected to face considerable pressure to raise compensation levels for new recruits, retain older salespeople for longer periods, or depend more on raiding their competition for the salespeople they will need to staff their organizations.[3] These factors are especially important for many leading firms, which would prefer to hire young, energetic, college-educated salespeople. As one research team puts it, "Tougher competition in the labor market, increasing turnover, and the high cost to attract and hire new talent all combine to provide a major challenge to recruiters."[4]

Today's sales manager's role in recruitment and selection will be explored in this chapter. Before examining a basic model of the process, the importance of recruitment and selection will be further discussed.

Importance of Recruitment and Selection

In most sales organizations, sales managers with direct supervisory responsibilities for salespeople have the ultimate responsibility for recruitment and selection. They may have the support of top management, or perhaps they coordinate their efforts with human resource personnel or other managers within the firm. But it is the sales manager who generally retains primary recruitment and selection responsibilities. To emphasize the importance of recruitment and selection, consider only a few of the potential problems associated with its inadequate implementation:

1. Inadequate sales coverage and lack of customer follow-up
2. Increased training costs to overcome deficiencies

3. More supervisory problems
4. Higher turnover rates
5. Difficulty in establishing enduring relationships with customers
6. Suboptimal total salesforce performance

Clearly, salesforce performance will suffer if recruitment and selection are poorly executed. Other sales management functions become more burdensome when the sales manager is handicapped by a multitude of "bad hires." The full costs of unsuccessful recruitment and selection are probably impossible to estimate. In addition to sales trainee salaries and employment agency fees, there are hidden costs associated with salesforce turnover and increased managerial problems that defy calculation. To get some perspective on the potential costs that might result from a single hiring mistake, recall from a previous chapter that it costs from $10,000 to $50,000 to hire, train, and supervise a salesperson until he or she has reached productive status. For a bad hire, such an investment represents sunk costs that may be nonrecoverable. And in view of studies that tell us that a significant number of salespeople should not be in sales for one reason or another,[5] it is apparent that recruitment and selection are among the most challenging and important responsibilities of sales management.

A Model of Recruitment and Selection

Figure 9.1 illustrates the steps in the recruitment and selection process. The first step involves **planning activities:** conducting a job analysis, establishing job qualifications, completing a written job description, setting recruitment and selection objectives, and developing a recruitment and selection strategy. These planning activities are conducted within the overall planning framework of the organization to ensure consistency with the objectives, strategies, resources, and constraints of the organization.

The second step is **recruitment,** which, simply put, is the procedure of locating a sufficient number of prospective job applicants. A number of internal (within the company) and external (outside the company) sources may be utilized to develop this pool of candidates.

The next step in the model is **selection,** the process of choosing which candidates will be offered the job. A variety of screening and evaluation methods are used in this step, including evaluation of resumes and job-application forms, interviews, tests, assessment centers, background investigations, and physical exams. A more detailed discussion of each step in the recruitment and selection process now follows.

Planning for Recruitment and Selection

Given the critical nature of recruitment and selection, it would be difficult to overstate the case for careful planning as part of the process. Sales managers are concerned with the current staffing needs of their organizations; but perhaps more importantly, they are also concerned with future staffing needs, which is what makes planning so essential.

FIGURE 9.1 ▪ *Recruiting and Selecting Salespeople*

Three main steps are involved in recruiting and selecting salespeople: planning activities are
followed by recruiting activities, which are followed by selection activities.

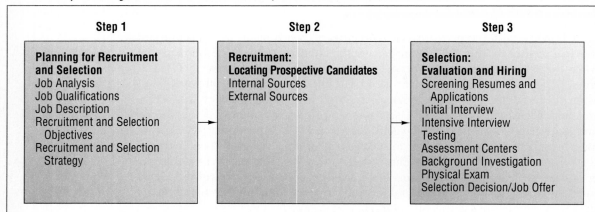

Proper planning provides more time for locating the best recruits. Upper
management can be alerted in advance to probable future needs, rather than having
to be convinced quickly when the need becomes imminent. Also, training can be
planned more effectively when the flow of new trainees into the organization is
known. Overall, the main benefit of adequate planning for the recruitment and
selection process is that it helps prevent the kind of poor decisions that often prove
so expensive in psychic and monetary terms. The key tasks in planning for
recruitment and selection will now be reviewed.

Job Analysis. To effectively recruit and select salespeople, sales managers must
have a complete understanding of the job for which candidates are sought. Since
most sales managers have served as salespeople in their companies prior to entering
management, it is reasonable to think that they would have a good understanding
of the sales jobs for which they recruit. Some, however, have lost touch with
changing conditions in the field and thus have an obsolete view of the current sales
task to be accomplished.

To assure an understanding of the sales job, the sales manager may need to
conduct, confirm, or update a **job analysis,** which entails an investigation of the
tasks, duties, and responsibilities of the job. For example, will the selling tasks
include responsibilities for opening new accounts as well as maintaining existing
accounts? Will the salesperson be responsible for collecting accounts receivable or
completing administrative reports? The job analysis defines the expected behavior
of salespeople, indicating which areas of performance will be crucial for success. In
most larger companies, the job analysis is completed by human resource managers
or other corporate managers, but even then, the sales manager may have input into
the job analysis.

Job Qualifications. The job analysis indicates what the salespeople are supposed
to do on the job, while **job qualifications** refer to the aptitude, skills, knowledge,
personal traits, and willingness to accept occupational conditions necessary to

A GLOBAL PERSPECTIVE

Recruiting a Multinational Salesforce Although recruiting for U.S. companies is complex on the domestic scene, it is even more complicated when these companies recruit in foreign markets. Salesperson selection practices in 45 countries were recently assessed in a study of multinational corporations such as American Hospital Supply, Pfizer, Honeywell, IBM, Kimberly-Clark, and Hewlett-Packard. Education tends to be a more important job qualification in foreign settings than in the United States.

Other criteria that are relatively unimportant in hiring salespeople for U.S. companies, yet that are important in hiring overseas, include social class and religious and ethnic background. It is interesting to note that when hiring in the United States it is illegal to discriminate on the basis of religious and ethnic backgrounds.

The differences in hiring criteria in foreign countries limit the usefulness of standardized hiring criteria, which have been developed by using high-performing U.S. salespeople as models. Sales recruiters in foreign markets must be more sensitive to ethnic segments, recognize the prominence of religion as an indicator of worth to society, and be prepared for a tough battle to recruit highly educated salespeople.

Source: John S. Hill and Meg Birdseye, "Salesperson Selection in Multinational Corporations: An Empirical Study," *Journal of Personal Selling and Sales Management* 9 (Summer 1989): 39–47.

perform the job. For example, is there a need for pharmaceutical salespeople to possess technical aptitude? The answer could be yes or no, depending on a particular company's approach to personal selling. Pharmaceutical giants Pfizer, Merck, and Baxter-Travenol do not insist on technical backgrounds for their sales applicants, while other leading firms such as Bristol-Meyers, Eli Lilly, Smith-Kline, and Parke-Davis like to see applicants with degrees in one of the hard sciences or in pharmacy.[6]

Common sales job qualifications address sales experience, educational level, willingness to travel, willingness to relocate, and ability to work independently. Consistent with our earlier discussion of the diversity of personal selling jobs, there is a corresponding variance in job qualifications for different sales jobs. For this reason, each sales manager should record the pertinent job qualifications for each job in the salesforce. A generic list of job qualifications for all the salespeople in the organization may not be feasible.

For a given sales job within the same company, the qualifications may vary in different selling situations. For example, a multinational company whose salespeople sell the same products to the same types of customers may require different qualifications in different countries. For more detail on this topic, see "A Global Perspective: Recruiting a Multinational Salesforce."

Job Description. Based on the job analysis and job qualifications, a written summary of the job, the **job description,** is completed by the sales manager or, in many cases, the human resource manager. Job descriptions for salespeople could contain any or all of the following elements:

1. Job title (e.g., sales trainee, senior sales representative)
2. Duties, tasks, and responsibilities of the salesperson

EXHIBIT 9.1   ▪   *Sales Representative's Job Description*

Job Description	
Position: Territory salesperson, Southern California	*Division:* Office Equipment

Summary:
Sell office staplers, paper shredders, and mail room supplies to office equipment dealers and major account end-users in Southern California territory.

Specific Responsibilities:
Cover Orange, Los Angeles, and Riverside counties. Call on dealers and important end-users. Meet quota projections. Check dealer inventory. Discuss promotions/incentives. Help train dealer sales staff. Product-train dealer, supply dealer literature. Work with dealer on store displays and advertising. Work product shows. Enter orders and follow through with order entry system. Call on major accounts. Make demos, surveys, and proposals. Report on competitive activity. Report calls and sales activity. Suggest new products.

Reporting Structure:
Report to District Sales Manager.

Knowledge, Skills, and Experience:
Requires two years college, some mechanical aptitude, good verbal and writing skills, and four years outside sales experience, preferably in office equipment industry. Experience calling on dealers mandatory. Experience calling on end-users highly desirable.

Source: Gene Garofalo, *Sales Manager's Desk Book* (Englewood Cliffs, N.J.: Prentice-Hall, 1989), 73.

3. Administrative relationships indicating to whom the salesperson reports
4. Types of products to be sold
5. Customer types
6. Significant job-related demands such as mental stress, physical strength or stamina requirements, or environmental pressures to be encountered

Job descriptions are an essential document in sales management. Their use in recruitment and selection is only one of their multiple functions. They are used to clarify duties and thereby reduce role ambiguity in the salesforce, to familiarize potential employees with the sales job, to set objectives for salespeople, and, eventually, to aid in evaluating performance. A typical job description for a sales representative is shown in Exhibit 9.1.

Recruitment and Selection Objectives. To be fully operational, recruitment and selection objectives should be specifically stated for a given time period. The following general objectives of recruitment and selection could be converted to specific operational objectives in a given firm:

- Determine present and future needs in terms of numbers and types of salespeople (as discussed in Chapter 8).
- Meet the company's legal and social responsibilities regarding composition of the salesforce.
- Reduce the number of underqualified or overqualified applicants.
- Increase the number of qualified applicants at a specified cost.
- Evaluate the effectiveness of recruiting sources and evaluation techniques.

By setting specific objectives for recruitment and selection, sales managers can channel resources into priority areas and improve organizational and salesforce effectiveness.

Recruitment and Selection Strategy.   After objectives have been set, a **recruitment and selection strategy** can be developed. Formulating this strategy requires the sales manager to consider the scope and timing of recruitment and selection activities, as follows:

- When will the recruitment and selection be done?
- How will the job be portrayed?
- How much time will be allowed for the candidate to accept or reject an offer?
- What are the most likely sources for qualified applicants?
- How will efforts with intermediaries such as employment agencies and college placement centers be optimized?

Recruitment and selection are perpetual activities in some sales organizations but in others are conducted only when a vacancy occurs. Most sales organizations could benefit by ongoing recruitment to facilitate selection when the need arises. Some recruit seasonally. For example, large companies often concentrate their efforts to coincide with spring graduation dates on college campuses.

A strategic decision must be made in terms of how the job will be portrayed, particularly in advertisements. Initial descriptions of the job in the media are necessarily limited. Should earnings potential be featured, or perhaps the opportunity for advancement? Or is this job correctly portrayed as ideal for the career salesperson? Consider how the magazine advertisement in Exhibit 9.2 portrays the office products salesperson's job.

Another strategic decision is the length of time a candidate will be given to accept an offer. This time element is important because other recruitment and selection activities may be temporarily suspended until the decision is made. Strategy also involves identifying the sources that look most promising for recruitment. This subject will be discussed in detail in the following section.

Recruitment: Locating Prospective Candidates

As Figure 9.1 showed, the next step in recruitment and selection is to locate a pool of prospective job candidates. This step, the actual recruiting, may utilize a variety of sources. Some of the more popular ones are newspaper advertising, employee referrals, and private employment agencies.

EXHIBIT 9.2 ▪ *Example of an Individual Company's Advertisement to Recruit Salespeople*

WE NEED SALES PROFESSIONALS WHO WILL MAKE THINGS HAPPEN

As the Industry Leader, companies turn to us for quality, reliable service and new solutions to their business needs. Due to unprecedented sales growth, Boise Cascade Office Products has openings for three experienced Sales Representatives in NYC.

The ideal candidate is a highly motivated, career-oriented professional with a successful track record in "repeat sales" business products or services.

Exceptional compensation package, including salary, auto allowance, expenses and the most complete benefits plan in the industry.

Forward resume with earnings history to: **Mr. Thomas Fields, Boise Cascade Office Products, Inc., 437 Madison Ave., 21st Floor, New York, NY 10022.** (No calls, please.) An Equal Opportunity Employer M/F.

 **Boise Cascade Office Products**

We're In Supply. You're In Demand.

Source: Reprinted with permission from Boise Cascade Office Products, Inc.

Internal Sources. One of the most popular methods of locating sales recruits is through **employee referral programs.** These programs are relatively quick and inexpensive compared to other recruiting methods such as newspaper advertising, utilizing employment agencies, and visiting college campuses. While the employee who furnishes the referral may be paid a "finder's fee," the cost is usually nominal. Existing salespeople are obviously good sources for referral programs, since they have a good understanding of the type of person sought for a sales position.

Purchasing agents within the company may also be helpful in identifying prospective sales candidates.

Other internal methods include announcing sales job openings through newsletters, in meetings, or on the bulletin board. Internal transfers or promotions may result from announcing an opening on the salesforce, as was the case with IBM in recent years, when many of its employees were transferred into marketing and sales to bolster its field efforts.

External Sources. While it is a good idea to include internal sources as part of a recruitment and selection program, there may not be enough qualified people inside the organization to meet the human resource needs of the salesforce. This is when the search is expanded to external sources.

Newspaper Advertisements. One way to produce a large pool of applicants in a short period of time is by newspaper advertising. On a cost-per-applicant basis, newspaper advertising is generally inexpensive. A large number of the applicants, however, may not be qualified for the job, even when the ads carefully dictate job qualifications. As a result, newspaper advertising usually requires extensive screening procedures to identify a reasonable number of prospective candidates. Exhibit 9.3 offers sound advice on how to use the newspaper to recruit salespeople.

Private Employment Agencies. A frequently used source is the **private employment agency.** The fee charged by the agency may be paid by the employer or the job-seeker, as established contractually before the agency commences work on behalf of either party. Fees vary but typically amount to 15 to 20 percent of the first-year earnings of the person hired through the agency. The higher the caliber of salesperson being sought, the greater the probability the employer will pay the fee.

Many agencies, such as SALESworld and Sales Consultants, specialize in the placement of salespeople and have offices across the country. Such agencies can be extremely useful in national searches, particularly if the sales manager is seeking high-quality, experienced salespeople. This is true because high-performing salespeople are usually employed but may contact an agency just to see if a better opportunity arises.

Employment agencies usually work from a job description furnished by the sales manager and can be instructed to screen candidates based on specific job qualifications. The professionalism of private employment agencies varies widely, but there are a sufficient number of good agencies that a sales manager should not tolerate an agency that cannot refer qualified candidates. The concern for professionalism and ethical conduct is featured in the magazine ad shown in Exhibit 9.4. Notice that the agency in this case requires that all fees be paid by the employer.

Colleges and Universities. A popular source for sales recruits, especially for large companies with extensive training programs, are the colleges and universities. College students usually can be hired at lower salaries than experienced salespeople, yet they have already demonstrated their learning abilities. Companies seeking future managers often look here for sales recruits.

EXHIBIT 9.3 ▪ *Writing Help-Wanted Ads for Salespeople*

THE SALES RECRUITING ads you run depend on the job, speed needed to fill it, availability of this applicant, and competition. If you want specific experience in your industry, business publications are effective. However, need for speed may rule this avenue out. For faster results, advertise in newspapers. Sundays are effective for classified. Provide a telephone number the reader can call on Sunday, if possible. Answer inquiries right away before they cool off. Display ads in the business pages are good for sales management and top selling posts. If the newspaper groups sales ads, don't start your ad with SALES. Flag them down with the experience required:

APPLIANCES

Major nationally advertised firm seeks salesperson for established territory to sell electrical appliances to department and discount stores. Experience required. Salary plus expenses plus company car plus commission. Call OX 7-3700.

If you are more interested in markets sold to than product sold, play that up in the headline:

VARIETY CHAINS

If you have sold to variety chains and have merchandising, POP, co-op advertising experience, here's opportunity to take over growing territory. Heavy travel. Company car. Draw against high commissions. Phone Mike Thomas at 800-222-3456 for appointment this week.

If you estimate earnings, do not exaggerate. Puffed-up estimates cause distrust.
If inexperienced applicants are fair game, advertise for sales trainees:

SALES TRAINEE:
WE WILL TRAIN

In sales techniques and product knowledge if you are college graduate with some technical or mechanical background. Nationally known manufacturer of valves and fittings sold to original equipment manufacturers offers $21,000 starting salary plus expenses and bonus. Send resume to Sales Manager, Acme Valve Co., 111 Second Street, Mineola, N.Y. 11501

This ad shows you want someone interested in learning sales. Copy shows established, well-known firm, starting salary, bonus opportunity. Restrictor—college grad with technical or mechanical background— prevents you from being flooded with unqualified trainees.
Here's how to attract trainees from another field:

ACCOUNTANTS

Tired of working with figures? If you have accounting background or education and prefer dealing with people rather than ledgers, we will train you to sell business forms and systems.

Our training program includes a step-by-step approach to mastering selling of our products which will lead to high earnings on a commission basis. Salary $2000 per month during training period. Phone Rod Mathews at 212-789-0987.

Using a box number allows you to screen unwanted applicants. They won't be able to bother you with phone calls or surprise visits. Disadvantage: many employed people won't answer box number ads.

Source: Arthur Pell, *Marketing Times* 30 (May–June 1983): 27.

EXHIBIT 9.4 ∎ *Example of a Private Employment Agency's Advertisement to Recruit Salespeople*

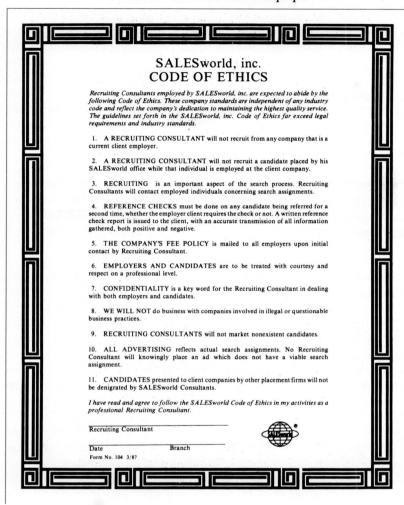

SALESworld, inc.
CODE OF ETHICS

Recruiting Consultants employed by SALESworld, inc. are expected to abide by the following Code of Ethics. These company standards are independent of any industry code and reflect the company's dedication to maintaining the highest quality service. The guidelines set forth in the SALESworld, inc. Code of Ethics far exceed legal requirements and industry standards.

1. A RECRUITING CONSULTANT will not recruit from any company that is a current client employer.

2. A RECRUITING CONSULTANT will not recruit a candidate placed by his SALESworld office while that individual is employed at the client company.

3. RECRUITING is an important aspect of the search process. Recruiting Consultants will contact employed individuals concerning search assignments.

4. REFERENCE CHECKS must be done on any candidate being referred for a second time, whether the employer client requires the check or not. A written reference check report is issued to the client, with an accurate transmission of all information gathered, both positive and negative.

5. THE COMPANY'S FEE POLICY is mailed to all employers upon initial contact by Recruiting Consultant.

6. EMPLOYERS AND CANDIDATES are to be treated with courtesy and respect on a professional level.

7. CONFIDENTIALITY is a key word for the Recruiting Consultant in dealing with both employers and candidates.

8. WE WILL NOT do business with companies involved in illegal or questionable business practices.

9. RECRUITING CONSULTANTS will not market nonexistent candidates.

10. ALL ADVERTISING reflects actual search assignments. No Recruiting Consultant will knowingly place an ad which does not have a viable search assignment.

11. CANDIDATES presented to client companies by other placement firms will not be denigrated by SALESworld Consultants.

I have read and agree to follow the SALESworld Code of Ethics in my activities as a professional Recruiting Consultant.

Recruiting Consultant

Date   Branch

Form No. 104 3/87

Source: Courtesy of SALESworld, Inc.

Campus placement centers can be helpful in providing resumes of applicants, arranging interviews, and providing facilities for screening interviews. Most placement centers also provide access to alumni in addition to the current student body. In some instances, contacts with faculty members may provide sales recruits. Another campus recruiting method is to offer sales internships, which allow both the company and the student an opportunity to see whether a match exists. The internship as a recruiting vehicle is gaining in popularity as major companies such as Procter & Gamble, Northwestern Mutual Life Insurance Company, and Automatic Data Processing are joined by hundreds of other large and small firms in sales internship programs.[7] College campuses are also frequent sites for career conferences in which multiple companies participate in trade show fashion to familiarize students with sales job opportunities.

On the international scene, college campuses are gaining in popularity as a source of sales recruits. College students in foreign countries are beginning to see U.S.-based firms as viable alternatives to home-country firms. Recall from the opening vignette to this chapter that Equitable Life is hiring only college graduates as it builds its Japanese subsidiary. Another firm that recruits extensively from college campuses in Japan is Digital Equipment Corporation. Digital has made considerable headway in the Japanese mainframe computer market by calling on college placement centers, professors, and students' parents, all of whom have an influence on where students will go to work after graduation.[8]

Advertising in Special Publications. Advertisements in trade publications can attract those already in a specified field. In the case of trade magazines, lead time to have an advertisement included in the next issue is longer than with newspapers— typically six to eight weeks. Other specialty publications are nationally distributed employment listings such as the one published by *The Wall Street Journal*.

Job Fairs. Several employers are brought together in one location for recruiting purposes by **job fairs.** Candidates visit the booths of employers they are interested in, or companies request a meeting with a candidate based on a favorable reaction to the candidate's resume. One organizer of job fairs, Career Concepts, usually arranges them for about 15 to 25 companies and hundreds of applicants. Career Concepts has conducted job fairs in 11 cities, charging a fee of $2,500 per company, paid whether or not a salesperson is hired as a result of the fair. Job fairs are best conducted in the evening hours so that currently employed salespeople can attend.[9]

Professional Societies. Another worthwhile source of sales recruits are professional societies. A primary reason sales executives join professional organizations is to establish a network of colleagues who have common interests. Organizations such as Sales and Marketing Executives International meet regularly and provide the opportunity to establish contacts with professional sales executives, who may provide the names of prospective salespeople. Some professional organizations publish newsletters or operate a placement service, which could also be used in recruiting.

Computer Rosters. Locating prospective salespeople through **computerized matchmaking** services is becoming a more important recruiting method as each day passes. Computer technology is being used by an increasing number of college placement centers and employment agencies. Independent computer recruiting services are also widely available. One example is the Denver-based consulting firm of Tracom Corporation, which assists New England Life Insurance (NEL) in locating and screening thousands of sales job candidates in multiple locations each year. NEL field managers record job interview data on personal computers, then transmit it to Tracom for processing, storage, and analysis. Over a period of years, the cumulative database has become capable of predicting future sales success more effectively than preexisting hiring practices. NEL management is now convinced that it has improved the ratio of successful salespeople to the total number hired.[10]

Selection: Evaluation and Hiring

The third step in the recruitment and selection model shown in Figure 9.1 is selection. As part of the selection process, various tools are employed to evaluate the job candidate in terms of job qualifications and provide a relative ranking compared with other candidates. In this section, we will present commonly used evaluation tools and discuss some of the key issues in salesforce selection.

Screening Resumes and Applications. The pool of prospective salespeople generated in the recruiting phase must often be drastically reduced prior to engaging in time-consuming, expensive evaluation procedures such as personal interviews. Initially, sales recruits may be screened based on a review of a resume or an application form.

In analyzing resumes, sales managers check job qualifications (for example, education or sales experience requirements), the degree of career progress by the applicant, and the frequency of job change. Depending on the format and extensiveness of the resume, it may be possible to examine salary history and requirements, travel or relocation restrictions, and reasons for past job changes. Also, valuable clues about the recruit may be gathered from the appearance and completeness of the resume.

A **job-application form** can be designed to gather all pertinent information and exclude unnecessary information. There are three additional advantages of application forms as a selection tool. First, the application form can be designed to meet antidiscriminatory legal requirements, whereas resumes often contain such information. For example, if some applicants note age, sex, race, color, religion, or national origin on their resumes while others do not, a legal question as to whether this information was used in the selection process might arise. A second advantage of application forms is that the comparison of multiple candidates is facilitated since the information on each candidate is presented in the same sequence. This is not the case with personalized resumes. Finally, job applications are usually filled out in handwriting, so the sales manager can observe the attention to detail and neatness of the candidate. In some sales jobs, these factors may be important for success.

Interviews. Interviews of assorted types are an integral part of the selection process. Since interpersonal communications and relationships are a fundamental part of sales jobs, it is only natural for sales managers to weigh interview results heavily in the selection process.

While sales managers agree that interviews are important in selecting salespeople, there is less agreement on how structured the interviews should be and how they should be conducted. For example, some sales managers favor unstructured interviews, which encourage the candidates to talk freely about themselves. Others favor a more structured approach in which particular answers are sought, in a particular sequence, from each candidate.

Initial Interviews. Interviews are usually designed to get an in-depth look at the candidate. In some cases, however, they merely serve as a screening mechanism to support or replace a review of resumes or application forms. These **initial interviews** are typified by the on-campus interviews conducted by most sales recruiters. They are brief, lasting less than an hour. The recruiter clarifies questions about job qualifications and makes a preliminary judgment on whether or not a match exists between the applicant and the company.

During this phase of selection, sales managers should be careful to give the candidate an accurate picture of the job and not oversell it. Candidates who are totally "sold" on the job during the first interview only to be rejected later suffer unnecessary trauma.

Intensive Interviews. One or more **intensive interviews** may be conducted to get an in-depth look at the candidate. Often, this involves multiple sequential interviews by several executives or several managers at the company's facilities. Another variation on the theme, employed less often, is to interview several job candidates simultaneously in a group setting.

When a candidate is to be interviewed in succession by several managers, planning and coordination are required to achieve more depth and to avoid redundancy. Otherwise, each interviewer might concentrate on the more interesting dimensions of a candidate and some important areas may be neglected. An interviewing guide such as the one in Exhibit 9.5 could be utilized with multiple interviewers, each of whom would delve into one or more of the seven categories of information about the candidate.

Interviews, like any other single selection tool, may fail to adequately predict applicants' future success on the job.[11] **Interviewer bias,** or allowing personal opinions, attitudes, and beliefs to influence judgments about a candidate, can be a particularly acute problem with some interviewers. Sales managers, like other human beings, tend to have preferences in candidates' appearances and personalities—and any number of other subjective feelings that may be irrelevant for a given interview situation.

Research confirms the subjective nature of interviewing, concluding that different interviewers will rate the same applicant differently unless there is a commonly accepted stereotype of the ideal applicant.[12]

Testing. To overcome the pitfalls of subjectivity and a potential lack of critical analysis of job candidates, many firms use tests as part of the selection process. Selection tests may be designed to measure intelligence, aptitudes, personality, and other interpersonal factors.

Historically, the use of such tests has been controversial. In the late 1960s, it appeared that testing would slowly disappear from the employment scene under legal and social pressure related to the lack of validity and possible discriminatory nature of some testing procedures. Instead, selection tests have changed, and perhaps managers have learned more about how to utilize them as a legitimate part of the selection process. Therefore, they are still used today. One survey found that approximately one-quarter of the large, industrial firms in the survey used tests in selecting salespeople.[13]

EXHIBIT 9.5 ▪ *Interview Guide*

Meeting the Candidate

At the outset, act friendly but avoid prolonged small talk—interviewing time costs money.

- Introduce yourself by using your name and title.
- Mention casually that you will make notes. (You don't mind if I make notes, do you?)
- Assure candidate that all information will be treated in confidence.

Questions:

- Ask questions in a conversational tone. Make them both concise and clear.
- Avoid loaded and/or negative questions. Ask open ended questions which will force complete answers: "Why do you say that?" (Who, what, where, when, how?)
- Don't ask direct questions that can be answered "Yes" or "No."

Analyzing:

- Attempt to determine the candidate's goals. Try to draw the candidate out, but let him/her do most of the talking. Don't sell—interview.
- Try to avoid snap judgments.

Interviewer Instructions

You will find two columns of questions on the following pages. The left hand column contains questions to ask yourself about the candidate. The right hand column suggests questions to ask the candidate. During the interview it is suggested that you continually ask yourself "what is this person telling me about himself or herself? What kind of person is he/she?" In other parts of the interview you can cover education, previous experience and other matters relating to specific qualifications.

Ask Yourself

Ask the Candidate

I. Attitude

- Can compete without irritation?
- Can bounce back easily?
- Can balance interest of both company and self?
- What is important to him/her?
- Is he/she loyal?
- Takes pride in doing a good job?
- Is he/she cooperative team player?

1. Ever lose in competition? Feelings?
2. Ever uncertain about providing for your family?
3. How can the American way of business be improved?
4. Do you feel you've made a success of life to date?
5. Who was your best boss? Describe the person.
6. How do you handle customer complaints?

II. Motivation

- Is settled in choice of work?
- Works from necessity, or choice?
- Makes day-to-day and long-range plans?
- Uses some leisure for self-improvement?
- Is willing to work for what he/she wants in face of opposition?

1. How does your spouse (or others) feel about a selling career?
2. When and how did you first develop an interest in selling?
3. What mortgages, debts, etc., press you now?
4. How will this job help you get what you want?
5. What obstacles are most likely to trip you up?

III. Initiative

- Is he or she a self-starter?
- Completes own tasks?
- Follows through on assigned tasks?
- Works in assigned manner without leaving own "trademark"?
- Can work independently?

1. How (or why) did you get into (or want) sales?
2. Do you prefer to work alone or with others?
3. What do you like most, like least about selling?
4. Which supervisors let you work alone? How did you feel about this?
5. When have you felt like giving up on a task? Tell me about it.

continued

EXHIBIT 9.5 ▮ *continued*

Ask Yourself	*Ask the Candidate*

IV. Stability

- Is he or she excitable or even-tempered?
- Impatient or understanding?
- Does candidate use words that show strong feelings?
- Is candidate poised or impulsive; controlled or erratic?
- Will he or she broaden or flatten under pressure?
- Is candidate enthusiastic about job?

1. What things disturb you most?
2. How do you get along with customers (people) you dislike?
3. What buyers' actions irritate you?
4. What were your most unpleasant sales (work) experiences?
5. Most pleasant sales (work) experiences?
6. What do you most admire about your friends?
7. What things do some customers do that are irritating to other people?

V. Planning

- Ability to plan and follow through? Or will he depend on supervisor for planning?
- Ability to coordinate work of others?
- Ability to think of ways of improving methods?
- Ability to fit into company methods?
- Will he or she see the whole job or get caught up in details?

1. What part of your work (selling) do you like best? Like least?
2. What part is the most difficult for you?
3. Give me an idea of how you spend a typical day.
4. Where do you want to be five years from today?
5. If you were Manager, how would you run your present job?
6. What are the differences between planned and unplanned work?

VI. Insight

- Realistic in appraising self?
- Desire for self-improvement?
- Interested in problems of others?
- Interested in reaction of others to self?
- Will he or she take constructive action on weaknesses?
- How does he/she take criticism?

1. Tell me about your strengths/weaknesses.
2. Are your weaknesses important enough to do something about them? Why or why not?
3. How do you feel about those weaknesses?
4. How would you size up your last employer?
5. Most useful criticism received? From whom? Tell me about it. Most useless?
6. How do you handle fault finders?

VII. Social Skills

- Is he/she a leader or follower?
- Interested in new ways of dealing with people?
- Can get along best with what types of people?
- Will wear well over the long term?
- Can make friends easily?

1. What do you like to do in your spare time?
2. Have you ever organized a group? Tell me about it.
3. What methods are effective in dealing with people? What methods are ineffective?
4. What kind of customers (people) do you get along with best?
5. Do you prefer making new friends or keeping old ones? Why?
6. How would you go about making a friend? Developing a customer?
7. What must a person do to be liked by others?

Source: "Interviewing the Candidate," Sales Consultants International, Inc., Cleveland, Ohio.

Those who remain reluctant to use tests ask three interacting questions: (1) Can selection tests really predict future job performance? (2) Can tests give an accurate, job-related profile of the candidate? (3) What are the legal liabilities arising from testing? In addressing the first question, one must admit it is sometimes difficult to correlate performance on a test at a given point in time with job performance at a later date. For example, how can sales managers account for performance variations caused primarily by changes in the uncontrollable environment, as might be the case in an unpredictable economic setting?

Question 2 is really concerned with whether or not the tests measure the appropriate factors in an accurate fashion. The precise measurement of complex behavioral variables such as motivation is difficult at best, so it is likely that some tests do not really measure what they purport to measure.

Answers to Question 3 depend largely on the complete answers to Questions 1 and 2. The capsule response to the third question is that unless test results can be validated as a meaningful indicator of performance, there is a strong possibility that the sales manager is in a legally precarious position.

Suggestions to improve the usefulness of tests to sales managers as selection tools follow:[14]

1. Do not attempt to construct tests for the purpose of selecting salespeople. Leave this job to the testing experts and human resource specialists.
2. If psychological tests are used, be sure the standards of the American Psychological Association have been met.
3. Utilize tests that have been based on a job analysis for the particular job in question.
4. Select a test that minimizes the applicant's ability to anticipate desired responses.
5. Use tests as part of the selection process, but do not base the hiring decision solely on test results.

Tests can be useful selection tools if these suggestions are followed. In particular, tests can identify areas worthy of further scrutiny if they are administered and interpreted before a final round of intensive interviewing. Sales managers may utilize commercial testing services in selecting salespeople. For example, E. F. Wonderlic Personnel Test Inc. offers a computer-scored test called the Comprehensive Personality Profile, to be "used in assessing personality in terms of sales potential."[15] According to Wonderlic, this test is extensively validated and offers insight into 24 different sales-job factors, including the applicant's ego drive, level of empathy, and objectivity.

Assessment Centers. The concept of an **assessment center** refers to a set of well-defined procedures for utilizing multiple techniques such as group discussion, business game simulations, presentations, and role-playing exercises for the purpose of employee selection or development. The participant's performance is evaluated by a group of assessors, usually members of management within the firm. Though somewhat expensive due to the high cost of managerial time to conduct the assessments, such centers are being used more often in the selection of salespeople.

An interesting report of the use of an assessment center to select salespeople comes from the life insurance industry, which is notorious for a continual need for new salespeople. Traditional selection methods used in this industry apparently leave something to be desired, as turnover rates are among the highest for salespeople. An assessment-center approach was used by one life insurance firm to select salespeople based on exercises simulating various sales skills such as prospecting, time management, and sales-presentation skills. Results of the study indicated that this program was superior to traditional methods of selecting salespeople in the insurance industry in terms of predicting which salespeople would survive and which would drop out within six months of being hired.[16]

Background Investigation. Job candidates who have favorably emerged from resume and application screening, interviewing, testing, and perhaps an assessment center may next become the subjects of **background investigations.** These may be as perfunctory as a reference check or quite comprehensive if the situation warrants it. In conducting background investigations, it is advisable to request job-related information only and to obtain a written release from the candidate before proceeding with the investigation.

If a reference check is conducted, two points should be kept in mind. First, persons listed as references are biased in favor of the job applicant. As one sales manager puts it, "Even the losers have three good references—so I don't bother checking them." Second, persons serving as references may not be candid or may not provide the desired information. This reluctance may stem from a personal concern (i.e., Will I lose a friend or be sued if I tell the truth?) or from a company policy limiting the discussion of past employees.

Despite these and other limitations, a reference check can help verify the true identity of a person and possibly confirm his or her employment history. With personal misrepresentation and resume fraud being very real possibilities, a reference check is recommended.[17]

Physical Exam. Requiring the job candidate to pass a physical exam is often a formal condition of employment. In many instances, the insurance carrier of the employing firm requires a physical exam of all incoming employees. The objective is to discover any physical problem that may inhibit job performance.

In recent years, drug and communicable-disease testing has made this phase of selection controversial. While the courts will undoubtedly have a major role in determining the legality of testing in these areas in the future, the current rules, at least in the case of drug testing of potential employees, are fairly simple. A company can test for drug use if the applicant is informed of the test prior to taking it, if the results are kept confidential, and if the need for drug testing is reasonably related to potential job functions.[18]

Selection Decision and Job Offer. After evaluating the available candidates, the sales manager may be ready to offer a job to one or more candidates. Some candidates may be "put on hold" until the top candidates have made their decisions. Another possibility is that the sales manager may decide to extend the search and begin the recruitment and selection process all over again.

In communicating with those offered jobs, it is now appropriate for the sales manager to "sell" the prospective salesperson on joining the firm. In reality, top salespeople are hard to find, and the competition for them is intense. Therefore, a sales manager should enthusiastically pursue the candidate once the offer is extended. As always, an accurate portrayal of the job is a must.

The offer of employment should be written but can be initially extended in verbal form. Any final contingencies, such as passing a physical exam, should be detailed in the offer letter. Candidates not receiving a job offer should be notified in a prompt, courteous manner. A specific reason for not hiring a candidate need not be given. A simple statement that an individual who better suits the needs of the company has been hired is sufficient.

Legal Considerations in Recruitment and Selection

Key Legislation

The possibility of illegal discrimination permeates the recruitment and selection process, and a basic understanding of pertinent legislation can be beneficial to the sales manager. Some of the most important legislation is summarized in Exhibit 9.6. The legislative acts featured in Exhibit 9.6 are federal laws, applicable to all firms engaged in interstate commerce. Companies not engaging in interstate commerce are often subject to state and local laws that are quite similar to these federal laws.

Guidelines for Sales Managers

The legislation reviewed in Exhibit 9.6 is supported by various executive orders and guidelines that make it clear that a sales manager, along with other hiring officials in a firm, have legal responsibilities of grave importance in the recruitment and selection process. In Step 1 of the process, planning for recruitment and selection, sales managers must take care to analyze the job to be filled in an open-minded way, attempting to overcome any personal mental biases. For example, in the 1980s, many sales organizations have overcome biases against women in sales positions. These organizations are practically unanimous in reporting that women have performed as well as, and in some cases better than, their male counterparts.

Job descriptions and job qualifications should be accurate and based on a thoughtful job analysis. The planning stage may also require that the sales manager consider fair-employment legislation and affirmative action requirements before setting recruitment and selection objectives.

In Step 2 of the process, recruitment, the sources that serve as intermediaries in the search for prospective candidates should be informed of the firm's legal position. It is also crucial that advertising and other communications be devoid of potentially discriminatory content. For example, companies that advertise for "young, self-motivated salesmen" may be inviting an inquiry from the EEOC.

Finally, all selection tools must be related to job performance. Munson and Spivey summarize legal advice for selection by stating, "At each step in the

EXHIBIT 9.6 ▪ *Legislation Affecting Recruitment and Selection*

Legislative Act	*Purpose*
Civil Rights Act (1964)	Prohibits discrimination based on age, race, color, religion, sex, or national origin.
Fair Employment Opportunity Act (1972)	Founded the Equal Employment Opportunity Commission to ensure compliance with the Civil Rights Act.
Equal Pay Act (1963)	Requires that men and women be paid the same amount for performing similar job duties.
Rehabilitation Act (1973)	Requires affirmative action to hire and promote handicapped persons if the firm employs 50 or more employees and is seeking a federal contract in excess of $50,000.
Vietnam Veterans Readjustment Act (1974)	Requires affirmative action to hire Vietnam veterans and disabled veterans of any war. Applicable to firms holding federal contracts in excess of $10,000.
Age Discrimination in Employment Act (1967)	Prohibits discrimination against people of ages 40 to 70.
Fifth and Fourteenth Amendments to the U.S. Constitution	Provides equal-protection standards to prevent irrational or unreasonable selection methods.

selection process, it would be advisable to be as objective, quantitative, and consistent as possible, especially since present federal guidelines are concerned with all procedures suggesting employment discrimination."[19]

To more fully appreciate the sensitivity necessary in these matters, consider the following list of potentially troublesome information often found on employment applications:[20]

▪ Age or date of birth
▪ Length of time at present address
▪ Height and/or weight
▪ Marital status
▪ Ages of children
▪ Occupation of spouse
▪ Relatives already employed by the firm
▪ Person to notify in case of an emergency
▪ Type of military discharge

Not only are these topics open to charges of discrimination, but so is a request for a photograph of the applicant, a birth certificate, or a copy of military discharge papers. Further questions to avoid are those concerning the original name of the

to illegally discriminate against some job candidates. Federal laws and guidelines provide the basic antidiscriminatory framework, and state and local statutes may also be applicable. The most important legislation that applies are the Civil Rights Act and the Equal Employment Opportunity Act.

4. Discuss the ethical concerns of salesforce recruitment and selection. Two primary ethical concerns are (1) misrepresentation of the job to be filled and (2) utilizing stress interviews in the selection stage.

5. Name some additional special issues to be aware of in salesforce recruitment and selection. Some special issues in recruitment and selection are (1) the increasing usage of part-time salespeople, (2) the use of market bonuses, and (3) assisting cooperative channel members in recruiting and selecting their salespeople.

6. Describe how recruitment and selection affects salesforce socialization and performance. Socialization, the process by which salespeople adjust to their jobs, begins when the recruit is first contacted by the hiring firm. Two stages of socialization should be accomplished during recruitment and selection: achieving realism and achieving congruence. Realism means giving the recruit an accurate portrayal of the job. Congruence refers to the matching process that should occur between the needs of the organization and the capabilities of the recruit. If realism and congruence can be accomplished, future job satisfaction, involvement, commitment, and performance should be improved. These relationships are shown in a model of the socialization process in Figure 9.2.

Key Terms

- **Planning activities**
- **Recruitment**
- **Selection**
- **Job analysis**
- **Job qualifications**
- **Job description**
- **Recruitment and selection strategy**
- **Employee referral programs**
- **Private employment agency**
- **Job fairs**
- **Computerized matchmaking**
- **Job-application form**
- **Initial interviews**

- **Intensive interviews**
- **Interviewer bias**
- **Assessment centers**
- **Background investigations**
- **Misrepresentation**
- **Stress interview**
- **Part-time salespeople**
- **Market bonus**
- **Salesforce socialization**
- **Achieving realism**
- **Achieving congruence**
- **Job preview**

Review Questions

1. What are some of the problems associated with improperly executed recruitment and selection activities?

2. Describe the relationship between conducting a job analysis, determining job qualifications, and completing a written job description.

3. What are the advantages of using employee referral programs to recruit salespeople? Can you identify some disadvantages?

4. How can private employment agencies assist in the recruitment and selection of salespeople? Who pays the fee charged by such agencies, the hiring company or the job candidate?

5. What can be learned about a job candidate from analyzing a job application that cannot be learned from the candidate's resume?

6. Refer to the block entitled "A Global Perspective: Recruiting a Multinational Salesforce." In what ways is the recruiting and selection process complicated when implemented in foreign countries?

7. Summarize the primary legislation designed to prohibit illegal discrimination in the recruitment and selection process.

8. Refer to the block entitled "An Ethical Perspective: Teachers as Salespeople." How does the process of salesforce socialization relate to hiring part-time, inexperienced salespeople?

9. To enhance salesforce socialization, recruitment and selection should assure realism and congruence. How can this be accomplished?

10. What is stress interviewing? How do some sales managers justify using stress interviews?

Application Exercises

1. Examine the newspaper advertisements in Exhibit 9.3, noting the different emphasis for each advertisement. Using a Sunday edition of a newspaper, locate an example of each of the following types of advertisements for salespeople:

- An ad that emphasizes product-specific sales experience
- An ad that emphasizes customers sold to, rather than products sold
- An ad for sales trainees without sales experience
- An ad designed to attract trainees from another field

What suggestions would you make for improving each of these advertisements?

2. Executives at Acme Fabrications estimate they lose approximately $25,000 on each fired sales representative in salary, training costs, and lost sales. They hire 100 people a year of the 500 they interview. On the average, 20 are fired per year, at a cost of $500,000. Acme recently contracted with an assessment service, who will analyze 200 "finalists" for the 100 jobs at a cost of $150 per candidate. How much reduction in the average turnover rate is necessary to recoup the costs of utilizing the assessment center?

3. Analyze the following three resumes. Assume you are a sales manager for a Fortune 500 consumer goods company whose customers include grocery chains, discount stores, and drug stores. Your product line is health and beauty aids. For each candidate, develop questions to be asked in the interview. Exhibit 9.5 may be helpful in planning the interviews.

```
                            THOMAS WILLIAM GROGAN

Current Address                              Permanent Address
212 Parkview Dr.                             1121 Bath Avenue
Lexington, Ky. 40503                         London, Ky. 41101
(606) 555-1302                               (606) 555-3340



JOB OBJECTIVE:    Entry-level sales position leading to advancement based
                  on performance.

EDUCATION:        University of Kentucky, Lexington, Kentucky
                  Bachelor of Business Administration, May 1992
                  Major: Marketing        Minor: Economics
                  GPA 3.51/4.00

HONORS &          American Marketing Association: President
ACTIVITIES:       Beta Gamma Sigma Honorary: President
                  Academic Excellence Scholarship
                  Sigma Alpha Epsilon Fraternity: Rush Chairman,
                      Assistant Treasurer, President of Pledge Class,
                      Editor of Summer Newsletter
                  Lances Junior Men's Honorary
                  Omicron Delta Kappa Leadership Honor Society
                  Mortar Board Senior Honor Society
                  Student Agencies Incorporated

EXPERIENCE:       Manager/Internship
                  Copy Cat Print Shop, Lexington, Kentucky
                      Hire, schedule and supervise employees. Develop
                      sales promotions and make personal sales calls.
                      Conduct inventory and order supplies. Maintain
                      financial records.
                  January 1991 to present
                  Servicing Clerk
                  First Security Mortgage Co., Lexington, Kentucky
                      Made deposits and daily journal entries. Filed
                      and copied loan information.
                  May 1991 to August 1991
                  Sales Clerk
                  Copy Cat Print Shop, Lexington, Kentucky
                      Operated printing machine. Sold supplies to
                      customers. Handled cash/credit transactions.
                  September 1990 to December 1990
                  Ophthalmic Assistant
                  Raymond V. Mecca, M.D., Ashland, Kentucky
                      Recorded patients' general medical history.
                      Measured visual acuity. Operated eye computer.
                  Summers of 1986 to 1990

REFERENCES:       Available on request.
```

LINDA A. BLACKBURN

School Address   Permanent Address
378 Summertree Road   730 Hemingway Road
Lexington, Kentucky 40802   Circleville, Ohio 43113
(606) 555-9842   (614) 555-9301

CAREER   A competitive position in the realm of marketing,
OBJECTIVE: customer service, or sales with career opportunities
                conducive to personal and professional growth.

EDUCATION: University of Kentucky   Lexington, Kentucky
                B.B.A. to be awarded in May 1992
                Major: Marketing
                G.P.A.: 3.2 (A=4.0)
                G.P.A. in major field of study: 3.83

RELATED   Salesforce Management   Computer Science
COURSEWORK: Retail and Distribution Management Managerial Accounting
                Marketing Research   Business Statistics
                Promotion Management   Industrial Communication
                Behavioral Systems in Marketing   Strategic Management
                Marketing Strategy and Planning   Corporation Finance

EMPLOYMENT: Office for Experiential Education   Lexington, KY
                September 1991-Present
                Marketing Intern: Responsibilities involve development of
                marketing strategies to increase awareness of the services
                offered by the Office of Experiential Education.
                RCA Corporation   Circleville, OH
                Summers 1991, 1990
                Assisted in the production of television picture tube parts
                on the production line.
                Container Corporation of America   Circleville, OH
                Summer 1988
                General labor pool which included training in the woodyard
                and work on a forklift truck.
                McDonald's Restaurant   Circleville, OH
                Summer 1987
                Operated cash register and assembled orders.

ACTIVITIES   Dean's Honor List
AND HONORS: Scholarship member of women's varsity track and
                cross-country teams
                1991 All-American Honors in track
                1991 Academic All-Southeastern Conference
                Member of American Marketing Association
                Member of Phi Beta Lambda
                Member of the Fellowship of Christian Athletes

REFERENCES: Furnished upon request.

STEVEN J. WICKHAM

Campus Address   **Permanent Address**
Box 642 Killian Hall   358 Mandino Circle
Lexington, KY 40526-0149   Edgewood, KY 41017
Phone: (606) 555-9165   Phone: (606) 555-7891

Objective   To obtain an entry-level position in corporate sales/
                 advertising/marketing, with potential advancement to
                 sales management.

Education   University of Kentucky, Lexington, KY
                 Bachelor of Business Administration (concentration in marketing)
                 Cumulative GPA: 3.45/4.0
                 Graduation: May 1992
                 Graduated with honors from Covington Catholic High School,
                     Park Hills, KY

Work Experience

August 1991-Present
                 Kentucky Kernel, University of Kentucky's student newspaper
                 Advertising Sales -Responsibilities include sales, servicing
                 existing accounts, making cold calls, handling invoices, ad
                 contracts, credit applications, and ad layouts. Requires
                 salesperson who is a self-starter, aggressive, and self-
                 motivated with commission-based pay.

August 1991-Present
                 Resident Advisor, using leadership skills to aid in student
                 development of 30 men. Coordinating service, charity, and
                 intramural programs. Also development of tournament
                 activities for 640 men.

May 1991-Present
                 Summit Hills Country Club. Responsibilities include retail
                 sales, supervising and maintaining club storage. Strong
                 membership service required.

Leadership Activities
                 Resident Advisor
                 Collegians for Academic Excellence 1990-92
                 American Marketing Association
                 Haggin Hall's House Council Representative
                 Charity Fundraising
                 Christian Awakening Program -Team Leader
                 Intramural Sports
Honors   Academic Excellence Scholarship
                 Beta Gamma Sigma Business Honorary
                 Dean's List
                 Business Award, C.C.H.S.

(References available on request.)

Notes

[1] J. Michael Munson and W. Austin Spivey, "Salesforce Selection That Meets Federal Regulation and Management Needs," *Industrial Marketing Management* 9 (February 1980): 12.

[2] See "The Graying of the Sales Force," *Sales and Marketing Management*, November 1989, 24; and Beth Brophy, "The Birth of a Saleswoman," *U.S. News & World Report*, February 6, 1989, 40–42.

[3] Thayer C. Taylor, "Meet the Sales Force of the Future," *Sales and Marketing Management*, March 10, 1986, 59–60.

[4] Thomas R. Wotruba, Edwin K. Simpson, and Jennifer L. Reed-Draznik, "The Recruiting Interview as Perceived by College Student Applicants for Sales Positions," *Journal of Personal Selling and Sales Management*, 9 (Fall 1989): 13.

[5]Jeanne Greenberg and Herbert Greenberg, *What it Takes to Succeed in Sales: Selecting and Retaining Top Producers* (Homewood, Ill.: Dow Jones–Irwin, 1990).

[6]Michael David Harkavy and the Philip Lief Group, *The 100 Best Companies to Sell For* (New York: John Wiley and Sons, 1989), 253–269.

[7]Elizabeth Hoffman, "A Selling Point: Sales Internship Program Gives Students an Advantage," *Insurance and Financial Services Careers 1990*, March 1990, 12–13.

[8]Vernon R. Alden, "Who Says You Can't Crack Japanese Markets?" *Harvard Business Review* 65 (January–February 1987): 52–56.

[9]"A Matchmaker for Sales Managers," *Sales and Marketing Management*, December 9, 1985, 52–53.

[10]"New England Life Takes Steps to Insure Its Future," *Sales and Marketing Management*, August 12, 1985, 74–77.

[11]Bruce G. Posner, "Hiring the Best," *INC.*, April 1989, 169–170.

[12]Wesley J. Johnston and Martha C. Cooper, "Industrial Sales Force Selection: Current Knowledge and Needed Research," *Journal of Personal Selling and Sales Management* 1 (Spring–Summer 1981): 49–57.

[13]Richard Nelson, *The Use of Psychological Tests in Selecting Sales Representatives* (monograph), National Society of Sales Training Executives, NSSTE Library, Center for Research and Management Services, Indiana State University, Terre Haute, Ind.

[14]Based on Samuel J. Maurice, "Stalking the High-Scoring Salesperson," *Sales and Marketing Management*, October 7, 1985,

63–64; George B. Salsbury, "Properly Recruit Salespeople To Reduce Training Cost," *Industrial Marketing Management* 11 (April 1982): 143–146; and Richard Kern, "IQ Tests for Salesmen Make a Comeback," *Sales and Marketing Management*, April 1988, 42–46.

[15]*Wonderlic Employment Tests and Procedures, 1990 Catalog* (E. F. Wonderlic Personnel Test Inc., Northfield, Ill., 1990).

[16]E. James Randall, Ernest F. Cooke, and Lois Smith, "A Successful Application of the Assessment Center Concept to the Salesperson Selection Process," *Journal of Personal Selling and Sales Management* 5 (May 1985): 53–61.

[17]Liz Murphy, "Did Your Salesman Lie to Get His Job?" *Sales and Marketing Management*, November 1987, 54–58.

[18]Kenneth H. Richman, "Laws Differ for Testing Potential, Present Employees," *Marketing News*, November 21, 1986, 9.

[19]Munson and Spivey, "Salesforce Selection," 15.

[20]For more discussion of what information should not be sought in a job interview, see John P. Steinbrink, ed., *The Dartnell Sales Manager's Handbook*, 14th ed. (Chicago: The Dartnell Press, 1989), 820–823.

[21]Jon M. Hawes, "How To Improve Your College Recruiting Program," *Journal of Personal Selling and Sales Management* 9 (Summer 1989): 51.

[22]Alan J. Dubinsky, Charles H. Fay, Thomas N. Ingram, and Marc J. Wallace, "Market Bonuses: How Effective Are They?" *Business Horizons*, May–June 1983, 11–14.

[23]"GA Helps Dealers Hire the Best," *Sales and Marketing Management*, May 19, 1986, 26.

CASE 9.1   *The Socialization of Nancy Jeffries*

Background

Nancy Jeffries was hired four months ago to sell plastic foam egg cartons for The Container Company (TCC), a large packaging manufacturer. Her territory included half the state of Tennessee; she had relocated from Atlanta to Nashville when she joined TCC. Nancy's qualifications included three years' sales experience with Microword, where she sold software packages to a variety of high-tech businesses in the Atlanta area. A graduate of the University of Georgia, Nancy had lived in Georgia her entire life prior to joining TCC.

Current Situation

Although she was doing quite well on the job and exceeding her sales targets, Nancy was unhappy with her new sales position. In fact, she was contemplating making another job change and probably would have already changed jobs had she not thought that such an early departure would negatively affect her chances of making a beneficial move. The problems that led Nancy to this point could be summarized in one statement: The job simply was not what she expected.

When Nancy interviewed for the job, Brad

Wade, TCC regional sales manager, spoke enthusiastically about the opportunities of calling on a diverse customer base including grocery store chain buyers, egg processing plant personnel, and even what Brad described as "good-ole-boy chicken farmers." What Brad did not describe, however, was the bureaucratic nature of chain store purchasing, the extensive travel required to cover the farms and processing plants, and the need to call on farmers at daybreak before they became involved in the day's activities.

In a typical day, Nancy would cover 150 miles, mostly on rural back roads. Furthermore, she would frequently change clothes in service stations and rest areas to be appropriately dressed for both the chain store buyers (more businesslike) and her other customers (from semicasual to absolutely down-home). In Nancy's opinion, her dry-cleaning and laundry bills were astronomical, since she ended nearly every day with two or three outfits in need of cleaning.

The driving had become a burden for Nancy, so she had asked Brad about increasing her expense allowance to include more overnight travel. Brad had granted her request, and Nancy had increased her overnight travel from one night a week to three nights a week.

Now, after four months in Nashville, she had little social life and each weekend became an exercise in boredom. It seemed that the people she had met in her apartment complex often made plans for the weekend while Nancy was out of town during the week. She was particularly depressed one Friday evening when she came home and saw a large group departing in convoy for a weekend of camping and water-skiing at a nearby lake. Nancy loved to water-ski but had little time for the sport since joining TCC.

Brad Wade was scheduled to visit Nancy's territory in one week. This would be Brad's second trip to her territory since she had joined TCC. One purpose of his trip was to congratulate Nancy on her fast start with TCC and to inform her that she was presently the leading candidate for TCC's Rookie of the Year designation. When Brad phoned Nancy to inform her of his trip, Nancy told him, "I'm glad you're coming to Nashville, Brad. We really need to talk about the way things are going, now that I have a good picture of the job." Brad asked Nancy to elaborate, but she responded that her thoughts were not fully developed yet. She politely asked Brad to wait until his visit for further discussion, a request that Brad reluctantly granted.

Questions

1. How are the key concepts of salesforce socialization related to this situation?
2. What responsibilities does a job applicant such as Nancy Jeffries have to find out for herself what the job is likely to involve?
3. What can Brad Wade do to prepare for his upcoming visit with Nancy?
4. What steps can Brad take in the future to improve the early stages of socialization with his newly hired salespeople?

CASE 9.2 *Jim Rutledge: A Man of Mystery*

Background

Jim Rutledge had been impressive in his quest to land a sales job with Scientific Research Services (SRS), a national firm specializing in consumer opinion surveys for the toy industry. Dave Ryan, district sales manager for SRS, would be Rutledge's immediate supervisor if he came to work for SRS. Ryan had been one of six SRS executives to interview Rutledge, and like the others, he found the candidate to be articulate, quick-witted, engaging, and immediately likable. On paper, Rutledge also appeared to be an ideal candidate. He met or exceeded all of the stated job qualifications regarding education and prior experience.

Among his qualifications, Rutledge had an undergraduate degree in marketing from Arizona State University and three years' sales experience with Mattel. He was nearing completion of an MBA degree from Tulane University, which he had been pursuing on a part-time basis over the past three years.

Current Situation

SRS has decided to offer Jim Rutledge a sales position. Dave Ryan has spoken with Rutledge on the telephone and advised him that a formal offer letter was mailed earlier in the day. He verbally outlined the offer to Rutledge, who seemed excited and agreed to accept the offer, pending receipt of the written offer.

After getting off the phone with Rutledge, Ryan began calling the individuals that Rutledge had listed as references. He called the company Rutledge had worked for prior to Mattel but did not get much information. Basically, the contact confirmed Rutledge's dates of employment and indicated that Rutledge would receive positive consideration if he should reapply for a job with the company. Next, he called a marketing professor at Arizona State University. When he reached the marketing department, however, he was told that no such professor was now or had ever been on the marketing faculty at the university.

Puzzled, Ryan called the next individual on the reference listing, Dr. Baskin, head of the MBA program at Tulane University. Dr. Baskin informed Ryan that he had no recollection of any student by the name of Jim Rutledge, but he checked the enrollment records to be certain. Dr. Baskin called Ryan back within the hour with the news — no student by the name of Jim Rutledge had ever been a student at Tulane. Dave Ryan hung up the phone and began pondering his next move.

Questions

1. What would you do at this point if you were Dave Ryan?
2. How reliable is information gained from references?
3. How could the content of the written offer letter (unknown in this case) affect Ryan's next move?

Continual Development of the Salesforce: Sales Training

SALES TRAINING: DEVELOPING COLLEGE GRADU-ATES FOR SALES JOBS Major corporations flock to college campuses each year in search of prime sales talent. After the new recruits are on board, sales trainers begin the task of molding yet another generation of productive salespeople. In the 1990s, several trends are affecting the design and delivery of initial sales training of newly hired salespeople. For example, the concept of quality is being emphasized by those who make buying decisions. This means that sales organizations must be sharp to avoid elimination from a customer's preferred vendor list. Salespeople must be able to provide accurate information in a timely fashion to be of value in the relationship between the customer and the sales organization. How will these developments affect sales training?

There will be a greater emphasis on listening as the key communication skill in selling. Training will be designed to stress customer and product knowledge rather than gimmicky sales techniques. Sales managers and sales trainers will increasingly provide sales training for employees who are not salespeople but are involved in the sales process.

Today's college graduates are ideal candidates for progressive sales training programs because they have proven that they can learn, yet they have not typically formed poor work habits. Terry Van Tell, a sales training consultant based in New York City, adds that recent college graduates "like to take risks, have a high energy level, are impatient and innovative; they like to challenge authority and be challenged." Van Tell says that trainers need to get young sales recruits to be patient enough to develop long-term customer relationships. She notes that some of the recruits will be uncomfortable with the complexities of selling. Summing up the recent college graduate as a sales trainee, Ms. Van Tell says, "They are more receptive than ever before. . . . If what you're saying makes sense, they'll listen and they'll do it. But it has to make sense to them."

Source: Compiled from Michael J. Major, "Sales Training Emphasizes Service and Quality," *Marketing News*, March 5, 1990, 5; and Arthur Bragg, "How to Avoid School Daze," *Sales and Marketing Management*, May 1989, 90.

Learning Objectives

After completing this chapter, you should be able to

1 *Explain the importance of sales training and the sales manager's role in sales training.*

2 *Describe the sales training process as a series of six interrelated steps.*

3 *Discuss five methods for assessing sales training needs and identify typical sales training needs.*

4 *Name some typical objectives of sales training programs, and explain how setting objectives for sales training is beneficial to sales managers.*

5 *Identify the key issues in evaluating sales training alternatives.*

As indicated in the opening vignette, sales training is indeed undergoing significant changes. Sales training is incorporating new topics that were rarely included in the 1980s. The widespread implementation of quality-improvement programs requires that sales organizations become aware of customers' expectations of quality and then assign well-prepared salespeople to meet those expectations. In an era of change and rapid dissemination of information, salespeople must be equipped with the latest skills and technologies.

Fielding a productive sales team is usually expensive, and sales training expenditures can be a large portion of the investment in a salesforce. In addition, it is often difficult to assess the effectiveness of the training. Nonetheless, many sales executives invest heavily in sales training. This passage illustrates the critical nature of sales training:

> Sales training is like motherhood and the flag. It's hard to find anyone who has a word to say against it. The reason is plain. For salespeople to perform successfully, they must be familiar with all aspects of their jobs. We hear much about "natural" salespeople, but they're more myth than reality. . . . Sales skills must be learned, and heaven help the company that allows its salesforce to learn them haphazardly.[1]

In this chapter, we will discuss a number of sales training issues and methods. First, we will consider the importance of sales training. Then a model of the sales training process will be discussed.

Importance of Sales Training

A comprehensive review of sales management research concludes that whom one recruits is important, but probably not as important in determining salesforce performance as what sales managers do with the recruits—and to the recruits— after they have been hired.[2]

The importance of sales training in achieving the highest levels of sales performance is shown in *Sales and Marketing Management* magazine's annual survey of the best salesforces in the United States. First, "quality of sales training" is one of seven criteria used to determine the top salesforces. Second, the accounts of sales successes for the top salesforces often reveal that the winning salesforces had to adapt to changes in marketing and sales strategies. This obviously requires some degree of salesforce training or retraining. United Parcel Service (UPS) received the highest marks for sales training, narrowly edging out Procter & Gamble in the survey standings. A significant amount of sales training at UPS is dedicated to learning the technological aspects of a continual stream of new services. Apparently, sales training is paying off at UPS, as the company added 70,000 new accounts during a highly competitive year.[3]

While there is a general need for sales training, other factors affect its relative importance in a given sales organization, namely, the size of the company, complexity of the product or service being sold, and level of competitiveness in the industry.

General Need for Sales Training

Most organizations have a need for sales training of some type. This enduring need exists in part due to inadequacies of current training programs and in part because new salespeople join the organization on a regular basis. The inadequacies of existing sales training programs are exposed in reports such as the following:

- According to a survey of 255 salespeople (not sales managers), salespeople are too talkative, are prone to overpromising in an attempt to please customers, and do a poor job of postsale follow-up.[4]
- Surveys of customers also indicate a need for improved sales training. For example, one survey asked customers, "Most salespeople do not know how to ask the right questions about my company's needs. True or false?" Eighty-seven percent of the responding customers answered "True."[5]
- Roy Chitwood, a Los Angeles-based sales trainer and consultant, sees a multitude of shortcomings in sales training in many companies: not enough sales training; a reliance on one-shot training programs, rather than ongoing programs; the use of nonqualified trainers; and programs that contain outdated material.[6]

These examples indicate an ongoing need to conduct sales training to improve salesforce performance. It should be stressed that the need for sales training is continual, if for no other reason than that the sales environment is constantly changing. For example, Converse has traditionally sold its athletic shoes through smaller retail outlets and recently began trying to gain additional distribution through large specialty retailers. Converse salespeople are encountering different types of buyers who deal in larger quantities. These buyers represent retail organizations that have different clientele than the smaller retailers, and special attention must be paid to developing tailored sales plans to gain the buyer's business.[7] This will require that the Converse sales organization be retrained in order to implement the changes in sales strategy.

As we have previously mentioned, customers appreciate, and sometimes demand, a well-trained salesforce from their vendors. It is also interesting to note that professional purchasing agents put a premium on sales-related topics in their own training programs. One survey of purchasing personnel found the most important topics covered in their training programs to be vendor relations and negotiation techniques.[8] At a minimum, this indicates a need to stay abreast of customers through sales training.

Company Size and Sales Training

As shown in Exhibit 10.1, there is a positive relationship between company size and whether or not the company offers *formalized* sales training (which is structured in some way) as opposed to *informal on-the-job* training. Approximately 54 percent of companies with 10,000 or more employees, and slightly over 46 percent of companies with 100 to 499 employees, offer formalized sales training. Large companies are more likely to have sales training programs, in part because they have outgrown the alternative of hiring skilled, capable salespeople from other firms. Smaller companies may choose to minimize training by hiring salespeople from other firms known for their excellent training programs. For example, the competition among smaller firms to hire salespeople from IBM, Procter & Gamble, and Xerox can be intense.

EXHIBIT 10.1   ▪   *Sales Training by Size of Organization*

No. of Employees	Percent Offering Formal Sales Training
100–499	46.2
500–999	47.9
1,000–2,499	48.2
2,500–9,999	51.5
10,000 or more	54.3

Source: Beverly Geber, "Who, How, and What," *Training*, October 1989, 60.

Product/Service Complexity and Sales Training

High technology companies place considerable emphasis on sales training to correspond with their often hectic pace of new-product or new-service development. The importance of sales training to high-technology companies is illustrated in the case of AT&T, when the company moved into the computer business in the mid-1980s. The 6,000 AT&T salespeople were well equipped to sell telephone systems but not computers. They had not been trained in tailoring computer systems to customer needs. When results were disappointing, a new sales training program was implemented to make the salesforce more competitive. Customers reacted favorably, as indicated by a J.C. Penney vice-president who commented, "I am impressed with the quality of the people I am seeing now. They understand they have to sell, and if they get some better products, they can do it."[9]

Until quite recently, service organizations clearly lagged behind industrial and consumer product companies in the amount of time and money dedicated to training new salespeople. This is no longer the case. Apparently, service organizations are beginning to see that sales training is just as important for them as it is for product companies and that, in addition, they require training which focuses on the unique challenges of selling intangibles.

Level of Competitiveness and Sales Training

Sales organizations in highly competitive markets, especially newly competitive markets, have a strong need for sales training. For example, the direct-sales industry, with companies such as Tupperware, Mary Kay, and Avon, has become a lot more competitive in recent years. To survive in this increasingly competitive market, many firms are upgrading their training methods. Avon has decided to push for improved salesforce productivity rather than continuing a strong reliance on simply increasing salesforce size.[10]

Deregulation in the financial services industries has created intensified levels of competition, and many of the leading firms rely heavily on sales training to build a competitive advantage. For example, IDS Financial Services, an American Express Company, trains nearly 2,000 new financial planners each year. The planners learn consultative selling skills through classroom training, independent study, and selling simulations. The initial training program for financial planners is 22 weeks long, and as IDS executives point out, that is only the beginning, as sales training is continual with the firm.[11]

Investment in Sales Training

The importance accorded sales training by most firms is not always matched by their investment in it. Recall from Exhibit 10.1 that although a majority of large firms (10,000 or more employees) offer formalized training, a majority of smaller firms do not; and when firms of all sizes are considered, it is estimated that only 37 percent of all salespeople receive formalized training.[12] In firms where sales training is offered, the investment in time and money is often considerable, however. Training periods for new salespeople commonly run from three to twelve months, during which time the company is usually paying the trainee a salary that could easily exceed $2,000 a month.[13]

One aspect of the investment in sales training is the amount of time required of the sales manager. Usually, sales managers are involved not only in the "big picture" of planning but also in the time-consuming details of implementing training, such as the following:[14]

- Arranging for salespeople to work with key personnel in various departments in the firm in order to familiarize them with the functions of those departments
- Selecting literature, sales aids, and materials for study
- Enrolling salespeople in professional workshops
- Accompanying salespeople in the field to critique their sales behavior and reinforce other training
- Conducting periodic training meetings and personal training conferences

The significant time investment required from sales management is, unfortunately, not always well spent. One study of 235 companies concluded that the "companies had not resolved some significant discrepancies between what they teach and what they believe a successful salesperson needs" to be successful.[15] This study found, for example, that salespeople's attitudes were thought to be critical for sales success, yet training programs tended to concentrate on skills and knowledge while virtually ignoring work attitudes.

Sales training is indeed expensive, and sales managers should take special care to see that time and money are wisely spent. With these thoughts in mind, let us examine a model for the judicious analysis, planning, and implementation of a sales training program.

A Model of the Sales Training Process

The sales training process is depicted as six interrelated steps in Figure 10.1: assess training needs, set training objectives, evaluate training alternatives, design sales training program, perform sales training, and conduct follow-up and evaluation.

FIGURE 10.1 ▪ *Sales Training Process*

The sales training process is performed in six steps, beginning with an assessment of training needs. The process is continual, with the follow-up and evaluation step providing feedback that may alter the other steps in future sales training activities.

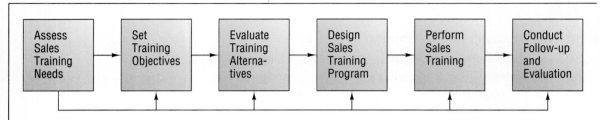

be willing to change or readjust. Don't keep the same needs or objec...

Assess Training Needs

The purpose of sales training **needs assessment** is to compare the specific performance-related skills, attitudes, perceptions, and behaviors required for salesforce success with the state of readiness of the salesforce. Such an assessment usually reveals a need for changing or reinforcing one or more determinants of salesforce performance.

All too often, the need for sales training becomes apparent only after a decline in salesforce performance is manifested by decreasing sales volume, rising expenses, or perhaps low morale. Sales training for correcting such problems is sometimes necessary, but the preferred role of sales training is to prevent problems and improve salesforce productivity on a proactive, not reactive, basis.

Needs assessment requires that sales managers consider the training appropriate for both *sales trainees* and regular salespeople. A sales trainee is an entry-level salesperson who is learning the company's products, services, and policies in preparation for a regular sales assignment. Another factor worth considering during needs assessment is each salesperson's career stage, as explained in Chapter 4. For example, salespeople in the exploration stage may need basic training in sales techniques, while the salespeople in the maintenance stage could benefit from training in advanced sales techniques.

Methods of Needs Assessment. Proactive approaches to determining sales training needs include a salesforce audit, performance testing, observation, salesforce survey, customer survey, and a job analysis.

Salesforce Audit. A comprehensive definition of **salesforce audit** is "a systematic, diagnostic, prescriptive tool which can be employed on a periodic basis to identify and address sales department problems and to prevent or reduce the impact of future problems.[16] The salesforce audit (discussed fully in Chapter 15) includes an appraisal of all salesforce activities and the environment in which the salesforce operates. In the sales training area, the audit examines questions such as

▪ Is the training program adequate in light of objectives and resources?
▪ Does the training program need revision?
▪ Is there an ongoing training program for senior salespeople?

Does the training program contribute in a positive manner to the socialization of sales trainees?

To be effective, a salesforce audit should be conducted annually. More frequent audits may be warranted in some situations, but the comprehensive nature of an audit requires a considerable time and money investment. As a result, other periodic assessments of sales training are suggested.

Performance Testing. Some firms use **performance testing** to help determine training needs. This method specifies the evaluation of particular tasks or skills of the salesforce. For example, salespeople may be given periodic exams on product knowledge to check retention rates and uncover areas for retraining. Salespeople may be asked to exhibit particular sales techniques such as demonstrating the product or using the telephone to set up sales appointments while the sales trainer evaluates their performance.

Observation. First-level sales managers spend a considerable amount of time in the field working with salespeople. They also may have direct responsibility for some accounts, acting as a salesperson or as a member of a sales team. Through these field selling activities, sales managers often *observe* the need for particular sales training. In some instances, the training need is addressed instantaneously by critiquing the salesperson's performance after the sales call has been completed. In other situations, frequent observation of particularly deficient or outstanding sales behavior may suggest future training topics.

Salesforce Survey. The salesforce may be surveyed in an attempt to isolate sales training needs. Such **salesforce surveys** may be completed as an independent activity or combined with other sales management activities such as field visits or even included as part of the routine salesforce reporting procedures. The reports submitted by many salespeople on a weekly basis to their sales managers frequently have sections dealing with problems to be solved and areas in which managerial assistance is requested. For example, a faltering new-product introduction may signal the need for more product training, additional sales technique sharpening, or perhaps training needs specific to an individual salesperson.

By surveying the salesforce, the task of assessing training needs may become more complex than if sales management alone determines training needs. To ignore the salesforce in this step of the training process, however, could be a serious sin of omission. Consider the results of the Sales Needs Analysis Survey (SNAS) conducted by the Stamford, Connecticut, consulting firm, Learning International. In this survey, salespeople and sales managers disagreed on which training topics were most important for improving sales effectiveness. Sales managers cited sales skills and knowledge as most important, while salespeople cited organizational factors such as improving marketing strategy, direct support, and customer service.[17] If sales managers and their salespeople should disagree on training needs, it is far better to discover this disagreement and resolve it prior to designing and delivering specific sales training programs.

Customer Survey. Intended to define customer expectations, a **customer survey** helps determine how competitive the salesforce is compared with other salesforces in the industry. If personal selling is prominent in the firm's marketing strategy, some sort of customer survey to help determine sales training needs is highly recommended.

Job Analysis. The job analysis, defined in Chapter 9, is an investigation of the task, duties, and responsibilities of the sales job. In a well-run sales organization, a job analysis will be part of the recruitment and selection process and then will continue to be used in sales training and other managerial functions. Since the job analysis defines expected behavior for salespeople, it is a logical tool to be employed in assessing training needs. Since sales jobs may vary within the same salesforce, job analyses may also help in determining individualized sales training needs or the needs of different groups of salespeople.

Typical Sales Training Needs. As the preceding discussion implies, the need for sales training varies over time and across organizations. The need for salesforce training on certain topics, however, is widespread. Some of the more popular sales training topics will now be discussed.

Orientation and Socialization. Newly hired salespeople usually receive a company orientation designed to familiarize them with company history, policies, facilities, procedures, and key people with whom salespeople interact. Some firms go well beyond a perfunctory company orientation in an effort to enhance salesforce *socialization*, a concept introduced at the conclusion of Chapter 9. By referring to Figure 9.2 in that chapter, you can see how sales training can affect salesforce socialization. During initial sales training, it is hoped that each salesforce member will experience a positive **initiation to task**—the degree to which a sales trainee feels competent and accepted as a working partner—and satisfactory **role definition**—an understanding of what tasks are to be performed, what the priorities of the tasks are, and how time should be allocated among the tasks.[18]

The need for socialization as part of the training process is supported by expected indirect linkages between socialization and beneficial job outcomes. As suggested in Figure 9.2, trainees who have been properly recruited and trained tend to be more confident on the job and have fewer problems with job conflicts, leading to higher job satisfaction, involvement, commitment, and performance.

The positive relationships between salespeople's job-related attitudes and perceptions and their commitment to their companies have been supported in empirical studies. For example, a study of 102 salespeople in the food industry found that "among approaches within a company's control, programs aimed at minimizing new salespeople's role ambiguity and improving their satisfaction are most likely to be most effective in building commitment to the company."[19] Another study of 120 manufacturers' salespeople found a positive relationship between job satisfaction and salespeople's commitment to the organization.[20] These studies reinforce the importance of sales managers taking an active role in socializing their salespeople to maximize overall salesforce productivity.

Newly hired salespeople should be extremely interested in learning about their jobs, peers, and supervisors. A basic orientation may be insufficient to provide all the information they desire, so more extensive socialization may be indicated. One company that emphasizes salesforce socialization as part of its training program is furniture manufacturer Knoll International. Knoll allows its new salespeople, much like investigative reporters, to interview the heads of various departments such as credit and shipping to learn how the departments interface with the salespeople. Afterward, the salespeople make presentations on what they learn to other members of the salesforce, and then salespeople and department heads meet in a social setting to get to know each other better. In the past, Knoll had relied on what Susan Onaitis, director of sales training, called the "talking heads" approach. This involved all of the department heads making formal presentations to the salespeople, which had been ineffective in fostering working relationships between salespeople and the departments.[21]

The need for salesforce socialization is especially likely to extend past the initial training period. This is particularly true if salesforce members have limited personal contact with peers, managers, and other company personnel.

Sales Techniques. There is a universal, ongoing need for training on "how to sell." Research has indicated that salespeople sometimes sell in spite of themselves; that is to say, many salespeople do not competently execute fundamental sales techniques.[22] Common mistakes identified in this research include

- Ineffective listening and questioning
- Failure to build rapport and trust
- Poor job of prospecting for new accounts
- Lack of preplanning of sales calls
- Reluctance to make cold calls (without an appointment)
- Lack of sales strategies for different accounts
- Failure to match call frequency with account potential
- Spending too much time with old customers
- Over-controlling the sales call
- Failure to respond to customer needs with related benefits
- Giving benefits before clarifying customer needs
- Ineffective handling of negative attitudes
- Failure to effectively confirm the sale

This rather lengthy list of common shortcomings is remarkable in that proper training could erase these problems entirely. In fact, most formal sales training programs do spend a considerable amount of time on sales techniques. One survey of sales trainers concluded that over 50 percent of the time spent in training programs for new salespeople was dedicated to sales skills, while almost two-thirds of the training time for more experienced salespeople was spent on sales skills.[23]

As we have previously mentioned, the basic nature of sales techniques training is changing, and more emphasis is being placed on developing trusting, enduring relationships with customers. Salespeople are receiving more training on listening and questioning skills so that they may do a more effective job of learning the customer's needs. Furthermore, high-pressure sales techniques are declining in popularity and being replaced with sales techniques based on need satisfaction, problem solving, and partnership forming with the customer's best interests as the focus.[24]

Product Knowledge. Salespeople must have thorough **product knowledge** including the benefits, applications, competitive strengths, and limitations of the product. Product knowledge may need updating in the event of new-product development, product modification, product deletions, or the development of new applications for the product.

Generally speaking, product knowledge is one of the most frequently covered topics in sales training programs. As expected, the more complex the product or service, the higher the likelihood that detailed knowledge about the offering will be stressed in the training program.

Although it is an essential requirement, adequate product knowledge will not necessarily lead to sales success. Studies have shown that product knowledge levels of high-performing salespeople are not significantly different than for moderate performers.[25] Having product knowledge is not enough—the salesperson must know the customer and have the necessary sales skills to apply the knowledge of the product to the customer's situation.

Customer Knowledge. Sales training may include information relating to customer needs, buying motives, buying procedures, and personalities. Faced with situational and individual differences among customers, some firms use classification methods to categorize buyers according to personality and the buying situation. An example of different types of buyers and suggested sales training topics is presented in Exhibit 10.2.

As companies expand their global selling efforts, training programs must address cultural differences and business protocol in foreign countries. For example, gift-giving is a sensitive area, since well-intentioned expressions of goodwill can backfire and instead become personal insults to a prospective customer. The rules of conduct given in "A Global Perspective: Training the Salesforce on Gift Giving" are illustrative of issues that could be included in sales training sessions.

Competitive Knowledge. Salespeople must know competitive offerings in terms of strengths and weaknesses to effectively plan sales strategy and sales presentations and be able to respond effectively to customer questions and objections. This area is extremely important for salespeople who are new to the industry, as the competitor's salespeople may have years of experience and be quite knowledgeable. Further, customers may exploit a salesperson's lack of competitive knowledge to negotiate terms of sale that may be costly to the selling firm. For example, salespeople who are not familiar with a competitor's price structure may unnecessarily reduce their own price to make a sale, thereby sacrificing more revenue and profits than they should have.

Time and Territory Management. The quest for an optimal balance between salesforce output and salesforce expenditures is a perennial objective for most sales managers. For this reason, training in time and territory management (TTM),

EXHIBIT 10.2   ▪   *Sales Training for Different Types of Buyers*

Kind of Buyer	*Sales Training Topic*
1. The Hard Bargainer (a difficult person to deal with)	1. Teach psychologically-oriented sales strategies (such as transactional analysis). 2. Teach sales *negotiation* strategies (such as the use of different bases of power). 3. Teach listening skills and the benefits of listening to the prospect. 4. Emphasize how to handle objections. 5. Emphasize *competitive* product knowledge.
2. The Sales Job Facilitator (attempts to make the sales transaction go smoothly)	1. Teach importance of a *quid pro quo*. 2. Communicate advantages of having a satisfied customer base. 3. Show how customers can assist salespeople (e.g., by pooling orders, providing leads).
3. The Straight Shooter (behaves with integrity and propriety)	1. Teach importance of selling the "substance" of the product offering and not just the "sizzle." 2. Teach straightforward techniques of handling objections (e.g., a direct denial approach).
4. The Socializer (enjoys personal interaction with salespeople)	1. Communicate company policy information about giving gifts and entertaining and socializing with customers. 2. Discuss ethical and legal implications of transacting business. 3. Emphasize importance of salespeople maintaining an appropriate balance between socializing with customers and performing job responsibilities.
5. The Persuader (attempts to "market" his or her company)	1. Communicate importance of qualifying prospects. 2. Teach techniques for qualifying customers.
6. The Considerate (shows compassion for salesperson)	1. Communicate importance of obtaining market information from customers. 2. Teach importance of a *quid pro quo*.

Source: Alan J. Dubinsky and Thomas N. Ingram, "A Classification of Industrial Buyers: Implications for Sales Training," *Journal of Personal Selling and Sales Management* 2 (Fall–Winter 1981–1982): 49.

introduced in Chapter 3 of this text, is often included in formal sales training programs. Essentially, the purpose of TTM training is to teach salespeople how to use time and efforts for maximum work efficiency.

TTM training is important for all sales organizations but especially for those in declining, stagnant, or highly competitive industries. In such situations,

A GLOBAL PERSPECTIVE

Training the Salesforce on Gift Giving   The suggestions for adapting to local cultures and laws sometimes appear to be trivial. Americans are often ethnocentric, and they should try to remember that what appears to be trivial to them may indeed be extremely important to other peoples of the world. For instance, in China, writing in red ink is not recommended, as it signals the end of a relationship. In Italy, chrysanthemums should not be given as a gift, as they are a symbol of mourning. Also in Italy, salespeople would be wise to avoid the color purple in gift giving, as it represents death. In Japan, gifts that consist of less than ten items should be given in odd numbers. For example, place settings and tea cups are sold in sets of five.

The legal system can also influence gift giving. In Australia, strict quarantine laws place a ban on all meats, wood products, straw articles such as baskets, and dairy products.

Salespeople operating in new foreign markets must learn how cultural differences dictate business protocol, including the proper role of entertaining and gift giving. Progressive firms do not treat such topics lightly, as they know that violations of cultural norms can impede sales results and that sales training can address these issues.

Source: Dawn Bryan, "Beware the Purple Pigskin Clock," *Sales and Marketing Management*, August 1990, 74–78.

salespeople are often overworked, and there comes a point when working harder to improve results is not realistic. Such circumstances call for "working smarter, not harder," an idea that is receiving considerable discussion in sales management circles.[26]

Ethical and Legal Issues.   Ethical and legal issues are being included in sales training programs more frequently than in the past. One catalyst for this change has been product-liability litigation that has awarded multimillion-dollar judgments to plaintiffs who have suffered as a result of unsafe products. Research has found that salespeople face a number of ethical and legal dilemmas on the job and that salespeople want more direction from their managers on how to handle such dilemmas.[27]

Training in the legal area is extremely difficult, since laws are sometimes confusing and subject to multiple interpretations. Training salespeople in ethics is even more difficult, as ethical issues are often "gray," not black or white. Companies who address ethics and legal issues in their sales training programs usually rely on straightforward guidelines that avoid complexity. Salespeople are given basic training on applicable legal dimensions and advised simply to tell the truth and seek management assistance should problems arise. This may sound simplistic, but such training can greatly reduce salesperson conflict on the job, help develop profitable long-term relationships with customers, and reduce the liability of the salesperson and the organization.

Interestingly, some of the stronger ethical and legal training programs are being conducted in firms that previously engaged in some unethical and illegal sales methods. One such firm is General Dynamics, which was charged with overbilling the government on defense contracts but now has a 20-page code of ethics telling salespeople how to conduct themselves.[28] Examples from this code of ethics are

EXHIBIT 10.3 ▪ *Example Items from General Dynamics Code of Ethics*

1. If it becomes clear that the company must engage in unethical or illegal activity to win a contract, that business will not be further pursued.

2. All information provided relative to products or services should be clear and concise.

3. Receiving or soliciting gifts, entertainment, or anything else of value is expressly prohibited.

4. In countries where common practice might indicate conduct lower than that to which General Dynamics aspires, salespeople will follow the company's standards.

5. Under no circumstance may an employee give anything to a customer's representative in an effort to influence him.

Source: Arthur Bragg, "Ethics in Selling, Honest!" *Sales and Marketing Management*, May 1987, 44.

shown in Exhibit 10.3. For some advice on how to emphasize ethics during sales techniques training, see "An Ethical Perspective: Gaining a Commitment from the Customer."

The legal framework for personal selling is quite extensive. Some of the key components of this framework are antitrust legislation, contract law, local ordinances governing sales practices, and guidelines issued by the Federal Trade Commission dealing with unfair trade practices. A partial listing of important legal reminders that should be included in a sales training program is shown in Exhibit 10.4.

AN ETHICAL PERSPECTIVE

Gaining a Commitment from the Customer Ron Willingham, a sales trainer and consultant whose clients include General Motors, has earned a reputation as one of the strongest proponents of ethical selling. One part of the sales process that often presents ethical dilemmas for salespeople is when a purchase decision is imminent and the salesperson feels the pressure to make the sale. This sometimes results in less-than-ethical sales techniques. For example, the salesperson might suggest that the customer place an order immediately to avoid an out-of-stock situation, even if ample inventory is on hand to meet the customer's requirements.

In his sales training program, Willingham reminds salespeople that bookstores are full of books that put the emphasis on "tricky, gimmicky maneuvers to outsmart people and get them to buy." Noting that such manipulative techniques are not effective in most situations anyway, Willingham encourages a customer-oriented approach for gaining customer commitment. Among his least-favorite suggestions are oft-encountered sales clichés such as "Close early and often" and "The sale begins when the customer says no." He suggests that salespeople ask for a commitment only when they are reasonably sure that all customer concerns have been met and that the customer will receive bona fide value by making the purchase.

Source: Ron Willingham, *Integrity Selling* (New York: Doubleday, 1987), 125–127.

EXHIBIT 10.4 ▪ *Legal Reminders for Salespeople*

1. Use factual data rather than general statements of praise during the sales presentation. Avoid misrepresentation.
2. Thoroughly educate customers before the sale on the product's specifications, capabilities, and limitations.
3. Do not overstep authority, as the salesperson's actions can be binding to the selling firm.
4. Avoid discussing these topics with competitors: prices, profit margins, discounts, terms of sale, bids or intent to bid, sales territories or markets to be served, rejection or termination of customers.
5. Do not use one product as bait for selling another product.
6. Do not try to force the customer to buy only from your organization.
7. Offer the same price and support to all buyers who purchase under the same set of circumstances.
8. Do not tamper with a competitor's product.
9. Do not disparage a competitor's product without specific evidence of your contentions.
10. Avoid promises that will be difficult or impossible to honor.

Set Training Objectives

Having assessed the needs for sales training, the sales manager moves to the next step in the sales training model shown in Figure 10.1: setting specific **sales training objectives.** Since training needs vary from one sales organization to the next, so do the objectives. In general, however, one or more of the following are included:

1. Increase sales or profits.
2. Create positive attitudes and improve salesforce morale.
3. Assist in salesforce socialization.
4. Reduce role conflict and ambiguity.
5. Introduce new products, markets, and promotional programs.
6. Develop salespeople for future management positions.
7. Ensure awareness of ethical and legal responsibilities.
8. Teach administrative procedures (e.g., expense accounts, call reports).
9. Ensure competence in the use of sales and sales support tools such as portable computers.
10. Minimize salesforce turnover rate.
11. Prepare new salespeople for assignment to a sales territory.
12. Improve teamwork and cooperative efforts.

These objectives are interrelated. For example, if salespeople gain competence in the use of a new sales tool, sales and profit may improve, salesforce morale may be positively affected, and other beneficial outcomes may occur. By setting objectives for sales training, the manager avoids the wasteful practice of training simply for training's sake. Further, objectives force the sales manager to define the reasonable expectations of sales training rather than to view training as a quick-fix panacea for all the problems faced by the salesforce. Additional benefits of setting objectives for sales training are:[29]

- Written objectives become a good communications vehicle to inform the salesforce and other interested parties about upcoming training.
- Top management is responsive to well-written, specific objectives and may be more willing to provide budget support for the training.
- Specific training objectives provide a standard for measuring the effectiveness of training.
- By setting objectives, the sales manager finds it easier to prioritize various training needs, and the proper sequence of training becomes more apparent.

Evaluate Training Alternatives

In the third step of the sales training process, the sales manager considers various approaches for accomplishing the objectives of training. Certainly many more alternatives exist today than in the past, thanks to technologies such as computer-assisted instruction, videotape, and videotext. The number of sales training professionals for hire also seems to be increasing, or perhaps such trainers are just doing a better job of promoting their services. Even a casual examination of a typical shopping mall bookstore will reveal a number of titles related to building sales skills, along with audiotapes and videotapes on the subject.

Critiquing all these alternatives is a monumental job, so it is recommended that fairly stringent criteria be established for preliminary screening, including cost, location of the training, flexibility of prepackaged materials, opportunity for reinforcement training, and time required to implement an alternative.

The evaluation of alternatives for training inevitably leads to three key questions. First, who will conduct the training? An answer to this question will require the consideration of internal (within the company) and external (outside the company) trainers. The second question deals with location for the training. Sales training may be conducted in the field, in the office, at a central training location, hotels and conference centers, or other locations. The third question is, Which method (or methods) and media are best suited for conducting the training?

Selecting Sales Trainers. In general, companies rely most heavily on their own personnel to conduct sales training. In this endeavor, the sales manager is the most important **sales trainer.** Senior salespeople are also frequently involved as trainers. In larger companies, a full-time sales trainer is often available. According to surveys of training practices, only a small percentage of firms use outside training consultants, and these are primarily larger firms. A survey of over 1,500 companies showed that only 5 percent of the respondents used outside trainers or consultants on a frequent basis, while 23 percent used them occasionally, and 35 percent reported that they never used them. Overall, it is estimated that slightly over 10 percent of sales training is conducted by external trainers or consultants.[30]

What factors lead to the dominance of internal sources in sales training? First, and perhaps most importantly, sales managers and senior salespeople are intimately aware of job requirements and can communicate in very specific terms to the sales trainee. On the other hand, outside consultants may be only superficially informed about a specific sales job and frequently offer generic sales training packages. Second, sales managers are the logical source for training to be conducted in the field, where valuable learning can occur with each sales call. It is extremely difficult to turn field training over to external trainers. Finally, using internal trainers simplifies control and coordination tasks. It is easier for sales managers to control the content of the program, coordinate training for maximum impact, and provide continuity for the program when it is the sales manager who does the training or who designates other company personnel to do the training.

At some point, a sales manager's effectiveness may be improved by using external trainers. Internal resources, including time, expertise, facilities, and personnel, may be insufficient to accomplish the objectives of the sales training program. Also, outside trainers might be looked to for new ideas and methods. One sales manager who strongly supports the use of external trainers is Mark Burrall of Pflow Industries, a $10 million company with four salespeople in the field. Burrall says that he encourages salespeople to let him know what type of training they desire, then he "shops around" to find the best commercially available program. He spends approximately $1,800 per salesperson per year for off-the-shelf programs and seminars, favoring some of the more expensive programs because he has found that "you get what you pay for."[31]

Many companies utilize outside trainers to get ideas or to learn new training methods, then conduct the actual sales training with internal personnel. One such company is Warner-Lambert, a large pharmaceutical firm. Warner-Lambert uses outside sources for virtually all of its training materials, including printed matter and video training materials, but never uses these materials for actual training until they have been customized for the salesforce.[32] Large training firms such as The Forum Corporation, U.S. Learning Inc., and Learning International frequently customize their generic programs for use within specific companies.

Evaluating Sales Training Locations. As shown in Figure 10.2, the large majority of sales training is conducted in home, regional, or field offices of the sales organization. Manufacturing plants are also popular training sites, and some firms use non-company sites such as hotels or conference centers to conduct training.

Central training facilities are another possibility, used extensively by Noxell Corporation, Xerox, IBM, General Electric, Armstrong World Industries, and scores of other large firms. Russ Stavig, introduced to you at the beginning of Chapter 4, oversees the Armstrong World Industries Floor Division initial sales training programs at a central facility in Lancaster, Pennsylvania. Sales trainees live dormitory-style in an updated country home called The Manor, where they can relax together after hours and, on frequent occasions, work together on training assignments. On a daily basis, the trainees will travel a short distance to Armstrong's headquarters for extensive sessions dealing with sales techniques, product knowledge, ethical and legal information, and various other topics. Armstrong's management team and their sales trainees agree that the centralized training facility allows the trainees to concentrate on the tasks at hand, but at least as importantly, it allows each training class to build camaraderie and learn more about how the company works. In other words, Armstrong believes their central

FIGURE 10.2 ■ *Sites Most Frequently Used for Sales Training*

Most sales training is conducted in company facilities. The field office is the most popular location for sales training, followed by the home office.

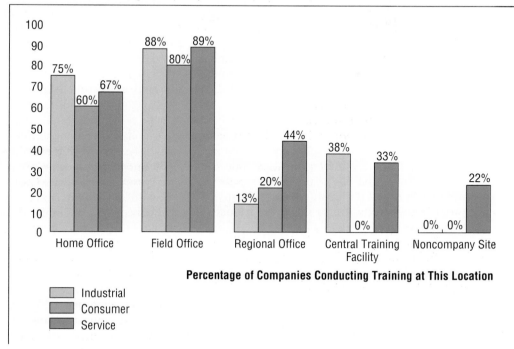

Source: "Survey of Selling Costs," *Sales and Marketing Management*, February 22, 1988, 49.

training facility improves salesforce socialization in addition to being an efficient way to train salespeople.[33]

As video broadcasting and teleconferencing become more prevalent, many firms are enjoying some of the benefits of a centralized training facility without incurring the travel costs and lost time to transport the salesforce to and from training. Field offices arrange for video hook-up, either in-house or at video-equipped conference hotels, and trainees across the country share simultaneously in training emanating from a central location.

Selecting Sales Training Methods. A variety of methods can be selected to fit the training situation. Indeed, the use of multiple methods is encouraged over the course of a training program to help maintain trainee attention and enhance learning. There are four categories of training methods: classroom/conference, on-the-job, behavioral simulations, and absorption.

Classroom/Conference Training. The classroom or conference setting features lectures, demonstrations, and group discussion with expert trainers serving as instructors. This method is frequently used for training on basic product knowledge, new-product introductions, administrative procedures, and legal and ethical issues in personal selling. The format often resembles a college classroom, with regularly scheduled exams and overnight homework assignments. In addition to using internal facilities and personnel, some companies send their salespeople to seminars sponsored by the American Management Association, American Marketing Association, Sales and Marketing Executives International, and local colleges and universities. These organizations offer training on practically any phase of selling and sales management, and there is even a graduate school of sales management co-sponsored by Syracuse University and Sales and Marketing Executives International.

On-the-Job Training. In the final analysis, salespeople can only be taught so much about selling without actually experiencing it. Consequently, **on-the-job training (OJT)** is extremely important. OJT puts the trainee into actual work circumstances, under the observant (it is hoped) eye of a supportive **mentor** or sales manager. Other OJT methods approximate a "sink or swim" philosophy and often produce disastrous results when the trainee is overwhelmed with unfamiliar job requirements.

The use of mentors is especially prevalent in larger companies, with approximately one-third of the nation's major companies reporting the use of mentors. Some of the better-known firms using mentors include Colgate, Schering-Plough, AT&T, and Georgia-Pacific.[34] The mentors have different objectives from company to company, but they usually strive to make the new hires feel at home in their jobs, relay information about the corporate culture, and be available for discussion and advice on topics of concern to the trainee. Coworker mentoring is popular among salesforces, and in some companies, such as Georgia-Pacific, the sales manager serves as the mentor. The use of the mentoring concept is yet another way that companies are striving to improve salesforce socialization, especially the role-definition and initiation-to-task steps explained earlier in this chapter.

Other than working with a senior salesperson or a mentor, common OJT assignments include the trainee's filling in for a vacationing salesperson, working with a sales manager who acts as a "coach," and job rotation. When senior salespeople act as mentors, they too are undergoing continual training as their ideas and methods are reassessed, and sometimes refined, with each trainee. The sales manager's role as *coach* will be discussed in a later chapter on supervision and leadership of the salesforce. **Job rotation,** the exposure of different jobs to the sales trainee, may involve stints as customer service representatives, distribution clerks, or perhaps other sales positions. Job rotation is frequently used to groom salespeople for management positions.

Behavioral Simulations. Methods that focus on behavioral learning by means of business games and simulations, case studies, and role playing, where trainees portray a specified role in a staged situation, are called **behavioral simulations.** They focus on defining desirable behavior or in correcting behavioral mistakes.

An example of a business game for salespeople has been developed by Management Campus Inc. in Atlanta. The game uses a "day in the life of a salesperson" approach to teach salespeople to develop selling strategies and skills. Salespeople compete with each other on prospecting, routing, and the ways they execute necessary sales tasks.[35] Another popular game format is the television-style quiz show, featuring customized questions and answers dealing with realistic selling situations and product knowledge. Teams of salespeople-contestants compete on a stage set complete with an emcee and a colorful electronic scoreboard, with an audience made up of peers, managers, and perhaps customers. Companies using the quiz-show format in sales training include Coca-Cola, Sherwin-Williams, Minolta, Nabisco, and Shearson Lehman Hutton.[36]

Along with OJT, **role playing** is extremely popular for teaching sales techniques. Typically, one trainee plays the role of the salesperson, and another trainee acts as the buyer. The role playing is videotaped or performed live for a group of observers who then critique the performance. This can be an extremely effective means of teaching personal selling, without the risk of a poor performance in the presence of a live customer. It is most effective when promptly critiqued with emphasis on the positive points of the performance as well as suggestions for improvement. A good way to maximize the benefits of the critique is to have the person who has played the role of the salesperson offer opinions first and then solicit opinions from observers. After role playing, the "salesperson" is usually quite modest about his or her performance, and the comments from observers may bolster this individual's self-confidence. In turn, future performance may be improved.[37]

Absorption Training. As the name implies, **absorption training** involves furnishing trainees or salespeople with materials that they peruse (or "absorb") without opportunity for immediate feedback and questioning. Product manuals, direction-laden memoranda, and sales bulletins are used in absorption training. This method is most useful as a supplement to update salesforce knowledge, reinforce previous training, or to introduce basic materials to be covered in more detail at a later date.

One method of absorption training that has become widespread in recent years is to furnish the salesforce with audiocassettes, so that driving time can be utilized as training time.[38] The salesforces of Digital Equipment Corporation, Pfizer Labs, Moore Business Forms, Johnson & Johnson, and Gillette all use audiocassettes as a routine part of their training programs. In some cases, companies produce their own cassettes, while in other instances they use rental tapes from services such as Tape Rental Library located in Charlottesville, Virginia.

Selecting Sales Training Media. Communications and computer technology have expanded the range of sales training media dramatically in the past decade. Sales trainers warn against the tendency to be overly impressed with the glamorous aspects of such training media, but they agree that it is advisable to evaluate new media on a continual basis to see if it should be incorporated into the sales training program. The most promising new media are found at the communications/computer technology interface.

An example of how video technology can improve sales training comes from Medtronics Inc., manufacturer of a prosthetic heart valve. Videotape of live surgery using the valve is used as a training film, replacing printed materials as the preferred training medium. Noting that live surgery cannot be conducted on a sales call, the training film is also promoted as an effective adjunct to the sales presentation to doctors.[39]

Computer and communications equipment are combined for training in the Simulation System Trainer developed by Performax Inc. This system features a personal computer, videodisc player, videotape camera and recorder, video monitor, equipment interfaces, and computer programs that enable the trainee to "talk" to a customer on the screen. Realistic dialogues are accomplished, and the trainee has the opportunity to analyze the outcomes of sales behaviors and improve presentation skills.

The Performax interactive video training system is being used by several major companies, including IBM, South Central Bell, and Ottaway Newspapers, a New York subsidiary of Dow-Jones. It is also being used to supplement instruction in sales fundamentals at Memphis State University.

In addition, interactive video is being used to conduct sales training in a teleconference setting. For example, Federal Express produces an in-house monthly satellite program called Salesline, which is broadcast over FXTV (Federal Express Television) to 750 locations. A typical broadcast features a Federal Express sales executive who handles questions on diverse topics such as pricing, the use of computer graphics in sales presentations, or on whatever the salespeople need information.[40]

There is also a growing supply of sales training software available for a few hundred dollars per program or less. Programs cover time and territory management, sales analysis, and the entire sales process. Popular programs include the Sales Edge and Sell! Sell! Sell![41]

Design the Sales Training Program

The fourth step in the sales training process is a culmination of, and condensation of, the first three steps shown in Figure 10.1. Working toward selected objectives based on needs assessment, and having evaluated training alternatives, the sales manager now commits resources to the training to be accomplished. At this point in the process, sales managers may have to seek budget approval from upper management.

In this step of designing the training program, the necessary responses to what, when, where, and how questions are finalized. Training is scheduled, travel arrangements made, media selected, speakers hired, and countless other details attended to. Certainly this can be the most tedious part of the sales training process, but attention to detail is necessary to ensure successful implementation of the process.

Perform Sales Training

The fifth step in the process, actually performing the training, may only take a fraction of the time required by the previous steps. This is particularly true in better sales training programs. As the training is being conducted, the sales manager's primary responsibility is to monitor the progress of the trainees and to ensure adequate presentation of the training topics. In particular, sales managers should assess the clarity of training materials. It is also recommended that some assessment of the trainees' continuing motivation to learn be made. Feedback from the trainees might be solicited on everything from the effectiveness of external trainers to the adequacy of the physical training site.

Conduct Follow-up and Evaluation

It is always difficult to measure the effectiveness of sales training. This is a long-standing problem, due in some cases to a lack of clearly stated sales training objectives. Even with clearly stated objectives, however, it is hard to determine which future performance variations are a result of sales training. Other factors such as motivation, role perceptions, and environmental factors may affect performance more or less than training in different situations.

Although scientific precision cannot be hoped for, a reasonable attempt must be nevertheless made to assess whether current training expenditures are worthwhile and whether future modification is warranted. Evaluations can be made before, during, and after the training occurs.[42] For example, the pre-training evaluation might include an exam for sales trainees to assess their level of knowledge, corroborate or deny the need for training, and further define the objectives of the training. As suggested earlier, training can be evaluated while it is being conducted, and adjustments may be made at any point in the delivery of training. Post-training evaluations might include reactions or critiques of the trainees, "final exams," retention exams at later dates, observations by sales managers as they work in the field with salespeople, and in some cases an examination of actual performance indicators such as sales volume. Exhibit 10.5 summarizes the sales training evaluation practices of 100 large and small companies. Note that formal evaluations of sales training are more likely to occur in larger companies, where training expenditures are generally higher.

Despite the inherent difficulty in relating subsequent sales performance to previously conducted sales training, the effectiveness of sales training is increasingly being measured in dollars and cents. This return-on-investment approach seeks to define training effectiveness in terms of incremental sales volume from existing accounts or volume generated by new accounts. According to one survey of over 1,500 companies, approximately 40 percent of companies use increased sales as a benchmark to gauge the effectiveness of sales training.[43]

An example of this approach is provided by the manager of training and development for James River–Dixie/Northern, marketer of Dixie cups, who claims concrete proof of the effectiveness of a sales strategy training program. The program required the salespeople to design a sales strategy for targeted accounts that they had been unable to sell and then to implement the strategy. A postprogram evaluation concluded that $2.1 million in new sales volume had been generated as a direct result of the training.[44] Did this mean the training was a success? While it would be difficult to prove conclusively that training alone produced these outcomes, most managers would agree that unless the training in this case was prohibitively expensive, it proved itself worthwhile.

In essence, this thinking pervades this entire chapter. A reasonable approach to sales training is to ensure that it is not prohibitively expensive by carefully

EXHIBIT 10.5 ▪ *Sales Training Evaluation Practices in Large and Small Companies*

Types/Methods	Large Companies	Small Companies
Trainee Reaction		
Written critique: content	76%	29%
Written critique: methods	61%	20%
Written critique: trainers	55%	22%
Discussion of training program	51%	45%
Knowledge		
Testing	53%	28%
Behavior		
Field evaluation: attitude	35%	45%
Results		
Field evaluation: performance	49%	65%
No evaluation conducted	2%	16%

*Multiple responses were allowed. Percentages denote proportion of companies using the various methods.
Source: Earl D. Honeycutt, Jr., and Thomas H. Stevenson, "Evaluating Sales Training Programs," *Industrial Marketing Management* 18 (August 1989): 218.

assessing training needs, setting objectives, and evaluating training alternatives before designing the training program and performing the training. Further, the sales training process is incomplete without evaluation and follow-up.

Summary

1.   **Explain the importance of sales training and the sales manager's role in sales training.** Most organizations have a continual need for sales training as a result of changing business conditions, the influx of new salespeople into the organization, and the need to reinforce previous training. Sizable investments in training are likely in larger companies and those companies involved in high technology industries and highly competitive industries. The sales manager has the overall responsibility for training the salesforce, although other people may also conduct sales training.

2.   **Describe the sales training process as a series of six interrelated steps.** Figure 10.1 presents the sales training process in six steps: assess sales training needs, set training objectives, evaluate training alternatives, design the sales training program, perform sales training, and conduct follow-up and evaluation. The time spent to perform sales training may be only a fraction of the time spent to complete the other steps in the process, especially in well-run sales organizations.

3.   **Discuss five methods for assessing sales training needs and identify typical sales training needs.** Sales managers may assess needs through performance testing, observation, a salesforce survey, customer survey, or a job analysis. It is recommended that salesforce training needs be assessed in a proactive fashion; that is, needs should be assessed before performance problems occur rather than after problems occur. Typical sales training needs include orientation and socialization of the salesforce; product, customer, and competitive knowledge; sales techniques; time and territory management; and ethical and legal issues.

4.   **Name some typical objectives of sales training programs, and explain how setting objectives for sales training is beneficial to sales managers.** The objectives of sales training vary over time and across organizations, but they often include preparing sales trainees for assignment to a sales territory, improving a particular dimension of performance, aiding in the socialization process, or improving salesforce morale and motivation. By setting objectives, the sales manager can prioritize training, allocate resources consistent with priorities, communicate the purpose of the training to interested parties, and perhaps gain top management support for sales training.

5.   **Identify the key issues in evaluating sales training alternatives.** evaluation of alternatives is a search for an optimal balance between cost and effectiveness. One key issue is the selection of trainers, whether from outside the company (external) or inside the company (internal). Another is the potential location or locations for training. Still another important factor is the method or methods to use for various topics. Sales training methods include classroom/conference training, on-the-job training (OJT), behavioral simulations, and absorption training. The sales manager must also consider whether to use various sales training media such as printed material, videotape, and computer-assisted instruction.

Key Terms

- **Needs assessment**
- **Salesforce audit**
- **Performance testing**
- **Salesforce survey**
- **Customer survey**
- **Initiation to task**
- **Role definition**
- **Product knowledge**
- **Sales training objectives**

- **Sales trainer**
- **Central training facility**
- **On-the-job training (OJT)**
- **Mentor**
- **Job rotation**
- **Behavioral simulations**
- **Role playing**
- **Absorption training**

Review Questions

1. What factors contribute to a general need for sales training?

2. Refer to the boxed insert entitled "A Global Perspective: Training the Salesforce on Gift Giving." How will the globalization of sales efforts affect the training programs of sales organizations that will operate outside their home countries?

3. What are five methods of assessing sales training needs? Can each of these methods be used in either a proactive or reactive approach to determining training needs?

4. How is sales training related to recruiting and selecting salespeople? How can sales training contribute to salesforce socialization?

5. What are some of the important ethical and legal considerations that might be included in a sales training program?

6. How is the process of setting objectives for sales training beneficial to sales managers?

7. When the sales manager is evaluating sales training alternatives, what four areas should he or she consider?

8. Refer to the boxed insert entitled "An Ethical Perspective: Gaining a Commitment from the Customer." Other than sales training, what factors influence the degree to which salespeople might use unethical sales techniques to gain a commitment from the customer?

9. Discuss four methods for delivering sales training.

10. What is the purpose of the follow-up and evaluation step in the sales training process? When should evaluation take place?

Application Exercises

1.   Assume you are a sales manager for a large manufacturer of gasoline-powered portable generators and that your firm sells directly to building contractors. As part of the initial training program for 50 newly hired salespeople, you are planning a week-long session on product knowledge. The director of human resources in your firm has suggested that the effectiveness of the product-knowledge training be evaluated and has asked you for suggestions on how this may be accomplished. She has suggested testing the trainees before and after the training, which would be a departure from past practices. Historically, new trainees have taken a "final exam" on product knowledge but have not been tested prior to receiving product training. The director has also suggested experimenting with different training methods and media to try to determine which is most effective. What ideas do you have for evaluating the effectiveness of the product-knowledge training?

2.   Visit the business section of an off-campus bookstore and locate the paperback books on selling. Select one of the books, read it, and answer the following questions:

a.   How effective do you think the book would be in teaching a novice how to sell?

b.   Does the book suggest any ethically questionable sales techniques? If so, cite examples.

c.   How could the book be incorporated into a formalized sales training program for professional salespeople?

3.   Refer to Exhibit 10.2, which suggests different types of sales techniques for different customer personality types. Companies who use this approach train their salespeople to observe their customer's office, dress, verbal and nonverbal behavior, and the content of their communications for the purpose of classifying them as one personality type or another. Once the customer has been classified, the salesperson proceeds with predetermined sales tactics. What are the benefits of such training? What are its shortcomings and potential problems?

Notes

[1] Gene Garofalo, *Sales Manager's Desk Book* (Englewood Cliffs, N.J.: Prentice-Hall, 1989), 173.

[2] Gilbert A. Churchill, Jr., Neil M. Ford, Steven W. Hartley, and Orville C. Walker, Jr., "The Determinants of Salesperson Performance: A Meta-Analysis," *Journal of Marketing Research* 22 (May 1985): 117.

[3] William Keenan, Jr., "America's Best Salesforces: Six at the Summit," *Sales and Marketing Management*, June 1990, 80.

[4] "How Do Salespeople Rate Themselves?" *Sales and Marketing Management*, March 1989, 17.

[5] Arthur Bragg, "Listen Up," *Sales and Marketing Management*, February 1990, 10.

[6] *The Seven Deadly Sins of Sales Training* (El Segundo, Calif.: Max Sacks International, 1989).

[7] Phil Anderson, "Refresher Sales Training," *Training*, May 1989, 20.

[8] Earl Naumann, "Purchasing Training Programs," *Journal of Purchasing and Materials Management* 18 (Summer 1983): 21.

[9] "AT&T Makes a Second Stab at the Computer Market," *Business Week*, April 1, 1985, 92.

[10] Amy Dunkin, "Big Names Are Opening Doors for Avon," *Business Week*, June 1, 1987, 96.

[11] Paula C. Kringle, "Training Salespeople To Sell Services," *Training*, May 1989, 15.

[12] Beverly Geber, "Who, How, and What," *Training*, October 1989, 50.

[13] "1990 Survey of Selling Costs," *Sales and Marketing Management*, February 26, 1990, 76.

[14] For an extensive review of how the sales manager might be involved in the details of sales training, see John P. Steinbrink, ed., *The Dartnell Sales Manager's Handbook*, 14th ed. (Chicago: The Dartnell Corporation, 1989), 850–926.

[15] Meg Kerr and Bill Burzynski, "Missing the Target: Sales Training in America," *Training and Development Journal* 42 (July 1988): 68.

[16] See Alan J. Dubinsky and Richard W. Hansen, "The Sales Force Management Audit," *California Management Review* 24 (Winter 1981): 86–95.

[17] "Salespeople and Sales Managers Disagree on How to Boost Sales," *Marketing Times*, July–August 1990, 3.

[18] Alan J. Dubinsky, Roy D. Howell, Thomas N. Ingram, and Danny N. Bellenger, "Salesforce Socialization," *Journal of Marketing* 50 (October 1986): 195.

[19] Mark W. Johnston, A. Parasuraman, Charles M. Futrell, and William C. Black, "A Longitudinal Assessment of the Impact of Selected Organizational Influences on Salespeople's Organizational Commitment During Early Employment," *Journal of Marketing Research* 27 (August 1990): 341.

[20] Jeffrey K. Sager, "How to Retain Salespeople," *Industrial Marketing Management* 19 (May 1990): 155–166.

[21] "Eliminate the Talking Heads," *Sales and Marketing Management*, March 1989, 17.

[22] See "Study Reveals Needs of Business Marketers," *Marketing News*, March 13, 1989, 6; *Success Factors in Selling* (Stamford, Conn.: Learning International, 1989); and "How Do Salespeople Rate Themselves?" *Sales and Marketing Management*, March 1989, 17.

[23] Kerr and Burzynski, "Missing the Target," 68–71.

[24] Michael J. Major, "Sales Training Emphasizes Service and Quality," *Marketing News*, March 1990, 5.

[25] Marc Hequet, "Product Knowledge: Knowing What They're Selling May Be the Key to How Well They Sell It," *Training*, February 1988, 18–22.

[26] Harish Sujan, Barton A. Weitz, and Mita Sujan, "Increasing Sales Productivity by Getting Salespeople to Work Smarter," *Journal of Personal Selling and Sales Management* 8 (August 1988): 9–20.

[27] Alan J. Dubinsky and Thomas N. Ingram, "Correlates of Salespeople's Ethical Conflict: An Exploratory Investigation," *Journal of Business Ethics* 3 (1984): 343–353; and Alan J. Dubinsky, Thomas N. Ingram, and William Rudelius, "Ethics in Industrial Selling: How Product and Service Salespeople Compare," *Journal of the Academy of Marketing Science* 13 (Winter 1985): 160–170.

[28] Arthur Bragg, "Ethics in Selling, Honest!" *Sales and Marketing Management*, May 1987, 44.

[29] Jared F. Harrison, ed., *The Sales Manager as a Trainer* (Orlando, Fla.: National Society of Sales Training Executives, 1983), 7.

[30] William Keenan, Jr., "Are You Overspending on Training?" *Sales and Marketing Management*, January 1990, 59; and Geber, "Who, How, and What," 51.

[31] Keenan, "Are You Overspending?"

[32] Keenan, "Are You Overspending?" 60.

[33] Observations made by one of the authors during a visit to Armstrong World Industries Inc. headquarters and to The Manor, both located in Lancaster, Pennsylvania.

[34]Arthur Bragg, "Is There a Mentoring Program in Your Future?" *Sales and Marketing Management*, September 1989, 54–63.

[35]"Learning Sales Tactics Is Like Playing a Game," *Marketing News*, May 23, 1986, 9.

[36]"To Reinforce and Motivate Your Sales Team, Use TV-Style Quiz Shows," *Personal Selling Power*, July–August 1990, 44–46.

[37]For an application of role playing in sales training, see Larry J. B. Robinson, "Role Playing as a Sales Training Tool," *Harvard Business Review* 65 (May–June 1987): 34–35. Also see Thomas N. Ingram, "Guidelines for Maximizing Role-Play Activities," in *Proceedings*, National Conference in Sales Management, Dallas, 1990.

[38]Jack Falvey, "The Most Neglected Training Tool," *Sales and Marketing Management*, January 1990, 51–54.

[39]"Videos Assist in Medical Product Sales, Training," *Marketing News*, October 10, 1986, 14.

[40]Gerhard Gschwandtner, "Secrets of Sales Success at Federal Express," *Personal Selling Power*, January–February 1990, 12–16.

[41]For reviews of these software packages, see Robert H. Collins, "Sales Training: A Microcomputer-Based Approach," *Journal of Personal Selling and Sales Management* 6 (May 1986): 71–76; and Robert H. Collins, "Artificial Intelligence in Personal Selling," *Journal of Personal Selling and Sales Management* 4 (May 1984): 58–66.

[42]Jon M. Hawes, Stephen P. Huthchens, and William F. Crittenden, "Evaluating Corporate Sales Training Programs," *Training and Development Journal* 36 (November 1982), 44–49.

[43]Keenan, "Are You Overspending on Training?" 60.

[44]Arthur Bragg, "Prove That You Produce Sales," *Sales and Marketing Management*, January 1989, 55–59.

CASE 10.1   *Statru Golf Clubs*

Background

Statru, a golf club manufacturing company, was planning to introduce a new line of graphite clubs on June 1. Regional sales meetings were scheduled for May 15 when the sales representatives would be given product knowledge and training, as well as sales strategy training for the new line, called Statru-TM, with "TM" meaning Tour Model.

Central Region Sales Manager Tom O'Neal knew the importance of a well-trained salesforce in the introduction of a new product. He had seen competitors' products fail completely because the sales representatives simply did not know enough about the product to sell it. In its history, Statru had experienced very few product failures due to poor training.

However, O'Neal was concerned with the training job to be done prior to the introduction of Statru-TM. He had held a sales meeting for the Central Region salesforce on January 10 and had been disappointed with the performance of six of the eight sales representatives during a role-playing training exercise.

The importance of the role playing had been minimized prior to the meeting, with the sales representatives being told to prepare a "routine" presentation on an assigned product. Each person presented a different product to another sales representative, who played the role of the prospective buyer.

The presentations were viewed by the rest of the salesforce, O'Neal, and Mike Cromwell, the regional marketing manager. After each of the presentations was completed, O'Neal had led an oral group critique of the presentation to point out areas of strength and weakness.

Cromwell had expressed his displeasure with the outcome of the role playing by telling O'Neal, "With the excellent record of your people in the field, I was shocked at their performance. I would like to see another role-playing exercise at the May 15 meeting, and I know that their performance will be improved."

Also, O'Neal felt the sales representatives would have done better had he stressed "doing a better job" on the presentations prior to the meeting. However, he had taken Mike Cromwell's advice, who told him, "Tom, don't build up the role playing prior to the meeting. I would like to see how your people respond on their *own* initiative."

EXHIBIT 10.A ▪ *January 10 Sales Meeting: Role-Playing Notes*

1. Greg Cochran—The best presentation of the group. Seemed a little nervous. Good use of sales literature. Listened to buyer attentively and asked the right questions.

2. Brenda Higgins—Poorly prepared. Unable to answer several questions. Prematurely asked the buyer for an order.

3. Tom Latham—Lackadaisical. Seemed to perform more for the viewers than for the buyer. Argued with the buyer rather than presenting facts to counter objections.

4. Joan Wade—Good presentation, although a little "low-key." Nervous at the outset, but settled down. Could have handled price objection in a more positive manner.

5. Jim Lawrence—Would have never known he was our top sales representative. No supporting material used. Tried to overcome objections in a superficial manner. Very relaxed—in fact, too relaxed. Slouched in his chair as he talked with buyer.

6. Ray Maless—Very ill at ease. Appeared slow to respond to buyer's questions. Seemed relieved when the presentation ended, even though buyer turned down his request for an order.

7. John Winder—Average presentation. No glaring weakness, but lacked John's usual creative flare in confirming the sale.

8. Dan Wilson—Followed all the right techniques, but seemed like he was "going through the motions." Made a statement about product performance that he knew not to be true.

Current Situation

As he drove into work on May 1, O'Neal reviewed the training each of his representatives had received in their respective careers. All had received formal training from Statru consisting of product knowledge, sales techniques, administrative procedures, and manufacturing methods. As part of his regular territory visits, O'Neal conducted critiques after each call with regard to the effectiveness and professionalism of the call.

Until the January meeting, O'Neal had felt that his salesforce was highly professional—a conclusion supported by their results during the last two years. He thought that possibly the sales representatives had a temporary letdown after a tough year and perhaps felt they did not need the role-playing exercise since they had experienced similar training in the past.

Since the January meeting, O'Neal had discussed the presentations with each of the representatives. Most expressed surprise at O'Neal's critical evaluations and seemed defensive about their shortcomings. O'Neal was not trying to revise the role-playing exercises in preparation for the May 15 meeting. He had reviewed his notes of each evaluation (see Exhibit 10.A) and was now trying to plan the specific points he wanted to pass on to the salespeople prior to the meeting.

O'Neal felt that the exercise must be designed to reinforce the enthusiasm of the group prior to the introduction of Statru-TM, since a successful program would be crucial in attaining this year's sales targets. However, O'Neal was still bothered by the numerous weaknesses revealed in his notes of January 10. He thought, What went wrong in the January presentations? What should I do before the May 15 meeting? Maybe I should just let the January sessions become "water under the bridge" and not worry about it—after all, they're all good salespeople.

Questions

1. How would you proceed to prepare for the May 15 meeting?

2. If you were Tom O'Neal, what types of communication would you attempt with your salesforce prior to the May 15 meeting? Would you want to discuss the role-playing plans for the meeting with Mike Cromwell? If so, what would you tell Cromwell?

3. What are the effects of sales training on salesforce motivation and morale?

CASE 10.2 *Aqua-Seal Products*

Background

Aqua-Seal, a regional firm located in Portland, Oregon, had been in business for 12 years, selling waterproofing services to contractors, home-builders, and homeowners. Targeting the new-home market, Aqua-Seal had formulated a product similar to Thompson's Water Seal, which they applied to sidewalks, patios, driveways, fences, and decks. Their product was designed to protect exposed surfaces by shielding them from water and sun, which could do considerable damage to unprotected surfaces.

Aqua-Seal did not sell the product separately, but rather arranged for one of their highly trained crews to do the work. By providing good service and guaranteed results, Aqua-Seal had enjoyed steady growth, which had slightly outpaced the rate of new-home construction in their geographic area. Recently, new-home construction had been somewhat flat, and Aqua-Seal sales had dropped considerably.

Current Situation

Bob Kellar, general sales manager for Aqua-Seal, had been reviewing the sales figures, and he was becoming quite alarmed. Of his ten field salespeople, eight were selling behind last year's pace and the other two were barely ahead of last year's numbers. The two inside salespeople and the two customer service representatives reporting to Kellar had just informed him that the current order-entry rate was "really slow." He directed them to give him more details, but Kellar was afraid that he already had the picture — business was way down, even worse than he had thought.

Within a couple of weeks, Kellar knew that his fears had been justified. New-home construction was down 10 percent for this quarter compared with last year, but Aqua-Seal sales were off 20 percent from last year for the same period. He had discovered that several large home-builder and contractor accounts had ceased purchasing, yet the salespeople involved had not reported this to Kellar. To the best of his knowledge, no new competitors had entered the Aqua-Seal market area. Kellar did recall, however, that Thompson's Water Seal was running a heavy advertising schedule on television. Also, when he made a trip to K-Mart recently, Thompson's had a huge end-of-the-aisle display and was offering a very attractive rebate program on purchases over $50. He had no way of really knowing, but Kellar wondered whether Thompson's sales push was at least partially responsible for Aqua-Seal's decline.

Kellar decided to call a meeting for Friday afternoon, after all of the salespeople had returned to Portland. Meanwhile, he began thinking about what he could do to turn the situation around. One thing he knew was that he was going to ask the salespeople for their views on what was happening. In fact, the more he thought about it, he couldn't believe that none of the salespeople had indicated any problems in their territories. Maybe, thought Kellar, I ought to read them the riot act during Friday's meeting. He entertained the thought that maybe nothing was basically wrong except that the troops had gotten a little complacent.

Bob Kellar decided to do a few other things to determine whether sales training might help alleviate the sales slump. He interviewed the customer service representatives for their ideas but did not get a lot of useful information. As far as the customer service representatives could tell, the salespeople were doing business as usual.

The inside salespeople, who handled routine reorders from established accounts, said that a few customers had mentioned that the field salespeople had not been around much lately, and this spurred Kellar's next move. He sent a letter to a large sample of Aqua-Seal's customers, asking them specific questions about sales coverage and whether or not their expectations were being met by the Aqua-Seal salesforce. In the letter, Kellar encouraged the customers to be frank in their responses, as he was simply trying to ensure that the customers received the best possible sales effort from the Aqua-Seal salesforce.

During the week, Kellar visited several of the territories without the knowledge of the salespeople. He called on some key accounts, including a few that had stopped buying from Aqua-Seal. He knew some of the people in these accounts, and they talked openly about why they no longer were buying from Aqua-Seal. In a few cases, the salesperson had made mistakes that directly led to the customer's decision to no longer buy from Aqua-

Seal. On the whole, however, customers reported that the salespeople had been doing a good job and that business was "just down, that's all."

Questions

1. What do you think of Bob Kellar's attempts to determine the causes of Aqua-Seal's decline in sales?
2. What would you advise Kellar to do at the upcoming Friday afternoon meeting?
3. To what extent to you think that sales training can address the Aqua-Seal problems?

CASES FOR PART FOUR

Allied Food Distributors

In April 1987, Ms. Elizabeth Ramsey, the district sales manager for the upper Midwest district of Allied Food Distributors, was preparing to hire a new salesperson for the southwest Indiana sales territory. The current salesperson in this territory was leaving the company at the end of June. Ms. Ramsey had narrowed the list of potential candidates to three. She wondered which of these applicants she should select.

Company Background

Allied Food Distributors was one of the largest food wholesalers in the United States. The company carried hundreds of different packaged food items (fruits, vegetables, cake mixes, cookies, powdered soft drinks, and so on) for sales to supermarkets and grocery stores. Allied carried items in two different circumstances. First, some small food companies had Allied carry their entire line in all areas of the United States. Allied was in essence their sales force. Second, some large good companies had Allied carry their lines in less populated parts of the country. These areas were not large enough to sustain a salesperson for each food company.

Allied operated in all 50 states. The country was divided into 20 sales districts. Ms. Ramsey's sales district included Michigan, Indiana, and Illinois. Each district was divided into a number of sales territories. A salesperson was assigned to each territory.

The Southwest Indiana Territory

The sales territory for which Ms. Ramsey was seeking a salesperson was located in the southwest corner of Indiana. Exhibit 1 presents a map of the territory. It was bordered on the south by the Ohio River and the state of Kentucky, on the west by the Wabash River and the state of Illinois, and on the east by the Hoosier National Forest. The northern boundary ran a few miles north of Highways 50 and 150 that ran from Vincennes in the west through Washington to

EXHIBIT 1 ■ **A Map of the Southwest Indiana Territory**

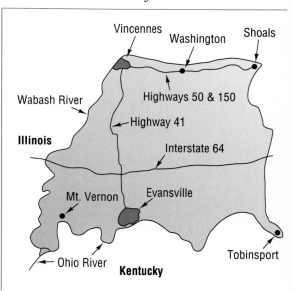

Shoals in the east. Evansville was the largest city in the area with a population of about 140,000. The salesperson for the territory was expected to live in Evansville, but would spend about three nights a week on the road. The only other reasonably large population concentration was in Vincennes with a population of about 20,000. Vincennes was located about 55 miles straight north of Evansville on Highway 41. Interstate Highway 64 ran the 80 miles east-west through the territory about 15 miles north of Evansville. Evansville was 165 miles southwest of Indianapolis, 170 miles east of St. Louis, Missouri, and 115 miles southwest of Louisville, Kentucky. The territory was very rural in character with agriculture being the dominant

Source: This case was written by Thomas C. Kinnear.
Copyright © 1987 Thomas C. Kinnear.

357

industry. The terrain was quite hilly, with poor soil. As a result, the farms in the area tended to be economically weak. There were many small towns and villages located throughout this basically rural environment.

The Selling Task

Allied maintained 75 active retail accounts in the southwest Indiana territory. About 10 of these accounts were medium- to large-sized independent supermarkets located in Evansville and Vincennes. The rest of the accounts were small, independent general food stores located throughout the territory.

The salesperson was expected to call on these accounts about every three weeks. The salesperson's duties included: checking displays and inventory levels for items already carried, obtaining orders on these items, informing retailers about new items, attempting to gain sales orders on these items, setting up special displays, and generally servicing the retailers' needs. Often, the salesperson would check the level of inventory on an item, make out an order, and present it to the retailer to be signed. The salesperson generally knew the store owner on a first name basis. The ordered goods were sent directly to the retailer from a warehouse located in Indianapolis.

The Selection Process

The responsibility for recruiting salespersons for the territories within a district was given to the district sales manager. The process consisted of the following steps:

1. An advertisement for the job was placed in newspapers in the state in question.
2. Those responding to the ad were sent job application forms.
3. The returned application forms were examined and certain applicants were asked to come to the district sales office for a full day of interviews.
4. The selection was then made by the district sales manager, or all applicants were rejected and the process started again.

Training

Allied did all its salesperson training on the job. The salesperson in the territory to which a new person would be assigned was given the task of training. Basi-

EXHIBIT 2 ▪ *Information on Mr. Michael Gehringer*

Personal Information

Born July 15, 1945; married; three children ages 14, 16, and 19; height 5 feet, 10 inches; weight 205; excellent health; born and raised in Indianapolis.

Education

High School graduate; played football; no extracurricular activities of note.

Employment record

1. Currently employed by Allied Food Distributors in the warehouse in Indianapolis; two years with Allied; job responsibilities include processing orders from the field and expediting rush orders; current salary $2,200 per month.
2. In 1984–85 employed by Hoosier Van Lines in Indianapolis as a sales agent; terminating salary was $550 per month; left due to limits placed on salary and lack of challenge in the job.
3. In 1982–84 employed by Main Street Clothiers of Indianapolis as a retail salesperson in the men's department; terminating salary $1,500 per month; left due to boring nature of this type of selling.
4. Between 1965 and 1982 held six other clerical and sales type jobs, all in Indianapolis.

Applicant's statement

I feel that my true employment interest lies in selling in a situation where I can be my own boss. This jobs seems just right.

Ms. Ramsey's comments

Seems very interested in job as a career.
Well recommended by his current boss.
Reasonably intelligent.
Good appearance.
Moderately aggressive.

cally, this involved having the new person travel the territory to meet the retailers and to be shown how to obtain and send in orders. The district sales manager usually assisted in this process by traveling with the new salesperson for a few days.

they chatted over a cup of coffee before beginning their calls.

When Murphy explained that he was helping to do a study for GBD on methods of training salesmen, Grace evidently interpreted this to mean that she should talk about her job, for she started explaining her daily call routine. Her suggested approach to the retailer was much the same as that of Bob Benton.

Grace and Murphy first visited the Petaluma TV and Radio store, which sold additionally a broad line of home appliances. Adams quickly introduced Murphy to Mrs. Smith (the owner's wife), listened to a complaint about a scratched cabinet on a television set, and checked the company's inventory. After discussing with Mrs. Smith the aggressive price cutting initiated by a local discounter, Grace took an order for two home video units. The call lasted about 20 minutes.

As they walked toward the second stop several blocks away, Grace confided:

I always try to get on a first-name basis with my retailers as soon as I can because it helps me establish rapport. We all like to do business with our friends. Another secret to calling in a territory that you haven't visited for a week or so is to walk along the main street and window shop and see who's got what bargains displayed. I also buy a local paper most every time I come into these little towns to see who's advertising what. I think that helps me to get a feel for my competition too.

The second call, which lasted about 45 minutes, was at a large home service center. As soon as they entered the store, Grace introduced Murphy to Joe, the owner. The following conversation took place:

Adams: I see you're featuring a couple of our home computer systems, Joe. Great—that should help to boost your sales.

Joe: Yeah, that's true. But the reason I'm promoting them is that I can't sell them at full retail. As long as I make some profit, though, I should care.

Adams: Joe, that business should be picking up pretty soon now—Christmas, you know. Over half of these sales should come in November and December.

Joe: What's good in the rest of your lines?

Adams: Everything, Joe.

Joe: (Looking at some promotional material) I've got some Sonys here, got them at a special price. But the last I sold was about three months ago.

Adams began to talk about a new warranty program on the food mixer. Joe explained he was aware of it.

Adams: Well, we do have a nice gift promotion on the mixers.

Joe: I don't need all that stuff. I've got plenty now.

Adams: We can send it to you prepaid you know, Joe, plus a 10 percent dating. These mixers will really go well . . .

Joe: I just don't need any.

Adams: Well, anything else? How about taking an ad in your local paper on the video player? I've never seen your newspaper feature any of our products. What's the cost over there anyway?

Joe: $2.60 a line.

Adams: Well, of course, we'd split the cost 50-50 with you, Joe, on any ads you'd like to run.

Joe: 50-50?

Adams: Yes, on all the lines you run with our mats.

Joe: On everything?

Adams: That's right. Just send us the tear sheets.

Joe: Why don't you mail me some mats then? I can use them.

Adams: OK. Now, how about the TVs, Joe?

Joe: Send me a couple of those new Sony portables—you know the ones I mean?

Adams: The FM-36B? A good choice. That's the popular one, Joe.

Joe: OK. I'll see you next week.

Adams: Fine, Joe, see you.

As they left the store, Grace remarked, "Gee, sure looks like a good day. You know, the personal approach means everything in this business. I'm trying to build goodwill so that when I leave a store, those retailers will want to sell GBD because of me. Now Joe there thinks that I'm a pleasant person, so he tries to sell my line. Incidentally, the reason I pushed some advertising is that he's got to advertise if he wants to sell. These dealers often look upon advertising as a cost instead of an investment. Or they think the manufacturer should do it all."

The next stop was a new TV dealer. Grace had taken an order from the dealer for a new combination stereo TV and home recording system on the promise

- GBD has inventory problem that can't deliver J.T. to satisfy customer.
   - ruin reputation.

that it would be delivered in two days. Three days after taking the order, she had received a phone call from the dealer who stated that unless the set was delivered that very day, Grace was to cancel the order. She commented to Murphy, "I checked with our people yesterday after I got the call, and they weren't sure the set would go out. If it isn't there now, I'll be in trouble with him. Seeing as how he's a new dealer, I don't want to rock the boat."

In the TV dealer's window was the system distributed by GBD. "Well," remarked Grace, "I guess it's safe to go in." As soon as they entered the store, a thin man greeted her with, "The set arrived just as I was closing last night." Grace explained some of the features of the set to the dealer and gave him some literature on several other models. Then she inquired about what other sets the dealer was planning to install. The dealer replied that he wouldn't carry any others until he had sold this one. After a few more words, Grace and Murphy left the store. Several minutes later she remarked, "You know, bringing people around with you hurts your sales . . . but he's a tough dealer to sell, anyway."

Murphy and Adams then drove 20 miles to another town further north. During the trip, Grace talked about why she had left the retail business and why she liked selling. When they arrived at the next stop, Grace explained, "I have to try to collect a check from the dealer and report my results back to the home office by telephone." Since the man she wished to see was not in, she made arrangements to call back later that afternoon.

During lunch at a small diner, Grace talked more about the retail business. She also expressed a desire to obtain a territory closer to the city. After lunch, as they began walking toward the next call, they passed a newly renovated electronics store. Grace paused, "This is a new store. I haven't gotten them for an account. It's just possible they don't have a computer line. I think I'll go in cold and see what I can do." They entered the store and looked around for a clerk. A

if co. has the IT system knows this information @ then let salesman knows.

woman came out, and Grace explained the purpose of her call, stating that her company had just started up with a new line of complete computer systems. When she mentioned the brand names, the woman remarked that the store carried one well-known brand and added that she could show it to them. In a corner of the store, a special display was devoted to the computer and peripherals. The shopkeeper explained that she and her husband had recently purchased the store, need didn't know much about personal computers, and were in the process of rethinking the business. Grace noted the inventory that she had and explained that, on her next call, she would supply some promotional materials. She also added that the distributor who formerly handled the line had gone out of business and that GBD would gladly provide the components from now on. The woman thanked her, and they left the store.

After similar experiences traveling with three other salespeople, Kevin Murphy felt that he had a good feeling for the GBD selling job and its requirements. Since two men were retiring soon from GBD's sales force, John Gray was very anxious that Murphy complete his recommendations for a sales training program before new recruits had to be hired to take over the territories. Thus, Murphy began outlining a training program for GBD which would include recommendations for training dealer sales personnel as well as the firm's own sales force.

Questions

1. What is the basic role of the distributors' salesmen in this situation?
2. What skills do these salesmen need?
3. What specific training program (coverage, subjects) do you recommend?
4. Elaborate upon one particular training subject in your program that you consider important—points to be covered, specific training technique to be used, measurement objectives, etc.

Plastic Piping Systems: Employee Turnover (A)

Introduction

In March 1983, Mr. George C. Mammola, Vice President of Sales of Plastic Piping Systems (PPS), was conducting a review of the company's performance for previous years. During the last three years, PPS has undergone significant expansion, increasing their number of sales offices from five to eight. The combination of the poor economy and high employee turnover has had a negative impact on PPS over the past six months; with sales even with the same period in 1981, PPS went from 5% profit to a 2% loss. Mr. Mammola will be meeting with the Board of Directors next week to discuss the situation and recommend a course of action. PPS is a distributor of plastic pipe, valves, and fittings to the industrial marketplace.

History

PPS was started in 1969 in Newark, New Jersey. Sales spiraled upward for the first four years with branches in seven cities by 1975. The rapid expansion of PPS resulted in an overextension of both assets and management. Consequently, in 1977 and 1978 management was changed and consolidated. Mr. Ted Vagell bought out the other partners and initiated the following actions: The Maryland branch was sold off with a restrictive agreement that PPS would not enter that marketplace for 10 years. Two other branches were closed, leaving PPS with branches in South Plainfield, New Jersey; Cleveland, Ohio; Charlotte, North Carolina; and Chicago, Illinois. The turnaround was successful.

PPS's sales and earnings grew at a rate of 25% per year from 1978 to 1981. This rapid increase is the result of PPS's concentration on the industrial marketplace, the talents of each branch manager, and the strict attention to asset management.

Product

PPS distributes plastic pipe, valves, and fittings used in manufacturing plants to transport fluids. These products are made from a variety of materials such as polyvinyl chloride, chlorinated polyvinyl chloride, polypropylene, and polyvinylidene fluoride. The advantage of plastic pipe is its exceptional chemical resistance to nearly all acids, alkalis, alcohols, halogens and other corrosive materials up to temperatures of 280°F. Industrial plastic pipe is different from the plastic pipe used in residential construction, with industrial pipe, valves, and fittings being thicker, therefore more durable and more expensive.

First introduced in 1935 for piping applications, plastic piping profited from intensive R&D during WW II. Since 1948, the plastic piping industry has sustained a remarkable growth rate of 25% per year in both industry and residential construction. PPS carries other products such as plastic pumps, tanks and fans, but 90% of sales are from pipe, valves, and fittings.

Industry Structure

Plastic pipe, valves, and fittings are manufactured by a variety of companies. There are eight companies which manufacture industrial plastic pipe of which three of these companies also manufacture valves and fittings. There are another four companies which only manufacture valves and fittings. These 12 manufacturers sell their products to industrial plants using distributors and/or reps. Historically, the manufacturers have not sold direct due to the large number of potential customers and the need for local inventory.

The three types of distributors are plastic piping specialists, plumbing supply houses and mill supply houses. Plastic piping specialists are smaller distributors, usually with less than 20 employees, which represent 2 or 3 manufacturers and sell to local plants. Plumbing supply houses sell primarily to local plumbers items used in residential construction such as water, sewer, and drain pipe, tubs, sinks, toilets, etc. Occasionally plumbing supply houses also carry industrial plastic pipe. Mill supply houses are usually large distributors specializing in metal pipe, valves and fittings for industrial use. In most cases the mill supply houses look at plastic pipe as a low cost alternative to metal pipe. Some mill supply houses carry plastic, others do not.

Over the past 20 years there has been a trend toward the use of plastic specialty distributors to sell industrial plastic pipe. The basis for this trend is, first, the technical knowledge needed to select which type of plastic pipe should be used and, second, the fact that the traditional metal pipe suppliers such as the mill

Source: Copyright © 1984. Prepared by Hubert D. Hennessey. Interviews of past and present salespeople were conducted by Kim Koehler and Anne Timson.

supply house view plastic pipe as competition and prefer not to offer it.

Distributor Operations

Plastic piping specialists provide an important function in the distribution channel. They maintain an inventory of plastic pipe, valves, and fittings from various manufacturers in a local location. The plastic piping specialist is technically competent to select a particular type of pipe based on the corrosive being carried, the temperature, and the pressure of the fluid.

The distributor fills a large volume of small and medium-sized orders which would be uneconomical for a manufacturer to supply from regional warehouses.

Distributors purchase from manufacturers based on price, availability, and credit terms. While most distributors carry competitive lines, each normally carries one main line, filling in with complementary lines. The distributor makes annual purchase agreements with manufacturers based on expected demand.

In addition to serving the needs of current customers, distributor salespeople are continually calling on plant engineers, plant maintenance supervisors, and consulting engineers to persuade them to recommend or use plastic pipe instead of the traditional metal piping such as stainless steel.

How Customers Buy

Industrial plastics are used in manufacturing plants. There are two different buying situations which will result in the sale of plastic piping products. Larger expansions to manufacturing plants are normally designed by consulting engineers and bid through mechanical contractors. These contractors will get prices from distributors to be used in their bids. The mechanical contractor with the lowest price is normally awarded the bid. Small additions to current facilities or maintenance and repair situations are normally handled by the maintenance staff; therefore, the buying is done by the plant purchasing agent. Piping products purchased directly by the plant personnel are normally less price competitive than piping products purchased by the mechanical contractors.

Customers normally purchase plastic piping based on performance requirements of the situation, i.e., material being handled, temperature, and pressure. In most cases the customer will not specify a particular manufacturer except in the case of some specialized

valves which are perceived to be significantly different than other valves.

The purchase decision for most small purchases is usually a function of availability. If a processing line is shut down because of a leaking valve or fitting, the cost of the item is insignificant to the cost of the line being shut down. Local suppliers are preferred for these situations, since someone from the plant will be sent to pick up the item.

Larger purchases are normally purchased based on price and availability. Two or more distributors are normally contacted to compare prices and availability with the order going to the lowest price.

PPS Long-term Strategy

PPS's primary objective is to maintain itself as a privately managed distributor organization providing quality products at competitive prices, serving industrial end users and contractors. Prior to the economic downturn in 1982, PPS had planned to double sales and profit between 1981 and 1985. To achieve these objectives, PPS implemented the following programs during 1981 and 1982: (1) geographic expansion, (2) selection and training of sales personnel, (3) annual branch planning, and (4) computerization.

(1) Geographic Expansion: To expand geographically, PPS opened a new office in Tampa, Florida. The office was opened in August, 1982. John Camp, formerly the branch manager for Charlotte, North Carolina, was promoted to Southeast Divisional Manager and given the responsibility for both North Carolina and Florida. Al Rubens, a seasoned pipe salesperson, was hired as the Florida branch manager, reporting to Camp. An inside salesperson was hired in August 1981 and is still located at the branch. Three outside salespeople had been hired to work out of the Florida branch. As of December 1982 all three had left.

In July of 1981 Plastic Piping Systems acquired Plastic Fluid Systems with offices in Houston and Austin for a reasonable price to be paid over a seven-year period. PFS's president was the founder and former owner of PPS and in 1978 sold his interest in PPS to Ted Vagell.

The Texas offices report to George Mammola, the Vice President of Sales. The Houston office was managed by Mr. Matthews when acquired. Matthews was given the responsibility of sales manager, and Patricia Minter, a recent graduate of Babson and PPS's eight-week training program, was appointed operations manager. Six months after the acquisition, Matthews left, and Rob Vernon, a star salesperson in the North Carolina office, was promoted to Sales Manager of the Houston office. Rob Vernon and Patricia Minter were married on February 5, 1983.

The Austin branch is managed by John Nevin, formerly a salesperson for PFS. He was promoted to branch manager just before the acquisition.

(2) Selection and Training: Since it is a distributor organization, the lifeblood of PPS is its salespeople. In 1980, PPS initiated a comprehensive training program. The first group of six trainees was given a four-week indoctrination and training in the summer of 1980. The second group of fourteen was given an eight-week program in the summer of 1981. Before 1980, most of the salespeople who were hired had some sales experience and limited college education. They received their training at the branch level. The new program was oriented toward hiring undergraduates, training them in a location, then sending them to their respective branches. Out of the first six trainees, two are left, and out of the second fourteen trainees, seven remain at PPS. No training program was held in the summer of 1982.

(3) Annual Branch Planning: Prior to 1980, much of the planning was superficial. In 1980, PPS initiated a detailed planning and control system which established objectives for each employee in the company, based on individual and branch performance. All salespeople received a salary plus commission, but the commission does not kick in until you meet a minimum gross profit for the month. The branch managers also participate in the bonus program, receiving up to 100% of their base salary, based on the profit of the branch.

(4) Computerization: The computerization of all invoicing, inventory, payables, accounts receivable, and mailing lists started in 1981. As of February 1983, most of the systems are up and running with the last of the sales offices just being connected with the home office in Cranford, New Jersey.

PPS Management

The home office staff consists of Ted Vagell, the President; George Mammola, the Vice President of Sales; Doug Sebesky, Manager of Corporate Accounting; Charles Windruff, Director of MIS; and approximately seven other accounting, computer, and secretarial peo-

ple. The tone of the home office is dominated by Mr. Vagell and Mr. Mammola, both major stockholders who are concerned about the short- and long-term future of PPS. Both have a friendly ongoing relationship with the home office employees.

The tone of the branch operations is set by the individual manager and in most cases the division manager—John Camp or Peter Vagell. John Camp has been with the company eight years. He opened the Charlotte, North Carolina branch, trained most of the current employees, and had a major input on its success. The Charlotte branch has grown every year since it started until 1982, which was the first year sales did not increase and profits were down. Peter Vagell, brother of the President, has also been with PPS for eight years. Mr. Peter Vagell has been the branch manager of the South Plainfield, New Jersey office for six years. Sales growth in New Jersey has been steady with an especially good performance expected this year. Both Peter Vagell and John Camp are shareholders in the corporation.

The organizational structure of PPS is shown in Exhibit 1.

Responsibilities of Field Force

The salesforce consists of telemarketers, customer service respresentatives and outside salespeople. The customer service representative is responsible for handling incoming calls, entering and processing orders, checking credit and selling via the telephone to low-volume customers. The telemarketer calls other distributors and accounts not assigned to outside salespeople. The outside salesperson handles personal calls to current and potential customers, mostly through visits but occasionally by phone.

Exhibit 2 contains a summary of interviews conducted of salespeople currently employed at PPS.

Salesperson Turnover

There was a major turnover of salespeople at each branch in 1982, ranging from 300% in Florida to 40% in New Jersey, with a company average of 50% turnover. According to branch managers it takes one to two years for a new salesperson to be productive for PPS. The long lead time is required to learn the technical knowledge, develop the sales skills, and locate, identify, and sell new accounts. During this start-up period, the salesperson earns a straight salary, and re-

EXHIBIT 1   ▪ *PPS — Organizational Chart*

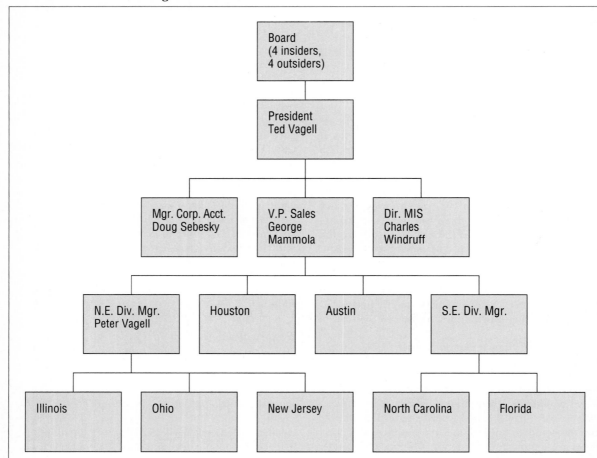

ceives a bonus commission only when the monthly gross margin minimum is reached.

The turnover of salespeople is a serious problem for PPS, due to the start-up cost of salespeople who leave and the cost of hiring and training new people. To help understand this problem, a graduate student interviewed via telephone four salespeople who left PPS in the last five months. A summary of the four salespeople who were interviewed is shown in Exhibit 3. The summary of each interview is shown in Exhibit 4. Exhibit 5 includes a letter written by an ex-salesperson in Chicago to the Branch Manager.

EXHIBIT 2 ▪ *Interviews with Current PPS Salespeople*

Frank Bower: New Jersey
College Degree: B.S. Marketing
Prior Sales Experience: No formal sales
Time with PPS: 3 years
Training Received: 3 months in Chicago upon graduation from college

Initial Perceptions: Frank knew about PPS through Ted Vagell. Upon [Frank's] graduating from college, Ted had asked Frank to come in for an interview. Frank was hired and went through the 3-month intensive training program which he felt was accurate. After training he went into telemarketing. He felt that the telemarketing gave him a firm understanding of the product line and he also learned how to allocate his time.

Present Position: After four months doing telemarketing, Frank moved into outside sales where he calls on regular customers and follows up on leads. He likes this position because it allows him to meet his customers face-to-face, and he enjoys the personal contact.

Frank realizes that PPS does not have the manpower to provide the technical expertise that is occasionally needed, but he feels the company does a good job given its size. On a scale from 1 to 10, Frank rates the technical support given to him by PPS as an 8.

Frank is quite content working for a small distributor and while he realizes that the other branches might have problems, his main objective is to better his branch. He feels that the product line is sufficient and the key to being good in this industry is to know what you can and cannot deliver.

Frank sees his primary responsibility as providing the best service to the customer. He feels the one area in which PPS can help him to enhance his service capabilities is to improve the delivery system. Frank feels that by adding trucks (instead of using common carriers and couriers), delivery will improve.

All in all, Frank is satisfied with his position at PPS and enjoys his work.

Contact: Alice Kopp
Office: Cleveland
College Degree: (Major) Marketing
Prior Sales Experience: Sold ski equipment in high school
Time with PPS: Started in June 1981
Training: 3 months in Chicago

Initial Perceptions: Alice had heard about PPS from a friend who had interviewed with the company. The friend was very enthusiastic about the job opportunity but wanted to live in Chicago. Prior to the interview, Alice attempted to research the company but could not find anything published on PPS. Although Alice did not know anything about pipes, valves, and fittings, she was assured that she could sell anything.

Present Status: Alice spent her first year in telemarketing. While she became well-versed in the product lines, she was discouraged by the rejections she received. She had originally been told that she would get established accounts, but found herself calling on dormant accounts and inquiries. She was further discouraged about telemarketing because she felt that as a female she did not have the credibility over the phone that her male counterparts had. She felt that the customers she called on perceived her as a secretary/clerk and not as a trained sales representative.

In her second year, Alice became a customer service representative. She enjoys this position, primarily because she has established accounts and receives incoming calls. Alice has received a tremendous amount of technical support from the home office and says the computer is a great asset for operations. She, however, is under time pressure to get out bids. Larger orders must go through the home office to get approved, and this takes longer than the 2 days most clients need. On smaller orders, which do not need home office approval, Alice must check into the financial background before she issues the bid. If the client company defaults on its payments, then the representative's salary is docked. While Alice realizes it is important to check up on the financial positions, she feels that it detracts both from her selling time and potential bids she can issue.

(continued)

EXHIBIT 2 ▪ *(continued)*

Alice has been out of the office to make calls. She would like to do more of this. Her office, however, has done so well in telemarketing, PPS is discouraging the representatives from making outside calls. As a result, Alice does not see herself in this position forever and would like to move into an outside sales career. She feels that there is limited potential for her to move into outside sales within PPS and might eventually leave the company for such a position.

Name: John Murphy

College Degree: Business Economics

Prior Sales Experience: none

Time with PPS: 3 years

Training Received: 3 months

Initial Perceptions: John heard about PPS through the placement service at his college in Illinois. He turned down the job offer he received from PPS because he would not be able to stay in the Chicago area. PPS later called informing him that he could work in the Chicago office. John feels the training program definitely helped him and was of great value in gaining product knowledge. After his training program, John spent six months in telemarketing, then six months in customer service. He then spent a year in telemarketing.

Present Position: John is now in customer service. He says that telemarketing and customer service were both easier the second time around, as telemarketing was, at first, hard and took getting used to. He has received a great deal of technical support from his office and while he does not deal regularly with the home office, he says that when he does, they are extremely helpful. He has had no major problems with PPS since he has been there.

Name: David Flynn, North Carolina

College Degree: B.S. Marketing

Prior Sales Experience: No prior

Time with PPS: 5 years

Training: 3 months

Initial Perceptions: David was interviewed by Ted Vagell at the placement office through his school. He wanted a sales position and had interviewed mostly with large computer companies. He, however, was impressed with the opportunities PPS offered. During David's training he learned the technical expertise required to sell the product but had no hands-on experience with respect to selling. He was very impressed by a sales seminar held in 1983 for the representatives at PPS.

Present Status: The first 2½ months David worked in the home office in North Carolina doing telemarketing, after which he was transferred to South Carolina. He works mostly in his home and is left on his own. Until just recently, David worked in the field 5 days a week, but now spends 2 days telemarketing. Although he is under the North Carolina office, he has been basically on his own since his move to South Carolina.

He finds the company to be supportive in fulfilling his needs. Because of its size, he feels free to call his boss at home if there is a problem, and/or the home office.

David almost left the company 2 years ago as a result of his branch manager who was extremely difficult to work with. He started to look for other jobs, but then found out his manager was leaving. David, therefore, decided to stay. He presently feels the company does not have any clear objectives (or they have not been communicated to the sales representatives). He also feels that the company has lost touch with what has been happening in the marketplace.

EXHIBIT 3 ▪ *Summary of Salespeople Having Left the Company*

	College Degree	Sales Experience	Time at PPS	New Job When Left Company	Training	Money Reason For Quitting	Office
Pat Owen	yes BS Bus. Ad.	no	18 mos.	no	Chicago (classroom)	no	N.J.
Mark Sands	no	no		yes	general	yes	Cleveland
Steve Robertson	yes BS Biology	yes	18 mos.	yes	California	no	Houston
Warren Smith	no 1 yr. college	yes	4 mos.	yes	California	no	Houston
Tim Neeley	yes Liberal Arts	no	16 mos.	yes	Chicago	no	North Carolina

Note: Names are fictitious.

EXHIBIT 4 ▪ *Interviews with Former PPS Salespeople*

Mark Sands, Cleveland
No college degree
First sales job

Initial Perception of Company: Mark was flown to New Jersey to get a tour of the company. He was impressed with the company's senior management. During his training he was flown around the country to view different offices of the company and vendors. Mark would have preferred some formal training in addition to this.

Problems on the Job: Mark said that PPS on the local level is vastly different from the company as a whole. He had trouble meeting obligations he made to his customers due to poor management in the lower level of the company. He said he was encouraged to make sales promises and then given no support in the follow through.

Mark claims that he would have stayed at PPS if he had not been approached by a competitor who offered more benefits and a much better base salary. He claims that some firefighting between salesmen and management is to be expected in industrial sales, and it didn't bother him too much at PPS; however, it did contribute to his leaving the company.

Mark said he would recommend a sales career at PPS, but not above others in the industry. He did emphasize that PPS is the leader in corrosive piping, and that the problems are localized at the branch management levels. He felt that as a first job, PPS was a good place to learn the business.

Pat Owen, New Jersey
BS Business Administration
18 months with PPS

Initial Perception of Company: Pat saw the sales job advertised in the classified section of the New York Times. He did not research the company or the industry before his interview. He believed that the company had a good reputation. In the interview he was given salary expectations that he claims were not lived up to.

Pat spent eight weeks in a training program for PPS salesmen in Chicago. The experience was interesting and fun, with a party-like atmosphere after hours. Pat said that the training program could have easily

(continued)

EXHIBIT 4   ▪   *(continued)*

been half as long. He would have preferred some office and field training in addition to the classroom instruction.

Problems on the Job: Pat's biggest problem was with his immediate superior. Pat did not believe him to be ethical. His boss's policy was to get an order and worry later if the company could fill it. Pat could not keep the deadlines he promised to his customers because sales quotas were being rammed down his throat. Pat was caught between a boss he claims would have wrung his neck if he didn't get the order, and many angry customers. In one instance, a contractor (over the phone) threatened to beat Pat up because of an order that was not delivered on time.

In spite of this, Pat claims that he was a very good salesman and that he exceeded his quota regularly.

Besides his discontent with work, Pat did not like the geographic area he moved to. He said that if only one of these aspects was positive, he might have stayed with PPS longer. After 18 months he was tired of being miserable at work, and then going home and being miserable. Pat left the company to move back with his parents, and look for a job in the area he grew up in.

Steve Robertson, Houston
BS Biology
Sales experience with 2 companies
18 months with PPS

Initial Perception of Company: Steve had learned about PPS from a friend. At the time of his interview Steve believed that PPS was a good, aggressive company. He decided to work there based on the money, benefits, and promotion opportunity he was promised.

Steve participated in the [California] training program, which he believed was good but could have been shortened.

Problems on the Job: Steve said that PPS tried to keep their incentive promises but couldn't due to personality conflicts that developed at the office. This resulted in a system that lacked incentives and was poor overall. Steve said that 80% of his time with the company was enjoyable while 20% he hated very much.

Steve had hoped to be promoted to sales manager some time in the future. But, when two of the middle managers (one his sales manager) made plans to marry each other, he expected that neither would be leaving the company soon, thereby leaving no room for promotion. This situation was 40% of the reason he left. His biggest sore spot was the animosity between the salesmen and their superiors, particularly the engaged couple at his office. Steve said that a large salary increase might have kept him at PPS for a while, but he would have left eventually. He now sells protective coatings to the same customer base. Steve, like all the salesmen, was often contacted by headhunters.

Steve would recommend a job at PPS as a learning experience. He would not recommend a career there, because the incentive system is poor.

Warren Smith, Houston
1 year college
8 years sales experience
4 months with PPS

Initial Perception of Company: Warren saw an employment ad for PPS in a large city newspaper. He had interviewed with PPS one year previous. Warren was leaving his job due to personality conflicts, and it was convenient to take the job at PPS. Warren said he was promised a lucrative job with good opportunities. At the time of the interview he thought the commission was good.

Warren participated in the California training program which he thought was very adequate.

Problems on the Job: Once he started selling, Warren realized that the company had colored things up in the interview. On a 10-point scale he rated PPS's honesty in hiring at 5, and most other companies at 7 to 8.

(continued)

EXHIBIT 4 ▪ *(continued)*

His main complaint was with the sales manager whom he described as young and unprofessional. Warren was adamant that the whole system from the bottom up needed to become more professionalized. He claimed his manager was a back-stabber who was afraid to call his boss, or give support to his salespeople. His perception was that the bosses were always pointing fingers at each other.

At one time the people in Warren's office tried to go to the sales manager's boss for a confidential meeting. The meeting was not held in confidence, and the sales manager knew which individuals had gone over his head.

Besides company politics, Warren resented that salesmen were expected to spend one day each week in the office doing telemarketing duties. He believed this hurt the income of both the salesmen and the company. Warren would have liked for other personnel to have the responsibility for telemarketing.

Warren views himself as a small sales business person and his top priority is to generate orders for the company. He did not think the system at PPS allowed for a professional salesman to do his job. Warren started looking for a new job after his second week at PPS.

Tim Neeley, North Carolina
4 year college degree
First industrial sales job
16 months with PPS

Initial Perception of Company: Tim spoke with a PPS recruiter on campus before graduation. Although PPS was not his first choice, he thought the company had strong potential and very good market penetration. He also liked the fact that he would be able to work in the southern part of the U.S. He believed the salary and benefits at PPS to be about equal to that offered by other companies. Tim received his sales training in Chicago. His main criticism was that the training did not prepare him for the managers with whom he would be working.

Problems on the Job: Tim said that there was a lot of friction between the branch manager and the sales manager. He elaborated that the branch manager was very secretive about what went on at the different offices. The salesmen were not really free to communicate with their counterparts at different PPS sales offices. Tim would have liked to have contacted salesmen he had trained with but was afraid of repercussions from his superiors.

Tim would not recommend a sales career at PPS unless the lower management system was changed. He said that upper management was not aware of what went on below the branch level of the company. He thought that the problem was due to a few people, who, for greed or other reasons, did not back up the salespeople.

Tim has taken another sales job that he describes as a very satisfying team effort, for a very good company.

EXHIBIT 5 ▪ *Exit Letter from Salesperson Who Left PPS*

Dear Sales Manager,

Plastic Piping Systems is a profitable company which obviously does many things correctly from the standpoint of its customers, vendors, managers and employees. For those reasons I am grateful to the company for having me as an employee. Upon resignation you asked me to comment in writing about the negative things which occurred at PPS rather than make a lot of patronizing comments. Following is the information you wanted. I sincerely hope that it is used in a positive manner to improve corporate relations and profits.

Commitments
Corporate commitments, to me, have never been taken seriously by the company or its managers. That is the most frustrating thing I have experienced at PPS. Before joining PPS the following commitments were made:
• Product and sales training was promised to prepare me for an outside sales territory after six months when it was available within the company. Training was a joke after my first three weeks. Requests for 20 minutes per day during my first year to review questions and problems were ignored. Organized product training was forgotten after the first three weeks with the exception of several days at AO-Smith. Outside sales training and preparation was non-existent during my first year.
• Quarterly reviews during my first year were promised to insure growth and progress. The second, third, and fourth reviews were never arranged.
• An inside sales commission program was supposed to be implemented early in the spring during my first year with the company. Nothing was implemented until the fall after the busy season. When it was implemented, we could not obtain anything in writing. What happened is that a program was set up to run for three months after which time it would be reviewed to make sure it was fair to the salesman and the company. The program was not given a chance. When we started earning some decent sales commissions the rules were unilaterally changed. Twice!

After six months a couple of outside sales territories were available. Instead of me being prepared to manage one, there were new, young, and less mature people hired and trained for the position.
    During my first year at PPS I was already interviewing for sales positions at other companies. When management at PPS discovered that I would be gone within two months, they offered me a geographical sales territory in Chicago with a fair car allowance and a review scheduled for July 1, 1981.
    Sales efforts and progress during my first year in Chicago were excellent despite the recession and limited inside sales support. (During the past one-and-a-half years the personnel responsible for inside support changed ten (10) times. This made it difficult to establish effective communication and teamwork.)
    After I called on a diversity of accounts in my territory as advised by management, the commissions in the territory grew. Without financial compensation, the company stopped giving me credit for two-hundred (200)+ accounts that I had worked with because they did not fit on an arbitrary list number of 100 which was now established.

(continued)

EXHIBIT 5 ▪ *(continued)*

When the new sales program was implemented we did not even understand the basic mechanics, such as how to add or subtract an account or get an engineering credit. *Before* changing the sales programs there should have been communication with the salesmen. Changes in base salary, minimum gross margin, etc., should have been clear. There was no increase in my base salary or decrease in the bogie—only less accounts from an existing territory to receive credit for.

July first, I was scheduled to have a salary and performance review. At this point I was the most profitable salesman in the midwest. Logic dictated that I would be rewarded and encouraged to achieve more. During the month of *October* my review was still not granted despite constant reminders and requests. When the review was given, it offered a modest increase in salary and a greater increase in minimum gross margin. This would have lowered my income based upon past average sales performance by almost $150.00 per month. A new package was then offered which increased my annual salary $3,000.00 per year and increased my minimum gross margin total $45,000.00 per year. What this means is that I am standing still at PPS. When a good salesman earns less than $30,000 per year in industrial sales he should consider changing companies. (My projected income this year is less than $25,000.)

Although Plastic Piping Systems has intelligent, hard-working people at all levels of operation, it is my opinion that positive reinforcement is severely lacking. For example, the bonus check earned by a warehouse worker was withheld by the office for more than three months. These actions develop negative attitudes in the company.

Better communication and teamwork should be encouraged.

Respectfully submitted,

Donald Larsen

Donald Larsen

Plastic Piping Systems: Employee Turnover (B)

Ted: Well, George and Peter, it looks as if 1984 is shaping up to be a good year. I was just examining our first quarter results and sales are up 14% over 1983, gross profit is up 13%, and net income is up.

George: Everything seems to be up!

Peter: Except the turnover among our field force.

Ted: I know, and that is because of your hard work.

Peter: Thanks, Ted, but quite honestly I think it was a result of a lot of internal changes.

George: The computer was sure a big help.

Ted: (Turns to a computer screen in his office) You're right. Let's see what Cleveland sold this morning. (Types on keyboard) They just sold a shipment of $42,000 to a contractor in Columbus.

George: Have we sold to him before?

Ted: (Punches some more keys) Yes, back in September 1982. Seems he basically deals in residential construction.

Peter: This computer system is our best asset. It provides us with a great deal of information and saves on excessive paperwork, which enables our field force to perform more effectively and efficiently.

George: It does so much that it allowed us to virtually eliminate middle management.

Peter: And consequently, the friction between the field force and middle management no longer exists.

Ted: I like the new organizational structure that we have created. (Exhibit 1).

George: And Peter is doing a fine job in his new position of overseeing all the branches.

Ted: I've got to hand it to you Peter, you have a difficult task, especially with those branches that do not have managers.

Peter: Well, because of the computer system it's easier for me to monitor those branches.

George: Under our old system, the branch managers spent 50% of their time managing the inventory to insure that it was at the appropriate levels.

Peter: Now with centralized purchasing and inventory management our remaining managers have more time to focus on key accounts and help their people with the selling function.

Ted: I'm also glad we stopped promising everyone in the world that they could all become branch managers. It seemed like some of the previous people we hired were disappointed when they didn't take over the branch after three months.

George: That's true, but to get and maintain good people we need to establish some sort of career path. Our present structure is tight, and rapid advancement is hard to provide.

Peter: Well, George, despite a lack of a lot of upward mobility we were able to hire three solid outside salesmen. We have an engineer, who was previously with a consulting firm in Tampa, and two men in Texas and New Jersey with a proven track record in outside sales, one with a college degree.

Ted: Sounds like a qualified group. How did we lure them to PPS?

George: Don't forget, Ted, we have an extensive product line and we've increased our compensation package so we are competitive within the industry.

Peter: I'm also pleased with the three people from the warehouse we promoted to inside sales. All six of the new recruits are getting on-the-job training.

Ted: With what you said before, George, about career mobility, I hope everyone in the warehouse doesn't think they will automatically be promoted to inside sales. Especially since we have been able to stabilize turnover.

George: I guess we never fully analyzed the various sales functions and the appropriate people for each position, but when you have good people you want to keep them.

Source: Copyright © 1984. Prepared by Hubert D. Hennessey with the assistance of Kim Koehler, Research Assistant.

EXHIBIT 1 ▪ *Organization Structure*

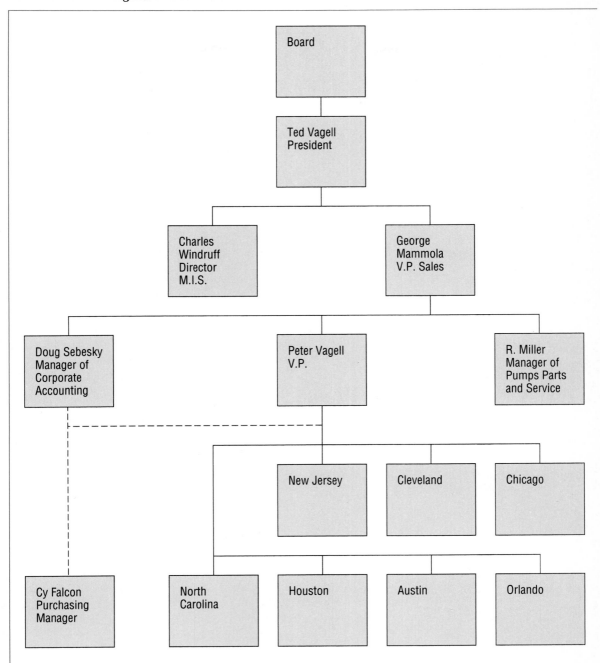

Peter: Yes, take Alice Kopp for example. We could tell she was anxious to move to outside sales and had offers from other companies. We hated to lose Alice so we were able to accommodate her.

George: And from the first quarter results, we might have some more openings in sales.

Ted: I guess it's not too early to start thinking about beginning our college recruitment program and reinstituting our formal training classes. What do you guys think about hiring more salespeople, one for each location? How should we hire and train them?

Part Five

DIRECTING THE SALESFORCE

This part contains three chapters dealing with the direction of the activities of the salesforce. Chapter 11 provides a summary of relevant salesforce motivation theories and examines several current issues related to motivating the salesforce. Guidelines for managing the motivation component are also presented.

Chapter 12 discusses the management of salesforce reward systems, with an emphasis on financial and nonfinancial compensation. Sales expenses and sales contests are among the other topics covered in this chapter.

Chapter 13 presents a model of sales management leadership. Important leadership functions such as coaching are discussed, and the always important topic of ethics in leadership is investigated. Problems that challenge sales managers as leaders are also treated in this chapter.

Salesforce Motivation: Theories and Current Issues

SALES MANAGEMENT CHALLENGE: MOTIVATING THE MOTLEY CREW It is a true pleasure to manage the self-motivated sales superstars. But how about the nonsuperstars? An article in *Personal Selling Power* introduces us to a cast of dubious sales characters with self-descriptive names: Grandstand George, Fearful Fred, Perfectionist Pete, Slumped Sally, Excited Eddie, Disorganized Debby, and Worried Walter. Even in the best salesforces, one or more of these characters may appear. Each represents a unique motivational challenge. Having a basic understanding of motivation theories can help the sales manager diagnose these problem salespeople and motivate them to greater successes.

Grandstand George is an individualistic, spotlight-seeking "hot dog." A sales manager may have special problems getting him to be a team player. How could he be motivated to sublimate his own ego and put the salesforce team interests first? Fearful Fred wants to be a team player but lacks enthusiasm. Grandstand George is motivated by big awards, while Fearful Fred is seeking emotional support.

Slumped Sally is burned out, and she may require the sales manager's personal attention to rebuild her positive attitude.

Chapter 11

At the other end of the spectrum, Excited Eddie is "wired" but often rushes past important relationship-building tasks such as customer follow-up. He might need to gain a clear understanding of how customer follow-up and paying attention to detail are keys for future success.

Worried Walter lacks self-confidence and is hesitant to contact new prospects. The sales manager may need to motivate him by building his job-related self-esteem. Both Disorganized Debby and Perfectionist Pete can be described as unfocused. They procrastinate and avoid the difficult parts of their jobs. Debby may be seeking true meaning and a sense of accomplishment, while Pete has a real need to control his life.

This rather motley crew of salespeople is not necessarily a group of hard-core losers. With the proper motivation, they can become valuable contributors to the sales effort. Managing these types of salespeople requires a versatile sales manager, one who understands how human behavior can be directed through various motivational methods.

Source: Donald J. Moine and Gerhard Gschwandter, "How to Manage Selling's Seven Most Difficult (but Promising) Personalities," *Personal Selling Power*, May–June 1990, 10–15.

Learning Objectives

After completing this chapter, you should be able to

1 *Define motivation in terms of intensity, persistence, and direction.*

2 *Discuss motivation as a process that begins with a perceived need deficiency.*

3 *Discuss the basic points of four content theories and four process theories of motivation.*

4 *Identify key issues in salesforce motivation.*

5 *Cite managerial guidelines for salesforce motivation.*

The salespeople described in the opening vignette appear from time to time in the lives of practically all sales managers. Indeed, it would be rare to manage a salesforce for any significant time and not encounter one of the characters just described. Sales managers often struggle with salesforce motivation problems, as they are not trained industrial psychologists. They typically rely on intuition and observations of salespeople's behaviors to gain clues about motivation levels and the appropriate course of action to maximally motivate their salesforces. To fully appreciate their role in salesforce motivation, sales managers should have a fundamental understanding of the theories of human motivation.

In this chapter, we provide a foundation for understanding the sales manager's role in salesforce motivation. Motivation will be defined, motivational theories will be discussed, and current issues in salesforce motivation will be presented. Guidelines for managerial actions regarding motivation will also be suggested.

Motivation Defined

Defining **motivation** has been a tedious job for psychologists, sales management researchers, and sales managers. After decades of study, the most commonly used definitions of motivation include three dimensions—intensity, persistence, and direction.[1] **Intensity** refers to the amount of mental and physical effort put forth by the salesperson. **Persistence** describes the salesperson's choice to expend effort over a period of time, especially when faced with adverse conditions. **Direction** implies that salespeople choose where their efforts will be spent among various job activities.[2]

Since salespeople are often faced with a diverse set of selling and nonselling job responsibilities, their choice of which activities warrant action is just as important as how hard they work or how well they persist in their efforts. The motivation task is incomplete unless salespeople's efforts are channeled in directions consistent with the overall strategic role of the salesforce within the firm. These ideas are supported in two studies of salespeople, one in the direct selling industry and the other of a national manufacturer's salesforce.[3] Both studies indicate that higher levels of effort, or intensity, are not necessarily associated with higher levels of performance.

A truly "motivated" salesforce does not need constant reminders to work hard on the right job dimensions and to persevere in the face of adversity. Rather, the ideal salesforce is self-motivated and requires only periodic direction from the sales manager.

Motivation is an unobservable phenomenon, and the terms intensity, persistence, and direction are concepts that help managers explain what they expect from their salespeople. It is important to note that although sales managers can observe salespeople's behavior, they can only infer their motivation. Indeed, it is the personal, unobservable nature of motivation that makes it such a difficult area of study.

Motivation can also be viewed as intrinsic or extrinsic. If salespeople find their job to be inherently rewarding, they are **intrinsically motivated.** If they are motivated by the rewards provided by others, such as pay and formal recognition, they are **extrinsically motivated.** Although a salesperson's overall motivation

FIGURE 11.1   ▪   *A Basic Model of the Motivational Process*

The motivational process begins when an individual perceives an unfulfilled need and begins to search for ways to meet the need. When people feel that needs can be partially or fully met through job behavior, they will set goals and direct their efforts accordingly. Subsequent performance is evaluated and perhaps reinforced through rewards or punishment. This may lead to reassessment of the need and the means for satisfying the need.

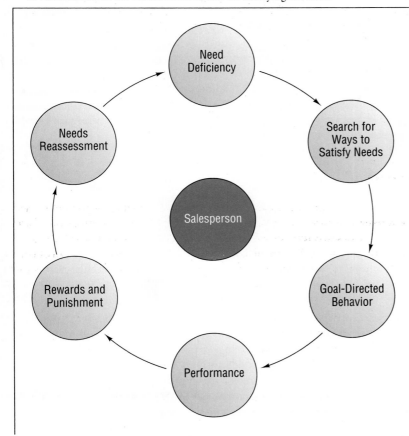

Source: Adapted from James L. Gibson, John M. Ivancevich, and James H. Donnelly, Jr., *Organizations: Behavior, Structure, Processes*, 8th ed. (Plano, Texas: Business Publications, Inc., 1990), 102.

could be a function of both intrinsic and extrinsic motivation, some will have strong preferences for extrinsic rewards such as pay and formal recognition awards while others will seek intrinsic rewards such as interesting, challenging work.[4]

Motivation and Behavior

As shown in Figure 11.1, the motivation process begins when the salesperson feels a deficiency in one or more needs. These needs may be economic, social, or self-actualizing.[5] In the salesforce context, **economic needs,** or *existence needs*, could relate to the pay, fringe benefits, and security offered by the job. **Social**

needs are relationship-oriented. They could be associated with the salesperson's interactions with the sales manager, coworkers, and customers or be affected by the nature of company policy and support. **Self-actualization needs** are essentially personal-growth needs such as interesting work and opportunities for job advancement.

The process shown in Figure 11.1 suggests several key points. First, normal human behavior is not a random process. It is **goal-directed behavior,** though not necessarily rational. Second, rewards and punishment contribute to an individual's learning experience, and need-satisfaction typically results from learned, not instinctive, behaviors. Third, consider how much the sales manager can influence salespeople at each step in the process. To some degree, sales managers have the opportunity to stimulate felt needs, identify ways to satisfy the need, direct the behavior of the salesperson, evaluate performance, reward or punish, and counsel the salesperson during the reassessment stage.

Theories of Motivation

A considerable number of sales managers are skeptical of theoretical approaches to salesforce motivation, as expressed in this review of standard motivation training for sales managers:

> Typically it has consisted of lengthy exposure to the motivational theories of Maslow, Herzberg, and others. In such sessions, almost everything presented is either theory or unrelated to the field manager's business and the realities of their organizations' cultures and policies. So nothing really changes.[6]

Such opinions indicate the misapplication of motivational theories by those who expect simple answers to complex questions. Theories do not purport to provide widesweeping prescriptions for motivating a salesforce but rather a basic understanding of the complex processes of motivation.

In fairness to sales managers who reject the inputs of motivation theories, it should be stressed that motivation theories focus on the individual and that the realities of the workplace often dictate a group orientation. Further, these theories were developed by psychologists who have specialized expertise in the application of the theories. Sales managers have expertise in running a sales organization, not in uncovering obscure dimensions of an individual's motivation.

As we proceed with our discussion of motivation theories, remember two cautionary points. First, none of the theories offers a universally accepted explanation of human behavior, either in or out of the salesforce setting. Second, the complexity of the human mind assures us that "theories will continue to be created, expounded, tried, revised, accepted, and rejected."[7] In other words, the theories to be discussed are obviously not infallible, but they are presented as tools useful for gaining a basic understanding of salesforce motivation.

Motivation theories can be classified as content theories or as process theories. **Content theories of motivation** are more concerned with inferring the factors that influence behavior and less concerned with how these factors influence behavior.[8] Content theories try to describe the types of needs people have, the rewards they seek, and the incentives that have the greatest impact on their behavior. Sales managers can benefit from a basic understanding of content theories in that these approaches emphasize the importance of understanding individual differences when trying to motivate a salesforce.

Process theories of motivation concentrate on the mental processes people go through in deciding on alternative courses of action and the effort that should be expended.[9] These theories attempt to explain how different variables interact to influence the expenditure of effort and behavior. Clearly, sales managers need to try to understand what the processes of motivation are and how salespeople make choices.

Content Theories of Motivation

Four content theories of motivation will be reviewed: Maslow's need-hierarchy theory, Alderfer's ERG theory, Herzberg's hygiene-motivation theory, and McClelland's learned-needs theory.

Maslow's Need Hierarchy. First presented over 50 years ago, **Maslow's need-hierarchy theory** has endured as a popular way to study salesforce motivation, despite a lack of convincing empirical support.[10] As shown in Figure 11.2, Maslow's theory proposes that people have five basic sets of needs: [11]

1. *Physiological needs.* The basic needs or drives that are satisfied by such things as food, water, and sleep.
2. *Safety and security needs.* The needs associated with producing a secure environment free of threats to continued existence.
3. *Love and belongingness needs.* Concerned with interpersonal factors; reflect a desire to have peer acceptance.
4. *Self-esteem needs.* Needs for self-respect and respect by others. Needs for strength, achievement, and recognition by others.
5. *Self-actualization needs.* Need for self-fulfillment; need for the individual to maximize potential.

According to Maslow, these basic needs are arranged in a hierarchy of prepotency such that the lower-order needs are of primary importance until they are satisfied. As the lower-order needs are satisfied, the higher-order needs become more important to the individual. When needs are met at the highest level, self-actualization, these needs become even more important to the individual. In summary, behavior is motivated by the need that is most important at a particular time. The strength of a need is a function of its position in the hierarchy and whether or not lower-ranked needs in the hierarchy have been satisfied.

Recent research indicates that of the five categories in Maslow's hierarchy, esteem needs may be more important in the motivation of salespeople than previously thought. Bagozzi found self-esteem to be a key determinant of sales performance, suggesting that sales managers should put a high priority on enhancing salesperson self-esteem through positive reinforcement in the form of recognition programs and monetary rewards.[12] Other researchers have suggested that esteem needs could be partially met through giving salespeople more prestigious job titles.[13]

FIGURE 11.2 ▪ *Maslow's Hierarchy of Needs*

Self-actualization is the highest-order need in Maslow's hierarchy of needs and is achieved by the fewest number of people.

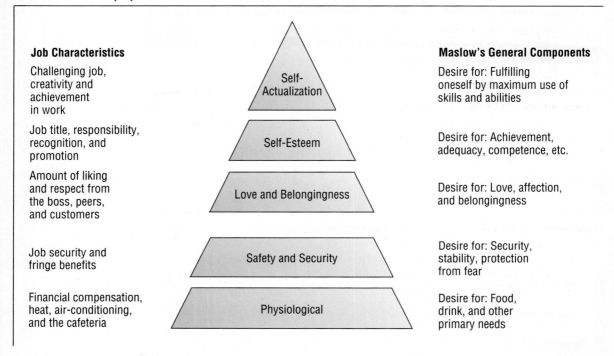

Source: Robert L. Berl, Nicholas C. Williamson, and Terry Powell, "Industrial Salesforce Motivation: A Critique and Test of Maslow's Hierarchy of Need," *Journal of Personal Selling and Sales Management* 4 (May 1984): 33. Used with permission.

Alderfer's ERG Theory. In contrast to Maslow's theory, **Alderfer's ERG theory** presumes that people have three sets of needs.[14]

1. *Existence needs.* Includes various forms of material and physiological desires; satisfied by environmental factors such as food, water, pay, and working conditions.
2. *Relatedness needs.* Needs concerning maintenance of interpersonal relationships with significant others such as coworkers, family, and friends.
3. *Growth needs.* Needs related to an individual's attempt to seek opportunities for unique personal development and full utilization of his or her capacities.

Alderfer's hierarchy differs from Maslow's hierarchy in the number of need categories it identifies and in the content of those categories, but both theories propose that higher-order needs become more important when lower-order needs have been satisfied. An important distinction between the two theories revolves around the issue of frustration in satisfying higher-order needs. Maslow says an individual will continue to "swim upstream" in the quest for unmet higher-order needs, while Alderfer contends that some people might decide to drop back down the hierarchy and attempt to maximize a lower-order reward. For example, a career salesperson may have unmet growth or self-actualization needs as a result of having been continually passed over for promotion into sales management. Maslow would argue that such a person will continue to be motivated by the unmet need to be promoted, while Alderfer would say that he or she might give up on the prospect of promotion and perhaps try to maximize a lower-order reward such as pay.

Herzberg's Hygiene-Motivation Theory.   Another content theory, **Herzberg's hygiene-motivation theory** postulates that the job environment can be separated into two dimensions: hygiene factors and motivation factors.[15] **Hygiene factors** are those that, if insufficient, can cause dissatisfaction on the job. Examples are pay, company policies, working conditions, and relationships with coworkers and supervisors. A sales manager may alleviate dissatisfaction by improving a hygiene factor, but the effects are thought to be temporary and lacking in lasting motivational benefit. For example, dissatisfaction with pay could be eliminated with a pay raise, but this might not motivate better performance or assure satisfaction beyond the short term. To gain some idea of the challenge associated with providing sufficient hygiene factors, consider that one survey found 80 percent of salespeople to be dissatisfied with company policy.[16]

Motivation factors in Herzberg's theory include achievement, recognition, challenging work, and opportunity for growth and advancement. These factors correspond to the esteem and self-actualization categories in Maslow's hierarchy and are thought to be related to long-term motivation, job satisfaction, and performance.

Although some studies have reported a lack of support for Herzberg's theory among salespeople,[17] the hygiene-motivation concept offers a solid principle of salesforce motivation. Pay and other hygiene factors are only partially sufficient to motivate the salesforce, and their effects are often fleeting.

McClelland's Theory of Learned Needs.   Another theory, **McClelland's learned-needs theory,** holds that people learn to strive for achievement, affiliation, and power.[18] It attributes the individual differences in motivation to whichever of these three needs is dominant at a given point in time. Salespeople who are high in the need for *achievement* may prefer higher-order rewards such as feelings of accomplishment and opportunities for personal growth. Further, they may avoid tasks where they believe the probability of failure is high.[19] The need for achievement has received considerable attention as a determinant of overall salesperson motivation. One study appearing in the *Harvard Business Review* identified *personality*, particularly the need to achieve, as one of the key determinants of motivation, along with the sales job itself and type of compensation plan.[20]

Salespeople whose need for *affiliation* dominates their behavior are motivated by being a part of a group or company organization. Interestingly, the stereotypical high-producing salesperson is often depicted as a loner who wants as little direction as possible. These salespeople are often described as "lone wolves," suggesting that they prefer independence of action as opposed to running with the pack (i.e., the rest of the sales team). They are not strongly committed to their employers but are highly involved in their sales activities; that is, they truly enjoy interacting with customers and the aspects of their jobs that deal with actual selling.[21] When we take a closer look at so-called lone-wolf salespeople, it is often apparent that they too have strong affiliation needs. Rather than meet these needs by affiliating with their peers and managers, they relate much more strongly with customers.

Some salespeople covet *power* and are extremely motivated in their pursuit of it. According to McClelland, a need for power is a need to influence other's behavior, and it can be a positive characteristic for successful sales management. Salespeople who seek promotion into management might be extremely motivated to sharpen their interpersonal sales skills, thinking that such skills will be a positive attribute in future management assignments.

Overlap of Content Theories. The content theories of motivation, while different, have considerable overlap. Since each has been derived in part from a preexisting theory, such overlap is to be expected. The similarities among the content theories discussed in this chapter are summarized in Figure 11.3.

Process Theories of Motivation

Four process theories of motivation will be briefly reviewed: expectancy theory, equity theory, attribution theory, and reinforcement theory.

Expectancy Theory. Building on the work of Vroom[22] and others, Walker, Churchill, and Ford introduced the **expectancy theory** of salesperson motivation over a decade ago.[23] According to expectancy theory, a salesperson's motivation to expend effort on a given task is a function of three interrelated factors: expectancies, instrumentalities, and valences.

Expectancies are the salesperson's perceptions of the linkages between effort and job performance. For example, one salesperson may perceive a strong connection between total hours worked and job performance. Conversely, another salesperson might see very little connection between incremental effort and improved performance.

Instrumentalities are the salesperson's perceptions about the correlation of performance and various rewards. For example, a salesperson can easily see that increasing sales volume leads to a financial reward if he or she is paid a commission on sales. A straight-salary salesperson, however, will probably be less certain of the nature of the reward, if any, for increased sales volume.

The **valence for rewards,** the third dimension of motivation according to expectancy theory, is the salesperson's perception of the desirability of receiving increased rewards for improved performance. While it is generally assumed that all rewards are desirable, in fact some rewards are only marginally effective, and some can actually have a negative effect on a salesperson's motivation. For example, we know of a high-performing sales representative who tried not to win a sales contest, since the grand prize was a trip to Hawaii, and he had a true fear of flying. His valence for the available reward was actually negative.

FIGURE 11.3 ▪ *Summary of Content Theories of Motivation*

Each of the four content theories of motivation attempts to explain behavior from similar but not identical perspectives. By following the arrows from left to right, you can compare the components of these theories.

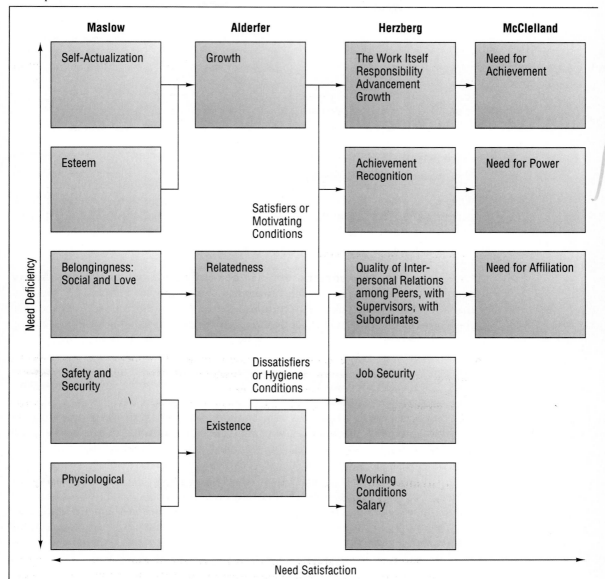

Source: James L. Gibson, John M. Ivancevich, and James H. Donnelly, Jr., *Organizations: Behavior, Structure, Processes*, 8th ed. (Plano, Texas: Business Publications, Inc., 1990), 123. Used with permission.

FIGURE 11.4 ▪ *Key Salesperson Questions in Expectancy Theory*

Salespeople's motivation level may be affected by their perceptions of the linkages between effort and performance and between performance and rewards. Motivation can also be affected by how much the salesperson values the reward being offered.

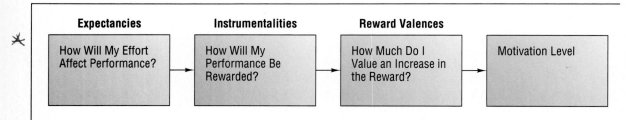

Expectancy theory holds that behavior is "purposeful, based on conscious behavior, and goal-directed."[24] By perceiving expectancies, instrumentalities, and valences for rewards, salespeople look into the future and adjust behavior based on what they expect to happen and how much they value the outcomes of their performance. This "future-gazing" can influence motivation positively, negatively, or leave it unchanged. The key questions asked of themselves by salespeople who behave according to the expectancy model of motivation are summarized in Figure 11.4.

One of the most versatile theories of motivation, expectancy theory offers commonsense guidelines for sales managers. For example, Figure 11.4 suggests that sales managers set clear expectations for achievement of realistic goals and that they provide valued rewards for achievement of the goals.[25]

Equity Theory. Introducing the concept of fairness into salesforce motivation, **equity theory** proposes that salespeople may evaluate their treatment as compared with "relevant others" in the salesforce and, if they perceive inequitable treatment, suffer detrimental motivational effects. Equity theory was developed by Adams, who proposed that employees use input/output ratios to determine relative equity.[26] Inputs to the organization might include educational level, job experience, or perhaps hours worked, while typical outputs would be pay, promotion opportunities, and other rewards. A salesperson sensitive to equity issues might say, "I don't mind making less money than Joe for doing basically the same job, since he has twice the sales experience that I do, but I really don't think it's fair for me to make less money than Bill just because he has an MBA and I don't."

According to Adams, individuals who perceive inequity may take one of several courses of action to rectify the situation. They may rationalize the situation by distorting their own perceptions (maybe an MBA is worth more after all), or they may alter their job inputs (I will cut down on the number of hours worked, since it doesn't really pay to work extra hours). They may also try to influence the "relevant other" person to alter his or her inputs or outcomes, select another person for comparison purposes, or perhaps leave the job. All of these actions could have negative effects on overall salesforce motivation and performance. The primary processes in equity theory are illustrated in Figure 11.5.

FIGURE 11.5 ▪ *Equity Theory and Salesforce Motivation*

Equity theory suggests that salespeople will compare their efforts, performance, and rewards to others in the salesforce. If they feel they have been treated unfairly, their motivation may be diminished.

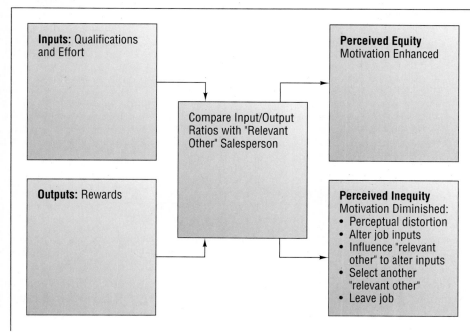

Sales managers can expect that job-related equity issues will become more important in the future. Employee expectations are being influenced by widespread discussions on topics such as providing comparable pay for comparable jobs and curtailing sexual harassment. The fair treatment of employees is viewed not only as a motivational tool but also as a basic responsibility of sales managers.

Attribution Theory. Based on the notion that people are motivated to understand the causes of their performance, **attribution theory** concentrates on the mental processes people utilize to understand why events occur as they do. In a review of attribution theory, Teas and McElroy reiterate the basic assumptions underlying the theory.[27]

1. Individuals will try to assign causes for important instances of behavior, sometimes seeking additional information to do so.
2. Individuals will assign causes in a systematic manner.
3. The particular cause that an individual attributes to a given event will affect subsequent behavior.

The attribution process might be initiated if a salesperson achieves an unexpected result or fails to perform satisfactorily on a well-defined routine task. The self-analysis will utilize past performance information and perhaps an

FIGURE 11.6   ▪   *Attribution Theory and Expectancy Estimates*

Attribution theory suggests that salespeople try to determine the causes of their successes and failures. After attributing performance results to a set of factors and circumstances, salespeople may change their expectancy estimates (the perceived linkage between effort and performance).

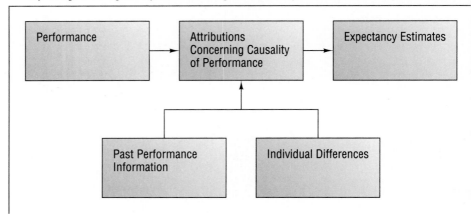

Source: R. Kenneth Teas and James C. McElroy, "Causal Attributions and Expectancy Estimates: A Framework for Understanding the Dynamics of Salesforce Motivation." Reprinted from *Journal of Marketing* 50 (January 1986): 76, published by the American Marketing Association.

assessment of how the salesperson differs from other salespeople. Further, future behavior and perceptions, including the effort-performance linkage (*expectancy*) may be altered. For example, a salesperson may attribute failure to poor strategy rather than to poor effort. In these situations, salespeople may be motivated to change their strategy, perhaps by using a different sales approach or asking more questions during the sales presentation. When failure is attributed to a lack of effort, salespeople may be motivated to work longer hours, but still follow the same strategies and tactics. [28]

A recent study of 146 business forms salespeople reinforces the role of salespeople's attributions in determining future effort intentions and expectancy estimates.[29] Salespeople in this study who blamed themselves for not making quota reported increased intentions for making quota in future months, while those who attributed their shortcomings to other factors reported a decrease in future effort intentions. This study reminds us of the importance of determining, as part of the salesforce motivation process, *why* salespeople think they have performed at a given level.

As the sales job becomes more sophisticated and competition intensifies, sales managers and salespeople will become more involved in the use of post-hoc analysis consistent with attribution theory to attempt to uncover the causes of success and failure. Attribution theory is summarized in Figure 11.6.

Reinforcement Theory.   Reinforcement theorists are not interested in explaining behavior by studying unobservable personality traits, inner drives and needs, or mental processes. In contrast to the other motivation theories we have discussed to this point, **reinforcement theory,** pioneered by B. F. Skinner, never moves its

EXHIBIT 11.1 ▪ *Behavior Modification through Reinforcement*

I. Behavior Modification Strategies to Increase Desired Behavior

Problem:	Desirable behavior does not occur frequently enough	
Behavior modification strategies:	1. Positive reinforcement	2. Negative reinforcement
Method:	When desirable behavior occurs, follow it with a pleasant consequence.	When desirable behavior occurs, allow the salesperson to avoid an unpleasant consequence.
Example:		
1. Desirable behavior	Gain a new customer.	Turn in expense accounts on time.
2. Consequence	Bonus for gaining new customer.	If expense account on time, allow salesperson to *avoid* a downgrading in performance review.

II. Behavior Modification Strategies to Decrease Undesirable Behavior

Problem:	Undesirable behavior occurs too frequently	
Behavior modification strategies:	1. Punishment	2. Extinction
Method:	When undesirable behavior occurs, follow it with an unpleasant consequence.	When undesirable behavior occurs, no positive reinforcement.
Example:		
1. Undesirable behavior	Sales order not complete.	Salesperson turns in incomplete expense reports.
2. Consequence	Loss of part of the commission on the order.	Sales manager stops correcting the reports for the salesperson and returns them to the salesperson for completion.[a]

[a]By correcting incomplete reports, the sales manager was inadvertently providing positive reinforcement for undesirable behavior.

Source: Robert A. Scott, John E. Swan, M. Elizabeth Wilson, and Jenny J. Roberts, "Organizational Behavior Modification: A General Tool for Sales Management," *Journal of Personal Selling and Sales Management* 6 (August 1986): 63–64. Used with permission.

---

focus from behavior. Moreover, Skinner believes that behavior can be explained solely on the principle of reinforcement.[30]

Basically, reinforcement theory proposes that specific behaviors can be initiated, encouraged, modified, or eliminated by utilizing the specific reinforcement strategies of positive reinforcement, negative reinforcement, punishment, and extinction. As shown in Exhibit 11.1, **positive reinforcement** provides a pleasant consequence for desirable behavior. **Negative reinforcement** allows the salesperson to avoid an unpleasant consequence if desirable behavior has occurred. **Punishment**, the provision of an unpleasant experience, or **extinction**, the

A GLOBAL PERSPECTIVE

Toyota Salesperson Janet Lim

At the age of nine, Janet Lim was helping her mother earn a living by cleaning airports. As a 14-year-old student, she worked part-time on a farm and in construction for $5 per day. At the age of 29, she has yet to earn a college degree yet earns over four times what the average college graduate earns in her home of Singapore. Janet Lim is a self-motivated, successful salesperson for Borneo Motors, a Toyota dealership.

Prior to beginning her career in automobile sales, Janet Lim had worked her way up to a $14,000-a-year job in a jewelry store. When she decided to take a job selling Toyotas primarily on commission (base salary of $190 per month), Janet identified three key conditions that would serve as her internal motivators. First, she felt she would have to have a genuine fondness for the industry. Second, she knew that she must possess a burning desire to learn a new business and the ways to sell within that business. Finally, she knew that potential financial gains must be important to her in order to succeed.

A dedicated goal setter, Janet Lim has become a great success story. She earns $80,000 a year, while the typical college graduate in Singapore earns between $12,000 and $18,000. She has constantly upgraded her selling skills by observing other productive salespeople, and then what she does, in her own words, is "copy, copy, copy."

Source: Christine Harvey, *Secrets of the World's Greatest Sales Performers* (Holbrook, Mass.: Bob Adams Publishers Inc., 1990), 13–24.

withholding of positive reinforcement, may be used following undesirable behavior.

Reinforcement theory's critics contend that it places too much reliance on "carrot and stick" dimensions of motivation. They charge that adherents to this theory may mistakenly believe that motivation is simply a matter of meting out rewards and punishments and thus ignore other important dimensions of motivation such as job design and providing necessary job training.

Another problem of relying on reinforcement procedures is that the sales manager may become a cue for the salesperson to perform the expected behavior. For example, the salesperson may devote time to an expected behavior (e.g., setting up merchandise displays) only when the sales manager is accompanying the salesperson in the field.[31]

Despite the shortcomings of reinforcement theory, it is commonly used to encourage specific salesperson behaviors. For example, Network Equipment Technologies in Redwood City, California, emphasizes customer satisfaction through its salesforce compensation plan.[32] When satisfaction with a transaction is verified by the customer, the salesperson receives the final installment of the commission due. In this instance, the company is using both negative reinforcement (withholding part of the commission if the customer is not satisfied) and positive reinforcement (paying full commission when the customer is satisfied), depending on whether or not the salesperson has taken steps to ensure satisfaction.

To the extent that salespeople are self-motivated and compliant with prescribed policies and procedures, reinforcement will be less important as a motivational tool. The self-motivated salesperson described in "A Global Perspective: Toyota Salesperson Janet Lim" would have little need for reinforcement from her sales manager.

Comment on Content and Process Motivation Theories

We would encourage any sales manager to become familiar with the basic concepts of all the motivation theories we have discussed. An experienced sales manager reflected on the usefulness of theoreticians such as Maslow, Vroom, Herzberg, and McClelland as follows:

> Although we will never know whether these famous scientists could ever have been as effective as you are in meeting a sales quota, the probability is they could identify your people-problems and guide you in a way that could help you develop highly effective solutions. Therefore, a good comprehension of their theories of human behavior can be quite valuable as you attempt to bring order to your potentially chaotic situations, provide incentives and motivation, and satisfy your own needs at the same time. After all, the title "manager" does not mean you are also not a human being.[33]

Sales managers and theorists would agree that there is still a lot to learn about what motivates salespeople, but at least some insights into the subject are offered by the major theories reviewed here. For a summary of how the thought-provoking suggestions of these theorists can be applied to salesforce motivation, refer to Exhibit 11.2.

Current Issues in Salesforce Motivation

Issues of particular interest in salesforce motivation today are usually phrased as questions, indicating that the answers are yet to be determined:

1. How individualized should motivation be?
2. What will be the effects of an aging population on salesforce motivation?
3. How should the expectations of today's emerging salesforce concerning the future be addressed in motivational programs?
4. Are traditional motivational practices still effective?

Motivation: Individual or Group Orientation

Motivation theories stress the individual nature of motivation and contend that group approaches to motivation will be suboptimal. Yet, in practice, it is rare to find individualized motivational programs, especially in large organizations. In fact, there is a fair amount of resistance to individualized programs, partly due to the inescapable fact that it is easier to implement one motivational program for the entire salesforce than to design individual ones for every salesperson. In some cases, greater overall productivity can be achieved through standardization. Furthermore, the utilization of a single program for everyone can reduce the firm's legal liabilities with regard to employee treatment.

There has been some discussion of developing a compromise approach to motivation that falls between the extremes of individual and mass approaches. The concept, called **salesforce segmentation,** suggests dividing the salesforce into groups based on motivational needs, then developing motivational programs for each group (which, of course, would share some common parts). This idea was first proposed by professors Moissen and Fram and has continued to spur discussion.[34]

EXHIBIT 11.2 ▪ *Sales Motivation Implications of Motivation Theories*

Theory	*Selected Managerial Implications*
Maslow's need-hierarchy theory	Recognize that different people are motivated by different needs; consider individual needs when designing motivational programs; offer a variety of rewards if individual needs cannot be explicitly considered.
Alderfer's ERG theory	Recognize that salespeople may become frustrated if they cannot fulfill higher-order needs and may seek instead to maximize a lower-order reward related to lower-order need fulfillment.
Herzberg's hygiene-motivation theory	Recognize that pay and other job hygiene factors, though important in salesforce motivation, may be insufficient to sustain high levels of motivation in the long run.
McClelland's learned-needs theory	In some cases, it may be worthwhile to attempt to increase a salesperson's need for achievement through training or counseling; teach salespeople to exercise self-control and demonstrate maturity to balance their need for power when dealing with customers.
Expectancy theory	Clearly communicate the linkages between (1) job effort and performance and (2) performance and rewards.
Equity theory	Offer rewards valued by the salesforce; reward each salesperson on an equitable basis compared with other salespeople.
Attribution theory	Help salespeople understand the cause-and-effect relationships between their behavior and performance; consider the importance of direction of effort along with intensity and persistence of effort.
Reinforcement theory	Be consistent in reinforcing desirable behavior and discouraging undesirable behavior.

One study of salespeople identified three segments for motivational purposes: **comfort seekers, spotlight seekers,** and **developers.**[35] The *comfort seekers* sought job security, a sense of accomplishment, and liking and respect from their sales jobs. The *spotlight seekers* wanted highly visible rewards such as pay and recognition awards. The *developers* valued opportunities for personal growth as a job reward. This study demonstrated that salespeople can be effectively segmented for motivational purposes and recommended that more organizations consider such segmentation.

As more women join the ranks in professional selling, there has been considerable discussion and debate concerning the similarities and differences of male and female salespeople in terms of many important job variables, including motivation. Some sales managers might consider segmenting their salesforces for motivational purposes into male and female groups, a practice not recommended by the authors. A recent study of almost 400 male and female salespeople uncovered far more similarities than differences between the two groups in terms of how they respond to rewards and punishment meted out by sales managers. [36]

Demographics: An Aging Workforce

By 1995 nearly three-fourths of the nation's workforce will be in the 25 to 54 age range, compared with approximately two-thirds in this range in 1984.[37] For sales managers, this demographic development is a mixed blessing. According to the research on salesperson career cycles (briefly reviewed in Chapter 4), older, more experienced salespeople are among the most satisfied with their jobs. Further, they are among the highest performers in the salesforce.

On the other hand, there are some concerns related to aging salesforces. For the younger salespeople in the 25 to 54 age group, opportunities for promotion into management are expected to be limited. Salespeople who have limited opportunities for future promotion may be facing what researchers call a **career plateau.** In a study of two large salesforces, approximately 65 percent of the salespeople were considered plateaued; that is, these salespeople had not received a promotion in the past five years.[38] Among the plateaued group, over half were considered "deadwood" in that their current performance was low.

Another study, conducted over a three-year period, found that performance remained essentially unchanged for plateaued salespeople but that important job attitudes changed for the worse.[39] When job attitudes decline, even if performance remains stable, a sales manager begins to think about two critical questions: How long will it be before sales performance declines? And how will the declining attitudes of the plateaued salespeople affect the morale and productivity of the remainder of the salesforce? Motivating the entire salesforce can be complicated by the presence of plateaued salespeople.

Career plateauing can occur for a variety of reasons, including a lack of intrinsic and/or extrinsic motivation. The sources of career plateaus, the way plateaus influence performance and job attitudes, and the way sales managers might intervene to reduce plateauing and its effects are summarized in Exhibit 11.3. The items in category III are also mentioned later in the chapter in the discussion of job design.

Even though the demand for salespeople and sales managers is expected to be strong, the number of new sales management positions will not accommodate all those who seek promotion. The problems arising from career plateauing could worsen if the current trend toward downsizing corporations continues.

As indicated in Exhibit 11.3, another issue related to motivating the maturing salesforces is job-related stress, which has been called a significant problem among salespeople.[40] While all age groups are potential victims of stress, there is some thought that career salespeople may be particularly vulnerable to it. Job pressures and increasingly competitive conditions can lead to **job burnout** (see Exhibit 11.4) or to undesirable coping behaviors such as alcohol and drug abuse. In one survey, over 50 percent of responding sales managers reported that alcohol abuse was at least a minor problem in their salesforce.[41] Another survey indicated that drug abuse is at least a minor problem in approximately 40 percent of the respondents'

EXHIBIT 11.3 ▪ *Career Plateaus*

Source of Career Plateaus	Impact on Performance and Attitudes	Managerial Interventions

I. Individual Skills and Abilities
    Selection system deficiencies
    Lack of training
    Inaccurate perceptions of feedback
	Poor performance
	Poor job attitudes
		Redesign of selection system
		Improved training
		Improved performance appraisal and feedback systems

II. Individual Needs and Values
    Low growth need strength
    Career anchors of security and autonomy
    Self-imposed constraints
	Solid performance
	Good job attitudes
		Continue to reward, contingent on no downturn in performance
		Career information systems

III. Lack of Intrinsic Motivation
    Lack of skill variety
    Low task identity
    Low task significance
	Minimally acceptable job performance
	Declining job attitudes
		Combining tasks
		Forming natural work units
		Establishing client relationships
		Vertical loading
		Opening feedback channels

IV. Lack of Extrinsic Rewards
    Small raises, few promotions
    Inequities in reward systems
    Uncontingent rewards
	Poor performance
	Poor job attitudes
		Redesign of compensation system
		Redesign of promotion policies
		Encourage highly dissatisfied to leave

V. Stress and Burnout
    Interpersonal relationships on job
    Organizational climate
    Role conflict
	Poor performance
	Poor job attitudes
		Job rotation
		Preventive stress management
		Sabbaticals, off-site training

VI. Slow Organizational Growth
    External business conditions
    "Defender" corporate strategy
    Inaccurate personnel forecasts
	Continued good performance in short-run
	Declining job attitudes
		Provide "stars" with increased resources
		Provide poorer performers with incentives to leave or retire

Source: Daniel C. Feldman and Barton A. Weitz, "Career Plateaus Reconsidered," *Journal of Management* 14 (1988): 71.

salesforces.[42] While these findings cannot be strictly attributed to job stress, it does suggest the possibility that stress-reduction programs will become a more important part of salesforce motivation programs in the future.

Salespeople's Job Expectations

There is a general feeling that the job expectations of today's salespeople differ from those of generations past. Certainly this is a natural process, as new generations often bring new values and norms to the workplace. One indication

EXHIBIT 11.4   ▪   *Salesperson Burnout Self-Test*

Burnout Signals

Are you burning out?

At the heart of burnout is increasing disability to handle stress and mounting dissatisfaction with your job and yourself. While all of us, on occasion, have been unhappy with our lives or jobs, the problem of burnout goes much deeper and is more prolonged.

After three years of conducting burnout and stress management workshops for sales representatives and others in the workforce, we have found the following self-test useful in determining just who may be burning out. Ask yourself these questions:

	Yes	No
▪ Do you feel you're working harder and accomplishing less?	☐	☐
▪ Are you unhappy during work hours and irritated with fellow workers?	☐	☐
▪ Do you feel powerless or helpless to change the situation?	☐	☐
▪ Are you using more of your sick leave or other kinds of leave to stay away from work?	☐	☐
▪ Do you find yourself frequently saying, "I don't give a damn anymore," "I just can't keep up," or "It doesn't ever really matter what I do, it will turn out the same anyway"?	☐	☐
▪ Do you find your relationships with others—family and friends—more agitated because of the frustrations of the job?	☐	☐
▪ Do you find you're ignoring or angry at your buyers because of your work-related tensions?	☐	☐

If you're answering "yes" more often than "no," you may be a candidate for burnout. Some people are able to cope with their job frustrations and stress, but this might be the time for you to take stock of where you are in your job, where you're heading, and what you would like to change for the better.

A person has to decide what is creating stress and how best to handle it. While you may try to change your organization or company, it might be easier and better if you change your attitudes, work habits, values, goals and the way you spend your time.

Source: Charles Larson, Ph.D., "Help! My Job Is Killing Me! Burnout among Sales Reps," *Personal Selling Power* 1 (no. 4, 1981): 2.

that work values may be changing comes from a survey of 964 college students interested in entering sales positions.[43] In this survey, students ranked "the job itself" as the most-sought reward, ahead of pay and opportunities for advancement. Further, when asked to project their preferences ten years into the future, the surveyed students said they still thought the job itself would be the most motivating factor to them. These findings are noteworthy, in that the preferences of salespeople usually lean more toward extrinsic rewards. More discussion of salespeople's reward preferences will follow in Chapter 12.

It is quite difficult to assess the extent of changing work values and job expectations in today's workforce, much less in the future workforce. Furthermore, it is often an unfair oversimplification to describe generalized values and expectations as if they apply to every salesperson. The key point is that sales managers must make genuine efforts to understand the legitimate needs of today's salespeople, who happen to be among the most highly educated, achievement-oriented occupational groups. Traditional viewpoints must be reevaluated and discarded if necessary.

Reevaluating Traditional Practices

As previously mentioned, there has been a historical reliance on rewards and punishment in salesforce motivation. While both rewards and punishment have important places in the motivational program, other dimensions are emerging as being at least as important as these traditional tools. For example, **job enrichment,** which involves designing the sales job to include more variety, responsibility for completing the entire job, feedback, and meaningful work experiences, can be used to stimulate motivation. For example, entrepreneurially oriented firms would benefit from structuring sales jobs to encourage innovative, risk-taking, and proactive behavior on the part of their salesforces.[44] This might be done by providing a strong link between performance and rewards and allowing independence of action.

Career pathing is another practice that is becoming more useful as a motivational tool. It involves acquainting the salesperson with potential routes for career development in the organization, being as specific as possible regarding the skills, behavior, and performance necessary to pursue various paths. Perhaps the use of job enrichment and career pathing will ultimately redefine the role of traditional rewards and punishment in salesforce motivation. Another aspect of

AN ETHICAL PERSPECTIVE

Preventing Burnout with Career Paths   Job burnout and plateauing can result in serious consequences, for both the salesperson and the sales organization. Burned-out salespeople may resort to undesirable coping behaviors such as drug and alcohol abuse, absenteeism, and withdrawal from the job. The sales organization may suffer declining performance, dissatisfied customers, and costly turnover in the salesforce.

Rather than taking a passive approach and accepting burnout as a given, some firms are taking positive steps to prevent burnout and thus protect their valuable human assets. One such firm is National Semiconductor of Santa Clara, California. National has established clear career paths for salespeople who do not move into management. According to the firm's executives, National thinks that plateaus are management's problem as well as the individual's. Management believes that salespeople are self-motivated and that they will continue to improve and remain motivated if they have a clear idea of how they can progress up a sales career ladder.

Ethically responsible sales managers will not allow their salespeople to self-destruct or vegetate from boredom on the job. Providing clear career paths is one way to combat job burnout and career plateauing.

Source: Milan Moravec, Marshall Collins, and Clinton Tripodi, "Don't Want to Manage? Here's Another Path," *Sales and Marketing Management,* April 1990, 70–76.

career pathing is introduced in "An Ethical Perspective: Preventing Burnout with Career Paths."

Another traditional practice undergoing evaluation is the use of "rah-rah" motivational speakers. While motivational speakers are still an integral part of the salesforce motivation programs of many firms, the role of these performers is being reevaluated and often redefined. Popular speakers of yesteryear relied more on inspirational talks, but the most popular speakers of today are increasingly being asked to deliver substance that salespeople can put to use in their jobs. With fees ranging from $10,000 (football coach Lou Holtz) to $30,000 (author Tom Peters), it is easy to see why sales organizations want to get useful content, not just a high-priced pep talk.[45]

Guidelines for Motivating Salespeople

Sales managers should realize that practically everything they do will influence salesforce motivation one way or another. The people they recruit, the plans and policies they institute, the training they provide, and the way they communicate with and supervise salespeople are among the more important factors. In addition, sales managers should realize that environmental factors beyond their control may also influence salesforce motivation. Like other managerial functions, motivating salespeople requires a prioritized, calculated approach, rather than a futile attempt to address all motivational needs simultaneously. If for no other reason, the complexity of human nature and changing needs of salesforce members will prohibit the construction of motivational programs that run smoothly without periodic adjustment. Guidelines for motivating salespeople follow:

1. Recruit and select salespeople whose personal motives match the requirements and rewards of the job.
2. Attempt to incorporate the individual needs of salespeople into motivational programs.
3. Provide adequate job information and assure proper skill development for the salesforce.
4. Use job design and redesign as motivational tools.
5. Concentrate on building the self-esteem of salespeople.
6. Take a proactive approach to seeking out motivational problems and sources of frustration in the salesforce.

Recruitment and Selection

The importance of matching the abilities and needs of sales recruits to the requirements and rewards of the job cannot be overstated. This is especially critical for sales managers who have little opportunity to alter job dimensions and reward structures. Investing more time in recruitment and selection to assure a good match is likely to pay off later in terms of fewer motivational and other managerial problems. A regional manager for a business products company echoes these sentiments: "Our motivational program is built around goals, evaluations, and hiring the right people. It is not unusual for an applicant to visit our office six or seven times before a hiring decision is made. I want to get to know each person as thoroughly as possible before I make a commitment."[46]

Incorporation of Individual Needs

At the outset of this chapter, motivation was described as a complex personal process. At the heart of the complexity of motivation is the concept of individual needs. While there is considerable pressure and, in many cases, sound economic rationale, for supporting mass approaches to salesforce motivation, there may also be opportunities to incorporate individual needs into motivational programs. As researchers learn more about the salesperson's career cycle, it is likely that more intrasalesforce diversity in motivational programs will occur. Salesforce segmentation offers some of the benefits of individualized approaches and may be a logical alternative in large salesforces.

Information and Skills

The importance of providing adequate job information is well documented in expectancy theory. If sales managers equip their salespeople to make accurate expectancy and instrumentality estimates, a major motivational task is accomplished. If the salespeople's estimates are accurate and in agreement with the sales managers, reasonable goals can be set that allow performance worthy of rewards. Providing adequate information to the salesforce and nurturing skill development can also enhance salesforce socialization (discussed in earlier chapters), thereby reducing role ambiguity and role conflict.

Job Design

Some of the more promising research into salesforce motivation is in the area of job design and redesign. For example, two studies found job skill variety, task significance, job autonomy, and job feedback to be significantly related to the intrinsic motivational levels of salespeople.[47] **Job skill variety** is the extent to which salespeople get a chance to use skills and abilities in a wide range of job behaviors. **Task significance** is the degree to which the salesperson feels the job makes a meaningful contribution and is important to the organization. **Job autonomy** is the ability of the person in a given job to determine the nature of the tasks and to chart a course of action. **Feedback** refers to the degree to which salespeople receive clear information concerning the effectiveness of their performance.

Given the nature of sales jobs, one would expect good opportunities to stimulate intrinsic motivation without major changes in the job. Job skill variety is already present in many sales jobs. And given the unique contributions of personal selling to the organization as discussed in Chapter 2, imparting a feeling of task significance to salespeople should be feasible. Certainly, time and territory management as practiced in many sales organizations contributes to a feeling of job autonomy. Finally, feedback from sales managers or through self-monitoring is fairly easy to arrange. In many ways, the motivational task of sales managers is much easier than for some of their managerial counterparts in the organization. The sales job itself can be a powerful motivator.

Building Self-Esteem

Researchers have emphasized the importance of building self-esteem to enhance motivation and performance of salespeople.[48] Practitioners have agreed. One sales executive who believes that nothing is more important than money in motivating salespeople adds,

> Equally important is helping salespeople meet their needs for self-esteem. Fewer occupational groups have stronger needs in this area . . . . Our experience shows that even where financial incentives are extraordinary, turnover is high when sales managers erode salespeople's self-esteem. There are limits to the financial incentives that can be offered. The supply of self-esteem incentives is unlimited, however, and sales managers would do well to use them more often.[49]

Sales managers can use the insights of reinforcement theorists to build self-esteem in the salesforce. Positive reinforcement for good performance should be standard procedure. This may be done with formal or informal communications or recognition programs designed to spotlight good performance. When performance is less than satisfactory, it should not be overlooked but addressed in a constructive manner.

Proactive Approach

Sales managers should be committed to uncovering potential problems in motivation and eliminating them before they develop. For example, if some members of the salesforce perceive a lack of opportunity for promotion into management and are demotivated as a result, the sales manager might take additional steps to clearly define the guidelines for promotion into management and review the performance of management hopefuls in light of these guidelines. If promotion opportunities are indeed limited, the matching function of recruitment and selection again shows its importance.[50]

Summary

1. Define motivation in terms of intensity, persistence, and direction. Motivation has been defined in a variety of ways. The definition we use incorporates the qualities of intensity, persistence, and direction. Intensity is the amount of mental and physical effort the salesperson is willing to expend on a specific activity. Persistence is a choice to expend effort over time, especially in the face of adversity. Direction implies that, to some extent, salespeople choose the activities on which effort is expended.

2. Discuss motivation as a process that begins with a perceived need deficiency. As shown in Figure 11.1, motivation begins when the individual perceives a need deficiency. Needs are classified differently by different theorists, but three rather generic types of human needs are economic, social, and self-actualizing needs. When a need deficiency is perceived, people search for ways to satisfy the need and then engage in goal-directed behavior. Their performance on the job is usually followed by some form of reward or punishment, after which needs are reassessed.

3.   **Discuss the basic points of four content theories and four process theories of motivation.** The four content theories of motivation discussed in this chapter were Maslow's need-hierarchy theory (Figure 11.2), Alderfer's ERG theory, Herzberg's hygiene-motivation theory, and McClelland's learned-needs theory. The four process theories of motivation presented were expectancy theory (Figure 11.4), equity theory (Figure 11.5), attribution theory (Figure 11.6), and reinforcement theory (Exhibit 11.1).

4.   **Identify key issues in salesforce motivation.** One important issue deals with the question of how individualized motivational programs can be. While there are obvious advantages to incorporating individual needs into such programs, there are also strong arguments for a mass approach. Salesforce segmentation can compromise between individualized and mass approaches. Other important issues are the aging workforce, the incidence of job burnout among salespeople, and the expectations of today's emerging salesforce, including an apparently increasing desire for material possessions. Still another issue is the current trend to reevaluate traditional practices of salesforce motivation, including a strong reliance on rewards and punishment and the use of motivational speakers.

5.   **Cite managerial guidelines for salesforce motivation.** Six managerial guidelines for motivating salespeople are as follows: First, match the recruit to the requirements and rewards of the job. Second, incorporate individual needs into motivational programs when feasible. Third, provide salespeople with adequate information and ensure proper skill development to facilitate job performance. Fourth, cultivate salespeople's self-esteem. Fifth, take a proactive approach to uncovering motivational problems. Sixth, try to eliminate problems before they become serious.

Key Terms

- **Motivation**
- **Intensity**
- **Persistence**
- **Direction**
- **Intrinsic motivation**
- **Extrinsic motivation**
- **Economic needs**
- **Social needs**
- **Self-actualization needs**
- **Goal-directed behavior**
- **Content theories of motivation**
- **Process theories of motivation**

- **Maslow's need-hierarchy theory**
- **Alderfer's ERG theory**
- **Herzberg's hygiene-motivation theory**
- **Hygiene factors**
- **Motivation factors**
- **McClelland's learned-needs theory**
- **Expectancy theory**
- **Expectancies**
- **Instrumentalities**
- **Valence for rewards**
- **Equity theory**
- **Attribution theory**

- ▪ **Reinforcement theory**
- ▪ **Positive reinforcement**
- ▪ **Negative reinforcement**
- ▪ **Punishment**
- ▪ **Extinction**
- ▪ **Salesforce segmentation**
- ▪ **Comfort seekers**
- ▪ **Spotlight seekers**
- ▪ **Developers**

- ▪ **Career plateau**
- ▪ **Job burnout**
- ▪ **Job enrichment**
- ▪ **Career pathing**
- ▪ **Job skill variety**
- ▪ **Task significance**
- ▪ **Job autonomy**
- ▪ **Feedback**

Review Questions

1. Explain motivation in terms of intensity, persistence, and direction.
2. Explain the motivation process in terms of events that follow a perceived need deficiency.
3. How are the need hierarchies of Maslow and Alderfer alike? How do they differ?
4. Explain how McClelland's learned needs (achievement, power, and affiliation) correspond to dimensions of the other three content theories of motivation.
5. Explain the meanings of these terms: expectancies, instrumentalities, and valence for rewards.
6. How does attribution theory differ from the other three process theories of motivation?
7. Why should sales managers be concerned with theoretical approaches to motivation?
8. What is meant by salesforce segmentation? When might segmentation work for motivational purposes?
9. Review the blocked insert entitled "A Global Perspective: Toyota Salesperson Janet Lim." How important is self-motivation in determining sales success?
10. Review the blocked insert entitled "An Ethical Perspective: Preventing Burnout with Career Paths." Can you identify other areas in salesforce motivation where sales managers have ethical responsibilities?

Application Exercises

1. You are a national sales manager, with 150 salespeople in your organization. Your salespeople range in age from 22 to 67, with the average age being 36. Average earnings, including salary and bonuses, are $48,000 per year. Recently, you hired a consulting firm to assess the motivational level and reward preferences of your salesforce. You are now interpreting the findings of the consulting firm, and you are puzzled by one conclusion in particular.

According to the consultants, the older salespeople voiced stronger preferences for increased pay than did the younger salespeople. Since the older salespeople generally earn more money than do their younger counterparts, and you subscribe to the concepts of Maslow's need hierarchy, you find this surprising. You had always reasoned that since older salespeople earned more money, they probably placed more value on higher-order needs such as esteem and self-actualization. What are the possible explanations for this unexpected finding?

2. In his book, *Sales Manager's Problem-Solver*, Leon Wortman introduces us to a character called "no-no."[51] No-no is a malcontent, who never has a positive thing to say to other company personnel. He is a chronic complainer, but there is one good thing about him—he does a great job with his customers and regularly achieves high sales performance levels. When anyone suggests he adopt a more positive approach, he screams that he is not a robot and that he has a right to question the way things are done. Though highly intelligent, he has no idea of the disruptive effects he is having on his coworkers. At this point, assume you are no-no's sales manager, and your boss, having become aware of the problem, has asked you to present some options for dealing with no-no. You have come up with five options:

a.   Talk with the other salespeople and try to get them to be more tolerant of no-no.

b.   Ask one of his friends, or maybe someone from personnel, to take him aside and explain how his behavior is detrimental to the company.

c.   Apply some gentle pressure, much like a parent who tries to manage an unruly child.

d.   Assume others (family, peers, the company, or maybe you) are to blame for his behavior, and try to have a friendly conversation to uncover the underlying problem.

e.   Consider the possibility that he might be too intelligent for the job, and provide job enrichment to give him more challenging assignments.

Now that you have come up with these options, identify the advantages and disadvantages of each one.

3.   It is Monday morning, and Bill Jackson, the sales manager for a major-league baseball team, has the 15 members of the group ticket salesforce assembled for what promises to be an explosive meeting. Jackson is unhappy with last week's sales report, and he fully intends to do something about it. After a few preliminary announcements, he addresses the salesforce as follows:

> The numbers from last week are in, and I've got to wonder what you people did last week. I know one thing—you didn't sell enough to be called salespeople! How many of you sold at least 500 tickets last week? [A few hands go up, and Jackson continues.]
>
> Well, big deal! I could probably sell 500 tickets without getting out of bed. How many of you so-called salespeople sold 1,000 tickets last week—I know the answer, I just wanted to see if any of you know just how lousy you are. [This time, no one raises a hand, and Jackson concludes the meeting with these comments.]
>
> This week better be different. You get out there and call on every civic organization, corporation, and social club in town, and I mean *sell, sell, sell* huge blocks of tickets! Bat day is coming up, and I want a full house. Let me make one thing crystal clear—if you do not personally sell 1,000 tickets this week, don't bother to come to work next Monday. Now, hit the streets!

How would you react to Mr. Jackson's exhortations if you were one of the salespeople? What type of person would react most negatively? Most positively?

Notes

[1]Orville C. Walker, Jr., Gilbert A. Churchill, Jr., and Neil M. Ford, "Where Do We Go from Here? Selected Conceptual and Empirical Issues Concerning the Motivation and Performance of the Industrial Salesforce," in *Critical Issues in Sales Management: State-of-the-Art and Future Research Needs*, eds. Gerald Albaum and Gilbert A. Churchill, Jr. (Eugene, Ore.: Division of Research, College of Business Administration, University of Oregon, 1979), 25.

[2]Barton A. Weitz, Harish Sujan, and Mita Sujan, "Knowledge, Motivation, and Adaptive Behavior: A Framework for Improving Selling Effectiveness," *Journal of Marketing* 50 (October 1986): 180–181.

[3]See Thomas R. Wotruba, "The Effect of Goal-Setting on the Performance of Independent Sales Agents in Direct Selling," *Journal of Personal Selling and Sales Management* 9 (Spring

1989): 22–29; and Jeffrey K. Sager and Mark W. Johnston, "Antecedents and Outcomes of Organizational Commitment: A Study of Salespeople," *Journal of Personal Selling and Sales Management* 9 (Spring 1989): 30–41.

[4] A study of salespeople that illustrates the interrelationship, yet distinctiveness, of intrinsic and extrinsic dimensions of motivation is Thomas N. Ingram, Keun S. Lee, and Steven J. Skinner, "An Empirical Assessment of Salesperson Motivation, Commitment, and Job Outcomes," *Journal of Personal Selling and Sales Management* 9 (Fall 1989): 25–33.

[5] Z. S. Demirdjian, "A Multidimensional Approach to Motivating Salespeople," *Industrial Marketing Management* 13 (February 1984): 25–32.

[6] Robert Whyte, "So You Think You're Motivating," in *Sales Training and Motivation: A Special Report* (New York: Sales and Marketing Management, 1977), 2.

[7] Leon A. Wortman, *Sales Manager's Problem-Solver* (New York: John Wiley and Sons, 1983), 208.

[8] Walker, Churchill, and Ford, "Where Do We Go from Here?" 40.

[9] Ibid.

[10] Robert L. Berl, Nicholas C. Williamson, and Terry Powell, "Industrial Salesforce Motivation: A Critique and Test of Maslow's Hierarchy of Need," *Journal of Personal Selling and Sales Management* 4 (May 1984): 33–39.

[11] Abraham H. Maslow, "A Theory of Human Motivation," *Psychological Review* 50 (July 1943): 370–396.

[12] Richard P. Bagozzi, "Performance and Satisfaction in an Industrial Sales Force: An Examination of Their Antecedents and Simultaneity," *Journal of Marketing* 44 (Spring 1980): 65–77.

[13] Robert T. Adkins and John E. Swan, "Increase Salespeople's Prestige with a New Title," *Industrial Marketing Management* 9 (February 1980): 1–9.

[14] Clayton P. Alderfer, "An Empirical Test of a New Theory of Human Needs," *Organizational Behavior and Human Performance* 4 (May 1969): 142–175.

[15] Frederick Herzberg, Bernard Mauser, and R. Snyderman, *The Motivation to Work* (New York: John Wiley and Sons, 1959).

[16] Leon Winer and J. S. Schiff, "Industrial Salespeople's Views on Motivation," *Industrial Marketing Management* 9 (October 1980): 319–323.

[17] See Robert Berl, Terry Powell, and Nicholas C. Williamson, "Industrial Salesforce Satisfaction and Performance with Herzberg's Theory," *Industrial Marketing Management* 13 (February 1984): 11–19; and David D. Shipley and Julia A. Kiely, "Industrial Salesforce Motivation and Herzberg's Dual Factor Theory: A UK Perspective," *Journal of Personal Selling and Sales Management* 6 (May 1986): 9–16.

[18] David C. McClelland, "Business Drive and National Achievement," *Harvard Business Review* 40 (July–August 1962): 99–112. For a discussion of McClelland's theory of learned needs in sales management, see Leon A. Wortman, "Does Practice Support Theory?" *Business Marketing*, November 1988, 81–83.

[19] Walker, Churchill, and Ford, "Where Do We Go from Here?" 44–45.

[20] Stephen X. Doyle and Benson P. Shapiro, "What Counts Most in Motivating Your Sales Force?" *Harvard Business Review* 58 (May–June 1980): 133–140.

[21] Keun S. Lee, "A Typology of Industrial Salespeople Using Organizational Commitment and Job Involvement: A Framework of Predicting Behavioral Dimensions," in *1989 AMA Educators' Proceedings: Enhancing Knowledge Development in Marketing*, ed. Paul Bloom et al. (Chicago: American Marketing Association, 1989), 56–61.

[22] Victor H. Vroom, *Work and Motivation* (New York: John Wiley and Sons, 1964).

[23] Orville C. Walker, Jr., Gilbert A. Churchill, Jr., and Neil M. Ford, "Motivation and Performance in Industrial Selling: Present Knowledge and Needed Research," *Journal of Marketing Research* 14 (May 1977): 156–168.

[24] Kenneth R. Evans, Loren Margheim, and John L. Schlacter, "A Review of Expectancy Theory Research in Selling," *Journal of Personal Selling and Sales Management* 2 (November 1982): 34.

[25] For an illustration of how sales managers can use expectancy theory to motivate their salesforces, see Thomas L. Quick, "The Best-Kept Secret for Increasing Productivity," *Sales and Marketing Management*, July 1989, 34–38.

[26] J. Stacy Adams, "Toward an Understanding of Inequity," *Journal of Abnormal and Social Psychology* 67 (November 1963): 422–436.

[27] R. Kenneth Teas and James C. McElroy, "Causal Attributions and Expectancy Estimates: A Framework for Understanding the Dynamics of Salesforce Motivation," *Journal of Marketing* 50 (January 1986): 75–86.

[28] Weitz, Sujan, and Sujan, "Knowledge, Motivation, and Adaptive Behavior," 181–182.

[29] Gordon J. Badovick, "Emotional Reactions and Salesperson Motivation: An Attributional Approach Following Inadequate Sales Performance," *Journal of the Academy of Marketing Science* 18 (Spring 1990): 123–130.

[30] B. F. Skinner, *Beyond Freedom and Dignity* (New York: Alfred Knopf Inc., 1971).

[31] Daniel A. Sauers, James B. Hunt, and Ken Bass, "Behavioral Self-Management as a Supplement to External Sales Force Controls," *Journal of Personal Selling and Sales Management* 10 (Summer 1990): 17–28.

[32]"If the Customer Isn't Satisfied, the Salesman Isn't Paid," *Sales and Marketing Management*, April 1990, 136.

[33]Wortman, *Sales Manager's Problem-Solver*, 229.

[34]Herbert Moissen and Eugene H. Fram, "Segmentation for Sales Force Motivation," *Akron Business and Economic Review* (Winter 1973): 5–12.

[35]Thomas N. Ingram and Danny N. Bellenger, "Motivational Segments in the Salesforce," *California Management Review* 24 (Spring 1982): 81–88.

[36]Patrick L. Schul, Steven Remington, and Robert L. Berl, "Assessing Gender Differences in Relationships Between Supervisory Behaviors and Job-Related Outcomes in the Industrial Sales Force," *Journal of Personal Selling and Sales Management* 10 (Summer 1990): 1–16.

[37]Thayer C. Taylor, "Meet the Sales Force of the Future," *Sales and Marketing Management*, March 10, 1986, 59–60.

[38]John W. Slocum, Jr., William L. Cron, Richard W. Hansen, and Sallie Rawlings, "Business Strategy and the Management of Plateaued Employees," *Academy of Management Journal* 28 (March 1985): 133–154.

[39]Suzanne K. Stout, John W. Slocum, Jr., and William L. Cron, "Dynamics of the Career Plateauing Process," *Journal of Vocational Behavior* 32 (February 1988): 74–91.

[40]Frances Meritt Stern and Ron Zemke, *Stressless Selling*, rev. ed., (New York: American Management Association, 1990).

[41]W. E. Patton III and Michael Questell, "Alcohol Abuse in the Sales Force," *Journal of Personal Selling and Sales Management* 6 (November 1986): 39–51.

[42]W. E. Patton III, "Drug Abuse in the Sales Force," *Journal of Personal Selling and Sales Management* 8 (August 1988): 21–33.

[43]Stephen B. Castleberry, "The Importance of Various Motivational Factors to College Students Interested in Sales Positions," *Journal of Personal Selling and Sales Management* 10 (Spring 1990): 67–72.

[44]Michael H. Morris, Ramon Avila, and Eugene Teeple, "Sales Management as an Entrepreneurial Activity," *Journal of Personal Selling and Sales Management* 10 (Summer 1990): 1–11.

[45]Speakers' fees as appearing in Melissa Campanelli, "Finding a Speaker Who'll Set 'Um Cheering," *Sales and Marketing Management*, November 1989, 100–102.

[46]Doyle and Shapiro, "What Counts Most?" 136.

[47]See Richard C. Becherer, Fred W. Morgan, and Lawrence M. Richard, "The Job Characteristics of Industrial Salespersons: Relationship to Motivation and Satisfaction," *Journal of Marketing* 46 (Fall 1982): 125–135; and Pradeep K. Tyagi, "Relative Importance of Key Job Dimensions and Leadership Behaviors in Motivating Salesperson Work Performance," *Journal of Marketing* 49 (Summer 1985): 76–86.

[48]See Alan J. Dubinsky, Roy D. Howell, Thomas N. Ingram, and Danny N. Bellenger, "Salesforce Socialization," *Journal of Marketing* 50 (October 1986): 192–207; and Bagozzi, "Performance and Satisfaction in an Industrial Sales Force."

[49]Nicholas H. Ward, "Drop Those Salesman Psychology Myths," *Industrial Marketing*, July 1981, 91.

[50]Alan J. Dubinsky and Mary E. Lippit, "Managing Frustration in the Sales Force," *Industrial Marketing Management* 8 (July 1979): 200–206.

[51]Wortman, *Sales Manager's Problem-Solver*, 41–46.

CASE 11.1   *Medical Rentals Inc.*

Background

Medical Rentals Inc. (MRI) is a multilocation operation in the Midwest, with branch offices in Chicago, Indianapolis, Milwaukee, and Detroit. MRI provides convalescent care equipment for leasing to hospitals, clinics, home-health agencies, and the general public. Equipment available from MRI includes dialysis machines, various forms of monitoring devices, and respiratory equipment.

Betty Crenshaw is the general sales manager for MRI. She lives in Chicago and spends about half of her time there. The remainder of her time is divided between the other three branch offices. Each of the branches, including Chicago, has six salespeople. In each branch, the salespeople report to a sales supervisor, each of whom report directly to Betty.

Current Situation

MRI salespeople are paid on a straight salary plus bonus, which is based on achieving a dollar-volume sales quota. Salespeople receive a 10 percent bonus for making quota and an additional percentage point for every percentage point over quota that they achieve. There is a cap on total bonus of 35 percent. In other words, salespeople would "max" bonus by exceeding their quotas by 25 percent.

Five years ago, MRI had instituted two policies that were now having some interesting effects on the morale of the salesforce. First, MRI began to hire only college graduates for its sales positions. In the past, a college degree was not a strict job qualification, and many of the veteran MRI salespeople did not have a college education.

Next, MRI formulated a formal salary administration plan. The firm paid competitive entry-level salaries to attract college graduates, then granted annual increases based on performance. While "performance" was assessed on several dimensions, the sales versus quota performance was by far the most important determinant of any increase in pay. Strictly speaking, a salesperson need not make quota in a given year to receive some form of a raise. Salary increases were limited by company policy to 10 percent per year and typically averaged about 6 percent.

During the past few months, Betty has been hearing a lot of complaints from her veteran salespeople, who feel they are underpaid relative to the more recent hires. They feel that the salary administration plan has constrained their earnings, making it difficult to realize any gains in their real income or spending power. They also point out that MRI is more than happy to pay whatever the market dictates to hire its new salespeople off the college campuses and that some of the recent hires are earning almost as much as some of the veteran salespeople.

Betty is thinking about several alternatives to address the situation. She is considering the establishment of a "senior sales representative" designation for those salespeople who have performed well over a period of several years. Salespeople earning this designation would get an automatic pay increase, though she had not yet determined the appropriate amount for the increase. She is also considering a "do-nothing" strategy, reasoning that there is really little she could do to permanently solve the problem. After all, entry-level salaries have historically increased from year to year, while the salary administration program placed hard limits on how much existing salaries could increase.

Questions

1. What other alternatives should Betty consider?
2. How could equity theory be useful to Betty as she formulates and implements a plan of action?
3. What do you recommend that Betty do?

CASE 11.2 *Metropolitan Transportation Maintenance Inc.*

Background

Metropolitan Transportation Maintenance Inc. (MTM) is a contracting company that specializes in road, bridge, and overpass repair. The company has experienced tremendous growth in recent years, as many of the nation's roads are requiring major repairs. MTM concentrates its sales efforts in selected metropolitan areas with populations in excess of 750,000. Generally speaking, MTM has one sales representative per metro area, with as many as three salespeople in areas such as New York and Los Angeles. MTM has a total of 30 salespeople.

Fred Donnelly is the MTM national sales manager, with all of the salespeople reporting directly to him. He travels four out of five days each week, spending Monday in his New York office. With such a large salesforce, he relies on weekly reports from the field to keep him informed on key developments. These reports are submitted via an electronic mail system, which is also used by Donnelly and his salespeople to keep each other informed of late-breaking opportunities and problems.

Current Situation

Fred Donnelly is having some problems with one of his salespeople. Ron Tremaine, the sales representative in New Orleans, has been chronically late with his weekly reports over the past two months. He failed to submit reports on two occasions, causing Donnelly to arrange an unscheduled trip to New Orleans to get Tremaine back on track.

When questioned about the sloppy reporting, Tremaine seemed lackadaisical. He told Donnelly that he did not really see the need for weekly reports, since he could notify Donnelly of any "really important" news at any time via the electronic mail system. Donnelly had explained that he needed the reports to get a complete picture of competitive activity and sales performance across the country. Further, he pointed out to Tremaine that the weekly reports were used for planning his visits to the sales territories.

As he prepared to leave New Orleans, Donnelly told Tremaine: "Look, Ron, I need those reports on time. Let's make a deal — you get me the reports on time for the next 90 days, and the next time I get to New Orleans, you and your financée will be my guests for dinner. You pick the spot — Arnaud's, Commander's Palace, Le Ruth's — anywhere you want to go."

Ron got his reports in on time for the next six weeks, then sent them in late two weeks in a row.

The next week, the reports did not arrive at all. He left a couple of rather cryptic messages on the electronic mail system to the effect of, "Sorry I am late, nothing much going on anyway, details to follow." But the details were not forthcoming. Although Donnelly was extremely busy, it looked like he would have to make time to work Ron Tremaine into his schedule.

Questions

1. Can you offer some possible explanations for why Tremaine does not submit his weekly reports on time?
2. How does reinforcement theory relate to this situation?
3. What should Fred Donnelly do next?

Managing Salesforce Reward Systems

MERRILL LYNCH FACES THE FUTURE WITH A NEW BROKER REWARD SYSTEM   Some time-honored traditions in the brokerage business may soon become extinct. Merrill Lynch, the nation's largest and most visible securities company, has announced major changes in the way its brokers will be paid. Hoping to reduce turnover rates in its salesforce and improve overall performance, the company will pay longevity bonuses to certain brokers, improved commissions to new brokers, and a base salary to trainees.

The longevity bonus is designed to encourage productive brokers to stay with the firm for a minimum of 10 years. After this period, if certain performance targets are achieved and the broker has complied with company directives, a bonus of $100,000 will be paid. The payment of the bonus, however, is not assured merely by completing 10 years of service, for, as company officials estimate, if the program had been in place during the past decade, 20 to 25 percent of the salesforce would have been eligible.

Paying new brokers a base salary while they complete a two-year training program is unique, as is Merrill's plan to allow trainees to earn bonuses. A spokesperson for the company says that trainees will learn their business in more depth, rather than placing emphasis on short-term sales volume.

Obviously, this program could cost Merrill Lynch a fair amount of money, although the firm is not disclosing its cost estimates. Clearly, the company hopes to offset the incremental expenses with improved performance. As one industry analyst says: "Retaining the high-end broker is very important. To provide incentives to keep higher-end people around probably does have a beneficial impact on the bottom line."

The logic of Merrill's plan seems quite sound, given the customer fallout after the market crash of 1987. Merrill Lynch is banking on the investment consumer's ability to recognize and appreciate the increased performance and knowledge of their brokers, and, apparently, the firm is willing to pay a price for improved customer perceptions.

Source: Michael Scionolfi, "Merrill Revamps Broker's Training, Pay," *The Wall Street Journal*, December 11, 1990, Cl.

Learning Objectives

After completing this chapter, you should be able to

1 *Explain the difference between compensation rewards and non-compensation rewards.*

2 *Describe the primary financial and nonfinancial compensation rewards available to salespeople.*

3 *Describe salary, commission, and combination pay plans in terms of their advantages and disadvantages.*

4 *Explain the fundamental concepts in sales-expense reimbursement.*

5 *Discuss issues associated with the use of sales contests, pay secrecy versus pay disclosure, equal pay for equal work, and changing a reward system.*

6 *List the guidelines for managing a reward system.*

The opening vignette introduces several topics regarding the management of salesforce job rewards. A salesforce reward system, because of its impact on motivation and job satisfaction, is one of the most important determinants of both short- and long-term sales performance. The Merrill Lynch vignette reminds us, furthermore, that salesforce reward systems can also affect customer satisfaction with a company and its salespeople. Reward systems must be linked to the entire sales management system in a logical manner; otherwise, enormous waste is possible. To complement the changes in the reward system, Merrill Lynch is also investing heavily in an expanded broker training program. Substantial investments such as those being made by Merrill Lynch must provide appropriate returns if additional changes are to be avoided.

To illustrate the challenges inherent in managing salesforce reward systems, consider the findings of national consulting firms. Russell Roberts of Sibson & Company, a major consulting firm, asserts that most major companies fail to maximize salesforce productivity due to shortcomings in their reward systems. He says that some of the reward systems are too complex, some are too simple and narrow in scope, and many are not coordinated with the company's marketing and financial objectives.[1]

Another consultant, Suzanne Minken of A.S. Hansen Inc., points out that 60 percent of large companies surveyed are using a single performance measure—overall sales growth—in incentive programs, when they should be using a variety of criteria, including new accounts and mix of products sold, that reflect the firm's marketing plan.[2]

In the first section of this chapter, the characteristics of an effective reward system will be discussed along with the reward preferences of salespeople in general. The next section will concentrate on financial rewards such as salaries, commissions, and bonuses. Expense reimbursement will also be covered. As illustrated in Figure 12.1, expenditures for financial rewards are quite substantial, often being the largest component of the sales organization's budget.

Nonfinancial rewards such as opportunities for growth, recognition, and promotion will be reviewed. Current issues in reward system management such as the use of sales contests, pay secrecy versus pay disclosure, equal pay for equal work, and changing reward systems will be presented. The chapter will conclude with summary guidelines for managing salesforce reward systems.

Before addressing these topics, we should explain that **reward system management** involves the selection and utilization of organizational rewards to direct salespeople's behavior toward the attainment of organizational objectives. An organizational reward could be anything from a $5,000 pay raise to a pat on the back for a job well done.

Organizational rewards can be classified as compensation and non-compensation rewards. **Compensation rewards** are those that are given in return for acceptable performance or effort. It is important to note that compensation rewards can include nonfinancial compensation, such as recognition, and opportunities for growth and promotion.

Non-compensation rewards include factors related to the work situation and well-being of each salesperson. Job-design factors as discussed in Chapter 11 (skill variety, task significance, autonomy, and feedback) can certainly be viewed as

FIGURE 12.1 ▪ *Average Costs of Financial Compensation for Salespeople*

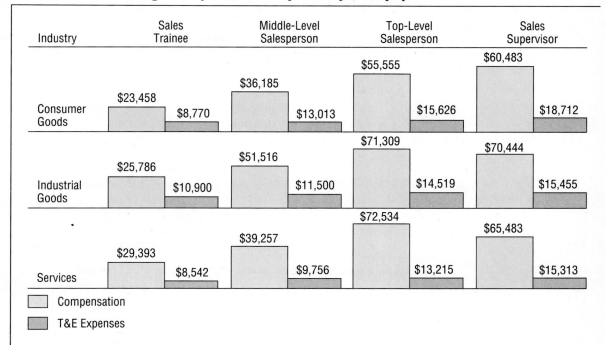

Notes: Financial compensation includes base salary, commission, and bonus. T&E expenses include travel, entertainment, food, and lodging costs.
Source: "Hey, Where's My Survey of Selling Costs?" *Sales and Marketing Management*, March 1991, 43.

non-compensation rewards when properly utilized. Other examples of non-compensation rewards are (1) providing adequate resources so that salespeople can accomplish their jobs and (2) practicing a supportive sales management leadership style. In this chapter, the focus is on compensation rewards, including financial and nonfinancial compensation.

The Optimal Salesforce Reward System

The optimal reward system balances the needs of the organization, its salespeople, and its customers against one another. From the organization's perspective, the reward system should help accomplish these results:

1. Provide an acceptable ratio of costs and salesforce output in volume, profit, or other objectives.
2. Encourage specific activities consistent with the firm's overall, marketing, and salesforce objectives and strategies. For example, the firm may use the reward system to encourage selling particular products or to conduct important follow-up after the sale.

3. Attract and retain competent salespeople, thereby enhancing long-term customer relationships.

4. Allow the kind of adjustments that facilitate administration of the reward system. A clearly stated, reasonably flexible plan assists in the administration of the plan.

On the surface, these characteristics sound reasonable, logical, and feasible for most sales organizations. Recall, however, the remarks of consultants in the opening part of this chapter indicating that many companies are struggling with their reward systems. Consider environmental pressures that sometimes cause pay freezes, pay reductions, cutbacks in formal recognition programs, and limited opportunities for promotion into management. Further consider the seemingly insatiable desires of even the best-paid salespeople. Surveys have indicated that dissatisfaction with pay is a rather widespread phenomenon among salespeople.[3] Obviously, the management of salesforce reward systems is a difficult job.

From the perspective of the salesperson, reward systems are expected to meet a somewhat different set of criteria than from the sales manager's perspective. As indicated in the previous chapter, salespeople expect to be treated equitably, with rewards comparable to those of others in the organization doing a similar job—and to the rewards of competitors' salespeople. Most salespeople prefer some stability in the reward system, but they simultaneously want incentive rewards for superior performance. The desire for stabilizing and incentive components was borne out by a study that found 89 percent of salespeople preferred to be paid by a combination of a salary plus incentives in commission or bonus.[4] Since the most productive salespeople have the best opportunities to leave the firm for more

AN ETHICAL PERSPECTIVE

Salesperson Rewards and Customer Trust   During the 1980s, Prudential-Bache experienced impressive sales growth in the area of real estate investments. When George Ball took over as president of the firm in 1982, the company's brokers were lagging behind industry standards in terms of gross commissions. Ball began recruiting the best brokers from rival firms, often using generous hiring bonuses as the main attraction. Once on board, the brokers were pressured to sell Prudential-Bache products, since in-house products returned commissions as high as 7 percent, compared with 2 percent or less on stock trading.

As time passed, the salesforce showed some resistance to push the in-house products, and several former executives allege that the salesforce is at a near-mutiny stage over the lack of product quality. The word spread that branch managers who were unwilling to aggressively sell the more profitable products should leave the company. Customers began complaining in significant numbers. By 1990, a number of class action suits had been filed by angry customers, who charged that they had been misled by Prudential-Bache salespeople.

Sales managers must realize the power of the salesforce compensation plan and must use that power judiciously. In many cases, reward systems that emphasize short-term sales results may ultimately damage customer trust and sales performance.

Source: Aaron Bernstein, "How Pushing Real Estate Backfired on Pru-Bache," *Business Week*, February 26, 1990, 88–91.

attractive work situations, the preferences of the salesforce regarding compensation must be given due consideration.

In recent years, the needs of the customer have become more important than the needs of the salesforce in determining the structure of reward systems in sales organizations. Recognizing the strength of long-term alliances with customers as a key to survival, some firms have reacted by changing salesforce reward systems. For example, some automobile dealers have tried to reduce customer dissatisfaction stemming from high-pressure sales techniques by paying their salespeople a salary instead of a commission based on sales volume. A few years ago, Metropolitan Insurance converted a portion of its salesforce to straight salary in order to better control follow-up activities, which had been neglected in favor of selling new policies. Network Equipment Technologies in Redwood City, California, pays its salespeople a full commission only after customer satisfaction has been verified.[5] Interestingly, Network Equipment's salespeople report that a commission based on customer satisfaction is a strong selling point. For more on salesforce rewards as they affect customers' interests, see "An Ethical Perspective: Salesperson Rewards and Customer Trust."

Meeting the needs of customers, salespeople, and the sales organization simultaneously is indeed a challenging task. As you might suspect, compromise between sometimes divergent interests becomes essential for managing most salesforce reward systems. As noted by Greenberg and Greenberg, "A salesforce is comprised of individual human beings with broadly varying needs, points of view, and psychological characteristics who cannot be infallibly categorized, measured, and punched out to formula."[6]

Types of Salesforce Rewards

For discussion purposes, the countless number of specific rewards available to salespeople will be classified into six categories (ranked in order of salespeople's preferences), as shown in Exhibit 12.1: pay, promotion, sense of accomplishment, personal growth opportunities, recognition, and job security. Each of these reward

---

EXHIBIT 12.1 ▪ *Salesforce Rewards Ranked in Order of Preference*

Pay

Promotion

Sense of Accomplishment

Personal Growth Opportunities

Recognition

Job Security

Source: Compiled from two studies: Thomas N. Ingram and Danny N. Bellenger, "Personal and Organizational Variables: Their Relative Effect on Reward Valences of Industrial Salespeople," *Journal of Marketing Research* 20 (May 1983): 198–205; and Neil M. Ford, Gilbert A. Churchill, Jr., and Orville C. Walker, Jr., "Differences in the Attractiveness of Alternative Rewards Among Industrial Salespeople: Additional Evidence," *Journal of Business Research* 13 (April 1985): 123–138.

EXHIBIT 12.2   ▪   *Types of Financial Compensation for Salespeople*

Salary plans	27%
Straight salary	
All commission plans	27%
Straight commission	24%
Commission + bonus	3%
All combination plans	50%
Salary + commission	11%
Salary + bonus	28%
Salary + commission + bonus	11%

Note: Total may exceed 100% because more than one plan may be used by a company.

Source: John P. Steinbrink, ed., *The Dartnell Sales Manager's Handbook* (Chicago: The Dartnell Corporation, 1989), 1024.

categories will be discussed in the next two sections of this chapter. The financial-compensation section will focus on pay, and the nonfinancial-compensation section on the other rewards shown in Exhibit 12.1.

Financial Compensation

In many sales organizations, financial compensation is composed of current spendable income, deferred income or retirement pay, and various insurance plans that may provide income when needed. Our discussion will be limited to the current spendable income, as it is the most controllable, and arguably most important, dimension of a salesforce reward system. The other components of financial compensation tend to be dictated more by overall company policy rather than by sales managers.

Current spendable income includes money provided in the short term (weekly, monthly, and annually) that allows salespeople to pay for desired goods and services. It includes salaries, commissions, and bonuses. Bonus compensation may include noncash income equivalents such as merchandise and free-travel awards. A comprehensive study of salesforce financial-compensation practices found salaries, commissions, and bonuses to be widely used to pay salespeople. The study concluded that financial-compensation plans including a salary and one or more incentives (commission and/or bonus) are the most popular among consumer and industrial firms.[7] These conclusions were supported in another survey of financial-compensation practices, as summarized in Exhibit 12.2.

The three basic types of salesforce financial-compensation plans are straight salary, straight commission, and a salary plus incentive, with the incentive being a commission and/or a bonus. A discussion of each type follows (summarized in Exhibit 12.3).

Straight Salary

As indicated in Exhibit 12.2, slightly over one-fourth of the surveyed companies pay at least some of their salespeople **straight salary** (exclusively by a salary). Such plans are well suited for paying sales support and existing-business salespeople,

EXHIBIT 12.3 ▪ *Summary of Financial-Compensation Plans*

Type of Plan	Advantages	Disadvantages	Common Uses
Salary ¼ used	Simple to administer; planned earnings facilitates budgeting and recruiting; customer loyalty enhanced; more control of nonselling activities	No financial incentive to improve performance; pay often based on seniority, not merit; salaries may be a burden to new firms or to those in declining industries	Sales trainees; team selling; sales support; seasonal sales
Commission ¼ used	Income linked to results; strong financial incentive to improve results; costs reduced during slow sales periods; less operating capital required	Difficult to build loyalty of salesforce to company; less control of nonselling activities	Real estate; insurance; wholesaling; securities; automobiles
Combination ½ used.	Flexibility allows frequent reward of desired behavior; may attract high-potential but unproven recruits	Complex to administer; may encourage crisis-oriented objectives	Widely used—most popular type of financial pay plan

those in seasonal or high-technology industries, those involved in team selling, and sales trainees.[8]

Sales support personnel, including missionaries and detailers, are involved in situations where it is difficult to determine who really makes the sale. Since missionaries and detailers are primarily concerned with dissemination of information rather than direct solicitation of orders, a salary can equitably compensate for effort. Compensation based on sales results would not be fair.

Salespeople who specialize in maintaining existing business, such as order-takers and route salespeople, are frequently paid by salary. These salespeople are not engaged in creative selling to a significant degree, and they are not usually expected to influence the size of the orders they are taking. Advertising may be more important in the sale of their products than personal selling, and incentives paid to these salespeople are likely to be an inefficient use of funds.

One example of a salesperson who specializes in maintaining existing business is the Exxon Dealer Sales Representative who sells to independent service station operators. Although some creative selling is required, the emphasis is on order-taking and performing a number of nonselling activities, as detailed in Exhibit 12.4. A straight-salary compensation plan is appropriate in such cases.

Salespeople who sell highly seasonal products such as college graduation rings make the large majority of their sales in the spring and spend the rest of the year developing new accounts. If these salespeople were paid by commission instead of salary, they would suffer a prolonged absence of income.

Sales engineers working in high-technology industries are another type of candidate for a salary plan, since they are frequently involved in advising customers, installing systems, training the customer's employees, and assisting in

EXHIBIT 12.4   ▪   *Primary Duties of an Exxon Dealer Sales Representative*

Company: Exxon Company, USA
Position: Dealer Sales Representative
Customers: Independent Service Station Operators

Primary Duties:

1. Achieve sales quota for gasoline, motor oil, tires, batteries, and automotive accessories by taking dealer orders on a regular basis.
2. Recruit new dealers on an as-needed basis.
3. Prepare documents to arrange financing for new dealers.
4. Provide training for service station personnel.
5. Provide business counseling for service station operators in the areas of merchandising and retail accounting practices.
6. Ensure that appearance standards of service stations are maintained, including having necessary repairs completed by outside contractors.
7. Maintain financial vigilance to ensure that dealers promptly remit proper lease payments to Exxon.

---

the diffusion of innovative products to the marketplace, sometimes over a period of years, making it difficult to assess their short-term sales performance.

Salary plans are also warranted when group, or team, selling is utilized. For example, if a field salesperson locates prospective customers, then works in concert with a team of financial, technical, and training specialists to confirm the sale, it is impossible to assess the relative contribution of each team member for incentive-pay purposes. Instead, each team member should receive a salary.

Finally, salaries are appropriate for sales trainees, who are involved in learning about the job rather than producing on the job. In most cases, a firm cannot recruit sales trainees on a college campus without the lure of a salary to be paid at least until training is completed.

Advantages of Salary Plans.   One advantage of using salary plans is that they are the simplest ones to administer, with adjustments usually occurring only once a year. Since salaries are fixed costs, **planned earnings** for the salesforce are easy to project, which facilitates the salesforce budgeting process. The fixed nature of planned earnings with salary plans may also facilitate recruitment and selection. For example, some recruits may be more likely to join the sales organization when their first-year earnings can be clearly articulated in salary terms rather than less certain commission terms.

Salaries can provide control over salespeople's activities, and reassigning salespeople and changing sales territories is less a problem with salary plans than with other financial-compensation plans. There is general agreement that salesforce loyalty to the company may be greater with salary plans and that there is less chance that high-pressure, non-customer-oriented sales techniques will be used.

Salaries are also used when substantial developmental work is required to open a new sales territory or introduce new products to the marketplace. Presumably, the income stability guaranteed by a salary allows the salesperson to concentrate on job activities rather than worry about how much the next paycheck will be. In general, salary plans allow more control over salesforce activities, especially nonselling activities.

Disadvantages of Salary Plans. The most serious shortcoming of straight-salary plans is that they offer little financial incentive to perform past a merely acceptable level. As a result, the least productive members of the salesforce are, in effect, the most rewarded salespeople. Conversely, the most productive salespeople are likely to think salary plans are inequitable.

Differences in salary levels among salespeople are often a function of seniority on the job instead of true merit. Even so, the constraints under which many salary plans operate may cause **salary compression,** or a narrow range of salaries in the salesforce. Thus, sales trainees may be earning close to what experienced salespeople earn, which could cause perceptions of inequity among experienced salespeople.

Salaries represent fixed overhead in a sales operation. If the market is declining or stagnating, the financial burden of the firm is greater with salary plans than with a variable expense such as commissions based on sales.

Straight Commission

Unlike straight-salary plans, commission-only plans, or **straight commission,** offer strong financial incentives to maximize performance. They also limit control of the salesforce, however. Some industries—real estate, insurance, automobiles, and securities—have traditionally paid salespeople by straight commission. In these industries, the primary responsibility of the salespeople is quite simply to close sales; nonselling activities are less important to the employer than in some other industries.

Manufacturers' representatives, who represent multiple manufacturers, are also paid by commission. Wholesalers, many of whom founded their businesses with limited working capital, also traditionally pay their salesforces by commission.

The huge direct-sales industry, including companies such as Mary Kay Cosmetics, Tupperware, and Avon, also pays by straight commission. The large number of salespeople working for these organizations makes salary payments impractical from an overhead and administrative standpoint. Avon, for example, has over 400,000 salespeople and simply could not afford to pay each of them a salary.[9]

Commission Plan Variations. There are several factors to be considered in developing a commission-only plan:

1. **Commission base**—volume or profitability.
2. **Commission rate**—constant, progressive, regressive, or a combination.
3. **Commission splits**—between two or more salespeople or between salespeople and the employer.

4. **Commission payout event** — when the order is confirmed, shipped, billed, paid for, or some combination of these events.

Commissions may be paid according to sales volume or some measure of profitability such as gross margin, contribution margin, or, in rare instances, net income. In recent years, there has been more experimentation with profitability-oriented commission plans in an effort to improve salesforce productivity.

Jerome A. Coletti, president of The Alexander Group Inc., a sales management consulting firm, advocates the use of profitability-based compensation programs but notes some common barriers to their use, including the strength of traditional sales management practices, which focus on sales volume in any form that it can be garnered. Coletti also observes that many sales departments lack the support functions to accurately conduct profitability analysis at the individual salesperson level.[10] Despite the gradual adoption of profitability-based commission plans by various companies, the most popular commission base appears to be sales volume.

Commission rates vary widely, and determining the appropriate rate is a weighty managerial task. The commission rate, or percentage paid to the salesperson, may be a **constant rate** over the pay period, which is an easy plan for the salespeople to understand and does provide incentive for them to produce more sales or profits (since pay is linked directly to performance). A **progressive rate** increases as salespeople reach prespecified targets. This provides an even stronger incentive to the salesperson, but it may result in overselling and higher selling costs. A **regressive rate** declines at some predetermined point. Regressive rates might be appropriate when the first order is hard to secure but reorders are virtually automatic. Such is the case for many manufacturer salespeople who sell to distributors and retailers.

Some circumstances might warrant a combination of a constant rate with either a progressive or regressive rate. For example, assume that a manufacturer has limited production capacity. The manufacturer wants to fully utilize capacity (i.e., sell out) but not oversell, because service problems would hamper future marketing plans. In such a case, the commission rate might be fixed, or perhaps progressive up to the point where capacity is almost fully utilized, then regressive to the point of full utilization.

When salespeople are paid on straight commission, the question of splitting commissions is of primary concern. To illustrate this point, consider a company with centralized purchasing, such as Delta Airlines. Delta may buy from a sales representative in Atlanta, where its headquarters are located, and have the product shipped to various hubs across the country. The salespeople in the hub cities are expected to provide local follow-up and be sure the product is performing satisfactorily. Which salespeople will receive how much commission? Procedures for splitting commissions are best established before such a question is asked.

There are no general rules for splitting commissions; rather, company-specific rules must be spelled out to avoid serious disputes. A company selling to Delta Airlines in the situation just described might decide to pay the salesperson who calls on the Atlanta headquarters 50 percent of the total commission and split the remaining 50 percent among the salespeople who serve the hub cities. The details of how commissions are split depend entirely on each company's situation.

Another issue in structuring straight-commission plans is when to pay the commission. The actual payment may be at any time interval, although monthly and quarterly payments are most commonplace. The question of when the commission is earned is probably just as important as when it is paid. The largest proportion of companies operating on the basis of sales-volume commissions declare the commission earned at the time the customer is billed for the order, rather than when the order is confirmed, shipped, or paid for.

Advantages of Commission Plans. One advantage of straight-commission plans is that salespeople's income is linked directly to desired results and therefore may be perceived as more equitable than salary plans. In the right circumstances, a strong financial incentive can provide superior results, and commission plans provide such an incentive.

From a cost-control perspective, commissions offer further advantages. Since commissions are a variable cost, operating costs are minimized during slack selling periods. Also, working capital requirements are lessened with commission-only pay plans. Before choosing a straight commission plan, however, the disadvantages of such plans should be considered.

Disadvantages of Commission Plans. Perhaps the most serious shortcoming of straight-commission plans is that they contribute little to company loyalty, which may mean other problems in controlling the activities of the salesforce, particularly nonselling and administrative activities. A lack of commitment may lead commission salespeople to leave the company if business conditions worsen or sales drop. Another potential problem can arise if commissions are not limited by an earnings cap, in that salespeople may earn more than their managers. Not only do managers resent this outcome, but the salespeople may not respond to direction from those they exceed in earnings.

Performance Bonuses

The third dimension of current spendable income is the **performance bonus,** either group or individual. Both types are prevalent, and some bonus plans combine them. As an example, the Plastics Division of Mobil Chemical pays a cash bonus of 10 percent of salary to any salesperson achieving his or her sales-volume target. If the operating group achieves its overall profit objectives, the salesperson receives another percentage point in bonus for every percentage point by which he or she exceeds the sales-volume target.

Bonuses are typically used to direct effort toward relatively short-term objectives such as introducing new products, adding new accounts, or reducing accounts receivable. They may be offered in the form of cash or income equivalents such as merchandise or free travel. While commissions or salary may be the financial-compensation base, bonuses are used strictly in a supplementary fashion.

Combination Plans (Salary plus Incentive)

The limitations of straight-salary and straight-commission plans have led to an increasing usage of plans that feature some combination of salary, commission, and bonus—in other words, **salary plus incentive.** Exhibit 12.2 indicates that salary-plus-bonus and commission-plus-bonus plans are extremely popular.

When properly conceived, combination plans offer a balance of incentive, control, and enough flexibility to reward important salesforce activities. The most difficult part of structuring combination plans is determining the **financial-compensation mix,** or the relative amounts to be paid in salary, commission, and bonus. Exhibit 12.5 enumerates a number of factors related to determining the appropriate ratio of salary to total financial compensation.

As indicated in Exhibit 12.5, the compensation mix should be tilted more heavily toward the salary component when individual salespeople have limited control over their own performance. When well-established companies rely heavily on advertising to sell their products in highly competitive markets, the salesforce has less direct control over job outcomes. Then a salary emphasis is quite logical. Further, if the provision of customer service is crucial as contrasted with maximizing short-term sales volume, or if team selling is utilized, a compensation mix favoring the salary dimension is appropriate. As suggested in Exhibit 12.5, conditions contrary to those favorable to a high salary-to-total-compensation ratio would dictate an emphasis on commissions in the compensation mix.

Combination pay plans usually feature salary as the major source of salesperson income. A recent survey indicates that the most popular plans contain approximately 60 percent salary and 40 percent incentive (commission and/or bonus) pay.[11]

Advantages of Combination Plans. The primary advantage of combination pay plans is their flexibility. Sales behavior can be rewarded frequently, and specific behaviors can be reinforced or stimulated quickly. For example, bonuses or additional commissions could be easily added to a salary base to encourage activities such as selling excess inventory, maximizing the sales of highly seasonal products, introducing new products, or obtaining new customers. A video distribution company, for example, wanted to focus on midsize retail stores, which had proven to be the most profitable market segment for the company. The large-size segment was dominated by chain stores and was characterized by highly competitive pricing and low margins. On the other end of the spectrum, the smaller, mom-and-pop video rental stores did not generate enough volume for the company to make a sufficient profit. An incentive plan was put into place that rewarded salespeople for selling to the midsize stores rather than to the less-profitable segments.[12]

Combination plans can also be used to advantage when the skill levels of the salesforce vary, assuming that the sales manager can accurately place salespeople into various skill level categories and then formulate the proper combination for each category.[13] In effect, this is done with sales trainees, regular salespeople, and senior salespeople in some companies, with each category of salespeople having a different combination of salary and incentive compensation.

EXHIBIT 12.5 ▪ *Conditions Influencing the Proportion of Salary to Total Pay for Salespeople*

Condition	Proportion of Salary to Total Pay Should Be	
	Lower	*Higher*
1. Importance of salesperson's personal skills in making sales	Considerable	Slight
2. Reputation of salesperson's company	Little known	Well known
3. Company's reliance on advertising and other sales promotion activities	Little	Much
4. Competitive advantage of product in terms of price, quality, etc.	Little	Much
5. Importance of providing customer service	Slight	Considerable
6. Significance of total sales volume as a primary selling objective	Greater	Lesser
7. Incidence of technical or team selling	Little	Much
8. Importance of factors beyond the control of salesperson which influence sales	Slight	Considerable

Source: Amiya K. Basu, Rajiv Lal, V. Srinivasan, and Richard Staelin, "Salesforce Compensation Plans: An Agency Theoretic Perspective," *Marketing Science* 4 (Fall 1985): 270. Reprinted by permission. Copyright 1985, The Institute of Management Sciences and the Operations Research Society of America.

Combination pay plans are attractive to high-potential, but unproven, candidates for sales jobs. College students nearing graduation, for example, might be attracted by the security of a salary and the opportunity for additional earnings from incentive-pay components.

Disadvantages of Combination Plans. As compared with straight-salary and straight-commission plans, combination plans are more complex and difficult to administer. Their flexibility sometimes leads to frequent changes in compensation practices to achieve short-term objectives. While flexibility is desirable, each change requires careful communication with the salesforce and precise coordination with long-term sales, marketing, and corporate objectives. A common criticism of combination plans is that they tend to produce too many salesforce objectives, many of which are of the crisis-resolution, "fire-fighting" variety. Should this occur, the accomplishment of more important long-term progress can be impeded.

Nonfinancial Compensation

As indicated early in this chapter, compensation for effort and performance may include nonfinancial rewards. Examples of **nonfinancial compensation** include career advancement through promotion, a sense of accomplishment on the job, opportunities for personal growth, recognition of achievement, and job security. Sometimes nonfinancial rewards are coupled with financial rewards—for example, a promotion into sales management usually results in a pay increase—so one salesperson might view these rewards as primarily financial, while another might view them from a nonfinancial perspective. The value of nonfinancial compensation is illustrated by the considerable number of salespeople who knowingly take cuts in financial compensation to become sales managers. The prevalence of other nonfinancial rewards in salesforce reward systems also attests to their important role.

Opportunity for Promotion

As shown in Exhibit 12.1, **opportunity for promotion** ranks second only to pay as the most preferred reward among salespeople. Among younger salespeople, it often eclipses pay as the most valued reward.[14] Given the increasing number of young to middle-age people in the workforce, the opportunities for promotion may be severely limited in non-growth industries. (Growth industries, such as financial services and direct sales, offer reasonably good opportunities for advancement through promotion.) Since opportunities for promotion are not easily varied in the short run, the importance of matching recruits to the job and its rewards is again emphasized. Other tactics being used by an increasing number of firms include offering top performers higher pay raises to keep them satisfied until promotions become available and using temporary assignments to develop salespeople for future managerial positions.[15]

It should be noted that a promotion need not involve a move from sales into management. Recall from Chapter 4 that some career paths may extend from sales into management, while others progress along a career salesperson path.

Sense of Accomplishment

Unlike some rewards, a **sense of accomplishment** cannot be delivered to the salesperson from the organization. Since a sense of accomplishment emanates from the salesperson's psyche, all the organization can do is to facilitate the process by which it develops. While organizations cannot administer sense-of-accomplishment rewards as they would pay increases, promotions, or formal recognition rewards, the converse is not true—they do have the ability to withhold this reward, to deprive individuals of feeling a sense of accomplishment. Of course, no organization chooses this result; it stems from poor management practice.

Several steps can be taken to facilitate a sense of accomplishment in the salesforce. First, assure that the salesforce members understand the critical role they fulfill in revenue production and other key activities within the company. Second, personalize the causes and effects of salesperson performance. In expectancy-theory terms, this means that each salesperson should understand the linkages between effort and performance (expectancies) and between performance and rewards (instrumentalities). Third, strongly consider the practice of management by objectives and/or goal setting as a standard management practice. Finally, reinforce feelings of worthwhile accomplishment in communications with the salesforce.

Opportunity for Personal Growth

Opportunities for personal growth are routinely offered to salespeople. For example, college-tuition reimbursement programs are commonplace, as are seminars and workshops on topics such as physical fitness, stress reduction, and personal financial planning. Interestingly, many sales job candidates think the major reward available from well-known companies is the opportunity for personal growth. This is particularly true of entrepreneurially oriented college students who hope to "learn then earn" in their own business. In a parallel development, many companies showcase their training program during recruitment and selection as an opportunity for personal growth through the acquisition of universally valuable selling skills.

Recognition

Recognition, both informal and formal, is an integral part of most salesforce reward systems. Informal recognition refers to "nice job" accolades and similar kudos usually delivered in private conversation or correspondence between a sales manager and a salesperson. Informal recognition is easy to administer, costs nothing or practically nothing, and can reinforce desirable behavior immediately after it occurs.

Long a tradition in most sales organizations, formal-recognition programs are becoming even more popular.[16] Examples include the Million Dollar Roundtable designation in the insurance industry, Stroh Brewery's Top Performer award for sales improvement, and numerous 100% Clubs for those who reach or exceed 100 percent of their sales quota. One particularly successful 100% Club program has been reported by Norwest Corp., a Minneapolis-based bank.[17] Stephen Byrnes, Norwest's director of marketing and product management, commented, "Much to our surprise, the element of recognition became more important than anything else we did" to spur sales.

Formal-recognition programs are typically based on group competition or individual accomplishments representing improved performance. Formal recognition may also be associated with monetary, merchandise, or travel awards but are distinguished from other rewards by two characteristics. First, formal recognition implies public recognition for accomplishment in the presence of peers and superiors in the organization. Second, there is a symbolic award of lasting psychological value, such as jewelry or a plaque.[18] Sound advice for conducting formal recognition programs is offered in Exhibit 12.6.

As formal-recognition programs grow in popularity, there seems to be an accompanying trend toward lavish awards banquets and ceremonies to culminate the program and set the stage for future recognition programs. Since lavish expenditures for any salesforce activity must ultimately be well justified in this era of emphasis on productivity improvement, it is evident that many companies believe that money spent on recognition is a good investment.

Formal-recognition programs are often linked with financial rewards or rewards that have monetary value such as trips for winners and their families. For a description of one type of travel incentive that could be part of a recognition program, see "A Global Perspective: Unique Travel Incentives."

A GLOBAL PERSPECTIVE

Unique Travel Incentives

Trips to exciting places have long been a tradition in salesforce recognition programs. For example, trips to Hawaii, the Caribbean, or perhaps the Super Bowl are rather standard awards for top sales performance. As world travel becomes more accessible, destinations for such trips now include more intriguing places such as the Swiss Alps for skiing or maybe a safari to Nairobi.

Should a safari be the reward for a winner, here is what he or she could expect. Close encounters with wildlife such as gazelles and hippos would be part of the trip, as would beautiful views of snow-capped Mount Kilimanjaro, complete with Masai tribesmen tending cattle nearby. Maybe a hot-air bal-

loon ride would be nice before retiring for the evening into a specially designed safari tent, complete with a four-poster bed.

Do such trips sound irrelevant in today's competitive environment, especially when political and social unrest is spread throughout the world? Perhaps, unless you are a sales manager trying to design exciting recognition programs to spur your people on to greater heights. In that case, such global travel as an incentive may be exactly right for providing lasting memories and, not coincidentally, improved performance.

Source: Abner Littel, "The Far Off, the Unique, the Exotic: An Incentive to Make Your Selling Soul Happy," *Personal Selling Power*, January–February 1991, 28–30.

EXHIBIT 12.6 ▪ *Guidelines for Formal Recognition Programs*

A Program That Will Do the Job

Regardless of its size or cost, any recognition program should incorporate the following features, says consultant Dr. Richard Boyatiz of McBer and Co.:

▪ The program must be strictly performance-based with no room for subjective judgments. If people suspect that it is in any way a personality contest, the program will not work. Says Boyatiz: "It should be clear to anyone looking at the data that, yes, these people won."

▪ It should be balanced. The program should not be so difficult that only a few can hope to win, or so easy that just about everyone does. In the first case, people will not try; in the second, the program will be meaningless.

▪ A ceremony should be involved. If rings are casually passed out, or plaques sent through the mail, a lot of the glamour of the program will be lost.

▪ The program must be in good taste. If not, it will be subject to ridicule and, rather than motivate people, leave them uninspired. No one wants to be part of a recognition program that is condescending or tacky. Says Boyatiz: "The program should make people feel good about being part of the company."

▪ There must be adequate publicity. In some cases, sales managers do such a poor job of explaining a program or promoting it to their own salespeople that no one seems to understand or care about it. Prominent mention of the program in company publications is the first step to overcoming this handicap.

Source: Bill Kelley, "Recognition Reaps Rewards," *Sales and Marketing Management*, June 1986, 104.

Job Security

Job security, though valued highly by salespeople nearing retirement age, is the least-valued reward among those shown in Exhibit 12.1. High-performing salespeople may sense they have job security, if not with their present employer then with another employer. According to Maslow's need hierarchy, these salespeople may value some other reward higher in the hierarchy. Low performers may not enjoy their sales jobs and thus place a low premium on job security.

With the current wave of mergers, acquisitions, and general downsizing of corporations, it is becoming more difficult to offer job security as a reward. In the past, job security was easier to assure, at least as long as performance contingencies were met. Another factor that will make it difficult to offer job security with a given company is the lack of unionization of salespeople in most fields.

Sales Expenses

A large majority of sales organizations provide full reimbursement to their salespeople for legitimate **sales expenses** incurred while on the job. As shown in Exhibit 12.7, typical reimbursable expenses include travel, lodging, meals, entertainment of customers, telephone, and incidentals such as tips. Some companies also reimburse laundry and dry cleaning expenses if the salesperson is required to be away from home for prolonged periods. Note in Exhibit 12.7 that companies that pay on a commission basis are less likely to pay salesperson expenses than are companies that pay on salary or combination plans.

Sales expenses can be substantial. According to compensation expert Bill Ryckman, "Eliminating the extremes, we feel safe in suggesting that expenses can average between 20 and 30 percent of compensation."[19] A review of the data in Figure 12.1 confirms Ryckman's conclusion. Given the magnitude of sales expenses, it is easy to understand why most companies impose tight controls to ensure judicious spending by the salesforce.

Controls used in the sales-expense reimbursement process include (1) a definition of which expenses are reimbursable, (2) the establishment of expense budgets, (3) the use of allowances for certain expenditures, and (4) documentation of expenses to be reimbursed.

Covered expenses vary from company to company, so it is important for each company to designate which expenses are reimbursable and which are not. For example, some firms reimburse their salespeople for personal entertainment such as the cost of movies and reading material while traveling, and others do not.

Expense budgets may be used to maintain expenses as a specified percentage of overall sales volume or profit. Expenditures are compared regularly to the budgeted amount, and expenditure patterns may change in response to budgetary pressures.

Allowances for automobile expenses, lodging, and meal costs are sometimes used to control expenditures. For example, one common practice is to reimburse personal automobile usage on the job at a cents-per-mile allowance. Many firms use a per-diem allowance for meals and lodging. In an unusual use of allowances,

EXHIBIT 12.7 ▪ *Percentage of Companies Paying All or Part of Expenses (All Companies and by Compensation Plan)*

	All Companies	Salary	Commission	Combination
Automobile (Company-Owned/ Leased/Personal)	76%	90%	49%	86%
Commercial Airlines	71%	90%	44%	80%
Railroads	37%	46%	19%	44%
Company Plane	21%	27%	11%	24%
Lodging	75%	92%	46%	84%
Telephone	83%	95%	66%	89%
Entertainment	75%	86%	48%	88%
Samples	65%	73%	51%	70%
Promotion	74%	80%	59%	81%
Office and/or Clerical	75%	84%	55%	83%

Source: John P. Steinbrink, ed., *The Dartnell Sales Manager's Handbook* (Chicago: The Dartnell Corporation, 1989), 946.

Timex reimburses its salespeople for two-thirds of their clothing expenditures as long as the clothing conforms to corporate standards of attire.[20]

Because of more stringent tax laws, extensive documentation in the form of receipts and other information concerning the what, when, who, and why of the expenditure has become standard procedure. Salespeople whose companies do not reimburse expenses must also provide such documentation in order to deduct sales expenses in calculating their income taxes. A typical form for documenting sales expenses is shown in Exhibit 12.8.

The area of expense reimbursement is the cause of some ethical and legal concern in sales organizations. Certainly **expense account padding,** in which a salesperson seeks reimbursement for ineligible or fictional expenses, is not unknown. There are countless ways for an unscrupulous salesperson to misappropriate company funds. A common ploy of expense account "padders" is to entertain friends rather than customers, then seek reimbursement for customer entertainment. Another tactic is to purchase equipment such as video players or slide projectors for personal use by applying company-paid rental fees in a lease-to-buy agreement with the dealer.

Tight financial controls, requirements for documentation of expenditures, and periodic visits by highly trained financial auditors help deter expense account abuse. While it may sound extreme, many companies have a simple policy regarding misappropriation of company funds—the minimum sanction is termination of employment, and criminal charges are a distinct possibility. For an interesting ethical scenario involving questionable sales management action in the area of expense accounts, see Case 12.1 at the end of the chapter.

EXHIBIT 12.8   ▪   *Sales Expense Report Form*

D A Y	City and State	Lodging	Transportation		Automobile Expenses	Meals — Itemize Business Meals Below			Local Taxi, Carfare, Tolls, Etc.	Entertain- ment	Miscellaneous Expenses	Daily Total
			Air, Rail, Etc.	Limousine Car Rental, Etc	Itemize Below	Breakfast	Lunch	Dinner		Itemize Below	Itemize Below	
S U N												
M O N												
T U E												
W E D												
T H U												
F R I												
S A T												
	Totals											

Entertainment and Business Meals

Date	Name of Person(s) Entertained Company, Title	Time and Place	Nature and Purpose of Entertainment	Amount	% or $ Allocated to Business

Total Expenses Paid by Employee

Itemize Below Those Expenses
Charged Directly to the Company

[ ]   Deduct from My Advance
[ ]   Mail to Home Address
[ ]   Mail to Branch Office

REMARKS:

Automobile and Miscellaneous Expenses

Date	Items	Amount

Expenses Charged Directly to the Company
(Air Fare, Auto Rental, Etc.)

Date	Items	Amount

Signature

Approved

Source: Gene Garofalo, *Sales Manager's Desk Book* (Englewood Cliffs, N.J.: Prentice-Hall, 1989), 128.

Additional Issues in Managing Salesforce Reward Systems

In addition to the managerial issues raised thus far, four other areas of salesforce reward systems are currently receiving considerable attention: sales contests, pay secrecy versus disclosure, equal pay for equal work, and changing an existing reward system.

Sales Contests

Sales contests are temporary programs that offer financial and/or nonfinancial rewards for accomplishing specified, usually short-term, objectives. Contests may involve group competition among salespeople, individual competition whereby each salesperson competes against past performance standards or new goals, or a combination of group and individual competition. Sales contests can be instituted without altering the basic financial-compensation plan.

Despite the widespread use of sales contests and the sizable expenditures for them, very little is known about their true effects. In fact, many contests are held to correct bad planning and poor sales performance, and others are held with the belief that contests must have positive effects, despite the difficulty in pinpointing these effects. While some researchers have found sales contests to be positively related to sales and profitability, others have pointed out the great number of questions that remain unanswered about them. For example, salespeople themselves have mixed feelings about sales contests. One survey revealed that salespeople enjoyed certain aspects of sales contests, such as the honor and recognition associated with winning, yet found fault with other aspects such as unrealistic expectations and lack of fairness often associated with contests.[21]

Sales managers also hold some reservations about the use of sales contests. One survey of 254 sales executives found that less than half were convinced that sales contests were "effective" or "very effective" in achieving set goals. Nonetheless, almost 75 percent were planning to continue sales contests at current levels.[22]

Though not supported by conclusive research, several guidelines for conducting sales contests have emerged from experienced practitioners:[23]

1. Minimize potential motivation and morale problems by allowing multiple winners. Salespeople should compete against individual goals and be declared winners if those goals are met.
2. Recognize that contests will concentrate efforts in specific areas, often at the temporary neglect of other areas. Plan accordingly.
3. Consider the positive effects of including nonselling personnel in sales contests.
4. Use variety as a basic element of sales contests. Vary timing, duration, themes, and rewards.
5. Ensure that sales contest objectives are clear, realistically attainable, and quantifiable to allow performance assessment.

It is hard to design a sales contest that will maximally motivate every member of the salesforce. It is even more difficult to precisely measure the effectiveness of most sales contests. Even so, sales contests will doubtless continue to be a frequently used tool. By following the five guidelines previously mentioned, sales managers can improve the odds of making justifiable investments in sales contests.

Secrecy versus Disclosure

Most companies use **closed pay systems,** meaning that critical financial-compensation information is kept secret from the employees. They are not told how much other salespeople earn, nor the amount of pay raises received by others. Even the way that pay raises are determined might not be revealed to the employees. In contrast, **open pay systems** are characterized by disclosure of pay information, including earnings of other employees and explanations of the way pay levels are determined.

Closed pay systems presumably reduce tension among employees and keep petty complaints to a minimum. As a result, sales managers spend less time explaining financial-compensation decisions than with an open pay system. In recent years, however, a growing number of companies have opened their pay systems to some degree.[24]

For sales organizations in which there is a strong correlation between performance and pay, open pay systems may be preferable. Salespeople paid a straight commission on sales volume may find it to be extremely motivating to know how much their peers earn. A study of pharmaceutical salespeople found that an open pay system was positively related to salesforce performance, as well as satisfaction with pay, company promotional policies, and the job itself.[25]

Another argument for open pay systems is rooted in the equity-theory concepts discussed in Chapter 11. If a sales manager believes that overall equity in the financial-compensation system contributes to motivation, performance, and retention of salespeople, then strong consideration should be given to implementing an open system. With a closed system, the necessary comparisons with relevant other salespeople are extremely difficult or impossible, and the information used for comparisons is likely to be inaccurate.

Equal Pay

In addition to the motivational aspects of equity in financial-compensation systems, there is a legal responsibility to assure that salespeople are paid on an equitable basis. The Equal Pay Act, mentioned in Chapter 9, requires that equal pay be given for jobs requiring the same skills, efforts, responsibilities, and working conditions.

Sad to say, some sales managers attempt to pay female salespeople less than males because they think women's family responsibilities will cause them to leave the salesforce, or they think women will be less willing to travel or relocate than male salespeople. The dangers of such thinking are not limited to legal ramifications, but the Equal Pay Act of 1963 does provide a strong reminder for those who consider paying one group of people less than another.

Changing the Reward System

The need to change the salesforce reward system for a given company may arise periodically as companies strive for improved performance and productivity. IBM changed its compensation structure in the late 1980s to encourage overall sales volume, whether of hardware, software, or services. In the past, commissions had been paid on an arbitrary, rather complicated point system that primarily encouraged the sale of selected hardware components.[26] Colgate-Palmolive, in contrast with IBM, moved away from a total-volume orientation for compensation to one that also rewards return-on-sales and selling a certain mix of products.[27]

The IBM and Colgate-Palmolive examples are not unusual. Reward systems should be closely monitored and should be changed when conditions warrant.

Minor adjustments in reward systems can be made relatively painlessly, and sometimes even pleasurably, for all concerned parties. For example, the sales manager might plan three sales contests this year instead of the customary two, or he (or she) might announce a cash bonus instead of a trip to Acapulco for those who make quota.

Making major changes in reward systems, however, can be traumatic for salespeople and management alike if not properly handled. Any major change in financial-compensation practices is likely to produce a widespread fear among the salesforce that their earnings will decline. Since many changes are precipitated by poor financial performance by the company or inequitable earnings among salesforce members, this fear is often justified for at least part of the salesforce.

To implement a new or modified reward system, sales managers must, in effect, sell the plan to the salesforce. To do this, the details of the plan must be clearly communicated well in advance of its implementation. Feedback from the salesforce should be encouraged and questions promptly addressed. Reasons for the change should be openly discussed, and any expected changes in job activities should be detailed.

It is recommended that, if possible, major changes be implemented to coincide with the beginning of a new fiscal year or planning period. It is also preferable to institute changes during favorable business conditions, rather than during recessionary periods.

The dynamic nature of marketing and sales environments dictates that sales managers constantly monitor their reward systems. It is not unreasonable to think that major changes could occur every few years or even more frequently.

Guidelines for Managing Salesforce Reward Systems

Several guidelines have been proposed for managing salesforce reward systems.[28] First, the reward system should be a direct reflection of corporate, business-unit, and marketing department priorities. The examples of the changes in the reward systems at IBM and Colgate-Palmolive illustrate this thinking. As a Harvard Business School professor puts it: "Despite the importance of individual abilities in sales, the sales rep is, ultimately, not an 'individual contributor' within the organization; he or she should be viewed as the agent of the firm's marketing strategy, and the compensation plan designed accordingly."[29]

The reward system should be based on what a particular company wants to accomplish, not necessarily what has been the industry tradition. Success stories are circulating about automobile dealers who have changed from straight-commission to salary-based compensation to improve customer-oriented sales behavior.

Strong consideration should be given to rewarding teamwork rather than relying solely on individual effort. While some internal competition can be healthy, the notion of building a strong sales team may serve long-term purposes better, especially if some of the top performers leave the organization.

There should be a strong emphasis on pay for performance, rather than paying according to competitive pay levels or seniority. This suggests the importance of incentive pay in the form of bonuses and/or commissions for paying salespeople in most situations.

comfortable in her role as a sales representative. Upon returning to the office late one Friday afternoon, Gina was summoned to O'Connor's office. The following conversation ensued.

Mike: Come in Gina, and grab a chair. I need to go over a few things with you.

Gina: Fine, Mike, what's on your mind?

Mike: Well, for openers I was reviewing your sales numbers, and it looks like you have really gotten off to a good start. How do you feel about your progress so far?

Gina: Pretty good, but I'm not sure my sales numbers are directly related to what I've been doing. You know we had a good base of customers, and maybe I'm just reaping the benefits.

Mike: Believe me, Gina, you're making a real difference. I've had some unsolicited calls from a few of your customers, and I hear a lot of good things about the way you're running your territory. Also, I was impressed the last time I visited with you in the field. Are there any particular problems that you are having . . . I mean, can I help you do even better?

Gina: Well, not that I know of, but you might be in a better position to spot areas for improvement than I am. What do *you* think, Mike?

Mike: On the sales end, I simply want you to keep doing what you're doing — everything's fine. Administratively, all's fine, but I did want to ask you about your expense account.

Gina: My expense account? Is there a problem? I've tried to fill out the forms and get them in on time . . .

Mike: True, true. In fact, there are no problems with when your expense accounts have been submitted, and you seem to be conscientious about providing all the receipts and documentation.

Gina: So, what's the problem? Am I spending too much?

Mike: No way! In fact, the opposite is true.

Gina: I don't understand. I've heard you say that we have to spend money to make money, and I agree. I'm on the road seeing my customers just like everybody else, but apparently not enough. Are you saying that you want me to travel more? Make more long-distance calls? More customer entertainment?

Mike: No, Gina, I'm not saying you should necessarily spend more money. The fact is, however, that your expenses are the lowest in the company, and I simply wonder why. As you know, our territories are fairly comparable in terms of numbers of customers and travel required, so it seems to me that your expenses should be in line with the others'. Are you sure you're claiming all of your eligible expenses for reimbursement? You're not losing money on your expense account, are you?

Gina: I don't think so, Mike. In fact, I'm pretty careful with my finances, and I'm sure my expenses are being covered.

Mike: Well, I hope so, Gina. Please understand my position. If you are consistently lower than the other sales reps on expenses, it's just a matter of time until Bill Michiletti [the company president] will ask me why. Either you're not spending enough or all the others are spending too much — that's how it looks. Just be sure you're claiming everything you're entitled to.

Afterward, Gina began to rethink her conversation with Mike O'Connor. She tried to resist the thought but, nonetheless, wondered if some of the other sales reps were padding their expense accounts.

Questions

1. How would you assess the manner in which Mike O'Connor handled this situation?

2. How should Gina proceed? Do you recommend that she increase her sales expenditures?

CASE 12.2 *Doubletree Door Company*

Background

Doubletree Door Company is one of the nation's leading manufacturers of high-quality residential and commercial security doors. Founded in 1940, the company had consistently experienced sales growth well beyond what its competitors had achieved. The Doubletree salesforce consists of 110 sales representatives, about half of whom call on residential home-builders and building supply outlets (both wholesale and retail). The other half of the Doubletree salesforce calls on large construction firms whose primary business is commercial development projects. Doubletree organizes its operation into five sales regions, each headed by a regional sales manager. Reporting to each regional sales manager are two residential district sales managers and two commercial district sales managers. Sales representatives, in groups of three to eight, report directly to the district sales managers.

All Doubletree salespeople are paid on a salary-plus-commission basis, with total dollar sales serving as the commission base. Typically, Doubletree salespeople's salaries account for approximately 60 percent of their total earnings. There is quite a bit of variance in total earnings, from a low of $28,000 to a high of $110,000.

Current Situation

Maxine Caldwell, Doubletree's national sales manager, is unhappy with year-to-date sales. She has asked Bill Kent, the residential sales director, and Laurel Hall, the commercial sales director, to meet with her to discuss ways of increasing sales.

As the meeting began, Bill Kent and Laurel Hall questioned just how realistic it would be to expect an increase in sales under current operating conditions. Most economists and industry analysts agree that the country is experiencing a recession. Housing starts are down approximately 8 percent compared with last year, and commercial development projects are down by approximately the same figure.

After an hour of heated discussion, Caldwell had heard enough. She told Kent and Hall: "Either we do something fast, or we won't make our targets for the year. We need a sales contest to boost

our numbers." Caldwell instructed Kent and Hall to work together on a draft of a sales contest plan and to present their ideas to her the following morning.

At 8:30 the next morning, Kent and Hall presented the following guidelines for their program:

1. Program is to commence 30 days from today and proceed for 90 days, with conclusion to coincide with ending of Doubletree's fiscal year.
2. Program is to be called the Doubletree Moneytree Extravaganza, with all written communications to the salesforce during the program to be placed on special custom-printed Moneytree stationery.
3. The objective of the program is to increase sales by 15 percent during the next 90 days, enabling Doubletree to achieve its originally planned annual sales objective of $100 million.
4. Each salesperson is to be given an incremental target to increase sales. Individual targets are to be left to the discretion of the regional sales managers. Regional sales managers are to be given incremental sales targets and, after consultation with the district sales managers, are to break their targets down into individual targets for each salesperson.
5. Each salesperson achieving his or her sales target is to receive a $1,000 cash bonus, plus an additional $100 bonus for every percentage point achieved over the target.
6. District sales managers are to receive a bonus of $3,000 for achieving their overall sales target. Regional sales managers are to receive a cash bonus of $5,000 for achieving their sales targets.
7. The salesperson with the highest percentage over target is to receive an additional $5,000 bonus. The district sales manager with the highest percentage over target is to receive an additional $3,000 Doubletree Double-Your-Money bonus. Likewise, the regional sales manager with the highest percentage over target is to receive a $5,000 Doubletree Double-Your-Money bonus.
8. The national sales manager and the sales directors are not to be eligible for cash awards.

However, the sales director achieving the highest percentage over target is to be the recipient of a Distinguished Sales Management Award at the next annual sales meeting in June. This award is to carry with it an all-expenses-paid trip for the winner and a guest to next year's NFL Super Bowl.

Questions

1. What are the strengths and weaknesses of the program at this stage in its development?
2. What questions would you recommend that Maxine Caldwell ask of Bill Kent and Laurel Hall?

Sales Management Leadership and Supervision

SUPERVISION AND LEADERSHIP OF NEW SALES-PEOPLE Bill Russell is a district sales manager for Pitney Bowes, one of the leading office products companies. He thinks that new salespeople are a very special part of the salesforce and that they require special handling by sales managers. Russell feels that experienced salespeople may take a few shortcuts and learn special sales techniques that work for them but that new salespeople must learn "by the numbers." Mr. Russell's approach to managing new salespeople is what he calls "forceful direction."

On Monday mornings, Bill personally visits with each new salesperson. During these meetings he asks a lot of questions, such as, "How come only 10 calls on Thursday?" "Why not 15 or 16 like you made on all the other days?" "Where's your prospect list?" "What's hot?" and "What are you going to do about it?"

Russell also travels extensively with new salespeople so that he can teach them the merits of having extensive product knowledge and a strong work ethic. He also tries to build their confidence by showing them they have nothing to fear in dealing with any customer as long as they have adequately prepared for their sales calls.

Sales managers like Bill Russell believe in spending an inordinate amount of time with new salespeople. They recognize the importance of the sales manager's role in developing a self-sustaining professional sales representative. Furthermore, they realize that a salesperson is extremely sensitive to massive criticism during the critical first year on the job. In effect, such sales managers are trying to protect their investment by maximizing performance and job satisfaction of the new salespeople, while building the salesperson's loyalty to the company.

Source: Jack Falvey, "The Care and Feeding of New Salespeople," *Sales and Marketing Management*, February 1990, 22–24.

Learning Objectives

After completing this chapter, you should be able to

1 *Distinguish between salesforce leadership and supervision.*

2 *Discuss how salesforce socialization can be enhanced through supervision and leadership.*

3 *List the six components of a sales leadership model.*

4 *Discuss five bases of power that affect leadership.*

5 *Explain five influence strategies used in leadership.*

6 *Describe the style of sales management preferred by salespeople.*

7 *Discuss issues related to coaching the salesforce, holding integrative meetings, and practicing ethical management.*

8 *Identify some of the problems encountered in leading and supervising a salesforce.*

This chapter deals with the leadership and supervisory roles of sales managers. With strong supervision and leadership obvious necessities, it is sometimes amazing to see sales managers who neglect to systematically plan and implement their activities to protect, and hopefully maximize, the investments made in a salesforce. Sadly, some managers think that sales management supervision and leadership are rather irrelevant, supposedly since true sales professionals cherish job freedom above all else, and they conclude that the sales manager's role is to "get out of the way" and let the salesforce run itself. In today's environment, such thinking can be deadly.

Leadership involves the use of influence with other people through communications processes to attain specific goals and objectives. Even though sales managers have a fair amount of authority by virtue of their positions in the organizational hierarchy, it is their skill to influence rather than dictate the actions of others that determines whether or not they are effective leaders. For example, in the previous chapter we discussed the necessity to "sell" the salesforce on major changes in the financial-compensation system. A poor leader would ignore the need to gain the support of the salesforce and would simply dictate the terms of the new system and hope for the best.

Supervision is the day-to-day control of the salesforce under routine operating conditions. It is obviously an integral part of leadership; however, it is not the sum total of leadership. For one thing, supervision is only concerned with the sales manager–salesperson relationship, whereas leadership extends to all interpersonal relationships in which the sales manager is engaged. Further, leadership requires more foresight and intuition than supervision. This is true because supervision deals more with maintenance and improvement of the status quo, while leadership often requires redefinition of major objectives and operations of the salesforce.

This chapter is organized into four sections. First, the previously discussed concept of salesforce socialization will be reviewed to see how it relates to supervision and leadership. Next, a leadership model is discussed. The third section deals with three important leadership functions: coaching, holding integrative meetings, and practicing ethical sales management. The last section addresses some problems in leading and supervising a salesforce—namely, conflicts of interest; chemical abuse and dependency; disruptive, rule-breaking salespeople; termination of employment; and sexual harassment.

Salesforce Socialization Revisited

As you will recall, a model of salesforce socialization (the process by which salespeople acquire the knowledge, skills, and values essential to do their job) was introduced as Figure 9.2. Note that recruiting/selection and training objectives that relate to salesforce socialization have been discussed in chapters 9 and 10, respectively. Through motivation, supervision, and leadership, sales managers can further socialize the salesforce, contributing to positive job-related outcomes. For example, research has demonstrated the importance of salespeople having high levels of job-related, **task-specific self-esteem,** which has been linked to improved performance and job satisfaction.[1]

Sales managers can positively affect their salesforce by reducing on-the-job conflicts and role stress (introduced in Chapter 2) for their salespeople (i.e., they can help achieve the congruence objective shown in Figure 9.2). For example, one study of salespeople who sold food found that by reducing salespeople's stress on the job, sales managers could increase not only salespeople's job satisfaction but, ultimately, their **organizational commitment** as well.[2] Organizational commitment can be defined variously but is usually thought of in one of two ways: (1) as a psychological bond to the organization or (2) as demonstrated through behavior over a period of time.

Despite whether salespeople might like to have freedom on the job, one study suggests that salespeople's job stress was reduced by higher levels of **formalization**—the extent to which work activity is directed by rules, regulations, and directives. The reduction in job stress led to higher levels of organizational commitment and lower levels of **work alienation,** which is described as an individual's psychological separation from the activities of the job.[3] Work alienation might be thought of as the opposite of **job involvement,** which is a strong attachment by the salesperson to the job itself.

Quite understandably, most sales managers would like to have a salesforce composed of people who are highly committed to the organization and highly involved in the job itself. In this chapter, we will consider how sales managers, through effective supervision and leadership, can impact overall salesforce performance and other desirable job outcomes such as satisfaction, involvement, and commitment on the part of their salespeople.

A Leadership Model for Sales Management

Figure 13.1 shows a leadership model for sales management with six components:

1. *Power*—of the salesperson, salespeople, or other party with whom the sales manager is interacting.
2. *Power*—of the sales manager.
3. *Situation*—including time constraints, nature of the task, organizational history, and group norms.
4. *Needs and wants*—of the salesperson, salespeople, or other people with whom the sales manager is interacting.
5. *Goals and objectives*—of the individuals and the organization.
6. *Leadership skills*—anticipation, diagnostic, selection and matching, and communications.

Power and Leadership

In most job-related interpersonal situations, sales managers and the parties with whom they interact hold power in some form or another. As the model in Figure 13.1 suggests, the possession and use of this power will have a major impact on the quality of leadership achieved by a sales manager. To simplify discussion, we will focus on the sales manager–salesperson relationship, but keep in mind that sales managers must use their leadership skills in dealing with other personnel in

FIGURE 13.1 ▪ *A Leadership Model for Sales Management*

A sales manager's leadership effectiveness is a function of six factors: the power of the salesperson and other people, the power of the sales manager, the situation, human needs and wants, individual and organizational goals and objectives, and the leadership skills of the sales manager.

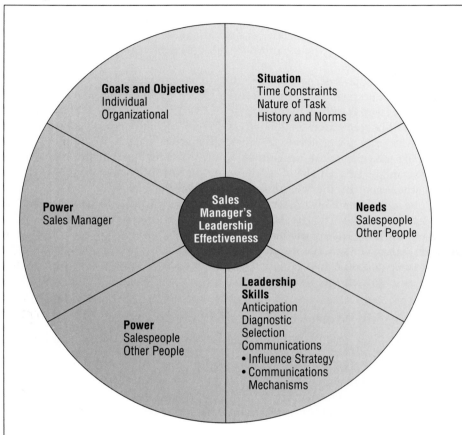

the firm, as well as outside parties such as employment agencies, external trainers, customers, and suppliers.

The power held by an individual in an interpersonal relationship can be of one or more of the following five types.[4] For each type, a sample comment from a salesperson recognizing the sales manager's power is shown in parentheses.[5]

1. **Expert power**—based on the belief that a person has valuable knowledge or skills in a given area. ("I respect her knowledge and good judgment because she is well trained and experienced.")

2. **Referent power**—based on the attractiveness of one party to another. It may arise from friendship, role modeling, or perceived similarity of personal background or viewpoints. ("I like him personally and regard him as a friend.")

3. **Legitimate power**—associated with the right to be a leader, usually as a result of designated organizational roles. ("She has a legitimate right, considering her position as sales manager, to expect that her suggestions be followed.")
4. **Reward power**—stems from the ability of one party to reward the other party for a designated action. ("He is in a good position to recommend promotions or permit special privileges for me.")
5. **Coercive power**—based on a belief that one party can remove rewards and provide punishment to affect behavior. ("She can apply pressure to enforce her suggestions if they are not carried out fully and properly.")

It should be stressed that it is the various individuals' perceptions of power, rather than a necessarily objective assessment of where the power lies, that will determine the effects of power in interpersonal relationships. For example, a newly appointed district sales manager may perceive the legitimate power associated with being a manager to be extremely high, while the salespeople may not share this perception in the least. Such differences in perceptions regarding the nature and balance of power are frequently at the root of the problems that challenge sales managers.

Many sales managers have been accused of relying too much on reward and coercive power. This is disturbing for three reasons. First, coercive actions are likely to create strife in the salesforce and may encourage turnover among high-performing salespeople who have other employment opportunities. Second, as salespeople move through the career cycle, they tend to self-regulate the reward system. Senior salespeople are often seeking intrinsic rewards that cannot be dispensed and controlled by sales managers. As a result, rewards lose some of their impact. Third, research has demonstrated that other power bases (expert and referent) are positively related to salespeople's satisfaction with supervision and with sales managers.[6] Thus, it is recommended that sales managers who wish to become effective leaders develop referent and expert power bases.

At times, salespeople have more power in a situation than the sales manager. For example, senior salespeople may be extremely knowledgeable and therefore have dominant expert power over a relatively inexperienced sales manager. Or a sales manager with strong esteem needs may be intent on winning a popularity contest with the salesforce, which could give salespeople a strong referent power base. When a sales manager senses that the salesperson is more powerful in one of these dimensions, there is a strong tendency to rely on legitimate, coercive, or reward power to gain control of the situation. Again, it is suggested that these three power bases be used sparingly, however, and that the sales manager work instead toward developing more expert and referent power.

This recommendation seems to be consistent with the views of top executives who say that today's workplace is quite different from that of the past. A typical comment comes from Reuben Mark, CEO of Colgate-Palmolive, who says: "You consolidate and build power by empowering others."[7] The concepts of teamwork and employee participation in management decision making are gaining popularity and are largely incompatible with the heavy-handed use of coercive and legitimate power. Sales managers interested in developing an effective power base might

EXHIBIT 13.1   ▪   *How Sales Managers Can Develop Power*

The president of Hill and Knowlton, the world's largest public relations firm, offers sales managers several suggestions for developing their power bases:

▪ Decide on overall objectives

▪ Listen to your sales team's wants, needs, and dreams

▪ Align the sales team with the firm's corporate culture

▪ Meet key customers and industry leaders

▪ Make appearances at image-enhancing events

▪ Secure support of upper management for sales management programs and activities

▪ Use one-on-one meetings to motivate salespeople

▪ Develop an information management system to minimize the flow of irrelevant information

Source: Adapted from L. B. Gschwandtner, "Personal PR Strategies for Creating Power and Influence," *Personal Selling Power*, October 1990, 20.

consider the advice given in Exhibit 13.1 by Robert Dilenschneider, president of Hill and Knowlton, the world's largest public relations firm.

One additional point on sales managers' use of power is that a combination of power bases may be employed in a given situation. For example, it might be a sales manager's referent and expert power that allow him or her to conduct a highly effective leadership function, such as an annual sales meeting. Previous research that focused on food brokers suggests that the use of combinations of power bases more accurately reflects reality than does the exclusive use of one power base in a given situation.[8]

Situational Factors

Scores of studies have tried to uncover what makes an effective leader. One popular category of this research is called the **trait approach,** which attempts to determine the personality traits of an effective leader. To date, trait research, however, has not been enlightening. The **behavior approach,** which seeks to catalog behaviors associated with effective leadership, has likewise failed to identify what makes an effective leader. As the behavior and trait studies continue inconclusive, it has become increasingly apparent that the *situation* could have a strong impact on leadership. The model in Figure 13.1 of a **contingency approach** to leadership recognizes the importance of the interaction between situational factors and other factors. Situational factors include time constraints, the nature of the task, and the history and norms of the organization. When time is at a premium, crisis management is called for, which requires totally different leadership behaviors than usual. For example, a sales manager might rely on legitimate power, or even coercive power, to get immediate, undisputed support of the salesforce if time is constrained.

A GLOBAL PERSPECTIVE

Supervising Independent Sales Agents   Tom Day is regional manager of Far East and Latin American sales for Procter & Gamble Cellulose, one of the world's largest pulp manufacturers. Mr. Day, who also has had sales management experience in the United States, works with independent sales agents in diverse markets such as Japan and Brazil. In noting the differences between global sales intermediaries and a domestic salesforce, Day points out that conventional management-by-objectives techniques can be utilized as long as the sales manager realizes that the sales agent's inputs into the process must be heavily weighed. He further suggests that sales managers must be much more willing to relinquish absolute control over every aspect of the sales agent's behavior and be willing to trust the agent on important matters.

Mr. Day stresses that the job of supervising a worldwide sales organization has become much more efficient in recent years with the advent of technological innovations such as fax transmissions and electronic data interchanges. Nonetheless, he cautions sales managers to extend their time horizons, as cultural differences dictate a slower pace of business than is usually the case in the United States.

Source: Personal interview on January 10, 1991, with Thomas R. Day, Regional Manager, Far East and Latin American Sales, Procter & Gamble Cellulose, Memphis, Tenn.

Certainly the nature of the task is an important part of the situation. If the situation is concerned with the top priority of the sales organization, a more calculated approach to leadership may be called for than when the situation is of minor importance.

The norms established either formally or informally in the workplace are another situational factor. Research on work groups indicates that groups will form on the job, that the norms of the group will exert a strong influence on group members, and that managers must be aware of group processes to be effective leaders.[9]

The history, culture, and policies of the company may also affect a particular situation and thus the leadership action that would be most suitable. For example, Oscar Mayer has a long-standing history as a market leader offering high-quality products at premium prices. Despite intense competitive pressures to reduce prices, Oscar Mayer sales leadership is bolstered by the tradition of high-quality products, and what might be viewed as a crisis in price competition by another firm is hardly worthy of managerial attention at Oscar Mayer.

As sales management increasingly takes on global dimensions, the necessity for considering situational factors will become more crucial. For some thoughts on this, see "A Global Perspective: Supervising Independent Sales Agents."

Needs and Wants of Salespeople

Continuing the discussion of the model shown in Figure 13.1, it should be stressed that leadership is an interactive process requiring one or more individuals to assume the role of followers or constituents. If coercive power-based behavior is cast aside, the needs and wants of salespeople must be given due consideration to ensure a supporting constituency for effective sales management leadership. Obviously, the needs and wants of salespeople cannot be met on a carte blanche basis. Further, a sales manager cannot become overly sensitive to the point of paranoia or managerial paralysis brought on by the fear that necessary actions will alienate the salesforce. But, on balance, the needs and wants of salespeople must be constantly weighed as an important determinant of leadership behavior.

In assessing the needs and wants of salespeople, it is important to consider each salesperson as a unique individual. While it is true that individual salespeople are typically part of a work group (i.e., the salesforce), sales managers should attempt to tailor their actions to individual salespeople when feasible. A recent study of retail and insurance salespeople provides support for these ideas, concluding that sales managers' supervisory behaviors are related to sales performance and that sales managers should manage salespeople individually in terms of supervisory behaviors.[10]

Goals and Objectives

If salespeople's needs and wants are consistent with the organization's goals and objectives, leadership is an easier task for sales managers. To this end, some companies hold extensive training and development sessions on "life planning" for their salespeople. In these sessions, salespeople define their short-term and long-term personal goals. In subsequent sessions, company management attempts to show how the salespeople's personal goal achievement can also assist in organizational goal achievement.

One firm that uses life planning is Combustion Engineering, a large industrial company. Combustion Engineering conducts these sessions on college campuses such as MIT with the assistance of industrial psychologists. The sessions are taken seriously. Company management feels that such goal clarification is beneficial not only to the personal development of their employees, but also because it helps produce a supportive constituency for the leaders of the firm.

Leadership Skills

As previously suggested, no one has been able to identify the exact personality traits or leadership behaviors that make an effective sales management leader. Likewise, there is no magic combination of skills that assures effective leadership. In this section, several skill areas will be reviewed that may be related to effective leadership; but keep in mind that possession of a particular skill is no more important than knowing when to employ it. The skill areas to be covered include anticipation and seeking feedback, diagnostic skills, selection and matching, and communications skills.

Anticipation and Seeking Feedback. The business press is full of examples of leadership crises that could have been avoided by *anticipation* of a potential problem. As mentioned in Chapter 5, Tandy has experienced extreme difficulty in trying to establish an outside salesforce to sell to business customers. While its Radio Shack retail stores are flourishing, the non-store salesforce is plagued with high turnover and a flat sales curve. Some observers feel that a major part of the problem is that Tandy took a "bargain basement" approach to developing its outside salesforce, which meant low salaries for the salespeople. Presumably, Tandy management did not anticipate the problems that could arise from such a stringent, budget-driven approach. It had a hard time attracting knowledgeable salespeople, and apparently those who did go to work for Tandy were ineffective against IBM and Apple. Many of these salespeople left, and Tandy faced a sales leadership crisis.[11]

The Tandy case illustrates how even the best-run companies can benefit from better anticipation of problems to avert leadership crises. It is not fair to expect unerring clairvoyance of sales managers, but it is reasonable to expect that responsible leaders will try to extend their vision into the future. One way they can do this is to *seek feedback* from customers, salespeople, and other important sources on a regular basis. An application of this idea that has become popular in recent years is called "management by wandering around" **(MBWA).** Key concepts of MBWA include listening, empathizing, and maintaining contact with customers and salespeople. As one executive puts it, MBWA helps to "uncover problems before they become major irritants" and to "give management a daily reminder of where the real world is—with our field reps and our customers."[12]

Feedback can also be regularly gathered through field visits, salesforce audits, and conscientious reviews of routine call reports submitted by salespeople. The idea of sales managers spending more time in the field, whether or not they are accompanied by salespeople, is increasingly being advocated. Harvey Mackay, a best-selling author of business books, suggests that sales managers who put in "windshield time" in the field can gain valuable insights into how well salespeople interact with customers and carry out their assigned duties.[13]

Another interesting variation of MBWA is for the sales manager to actually spend time in the field in the role of the salesperson. Some sales managers can have actual sales responsibilities; others can visit the field as temporary salespeople. While in the sales role, the manager can assess sales support, customer service, availability of required information, job stress, work load factors, and other variables of interest. This practice is followed in companies such as Xerox and Union Pacific, not only by sales managers but also by top executives.[14]

Diagnostic Skills. Effective leaders must be able to determine the specific nature of the problem or opportunity to be addressed. While this sounds simple, it is often difficult to distinguish between the real problem and the more visible symptoms of the problem. Earlier it was noted that sales managers have relied too heavily on reward and coercive power to direct their salesforces. A primary reason for this is a recurring tendency to attack easily identified symptoms of problems, not the core problems that need resolution. Reward and coercive power are also expedient ways to exercise control, and they suit the manager who likes to react without deliberation when faced with a problem.

For example, a sales manager may react to sluggish sales volume results by automatically assuming the problem is motivation. What follows from this hasty conclusion is a heavy dose of newly structured rewards, or just the opposite, a strong shot of coercion. Perhaps motivation is not the underlying problem; perhaps other determinants of performance are actually the source of the problem. But a lack of *diagnostic skills* (discussed further in Chapter 16) has led the sales manager to attack the easiest target, the symptom of the problem, rather than fully examine the root cause of the problem. As we all know from our experiences with the common cold, treating the symptoms will not permanently solve the problem.

Selection and Matching. As we have already mentioned, no specific inventory of skills exists for effective leadership. Rather, there is a range of behaviors that should be matched to a particular situation. For example, we have cast dispersions on the use of coercive power in sales management, but its use may be entirely appropriate in some situations. In the case of a problem employee whose insubordination is creating morale problems for the remainder of the salesforce, for example, a "shape up or ship out" ultimatum may be the best response.

The importance of *selecting* appropriate leadership responses to *match* the situation is highlighted in the research dealing with salespeople's concerns as they move through career stages. A study of one company's salespeople found those in the exploration stage to be unhappy with their sales managers and the aspects of the sales jobs over which the manager had considerable control.[15] For example, they did not perceive their sales managers to be open and supportive, and they felt they had little opportunity to make important decisions. Salespeople in the other career stages (establishment, maintenance, and disengagement) in this company held positive perceptions toward their sales managers and toward aspects of their jobs heavily influenced by management. Obviously, either a change in managerial behavior toward the discontented salespeople in the exploration stage was called for in this case, or the company's recruitment and selection methods should have been changed. Either way, being able to match managerial actions to the situation, rather than responding within a narrowly defined range of behaviors, would be a big advantage to effective leadership.

Communications

Recall the definition of leadership from the beginning of this chapter. At the heart of the definition is the phrase "the use of influence through communications processes." In this section, we will discuss various influence strategies and communications mechanisms involved in leadership and supervision. Effective leaders deliver clear, timely information through appropriate media or interpersonal communications. In contrast, the best plans and intentions can be destroyed by faulty communications. All too often, sales operations are damaged by premature leakage of information, inconsistent and conflicting communications, tardy messages, or poorly conceived strategies for influencing the salesforce.

Influence Strategies. Since sales managers have power from different sources to use in dealing with salespeople, peers, and superiors, they have the opportunity to devise different **influence strategies** according to situational demands. Influence strategies can be based on threats, promises, persuasion, relationships, and manipulation.[16] All are appropriate at some time with some salespeople but not necessarily with superiors or peers.

Threats. In a strategy based on **threats,** a manager might specify a desired behavior and the punishment that will follow if the behavior is not achieved. "If you do not call on your accounts at least once a week, you will lose your job," is an example. Since threats are used only in cases of noncompliance to operational guidelines, their use requires a monitoring system to see if the threatened person is engaging in the desired behavior. This can be time-consuming and annoying for the manager. Threats should be viewed as a last resort, but they should not be eliminated as a viable influence strategy. Research has indicated that salespeople, contrary to common wisdom, do not appear to react unfavorably to appropriate punishment and that managers "need to overcome their own reluctance in meting out punishment."[17]

Promises. Sales managers can utilize reward power as a basis for developing influence strategies based on **promises.** Research has indicated that promises produce better compliance than threats.[18] This would seem to be especially true for well-educated, mobile employees as typified by a large portion of professional salespeople. Further, influence strategies based on promises as opposed to threats help foster positive feelings among salespeople and boost salesforce morale.

Persuasion. An influence strategy based on **persuasion** can work without the use of reward or coercive power. Since persuasive messages must be rational and reasonable, however, expert and referent power bases are necessary to make them effective. Persuasion implies that the target of influence must first change his or her attitudes and intentions in order to produce a subsequent change in behavior. For example, a sales manager might persuade the salesforce to submit weekly activity reports by first convincing them of the importance of the reports in the company's marketing information system.

Sales managers are almost always former salespeople and therefore are quite comfortable with influence through persuasion. Generally speaking, persuasion is preferred to threats and promises, but it does require more time and skill.

Relationships. Two types of **relationships** can affect influence processes. The first type is based on referent power. It builds on personal friendships, or feelings of trust, admiration, or respect. In short, one party is quite willing to do what the other party desires, simply because the former likes the latter. In a salesforce setting, these kinds of relationships are consistent with the notion of the salesforce as a cooperative team. According to noted author Ken Blanchard, team members should be committed to open communication, and differences of opinion are resolved in a constructive manner. Blanchard notes that such work settings create an atmosphere of trust and acceptance, along with a sense of community among salesforce members and management.[19]

To develop relationships based on referent power, sales managers can take several actions. First, they should recognize that, generally speaking, they will be better liked by others if they can effectively cope with their own job pressures. Being calm and pleasant under pressure will bring a sales manager more power than caving in to the pressure, which might result in temper tantrums and impulsive reactions. Second, sales managers can take a genuine interest in the people with whom they interact and can learn to show that interest through conversation and other means of communication. Another suggestion is to initiate reciprocation with other parties by being the first to offer information or to provide a service.[20] For example, a sales manager might provide a production manager with a timely sales forecast on a voluntary basis to help schedule future manufacturing processes. In turn, this may lead the production manager to reciprocate with valuable information for the sales manager at some future date.

The second type of relationship is where one party has legitimate power over the other party by virtue of position in the organizational hierarchy. Sales managers have legitimate power in dealing with salespeople. As a result, they can influence salespeople in many situations without the use of threats, promises, or persuasion.

One interesting way of classifying salespeople according to the type of relationship they have with their sales manager is to think of salespeople as either **cadre** or **hired hands.**[21] According to theory, cadre are chosen by sales managers because they are skilled and can be trusted. Thus, cadre enjoy high-quality, trust-based relationships with their managers, and they receive more support from management. At the other theoretical extreme, hired hands are less skilled, less trusted, and thus not as valuable to the salesforce as are cadre. This conceptual distinction between cadre and hired hands is interesting, but it is important to remember that progressive sales managers usually concentrate their efforts on converting hired hands to cadre status or on replacing them in the salesforce.

Manipulation. Unlike the other influence strategies, **manipulation** does not involve direct communications with the target of influence. Rather, circumstances are controlled to influence behavior. For example, a salesperson lacking self-confidence might be assigned to work on temporary assignment with a confident senior salesperson. In team selling, the sales manager might control the group dynamics within teams by carefully selecting compatible personality types to compose the teams. Manipulation might also involve "office politics" and the use of third parties to influence others. For example, a sales manager might use the backing of his or her superior in dealing with peers on the job.

Communications Mechanisms. A critical part of using communications in leadership processes is knowing how to effectively use appropriate **communications mechanisms.** It is beyond the scope of this book to fully discuss fundamental business communications topics such as letter and memo writing and report writing. Instead, consider how a recently developed communications mechanism called the *hub concept* could contribute to effective leadership. This concept is contrasted with the traditional linear approach to communications in Figure 13.2.

The hub concept is only one example of how communications mechanisms can facilitate leadership functions. In today's productivity-driven environment, sales managers are using every conceivable device to improve the efficiency of their communications with the salesforce. Car phones, pagers, fax machines, voice mail, electronic bulletin boards, and companywide video networks are some of the more popular tools being used to speed communications to salesforces in far-flung

FIGURE 13.2 ▪ *The Hub Concept and Salesforce Communications*

The traditional linear approach to salesforce communications is frequently plagued by inefficiencies, or so-called bottlenecks. The hub concept allows direct communication between all parties.

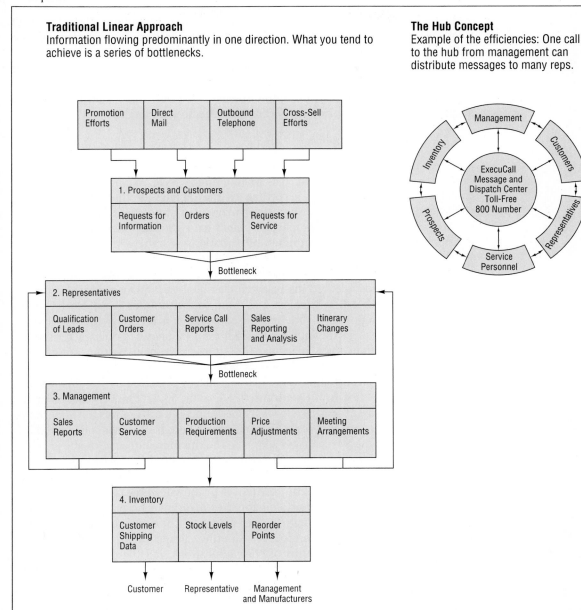

Traditional Linear Approach
Information flowing predominantly in one direction. What you tend to achieve is a series of bottlenecks.

The Hub Concept
Example of the efficiencies: One call to the hub from management can distribute messages to many reps.

Source: ExecuCall Incorporated, Cincinnati, Ohio. Used with permission.

locations. Well aware that salespeople's time is a valuable commodity, some companies are attempting to use otherwise-unproductive travel time to communicate with their salespeople. For example, Digital Equipment Corporation puts memos, announcements, and reports that may be pertinent to salespeople on audiotapes, which salespeople may request weekly by topic. Thus far, over two-thirds of Digital's salesforce has elected to receive their paperwork via audiotape.[22]

All communications with the salesforce must be carefully planned to ensure accuracy and clarity. And, remember, while the latest developments such as the hub offer exciting features, the simple spoken word between a sales manager and a salesperson is still of prime importance in effective leadership.

Management Style

The combination of two highly visible facets of leadership, power and communications, are sometimes referred to as **management style.** We have suggested that management style may vary according to the dictates of the situation, which contradicts the notion that a singular management style could be optimal. It is possible, however, that a sales manager might have a *primary management style* that is appropriate for a large number of situations—perhaps a majority of the situations typically encountered by sales managers.

Some interesting research has explored the type of management style preferred by salespeople.[23] This research classified sales managers' use of power according to whether the manager was dominant or submissive in dealing with salespeople. Communications methods used by sales managers were also divided into two categories, hostile and warm. Exhibit 13.2 shows the characteristics of each of the resultant four management styles: dominant-hostile, submissive-hostile, submissive-warm, and dominant-warm.

Salespeople who participated in a national survey preferred the dominant-warm management style shown in Quadrant 4 of Exhibit 13.2. The type of leader described in this quadrant seeks feedback from salespeople and realizes the importance of goal setting in controlling salesforce efforts. There is also evidence in Exhibit 13.2 that this type of sales manager adapts to the situation in that he or she provides more structure for those salespeople who cannot supervise their own efforts.

A valid question that arises from this research is, to what extent should a sales manager's style be determined by the desires of the salesforce? Since research has shown that salespeople prefer a dominant sales manager who provides fairly close supervision rather than a submissive sales manager,[24] it does not appear that sales management would be compromised by adopting salespeople's generally preferred management style. And in terms of communications, it is hard to argue against warm, open communications with the salesforce instead of hostile communications as general operating procedure.

Selected Leadership Functions

In this section, three particularly important leadership functions of sales management will be discussed: coaching the salesforce, planning and conducting integrative sales meetings, and striving for ethical (or moral) leadership behavior.

EXHIBIT 13.2 ▪ *Sales Management Styles*

DOMINANCE

Quadrant 1

Planning: Rarely involves salespeople ("Why should it? Planning is my prerogative. I make the plans, they carry them out. That's as it should be.")

Organizing: Tight organization. Patterns of relationship emphasize one-to-one interaction ("I make sure everyone knows what to do and how to do it. I call the shots.")

Controlling: Very close supervision ("Any sales manager who isn't vigilant is asking for trouble. Salespeople must know they're being closely scrutinized.")

Leading: Pushes, demands, drives ("Most people want a strong leader to tell them what to do. My people know who's boss.")

Quadrant 4

Planning: Consults salespeople whenever their thinking might help ("I want the best plans possible. That frequently requires ideas from others. I don't have all the answers.")

Organizing: Patterns of relationship designed to stimulate collaboration and interdependence ("I try to get synergism through pooling of resources.")

Controlling: Tries to develop salespeople who control themselves ("Get people committed to their goals, and they'll supervise their own efforts.") Provides more structure for those who can't.

Leading: Tries to make salespeople aware of their potential ("Leadership is helping people do what they have in them to do. A leader develops people.")

HOSTILITY ◄————————————————————► WARMTH

Quadrant 2

Planning: Relies heavily on own manager ("I prefer to pass along her plans. That way, my people know they'd better follow through.") Or leans heavily on tradition ("It's worked before; it should work again.")

Organizing: Patterns of relationship vague, indefinite. Doesn't encourage interaction ("Just do your own job and stay out of trouble.")

Controlling: Sees self mainly as a caretaker ("I'm paid to keep things stable. I exert enough control to make sure nobody disrupts routines. There's no point in doing more.")

Leading: Passive, indifferent. Downplays own influence ("Don't kid yourself. No matter how hard you try to lead people, they'll end up doing pretty much as they please.")

Quadrant 3

Planning: More concerned with generalities than details ("If you fence people in with too much planning, you'll demoralize them. I'm flexible; I give my people plenty of leeway.")

Organizing: Patterns of relationship emphasize loosely structured sociability ("If people feel good about their jobs, they'll do their best without lots of regulation. My job is to make sure they feel good.")

Controlling: Relies on high morale to produce hard work ("Control is secondary. What salespeople need most is a good feeling about their jobs.")

Leading: Believes optimism and encouragement get results ("Being a sales manager is like being a cheerleader. You can't let your people get discouraged.")

SUBMISSION

Source: Reprinted by permission of the publisher from Robert E. Hite and Joseph A. Bellizzi, "A Preferred Style of Sales Management," *Industrial Marketing Management* 15 (August 1986): 217. Copyright 1986 by Elsevier Science Publishing Co., Inc.

Coaching

In the **coaching** role, a sales manager concentrates on continuous development of salespeople. The importance of coaching is illustrated in this passage:

> To many a sales manager, a seller either has or hasn't got what it takes to sell. This attitude reduces sales management to a problem of finding the right seller. The difficulty with that approach is that seller turnover rates are often horrendous, leaving many territories poorly covered or not covered at all. . . . Sales managers should be in the field with their low producers, and their new sellers, as much as possible. Like good athletic coaches, they should constantly remind the sellers of the fundamentals, constantly encourage, and constantly praise good performance.[25]

Although coaching may entail the sales manager's interactions with a group of salespeople, its most crucial activities are those conducted with individual salespeople. Coaching sessions may take place in the office or during the sales manager's field visits with salespeople. In the field, such sessions often take the form of "curbstone conferences" immediately prior to or following each sales call.

Coaching is especially important for sales managers, as compared to other managers in a given company. As Peters and Austin have concluded, "Perhaps surprisingly, the more elbowroom a company grants to its people, the more important on-the-job coaching becomes."[26] Since salespeople often have considerable latitude to plan and execute work activities, coaching is extremely important for most sales managers. Further, the boundary-role demands of sales jobs, and the frequent geographic isolation of salespeople from other company personnel, add to the significance of coaching activities.

The essence of coaching is providing guidance and feedback in close time proximity to the occurrence of an appropriate event related to developing salespeople's skills, attitudes, or behaviors. By assuring a close link between the coaching session and the appropriate event (for example, a sales call), the sales manager is using the principle of *recency* to assist the developmental, or learning, process. Essentially, this is the principle that learning is facilitated when it is immediately applied. By making a practice of holding coaching sessions before and after each sales call, sales managers are also using *repetition*, another powerful learning tool.

In addition to using repetition and recency to facilitate learning, sales managers should consider the type of feedback they offer to salespeople during coaching sessions. Feedback can be described as either outcome feedback or as cognitive feedback.[27] **Outcome feedback** is information on whether or not a desired outcome is achieved. In contrast, **cognitive feedback** is information on how and why the desired outcome is achieved. Post-sales-call coaching focusing on outcome feedback might feature comments such as, "Your response to the question on pricing was totally inadequate," while cognitive feedback might focus on why the pricing question was poorly handled, how a better response could have been made, and how the proper handling of the question could have facilitated the desired outcome for the sales call.

Researchers have suggested that the use of cognitive feedback can be helpful to salespeople and that outcome feedback can be dysfunctional in the complex dynamic environments faced by many salespeople.[28] The importance of cognitive feedback is reaffirmed in several of the points in Exhibit 13.3.

EXHIBIT 13.3   ▪   *Coaching Suggestions*

1. Take a "we" approach instead of a "you" approach. Instead of telling the salesperson, "You should do it this way next time," try, "On the next call, we can try it this way."

2. Address only one or two problems at a time. Prioritize problems to be attacked, and deal with the most important ones first.

3. Instead of criticizing salespeople during coaching, help them improve by giving "how to" advice. Repeatedly tell them what you like about their performance.

4. Ask questions to maximize the salesperson's active involvement in the coaching process.

5. Insist that salespeople evaluate themselves. Self-evaluation helps develop salespeople into critical thinkers regarding their work habits and performance.

6. Reach concrete agreements about what corrective action is to be taken following each coaching session. Failure to agree on corrective action may lead to the salesperson's withdrawal from the developmental aspects of coaching.

7. Keep records of coaching sessions specifying corrective action to be taken, objectives of the coaching session, and a timetable for accomplishing the objective. Follow up to ensure objectives are accomplished.

Source: Compiled from Barry J. Farber, "Sales Managers: Do Yourself a Favor," *Personal Selling Power*, April 1990, 33; and "First Train Them, Then Coach Them," *Sales and Marketing Management*, August 1987, 64–65.

Planning and Conducting Integrative Meetings

One of the best opportunities for sales managers to demonstrate leadership ability comes when they plan and execute an **integrative meeting,** one in which several sales and sales management functions are achieved. Although multiple objectives are accomplished at such meetings, their overall purpose is to unite the salesforce in the quest for common objectives, a key part of the leadership model discussed earlier in the chapter. Such meetings may combine training, strategic planning, motivational programs, recognition of outstanding sales performance, and recreation and entertainment for the attendees. In large sales organizations, the entire salesforce may attend a major integrative sales meeting each year to review the past year's performance and unite for the upcoming year. According to John Mackenzie, a meeting consultant for Coca-Cola, Du Pont, and General Foods, such events allow "psychic bonding" among salespeople; that is, salespeople can share common experiences and feel more like team members than isolated employees.[29] Sales managers can use integrative meetings to ensure that salespeople gain a better understanding of their important revenue-production role. Mackenzie also stresses that such meetings provide an excellent means for sales managers to reinforce their own visibility, reputation, and image with top management and the salesforce.

To maximize the impact of a sales meeting, consultant George Schenk suggests that sales managers remember that "the word 'meeting' implies interaction among participants, but often it is just an opportunity for managers to coerce,

EXHIBIT 13.4 ▪ *Suggestions from Salespeople on Conducting Meetings*

1. Keep technical presentations succinct, and use visual aids and breakout discussion groups to maintain salespeople's interest.
2. Keep salespeople informed of corporate strategy and their role in it.
3. Minimize operations reviews unless they are directly related to sales. Use a combination of face-to-face exchanges and written handouts to introduce key people in advertising and customer service.
4. Set a humane schedule. Overscheduling can deter learning. Allow time for salespeople to share experiences so they learn from each other.
5. Let salespeople know what's planned. Be sure they are briefed on the purpose and content of the meeting.
6. Ask salespeople for their ideas of topics, speakers, and preferred recreational activities, if applicable.

Source: Rayna Skolnik, "Salespeople Sound Off on Meetings," *Sales and Marketing Management*, November 1987, 108.

browbeat, or preach to salespeople."[30] Mr. Schenk points out that a more effective use of time is to allow salespeople to be active participants in the meeting through group discussions, presentations, and role playing.

One company that believes in heavy participation by the salespeople during meetings is Merck Sharpe & Dohme. According to Douglas Durand, senior director of sales and marketing development:

Effective meetings are prepared as carefully as a major account presentation. Participants get meeting agendas and objectives in advance. Group members are assigned to make presentations, lead role-playing sessions, or report on how they solved a problem or grasped an opportunity. Each of these things encourages contribution and interaction. There's a lot of "meet" in these meetings.[31]

As is true with all leadership functions, the needs and wants of the salesforce should be given some consideration in the planning and execution of integrative meetings. Some suggestions from salespeople are given in Exhibit 13.4.

Planning and conducting an integrative sales meeting involves creative, sometimes glamorous activities such as selecting a theme for the meeting, arranging for the appearances of professional entertainers, or even assisting in the production of special films and other audiovisual materials. The ultimate success of all meetings, however, depends on the planning and execution of rather detailed activities such as communicating with all parties before the meeting, checking site arrangements, preparing materials for the meeting, arranging for audiovisual support, and being sure that all supplies are on hand when the meeting begins. To increase the effectiveness of a major meeting, sales managers would be well served to heed the advice given in Exhibit 13.5.

Meeting Ethical/Moral Responsibilities

In recent years, there has been increased attention paid to the subject of ethical responsibilities of business leaders. As pointed out in a prize-winning *Harvard Business Review* article, "Most business decisions involve some degree of ethical

EXHIBIT 13.5 ▪ *Sales Manager's Meeting Review List*

Before your meeting
1. Distribute meeting notice/agenda.
2. Plan and prepare the meeting content, both words and visuals, in terms of the needs of your audience.
3. Rehearse.
4. Check out room and equipment.

At the start of the meeting
1. Review the agenda.
2. Review meeting objectives.
3. Explain what role the participants will have in the meeting.

During the meeting (encouraging participation)
1. Ask open-end questions . . . that is, questions that can't be answered with a yes or no.
2. Ask one or two participants to bring specific relevant information to share at the meeting.
3. Reinforce statements that are on-target with meeting objectives.
4. When questions are asked of you, redirect them to the group or to the questioner.
5. Use examples from your own personal experience to encourage the group to think along similar lines.

During the meeting (maintaining control)
1. Ignore off-target remarks. Do not reinforce.
2. Ask questions specifically related to the task at hand.
3. Restate relevant points of the agenda when the discussion veers from objectives.
4. When one person is dominating the discussion, tactfully, but firmly, ask him/her to allow others to speak.
5. Ask the group's opinion as to whether or not a certain subject is on-target or not with the agenda.

At the end of the meeting
1. Summarize.
2. State conclusions and relate to original meeting objectives.
3. Outline actions to be taken as a result of the meeting. (Who is expected to do what and by when.)

Cautions
1. Encourage, don't resent, questions.
2. Be a facilitator and not a monopolizer of discussion.
3. A little humor is welcome at most any meeting, but don't attempt to be a constant comic.
4. Don't put anybody down in public. If you have a problem participant, take him or her aside at a break and ask for cooperation.
5. Coming unprepared is worse than not coming.

Source: From "Six Secrets to Holding a Good Meeting," furnished by 3M Visual Systems Division. Reproduced by permission of and copyrighted by Minnesota Mining and Mfg. Co.

judgment; few can be taken solely on the basis of arithmetic."[32] In previous chapters, ethical concerns have been highlighted to stress their importance in practically every sales management function. In this section, we will discuss three approaches to management ethics: **immoral management, amoral management, and moral management.** The key points distinguishing these three approaches are shown in Exhibit 13.6. The author of the material shown in the exhibit contends

EXHIBIT 13.6 ▪ *Approaches to Management Ethics*

Organizational Characteristics		*Immoral Management*	*Amoral Management*	*Moral Management*
	Ethical Norms	Management decisions, actions, and behavior imply a positive and active opposition to what is moral (ethical). Decisions are discordant with accepted ethical principles. An active negation of what is moral is implied.	Management is neither moral nor immoral, but decisions lie outside the sphere to which moral judgments apply. Management activity is outside or beyond the moral order of a particular code. May imply a lack of ethical perception and moral awareness.	Management activity conforms to a standard of ethical, or right, behavior. Conforms to accepted professional standards of conduct. Ethical leadership is commonplace on the part of management.
	Motives	Selfish. Management cares only about its or the company's gains.	Well-intentioned but selfish in the sense that impact on others is not considered.	Good. Management wants to succeed but only within the confines of sound ethical precepts (fairness, justice, due process).
	Goals	Profitability and organizational success at any price.	Profitability. Other goals are not considered.	Profitability within the confines of legal obedience and ethical standards.
	Orientation toward Law	Legal standards are barriers that management must overcome to accomplish what it wants.	Law is the ethical guide, preferably the letter of the law. The central question is what we can do legally.	Obedience toward letter and spirit of the law. Law is a minimal ethical behavior. Prefer to operate well above what law mandates.
	Strategy	Exploit opportunities for corporate gain. Cut corners when it appears useful.	Give managers free rein. Personal ethics may apply but only if managers choose. Respond to legal mandates if caught and required to do so.	Live by sound ethical standards. Assume leadership position when ethical dilemmas arise. Enlightened self-interest.

Source: Archie B. Carroll, "In Search of the Moral Manager," *Business Horizons* 30 (March–April 1987): 12. Copyright 1987 by the Foundation for the School of Business at Indiana University. Reprinted by permission.

that the majority of managers fit into the amoral category and that the number of moral managers roughly equals the number of immoral managers.[33]

As you review the information in Exhibit 13.6, examples of immoral management may come to mind quite easily, while examples of amoral and moral management are probably harder to recall. This is partially a function of what types of business practices have been deemed most topical by the business and popular press. However, that press coverage could also indicate a deep concern throughout society about ethics in management.

Before discussing the features of moral, or ethical, sales management, some examples of seemingly immoral management (as described in Exhibit 13.6) might be helpful:

- Lincoln Savings & Loan sold thrift investors $250 million of junk bonds in its parent company; the bonds are now worthless and the parent company bankrupt. In a written directive to its bond salespeople, Lincoln management said, "Remember the weak, meek, and ignorant are always good targets."[34]
- Oracle Systems Corporation, the largest supplier of relational data-based software, encouraged salespeople to sell products not yet developed and to collect on sales before delivery of products to customers. Unhappy customers claim that when they tried to complain, they received the "runaround." Analysts say that overaggressive sales policies have led to losses and have put Oracle in danger of violating loan covenants.[35]
- The FBI is investigating charges that one insurance company tried to sabotage another by having its agents join the other company and proceed to write fictitious policies, for which they received generous commissions. The policies allegedly were to be cancelled, creating a financial hardship for the victimized company.[36]
- The Boston office of Dean Witter is being investigated by the Massachusetts Securities Division after allegations that some of its brokers "churned" customer accounts to generate higher commissions and improperly invested customer money in a high-risk stock index option. One broker has been arrested on bank and mail fraud charges. A company spokesperson, speaking of the Boston branch office, says: "I don't think that place is out of control at all."[37]

These examples are in sharp contrast to moral management as described in Exhibit 13.6. Corporate training can help sensitize managers to ethical issues and may be able to convert amoral, and even immoral, managers to the moral school of thought. For example, Phillip Morris USA has trained 500 field managers in its salesforce on issues dealing with sexual harassment in a series of workshops involving group discussions and a video entitled "Shades of Gray."[38]

Tighter financial controls and closer supervision of sales activities may help achieve ethical sales management practices. Bribery, for example, is hard to commit when sales expenditures are closely monitored. Many sales organizations are adopting a **code of ethics.** An example of a company-specific code of ethics, that of General Dynamics, was presented in Chapter 10. Associations also develop ethical codes and urge members to adhere to standards of ethical business behavior. Sample items from the American Marketing Association's code of ethics for sales managers and salespeople are shown in Exhibit 13.7.

Certainly, the development of a code of ethics is a positive action, though it is probably not enough to ensure ethical management. Sales managers must be willing to evaluate their own behavior and ask themselves if they consistently act in an ethical manner in dealing with their coworkers, employees, customers, and

EXHIBIT 13.7 ■ *Excerpts from the American Marketing Association's Code of Ethics*

1. Reject the use of high-pressure manipulations or misleading sales tactics.
2. Disclose the full price associated with any purchase.
3. Disclose all substantial risks associated with product or service usage.
4. Do not manipulate the availability of a product for the purpose of exploitation.
5. Do not use coercion in the marketing channel.
6. Refrain from exerting undue influence over the reseller's choice to handle a product.
7. Prohibit selling under the guise of conducting research.
8. Communicate in a truthful and forthright manner.
9. Avoid manipulation to take advantage of situations to maximize personal welfare in a way that unfairly deprives or damages the organization of others.

Source: "AMA Adopts New Code of Ethics," *Marketing News*, September 11, 1987, 1, published by the American Marketing Association.

other parties.[39] This process of self-evaluation could be very revealing, as suggested in a study of how sales managers react to unethical sales behavior.[40] The study concluded that sales managers would be more likely to use harsher disciplinary measures if the salesperson were male instead of female or a poor performer rather than a top performer and if negative consequences (such as losing a major account) were to follow the unethical action by the salesperson. In an ideal world, sales managers would react to unethical sales behavior without regard for individual characteristics of the salesperson involved or the consequences of the unethical act.

In examining their own behavior and that of the salesforce, sales managers should be aware of three particularly relevant types of unethical acts, as shown in Exhibit 13.8. The first type of unethical act is termed a **non-role act.** This type of act (e.g., cheating on an expense account) would not relate to a sales manager's or a salesperson's specific job role but rather is a calculated attempt to gain something at the expense of the company. A **role-failure act** involves a failure to perform job responsibilities. For example, a sales manager may do a superficial job on a salesperson's performance appraisal. The third type of unethical act is the **role-distortion act** (e.g., committing bribery), which may put the individual at risk, presumably to benefit the company and the individual's own job objectives.

Researchers suggest that it is most likely that a given organization will concentrate attention on non-role acts by implementing financial controls and employee monitoring systems. Interestingly, these researchers conclude that role-distortion and role-failure acts seldom receive systematic attention in most organizations.[41] Perhaps these findings offer direction to sales managers who are determined to manage their salesforces according to principles of moral, or ethical, principles.

EXHIBIT 13.8 ▪ *Types of Morally Questionable Managerial Acts*

Type	Direct Effect	Examples
Non-role	Against-the-firm	▪ Expense account cheating ▪ Embezzlement ▪ Stealing supplies
Role-failure	Against-the-firm	▪ Superficial performance appraisal ▪ Not confronting expense account cheating ▪ Palming off a poor performer with inflated praise
Role-distortion	For-the-firm	▪ Bribery ▪ Price fixing ▪ Manipulation of suppliers

Source: Adapted from James A. Waters and Frederick Bird, "Attending to Ethics in Management," *Journal of Business Ethics* 8 (June 1989): 494.

Those interested in achieving moral management will undoubtedly face some challenges, since competitive pressures and the premium placed on expedient action often encourage unethical behavior. As one observer puts it,

> The central nature of selling—a negotiation between buyer and seller—is inherently a laboratory of ethical scenarios. Sales managers likewise face many ethical issues stemming from the discretion they must exercise in adjusting resources for variations in territories, salesperson ability, competitor strength, and social, political, and regulatory climates in the various markets served.[42]

For a long-term horizon for success, we urge you to use a framework for moral, ethical management as described in the last column of Exhibit 13.6 and to embrace, where available, codes of ethics, training to sensitize salespeople and their managers to ethical issues, and legal instruction. Those who become sales managers will have the added responsibility of providing ethical leadership by setting an example. Several suggestions for providing guidance to salespeople in their dealings with customers are given in "An Ethical Perspective: Guidance for Sales Presentations."

Problems in Leadership

Any managerial position involving the direct supervision of employees will require periodic handling of personnel management problems. As indicated earlier, personnel problems can be minimized through proper recruitment and selection, training, motivation and compensation and the establishment of clearly stated salesforce plans, policies, and procedures.

Examples of the problems that sales managers may have to deal with include conflicts of interest, chemical abuse and dependency, salespeople who will not conform to guidelines, salespeople whose employment must be terminated, and sexual harassment.

Conflicts of Interest

Since salespeople assume a boundary-role position, they cannot help but encounter **conflicts of interest.** Such conflicts are part of the job, and problem-solving skills are often tested. In some cases, meeting customer demands could violate company policy. In an even more serious vein, the salesperson could have a vested interest or ownership in a customer's business, or even in a competitor's business. The use of confidential information for individual profit, as in the case of Wall Street insider trading, is also an example of serious—in fact, criminal—conflict of interest. Many companies require that employees periodically sign an agreement not to engage in specified situations that may represent conflicting interests.

Chemical Abuse and Dependency

Salespeople may be no more susceptible to chemical dependency than any other occupational group, nor is there any hard evidence that chemical abuse and dependency are worse among their ranks now than in the past. However, awareness of this problem is increasing, and sales managers are taking a more active role in identifying individuals with problems and in assisting rehabilitative efforts.

One survey found that over 40 percent of the policies for dealing with alcohol abuse in the salesforce were set by the sales manager, not someone else in the company. The same survey found that the most common response to alcohol abuse was counseling by the sales manager, and the next most frequent response was

---

AN ETHICAL PERSPECTIVE

Guidance for Sales Presentations A review of legal cases since 1940 reveals that salespeople can create legal problems for their firms through various indiscretions. For example, punitive damages have been paid to customers for salespeople's overstating a product's technical capabilities, downplaying the importance of warning messages, making false negative claims about competitors, and promising warranties that were actually prohibited by a written sales agreement.

One important aspect of sensitizing salespeople to their legal and ethical responsibilities is for the sales manager to lead by example and routinely remind salespeople of potential legal issues during coaching sessions. Sales managers who encourage salespeople to adhere to ethical and legal standards yet who violate the standards themselves are probably adding to salespeople's role stress by increasing their feelings of role ambiguity. Since research has shown that employees' ethical standards are strongly influenced by their managers, it is important to supplement codes of ethics and written policies with consistent reinforcement in the field. Failure to correct an unethical act may serve as a sales manager's tacit approval.

Source: Karl A. Boedecker, Fred W. Morgan, and Jeffrey J. Stoltman, "Legal Dimensions of Salesperson's Statements: A Review and Managerial Suggestions," *Journal of Marketing* 55 (January 1991): 70–80.

referral to a formal alcohol-abuse program outside the firm.[43] An overwhelming majority (75 percent) of the sales managers in the survey felt that, in general, alcohol abuse was at least a "somewhat serious" problem.

A national survey of 463 sales managers revealed that approximately one-third of the respondents felt there was at least a "somewhat serious" problem regarding drug abuse as well among salespeople.[44] Consistent with the survey on alcohol abuse, sales managers reported playing an active role in determining the policies for dealing with drug abuse. According to this survey, sales managers were more likely to respond to salespersons' drug abuse by referring them to a formal drug abuse program outside the firm.

Problem Salespeople: A Disruptive Influence

Perhaps the most infamous of the "problem salespeople" is the nonconforming "maverick" who breaks all the rules in the quest for sales results. While mavericks often are high achievers, their flaunting of the rules can be disruptive to sales managers and can adversely affect the remainder of the salesforce. A maverick who fails to produce will not survive in most sales organizations, but a rule-breaker who can produce often thrives as the center of attention. Why is this true?

One defense often heard on behalf of mavericks is that they are merely being creative. A typical defense is expressed by Jack Falvey, a sales management consultant, who points out that "there's a place for creative sales reps in every kind of selling. . . . Let's be honest. Rules really are meant to be broken."[45]

In terms of organizational commitment and job involvement, discussed earlier in the chapter, mavericks are often very enthusiastic about their selling jobs (high involvement) but are not bound to their organizations (low commitment). This high/low combination in terms of involvement and commitment produces a salesperson type sometimes called a **lone wolf.**[46] In some sales environments, for example, if the company sold through independent sales contractors, so-called lone wolves would not present substantial problems. In others, especially where team efforts are required, they would represent a sales management challenge.

Salespeople who are highly committed to the organization but who do not strongly identify with their selling roles might be called **corporate citizens.** They, too, may represent supervisory problems for sales managers, particularly if aggressive sales growth objectives are in place.

Most sales managers would prefer to have a high proportion of salespeople who are both highly committed to the organization and highly involved in their selling jobs. Such salespeople have been called **institutional stars,** and they are the primary targets of retention and reward programs.

Continuing the involvement/commitment typology, salespeople who are low on both dimensions would represent another problem category for sales managers. These salespeople have been referred to as **apathetics** and may be candidates for termination of employment if they cannot be resurrected.

Termination of Employment

In some cases, problems cannot be overcome, and it is necessary to terminate the employment of a salesperson. When performance consistently fails to meet standards, and coaching, training, and retraining are unsuccessful, termination or reassignment may be the only remaining alternatives. Also, a salesperson's insubordination or lack of effort may damage the overall effectiveness or morale of the salesforce, in which case termination could be justified.

The current environment dictates that sales managers pay close attention to the legal ramifications of terminating a salesperson's employment. A permanent record of performance appraisals, conditions of employment, and any deviations from expected performance or behavior should be carefully maintained throughout the salesperson's term of employment. Attempts to correct performance deficiencies should be noted and filed when they occur.

Before firing the salesperson, the sales manager should carefully review all relevant company policies to ensure his or her own adherence to appropriate guidelines. Finally, the actual communication of termination should be written, and any verbal communication of the termination should be witnessed by a third party. At all times, sales managers should respect the dignity of the person whose employment is being terminated while firmly communicating the termination notice.

Sexual Harassment

In 1980, the Equal Employment Opportunity Commission (EEOC) formally addressed a long-standing workplace problem by issuing guidelines for minimizing **sexual harassment.** Defining this term is not an easy matter, but EEOC guidelines indicate that sexual harassment could include lewd remarks, physical and visual actions, and sexual innuendos. Companies are expected to have guidelines for dealing with this offense, including policies for prohibiting sexual harassment and disciplining offenders.

Since the establishment of EEOC guidelines, there have been numerous instances of reported sexual harassment, most often with a woman being the target of the harassment. One observer notes that "if you are a sales manager, the probability of being asked to help one of your saleswomen deal with sexual abuse is greater than ever before, because more women are entering the sales field every day."[47]

Policies and procedures for dealing with sexual harassment should be developed for the entire company, and sales managers must strive to implement them in a conscientious manner. Furthermore, sales managers must become familiar with EEOC guidelines in order to serve as role models and to communicate clearly to their salespeople the important issues involved in sexual harassment. The job of protecting salespeople from sexual harassment is complicated by the fact that salespeople work with customers away from the office and in social situations.

Dealing with sexual harassment is a serious responsibility of all managers. One expert reminds sales managers that "if he—or she—doesn't take proactive steps to remedy a problem, immense heat can arise. If a manager has knowledge of an alleged incident, he or she must, by law, investigate and resolve the matter, or the liability can fall to him or her."[48]

The examples of conflicts of interest, chemical dependency, rule-breaking salespeople, the need to terminate employment of unsatisfactory salespeople, and sexual harassment are offered here to remind the reader of the complex human issues of managing a salesforce. Realities dictate that sales managers be able to confront and handle personnel problems as adeptly as strategic sales management issues in order to be effective leaders of their salesforces.

Summary

1. **Distinguish between salesforce leadership and supervision.** Supervision is part of leadership. It deals with the day-to-day operations of the salesforce and is primarily concerned with the maintenance and improvement of the status quo. Leadership requires more foresight and intuition than mere supervision, however, and may involve major changes in salesforce objectives and operations. Leadership involves the sales manager's interactions with a variety of parties, including salespeople, customers, other company personnel, external trainers, and employment agencies. Supervision, on the other hand, is concerned only with the relationships between the sales manager and the salesforce.

2. **Discuss how salesforce socialization can be enhanced through supervision and leadership.** The concept of salesforce socialization was first introduced in Chapter 9 (refer to Figure 9.2). Through effective supervision and leadership, sales managers can build the task-specific self-esteem of their salespeople and help resolve on-the-job conflicts. This should lead to desirable job outcomes: higher levels of organizational commitment, job involvement, job satisfaction, and performance.

3. **List the six components of a sales leadership model.** A model for sales leadership, shown in Figure 13.1, identifies six components: power of the sales manager, power of salespeople, situational factors, needs and wants of salespeople and other parties, goals and objectives, and leadership skills.

4. **Discuss five bases of power that affect leadership.** Five power bases are coercive, reward, legitimate, referent, and expert. Coercive power is associated with punishment and is the opposite of reward power. Legitimate power stems from the individual's position in the organizational hierarchy. Referent power is held by one person when another person wants to maintain a relationship with that person. Expert power is attributed to the possession of information. A sales manager and those with whom he or she interacts may utilize one or more power bases in a given situation.

5. **Explain five influence strategies used in leadership.** Influence strategies used by sales managers could be based on threats, promises, persuasion, relationships, or manipulation. Unlike the other four strategies, manipulation does not involve face-to-face interactions with the target of influence. Threats utilize coercive power, while promises stem from the reward power base. Persuasion employs expert and referent power. Legitimate and referent power are used when influence strategy is based on interpersonal relationships.

6. **Describe the style of sales management preferred by salespeople.** Although leadership requires adapting to varying situational demands, research

suggests that salespeople prefer a style of management described as dominant (as opposed to submissive) in terms of power utilization and warm (as opposed to hostile) in terms of communication with the salesforce. Four management styles are summarized in Exhibit 13.2.

7.   **Discuss issues related to coaching the salesforce, holding integrative meetings, and practicing ethical management.** Coaching involves the continual development of the salesforce. A most critical part of coaching is one-on-one sessions with a salesperson. Coaching relies on the learning principles of recency and repetition and is often conducted in the field before and after sales calls. Integrative meetings accomplish multiple sales management functions. Sales managers are involved in creative aspects of planning integrative meetings, but paying attention to detail is the key to successful meetings. Meeting ethical responsibilities is not necessarily easy but is essential to long-term success in a sales career.

8.   **Identify some of the problems encountered in leading and supervising a salesforce.** Some of the problems encountered in salesforce management are conflicts of interest; chemical abuse and dependency; disruptive, rule-breaking salespeople; salespeople whose employment must be terminated; and sexual harassment.

Key Terms

- **Leadership**
- **Supervision**
- **Task-specific self-esteem**
- **Organizational commitment**
- **Formalization**
- **Work alienation**
- **Job involvement**
- **Expert power**
- **Referent power**
- **Legitimate power**
- **Reward power**
- **Coercive power**
- **Trait approach**
- **Behavior approach**
- **Contingency approach**
- **MBWA**
- **Influence strategies**
- **Threats**
- **Promises**
- **Persuasion**
- **Relationships**
- **Cadre**
- **Hired hands**
- **Manipulation**
- **Communications mechanisms**
- **Management style**
- **Coaching**
- **Outcome feedback**
- **Cognitive feedback**
- **Integrative meeting**
- **Immoral management**
- **Amoral management**

- **Moral management**
- **Code of ethics**
- **Non-role act**
- **Role-failure act**
- **Role-distortion act**
- **Conflicts of interest**

- **Lone wolf**
- **Corporate citizens**
- **Institutional stars**
- **Apathetics**
- **Sexual harassment**

Review Questions

1. Briefly describe the six components of the sales leadership model shown in Figure 13.1.
2. Describe five types of power that affect leadership. What are the problems associated with overreliance on reward and coercive power?
3. How does the contingency approach to leadership differ from the trait approach and the behavior approach?
4. What are four categories of skills that could be useful in leadership?
5. Which power base (or bases) is important when practicing "management by wandering around"?
6. Describe five influence strategies, including the power bases related to each strategy.
7. What is the difference between outcome feedback and cognitive feedback? Which is most important in coaching?
8. Which management style is generally most preferred by salespeople? Can a sales manager use this style without abdicating his or her management responsibilities?
9. Review the boxed insert entitled "A Global Perspective: Supervising Independent Sales Agents." Can a sales manager based in the United States really control the activities of an independent (nonemployee) sales agent in a distant country?
10. Review the boxed insert entitled "An Ethical Perspective: Guidance for Sales Presentations." In addition to the suggestions made, what else can sales managers do to ensure that their salespeople properly conduct themselves while making sales calls?

Application Exercises

1. Assume you are a newly appointed sales manager, responsible for eight salespeople in a 10-state area. You have completed your initial field visits with each of the salespeople and are now beginning your second month on the job. In yesterday's mail, an anonymous letter arrived, charging one of your salespeople with a conflict of interest. The letter claimed that Fred, a 55-year-old senior salesperson, was a silent owner in a newly established wholesaler in his territory. The letter also alleged that Fred was giving the new wholesaler preferential treatment on pricing. You suspect the letter must have come from another wholesaler or from a disgruntled competitor. How would you proceed in this matter?

2. Which power bases are in evidence in the following statements from a sales manager to a salesperson?

a. "If you come through with the Holiday Inn account, I guarantee you will be the next person promoted."

b. "Don't ask me why—just do it, please."

c. "You have always been one of my favorites, and I am depending on you to hit it big in the new territory. As a personal favor, will you accept the transfer?"

d. "There are some logistics of the situation that will not allow me to accept your proposal. I will be glad to lay out the details if you wish."

e. "If you don't improve your sales volume by the end of the year, your friends are going to be asking you how you liked being a sales rep for us."

3. Ron Tabor, a sales manager, has just received a letter from Mack Wides, an experienced salesperson. Mack has heard through the grapevine that an opportunity for a management position is opening up in another division, and he is anxious to get the job. In his letter, Mack points out that he has always exceeded his sales quotas and received excellent performance reviews. He states that he is ready to be promoted into sales management and concludes his letter by saying, "If this company can't use my talents I will have only one choice to make. What do you say?" Tabor believes the letter is basically an ultimatum—promote Mack Wides or he will resign. While Wides is a good performer as a salesperson, Tabor does not view him as management material at the present time. Furthermore, contrary to the grapevine, there is no sales management opening at the present time.

Identify at least three options for dealing with this situation. Discuss the advantages and disadvantages of each option you identify.

Notes

[1]Alan J. Dubinsky, Roy D. Howell, Thomas N. Ingram, and Danny N. Bellenger, "Salesforce Socialization," *Journal of Marketing* 50 (October 1986): 192–207; and Richard P. Bagozzi, "Performance and Satisfaction in an Industrial Sales Force: An Examination of Their Antecedents and Simultaneity," *Journal of Marketing* 44 (Spring 1978): 65–77.

[2]Mark W. Johnston, A. Parasuraman, Charles M. Futrell, and William C. Black, "A Longitudinal Assessment of the Impact of Selected Organizational Influences on Salespeople's Organizational Commitment During Early Employment," *Journal of Marketing Research* 27 (August 1990): 333–344.

[3]Ronald E. Michaels, William L. Cron, Alan J. Dubinsky, and Erich A. Joachimsthaler, "Influence of Formalization on the Organizational Commitment and Work Alienation of Salespeople and Industrial Buyers," *Journal of Marketing Research* 25 (November 1988): 376–383.

[4]Based on John French, Jr., and Bertram Raven, "The Bases of Social Power," in *Studies in Social Power,* ed. D. Cartwright (Ann Arbor, Mich.: The University of Michigan Press, 1959).

[5]Paul Busch, "The Sales Manager's Bases of Social Power and Influence upon the Sales Force," *Journal of Marketing* 44 (Summer 1980): 95.

[6]Ibid., 98–99.

[7]Wilton Woods, "New Ways to Exercise Power," *Fortune,* November 6, 1989, 52.

[8]Janet E. Keith, Donald W. Jackson, Jr., and Lawrence A. Crosby, "Effects of Alternative Types of Influence Strategies Under Different Channel Dependence Structures," *Journal of Marketing* 54 (July 1990): 30–41.

[9]Stephen X. Doyle, Charles Pignatelli, and Karen Florman, "The Hawthorne Legacy and the Motivation of Salespeople," *Journal of Personal Selling and Sales Management* 5 (November 1985): 1–6.

[10]Francis J. Yammarino and Alan J. Dubinsky, "Salesperson Performance and Managerially Controllable Factors: An Investigation of Individual and Work Group Effects," *Journal of Management* 16 (1990): 87–106.

[11]Todd Mason and Geoff Lewis, "Tandy Finds a Cold, Hard World Outside the Radio Shack," *Business Week,* August 31, 1987.

[12]Thomas J. Peters and Nancy K. Austin, *A Passion for Excellence* (New York: Random House, 1985): 9.

[13]Harvey B. Mackay, "The CEO Hits the Road (and Other Sales Tales)," *Harvard Business Review* 90 (March–April 1990): 32–42.

[14]George J. Schenk, "Are You Abusing Your Salespeople?" *Sales and Marketing Management,* April 1990, 39.

[15]William L. Cron and John W. Slocum, Jr., "Career Stages Approach to Managing the Sales Force," *Journal of Consumer Marketing* 3 (Fall 1986): 11–20.

[16]This discussion of influence strategies is largely based on Madeline E. Heilman and Harvey Hornstein, *Managing Human Forces in Organizations* (Homewood, Ill.: Irwin, 1982): 116–126.

[17]Ajay K. Kohli, "Some Unexplored Supervisory Behaviors and Their Influence on Salespeople's Role Clarity, Specific Self-esteem, Job Satisfaction, and Motivation," *Journal of Marketing Research* 22 (November 1985): 424–433.

[18]Ibid., 118.

[19]Ken Blanchard, "Your Group Should Perform Like a Team," *Personal Selling Power*, October 1990, 22–23.

[20]L. B. Gschwandter, "How to Influence with Integrity," *Personal Selling Power*, January–February 1990, 40–43.

[21]For an interesting discussion, see Stephen B. Castleberry and John F. Tanner, Jr., "The Manager-Salesperson Relationship: An Exploratory Examination of the Vertical-Dyad Linkage Model," *Journal of Personal Selling and Sales Management* 6 (November 1986): 29–37; Rosemary R. Lagace, "Leader-Member Exchange: Antecedents and Consequences of the Cadre and Hired Hand," *Journal of Personal Selling and Sales Management* 10 (Winter 1990): 11–20; and John F. Tanner, Jr., and Stephen B. Castleberry, "Vertical Exchange Quality and Performance: Studying the Role of the Sales Manager," *Journal of Personal Selling and Sales Management* 10 (Spring 1990): 17–28.

[22]"If Your Salespeople Put in a Lot of Travel Time," *Sales and Marketing Management*, February 1990, 32.

[23]Robert E. Hite and Joseph A. Bellizzi, "A Preferred Style of Sales Management," *Industrial Marketing Management* 15 (August 1986): 215–223.

[24]In addition to the Hite and Bellizzi study discussed in the text, see Gilbert A. Churchill, Jr., Neil M. Ford, and Orville C. Walker, Jr., "Organizational Climate and Job Satisfaction in the Salesforce," *Journal of Marketing Research* 13 (November 1976): 323–332.

[25]Saul W. Gellerman, "The Tests of a Good Salesperson," *Harvard Business Review* 68 (May–June 1990): 68.

[26]Peters and Austin, *A Passion for Excellence*, 329.

[27]Barton A. Weitz, Harish Sujan, and Mita Sujan, "Knowledge, Motivation, and Adaptive Behavior: A Framework for Improving Sales Effectiveness," *Journal of Marketing* 50 (October 1986): 183.

[28]Ibid.

[29]Elaine Evans, "How to Create Sales Meeting Magic," *Personal Selling Power*, September 1990, 34–35.

[30]Schenk, "Are You Abusing Your Salespeople?" 39.

[31]Ibid.

[32]Sir Adrian Cadbury, "Ethical Managers Make Their Own Rules," *Harvard Business Review* 65 (September–October 1987): 70.

[33]Archie B. Carroll, "In Search of the Moral Manager," *Business Horizons* 30 (March–April 1987): 7–15.

[34]Scott McCartney, "Lincoln Memo: Aim at Ignorant," *The Commercial Appeal*, September 9, 1990, C2.

[35]Richard Brandt and Evan I. Schwartz, "The Selling Frenzy That Nearly Undid Oracle," *Business Week*, December 3, 1990, 156–157.

[36]Chuck Hawkins and Jon Friedman, "Did Art Williams Take a Walk on the Wild Side?" *Business Week*, August 6, 1990, 31.

[37]Keith H. Hammonds and Jon Friedman, "Dean Witter Braces for a Backlash in Boston," *Business Week*, March 6, 1989, 86.

[38]Cathy Trost, "With Problem More Visible, Firms Crack Down on Sexual Harassment," *The Wall Street Journal*, August 28, 1986, 17.

[39]Michael R. Hyman, Robert Skipper, and Richard Tansey, "Ethical Codes Are Not Enough," *Business Horizons* (March–April 1990): 15–22.

[40]Joseph A. Bellizzi and Robert E. Hite, "Supervising Unethical Salesforce Behavior," *Journal of Marketing* 53 (April 1989): 36–47.

[41]James A. Waters and Frederick Bird, "Attending to Ethics in Management," *Journal of Business Ethics* 8 (June 1989): 493–497.

[42]Thomas R. Wotruba, "A Comprehensive Framework for the Analysis of Ethical Behavior, with a Focus on Sales Organizations," *Journal of Personal Selling and Sales Management* 10 (Spring 1990): 30.

[43]W. E. Patton III and Michael Questell, "Alcohol Abuse in the Sales Force," *Journal of Personal Selling and Sales Management* 6 (November 1986): 39–51.

[44]W. E. Patton III, "Drug Abuse in the Sales Force," *Journal of Personal Selling and Sales Management* 8 (August 1988): 21–34.

[45]Jack Falvey, "Managing the Maverick Salesperson," *Sales and Marketing Management*, September 1990, 12.

[46]Thomas N. Ingram, Keun S. Lee, and George H. Lucas, Jr., "Commitment and Involvement: Assessing a Salesforce Typology," *Journal of Academy of Marketing Science* 19 (Summer 1991), 187–197.

[47]Linda Lynton, "The Dilemma of Sexual Harassment," *Sales and Marketing Management*, October 1989, 67.

[48]Ibid., 69.

CASE 13.1   *Westchester Business Forms*

Background

Art Collier, National Sales Manager for Westchester Business Forms, had spent the better part of the past 30 days finalizing the annual sales meeting, which was to be held in Miami. It had been an excellent year for Westchester, and overall sales and profit goals had been exceeded. The meeting was meant to be a reward for the salespeople, with scheduled recreation and lavish dinners to offset rigorous training and planning sessions.

Collier was pleased with the plans for the meeting, except that the attendees were scheduled to travel on Super Bowl Sunday. Since Westchester's salesforce of 50 was scattered across the country, Collier had decided to have the entire group rendezvous in a designated hospitality suite in the Atlanta airport. This meant that some of the salespeople would have several hours to kill in Atlanta prior to the ultimate departure at 3:00 p.m. Collier didn't like this extended waiting time, but he did want the entire salesforce to travel to Florida together, since they could then travel to the resort meeting site on a single chartered bus.

Current Situation

The day after the flight to Miami, Art Collier found out he was in trouble. Bob Davidson, Senior Vice-President for Marketing and also Collier's boss, had angrily summoned Art to his suite for what turned out to be an old-fashioned tongue-lashing. It seems that events of the night before had gotten out of control, and there had been some rather serious consequences. It all started in the Atlanta airport, where several of the Westchester salespeople had apparently consumed a few too many cocktails as they impatiently awaited departure to Florida. Conduct on the flight had been somewhat out of line. When the flight made an intermediate stop in Orlando, the pilot had approached the group and advised them to "hold it down," or else he would lodge a complaint with authorities upon touchdown in Miami.

When the group arrived at the resort, spirits were truly high, in part because the bus driver had been cajoled into stopping along the way so the group could purchase beer and snacks for the ride.

By the time the group convened for dinner, many were irritable, especially those who had missed lunch because of tight connections in Atlanta. Others were frankly too drunk to care about eating, so they skipped dinner in favor of setting up poker games in various condominiums.

At 7:00 a.m. the next day, Bob Davidson received a call from the resort security director, who informed him of two disturbing developments. First, a distinguished guest of the hotel, a former Washington Cabinet member, had lodged a formal complaint with law enforcement authorities as a result of an incident in the lounge the prior evening. It seems that a Westchester salesperson had gotten into a heated argument with the guest, and a brawl had been narrowly averted. Now, security wanted Davidson to help identify the Westchester salesperson in the event formal charges were lodged.

The second problem was that security had located a station wagon almost fully submerged in a small lake on the golf course. The wagon had been leased from Hertz by a Westchester staff assistant, who had been using the vehicle to run errands in connection with the sales meeting.

After venting his anger, Davidson placed a call to the staff assistant to inquire about the station wagon. According to the staff assistant, the car had been parked at 6:00 the night before, and he didn't know it had been found in the lake. Davidson now addressed Collier: "Art, I hope you know how serious this is. I want you to account for all your people immediately. Let's hope none of them are at the bottom of the lake. Next, we have to figure out how to handle this flap with the politician. The first session of the meeting begins in less than half an hour. I want your action plan in five minutes."

Questions

1. Who is at fault here?
2. Can you identify things that could have been done differently to minimize the chances of these events occurring?
3. What should Art Collier do at this point?

CASE 13.2 *Successful Selling Incorporated*

Background

Successful Selling Incorporated (SSI) is a ten-year-old firm specializing in providing sales training materials such as videotapes, software, and custom-designed sales seminars to small and medium-sized firms in the Midwest. Headquartered in Minneapolis, the firm employs five salespeople who report directly to Director of Sales Karen Maxwell. Karen also does some direct selling in addition to her sales management duties.

Business has been a bit slow, and Karen has planned a target account program to increase sales. Essentially, each salesperson has been assigned three target accounts, and sales volume targets have been set for each account. There are no special incentives for securing the target accounts, as Karen believes that SSI's straight commission compensation plan should provide plenty of incentive to the salespeople.

Current Situation

Karen has reviewed the target account program, and she is upset at the lack of progress. She has met individually with each salesperson to discuss the situation, and nothing concrete has emerged from the meetings. The basic message from the salespeople is that they are indeed trying to add the target accounts but current business conditions are unfavorable for expanding the customer base. Some of their comments are still troubling Karen:

> "Look, Karen, just because we both want this to happen doesn't mean it will — at least not on your schedule."
>
> "Sorry, Karen, I simply haven't gotten to first base with any of my target accounts. Maybe I'm wasting my time."
>
> "Hey, whose idea was this anyway? I never said I could get those accounts!"

After concluding her meetings with each salesperson, Karen decided the salesforce had pretty much given up on the target account program. This conclusion gave her even more resolve to make the program work. As a result, she wrote a memo to the salesforce, as shown in Exhibit 13.A.

Questions

1. How would you assess Karen's sales management performance in this situation?
2. How do you think the SSI salespeople will react to Karen's memo?
3. How would you have handled this situation?

EXHIBIT 13.A ▪ *Memorandum*

To:	SSI Sales Representatives
From:	Karen Maxwell Director of Sales
Subject:	Target Account Program

As you know, I am disappointed at the lack of progress with our target account program. Here we are, 90 days into the program, with only 30 days to go, and not one target account has been secured. Not one! This is fairly serious, don't you agree?

As of this moment, be advised that your daily efforts should be redoubled to secure these accounts. Failure to accomplish the goals of the target account program will result in a review of your employment status. I know that each of you has been successful in the past, but my question is, "What have you done for SSI lately?" We cannot afford the no-growth position that you are apparently satisfied with, and we will do whatever is necessary to get things headed in the right direction.

If you would like to discuss this further with me, fine. But I must tell you that the time has come for action, not a lot of talk. I look forward to seeing your immediate progress and to the achievement of our goals.

Western Industrial Supply Company

Western Industrial Supply Company, located in Los Angeles, distributed janitorial supplies—waxes, cleaners, paper toweling, and the like—to industrial and institutional users in California from San Diego to Fresno and east as far as Needles. Salesmen called mainly on custodians who, if sold on the product(s), requisitioned the purchase through the firm's purchasing department. Western was one of the larger companies of its type in the state and, within its sales area, competed with some 30 to 40 other companies—many of which were small, local distributors. In both the Los Angeles and San Diego metropolitan areas, competition came mainly from distributors of a size similar to Western.

Population and industrial growth had increased the demand for janitorial supplies substantially during the early and mid-1970s. In more recent years, market growth had slowed, and competition had become more intense with the result that profits had declined when measured in real dollar terms. Mr. Randy Cross, the company's president and chief executive officer, felt that a new sales strategy was needed which included a different way of compensating the sales force.

In the past, Western had tried to minimize competition by emphasizing proprietary products through aggressive selling. Over the years, the company had increased the number of its proprietary products which yielded a gross margin considerably higher than did jobbed items. Such products were manufactured under contract by a variety of small manufacturers located in southern California. The company had a laboratory which developed the product's specifications, tested it against competitive products under a variety of use conditions, and made certain that it was produced to specification. Proprietary products represented about 18 percent of total sales but nearly 35 percent of total gross margin.

Western Industrial salesmen were expected to call regularly on their accounts, although their call frequency by account type and size was not known, since salesmen did not make out call reports. Once on the premises, they were expected to demonstrate items—

especially proprietary ones—whenever possible in an effort to call attention to those features which made the product unique. This required them to have a good technical knowledge of the product and a willingness to "get their hands dirty." Salesmen were trained to work with custodians to show them how to make their jobs easier and at the same time to improve the hygiene and cleanliness of the facilities they maintained.

The company employed 14 salespersons working under a vice-president in charge of sales. Each salesperson had an assigned territory the size of which depended upon the number, size, and density of accounts. Outside salespersons were paid on a commission basis backed by a monthly guarantee based on the individual's earnings record. In addition, each member of the sales force received either a $250 or $150 monthly car allowance (depending upon the size of the territory) plus fringe benefits. Three members of the sales force were "insiders" in that they handled phone orders and service requests. These persons were paid on a salary basis. Of the 11 outside salespersons, 4 were still on monthly guarantee, having been with the company less than one year. An average salesperson earned $1,500 per month while the better ones exceeded $2,000. Most of the better salespersons had been with the company a long time.

A number of trends had conspired to make the industry increasingly competitive. One was the growing consolidation of supply distributors. The small local distributor was fast becoming extinct. Cost of capital associated with inventories and accounts receivable coupled with high inflation had forced many small firms to exit the industry. A second trend was that an impressive number of medium to large customers had contracted out their cleaning activities, thereby reducing their direct purchases of janitorial supplies substan-

Source: This case was written by Professor Harper Boyd, College of Business Administration, University of Arkansas. Included in *Stanford Business Cases 1983* with permission. Reprinted with permission of Stanford University Graduate School of Business © 1983 by the Board of Trustees of the Leland Stanford Junior University.

tially. The larger contract cleaning firms either bought direct from manufacturers or acquired their supplies from distributors on a bid basis. A third trend was the increased importance of the purchasing department in the purchase of janitorial supplies. This tended to downplay the role of the custodian in the purchasing decision. Yet another trend was that more and more of the larger accounts were requesting bids on major supply items.

In view of the above, Mr. Cross thought that Western had to make some important decisions near term if the company was to survive and prosper. In commenting on the situation he said:

> The basic trends have dried up a number of our larger accounts since our company has never learned how to bid successfully. We really do very little bidding, but we've got to start learning how soon. Also, we're stuck with an increasing number of small accounts which means lots of small orders. These have increased our sales, order processing and fulfillment, delivery, and bad debt costs to a point where something significant has to be done. And we're having trouble holding our better salesmen. Our turnover here is not good.

Mr. Cross outlined his tentative corrective plan as follows:

1. Price the company's proprietary products more competitively. This meant that prices on present proprietary products would be reduced by as much as 10 to 20 percent through the use of quantity discounts.
2. Increase the number of new products. To accomplish this, two new technicians would be added to the company laboratory.
3. Divest in the very small accounts by using a minimum order size requirement in an effort to lower costs and allocate more resources to the larger accounts. These actions would likely result in a substantial shift in the composition and size of the sales territories.
4. Undertake aggressive bidding which would be accomplished by establishing a special inside unit to work with the sales force in the preparation of bids.
5. Better service to a point "where it is at least as good as any competitor and better than most." The plan called for all orders to be shipped within 72 hours after receipt. This was to be made possible mainly by a computerized order processing system which prepared all necessary documents and identified the exact warehouse location (bin number) of each invoice line item. In addition, a computerized inventory model would be installed which would hopefully reduce out-of-stocks to less than 2 percent of all items stocked.
6. Professionalization of the sales force. Given the actions cited above, it seemed clear that a different kind of salesperson would be needed. Some of the present sales force could be retrained, but it was anticipated that probably half would need to be replaced. It was likely that a new sales manager would have to be hired; further, that the infrastructure within the sales department would have to be improved (e.g., addition of the estimating unit and an increase in the number of inside salesmen).

Mr. Cross recognized that considerable fact-finding had to take place before he could make his plan operational. He also recognized that he should move slowly in this regard, perhaps taking several years to implement it. He thought the place to start was with the sales force. In this regard, he reasoned that since several salespersons needed replacing in the near future, the first step would be to draw up a new compensation plan which would retain the loyalty of those asked to stay while attracting the caliber of person desired. If a satisfactory plan could be developed which could accommodate both the present and the future, Mr. Cross was willing to install it for the next fiscal year, which started some five months hence.

The present outside sales force was paid a 10 percent commission on the sales of all proprietary items and a 5 percent commission on all jobbed items. In addition, each had a car allowance and received fringe benefits mostly in the form of health and life insurance and social security. Each had a monthly guarantee which was expected to be equaled or bettered by commissions. The company paid no bonus to the sales force, although all other workers received one in those years when before-tax profits exceeded a certain percent of sales. This was distributed on the basis of an employee's annual wages. Typically, this amounted to a week's salary.

The new compensation plan called for the setting of a dollar quota for each outside salesperson in three product categories—proprietary, high-margin jobbed products, and low-margin jobbed products. The quotas would be based on an extrapolation of sales from the three previous years with the last year carrying a double weight. This result would then be subject to adjustment based on the forecast for the coming year. The forecast would take into account new products, price changes, general economic conditions in the territory, and any change in competition. Adjustments would also need to be made to accommodate territorial shifts or realignments.

All salespersons would be paid a monthly salary in the future. This would be calculated by applying the present commission system to the quota for proprietary products and a total of the high- and low-margin jobbed items. Every effort would be made to approximate the present remuneration of a salesperson, although it was recognized that this could prove difficult when substantial territorial adjustments had to be made. In addition to salaries, salespersons would receive car mileage and the company's fringe benefit package and participate in the annual bonus plan. Quotas were to be set for each month of the year.

In addition to the base compensation plan, salespersons had the opportunity of earning an "improvement over standard bonus" each quarter for the three product categories as follows:

Percent improvement over standard (quota)	Commission rate to be paid
Category A—proprietary (18 percent of sales):	
0 and under 5	8%
5 and under 10	9
10 and under 15	10
15 and under 20	11
20 and over	12
Category B—high-margin jobbed items (26 percent of sales):	
0 and under 5	4.0
5 and under 10	4.5
10 and under 15	5.0
15 and under 20	5.5
20 and over	6.0
Category C—low-margin jobbed items (56 percent of sales):	
0 and under 5	2.0
5 and under 10	2.5
10 and under 15	3.0
15 and under 20	3.5
20 and over	4.0

To ensure that the sales force did not neglect the high-volume but low-margin items completely, the plan provided that *no* improvement over standard bonus would be paid unless the quotas were met in each of the three product categories. This seemed critical, given the relatively high fixed costs associated with the company's warehouse and delivery operations.

A possible alternative to the above was to set up a point system whereby an underage in one category could be offset by an overage elsewhere. Points would be assigned to each category based on its percent of the total quota which equaled 100 points. In the case of Category A, any deficit would be translated into a gross margin dollar figure which would have to be equaled by some combination of gross margin overages from the other two categories. A deficit in Category B could only be made up from a gross margin overage in Category C, while a deficit in the latter could only be accommodated by an overage in Category B. Average margins would be used to calculate overages and underages and were expected to be approximately 54 percent for Category A, 26 percent for Category B, and 16 percent for Category C.

While quota by product category was to be set monthly, commissions would be based on a quarterly basis, thereby enabling the salesperson to make up for a bad month; i.e., there would be four chances during the year for a salesperson to earn extra compensation in the form of a commission bonus since a failure to meet or exceed quota for any one quarter would not be cumulative.

Bidding posed a special problem. Since the company had little experience here, there was some question as to how best to handle it in terms of the new compensation plan. Sales from successful bidding activities could be large, but margins would be reduced. Thus, if successful, the sales force could meet the sales quotas but at a considerably lower average gross margin. One possibility was to credit sales on the basis of gross margin; e.g., if the company made a successful bid by cutting its margins by half, then the salesperson would receive credit for 50 percent of the dollar sales involved. The objection here was that, under such conditions, salesmen would shy away from bidding situations. Much the same would happen if quotas were established on the basis of gross margin dollars and not sales dollars. Once the company had developed a history of bidding, then the problem would be less acute.

Another problem was whether the new compensation plan would in any way inhibit the motivation of the inside sales force. A smart outside salesperson would likely use the insiders to do as much of his/her follow-up work as possible and would set high service standards. This could generate the feeling by the in-side sales personnel that they were making a significant contribution to company sales and profits and yet [were not participating] in the rewards.

Northern New Jersey Manufacturing Company

Northern New Jersey Manufacturing Company was a producer of several kinds of industrial equipment listed in Exhibit 1. It developed from the efforts in the late 1940s of a gifted engineer and inventor, Sidney Hovey, who patented several of his ideas for variations on standard products. He founded and was active in the firm for more than twenty-six years until his death.

Hovey had been very interested in the selling activity of his company and had a strong sense of professionalism that he used in personally selecting people for his sales force. He managed the sales force until it grew to a size of three men, at which time he secured the services of Herbert Staley as sales manager.

Before Staley's arrival and for several years thereafter, Hovey told the salesmen expressly the names of firms he wanted them to call on. The founder was acutely interested in the reputation of his young company. His concern with reputation included product characteristics as promised, delivery on time (critical to customers for these goods), and ethical, highly reserved business conduct by the salesmen. However, this concern for reputation was not restricted to these factors. Hovey also wanted to have as his customers those who enjoyed the finest reputations. For example, he told his salesmen never to solicit the orders of a small firm then known by the name of Reihnan and Loykas, for he considered the owners to be social climbers without proper backgrounds. In addition, he did not like an advertisement of theirs he once saw in a weekly business newspaper. He also instructed his salesmen not to call on Heather Glow, Inc., because it had been turned down for a loan at the bank that Hovey used. This was despite the fact Heather Glow found credit at another bank.

Not all the instructions were negative, however. Hovey had the salesmen, all of whom were engineers, visit Camden Mills, Stone & Kruger, and South Coast Metals time after time even though all three were committed to other sellers and other product designs. He wanted Northern New Jersey Manufacturing Company to be a name that such firms knew and respected. He also cultivated several large national companies, such as Combustion Engineering, American Machine and Foundry, Kaiser Industries, Westinghouse, and Melpar.

After Hovey's death, Staley continued these policies for the better part of a year. At that point James Watts, the new president hired from the outside, had a long talk with the sales manager and explained that he thought some changes were desirable. The firm should try to maximize sales and abandon all the "notions and pretentions," as he termed them. The salesmen should be put on a combination salary plus commission. The two other executives in the company, the finance man and the production man, spoke up with thorough endorsements of such changes. The existing policy was straight salary.

With some misgivings, Staley devised a new compensation structure for his four salesmen. Under this plan he estimated that a salesman would earn about 80 percent of his compensation through salary and about 20 percent through commissions. The plan was announced on August 1 and the men were told it would go into effect in thirty days. Sales in August slumped

Source: Reprinted with permission of Macmillan Publishing Company from *Cases in Marketing*, fourth edition by Thomas V. Greer. Copyright © 1987 by Thomas V. Greer.

EXHIBIT 1 ▪ *Northern New Jersey Manufacturing Company Sales by Product, Selected Months*

Product	September	July	September Last Year	September Two Years Before
Dryers	$21,000	$34,500	$35,000	$32,200
Sprayers	7,700	7,500	8,000	7,800
Planers	4,100	4,300	4,000	3,900
Power saws	3,200	3,000	3,000	3,100
Drills	4,200	4,100	4,000	3,900
Sanders	9,500	7,300	7,200	7,000
Metal buffers	7,500	4,900	5,000	4,800

about 17 percent from the same month one year earlier and 14 percent from the same month two years earlier.

After one month of use, the sales manager conducted a preliminary inquiry into the results of the new compensation policy. The results appeared to be that the easier to sell items in the product line were moving well, those of average difficulty to sell were moving adequately, and the one item that was rather difficult to sell (the dryer) was moving very poorly. Exhibit 1 gives the comparisons of September to the last month under the old policy (July) and to September one year before. Staley presented his analysis to Watts but cautioned him about premature inferences from these data. The sales manager said that he would repeat his comparisons after another month. In the meanwhile, the president told the sales manager to urge the salesmen to solicit orders for dryers.

At the beginning of November, Staley anxiously studied the results for October, as presented in Exhibit 2. He had taken a preliminary look at some frag-

mentary data about October 16 but knew that those data were undependable. In addition, the company had usually experienced a mild upswing in the fall season.

Staley was in his office reflecting on the figures in Exhibits 1 and 2 when Douglas Guglielmi, the production manager, and Richard Acker, the finance and accounting manager, both walked in. After several minutes of friendly conversation about sports and the weather, Guglielmi said that he and Staley jointly had a problem. To be specific, the mix of sales was apparently changing radically, which was upsetting his production schedule, company general plans, and deliveries. Richard Acker then added what Staley already knew, that the dryers had been earning the highest unit margin, whereas the sanders and metal buffers had been earning the lowest unit margin. Total profits were beginning to go down.

Advise Herbert Staley, sales manager for the Northern New Jersey Manufacturing Company.

EXHIBIT 2 ▪ *Northern New Jersey Manufacturing Company Sales by Product, Selected Months*

Product	October	October Last Year	October Two Years Before
Dryers	$23,000	$36,000	$35,400
Sprayers	7,900	8,400	8,200
Planers	4,300	4,200	4,000
Power saws	3,300	3,200	3,000
Drills	4,200	4,300	4,100
Sanders	11,500	7,500	7,200
Metal buffers	9,700	5,300	5,100

Liberty Statesman Corporation

Liberty Statesman Corporation was a large life insurance company operating throughout the United States and Canada. The manager of the Louisiana-Mississippi district, Cyrus Baker, had just retired after eight years in that post. His replacement was thirty-six-year-old Lyman Danner, who had been with the company six years and with a competitor for about seven years before that. For the past two years Danner, a native of New Jersey, had been manager for his home state for Liberty Statesman. The results in that territory had pleased top management. Danner, his wife, and three young children immediately moved to New Orleans, where district headquarters was located.

The first thing Danner did on arrival was to order the district office refurbished at a cost of about $7,500. He conferred at length during a series of meetings with an interior decorator on how the project was to be done. After about ten days he started a task that he described to many persons as "the most important for any new district manager, learning the sales force." Simultaneously he investigated the paper handling and limited bookkeeping activities the district office engaged in, for his observations indicated that things were not smoothly or efficiently handled and that applicable services of Liberty Statesman's national office were not being fully utilized. Using the national office for any available service might increase the expertise with which it was done and might save the district office some money, he explained.

Danner was accustomed to being in charge of one of the seven leading districts in terms of sales volume. As he discovered when he began to study the records in his new office, the Louisiana-Mississippi district had never finished in this elite group in any year. The best it had ever done was nineteenth among the thirty-eight districts and that was four years ago. The past year it had been twenty-fourth. It had been rumored in the company that Cyrus Baker was winding down toward his retirement the past two years. Therefore, Danner took the view that his new district had much more potential than the actual sales figures of the past implied. He wondered about trying to transfer in some of the highly able and motivated sales representatives he knew from his old district. He discussed the idea briefly with Sam Autier, his assistant district manager and right-hand man. Autier advised him not to waste valuable time and psychic energy even considering it, because insurance sales representatives do not transfer as readily as many other types of sales representatives.

They are on their own most of the time and can benefit handsomely from a detailed knowledge of and "feel" for the area in which they work. They need networks of contact and referrals from friends, acquaintances, and customers. Many sales require periodic visits for several years before the sale is consummated. Insurance on one member of the family may lead to insurance on another member.

Danner began to think. He knew all of this as well as Autier did and was embarrassed that he had even brought up such an idea. Perhaps, he reflected to himself, it was symptomatic of his anxiety. But he considered that Sam Autier was a good listener and he had to have someone with whom to "bat ideas around." After all, every manager had some ideas that could be improved on. And everyone in a position of responsibility needs people around him with whom he can talk without entering into commitments and promises.

What he actually said to Autier was: "Of course, you are so right. I was daydreaming. But if I had my druthers, that is about what I would do."

A few days later Danner and Autier set up a contest to furnish additional incentive for the twenty-eight sales representatives in the district. These salesmen did not represent any other company. There had been no contest in this district for about eighteen months. This one would last three months during the slow season and would be based on percentage increases over the same three months and previous year. There were to be three prizes. First prize was an all-expense-paid five-day vacation in Montego Bay, Jamaica. The second prize was a $100 U.S. savings bond, and the third prize was a bond of $50. All three winners would be presented handsome certificates on Danner's next field visit to their vicinity.

As soon as the three-month period was over, Danner eagerly began to examine the results, which are shown in Exhibit 1 for the ten persons with the highest percentage increases. He had never conducted a contest with such an outcome. Aggregate sales had gone up only about 4 per cent. He was surprised and keenly disappointed and said so, but he gave the three awards anyway. Moreover, he immediately announced to the sales force that there would be another contest,

Source: Reprinted with permission of Macmillan Publishing Company from *Cases in Marketing*, fourth edition by Thomas V. Greer. Copyright © 1987 by Thomas V. Greer.

EXHIBIT 1   ▪   *Selected Results of Sales Contest: The Ten Sales Representatives*
with the Highest Percentage Increases

Salesperson	Location	Sales During Contest	Sales, Same Period Last Year	Percentage Increase
Leary	Shreveport	$800,000	$705,000	13.4%
Caruthers	New Orleans	720,000	650,000	[10.8%]
Bymel	Baton Rouge	640,000	590,000	[8.5%]
Beatty	Jackson	635,000	590,000	[7.6%]
Verier	Lafayette	620,000	581,000	[6.7%]
Sutkin	Lake Charles	481,000	455,000	[5.7%]
Hemingway	Monroe	422,000	400,000	[5.5%]
Rymanson	Ruston	430,000	409,000	[5.1%]
Breaux	Hammond	430,500	410,000	[5.0%]
Belton	Natchitoches	435,750	415,000	[5.0%]

the details of which would be given out in a few weeks.

A few days later Danner made a field visit swing through Jackson, Oxford, Starkville, Hattiesburg, and Gulfport. At a party in his honor on this trip there was enough conversation, some of it oblique and some overheard, for him to realize that his remarks about wanting to transfer in some sales representatives from his former territory had gotten out and had apparently been repeated with some enlargement. There were no scenes at the party and Danner deftly avoided saying anything awkward or embarrassing, despite the strong temptation. Nevertheless, he returned to New Orleans perplexed.

Advise Lyman Danner of Liberty Statesman Corporation.

DETERMINING
SALESFORCE
PERFORMANCE

The three chapters in Part Six focus on determining salesforce performance. Chapter 14 presents different forecasting methods used by sales managers and discusses the use of forecasts as a basis for establishing sales quotas and selling budgets. Chapter 15 addresses the evaluation of sales organization effectiveness. Methods for analyzing sales, costs, profitability, and productivity at different sales organization levels are reviewed. Chapter 16 addresses the evaluation of salespeople's individual performance and job satisfaction. Ways of determining the appropriate performance criteria and methods of evaluation, and of using the evaluations to improve salesperson performance and job satisfaction, are discussed.

Developing Forecasts and Establishing Sales Quotas and Selling Budgets

SALES FORECASTING: METIER MANAGEMENT SYSTEMS Metier Management Systems is the dollar-volume leader in the project management systems marketplace. Established in 1977, the company has grown to annual sales in excess of $100 million, with average sales of $300,000 and average sales cycles of 3 to 18 months. The success of Metier is largely due to a systematic sales management philosophy that allows the company to respond quickly to turbulent changes in its markets and products.

The systematic sales management philosophy places heavy emphasis on sales training and a disciplined focus on developing accurate sales forecasts. The sales forecasting process consists of monthly sales prospect review meetings between each salesperson and his or her sales manager. These meetings typically last 4 to 6 hours per salesperson and are used to examine all prospects in detail. Information about the stage in the buying process, strategies for closing the sale, the expected size of the sale, and the time the sale should be completed are examined for each prospect. Although these

486

meetings are grueling, they provide the basis for the development of accurate sales forecasts.

After the sales prospect review meetings are completed, all salespeople and sales managers participate in a day-long meeting to develop final sales forecasts. Each salesperson presents and defends the information about each of his or her prospects. Then, the sales managers summarize this information into a company sales forecast for the next three months. These forecasts are compared with previous forecasts, and necessary adjustments are made. The final sales forecasts are then submitted to top management.

This systematic forecasting process produces extremely accurate sales forecasts. Sales managers are evaluated on the accuracy of their sales forecasts as well as the sales results achieved by their region. Thus, a sales manager from a region generating low sales volume can still be evaluated highly on sales forecasting if the actual sales volume is accurately predicted.

Source: Adapted from William E. Gregory, Jr., "Time to Ask Hard-Nosed Questions," *Sales and Marketing Management*, October 1989, 88–93.

Learning Objectives

After completing this chapter, you should be able to

1 *Discuss the different types of forecasts used by sales managers.*

2 *Describe the top-down and bottom-up forecasting approaches used by sales managers.*

3 *Explain the use of different forecasting methods in the top-down and bottom-up approaches.*

4 *Describe how sales quotas are established, including the use of regression procedures.*

5 *Discuss the importance of and methods for establishing selling budgets.*

A meteorologist used all of the latest technology to predict a bright and sunny day in the mid 80s. It rained most of the day and never got above 70 degrees. The weather forecast missed the mark on this particular occasion, but the meteorologist will continue to make weather forecasts and to work on improving weather forecasting procedures.

Sales managers face a situation similar to that of the meteorologist. The business environment is complex and dynamic, there are a number of forecasting methods available, and oftentimes forecasts are incorrect. Nevertheless, sales managers must continue to forecast and to work on improving their forecasting procedures. The Metier Management Systems example discussed in the opening vignette illustrates one firm's successful approach to the forecasting task.

Why is forecasting so important to sales managers? In one sense, all sales management decisions are based on some type of forecast. The sales manager decides on a certain action because he or she thinks it will produce a certain result. This expected result is a **forecast,** even though the sales manager may not have quantified it or may not have used a mathematical forecasting procedure. More specifically, forecasts provide the basis for the following sales management decisions:

1. Determining salesforce size
2. Designing territories
3. Establishing sales quotas and selling budgets
4. Determining sales compensation levels
5. Evaluating salesperson performance
6. Evaluating prospective accounts

The purpose of this chapter is to discuss forecasting, first from the perspective of a firm and then from the perspective of sales managers. Finally, we will investigate the use of forecasts in establishing sales quotas and selling budgets.

Forecasting from the Perspective of the Organization

Forecasts are important to all business functional areas and all management levels. Some of the key questions addressed in determining their use follow:[1]

1. What forecasts are needed (e.g., sales, market share, costs, competitive reactions, etc.)?
2. What are the circumstances surrounding the forecast (e.g., stage of the product life cycle, state of the economy, degree of regulation in the industry, etc.)?
3. What forecast horizon is appropriate (e.g., short-, medium-, long-term, etc.)?
4. What data are relevant and available?
5. With what frequency must the forecast be prepared?
6. Who will prepare the forecast, and how much time and resources will be committed to the task?
7. Who will use the forecast and in what manner?
8. What process and forecasting methods are to be used?
9. How soon is the forecast needed?

A GLOBAL PERSPECTIVE

Forecasting in International Markets Firms operating globally must determine the specific international markets for their products. One suggested approach is to identify a tentative list of potential international markets and then estimate the probable return on investment for each market. Estimating the probable return on investment for different international markets requires a number of different forecasts for each market, including

1. Estimate of current market potential
2. Forecast of future market potential and risk
3. Forecast of sales potential
4. Forecast of costs and profits
5. Estimate of rate of return on investment

Developing the required forecasts is extremely important, but it is often very difficult because of the lack of available data for some international markets and the lack of experience in these markets.

Source: Philip Kotler, *Marketing Management: Analysis, Planning, Implementation, and Control* (Englewood Cliffs, N.J.: Prentice-Hall, Inc., 1991), 411–412.

Although it is beyond the scope of this chapter to address all of these questions in detail, several comments are in order. The term *forecast* implies some prediction of a future state. Many different types of predictions (forecasts) are typically important (sales, market share, costs, etc.). These forecasts require some assumptions about the future situation that will be facing the firm (economic situation, regulatory environment, etc.). Thus, the forecasts of expected results desired by management are based on assumptions, or forecasts, of the expected environment within which the firm will be operating. The forecasting task is especially difficult for firms operating in international markets, as indicated in "A Global Perspective: Forecasting in International Markets."

This complex situation is illustrated in Figure 14.1. Management is typically most interested in forecasts of market share, sales, costs, and profits. Generating these forecasts, however, requires some assumptions, or forecasts, concerning the environment; market; actions by suppliers, distributors, and government; competitors' actions; and company actions. Firms that have the best information and insight concerning these situational factors are in the best position to forecast expected results.

One study of sales forecasting provides a snapshot of the company forecasting process used by U.S. firms.[2] This study found that 88 percent of responding firms prepared annual forecasts that were typically updated on a monthly or quarterly basis. Only 10 percent of the firms prepared two-year forecasts, while 26 percent forecasted sales on a five-year basis. Managers from different functional areas participated in the forecasting process. Respondent firms indicated major forecasting responsibility for the top marketing executive (41 percent) and for sales managers (19 percent). Many firms distribute the final forecast to field sales managers (34 percent) and to salespeople (19 percent). The sales forecasts are most often used in budget preparation (89 percent) and setting quotas (67 percent). The biggest problems in obtaining accurate sales forecasts were listed as the inability of salespeople or their sales managers to judge their sales prospects accurately (33 percent), difficulty in predicting the actions of competitors (31 percent), and

FIGURE 14.1 ▪ *Forecasting Framework*

The forecasting process is extremely complex. Forecasts of market share, sales, costs, and/or profits are typically desired. Preparing these forecasts requires information and understanding concerning the environment, market, competitors, channel members, and company actions.

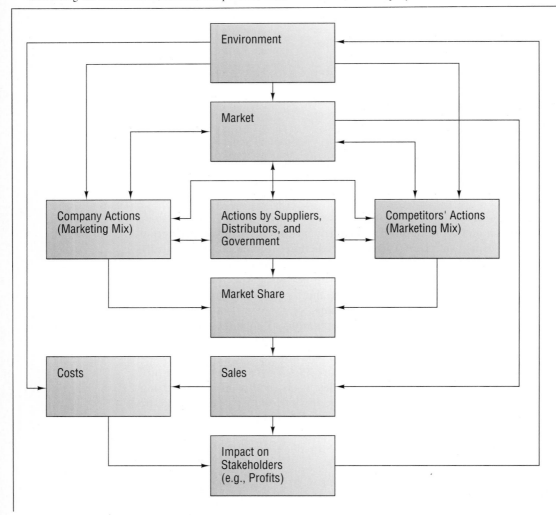

Source: J. Scott Armstrong, Roderick J. Brodie, and Shelby McIntyre, "Forecasting Methods for Marketing: Review of Empirical Research," *International Journal of Forecasting* 3 (1987): 357.

difficulty in predicting the state of the economy (30 percent). Despite these problems, 50 percent of the firms reported that their forecasts had been at least 90 percent accurate. Only 11 percent of the firms indicated forecast accuracy of less than 50 percent.

This overview of forecasting is intended to highlight both the importance and the complexity of the forecasting process. Although sales managers are often

FIGURE 14.2 ▪ *Defining the Forecast*

Many different types of forecasts are possible. Every forecast should be defined in terms of geographic area, product level, and time period.

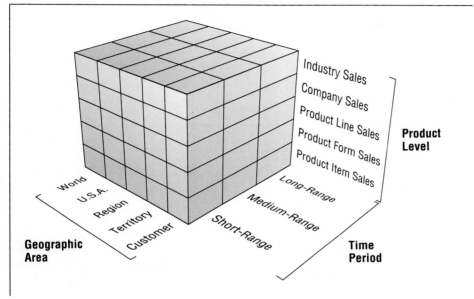

Source: Philip Kotler, *Marketing Management: Analysis, Planning, Implementation, and Control*, 7/e, © 1991, p. 242. Adapted by permission of Prentice-Hall, Inc., Englewood Cliffs, New Jersey.

involved with company forecasting, sales management activities require a different forecasting perspective.

Forecasting from the Perspective of Sales Management

Although top management levels are most concerned with total firm forecasts, sales managers are typically interested in developing and using forecasts for specific areas such as accounts, territories, districts, regions, and/or zones. For example, a district sales manager would be concerned with the district forecast as well as forecasts for individual territories and accounts within the district. There are, however, different types of forecasts that sales managers might use in different ways, and different approaches and methods might be employed to develop these forecasts.

Types of Forecasts

The term *forecast* is ordinarily used to refer to a prediction for a future time period. Although this usage is technically correct, it is too general for managerial value. As illustrated in Figure 14.2, at least three factors must be defined when referring to a forecast: the product level, the geographic area, and the time period. The figure presents 90 different forecasts that might be made, depending upon these factors.

EXHIBIT 14.1 ▪ *Types of Forecasts*

Four different types of forecasts are typically important to sales managers, depending upon whether a forecast is needed for the industry or the firm and whether the best possible or expected results are to be forecast.

	Best Possible Results	*Expected Results for Given Strategy*
Industry Level	Market Potential	Market Forecast
Firm Level	Sales Potential	Sales Forecast

Thus, when using the term *forecast*, sales management should be very specific in defining exactly what is being forecast, what geographic area is being targeted, and what time period is being forecast.

A useful way for viewing what is being forecast is presented in Exhibit 14.1. This exhibit suggests that it is important to differentiate between industry and firm levels and to determine whether the prediction is for the best possible results or for the expected results given a specific strategy. Four different types of forecasts emerge from this classification scheme:

1. **Market potential**—the best possible level of industry sales in a given geographic area for a specific time period.
2. **Market forecast**—the expected level of industry sales given a specific industry strategy in a given geographic area for a specific time period.
3. **Sales potential**—the best possible level of firm sales in a given geographic area for a specific time period.
4. **Sales forecast**—the expected level of firm sales given a specific strategy in a given geographic area for a specific time period.

Notice that the geographic area and time period are defined for each of these terms and that a true *sales forecast* must include the consideration of a specific strategy. If a firm changes this strategy, the sales forecast should change also.

As an example, assume that you are the district sales manager for a firm that markets microcomputers to organizational buyers. Your district includes Oklahoma, Texas, Louisiana, and Arkansas. You are preparing forecasts for 1992. You might first try to assess market potential. This market potential forecast would be an estimate of the highest level of microcomputer sales by all brands in your district for 1992. Then, you might try to develop a market forecast, which would be the expected level of industry microcomputer sales in your district for 1992. This forecast would be based on an assumption of the strategies that would be used by all microcomputer firms operating in your district. If you think that new firms are going to enter the industry or that existing firms are going to leave it or change their strategies, your industry forecast will change. Another type of forecast might be a determination of the best possible level of 1992 sales for your firm's microcomputers in the district. This would be a sales potential forecast. Finally, you would probably want to predict a specific level of district sales of your firm's microcomputers given your firm's expected strategy. This would result in a sales forecast that would have to be revised whenever strategic changes were made.

Uses of Forecasts

Since different types of forecasts convey different information, sales managers use specific types for specific sales management decisions. Forecasts of market potential and sales potential are most often used to identify opportunities and to guide the allocation of selling efforts. Market potential provides an assessment of overall demand opportunity available to all firms in an industry. Sales potential adjusts market potential to reflect industry competition and thus represents a better assessment of demand opportunity for an individual firm. Both of these forecasts of potential can be used by sales managers to determine where selling effort is needed and how selling effort should be distributed. For example, as discussed in Chapter 8, designing territories requires an assessment of market potential for all planning and control units. Specific territories are then designed by grouping planning and control units together and evaluating the equality of market potential across the territories.

Market forecasts and sales forecasts are used to predict the expected results from various sales management decisions. For example, once territories are designed, sales managers typically want to forecast expected industry and company sales for each specific sales territory. These forecasts are then used to set sales quotas and selling budgets for specific planning periods.

Top-Down and Bottom-Up Forecasting Approaches

Forecasting methods can be classified in a variety of ways.[3] Specific examples of two basic approaches are presented in Figure 14.3. **Top-down approaches** typically consist of different methods for developing company forecasts at the business unit level. Sales managers then break down these company forecasts into zone, region, district, territory, and account forecasts. **Bottom-up approaches,** in contrast, consist of different methods for developing sales forecasts for individual accounts. Sales managers then combine the account forecasts into territory, district, region, zone, and company forecasts. The top-down and bottom-up approaches represent entirely different perspectives for developing forecasts, although some forecasting methods can be used in either approach. We will, however, focus on the most popular forecasting methods for each approach.

Top-Down Approach. Implementing the top-down approach requires the development of company forecasts and their breakdown into zone, region, district, territory, and account levels. Different methods are used to develop company forecasts and break them down to the desired levels.

Company Forecasting Methods. Although there are a variety of methods available for developing company forecasts, we will limit our discussion to three popular time series methods: moving averages, exponential smoothing, and decomposition methods.

FIGURE 14.3   ▪   *Forecasting Approaches*

In top-down approaches, company personnel provide aggregate company forecasts that sales managers must break down into zone, region, district, territory, and account forecasts. In bottom-up approaches, account forecasts are combined into territory, district, region, zone, and company forecasts.

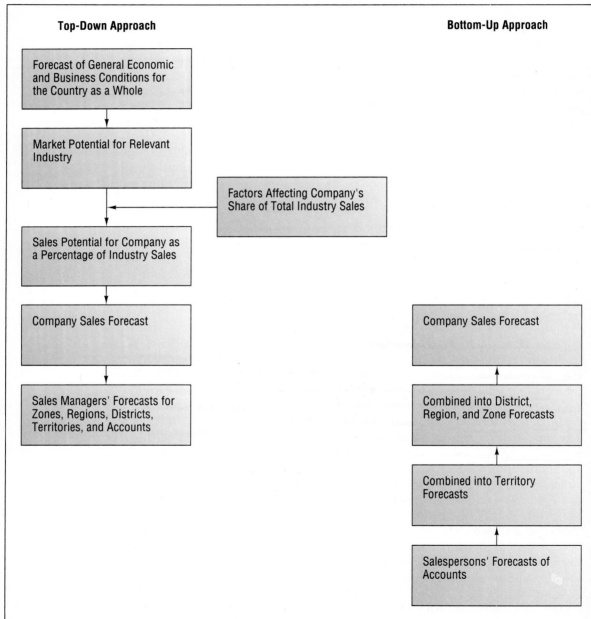

Source: Adapted from C. Robert Patty and Robert Hite, *Managing Salespeople* (Englewood Cliffs, N.J.: Prentice-Hall, Inc., 1988), 71.

EXHIBIT 14.2 ▪ *Moving Averages Example*

		Moving Averages Forecast	
Year	Actual Sales	Two-Year	Four-Year
1984	$ 8,400,000		
1985	8,820,000		
1986	8,644,000	$8,610,000	
1987	8,212,000	8,732,000	
1988	8,622,000	8,428,000	$8,520,000
1989	9,484,000	8,418,000	8,574,000
1990	9,674,000	9,054,000	8,740,000
1991	10,060,000	9,579,000	8,998,000
1992		9,868,000	9,460,000

where

$$\text{Sales forecast for next year} = \frac{\text{Actual sales for past two or four years}}{\text{Number of years (two or four years)}}$$

Moving averages is a relatively simple method that develops a company forecast by calculating the average company sales for previous years. Thus, the company sales forecast for next year is the average of actual company sales for the last three years, last six years, or some other number of years. An example of calculating a moving averages company sales forecast for two- and four-year time frames is presented in Exhibit 14.2. As illustrated in this example, the moving averages method is straightforward and requires very simple calculations. Management must, however, determine the appropriate number of years to include in the calculations. In addition, this method weights actual company sales for previous years equally in generating the forecast for the next year. This equal weighting may not be appropriate if company sales vary substantially from year to year or if there are major differences in the business environment between the most recent and past years.

Exponential smoothing is a type of moving averages method, except that company sales in the most recent year are weighted differently than company sales in past years.[4] An example of the exponential smoothing method is provided in Exhibit 14.3. A critical aspect of this method involves determining the appropriate weight (α) for this year's company sales. This is typically accomplished by examining different weights for historical sales data to determine which weight would have generated the most accurate sales forecasts in the past. Based on the analysis in Exhibit 14.3, management should probably use a weight of 0.8 for this year's company sales.

Decomposition methods involve different procedures that break down previous company sales data into four major components: trend, cycle, seasonal, and erratic events. These components are then reincorporated to produce the sales forecast. An example of a decomposition method is presented in Exhibit 14.4. Notice that the trend, cycle, and erratic events components are incorporated into

EXHIBIT 14.3 ∎ *Exponential Smoothing Example*

		Sales Forecast for Next Year		
Year	*Actual Sales*	$\alpha = 0.2$	$\alpha = 0.5$	$\alpha = 0.8$
1984	$ 8,400,000			
1985	8,820,000	$8,400,000	$8,400,000	$8,400,000
1986	8,644,000	8,484,000	8,610,000	8,736,000
1987	8,212,000	8,516,000	8,626,000	8,664,000
1988	8,622,000	8,456,000	8,420,000	8,302,000
1989	9,484,000	8,488,000	8,520,000	8,558,000
1990	9,674,000	8,686,000	9,002,000	9,298,000
1991	10,060,000	8,882,000	9,338,000	9,600,000
1992		9,118,000	9,698,000	9,968,000

where

Sales forecast
for next year $= (\alpha)$ (actual sales this year) $+ (1 - \alpha)$ (this year's sales forecast)

EXHIBIT 14.4 ∎ *Decomposition Method Example*

Assume that various analyses have decomposed previous sales data into the following components:

A 5 percent growth in sales is predicted due to basic developments in population, capital formation, and technology (trend component). A 10 percent decrease in sales is expected due to a business recession (cycle component). Increased tensions in the Middle East are expected to reduce sales by an additional 5% (erratic events component). Sales results are reasonably consistent throughout the year except for the fourth quarter, where sales are expected to be 25 percent higher than the other quarters (seasonal component).

A marketer of consumer products might recombine the different components in the following manner to forecast sales for 1992:

Sales in 1991 were $10,060,000. The trend component suggests that 1992 sales will be $10,563,000 ($10,060,000 × 1.05). However, incorporating the expected business recession represented in the cycle component changes the sales forecast to $9,506,700 ($10,563,000 × 0.90). The annual sales forecast is reduced to $9,031,365 when the erratic events component is introduced ($9,507,700 × 0.95). Quarterly sales forecasts would initially be calculated as $2,257,841 ($9,031,365 / 4). However, incorporating the seasonal component suggests fourth-quarter sales of $2,822,302 ($2,257,841 × 1.25) and sales for the other three quarters of $2,069,688 ($9,031,365) − $2,822,302 / 3).

Source: This example is based on an example presented in Philip Kotler, *Marketing Management: Analysis, Planning, Implementation, and Control* (Englewood Cliffs, N.J.: Prentice-Hall Inc., 1991), 255.

the annual forecast but that the seasonal component is used only when forecasting sales for periods of less than a year, such as months or quarters. Decomposition methods are sound conceptually but often require complex statistical approaches for breaking down the company sales data into the trend components. Once this decomposition has been completed, it is relatively easy to reincorporate the components into the development of a company forecast.

Breakdown Methods. Once sales managers receive a company forecast, they can use different market factor methods to break it down to the desired levels. **Market factor methods** typically involve identifying one or more factors that are related to sales at the zone, region, district, territory, or account levels and using these factors to break down the overall company forecast into forecasts at these levels.

A typical approach is to use the **Buying Power Index (BPI)** supplied by *Sales and Marketing Management.*[5] The BPI is a market factor calculated for different areas in the following manner:

$$BPI = (5I + 2P + 3R) / 10$$

where

> I = Percentage of U.S. disposable personal income in the area
> P = Percentage of U.S. population in the area
> R = Percentage of U.S. retail sales in the area

Performing these calculations for any area produces a BPI for the area. This BPI can be translated as the percentage of U.S. buying power residing in the area. The higher the index is, the more buying power in the area. Fortunately, *Sales and Marketing Management* provides these calculations for areas in the United States on an annual basis.

An example of the BPI data provided by *Sales and Marketing Management* is presented in Exhibit 14.5. BPIs and other data are available for all counties in a state and for the major cities and metropolitan areas. The information in the exhibit suggests that the BPI for the Louisville metropolitan area is 0.3752, for Jefferson County, 0.2765, and for the city of Louisville, 0.1056. This means that 0.3752 percent, 0.2765 percent, and 0.1056 percent of total U.S. buying power resides in the Louisville metro area, Jefferson County, and the city of Louisville, respectively.

Sales managers can use the BPI data to divide the overall company forecast into more disaggregate forecasts. For example, assume that you are the Kentucky district sales manager for a marketer of cosmetics. Management has used various methods to forecast total company sales in the United States of $500 million for 1992. The calculations necessary to break down this company forecast into sales forecasts for areas within your district are illustrated in Exhibit 14.6. Using the appropriate BPIs, you are able to forecast 1992 sales of $1,876,000, $1,382,500, and $528,000 for the Louisville metro area, Jefferson County, and the city of Louisville, respectively.

The BPI is an extremely useful tool for forecasting, since it is readily available and updated on an annual basis. It is most appropriate for often-purchased consumer goods because of the factors used in calculating the index for each area.

EXHIBIT 14.5 ▪ *BPI Data*

METRO AREA *County* *City*	Total EBI ($000)	Median Hsld. EBI	% of Hsls. by EBI Group: (A) $10,000–$19,999 (B) $20,000–$34,999 (C) $35,000–$49,999 (D) $50,000 & Over				Buying Power Index
			A	B	C	D	
CLARKSVILLE–HOPKINSVILLE..	**1,624,275**	**20,213**	**29.0**	**27.5**	**13.5**	**9.5**	**.0553**
Christian.........................	608,230	18,096	31.4	23.7	12.1	9.3	.0205
•Hopkinsville	329,203	19,553	26.6	23.5	14.4	11.2	.0128
Montgomery, Tenn.	*1,016,045*	*21,458*	*27.7*	*29.8*	*14.2*	*9.6*	*.0348*
• *Clarksville*	*871,471*	*21,096*	*29.2*	*30.1*	*13.5*	*9.4*	*.0308*
SUBURBAN TOTAL	423,601	18,390	30.7	25.3	12.7	8.3	.0117
HUNTINGTON–ASHLAND	**3,126,629**	**18,771**	**24.9**	**27.2**	**13.0**	**7.2**	**.1058**
Boyd	571,216	21,497	22.2	26.4	16.4	9.8	.0205
• Ashland	299,365	19,314	23.3	24.2	13.9	10.5	.0132
Carter	181,075	14,117	27.4	24.0	8.1	4.1	.0062
Greenup	353,895	21,012	23.8	32.5	13.3	6.5	.0102
Lawrence, Ohio	*633,492*	*21,235*	*22.7*	*29.1*	*15.0*	*8.5*	*.0187*
Cabell, W. Va.	*967,782*	*16,728*	*27.3*	*25.6*	*10.8*	*6.1*	*.0384*
• *Huntington*	*548,402*	*14,759*	*27.9*	*22.8*	*8.9*	*5.8*	*.0220*
Wayne, W. Va.	*419,169*	*19,017*	*25.0*	*26.8*	*14.0*	*7.0*	*.0118*
SUBURBAN TOTAL	2,278,862	20,001	24.2	28.9	14.0	7.2	.0706
LEXINGTON–FAYETTE	**4,324,044**	**23,146**	**23.6**	**26.7**	**15.6**	**14.3**	**.1442**
Bourbon	175,804	17,069	26.9	25.6	10.0	7.8	.0058
Clark..	345,034	23,473	20.6	26.7	17.0	13.1	.0111
Fayette..	2,936,049	23,330	23.9	26.3	15.3	15.3	.1020
• Lexington-Fayette	2,936,049	23,330	23.9	26.3	15.3	15.3	.1020
Jessamine	360,789	23,887	22.8	28.6	17.4	13.1	.0107
Scott	249,042	22,214	24.4	29.8	15.7	9.2	.0076
Woodford.....................................	257,326	27,610	20.8	25.5	19.2	18.9	.0070
SUBURBAN TOTAL	1,387,995	22,812	22.9	27.4	16.1	12.4	.0422
LOUISVILLE	**11,688,076**	**24,505**	**22.0**	**28.3**	**17.0**	**13.8**	**.3752**
Bullitt	475,028	26,293	20.3	34.9	20.4	9.5	.0131
Jefferson	8,578,892	24,506	21.8	27.2	16.6	15.0	.2765
• Louisville	3,137,839	18,179	25.7	23.9	11.8	10.2	.1056
Oldham	431,356	31,848	18.3	26.4	22.3	21.4	.0119
Shelby...	275,632	23,365	21.4	27.3	17.1	11.9	.0083
Clark, Ind.	*928,417*	*23,206*	*24.2*	*32.8*	*16.2*	*8.5*	*.0351*
Floyd, Ind.	*705,724*	*23,897*	*22.5*	*30.4*	*17.9*	*10.7*	*.0211*
• *New Albany*	*396,797*	*21,138*	*25.2*	*29.7*	*14.4*	*8.6*	*.0136*
Harrison, Ind.	*293,027*	*22,475*	*25.1*	*33.4*	*14.8*	*8.2*	*.0092*
SUBURBAN TOTAL	8,153,440	27,826	19.8	30.7	19.7	16.0	.2560

Source: "Survey of Buying Power," *Sales and Marketing Management*, August 13, 1990, C77.

EXHIBIT 14.6 ▪ *Market Factor Calculations*

	Louisville Metro Area	Jefferson County	Louisville City
1992 company sales forecast	$500,000,000	$500,000,000	$500,000,000
BPI	0.3752%	0.2765%	0.1056%
1992 area sales forecast	$1,876,000	$1,382,500	$528,000

Marketers of durable consumer goods or industrial products may not find the BPI sufficiently accurate for their needs. In these situations other market factors must be identified and used. For example, Pitney Bowes's U.S. Business Systems Division uses *growth in business employment* as a market factor for forecasting purposes.[6]

Another approach is for a firm to develop a buying power index for its specific situation. For example, a general aviation aircraft marketer developed a buying power index for its products in each county in the United States. The basic formula was

$$Index = (5I + 3AR + 2P) / 10$$

where

I = Percentage of U.S. disposable income in county
AR = Percentage of U.S. aircraft registrations in county
P = Percentage of U.S. registered pilots in county

These calculations produced an index for each county that could be translated and used like the BPI. The firm could take U.S. forecasts provided by the industry trade association and convert them to market and sales forecasts for each county using their calculated indices and market shares.

The use of market factor methods is widespread in the sales management area. Indices such as the BPI or those developed by specific firms and other market factor methods can be extremely valuable forecasting tools for sales managers. These indices and market factors should be continually evaluated and improved over time. They can be assessed by comparing actual sales in an area to the market factor value for the area. For example, the general aviation aircraft marketer found high correlations between actual aircraft sales in a county and the county indices. This finding provided support for the use of the calculated index as an indirect forecasting tool.

Bottom-Up Approach. Implementing the bottom-up approach requires various methods to forecast sales to individual accounts and the combination of these account forecasts into territory, district, region, zone, and company forecasts. We will focus on the survey of buyer intentions, jury of executive opinion, Delphi, and salesforce composite methods as used in a bottom-up approach.

The **survey of buyer intentions method** is any procedure that asks individual accounts about their purchasing plans for a future period and translates these responses into account forecasts. The intended purchases by accounts might be obtained through mail surveys, telephone surveys, personal interviews, or other approaches. For example, salespeople in Gillette's Safety Razor Division meet with each of their major accounts and work out mutually agreeable purchasing goals with these accounts.[7] Similarly, sales executives from Aldus Corporation, which sells strictly through resellers, meet annually with their top dealers and distributors to develop sales projections. The executives then consult with the same resellers to update the sales forecasts on a quarterly basis.[8]

Top down method

The **jury of executive opinion method** involves any approach where executives of the firm use their expert knowledge to forecast sales to individual accounts. Separate forecasts might be obtained from managers in different functional areas. These forecasts are then averaged or discussed by the managers until a consensus forecast for each account is reached. An interesting example of this method is used by Lockheed Aircraft Corporation. A group of Lockheed executives pose as different major customers and evaluate the company's products in relation to those of competitors. They try to simulate each account's purchasing process and use the results to forecast sales to each account.[9]

The **Delphi method** is a structured type of jury of executive opinion method. The basic procedure involves selection of a panel of managers from within the firm. Each member of the panel submits anonymous forecasts for each account. These forecasts are summarized into a report that is sent to each panel member. The report presents descriptive statistics concerning the submitted forecasts with reasons for the lowest and highest forecasts. Panel members review this information and then again submit anonymous individual forecasts. The same procedure is repeated until the forecasts for individual accounts converge into a consensus.

The **salesforce composite method** involves various procedures where salespeople provide forecasts for their assigned accounts, typically on specially designed forms (see Figure 14.4) or electronically via computer. For example, salespeople at Schlage Electronics send account forecasts to their sales managers each Monday through an electronic mail (E-mail) network. The sales managers combine their salesperson forecasts into a spreadsheet and send the results via E-mail to the national sales manager.[10] Research results suggest that salesperson forecasts can be improved by developing detailed instructions about the forecasting procedures and providing salespeople with detailed information about their accounts and feedback concerning the accuracy of previous forecasts.[11]

Using Different Forecasting Approaches and Methods

Our discussion of top-down and bottom-up approaches and several forecasting methods is illustrative of the forecasting procedures used by many sales organizations. However, we have not introduced all available forecasting methods, and some sales organizations may use the approaches and methods in different ways than we have discussed. For example, some sales organizations use statistical methods, such as regression analysis, to develop sales forecasts for accounts, territories, districts, regions, zones, and/or the company. The use of regression procedures for developing sales forecasts is examined as a means for establishing sales quotas in the next section of this chapter.

FIGURE 14.4 ▪ *Quarterly Forecasting Form for Salespeople*

This is an example of a form used by a firm to get salespeople to forecast sales for each account and product group.

| Account | Projected Sales By Product Group For Quarter Beginning 7/5/92 | | | | | | | Totals |
	364-60	364-80	28B	460	28			
Ace	1250	960	1400	2100	160			5870
Sentry	950	1250	1930	470	968			5568
Cutter	—	2110	—	960	1750			4820
Grossman	—	—	—	—	364			364
Paycass	400	1800	—	—	720			2920
American	—	—	—	—	1230			1230
Pro	—	700	—	—	—			700
Totals	2600	6820	3330	3530	5192			21,472

Source: Adapted from Stewart A. Washburn, "Don't Let Sales Forecasting Spook You," *Sales and Marketing Management*, September 1988, 118.

The actual usage of specific forecasting methods is presented in Exhibit 14.7. Interestingly, the results of this study suggest that all of the methods are used by some firms and only two methods (jury of executive opinion and salesforce composite) are used by a majority of the firms. Notice also the differences in the perceived accuracy among the forecasting methods.

Since forecasting is such a difficult task and each approach and method has certain advantages and disadvantages, most firms employ multiple forecasting approaches and methods. One study found that firms employ an average of 2.7 forecasting methods on a regular basis.[12] Then, various approaches are used to combine the results from each method into a final forecast.[13] If different approaches and methods produce similar sales forecasts, sales managers can be more confident in the validity of the forecast. If extremely divergent forecasts are generated from the different approaches and methods, additional analysis is required to determine the reasons for the large differences and to make the adjustments necessary to produce an accurate sales forecast.

Even though firms employ multiple forecasting methods, research evidence indicates that several criteria are used to select specific forecasting methods.[14] The most important criterion identified in this study was the accuracy of the forecasting method. Other criteria that were considered in decreasing importance were ease of use, data requirements, time horizon of the forecast, data pattern, number of items to be forecast, and availability of software. These results suggest that the selection of forecasting methods often represents a trade-off between the accuracy of the method and the ease with which it can be implemented. Some of the more accurate forecasting methods are difficult to use and have substantial data requirements.

EXHIBIT 14.7   ▪   *Usage of Forecasting Methods*

Forecasting Method	Percentage of Firms Using	Accuracy
Survey of buyer intentions	40	3.22
Jury of executive opinion	60	3.32
Delphi method	27	2.73
Salesforce composite	61	2.81
Moving averages	28	2.92
Exponential smoothing	17	3.20
Decomposition methods	10	3.50
Regression	41	3.40

Accuracy was measured by respondent perceptions on a scale of 1 to 5 where 1 = not accurate and 5 = very accurate.

Source: Adapted from Essam Mahmoud, Gillian Rice, and Naresh Malhotra, "Emerging Issues in Sales Forecasting and Decision Support Systems," *Journal of the Academy of Marketing Science*, Fall 1988, 56.

Thus, firms may have to sacrifice some accuracy by selecting methods that they are able to readily implement. This situation is illustrated in Exhibit 14.7, where some of the more accurate methods (e.g., decomposition) are not used by many firms.

Establishing Sales Quotas

Sales managers need valid and timely forecasts for establishing sales quotas and selling budgets. *Quotas* are organizational objectives that are to be achieved by sales managers and salespeople. The use of different types of quotas for evaluating salesperson performance will be discussed in detail in Chapter 16. Our discussion in this section focuses on the development of sales quotas throughout the sales organization.

A **sales quota** represents a reasonable sales objective for a territory, district, region, or zone. Since a sales forecast represents an expected level of firm sales for a defined geographic area, time period, and strategy, there should be a close relationship between the sales forecast and the sales quota. Bottom-up and/or top-down approaches might be used to develop sales forecasts that are translated into sales quotas. The use of judgmental forecasting methods can result in complex ethical situations, as discussed in "An Ethical Perspective: Ethical Considerations in Sales Forecasting."

Another recommended approach is to use statistical methods such as regression.[15] A market response framework to guide this type of approach is presented in Figure 14.5. Depending upon the planning and control unit of interest (territory, district, region, or zone), different determinants of market response (sales, market share, etc.) might be important. However, these determinants can be classified as either environmental, organizational, or salesperson factors. Once the determinant and market response factors are identified, their values for each planning and control unit in the previous period must be measured.

Statistical packages can then be used to estimate the parameters of the regression equation. For example, if you are a district sales manager interested in forecasting territory sales, you would identify and measure specific environmental, organizational, and salesperson factors as well as sales for each territory in the previous year. You could then develop a regression model of the following form:

$$\text{Territory sales} = a + (b1)(\text{environmental factor}) \\ + (b2)(\text{organizational factor}) + (b3)(\text{salesperson factor})$$

The a, b1, b2, and b3 values are the model parameters supplied by the regression procedure to define the relationship between the determinant factors and territory sales.

Although this type of model might be useful, it suffers from two basic weaknesses. First, it incorporates only the independent effects of the determinant variables, yet these variables are highly interrelated. Second, this type of equation is linear, yet the determinant variable relationships are probably nonlinear. These weaknesses can be addressed by performing the linear regression on the logarithms of the actual data, producing a multiplicative power function of the following form:

$$\text{Territory sales} = (a)(\text{environmental factor}^{b1})\,(\text{organizational factor}^{b2}) \\ (\text{salesperson factor}^{b3})$$

This function is nonlinear and incorporates interactions through the multiplication of determinant variables.

A specific example illustrating this type of function is presented in Exhibit 14.8. The environmental factors are *potential* and *concentration*, the salesperson factor is *experience*, and the organizational factor is *span of control*. The data are for

AN ETHICAL PERSPECTIVE

Ethical Considerations in Sales Forecasting Since sales forecasts provide the basis for establishing sales quotas, and since salespeople's and sales managers' compensation is often related to the achievement of these quotas, ethical problems may arise when the jury of executive opinion or the salesforce composite forecasting methods are employed. These methods are based on direct judgments of sales managers and/or salespeople, who can be torn between providing accurate judgments and tempering their estimates to produce low forecasts that would lead to lower sales quotas. Lower sales forecasts would be easier to achieve and thus would make it easier for them to earn higher compensation.

One way to overcome these potential ethical problems is to tie compensation levels to the accuracy of sales forecasts provided by salespeople and sales managers. The Metier Management Systems example described in the opening vignette illustrates one approach. Another successful example is provided by Ampertif, which compensates salespeople based on both their sales results and sales forecasts. This approach has produced sales forecasts that have been within 3 percent of actual sales for the past three years.

Source: "Ampertif Tolerates No Surprises," *Sales and Marketing Management*, February 1987, 18–19.

FIGURE 14.5 ▪ *Market Response Framework*

These are the types of factors that affect market response for any planning and control unit, whether it be accounts, territories, districts, regions, or zones. Market response might be profits, market share, or some other response, but sales is usually the market response variable of interest to sales managers.

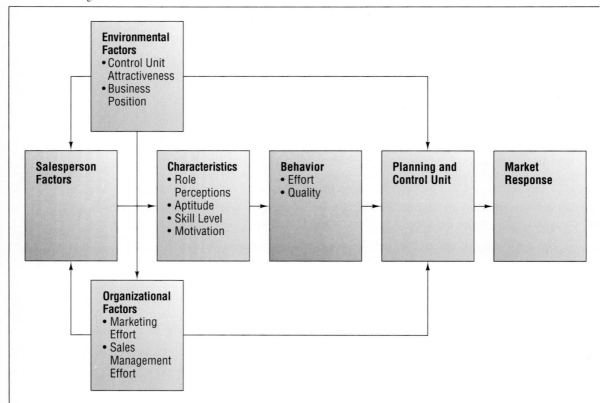

Source: Raymond W. LaForge and David W. Cravens, "A Market Response Model for Sales Management Decision Making," *Journal of Personal Selling and Sales Management*, Fall/Winter 1981–1982, 14. Used with permission.

three territories and are used in the model to generate sales forecasts for each territory individually. This regression model indicates that the higher the territory potential, account concentration, and level of salesperson experience are, the higher the territory sales will be. The larger the span of control is, the lower the territory sales. The exponents in the model suggest that territory sales are most affected by territory potential and span of control. Thus, the regression model generates a specific sales forecast for each territory, and it also provides information concerning relationships between determinant factors and sales.

The regression forecasting approach develops sales forecasts that explicitly consider the characteristics of a territory or other planning and control unit. Thus, these regression forecasts can be translated directly into sales quotas. For example, the sales forecasts for the three territories in Exhibit 14.8 ($586,000, $238,400, and

EXHIBIT 14.8   ▪   *Regression Model Example*

Territory sales = $(800.82)(\text{potential}^{.53})(\text{concentration}^{.03})(\text{experience}^{.08})(\text{span of control}^{-.55})$

	Territory 1	Territory 2	Territory 3
Potential (no. of persons employed by firms in customer industry located in territory)	114,000	125,000	87,000
Concentration (no. of persons employed by the large plants in customer industry located in territory)	94,000	52,000	12,000
Experience (months salesperson has been with company)	30	10	20
Span of control (no. of salespeople supervised by sales manager)	5	8	10
Territory sales forecast	$586,000	$238,400	$173,200

Source: Adapted from Adrian B. Ryans and Charles B. Weinberg, "Territory Sales Response Models: Stability Over Time," *Journal of Marketing Research*, May 1987, 231, published by the American Marketing Association.

$173,200), represent expected sales levels given the potential, concentration, experience, and span of control evaluations for each territory. Sales management might use these regression sales forecasts as sales quotas for each territory. Alternatively, sales management might adjust the forecasts up or down based on information about the territories not incorporated in the regression model. In any case, the territory sales forecasts provide the basis for establishing the territory sales quotas.

The regression approach can be used to develop sales forecasts and establish sales quotas at all sales organization levels.[16] The determinant variables and measures are typically different depending upon whether the control unit is a territory, district, region, or zone. Nevertheless, accurate sales forecasts are critical for establishing valid sales quotas at all sales organization levels.

Establishing Selling Budgets

Budgeting takes place throughout a corporate organization. A corporation has limited resources that must be allocated to business units, which in turn must assign resources to the functional departments of each business unit. Within the marketing function the available resources must be allocated across the different elements of the marketing mix. Of special interest to us is the allocation of promotional resources between advertising and personal selling. The resources earmarked for personal selling represent the total **selling budget.** Sales management must then determine the best way to allocate these sales resources throughout the sales organization and across the different selling activities. This is the key sales management budgeting task.

This budgeting process typically takes place after sales forecasts have been generated. The sales forecasts provide sales management with the expected level of sales for the next planning period, usually a year. These forecasts are then translated into sales quotas for each territory, district, region, and zone. The quotas represent a plan for sales results for the next period. Selling budgets represent a plan for selling expenses for the next period. Combining the sales quotas and selling budgets results in a profit plan for the next period. The budgeting process is intended to instill cost consciousness and profit awareness throughout the sales organization.

Selling budgets are developed at all levels of the sales organization and for all key expenditure categories. Our discussion will focus on the major selling expense categories and methods for establishing specific expenditure levels within the budget.

Selling Expense Categories

Firms differ considerably in how they define their selling expense categories. Nevertheless, all sales organizations should carefully plan expenditures for the major selling and sales management activities and for the different levels in the sales organization structure. The selling budget addresses controllable expenses, not uncontrollable ones. Typical selling budget expense categories are presented in Exhibit 14.9.

Both the total expenditures for each of these categories and sales management budget responsibility must be determined. Sales management budget responsibility depends upon the degree of centralization or decentralization in the sales organization. In general, more centralized sales organizations will place budget responsibility at higher sales management levels. For example, if salesforce recruitment and selection takes place at the regional level, then the regional sales managers will have responsibility for this budget category. A typical situation is where the sales management activity occurs at all management levels. For example, training activities might be performed at national, zone, regional, and district levels. In this case, the budgeting process must address how much to spend on overall training and how to allocate training expenditures to the different organizational levels.

The basic objective in budgeting for each category is to determine the lowest expenditure level necessary to *achieve the sales quotas.* Notice that we did not say the lowest possible expenditure level. Sales managers might cut costs and improve profitability in the short run, but if expenditures for training, travel, and so forth are too low, long-run sales and profits will be sacrificed. If, however, expenses can be reduced by more effective or more efficient spending, then these productivity improvements can produce increased profitability in the long run. Achieving productivity improvements has been one of the most demanding tasks facing sales

EXHIBIT 14.9 ▪ *Selling Expense Categories in Budget*

Classification	Actual 1991	Original 1992 Budget	April Revision	July Revision	October Revision

Compensation expenses
  Salaries
  Commissions
  Bonuses
    Total					

Travel expenses
  Lodging
  Food
  Transportation
  Miscellaneous
    Total					

Administrative expenses
  Recruiting
  Training
  Meetings
  Sales offices
    Total					

managers in recent years, since increases in field selling costs and extremely competitive markets have put tremendous pressure on firm profitability.

Methods for Determining the Selling Budget

Determining expenditure levels for each selling expense category is extremely difficult. Although there is no perfect way to arrive at these expenditure levels, two approaches warrant our attention: the percentage of sales method and the objective and task method.[17]

Probably the most often used, the **percentage of sales method** calculates an expenditure level for each category by multiplying an expenditure percentage times forecasted sales. The effectiveness of the percentage of sales method depends upon the accuracy of sales forecasts and the appropriateness of the expenditure percentages. If the sales forecasts are not accurate, the selling budgets will be incorrect, regardless of the expenditure percentages used. If sales forecasts are accurate, then the key is determining the expenditure percentages. Fortunately, typical expenditure percentages for different industries are available from published sources. Some general industry information is presented in Exhibit 14.10. These typical percentages should be viewed as guidelines only. Sales management should adjust them up or down to reflect the unique aspects of their sales organization.

The **objective and task method** takes an entirely different approach. In its most basic form, it is a type of zero-based budgeting. In essence, each sales manager prepares a separate budget request that stipulates the objectives to be

EXHIBIT 14.10 ▪ *Typical Sales Costs by Industry*

Industry Group	Cost per Call	Number of Calls Needed to Close a Sale	Salesforce Costs as a Percentage of Total Sales
Business services	$ 46.00	4.6	19.3%
Chemicals	165.80	2.8	3.0
Communications	40.60	4.0	21.6
Construction	111.20	2.8	3.2
Electronics	133.30	3.9	12.0
Fabricated metals	80.80	3.3	6.4
Food products	131.60	4.8	9.6
Instruments	226.00	5.3	10.3
Insurance	53.00	3.4	15.6
Machinery	68.50	3.0	13.0
Misc. manufacturing	85.90	2.8	13.2
Office equipment	25.00	3.7	15.0
Printing/publishing	70.10	4.5	8.3
Retail	25.00	3.3	23.5
Rubber/plastics	248.20	4.7	2.8
Utilities	89.90	4.8	17.3
Wholesale (consumer)	84.10	3.0	7.0
Wholesale (industrial)	50.00	3.3	12.6
Average	**96.39**	**3.8**	**11.9%**

Source: "Survey of Selling Costs," *Sales and Marketing Management*, February 26, 1990, 79.

achieved, the tasks required to achieve these objectives, and the costs associated with performing the necessary tasks. These requests are reviewed, and, through an iterative process, selling budgets are approved. Many variations of the objective and task method are used by different sales organizations.

In reality, the process of establishing a selling budget is an involved one that typically incorporates various types of analysis, many meetings, and much politicizing. The process has, however, been streamlined in many firms through the use of computer technology to rapidly evaluate alternative selling budgets.

Summary

1. **Discuss the different types of forecasts used by sales managers.** There are four types of forecasts of most interest to sales managers. A market potential forecast predicts the best possible level of total industry sales, while a market forecast predicts the expected level, assuming a specific industry structure and strategy. Similarly, a sales potential forecast predicts the best possible level of firm sales, while a sales forecast predicts the likely firm sales given a specific

strategy. All of these forecasts must include a geographic area and time period definition.

2.   Describe the top-down and bottom-up forecasting approaches used by sales managers. In top-down approaches, company forecasts are made at the business unit level and then are broken down by sales managers into zone, region, district, territory, and account forecasts. In bottom-up approaches, forecasts are initially made at the account level, then sales managers combine them into territory, district, region, zone, and, ultimately, company forecasts.

3.   Explain the use of different forecasting methods in the top-down and bottom-up approaches. Different forecasting methods can be used when employing the top-down and bottom-up approaches. The top-down approach requires the use of methods such as moving averages, exponential smoothing, or decomposition methods to develop a company sales forecast. Various types of market indices, such as the BPI, are then used to break down the company forecast into forecasts at the zone, region, district, territory, and/or account, levels. The bottom-up approach requires the use of forecasting methods to generate forecasts at the account level that are then aggregated into company sales forecasts. Typical forecasting strategies include the survey of buyer intentions, jury of executive opinion, Delphi method, and salesforce composite methods.

4.   Describe how sales quotas are established, including the use of regression procedures. Sales quotas are sales objectives at the territory, district, region, or zone levels. Sales forecasts provide a basis for establishing sales quotas, and they can also be established using bottom-up or top-down approaches. When regression procedures are used, different determinants of market response are chosen, depending on the planning and control unit of interest.

5.   Discuss the importance of and methods for establishing selling budgets. Sales forecasts provide a direct basis for establishing selling budgets. Whereas the sales forecast predicts sales, the selling budget helps to control the selling costs needed to generate these sales. Selling budgets should be established for the major categories of controllable selling expenses and assigned to different sales management levels throughout the sales organization. The percentage of sales and objective and task methods are often used to set the selling budgets. The basic objective of these budgets is to keep selling costs at the lowest level that will still achieve sales quotas. Long-run profitability depends upon sales management's ability to allocate selling expenditures in more productive ways.

Key Terms

- **Forecast**
- **Market potential**
- **Market forecast**
- **Sales potential**
- **Sales forecast**
- **Top-down approaches**

▪ **Bottom-up approaches**

▪ **Moving averages**

▪ **Exponential smoothing**

▪ **Decomposition methods**

▪ **Market factor methods**

▪ **Buying Power Index (BPI)**

▪ **Survey of buyer intentions methods**

▪ **Jury of executive opinion methods**

▪ **Delphi method**

▪ **Salesforce composite methods**

▪ **Sales quota**

▪ **Selling budget**

▪ **Percentage of sales method**

▪ **Objective and task method**

Review Questions

1. What is meant by the statement, "All sales management decisions are based on some type of forecast"?

2. Why is it important to differentiate between market potentials, market forecasts, sales potentials, and sales forecasts?

3. Referring to "A Global Perspective: Forecasting in International Markets," discuss the methods you would recommend for each type of forecast listed.

4. Discuss the basic differences in the top-down and bottom-up forecasting approaches.

5. What is the market factor method for forecasting? How would you develop a market factor method in any selling situation?

6. What is the general approach for using regression analysis to establish sales quotas? What are the advantages and disadvantages of the regression method?

7. Referring to "An Ethical Perspective: Ethical Considerations in Sales Forecasting," discuss what you would do to reduce ethical problems associated with the judgmental forecasting methods.

8. Why should sales managers use multiple forecasting approaches and methods? What should be done when these multiple approaches and methods produce consistent forecasts? Inconsistent forecasts?

9. Why are accurate forecasts necessary for establishing sales quotas and selling budgets? What effect will inaccurate forecasts have on the process of establishing quotas and budgets?

10. Compare and contrast the percentage of sales and the objective and task methods for establishing selling budgets.

Application Exercises

1. You are a sales manager for a manufacturer and marketer of construction equipment. Your firm has reasonably good data concerning its market share in different areas throughout the country. In addition, the trade association for the construction equipment industry has been able to develop accurate market forecasts. Your firm, however, is having trouble developing sales forecasts for specific sales districts. Describe how you would develop a market factor index that could be used by your firm to translate market forecasts and market share data into sales forecasts for each sales district. Discuss what would be included in the index and how it would be used once developed.

2. Contact three different sales organizations about their selling budget process. Compare and contrast their methods. Evaluate the three approaches.

3. Contact three different sales organizations about their process for establishing sales quotas. Compare and contrast their methods. Evaluate the three approaches.

Notes

[1] Taken from J. Scott Armstrong, Roderick J. Brodie, and Shelby McIntyre, "Forecasting Methods for Marketing: Review of Empirical Research," *International Journal of Forecasting* 3 (1987): 355–376.

[2] Reported in Harry R. White, *Sales Forecasting: Timesaving and Profit-Making Strategies That Work* (Glenview, Ill.: Scott, Foresman and Company, 1984), 6–19.

[3] For different classification schemes and more detailed discussion of individual forecasting methods, see White, *Sales Forecasting;* David M. Georgoff and Robert G. Murdick, "Manager's Guide to Forecasting," *Harvard Business Review*, January–February 1986, 113–118; and Armstrong, Brodie, and McIntyre, "Forecasting Methods."

[4] See John T. Mentzer, "Forecasting with Adaptive Extended Exponential Smoothing," *Journal of the Academy of Marketing Science*, Fall 1988, 62–70, for discussion and examples of different exponential smoothing methods.

[5] See "Survey of Buying Power," *Sales and Marketing Management*, August 13, 1990, for a discussion of the Buying Power Index and for the calculated indices throughout the United States.

[6] "And Now, the Home-Brewed Forecast," *Fortune*, January 20, 1986, 54.

[7] Reported in "Gillette Turns Planning into a Partnership," *Sales and Marketing Management*, February 1988, 24–25.

[8] Reported in Kate Bertrand, "Sales Forecasts: Getting There From Here," *Business Marketing*, October 1988, 36–37.

[9] Reported in Philip Kotler, *Marketing Management: Analysis, Planning, Implementation, and Control* (Englewood Cliffs, N.J.: Prentice-Hall, Inc., 1991), 254.

[10] Reported in Thayer C. Taylor, "Give Togetherness a Competitive Edge," *Sales and Marketing Management*, October 1989, 98–99.

[11] These and other recommendations are available in Robin T. Peterson, "Sales Force Composite Forecasting—An Exploratory Analysis," *The Journal of Business Forecasting*, Spring 1989, 23–27; and James E. Cox, Jr., "Approaches for Improving Salespersons' Forecasts," *Industrial Marketing Management* 18 (1989): 307–311.

[12] Reported in Essam Mahmoud, Gillian Rice, and Naresh Malhotra, "Emerging Issues in Sales Forecasting and Decision Support Systems," *Journal of the Academy of Marketing Science*, Fall 1988, 53.

[13] See Benito E. Flores and Edna M. White, "A Framework for the Combination of Forecasts," *Journal of the Academy of Marketing Science*, Fall 1988, 95–103, for an examination of different combination approaches.

[14] Reported in Mahmoud, Rice, and Malhotra, "Emerging Issues in Sales Forecasting," 57.

[15] For a review and more complete discussion of this approach, see Adrian B. Ryans and Charles B. Weinberg, "Territory Sales Response," *Journal of Marketing Research*, November 1979, 453–465; and Adrian B. Ryans and Charles B. Weinberg, "Territory Sales Response Models: Stability Over Time," *Journal of Marketing Research*, May 1987, 229–233.

[16] For specific examples of regression analysis used to establish territory sales quotas, see David W. Cravens, Robert B. Woodruff, and James C. Stamper, "An Analytical Approach for Evaluating Sales Territory Performance," *Journal of Marketing*, January 1972, 31–37; and David W. Cravens and Robert B. Woodruff, "An Approach for Determining Criteria of Sales Performance," *Journal of Applied Psychology*, June 1973, 240–247.

[17] See Nigel F. Piercy, "The Marketing Budgeting Process: Marketing Management Implications," *Journal of Marketing*, October 1987, 45–59, for results from a study of the overall marketing budgeting process.

CASE 14.1   *Simpson Business Forms*

Simpson Business Forms is a national marketer of business forms to small and midsized firms. The business forms industry is fiercely competitive, with several firms going out of business in the past few years and other firms consolidating through mergers and acquisitions. Simpson is a private firm that wants to maintain its independence. Management thinks that the best way to achieve this objective is to increase profitability by strengthening relationships with its small and midsized business customers.

Most of the responsibility for strengthening customer relationships has been given to the salesforce. The national sales manager, Ben Palmer, has called a meeting of all district sales managers for mid-December. The purpose of this meeting is to develop specific sales plans for 1992. Of particular importance is establishing sales quotas for salespeople that would ensure the sales levels needed to reach profit objectives. In addition, Ben is considering a restructuring of the sales organization to give district sales managers fewer salespeople to supervise. This close supervision is expected to help salespeople strengthen their relationships with customers.

District sales manager, Fred Nicklaus, is preparing for the mid-December sales meeting. He has asked each of his eight salespeople to submit what they think their sales quota should be for 1992. He also scheduled a meeting with each salesperson to discuss their plans for 1992 and their recommended sales quotas and to agree on quotas for 1992. The recommended sales quotas provided by the salespeople were

Salesperson A — $165,500

Salesperson B — $175,000

Salesperson C — $182,500

Salesperson D — $190,000

Salesperson E — $150,000

Salesperson F — $220,000

Salesperson G — $210,000

Salesperson H — $215,000

Prior to meeting with the salespeople, Fred decided to calculate sales forecasts for each territory using the statistical model and data provided by the company. The model and data are as follows:

$$\text{Territory sales} = (800)(\text{potential}^{.53})$$
$$(\text{concentration}^{.03})(\text{experience}^{.08})(\text{span of control}^{-.55})$$

Salesperson	Potential	Concentration	Experience	Span of Control
A	75,000	10,000	5	8
B	100,000	50,000	24	8
C	85,000	40,000	12	8
D	110,000	80,000	18	8
E	90,000	20,000	8	8
F	105,000	30,000	36	8
G	120,000	60,000	20	8
H	115,000	85,000	24	8

Fred wants to compare the sales forecast generated by the statistical model with the recommended sales quotas suggested by each salesperson.

Fred is also concerned about the potential restructuring of the sales organization. Although he is certain that closer supervision of his salespeople will help them strengthen their relationships with customers and increase sales, he is not sure that the increase in sales will cover the extra costs required to achieve closer salesperson supervision. A rumor circulating around the company is that Salesperson A and Salesperson B will be assigned to a new district sales manager. This will leave Fred with only six salespeople to supervise. He decided to use the statistical model to predict the expected increase in sales if this restructuring were to take place.

Questions

1. What should Fred discuss in his meetings with each of his salespeople?
2. What should Fred recommend about the restructuring of his sales district during the district sales manager meeting in mid-December?

CASE 14.2 *Barton Valves*

Mary Washington is the regional sales manager for the Southeast Region of Barton Valves. She is preparing for the national sales meeting, where all of the regional managers meet to develop sales forecasts for their regions and each state within their region. These state and regional forecasts will then be combined into a company forecast for 1992.

The company provides all regional sales managers with the national forecast for industry sales for 1992 as calculated by the industry trade associa-

tion. In addition, a market factor index model is developed along with specific data for each state in the sales manager's region. The information given to Mary is as follows:

Market factor index = (6MS + 4 ME) / 10

where

MS = Percentage of U.S. manufacturing sales in area

A GLOBAL PERSPECTIVE

The Effectiveness of Australian Sales Organizations   A study of 99 Australian sales organizations found differences in the more- and less-effective sales organizations similar to those reported in the U.S. sales organization study discussed earlier. However, some interesting differences were identified when the more-effective sales organizations in Australia and the United States were compared. For example, the more-effective U.S. sales organizations had much lower selling expenses as a percentage of sales (8 percent versus 15 percent) and much lower salesforce turnover (9 percent versus 17 percent) than the more-effective Australian sales organizations.

Some of the differences appear to be due to cultural factors, while others seem to be the result of differences in sales management practice. An Australian sales expert suggested that the higher salesforce turnover rates were probably due to the low status of sales jobs in Australia. Thus, entry-level salespeople are quickly moved into other positions within their firm. The differences in selling expenses are at least partially the result of closer supervision of salespeople (6 versus 8 span of control) and a higher percentage of fixed salary in salesforce compensation (84 percent versus 64 percent) in the Australian salesforces.

Source: David W. Cravens, Ken Grant, Thomas N. Ingram, Raymond W. LaForge, and Clifford E. Young, "Comparison of Field Sales Management Activities in Australian and American Sales Organizations," *Journal of Global Marketing*, 1992.

---

salesperson. Generally, different actions are warranted for different salespeople, depending upon the areas that need improvement.

Evidence for the difference between sales organization effectiveness and salesperson performance is provided in a study of 144 sales organizations in the United States. A comparison of the more-effective and less-effective sales organizations indicated that those that were more effective had achieved much better results in many areas, compared with their less-effective counterparts. For example, the more-effective sales organizations generated much higher sales per salesperson ($3,988,000 versus $1,755,000) and much lower selling expenses as a percentage of sales (13 percent versus 18 percent) than the less-effective sales organizations. The salespeople in the more-effective organizations also outperformed salespeople in the less-effective ones in several areas. However, the differences in salesperson performance were not sufficient to completely explain the differences in sales organization effectiveness. Thus, sales organization effectiveness is the result of salesperson performance as well as many other factors (e.g., sales organization structure and deployment, sales management performance, etc.).[2] As discussed in "A Global Perspective: The Effectiveness of Australian Sales Organizations," a study of Australian sales organizations produced similar results.

This chapter addresses the evaluation of sales organization effectiveness, and Chapter 16 addresses the evaluation of salesperson performance. This chapter begins with a discussion of a sales organization audit, then describes more specific analyses of sales, costs, profits, and productivity to determine sales organization effectiveness.

Sales Organization Audit

Although the term *audit* is most often used in reference to financial audits performed by accounting firms, the audit concept has been extended to different business functions in recent years. In Chapter 10, a **sales organization audit** was described as a comprehensive, systematic, diagnostic, and prescriptive tool.[3] The purpose of a sales organization audit is

> . . . to assess the adequacy of a firm's sales management process and to provide direction for improved performance and prescription for needed changes. It is a tool that should be used by all firms whether or not they are achieving their goals.

This type of audit is the most comprehensive approach for evaluating sales organization effectiveness.

A framework for performing a sales organization audit is presented in Figure 15.2. As indicated in the figure, the audit addresses four major areas: sales organization environment, sales management evaluation, sales organization planning system, and sales management functions. The purpose of the audit is to investigate each of these areas in a systematic and comprehensive way to identify existing or potential problems, determine their causes, and take the necessary corrective action.

The sales organization audit should be performed on a regular basis, not just when problems are evident. One of the major values of an audit is its generation of diagnostic information that can help management correct problems in early stages or eliminate potential problems before they become serious. Since auditing should be of an objective nature, it should be conducted by someone from outside the sales organization. This could be someone from another functional area within the firm or an outside consulting firm.

Although outsiders should conduct the audit, members of the sales organization should be active participants in it. Both sales managers and salespeople often provide much of the information collected. Exhibit 15.1 presents some sample questions that should be addressed in a sales organization audit. Answers to these types of questions typically come from members of the sales organization as well as from company records.

Though obviously an expensive and time-consuming process, the sales organization audit generates benefits that usually outweigh the monetary and time costs. This is especially true when they are conducted on a regular basis, since the chances of identifying and correcting potential problems before they become troublesome increases with the regularity of the auditing process.

Evaluations of Sales Organization Effectiveness

There is no one summary measure of sales organization effectiveness. Sales organizations have multiple goals and objectives and thus multiple factors must be assessed. As illustrated in Figure 15.3, four types of analyses are typically necessary to develop a comprehensive evaluation of any sales organization. Conducting analyses in each of these areas is a complex task for two reasons. First, many different types of analyses can be performed to evaluate sales, cost,

FIGURE 15.2 ▪ *Sales Organization Audit Framework*

The sales organization audit is the most comprehensive evaluation of sales organization effectiveness. The audit typically provides assessments of the sales organization environment, sales management evaluation, sales organization planning system, and sales management functions.

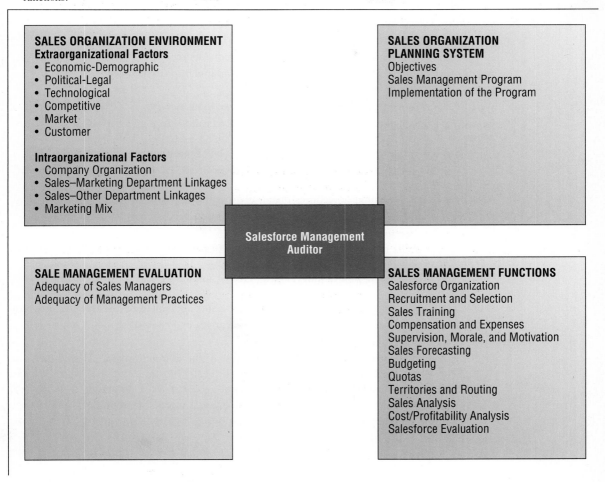

SALES ORGANIZATION ENVIRONMENT
Extraorganizational Factors
- Economic-Demographic
- Political-Legal
- Technological
- Competitive
- Market
- Customer

Intraorganizational Factors
- Company Organization
- Sales–Marketing Department Linkages
- Sales–Other Department Linkages
- Marketing Mix

SALES ORGANIZATION PLANNING SYSTEM
Objectives
Sales Management Program
Implementation of the Program

Salesforce Management Auditor

SALE MANAGEMENT EVALUATION
Adequacy of Sales Managers
Adequacy of Management Practices

SALES MANAGEMENT FUNCTIONS
Salesforce Organization
Recruitment and Selection
Sales Training
Compensation and Expenses
Supervision, Morale, and Motivation
Sales Forecasting
Budgeting
Quotas
Territories and Routing
Sales Analysis
Cost/Profitability Analysis
Salesforce Evaluation

Source: © 1981 by the Regents of the University of California. Adapted from Alan J. Dubinsky and Richard W. Hansen, "The Sales Force Management Audit," *California Management Review*, Winter 1981, 87, by permission of The Regents.

profitability, and productivity results. For example, a sales analysis might focus on total sales, sales of specific products, sales to specific customers, or other types of sales and might include sales comparisons to sales quotas, to previous periods, to competitors, or other types of analyses. Second, separate sales analyses need to be performed for the different levels in the sales organization. Thus, a typical evaluation would include separate sales analyses for sales zones, regions, districts, and territories.

EXHIBIT 15.1 ▪ *Sample Questions from a Sales Organization Audit*

IV. Sales Management Functions

A. Salesforce Organization

1. How is our salesforce organized (by product, by customer, by territory)?
2. Is this type of organization appropriate, given the current intraorganizational and extraorganizational conditions?
3. Does this type of organization adequately service the needs of our customers?

B. Recruitment and Selection

1. How many salespeople do we have?
2. Is this number adequate in light of our objectives and resources?
3. Are we serving our customers adequately with this number of salespeople?
4. How is our salesforce size determined?
5. What is our turnover rate? What have we done to try to change it?
6. Do we have adequate sources from which to obtain recruits? Have we overlooked some possible sources?
7. Do we have a job description for each of our sales jobs? Is each job description current?
8. Have we enumerated the necessary sales job qualifications? Have they been recently updated? Are they predictive of sales success?
9. Are our selection screening procedures financially feasible and appropriate?
10. Do we use a battery of psychological tests in our selection process? Are the tests valid and reliable?
11. Do our recruitment and selection procedures satisfy employment opportunity guidelines?

C. Sales Training

1. How is our sales training program developed? Does it meet the needs of management and sales personnel?
2. Do we establish training objectives before developing and implementing the training program?
3. Is the training program adequate in light of our objectives and resources?
4. What kinds of training do we currently provide our salespeople?
5. Does the training program need revising? What areas of the training program should be improved or deemphasized?
6. What methods do we use to evaluate the effectiveness of our training program?
7. Can we afford to train internally or should we use external sources for training?
8. Do we have an ongoing training program for senior salespeople? Is it adequate?

D. Compensation and Expenses

1. Does our sales compensation plan meet our objectives in light of our financial resources?
2. Is the compensation plan fair, flexible, economical, and easy to understand and to administer?
3. What is the level of compensation, the type of plan, and the frequency of payment?
4. Are the salespeople and management satisfied with the compensation plan?
5. Does the compensation plan ensure that the salespeople perform the necessary sales job activities?
6. Does the compensation plan attract and retain enough quality sales performers?
7. Does the sales expense plan meet our objectives in light of our financial resources?
8. Is the expense plan fair, flexible, and easy to administer? Does it allow for geographical, customer, and/or product differences?
9. Does the expense plan ensure that the necessary sales job activities are performed?
10. Can we easily audit the expenses incurred by our sales personnel?

Source: © 1981 by the Regents of the University of California. Reprinted from Alan J. Dubinsky and Richard W. Hansen, "The Sales Force Management Audit," *California Management Review*, Winter 1981, 90, by permission of The Regents.

FIGURE 15.3   ▪   *Sales Organization Effectiveness Framework*

Evaluating sales organization effectiveness requires analyses of sales, cost, profitability, and productivity. Each type of analysis can be performed in different ways, should be performed at different sales organization levels, and produces different evaluative and diagnostic information for sales managers.

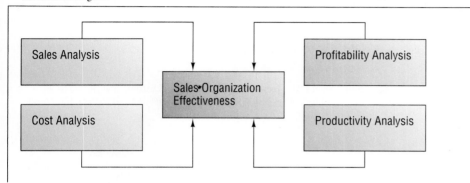

Many sales organizations focus their sales organization assessments on sales analysis.[4] The results from one study are presented in Exhibit 15.2. Almost all of the firms in this study employed different types of sales analyses. However, relatively small percentages of firms reported the use of cost, profit contribution, net profit, or return on assets analyses. Each area that should be addressed to evaluate sales organization effectiveness is discussed separately here.

Sales Analysis

Since the basic purpose of a sales organization is to generate sales, **sales analysis** is an obvious and important element of evaluating sales organization effectiveness. The difficulty, however, is in determining exactly what should be analyzed. One key consideration is in defining what is meant by a *sale*. Definitions include a placed order, a shipped order, and a paid order. Defining a sale by when an order is shipped is probably most common. Regardless of the definition used, the sales organization must be consistent and develop an information system to track sales based on whatever sales definition is employed.

Another consideration is whether to focus on *sales dollars* or *sales units*. This can be extremely important during times when prices increase or when salespeople have substantial latitude in negotiating selling prices. The sales information in Exhibit 15.3 illustrates how different conclusions may result from analyses of sales dollars or sales units. If just sales dollars are analyzed, all regions in the exhibit would appear to be generating substantial sales growth. However, when sales units are introduced, the dollar sales growth for all regions in 1990 can be attributed almost entirely to price increases, since units sold increased only minimally during this period. The situation is somewhat different in 1991, because all regions increased the number of units sold. However, sales volume for Region 2 is relatively flat, even though units sold increased. This could be caused by either selling more lower-priced products or by using larger price concessions than the other regions. In either case, analysis of sales dollars or sales units provides

EXHIBIT 15.2 ▪ *Use of Sales Organization Effectiveness Analyses*

	Sales Volume	Costs	Profit Contribution	Net Profit	Return on Assets Managed
Product Analysis	92%	40%	75%	57%	29%
Customer Analysis	91%	18%	41%	24%	10%
Geographic Analysis	92%	38%	26%	12%	7%

Source: Adapted from Donald W. Jackson, Jr., Lonnie L. Ostrom, and Kenneth R. Evans, "Measures Used to Evaluate Industrial Marketing Activities," *Industrial Marketing Management* 11, 1982, 269–274.

EXHIBIT 15.3 ▪ *Sales Dollars versus Sales Units*

	1989		1990		1991	
	Sales Dollars	Sales Units	Sales Dollars	Sales Units	Sales Dollars	Sales Units
Region 1	$40,000,000	400,000	$45,000,000	410,000	$52,000,000	475,000
Region 2	$45,000,000	450,000	$50,000,000	460,000	$52,000,000	500,000
Region 3	$35,000,000	350,000	$40,000,000	360,000	$48,000,000	420,000
Region 4	$50,000,000	500,000	$55,000,000	510,000	$63,000,000	620,000

different types of evaluative information, so it is often useful to include both dollars and units in a sales analysis.

Given a definition of sales and a decision concerning sales dollars versus units, many different sales evaluations can be performed. Several alternative evaluations are presented in Figure 15.4. The critical decision areas are the organizational level of analysis, the type of sales, and the type of analysis.

Organizational Level of Analysis. Sales analyses should be performed for all levels in the sales organization for two basic reasons. First, sales managers at each level need sales analyses at their level and the next level below for evaluation and control purposes. For example, a regional sales manager should have sales analyses for all regions as well as for all districts within his or her region. This makes it possible to assess the sales effectiveness of the region and to determine the sales contribution of each district.

Second, a useful way to identify problem areas in achieving sales effectiveness is to perform a **hierarchical sales analysis,** which consists of evaluating sales results throughout the sales organization from a top-down perspective. Essentially, the analysis begins with total sales for the sales organization and proceeds through each successively lower level in the sales organization. The emphasis is on identifying potential problem areas at each level and then using analyses at lower

FIGURE 15.4 ▪ Sales Analysis Framework

A sales analysis can be performed at different organization levels and for different types of sales and can employ different types of analysis.

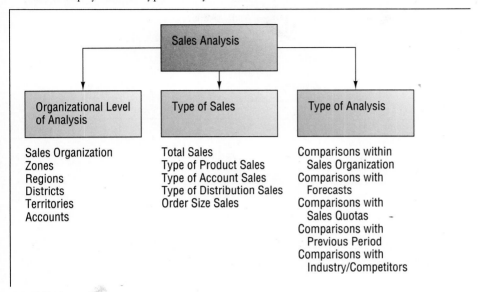

Organizational Level of Analysis	Type of Sales	Type of Analysis
Sales Organization	Total Sales	Comparisons within Sales Organization
Zones	Type of Product Sales	Comparisons with Forecasts
Regions	Type of Account Sales	Comparisons with Sales Quotas
Districts	Type of Distribution Sales	Comparisons with Previous Period
Territories	Order Size Sales	Comparisons with Industry/Competitors
Accounts		

levels to pinpoint the specific problems. An example of a hierarchical sales analysis is presented in Figure 15.5.

In this example, sales for Region 3 appear to be much lower than those for the other regions, so the analysis proceeds to investigate the sales for all of the districts in Region 3. Low sales are identified for District 4, then District 4 sales are analyzed by territory. The results of this analysis suggest potential sales problems within Territory 5. Additional analyses would be performed to determine why sales are so low for Territory 5 and to take corrective action to increase sales from this territory. The hierarchical approach to sales analysis provides an efficient way to conduct a sales analysis and to identify major areas of sales problems.

Type of Sales. The analysis in Figure 15.5 addresses only total firm sales at each organizational level. It is usually desirable to evaluate different types of sales, such as by

- Product type or specific products
- Account type or specific accounts
- Type of distribution method
- Order size

The hierarchical analysis in Figure 15.5 could have included sales by product type, account type, or other type of sales at each level. Or, once the potential sales problem in Territory 5 has been isolated, analysis of different types of sales could be performed to define the sales problem more fully. An example analysis is presented in Figure 15.6. This example suggests especially low sales volume for Product Type A and to Account Type B. Additional analyses within these product

FIGURE 15.5 ▪ *Example of Hierarchical Sales Analysis*

This multistage analysis proceeds from one sales organization level to the next by identifying the major deviations and investigating them in more detail at the next lower level. In the present example, Region 3 has the lowest sales, so all districts in Region 3 are examined. District 4 has poor sales results, so all of the territories in District 4 are examined. Additional analysis is indicated for Territory 5.

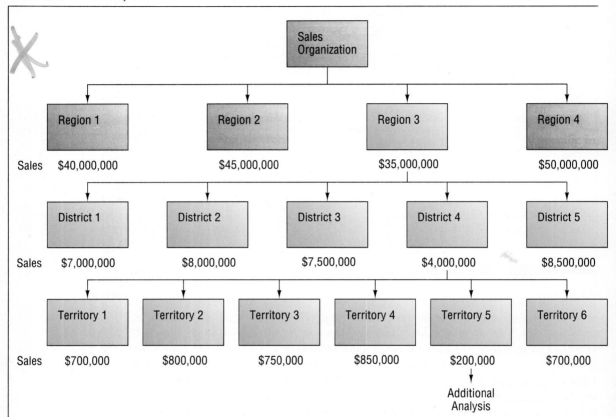

and account types would be needed to determine why sales are low in these areas and what needs to be done to improve sales effectiveness.

The analysis of different types of sales at different organizational levels increases management's ability to detect and define problem areas in sales performance. However, incorporating different sales types into the analysis complicates the evaluation process and requires an information system capable of providing sales data concerning the desired breakdowns.

Type of Analysis. Our discussion to this point has focused on the actual sales results for different organizational levels and for different types of sales. However, the use of actual sales results limits the analysis to comparisons across organizational levels and/or sales types. These within-organization comparisons provide some useful information but are insufficient for a comprehensive evaluation of sales

FIGURE 15.6 ▪ *Example of Type-of-Sales Analysis*

This is a continuation of the hierarchical sales analysis presented in Figure 15.5. Sales in Territory 5 are analyzed by both product type and account type. The analysis suggests poor sales results for Product Type A and Account Type B.

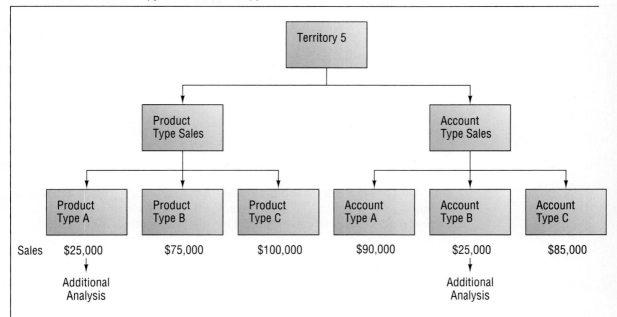

effectiveness. Several additional types of analysis are recommended and presented in Exhibit 15.4.

Comparing actual sales results to sales forecasts and quotas is extremely revealing. Remember from Chapter 14 that a *sales forecast* represents an expected level of firm sales for defined products, markets, and time periods and for a specified strategy. Based on this definition, a sales forecast provides a basis for establishing specific *sales objectives* and *sales quotas*. An **effectiveness index** can be computed by dividing actual sales results by the sales quota and multiplying by 100. As illustrated in Exhibit 15.4, sales results in excess of quota will have index values greater than 100, while results lower than quota will have index values less than 100. The sales effectiveness index makes it easy to compare directly the sales effectiveness of different organizational levels and different types of sales.

Another type of useful analysis is the comparison of actual results to previous periods. As illustrated in Exhibit 15.4, this type of analysis can be used to determine sales growth rates for different organizational levels and for different sales types. And incorporating sales data for many periods make it possible to assess long-term sales trends.

A final type of analysis to be considered is a comparison of actual sales results to those achieved by competitors. This type of analysis can again be performed at different organizational levels and for different types of sales. If the comparison is extended to overall industry sales, various types of market share can be calculated. Examples of these comparisons are presented in Exhibit 15.4.

EXHIBIT 15.4   ▪   *Types of Analysis Examples*

	District 1	District 2	District 3	District 4	District 5
Sales	$7,000,000	$8,000,000	$7,500,000	$4,000,000	$8,500,000
Sales Quota	$7,250,000	$7,500,000	$7,250,000	$7,000,000	7,500,000
Effectiveness Index	97	107	104	57	113
Sales Last Year	$6,750,000	$7,250,000	$7,000,000	$3,850,000	7,250,000
Sales Growth	4%	10%	7%	4%	17%
Industry Sales	$22,000,000	$22,000,000	$25,000,000	$20,000,000	$25,000,000
Market Share	32%	36%	30%	25%	34%

Sales analysis is the approach used most often for evaluating sales organization effectiveness. Sales data are typically more readily available than other data types, and sales results are extremely important to sales organizations. However, developing a sales analysis approach that will produce the desired evaluative information is a complex undertaking. Sales data must be available for different organizational levels and for different types of sales. Valid sales forecasts are needed to establish sales quotas for evaluating sales effectiveness in achieving sales objectives. In addition, industry and competitor sales information is also useful. Regardless of the comprehensiveness of the sales analysis, sales organizations need to perform additional analyses to evaluate sales organization effectiveness adequately.

Cost Analysis

A second major element in the evaluation of sales organization effectiveness is **cost analysis.** The emphasis here is on assessing the costs incurred by the sales organization to generate the achieved levels of sales. Just as sales quotas provide benchmarks for evaluating sales results, *selling budgets* set the benchmarks for evaluating selling costs. The general approach is to compare the costs incurred with planned costs as defined by selling budgets. However, as indicated in "An Ethical Perspective: Ethical Problems with Selling Budgets," the accuracy of this analysis depends upon the ethical behavior of salespeople and sales managers.

Examples of two types of cost analyses are presented in Exhibit 15.5. The first analysis calculates the variance between actual costs and budgeted costs for the regions in a sales organization. Regions with the largest variation, especially where actual costs far exceed budgeted costs, should be highlighted for further analysis. Large variations are not necessarily bad, but the reasons for the variations should be determined. For example, the ultimate purpose of selling costs is to generate sales. Therefore, the objective is not necessarily to minimize selling costs but to ensure that a specified relationship between sales and selling costs is maintained.

One way to evaluate this relationship is to calculate the various selling costs as a percentage of sales achieved. As discussed in Chapter 14, the *percentage of sales*

EXHIBIT 15.5 ▪ *Cost Analysis Examples*

	Compensation Costs			Training Costs		
	Actual Cost	*Budgeted Cost*	*Variance*	*Actual Cost*	*Budgeted Cost*	*Variance*
Region 1	$2,650,000	$2,600,000	+$ 50,000	$ 975,000	$1,040,000	−$ 65,000
Region 2	$2,500,000	$2,600,000	−$100,000	$1,100,000	$1,040,000	+$ 60,000
Region 3	$2,100,000	$2,400,000	−$300,000	$ 750,000	$ 960,000	−$210,000
Region 4	$3,150,000	$2,900,000	+$250,000	$1,300,000	$1,160,000	+$140,000

	Compensation Costs		Training Costs	
	Actual % Sales	*Budgeted % Sales*	*Actual % Sales*	*Budgeted % Sales*
Region 1	5.1%	5%	1.9%	2%
Region 2	4.8%	5%	2.1%	2%
Region 3	4.4%	5%	1.6%	2%
Region 4	5.0%	5%	2.1%	2%

method is often used to establish initial selling budgets. Translating actual selling costs into percentages of sales achieved provides a means for assessing whether the cost–sales relationship has been maintained, even though the actual costs may exceed the absolute level in the selling budget. This situation is illustrated by Region 4 in Exhibit 15.5.

Sales and cost analyses are the two most direct approaches for evaluating sales organization effectiveness. Profitability and productivity analyses extend the

AN ETHICAL PERSPECTIVE

Ethical Problems with Selling Budgets The value of comparing actual expenses with budgeted expenses depends upon the accuracy of the expense information provided by salespeople. Although most sales organizations have prepared forms with the expense categories and instructions for salespeople, salespeople often face ethical problems in reporting their expenses. Consider the following situations:

▪ A salesperson has been on the road for a week and incurs laundry expenses. He knows that if he places the laundry expenses under the miscellaneous expense category in his expense report, he will have to provide receipts. He decides that he can include them under the meals category, since receipts are not required for this category as long as he stays under his per-diem allowance.

▪ A salesperson is trying to get a customer to purchase a new product. He decides to take three individuals from the customer firm to dinner and a basketball game, even though he knows that he has exceeded his entertainment budget for the month. He thinks about hiding these entertainment expenses in different categories in his expense report.

The decisions that salespeople make in these and similar situations affect the ability of sales managers to evaluate actual and budgeted expenses in an accurate manner.

EXHIBIT 15.6 ▪ *Full Cost versus Contribution Approaches*

Full Cost Approach		Contribution Approach	
	Sales		Sales
Minus:	Cost of goods sold	Minus:	Cost of goods sold
	Gross margin		Gross margin
Minus:	Direct selling expenses	Minus:	Direct selling expenses
Minus:	Allocated portion of shared expenses		
	Net profit		Profit contribution

evaluation by assessing relationships between sales and costs. These analyses can be quite complex but may provide very useful information.

Profitability Analysis

Sales and cost data can be combined in various ways to produce evaluations of sales organization profitability for different organizational levels or different types of sales. We will cover three types of **profitability analysis:** income statement analysis, return on assets managed analysis, and residual income analysis.

Income Statement Analysis. The different levels in a sales organization and different types of sales can be considered as separate businesses.[5] Consequently, income statements can be developed for profitability analysis. One of the major difficulties in **income statement analysis** is that some costs are shared between organizational levels or sales types.

Two approaches for dealing with the shared costs are illustrated in Exhibit 15.6. The **full cost approach** attempts to allocate the shared costs to individual units based on some type of cost allocation procedure. This results in a net profit figure for each unit. The **contribution approach** is different in that only direct costs are included in the profitability analysis; the indirect or shared costs are not included. The net contribution calculated from this approach represents the *profit contribution* of the unit being analyzed. This profit contribution must be sufficient to cover indirect costs and other overhead and to provide the net profit for the firm.

An example that incorporates both approaches is presented in Exhibit 15.7. This example employs the direct approach for assessing sales region profitability and the contribution approach for evaluating the districts within this region. Notice that the profitability calculations for each district include only district sales, cost of goods sold, and district direct selling expenses. A *profit contribution* is generated for each district. The profitability calculations for the region include district selling expenses, region direct selling expenses that have not been allocated to the districts, and an allocated portion of shared zone costs. This produces a net profit figure for a profitability evaluation of the region.

Although either approach might be used, there seems to be a trend toward the contribution approach, probably because of the difficulty in arriving at a satisfactory procedure for allocating the shared costs. Different cost allocation methods produce different results. Thus, many firms feel more comfortable with

EXHIBIT 15.7 ▪ *Profitability Analysis Example*

	Full Cost Approach	Contribution Approach		
	Region	District 1	District 2	District 3
Sales	$200,000,000	$100,000,000	$60,000,000	$40,000,000
Cost of Goods Sold	160,000,000	90,000,000	50,000,000	20,000,000
Gross Margin	40,000,000	10,000,000	10,000,000	20,000,000
District Selling Expenses	10,000,000	5,000,000	3,000,000	2,000,000
Region Direct Selling Expenses	9,000,000	—	—	—
Profit Contribution	21,000,000	5,000,000	7,000,000	18,000,000
Allocated Portion of Shared Zone Costs	15,000,000			
Net Profit	6,000,000			

the contribution approach, since it eliminates the need for cost allocation judgments and is viewed as more objective.

Return on Assets Managed Analysis. The income statement approach to profitability assessment produces net profit or profit contribution in dollars or expressed as a percentage of sales. Although necessary and valuable, the income statement approach is incomplete because it does not incorporate any evaluation of the investment in assets required to generate the net profit or profit contribution.

The calculation of **return on assets managed (ROAM)** can extend the income statement analysis to include asset investment considerations. The formula for calculating ROAM is

ROAM = Profit contribution as percentage of sales × Asset turnover rate
     = Profit contribution/sales × Sales/assets managed

Profit contribution can be either a net profit figure from a direct approach or profit contribution from a contribution approach. Assets managed typically include inventory, accounts receivable, or other assets at each sales organizational level.

An example of ROAM calculations is presented in Exhibit 15.8. The example illustrates ROAM calculations for sales districts within a region. Notice that District 1 and District 2 produce the same ROAM but achieve their results in different ways. District 1 generates a relatively high profit contribution percentage, while District 2 operates with a relatively high asset turnover. Both District 3 and District 4 are achieving poor levels of ROAM, but for different reasons. District 3 has an acceptable profit contribution percentage but very low asset turnover ratio. This low asset turnover ratio is due either to both inventory accumulations or problems in payments from accounts. District 4, on the other hand, has an acceptable asset turnover ratio but low profit contribution percentage.

EXHIBIT 15.8 ▪ *Return on Assets Managed (ROAM) Example*

	District 1	District 2	District 3	District 4
Sales	$12,000,000	$12,000,000	$12,000,000	$12,000,000
Cost of Goods Sold	6,000,000	6,000,000	7,000,000	7,000,000
Gross Margin	6,000,000	6,000,000	5,000,000	5,000,000
Direct Selling Expenses	3,600,000	4,800,000	2,600,000	4,400,000
Profit Contribution	2,400,000	1,200,000	2,400,000	600,000
Accounts Receivable	4,000,000	2,000,000	8,000,000	2,000,000
Inventory	4,000,000	2,000,000	8,000,000	2,000,000
Total Assets Managed	8,000,000	4,000,000	16,000,000	4,000,000
Profit Contribution Percentage	20%	10%	20%	5%
Asset Turnover	1.5	3.0	.75	3.0
ROAM	30%	30%	15%	15%

This low profit contribution percentage may be the result of selling low margin products, negotiating low selling prices, or accruing excessive selling expenses.

As illustrated in the preceding example, ROAM calculations provide an assessment of profitability and useful diagnostic information. ROAM is determined by both profit contribution percentage and asset turnover. If ROAM is low in any area, the profit contribution percentage and asset turnover ratio can be examined to determine the reason. Corrective action (reduced selling expenses, stricter credit guidelines, lower inventory levels, etc.) can then be taken to improve future ROAM performance.

Residual Income Analysis. Although ROAM evaluates profitability in relation to asset investment, it does not include any consideration of sales growth. Since most firms have both sales growth and profitability objectives, an approach that incorporates both of these elements is extremely useful to sales managers. **Residual income analysis** has been proposed as such an approach.[6]

The basic concept underlying residual income analysis is that sales organization effectiveness depends upon both sales growth and profitability. Sales growth is desirable as long as the return on sales exceeds the cost of capital for acquiring assets. The formula for residual income analysis is

$$\text{Residual income} = \text{Profit contribution} - \text{Accounts receivable cost} - \text{Inventory carrying cost}$$

Thus, as long as residual income is positive, the return on sales is greater than the cost of assets.

EXHIBIT 15.9 ▪ *Residual Income Example*

	District 1	District 2	District 3	District 4
Sales	$5,750,000	$5,750,000	$5,250,000	$5,250,000
Sales Growth	15%	15%	5%	5%
ROAM	35%	15%	35%	15%
Profit Contribution	$ 520,208	$ 323,437	$ 520,625	$ 295,312
Accounts Receivable Cost	47,917	71,875	43,750	65,626
Inventory Cost	178,500	107,812	157,500	98,438
Residual Income	293,791	143,750	319,375	131,248
Target Residual Income	282,792	282,792	282,792	282,792
Variance	+ 10,999	− 139,042	+ 36,583	− 157,544

Source: Adapted from William L. Cron and Michael Levy, "Sales Management Performance Evaluation: A Residual Income Perspective," *Journal of Personal Selling and Sales Management*, August 1987, 63. Used with permission.

One of the advantages of residual income analysis is that residual income targets can be set for different levels of the sales organization. These targets are based on sales organization goals for both sales growth and profitability. Typically, they would be calculated by top management and supplied to the sales organization as target goals. Therefore, calculating residual income targets is outside the realm of sales managers and beyond the scope of this text. However, sales managers can use the residual income approach and should understand that the target residual income levels are calculated by directly considering a firm's objectives for sales growth and profitability.

An example of residual income analysis is presented in Exhibit 15.9. The firm in this example desired sales growth of 10 percent and profitability expressed by a 10 percent return on assets. Based on the firm's cost of capital, inventory carrying costs of 15 percent and accounts receivable costs of 10 percent were estimated. These figures were used to derive a target residual income of $1,131,168 for the sales region. Because the four sales districts were considered to be similar, equal residual income targets were established for each district ($1,131,168/4 = $282,792).

A review of Exhibit 15.9 illustrates the value of residual income analysis. If these districts had been evaluated only on ROAM calculations, District 1 and District 3 would have outperformed the other districts and, accordingly, would have been viewed as equally effective from a profitability perspective. District 2 and District 4 would have also been evaluated as similar in profitability. However, the residual income analysis indicates that when sales growth is included, District 3 was clearly more effective than District 1, and District 2 was more effective than

District 4. These evaluations are the same for both total residual income and target residual income, since all districts had the same targets. If different targets had been set for each district, then the comparison of actual residual income to target residual income would be the most meaningful evaluation.

Although the residual income approach has been employed extensively in the retail sector, it is a relatively new approach for the sales management area. The basic advantage of residual income analysis is its integration of sales growth and profitability assessments into one analysis. Even though the computations are somewhat complex, sales managers do not have to perform these computations and merely need to understand what is included in calculating the residual income targets and how to calculate actual residual income and compare it with target residual income.

Productivity Analysis

Although ROAM and residual income calculations incorporate elements of productivity by comparing profits and asset investments, additional **productivity analysis** is desirable for thorough evaluation of sales organization effectiveness. Productivity is typically measured in terms of ratios between outputs and inputs. For example, as discussed in Chapter 8, one often-used measure of salesforce productivity is sales/salesperson. A major advantage of productivity ratios is that they can be compared directly across the entire sales organization and with other sales organizations. This direct comparison is possible because all of the ratios are expressed in terms of the same units.

Since the basic job of sales managers is to manage salespeople, the most useful input unit for productivity analysis is the salesperson. Therefore, various types of productivity ratios are calculated on a per salesperson basis. The specific ratios depend upon the characteristics of a particular selling situation but often include important outputs such as sales, expenses, calls, demonstrations, and proposals. An example of a productivity analysis is presented in Exhibit 15.10.

Exhibit 15.10 illustrates how productivity analysis provides a different and useful perspective for evaluating sales organization effectiveness. As the exhibit reveals, absolute values can be misleading. For example, the highest sales districts are not necessarily the most effective. Although profitability analyses would likely detect this also, productivity analysis presents a vivid and precise evaluation by highlighting specific areas of both high and low productivity. Take the information concerning District 2. Although sales/salesperson is reasonable and expenses/salesperson is relatively low, both calls/salesperson and proposals/salesperson are much lower than the other districts. This may explain why selling expenses are low, but it also suggests that the salespeople in this district may not be covering the district adequately. The high sales may be due to a few large sales to large customers.

In any case, the productivity analysis provides useful evaluative and diagnostic information that is not directly available from the other types of analyses discussed in this chapter. Sales productivity and profitability are highly interrelated. However, profitability analysis has a financial perspective, while productivity

EXHIBIT 15.10 ▪ *Productivity Analysis Example*

	District 1	District 2	District 3	District 4
Sales	$10,000,000	$12,000,000	$10,000,000	$12,000,000
Selling Expenses	$ 1,000,000	$ 1,200,000	$ 1,500,000	$ 1,500,000
Sales Calls	5,000	4,500	4,500	6,000
Proposals	100	105	120	120
Number of Salespeople	10	15	10	15
Sales/Salesperson	$ 1,000,000	$ 800,000	$ 1,000,000	$ 800,000
Expenses/Salesperson	$ 100,000	$ 80,000	$ 150,000	$ 100,000
Calls/Salesperson	500	300	450	400
Proposals/Salesperson	10	7	12	8

analysis is more managerially oriented. Improvements in sales productivity should translate into increases in profitability.

Productivity improvements are obtained in one of two basic ways:

1. Increasing output with the same level of input.
2. Maintaining the same level of output but using less input.

Productivity analysis can help determine which of these basic approaches should be pursued.

Concluding Comments

As is obvious from the discussion in this chapter, there is no easy way to evaluate the effectiveness of a sales organization. Our recommendation is to perform separate analyses of sales, costs, profitability, and productivity to assess different aspects of sales organization effectiveness. Each type of analysis offers a piece of the puzzle. Sales managers must put these pieces together for comprehensive evaluations. The objective underlying each of the analyses is to be able to evaluate effectiveness, identify problem areas, and use this information to improve future sales organization effectiveness.

Summary

1. **Differentiate between sales organization effectiveness and salesperson performance.** Sales organization effectiveness is a summary evaluation of the overall success of a sales organization in meeting its goals and objectives in total and at different organizational levels. In contrast, salesperson performance is a function of individual salesperson performance in individual situations.

2.   Define a sales organization audit and discuss how it should be conducted. The most comprehensive type of evaluation is a sales organization audit, which is a systematic assessment of all aspects of a sales organization. The major areas included in the audit are sales organization environment, sales management evaluation, sales organization planning system, and sales management functions. The audit should be conducted on a regular basis by individuals outside the sales organization. It is intended to identify existing or potential problems at an early date so that corrective action can be taken before the problems become serious.

3.   Describe how to perform different types of sales analysis for different organizational levels and types of sales. Sales analysis is the most common evaluation approach, but it can be extremely complex. Specific definitions of a sale are required, and both sales dollars and units should typically be considered. A hierarchical approach is suggested as a top-down procedure to address sales results at each level of the sales organization with an emphasis on identifying problem areas. Sales analysis is more useful when sales results are compared to forecasts, quotas, previous time periods, and competitor results.

4.   Describe how to perform a cost analysis for a sales organization. Cost analysis focuses on the costs incurred to generate sales results. Specific costs can be compared to the planned levels in the selling budget. Areas with large variances require specific attention. Costs can also be evaluated as percentages of sales and compared to comparable industry figures.

5.   Describe how to perform income statement, return on assets managed, and residual income analyses to assess sales organization profitability. Profitability analysis combines sales and cost data in various ways. The income statement approach focuses on net profit or profit contributions from the different sales organization levels. The return on assets managed approach assesses relationships between profit contributions and the assets used to generate these profit contributions. Residual income analysis combines the return on assets managed concept with sales growth objectives to produce a very useful evaluative tool. The different profitability analyses address different aspects of profitability that are of interest to sales managers.

6.   Describe how to perform a productivity analysis for a sales organization. Productivity analysis focuses on relationships between outputs and inputs. The most useful input is the number of salespeople, while relevant outputs might be sales, expenses, proposals, and so on. The productivity ratios calculated in this manner are versatile, since they can be used for comparisons within the sales organization and across other sales organizations. Productivity analysis not only provides useful evaluative information but also provides managerially useful diagnostic information that can suggest ways to improve productivity and increase profitability.

Key Terms

- Sales organization audit
- Sales analysis
- Hierarchical sales analysis
- Effectiveness index
- Cost analysis
- Profitability analysis
- Income statement analysis
- Full cost approach
- Contribution approach
- Return on assets managed (ROAM)
- Residual income analysis
- Productivity analysis

Review Questions

1. Discuss why it is important to differentiate between sales organization effectiveness and salesperson performance.
2. Discuss what is involved in conducting a sales management audit.
3. Referring to "A Global Perspective: The Effectiveness of Australian Sales Organizations," discuss potential reasons for the similarities and differences between the effectiveness of sales organizations in Australia and the United States.
4. What is meant by a hierarchical sales analysis? Can a hierarchical approach be used in analyzing costs, profitability, and/or productivity?
5. What is the difference between the full cost and contribution approaches to income statement analysis for a sales organization? Which would you recommend for a sales organization? Why?
6. What are the two basic components of return on assets managed? How is each component calculated, and what does each component tell a sales manager?
7. What is the value of residual income analysis? How should it be used by sales managers?
8. Recommend the appropriate ethical behavior in each situation mentioned in "An Ethical Perspective: Ethical Problems with Selling Budgets." What should sales managers do to ensure that salespeople report their expenses accurately?
9. Identify five different sales organization productivity ratios that you would recommend. Describe how each would be calculated and what information each would provide.
10. Discuss how you think new computer and information technologies will affect the evaluations of sales organization effectiveness in the future.

Application Exercises

	Territory 1	Territory 2	Territory 3
Sales	$2,200,000	$2,500,000	$2,000,000
Expenses	$1,979,000	$2,157,000	$1,783,000
Assets	$ 800,000	$ 890,000	$ 775,000
Sales Calls	1,250	1,300	1,275
Demonstrations	200	400	300

Assume that you are a district sales manager and have assembled the information provided above to evaluate the effectiveness of your district.

1. Evaluate the productivity of each territory and interpret the results of your analysis.

2. Evaluate the profitability of each territory listed above and interpret the results of your analysis.

3. Evaluate the productivity and profitability of your district and interpret the results of your analysis.

Notes

[1]For a more complete discussion of this issue, see Orville C. Walker, Jr., Gilbert A. Churchill, Jr., and Neil M. Ford, "Where Do We Go From Here? Selected Conceptual and Empirical Issues Concerning the Motivation and Performance of the Industrial Salesforce," in *Critical Issues in Sales Management: State-of-the-Art and Future Research Needs*, ed. Gerald Albaum and Gilbert A. Churchill, Jr. (Eugene, Ore.: University of Oregon, 1979).

[2]The study results are taken from David W. Cravens, Thomas N. Ingram, Raymond W. LaForge, and Clifford E. Young, "The Relationship Between Salesperson Performance and Sales Organization Effectiveness: An Empirical Analysis," 1991, working paper.

[3]Much of the discussion in this section comes from Alan J. Dubinsky and Richard W. Hansen, "The Sales Force Management Audit," *California Management Review*, Winter 1981, 86–95.

[4]For the results of empirical studies that support this point, see Alan J. Dubinsky and Thomas E. Barry, "A Survey of Sales Management Practices," *Industrial Marketing Management* 11, 1982, 133–141; and Donald W. Jackson, Jr., Lonnie L. Ostrom, and Kenneth R. Evans, "Measures Used to Evaluate Industrial Marketing Activities," *Industrial Marketing Management* 11, 1982, 269–274.

[5]For a more complete presentation of this concept, see J. S. Schiff, "Evaluate the Sales Force as a Business," *Industrial Marketing Management* 12, 1983, 131–137.

[6]For a comprehensive presentation of this approach, see William L. Cron and Michael Levy, "Sales Management Performance Evaluation: A Residual Income Perspective," *Journal of Personal Selling and Sales Management*, August 1987, 57–66.

CASE 15.1   *Anderson-Smith Co.*

Anderson-Smith Co. is a manufacturer and marketer of various types of diagnostic equipment for chemical laboratories. Major customers include industrial firms with chemical laboratories and educational institutions that use laboratories in teaching chemistry classes. The company operates throughout the United States and is divided into four regions, each consisting of five districts with a district sales manager in charge of each district. A regional sales manager is assigned ultimate responsibility for each region.

Terry Wynn is the regional sales manager for the southern region. Terry has just seen preliminary financial results for the fiscal year that just ended. These results indicate that Anderson-Smith had a banner year, with sales and profits reaching record levels. However, Terry noticed that his region was ranked below the other regions in almost every area in the preliminary report. He knew that he would be questioned about these results by the national sales manager, Ed Huggett. Therefore, Terry decided to perform a detailed analysis of his region and each of his districts. His objective was to identify problem areas and to implement solutions before meeting with Ed Huggett.

Terry assembled the following information to help him achieve his objective:

	District 1 ($000)	District 2 ($000)	District 3 ($000)	District 4 ($000)	District 5 ($000)
Sales	8,200	9,500	10,450	13,750	8,400
Cost of Goods Sold	4,920	5,510	6,479	8,250	4,620
Compensation	615	810	735	1,170	630
Transportation	41	67	42	70	50
Lodging and Meals	17	30	16	41	21
Telephone	8	10	12	14	9
Entertainment	10	8	15	12	12
Training	80	95	105	125	110
District Inventory	2,000	3,500	3,200	5,250	2,500
District Accounts Receivable	1,170	1,400	1,450	2,420	1,150
Number of Salespeople	8	9	11	12	10
Sales Quota	8,100	9,750	10,250	14,125	8,300
Sales Last Year	7,500	9,250	10,250	13,925	8,200

Questions

1. What analyses should Terry perform with this data? Perform these analyses.
2. What problems can you identify from your analyses?
3. What solutions do you recommend to solve these problems and improve results in the future?

CASE 15.2 *Southern Pharmacal Corp.*

Southern Pharmacal Corp. is a leading producer and marketer of prescription pharmaceutical products for dermatologists. Although the company markets its products only to dermatologists in a five-state area, it has achieved a strong market position and has been very profitable in recent years. Top management believes that the company must expand into other geographic markets for future growth. Since the company has accumulated a great deal of cash and has substantial borrowing capacity, management has decided to move into new geographic areas by acquiring another pharmaceutical firm.

Preliminary analysis of potential acquisition candidates suggests that the firm should try to acquire either Jones Dermatologicals or Dermatological Pharmaceuticals. Both companies would pro-vide Southern Pharmacal with access to similar markets and have dermatological products that would complement the Southern Pharmacal line nicely. Both firms have salesforces of 100. However, Southern Pharmacal management thinks that the quality of the sales organization is a critical factor in deciding which company to acquire and how much to pay for the acquisition.

Bill Smuthers, president of Southern Pharmacal, has just walked into the office of National Sales Manager Tom Anderson. They have the following conversation:

Bill: Tom, as you know, we're looking carefully at the potential acquisition of either Jones Dermatologicals or Dermatological Pharmaceuticals.

Tom: Well, I've heard the rumors but don't know any of the details.

Bill: We screened a large number of companies, and these two firms seemed to be the best for our purposes. We've also analyzed both companies in great detail but are having a hard time determining which company to acquire and how much we should pay for the acquisition.

Tom: I can appreciate how difficult this decision is.

Bill: It is difficult. However, we now think that the deciding factor should be the quality of the sales organizations. Our judgment is that both companies are very similar on the other factors we've examined. We think that the ultimate decision hinges on which company has the best sales organization.

Tom: That makes a lot of sense.

Bill: Our problem is that we're not sure how to analyze the sales organizations to determine which one is the best. Therefore, I'd like for you to develop a procedure that will guide us through the appropriate analysis. If you can tell us what to do and how to do it, we can have our staff perform the analyses.

Tom: This is a pretty tall order.

Bill: I know it is, but it's extremely important to our decision. I'd like for you to submit a report containing your recommended procedures and present these to the members of the acquisition team in two weeks.

Tom: I'll do my best.

Questions

1. What procedures should Tom recommend to evaluate the two sales organizations?
2. What would you include in Tom's written report?

Evaluating and Controlling Salesperson Performance and Job Satisfaction

EVALUATING SALESFORCE PERFORMANCE: US WEST US West Inc. was one of the seven regional telecommunications companies created during the Bell System breakup, prior to which the company had operated in a monopoly situation, telling customers what products and services they could have. US West now operates in an extremely competitive situation where customers can choose from a range of products and services.

US West developed a customer-oriented strategy to perform successfully in this fiercely competitive environment. One aspect of this strategy was to develop sales and marketing units that specialized by industry type so that they could understand and respond to specific customer problems and needs. Another important element of their strategy was to evaluate the current performance of their salesforce to improve future performance.

US West hired a consulting firm to perform a comprehensive analysis of salesforce performance. Specific areas investigated included the present level of salesperson knowledge of company products, competitors, and buyer needs. Information concerning the current level of salesforce selling skills was also obtained. The consulting firm collected information from customers, account teams, and model sales organizations and also observed live sales calls.

This information was analyzed and summarized into a statement of current salesforce strengths and weaknesses. US West management reviewed the results of the salesforce performance study and developed a specific action plan to improve the performance of the salesforce. The action plan included the development of a more effective account planning process, the establishment of an expanded sales training program, and an emphasis on sales management coaching sessions with salespeople to improve their selling skills. Improvements in salesforce performance have helped US West become customer-oriented and compete effectively in the telecommunications industry.

Source: Reported in Rod Kopp and John Faier, "Sizing Up Your Sales Force," *Business Marketing*, May 1990, 42–45.

Learning Objectives

After completing this chapter, you should be able to

1 *Discuss the different purposes of salesperson performance evaluations.*

2 *Differentiate between an outcome-based and a behavior-based perspective for evaluating and controlling salesperson performance.*

3 *Describe the different types of criteria necessary for comprehensive evaluations of salesperson performance.*

4 *Compare the advantages and disadvantages of different methods of salesperson performance evaluation.*

5 *Explain how salesperson performance information can be used to identify problems, determine their causes, and suggest sales management actions to solve them.*

6 *Discuss the measurement and importance of salesperson job satisfaction.*

Whereas Chapter 15 focused on evaluating sales organization effectiveness, this chapter examines the task of evaluating salesperson performance and job satisfaction. Evaluations of sales organization effectiveness concentrate on the overall results achieved by the different units within the sales organization, with special attention given to determining the effectiveness of territories, districts, regions, and zones and identifying strategic changes to improve future effectiveness. These effectiveness assessments examine sales organization units and do not directly evaluate people; however, sales managers are responsible for the effectiveness of their assigned units.

The US West example in the opening vignette illustrates a situation where a company employed a consulting firm to evaluate the performance of an entire salesforce. Although this situation is somewhat rare, the consulting firm did examine various aspects of the performance of salespeople and not the overall effectiveness of the sales organization. The more typical situation is where sales managers evaluate the performance of the salespeople assigned to them. This is a difficult process, since people (sales managers) examine the performance of other people (salespeople). For example, consider the difficult ethical situations that sales managers can face in the salesperson performance evaluation process (see "An Ethical Perspective: Ethical Problems in Salesperson Performance Evaluation").

The purpose of this chapter is to investigate the key issues involved in evaluating and controlling the performance and job satisfaction of salespeople. The different purposes of salesperson performance evaluations are discussed initially. Then, the performance evaluation procedures currently used by sales organizations are examined. This is followed by a comprehensive assessment of the different areas in salesperson performance evaluation. The assessment addresses the criteria to be used in evaluating salespeople, the methods for evaluating salespeople against these criteria, and the outcomes of salesperson performance

AN ETHICAL PERSPECTIVE

Ethical Problems in Salesperson Performance Evaluation

Brent Pennington, director of sales for the Virginia Lottery, developed the following scenario to illustrate one type of ethical problem sales managers face in the salesperson performance evaluation process:

Dan had been with the XYZ Company for five years. XYZ was offering retailers an incentive program for increasing the sales of XYZ products for a limited time period. Dan's financial situation was tight, and he saw the incentive program as a way to increase his bonus by convincing retailers to increase their inventories during the promotion period. Since he had a good relationship with many of the retailers, he told them about his personal financial situation as a way to get them to increase their orders, even if they already had sufficient inventory. Sure enough, many of the retailers increased their purchases of XYZ products substantially, and Dan was set to receive a large bonus because of his performance during the incentive program. However, shortly after the program ended, many of the retailers in Dan's territory returned much of the product they had previously ordered.

This scenario illustrates the types of ethical situations that can arise when salespeople focus on short-term objectives. Sales managers must balance short- and long-term perspectives in their evaluations of salesperson performance.

Source: Adapted from information provided by Brent Pennington on January 28, 1991.

evaluations. The chapter concludes by discussing the importance and measurement of salesperson job satisfaction and relationships between salesperson performance and job satisfaction.

Purposes of Salesperson Performance Evaluations

As the name suggests, the basic objective of salesperson performance evaluations is to determine how well individual salespeople have performed. However, the results of salesperson performance evaluations can be used for many sales management purposes:[1]

1. To ensure that compensation and other reward disbursements are consistent with actual salesperson performance.
2. To identify salespeople that might be promoted.
3. To identify salespeople whose employment should be terminated and to supply evidence to support the need for termination.
4. To determine the specific training and counseling needs of individual salespeople and the overall salesforce.
5. To provide information for effective human resource planning.
6. To identify criteria that can be used to recruit and select salespeople in the future.

These diverse purposes affect all aspects of the performance evaluation process. For example, performance evaluations for determining compensation and reward disbursements should emphasize activities and results related to the salesperson's current job and situation. Performance evaluations for the purpose of identifying salespeople for promotion into sales management positions should focus on criteria related to potential effectiveness as a sales manager and not just current performance as a salesperson. The best salespeople do not always make the best sales managers. Thus, salesperson performance appraisals must be carefully developed and implemented to provide the types of information necessary to accomplish all of the desired purposes.

Current Approaches to Salesperson Performance Evaluations

Although it is impossible to determine with precision all the performance evaluation approaches used by sales organizations, several studies have produced sufficiently consistent information to warrant some general conclusions:[2]

1. Most sales organizations evaluate salesperson performance on an annual basis, although many firms conduct evaluations on a semiannual or quarterly basis. Relatively few firms evaluate salesperson performance more often than quarterly.
2. Most sales organizations employ combinations of input and output criteria that are evaluated by quantitative and qualitative measures. However, emphasis seems to be placed on outputs, with evaluations of sales volume results the most popular.

EXHIBIT 16.1 ▪ *Information Sources for Salesperson Performance Evaluations*

Source	Percent Frequently Using	Percent Always Using
Printed form	12	46
Computer printout	44	31
Call reports	29	19
Supervisory calls	32	23
Client feedback	46	25

Source: Michael H. Morris, Duane L. Davis, Jeffrey W. Allen, Ramon A. Avila, and Joseph Chapman, "Assessing the Relationships between Performance Measures, Managerial Practices, and Satisfaction when Evaluating the Salesforce," *Journal of Personal Selling and Sales Management,* Summer 1991.

3. Sales organizations that set performance standards or quotas tend to enlist the aid of salespeople in establishing these objectives. The degree of salesperson input and involvement does, however, appear to vary across firms.

4. As indicated in Exhibit 16.1, most firms use more than one source of information in evaluating salesperson performance. Qualitative information is most often provided by using printed performance evaluation forms, while quantitative information typically comes from the analysis of computer printouts for each territory. An interesting trend appears to be the use of client feedback information.

5. Most salesperson performance evaluations are conducted by the field sales manager who supervises the salesperson. However, some firms involve the manager above the field sales manager in the salesperson performance appraisal.

6. Most sales organizations provide salespeople with a written copy of their performance review and have sales managers discuss the performance evaluation with each salesperson. These discussions typically take place in an office, although sometimes they are conducted in the field.

These results offer a glimpse of current practices in evaluating salesperson performance. The remainder of this chapter will address the key decision areas and alternative approaches for developing comprehensive evaluation and control procedures.

Key Issues in Evaluating and Controlling Salesperson Performance

A useful way to view different perspectives for evaluating and controlling salesperson performance is presented in Exhibit 16.2. An **outcome-based perspective** focuses on objective measures of results with little monitoring or